EX LIBRIS
Pace University
New York · Westchester
PACE UNIVERSITY
OPPORTVNITAS
MCMVI
NEW YORK
NEW YORK & WESTCHESTER
PACE PLAZA
NEW YORK

D1385383

MUSIC IN AMERICAN LIFE

Books in the series:

Only a Miner: Studies in Recorded Coal-Mining Songs
ARCHIE GREEN

Great Day Coming: Folk Music and the American Left
R. SERGE DENISOFF

John Philip Sousa: A Descriptive Catalog of His Works
PAUL E. BIERLEY

The Hell-Bound Train: A Cowboy Songbook
GLENN OHRLIN

Oh, Didn't He Ramble: The Life Story of Lee Collins as Told to Mary Collins
FRANK J. GILLIS AND JOHN W. MINER, EDITORS

American Labor Songs of the Nineteenth Century
PHILIP S. FONER

American Labor Songs of the Nineteenth Century

PHILIP S. FONER

American LABOR SONGS of the Nineteenth Century

UNIVERSITY OF ILLINOIS PRESS
Urbana Chicago London

© 1975 by the Board of Trustees of the University of Illinois
Manufactured in the United States of America

Library of Congress Cataloging in Publication Data

Foner, Philip Sheldon, 1910- comp.
American labor songs of the nineteenth century.

(Music in American life)
Without the music.
Bibliography: p.
Includes indexes.
1. Labor and laboring classes—Songs and music.
2. American ballads and songs. I. Title.
M1977.L3F74 784.6′8′3310973 74-20968
ISBN 0-252-00187-7

Grateful acknowledgment is made for permission to use the following copyrighted material.

"The Long Strike," "The Hard Working Miner," "The Knights of Labor Strike," and "Me Johnny Mitchell Man" from *Songs and Ballads of the Anthracite Miner* by George Korson (New York: Grafton Press, 1927); "W.B.A.," "Hugh McGeehan," and "Break the News to Morgan" from *Minstrels of the Mine Patch: Songs and Stories of the Anthracite Industry* by George Korson (1938; reprinted, Hatboro, Pa.: Folklore Associates, 1964); "Two Cent Coal," "The Coal Creek Rebellion," and "The Homestead Strike" from *Coal Dust on the Fiddle: Songs and Stories of the Bituminous Industry* by George Korson (1943; reprinted, Hatboro, Pa.: Folklore Associates, 1965); "The Avondale Mine Disaster," "The Old Miner's Refrain," "Down in a Coal Mine," "On Johnny Mitchell's Train," and "The Lonely Miner of Wilkes-Barre" from *Pennsylvania Songs and Legends* by George Korson (Philadelphia: University of Pennsylvania Press, 1949). All reprinted by permission of Rae Korson.

"The Plight of a Miner's Widow" from *Black Rock: Mining Folklore of the Pennsylvania Dutch* by George Korson (Baltimore: Johns Hopkins University Press, 1960). Copyright by The Johns Hopkins University Press.

"Father Was Killed by the Pinkerton Men" from *Weep Some More, My Lady* by Sigmund Spaeth (Garden City, N.Y.: Doubleday, Page & Co., 1927). Reprinted herein by permission of the Estate of Sigmund Spaeth.

M
1977
.L3
F74
1975

FOR HEINZ AND GUSTEL

Contents

Preface

The student of American labor history and American folklore has long believed that apart from the songs of the coal miners and a few associated with the Knights of Labor and the struggle for the shorter working day, the labor song and ballad in America began with the rise of the Industrial Workers of the World (IWW) after 1905. In 1913, when the *Little Red Song Book* was being distributed by the thousands, Harry F. Ward, writing of the labor protest song, observed that "American labor is just beginning to express itself."[1] Even a compiler of "songs for the toiler" in 1891 did not seem to know of the existence of labor songs prior to his decade, for he wrote in the preface: "Our poets have rhymed for the beautiful and wealthy, the authors have exhausted their skill to tickle the fancy of those who dwell in luxury and opulence. Our ministers have preached and prayed for the souls of men too often after the pocket of the influential, and let the bodies go; *but the single-handed farmer, mechanic, and day-laborer, has had to sing another's song*—if, by chance, he felt like singing at all after 'duties' were done—or go without that music all men love, and nature craves."[2]

By including a small selection of the labor songs and ballads of the nineteenth century in his *American Folksongs of Protest*, published in 1953, John Greenway revealed that there was a tradition of labor songs, apart from those of the miners, even before 1900. But the selection was extremely limited in scope, and the nineteenth century was still considered largely barren of labor songs.

American Labor Songs of the Nineteenth Century, then, is the first comprehensive collection of such material, and even the more than 550 examples reproduced in full or in fragment here have been selected from hundreds more of similar pieces.

In his foreword to the 1964 edition of George Korson's *Minstrels of the Mine Patch*, Archie Green, himself a noted collector of labor songs and folklorist, observed: "The union press from the Age of Jackson until today has always printed anecdotes, songs, and tales contributed directly by members or reported in secondary form. Many of these items are pure folklore by the severest standards of life in tradition, anonymity, and variation. (They await an anthologist's eye and hand.)"[3] Long before Green wrote this, I had been engaged in collecting the songs and ballads which appeared in the American labor press from the revolutionary period to the present. This volume mainly includes pieces which appeared originally in the press of nineteenth-century America and are now for the first time reprinted. Admittedly, some of the best labor songs of the nineteenth century have disappeared. A case in point is revealed by the following item published in *Truth* (San Francisco), November 8, 1882:

[1]Harry F. Ward, "Songs of Discontent," *Methodist Review*, Sept., 1913, p. 726. However, the January 3, 1914, issue of the *Survey*, the "Social Hymn Number," included "Songs for Labor," in which Elizabeth Balch showed some awareness of the existence of American labor songs in the nineteenth century.

[2]Leopold Vincent, comp., *The Alliance and Labor Songster* (Winfield, Kans., 1891). My emphasis.

[3]Archie Green, in George Korson, *Minstrels of the Mine Patch* (1938; reprinted, Hatboro, Pa., 1964), p. ix.

THE HYMN OF LABOR

Some time ago the N.Y. *Truth* asked who should write the Song of Labor, and the query was widely copied and discussed by the labor press of the United States.

A little while thereafter *Truth* brought to mind the stirring verses of Ralph Waldo Emerson and suggested that appropriate music be composed for them.

J. N. E. Wilson has responded to that suggestion by a composition which is peculiarly appropriate.

Hardly ever does music so well express the meaning of words as does this. It is in truth, "The Hymn of Labor."

It has been published in sheet music form and well distributed throughout the labor organizations of San Francisco.

It would be a good idea if a glee club could be formed in each L[ocal] A[ssembly] to sing it.

The Abolition movement gave birth to "John Brown's Body" and the singing of that air, helped on the cause of freedom wonderfully.

Should the "Hymn of Labor" become as popular it would have as great an effect in aid of the cause of Labor.

Since "The Hymn of Labor" was published in sheet music form, it did not appear in any labor paper of the period (at least in any still in existence). However, no copy of the sheet music exists in the Art and Music Department of the San Francisco Public Library. An inquiry to the Reference Section, Music Division, Library of Congress, brought the following disappointing reply:

Your letter of July 31 has led us into a situation that I don't recall ever coming upon before. The records of the Copyright Office contain an entry for a registration dated December 6, 1882: "The Hymn of Labor," words by Ralph Waldo Emerson, music by J. N. E. Wilson, registration number 1882-20639. We still have a great many copyright deposits of sheet music organized by copyright number, so we went to that year and number and found a piece of music with the Copyright Office stamp of December 6, 1882, and the Copyright Office number 20639. But instead of being Wilson's setting of Emerson's "The Hymn of Labor," it turns out to be "Anti-Monopoly / War / Song / composed for the Anti-Monopoly Party of California / Dedicated to R. J. Harris." There is no attribution of either the words or the music, but the copyright is in the name of R. J. Harris.

The obvious answer was that during the stamping or somewhere else along the way, this sheet music had gotten switched with the Wilson song, so we looked in the Copyright records for an "anti-monopoly registration." None was found. Since then we have searched in many different places in our collection, using all the catalogs we have, and we have still found no trace of the Emerson-Wilson song. Several labor songs were sent on the same day; there is a pencilled inscription on the ledger: "M. Gray, 117 Port St., S.F.," and "Mr. Gray" is listed as claimant of the item numbered directly following the Wilson entry. Perhaps he was an attorney. Anyway, he must inadvertently have sent in the wrong piece of music to go with the Wilson registration, and the clerk in the Copyright Office must have stamped it, written in the Wilson number, and sent it on—all without noticing, or at least objecting to, the mistake. Now, 85 years later, the mistake causes grief.

We are sorry, but there doesn't seem much we can do about it. I looked through the copyright ledger for pages before and pages following the Wilson entry, but without seeing any sign of another clue.[4]

It is difficult to estimate what percentage of the total songs published by the labor press between 1828, when the *Mechanics' Free Press* began publication in Philadelphia, and the end of the century is represented by those labor papers of which copies are still in existence. For one thing, not all labor papers ran songs or even poetry. The *National Labor Tribune*, to cite one example, appeared weekly for thirty years in Pittsburgh without publishing a single song or ballad, although it did carry an occasional poem. Some labor papers carried sentimental songs and poems in each issue but devoted little space to songs related to current labor issues. However, the majority of labor papers, which did devote space regularly to songs and ballads and, indeed, often solicited them from readers, are available, even if only in incomplete files in some cases. Thus the present collection can be viewed as including a large percentage of the songs published by the nineteenth-century labor press.

In selecting from the hundreds of songs and ballads in the surviving files of the labor press the ones that have gone into this collection, I have sought to choose songs not so much on the basis of literary merit—though those with the best literary quality usually chose themselves—but for how effectively they reflected the issues with which they dealt. No doubt purists who judge songs by their literary quality will find many in this collection execrable; but whatever

[4]William Lichtenwanger, Head, Reference Section, to author, Sept. 14, 1967. For the "Anti-Monopoly War Song," see pp. 256–59.

their literary merit, they do demonstrate that the American labor movement from its birth was rich in songs, especially protest songs.

Unfortunately, hardly any labor songs found their way into the popular songbooks of the nineteenth century. These songbooks, generally known as "songsters," appeared in increasing numbers after the 1780s.[5] Many were sacred songsters, but most were secular in nature and were advertised as containing "the everyday songs of the people." But workers seem not to have belonged to the category of "the people," for none of the songsters carried any of the songs or ballads which were appearing in growing quantity in the labor press. Moreover, the songs dealing with black workers included in many of the songsters were often grotesquely exaggerated dialect songs, presenting the Negro as a comic figure associated with undesirable traits of all kinds. Usually the only good blacks portrayed were slaves who were content with bondage and opposed being emancipated. Thus in the song "Picayune Butler," published around 1847, the slave sings:

De folks all preach 'bout abolition,
And say dey'll mend de nigger's condition
Yah! yah!
But if dey let de niggers alone,
De niggers will always have a home.

Again, in "Sambo's Opinion" (1863) there are these lines:

Some say de niggers shall be slaves some say dey shall be free
I'd like to know what difference all dis trouble makes to me
Freedom may be well enough, likewise emancipation,
But I guess dat I is better off down on de old plantation.[6]

The other group of workers about whom songs appeared in several of the songsters were the Chinese. These were invariably anti-Chinese songs, depicting the Chinese immigrants as racially inferior to white Americans and a menace to the living standards of American workers.[7]

Many of the songs and ballads of different occupational groups already in print—those of the cowboys, railroad workers, sailors, lumbermen and shanty boys, and whalers, for instance[8]—deal mainly with such issues as love, humor, and crime. The labor press did publish songs of this nature. An example of this type of song is the following, published in the *American Workman* (Boston), July 3, 1869:

FACTORY SONG
By Mrs. L. S. Goodwin

The spindles whirl, the bobbins fill,
A little maid tends the thread,
Singing a song of somebody,
And somebody's name is Fred.
She sings aloud, for none can hear,
So noisily goes the mill,
Telling her secret to many an ear,
And keeping her secret still.

The din to her has a goodly sound
Of a carpenter's hammer and saw,
And voice of raisers of cottage walls—
"Heave! heave! hurrah!"
Building a home for a married pair—
And somebody's name is Fred,
And somebody's wife is a factory girl,
Spinning the slender thread.

Oh, never she doubts but somebody thinks
Of her as she thinks of him;
Knowing what day their cup of bliss
Will be full to its very brim.
So, to and fro in the aisle she goes,
Light-hearted and light of tread,
Thinking how willingly ever she'll work
For the man whose name is Fred.

She doffs the bobbins, they fill again,
And so on all the day;
Then at the sound of the bell, the little maid
Trips down the stairs and away.
But whether by day or whether by night,
At work, or asleep in bed,
Her spirit is singing of somebody,
And somebody's name is Fred.

5Some of the titles were *The American Songster* (1788), *The National Songster* (1808), *The Patriotic Songster* (1816), *The American Naval and Patriotic Songster* (1836), *Christy's Panorama Songster* (1857).

6Cecil Lloyd Patterson, "A Different Drum: The Image of the Negro in Nineteenth Century Popular Song Books" (Ph.D. thesis, University of Pennsylvania, 1961), p. 126.

7See for example, *The California Songster* (San Francisco, 1855), p. 44, and *The Blue and Gray Songster* (San Francisco, 1877), pp. 16–17.

8None of these songs are included in the present collection since they are available elsewhere and lie outside the main scope of this work. Those who wish to read the songs and ballads of the occupational groups mentioned above will find collections listed in the Bibliography.

In the main, however, the songs and ballads in the labor papers dealt with the organizations and struggles of working people, their hatred for the oppressor, their affirmation of the dignity and worth of labor, their determination to endure hardships together and to fight together for a better life.[9] There is scarcely a single important labor issue or labor struggle in nineteenth-century America which is not represented in this collection by at least one song, some by several. Mainly these are songs and ballads of organized, unionized workers who, after all, had a labor press in which their literary and musical output could find its way into print. A small group, however, are expressions of workers who were unorganized, especially black workers, who, either because most were slaves for the first six decades of the century or even when free were excluded from nearly all unions, could not express themselves in the labor press.

To the oppressed workers the labor press was both an advocate and a symbol of hope, the only means through which they could voice their opposition to exploitation and their aspirations and demands. One worker used verse to express this idea, writing in the *Champion of Labor* of April 17, 1847:

Has stern oppression met a check?
Will not the Poor Man bend his neck
    Nor truckle unto might?
Has that strong advocate, the PRESS,
Proclaim'd his wrongs—advanc'd Redress
    And thundered forth his Right?

The answer was clearly "No!" In contrast, the labor press was

    LABOR'S warmest friend,
Success unto thy onward course
May tyrants feel thy moral force
    And to thy TRUTH'S attend!

A large part of this collection illustrates the fact that the central commitment of trade unionism was to the improvement of wages, hours, and working conditions for its own members. But there are also many songs which point up the concern of nineteenth-century unionism with the struggle to give the workers dignity as well as higher income and shorter hours and even with a new and better social system to replace the existing system.

It is often impossible to tell whether a printed stanza is a poem or a song. I have included in the collection those texts which either appear to have been written to be sung or which, judging from references in the labor press or later, were made into songs. A very few poems have also been included which emphasize an important issue or event. However, a whole book just of labor poems, apart from those included in the present collection, could be published.

The position of the labor song, like all songs of protest, in folk literature is debatable. Are they or are they not folksongs? Folksong scholars have tended to ignore them as unworthy of qualifying as folksongs.[10] In his introduction to *American Folksongs of Protest*, John Greenway has made a good case for including such songs in the category of folksongs, effectively criticizing folklorists who refuse to recognize them as such. There is little to be added to what he has said: "To understand the people who produce folksongs, and thereby to understand the songs themselves, it is essential to consider all the songs that emanate from them, the disturbing as well as the complacent, those that carry a message as well as those written simply for diversion."[11]

There is no way of knowing just how many of the songs written for the labor press were actually sung. The chances are that many never got off the printed page and entered oral tradition. But from evidence in reports of meetings, conventions, strikes, and political demonstrations, enough did to warrant the conclusion that a fairly large number were sung by the workers of the time. Since many of the demands for which the song or ballad was written disappeared,

9Jesse Lemisch and John K. Alexander observe: "Hindered by a relative scarcity of sources but ultimately done in by a hearing defect, historians have too often chosen to conclude that their inability to hear means that people were actually inarticulate" ("The White Oaks, Jack Tar, and the Concept of the 'Inarticulate,' " *William and Mary Quarterly*, XXIX [Jan., 1972], 131). Certainly the songs and ballads in this collection should do much to erase the idea that workers in American society were "inarticulate."

10In *An Introduction to Folk Music in the United States*, rev. ed. (Detroit, 1962), folklorist Bruno Nettl briefly discusses cowboy and coal-mining songs and the general failure of labor unions to create folksongs in the city (pp. 51–52, 67–68). His musical examples include only two labor songs: "The Jolly Lumberman" and a Slovak industrial song, "Aja Lejber Man" (pp. 96–97, 112).

11John Greenway, *American Folksongs of Protest* (Philadelphia, 1953), p. 4.

mainly because they were achieved in time, the songs themselves were most likely forgotten and remained only in the pages of the labor press or on broadsides which have been collected.[12] Yet even though these songs were ephemeral, their passing nature should not cause them to be underestimated. They provide us with insights into the causes of strikes and other labor issues from the viewpoint of the workers themselves, and they indicate what the composers—themselves often participants in the struggles—thought would be the most stirring way to mobilize workers in the movement for a better life. They are important social documents, for they served their causes well and were significant in helping advance the goals they were written to achieve. On December 3, 1847, the *Voice of Industry*, a labor paper published in Massachusetts, predicted that "if anything can arouse the masses in our country from the fearful state of apathy into which they are sunk, the thrilling tones of the songs of labor must do it. And they will do it, for greater than the Philosopher or the Legislator, is the Child of Song." Almost a half century later, A. W. Wright, editor of the *Journal of the Knights of Labor*, voiced a similar opinion: "Songs . . . will reach thousands to whom arguments would at first be addressed in vain, and even veterans in the movement will listen to an argument in a better mood for having drank in some familiar truth in the setting of a well-remembered air."[13] In the same vein, the editor of *Songs of Socialism* wrote:

> The masses may not so readily comprehend the scientific basis of Socialism, historical and class-conscious, when presented in a prosaic, argumentative form, however desirable and necessary; but every heart will quickly "feel a brother's care" through a plaintive song picture of his brother's woe, so often his own life story. So, likewise, will all easily see the wrongs, the truths and glorious possibilities of Socialism, and its easy consummation, when presented through enthusiastic song. And, most important of all, through this medium, everybody, including the children, may become active and efficient workers for Socialism, and thus greatly hasten the day of our redemption from injustice, want, and worry.[14]

Several decades later, John Steinbeck wrote: "Songs are the statement of a people. You can learn more about people by listening to their songs than any other way, for into the songs go all the hopes and hurts, the angers, fears, the wants and aspirations."[15]

As Wright indicated, most labor songs were set to a "well-remembered air." Musically, then, the majority of the songs in this collection are unoriginal; the words are set to old favorites or to popular tunes of the day. Duncan Emrich has contended, with considerable insight, that the lack of originality among labor songwriters results from their fatiguing occupations and from a scarcity of leisure time in which to create original music.[16] A small number of the songs in this collection, however, had music especially composed for them, and in some cases where such songs are included in the collection they are accompanied by the music.

Many of the songwriters who set their words to a "well-remembered air" did so anonymously or under a simple pseudonym, such as "A Worker," "A Miner's Wife," and so forth. But as the Index of Composers indicates, there were a large number of songwriters who signed their names to their contributions. Many wrote one song or ballad, but several, like Edward Earle, Robert Hume, A. J. H. Duganne, Edward R. Place, Phillips Thompson, Karl Reuber, B. M. Lawrence, and Morris Rosenfeld, contributed songs regularly to the labor press, and some even had their contributions published in a collection. A few, like John Siney, the mine union leader, Ira Steward, the eight-hour champion, and John A. Sovereign, grand master workman of the Knights of Labor, are well known. But we ought to know more about the other nineteenth-century composers and what their place was in the workers' organizations and struggles. They and the anonymous songwriters helped create a body of material which is an important part of the history of the so-called inarticulate.

[12]In this connection, the comment of Pete Seeger, the noted American folksinger and collector of labor songs, is interesting: "In my experience, songs arise during a crisis, and are almost forgotten between crises. But if even one or two people remember a song, it may be revived & become popular all over again, during the next crisis—with probably slight changes" (Pete Seeger to author, Feb. 10, 1967).

[13]Quoted by Phillips Thompson in his introduction to *The Labor Reform Songster* (Philadelphia, 1892).

[14]Harvey P. Moyer, ed., *Songs of Socialism* (Chicago, 1905), introduction.

[15]Quoted in Greenway, *American Folksongs of Protest*, p. vii.

[16]Duncan Emrich, "Songs of the Western Miners," *California Folklore Quarterly*, I (1942), 213–14.

Scores of the songs in this collections were composed by workers in America on patterns brought from the Old World.[17] Most of these were in English, but many also appeared in the language of the immigrant workers, especially the Germans. I have had a number of German songs translated; they appear here without the poetry in the original. It is, of course, impossible to convey in these English translations the exact meaning of the German and the spirit and resonance deriving from the German language.[18] But I thought it better to present a literal translation than to give an inferior one which retained the rhymes of the verses. Fortunately, in the case of the songs and ballads in the Yiddish language, excellent translations in verse do exist, and they have been included.

The songs have been grouped in chapters corresponding to their period and subject, although there is inevitably some overlapping. To enable the reader to understand the circumstances out of which the songs in this collection grew and the issues they dealt with, I have provided introductory sections and explanatory notes throughout. However, having published two lengthy volumes dealing with the history of the nineteenth-century labor movement in the United States, I cannot claim that these introductory and explanatory materials do more than offer a survey of the main trends. Those who wish to delve more deeply into the issues out of which the songs emerged will find a comprehensive bibliography to assist them. Sources for direct quotations, however, have been furnished throughout. I have reproduced the verses exactly as they were originally printed, calling attention in numbered footnotes to what are or may be errors. Notes in the original are indicated by symbols (*, †).

I hope that the publication of this work will help revive a worthy American labor tradition. Very few unions today encourage the creative work of their members. There are some noteworthy exceptions. Hospital Workers Local 1199 in New York maintains a permanent art gallery at its headquarters, publishes members' poetry regularly in the letters-to-editors section of its magazine, and has sponsored the publication of a volume of poetry by one of its members. The Fur Workers also publish poetry and have exhibited members' art and photography. The Farmworkers' paper, *El Malcriado*, features members' poetry in Spanish. But these are few and far between.[19]

In the preparation of this collection, I have had the assistance of numerous institutions and individuals. I particularly wish to express my gratitude to the staffs of the University Library, Brown University; the American Antiquarian Society; the Historical Society of Pennsylvania; the Kansas Historical Society; the New Hampshire Historical Society; the Wisconsin State Historical Society; the Tamiment Institute Library of New York University; the Library of Congress; the New York Public Library; the Boston Public Library; the Yale University Library; the Harvard University Library; the San Francisco Public Library; the New York State Library, Albany; the New York Historical Society; the Columbia University Library; the Labadie Collection, University of Michigan Library; the Library Company of Philadelphia; the library of the Institut für Marxismus-Leninismus, Berlin; the Lynn Historical Society, Lynn, Massachusetts; and the Lincoln University Library. Lenore Veltfort, Rudi Bass, and Brewster Chamberlin were of great assistance in translating songs from the German-

17"There is also a weaver's poetry," notes E. P. Thompson, "some traditional, some more sophisticated. The Lancashire 'Jone o' Grinfilt' ballads went through a patriotic cycle at the start of the Wars (with Jacobin counter-ballads) and continued through Chartist times to the Crimean War" (*The Making of the English Working Class* [New York, 1964], p. 292). Like the miners, who had a long tradition of songs and ballads, the British weavers who migrated to this country brought their ballads with them.

18In a few cases the labor press published good translations in verse of songs of the German-American workers, and these are included below.

19An interesting recent development which should encourage unions to pay more attention to their membership's creative talents is the publication in 1970 of *Time of the Phoenix*, a paperback volume, by the Young Patriots Organization, a radical group of poor whites in Chicago's Uptown section who were influenced by the Black Panthers. In addition to leading rent strikes and anti–Vietnam War demonstrations, the YPO encouraged poetry and song-making by their people. These songs and poetry comprised the first *Time of the Phoenix*, which, while ignored by the critics, was so successful in Chicago's Uptown that a second volume was published in 1972. In the introduction to the latter volume, the point is made: "Search the shelves of bookstore or library and you will find ample materials written for and about poor people but far and few in between are those written by the poor themselves. This anthology of song and poetry is written by poor people."

American press. Pete Seeger was generous in providing material from his personal collection. My brother, Henry Foner, both a trade union official and a writer of songs, was most helpful in reading the work and making useful suggestions. I wish to thank *Jewish Currents* for permission to quote songs and verse which appeared in *Jewish Life*, and the Jewish Youth Bund for permission to use material from their LP *Yiddish Songs of Work and Struggle.* I owe a special debt of gratitude to Judith McCulloh for the care with which she prepared the manuscript for the printer and the many valuable suggestions for improving the work.

1

Colonial, Revolutionary, and Early National Period

COLONIAL WORKERS

Although manufactures in the American colonies had to await release from British mercantilist restrictions before they were able to develop in earnest, there existed before the Revolution a number of leading commercial centers: Philadelphia, New York, Boston, Baltimore, Providence, Charleston. Here there emerged a large number of working people who produced such diverse items as ships, distilled spirits, paper, candles, soap, tobacco, cannon, muskets, anchors, nails, Windsor chairs, plows and other farm implements, carriages, shoes, saddlery, boots, leather goods, hosiery and other wearing apparel, coarse linens and woolens, some cotton wares, and metal products. Among these working people were many indentured servants who by law were supposed to labor without pay for five to seven years to defray the cost of their transportation. Another group comprised the Negro slaves who by law and custom were to labor without pay for life and whose children, in the case of female slaves, were also slaves for life. Once freed of his contractual obligations, the former indentured servant either became a farmer or joined the ranks of free labor as an artisan, mechanic, or journeyman.

By the eve of the Revolution, many workers were employed as weavers, shoemakers, and cabinetmakers in large shops in New York, Boston, Philadelphia, and elsewhere. The typical colonial shop, however, did not have many workers. In 1750 such a shop would consist of a master craftsman, who was the owner and employer; two or three journeymen; and a small number of apprentices. The master craftsman still worked side by side with his wageworkers. He provided the capital and the raw material and sold the finished articles.

While the shortage of labor made the lot of the free workers of the colonial period a better one than that of their European counterparts, they were often reduced to poverty by long periods of unemployment, high prices, and competition from indentured servants and black slaves. That all was not milk and honey in the life of a colonial wage earner is revealed in this 1770 song describing a craftsman:

A SQUIB
To the tune of "Miss Dawson's Hornpipe"
June 29, 1770

In yonder *Hutt* is to be seen,
A Hungry GIANT *lank and lean,*
With well patch'd threadbare Coat of Green;
To cover Round Shoulders;
With unfleg'd Chin, and foolish Face,
A Greasy Hat, with worsted Lace,
Poor NAT (tho' in a wretched Case)
Makes sport, for his beholders.[1]

Life for the colonial seaman was also difficult, as the following version of "Ye Gentlemen of England" indicates. The song was widely sung in the pubs and taverns where sailors gathered, both in Britain and in the colonies.

[1]Carl Bridenbaugh, *The Colonial Craftsman* (New York and London, 1950), p. 152.

A SEA SONG

You gentlemen of England who stay at home at ease
How little do you think of the Dangers of the Seas
Give ear unto any bold Mariners and they will plainly
Sho
The fears and the cares we poor Seamen undergo.

If you intend to be Seamen you must have a valliant
heart
And when your on the raging Seas you must think to
start
Neither be faint hearted at hail, rain, frost or snow
Or to think for to sink whilst the stormy winds do blow.

When we meet our Enemies as often times we do
We'll either drive them off our Coast or else we'll bring
them too
Our roaring guns shall teach them our vallor for to show
For we'll real on her keale while the stormy winds do
blow

Sometimes in absent Bosom our ship she is toss'd with
waves
Expecting every moment the Seas would prove our
graves
It's up aloft she mounts Boys then down again so low
For we'll real on her keale whilst the stormy winds do
blow.

When to Boston we return our wages for our pains
The tapster and the miller shall share in all our gains
We'll call for Licker round boys we'll pay before we go
For we'll rore on the shore while the stormy winds do
blow.[2]

COLONIAL WORKERS' POLITICAL ACTION

From time to time the free workers in colonial America undertook positive action to protect their rights. They formed organized groups, such as the mechanics' societies, which were primarily "benevolent and protective associations" open to both masters and journeymen. They even conducted a few strikes before the Revolution, and, in addition, they appreciated early the need for political action to supplement that on the economic front. This was not easy, however, for with the introduction of property qualifications for voting, suffrage was restricted to owners of land. Even where free workers could vote, their wishes were not consulted in political affairs. Thus, before the Revolution a Philadelphia mechanic wrote: "It has been customary for a certain company of leading Men to nominate persons, and to settle the ticket for Assemblymen, Commissioners, Assessors, etc., without even permitting the affirmative or negative voice of a Mechanic to interfere. . . . This we have so tamely submitted to so long, that those Gentlemen make no Scruple to say, that the Mechanics have no Right to *speak* or *think* for themselves. . . . I think it is absolutely necessary that one or two Mechanics be elected to represent so large a body of Inhabitants."[3]

Not all workers, however, "tamely submitted." Riots often took place on election days, when small shopkeepers, artisans, and laborers would march to the polls, armed with sticks and stones, and demand a voice in government. These demonstrations were supplemented by literary protests in prose and verse, such as

Now the pleasant time approaches;
Gentlemen do ride in coaches,
But poor men they don't regard,
That to maintain them labour hard.[4]

In New York City in the 1730s about 10 percent of the white population possessed the right to vote. Thus, while the government was controlled by merchants, crown officers, lawyers, and landowners, the opportunity existed for a political movement of the artisans. The opportunity came during the aldermanic campaign of 1734, when the Court party, representing Governor William Cosby and the merchants, was determined to retain control of the city government by reelecting its aldermen and councilmen. Arrayed against it was the Popular party, supported by the artisans and aided by John Peter Zenger's *New York Journal.* In a handbill distributed by the Popular party during the campaign, the workingmen of New York were urged "to chuse no Courtiers, or Trimmers; or any of that vain Tribe that are more fond of a Feather in their Hats, than the true interest of the City. Nor to chuse any dependents on them." It reminded the voters that "a poor honest Man [is] preferable to a rich Knave."[5] Towards the end of the campaign, the workingmen were rallied to

[2]George Carey, "Songs of Jack Tar in the Darbies," *Journal of American Folklore,* LXXXV (Apr.-June, 1972), 176.

[3]*Pennsylvania Gazette,* Sept. 27, 1770.

[4]Isaac N. P. Stokes, *The Iconography of Manhattan Island 1498 to 1909,* 6 vols. (New York, 1915–28), IV, 536.

[5]George W. Edwards, "New York Politics before the American Revolution," *Political Science Quarterly,* XXXVI (Dec., 1921), 589; see also the *New York Gazette,* May 27 and Oct. 14, 1734, and the *New York Journal,* Oct. 14, 1734.

the polls by the following songs printed on the press of John Peter Zenger:

A SONG MADE UPON THE ELECTION OF NEW MAGISTRATES FOR THIS CITY

To the tune of "To You Fair Ladies Now on Land"

To you good lads that dare oppose
All lawless power and might,
You are the theme that we have chose,
And to your praise we write:
You dar'd to shew your faces brave
In spite of every abject slave;
With a fa la la.

Your votes you gave for those brave men
Who feasling did dispise;
And never prostituted pen
To certify the lies
That were drawn up to put in chains,
As well our nymphs as happy swains;
With a fa la la.

And the great ones frown at this,
What need have you to care?
Still let them fret and talk amiss,
You'll shew you boldly dare
Stand up to save your Country dear,
In spight of usquebaugh and beer;
With a fa la la.

They beg'd and pray'd for one year more,
But it was all in vain:
No wolawants you'd have, you swore;
By jove you made it plain:
So sent them home to take their rest,
And here's a health unto the best;
With a fa la la.

A SONG MADE UPON THE FOREGOING OCCASION

To the tune of "Now, Now, You Tories All Shall Stoop"

Come on brave boys, let us be brave
For liberty and law,
Boldly despise the haughty Knave,
That would keep us in aw.
Let's scorn the tools bought by a sop,
And every cringing fool.
The man who basely bend's a fop,
A vile insipid tool.

Our Country's Rights we will defend,
Like brave and honest men;
We voted right and there's an end,
And so we'll do again.
We vote all signers out of place
As men who did amiss
Who sold us by a false adress,
I'm sure we're right in this.

Exchequer courts, as void by law,
Great grievances we call;
Tho' great men do assert no flaw
Is in them; they shall fall,
And be contemn'd by every man
That's fond of liberty.
Let them withstand it all they can,
Our Laws we will stand by.

The pettyfogging knaves deny
Us Rights of Englishmen;
We'll make the scoundrel raskals fly,
And ne'er return again.
Our Judges they would chop and change
For those that serve their turn,
And will not surely think it strange
If they for this should mourn.

Come fill a bumber, fill it up,
Unto our Aldermen;
For common-council fill the cup,
And take it o'er again,
While they with us resolve to stand
For liberty and law,
We'll drink their healths with hat in hand,
Whoraa! whoraa! whoraa![6]

The election was a triumph for the Popular party. John Fred (laborer), Johannes Burger (bricklayer), William Roome (painter), Henry Bogart (baker), and other artisans were elected to the common council. Infuriated by the victory of the people, Governor Cosby issued a proclamation on November 6, 1734, offering a reward of twenty pounds for the discovery of "the Author or Authors of the two Scandalous Songs or Ballads."[7] The "Author or Authors" were never discovered, but the governor got his revenge, first, by ordering the broadside containing the songs "to be burnt at the Hands of the common Hangman" and, second, by citing the two "Virulent, Scandalous and Seditious" songs in the charges against John Peter Zenger on November 17, 1734, accusing him of seditious libel. But the jury brought in a verdict of not guilty, and the precedent of freedom of the press was established in America.

SONS OF LIBERTY

During the two decades before the American Revolution, the resistance to British policies was

6Broadside, Rare Book Room, New York Public Library.

7Proclamation of Governor William Cosby, Nov. 6, 1734, Rare Book Room, New York Public Library.

led by organizations known as Sons of Liberty. Although directed by a few merchants and lawyers, the Sons of Liberty were made up in the main by groups of workingmen—masters, mechanics, day laborers, seamen, and other members of the urban lower classes. Wherever they appeared, they demonstrated against the oppressive measures of the British ministry, secured the repeal of the Stamp Act, fought the Townshend Act, and made possible the enforcement of the non-importation agreements and the boycott on English goods. In addition, the artisans and laborers saw in the struggle against British oppression an opportunity to weaken the domination of colonial life by the wealthy and wellborn. In 1772 the mechanics of Philadelphia formed a Patriotic Society (which two years later became the Mechanics' Association of Philadelphia) to preserve "our just Rights and Privileges to us and our Posterity against every attempt to violate . . . the same, *either here or on the other side of the Atlantic.*"[8]

Either through the Sons of Liberty or their benevolent societies, which often acted in collaboration with the Sons of Liberty, the colonial workers announced their determination to "fight up to their knees in blood" rather than be ruled by tyrants. They paraded to public meetings in military formation, with liberty tree medals suspended from their necks, and at singing festivals they raised their voices in revolutionary song, warning aristocrats that they dared to be free from domestic as well as British tyranny.

A NEW SONG

Address'd to the SONS OF LIBERTY, on the Continent of AMERICA; particularly to the illustrious, Glorious and never to be Forgotten NINETY-TWO of BOSTON.[9]

"The Americans are the Sons, not the Bastards of England; the *Commons* of *America*, represented in their several Assemblies, have ever been in Possession of the Exercise of *this their Constitutional Right*, of GIVING and GRANTING their OWN MONEY; they would have been SLAVES, if they had not enjoyed it."—Mr. Pitt's *speech*[10]

By a Son of Liberty

Tune—"Come Jolly Bacchus"
or "Glorious First of August"

Come jolly SONS of LIBERTY—
Come ALL with Hearts UNITED,
Our Motto is "WE DARE BE FREE"
Not easily affrighted!
Oppression's Band we must subdue,
Now is the Time, or never;
Let each Man PROVE this Motto True.
And SLAVERY from him sever.

Pale vissag'd *Fear*, let none possess!
Or Terrors e're perplex him,
POSTERITY will ever bless,
And nought hereafter vex him;
To *Freedom's Banner*, let's Repair;
When e're we see Occasion—
Nor WIVES nor CHILDREN, tho' most dear,
E're stop to look, or gaze on.

In *Freedom's Cause*, the slavish Knave,
'Twere better his Condition,
(That might his *Country's Ruin* save!)
To sink into Perdition;
Chain'd to a GALLEY, groan his Days,
And never be forgotten,
While Furies croak his *Bondage Lays*,
After he's Dead and Rotten.

Once shou'd *this* PRECEDENT take Place!
Tell, what you call your OWN Sir!
MAGNA CHARTA in Disgrace!
Your *Substance* now, all flown Sir!
No more shall *Peers* now try *your Cause!*
That Time is now *all over!*
What *need* have we pray now of *Laws?*
Now *Right* is *Wrong* in *Trover!*

See *Liberty* high poiz'd in Air,
Her *FREE BORN SONS* commanding,
"Come on, my Sons, without all fear;
"Your NAT'RAL RIGHTS demanding!
"Your CAUSE, the Gods proclaim, is *Just*,
"Can *tamely*, you, be *fetter'd?*
"In which, *disturb* your *Fathers* DUST!
"With S, be *ever* letter'd!"

Obey, my *Brothers*, *Nature's* call,
Your *Country* too demands it!
Let LIBERTY ne'er have a *Fall!*
'Tis Freedom that commands it.

8Philip Davidson, *Propaganda and the American Revolution, 1763–1783* (Chapel Hill, N.C., 1941), pp. 77–78.

9The song is dedicated to the Sons of Liberty of Boston who on August 14–15, 1765, leveled the stamp office to the ground, burned the stamp distributor in effigy, and forced him to resign his position.

10In a speech to Parliament on January 9, 1766, William Pitt denounced the Stamp Act, called for its immediate repeal, and, in addition to the statement quoted above, declared: "I rejoice that America has resisted. . . ." For the complete address, see J. Wright, *Parliamentary History of England . . .* (London, 1813), XVI, 97–108.

The *Ax*, now to *the Root is laid.*
Will you be, or BOND or FREE?
No *Time* to pause—then "Whose afraid?"
Live or *die* in *Liberty!*

Now FARMER, Dear, we'll fill to you,
May Heav'n its *Blessings* Show'r,
As on the Glorious NINETY-TWO,
But Seventeen devour—
Mean abject *Wretches!—Slaves in Grain!*
How dare ye shew *your Faces?*
To latest Days, *go dragg your Chain!*
Like *other* MULES or ASSES.[11]

LABOR AND JEFFERSONIAN DEMOCRACY

When the revolutionary war was over, the artisans, mechanics, and laborers organized to preserve the cause of freedom for which the American people had fought. In Philadelphia, coopers, watchmakers, ropemakers, brickmakers, saddlers, cordwainers (shoemakers), and other workers formed artisan clubs to support workingmen's candidates for public office. (Pennsylvania's constitution, adopted in 1777, made it one of the few states without property qualifications for voting.) They voiced their feelings in such songs as

Come each true-hearted Whig and each Jolly Mechanic
Who never knew fear or political panic
Come rally your forces and muster your bands
To support the Old Cause with your hearts and your hands.[12]

The artisan clubs represented the workingmen of Philadelphia during the processions held in that city on the adoption of the Constitution in 1788.[13] Here they joined in singing "The Raising: A New SONG for Federal Mechanics," the text of which was printed in the *Pennsylvania Gazette* on February 6 of that year:

By A.B.

Come muster my Lads, your mechanical Tools,
Your Saws and Your Axes, your Hammers and Rules;
Bring your Mallets and Planes, your Level and Line,
And Plenty of Pins of American Pine;
For our Roof we will raise, and our Song still shall be—
A Government firm, and our Citizens free.

Come, up with the *Plates*, lay them firm on the Wall,
Like the People at Large, they're the Ground-work of all,
Examine them well, and see that they're Sound,
Let no rotten Parts in our Building be found;
For our Roof we will raise, and our Song still shall be—
Our Government firm, and our Citizens free.

Now hand up the *Girders*, lay each in his Place,
Between them the *Joists* must divide all the Space,
Like Assembly-men, *these* should lye level along,
Like *Girders*, our Senate prove level and Strong;
For our Roof we will raise, and our Song still shall be—
A Government firm, over citizens free.

The *Rafters* now frame . . . your *King-Posts* and *Braces*,
And drive your Pins home, to keep all in their Places;
Let Wisdom and Strength in the Fabric Combine,
And your Pins be all made of American Pine.
For our Roof we will raise, and our Song still shall be—
A Government firm, and our Citizens free.

Our *King-Posts* are Judges—how upright they stand,
Supporting the *Braces*, the Laws of the Land—
The Laws of the Land, which divide Right from Wrong,
And Strengthen the Weak, by weak'ning the Strong;
For our Roof we will raise, and our Song still shall be—
Laws equal and just, for a People that's free.

Up! Up with the Rafters—each Frame is a State!
How nobly they rise! their Span, too, how great!
From the North to the South, o'er the Whole they extend,
And rest on the Walls, while the Walls they defend!
For our Roof we will raise, and our Song still shall be—
Combine in Strength, yet as Citizens free.

Now enter the *Purlins*, and your Pins through,
And see that your Joints are drawn home, and all true;
The *Purlins* will bind all the Rafters together,
The Strength of the Whole shall defy Wind and Weather;
For our Roof we will raise, and our Song still shall be—
United as States, but as Citizens free.

Come, raise up the Turret, our Glory and Pride—
In the Centre it stands, o'er the Whole to preside;
The Sons of Columbia shall view with Delight
Its Pillars, and Arches, and towering Height;
Our Roof is now rais'd, and our Song still shall be—
A Federal Head, o'er people still free.[14]

[11] Broadside, Historical Society of Pennsylvania.

[12] *Pennsylvania Packet*, Apr. 29, 1786.

[13] At the Grand Federal Procession of July 4, 1788, in Philadelphia, members of eighty-eight trades took part, carrying signs in favor of the Constitution and home industry. The brewers' banner read: "Home brew is best!" (*Columbian Magazine*, III [July, 1788], 400).

[14] When the song was reprinted in an abbreviated

Huzza! my brave Boys, our Work is complete,
The World shall admire *Columbia's* fair Seat;
Its Strength against Tempests and Time shall be Proof.
And Thousands shall come to dwell under our ROOF.
Whilst we drain the deep Bowl, our Toast still shall be—
A Government firm, and our Citizens free.

Although this song was written in behalf of the principles of federalism as opposed to anti-federalism, the vast majority of the artisans in the early years of the Republic supported the political principles of Thomas Jefferson against those of the Federalists. They took a leading part in the formation of the Democratic-Republican Societies which supported the French Revolution and opposed the attempts of Britain, the arch-foe of revolutionary France, to destroy the principles of republicanism emanating from France. The societies viewed with growing hostility the support the Federalist administrations rendered Britain in this endeavor, regarding it as a danger to the future of republicanism and democracy in the United States. The clubs favored popular education in the form of public schools and other democratic advances, but their essential aim was to make the opinion of the people known to the government so that its actions would be truly representative of popular will.

So numerous were the mechanics and workmen in the Democratic-Republican Societies of some cities, it was even suggested that the clubs unite themselves into a Labouring Society. While this did not take place, the societies of artisans cooperated and worked closely with the Democratic-Republican clubs, and the membership and leadership of the two often overlapped. A meeting in New York City on July 4, 1797, to celebrate the independence of the United States and the principles of the American Revolution, was jointly sponsored by the General Society of Mechanics and Tradesmen, the Democratic Society, and the Cooper (barrelmakers) Society. An ode composed for the occasion by Philip Freneau, "the poet of the American Revolution," was sung, "the *Musick* performed by the *Uranian Musical Society*." The ode went:

Once more our annual debt to pay
We meet on this auspicious day,
That shall through every coming age
The feelings of mankind engage;
Red war will soon be chang'd for peace,
All human woe for human bliss,
And nations that embrace again
Enjoy a long pacific reign.

Thou source of every pure delight,
Fair Peace! extend thy sway,
While to thy standard we invite
All nations on this day.

O dire effects of tyrant power,
How have ye darkened every hour,
And bade those years embitter'd flow
That nature meant for bliss below!
With sceptred pride and looks of awe
OPPRESSION gave the world her law;
And Man, that should such laws disdain,
Has bow'd to her malignant reign.

Thou source, &c.

Here, on our quiet native coast
No more we dread the warlike host
That once alarm'd, when Britons rose,
And made COLUMBIA's sons their foes—
Parent of every cruel art
That stains the soul, that steels the heart,
Dire War! with all thy bleeding band
Molest no more this happy land!

But source, &c.

May now all despots disappear
And man to man be less severe—
The ties of love more firmly bind
Than fetters that enchain mankind.—
But VIRTUE must her rights maintain,
Or short, too short, is FREEDOM's reign;
And when her precepts we despise
Tyrants and Kings again will rise.

O VIRTUE! source of pure delight,
Extend thy happy sway, &c.

No more a plundering, pageant race,
Man shall in every clime embrace:
And we, on this secluded shore,
Involv'd in horrid wars no more,
On this returning annual day,
To Heaven our grateful tribute pay,
That here the happy times began
That made mankind the friends of Man.

Thou source, &c.[15]

form in the *Popular National Songster* (Baltimore, 1816), under the title "The House Carpenter," this line was changed to read "A republican head, o'er people that's free."

[15]*Oration Delivered before the General Society of Mechanics and Tradesmen, the Tammany Society, or Columbian Order, the Democratic and New-York Cooper Societies and Other Citizens* (New York, 1797), pp. 21–22 (copy in New York Historical Society).

In an attack on Federalist Mayor Varick of New York City as the special enemy of workingmen, the cartmen sang a satirical ballad in 1796 in which it was made clear that *varick* meant "hog" in Dutch.

THE STRANGE AND WONDERFUL ACCOUNT OF A DUTCH HOG

Who Resides in New-York

COME Nathan, give a Penny Bill,
To NAB or BIJAH Kitchell,
We'll send for 'Lasses half a jill
And make a mug of Switchell;

For business now is at a stand,
And cash—there's no such thing Sir,
So take your comrade by the hand,
We'll drink about and sing Sir.

There is a man lives in our town,
Whose tricks are now in vogue Sir,
And though his name I can't set down
It sounds somewhat like HOG Sir,

And all the Dutch Men great and small
Who live beyond New-York Sir,
Or Pig, or Shoat, or Hog, do call
A Coochey or a V-rck Sir,

He is a Man of courage true,
A Quixatonian Knight Sir,
But as his teeth are rather few,
He'll neither bite nor fight Sir,

For once a certain Colonel White,
With fierce intent to flog Sir,
Did chace around a Waggon quite
This formidable Hog Sir.

He often ssts upon a bench,
Much like unto a Judge Sir,
And makes the wretches bosom wrench
To whom he owes a grudge Sir.

But now he does a great offence,
It is no thing to mock at,
He takes away the Cartmen's pence
And puts them in his pocket.

We all are friends to Liberty,
And he among the rest Sir,
But then he would that ONLY HE,
Should do as he thinks best Sir.

He acts as tho' he fancies POWER
Were made but for his use Sir,
And when it is—in luckless hour,
He'd turn it to abuse Sir.

For once two vulgar Ferrymen
Some thought let freely slip Sir,
But ah! he sent them to a Den,
And made them feel the whip Sir.

This Hog, I vow, it is not fit
That folks so well should feed him,
It would be right that they should let
A CERTAIN Doctor bleed him.

Or send him to his Pen so close,
'Twould be a funny joke Sir.
An iron ring upon his nose,
And on his neck a yoke Sir.[16]

Though most workers could not vote, their part in the presidential campaign of 1800 was crucial. In New York many mechanics and laborers could vote for members of the state assembly, and since the legislature of New York voted for the presidential electors, a victory in New York City for the Republicans would guarantee twelve electoral votes for Jefferson. "In New York," wrote Jefferson to James Madison on March 4, 1800, "all depends on the success of the city election." He went on to point out the significance of this election in the entire national campaign: "If the city election of New York is in favour of the republican ticket, the issue will be republican; if the federal ticket for the city of New York prevails, the probabilities will be in favor of a federal issue, because it would then require a republican vote both from Jersey and Pennsylvania to preponderate against New York, on which we could not count with any confidence."[17]

Victory in New York City depended on the vote of the artisans, mechanics, clerks, journeymen, and laborers. In order to win, the Federalists tried to coerce the workers by telling them to choose between Jefferson and their jobs. "Merchants, your ships will be condemned to rot in your harbours, for the navy which is their protection Jefferson will destroy," the Federalist *New York Daily Advertiser* beseeched. "Cartmen, you may burn your carts, for the merchants will no longer be able to give you employment. The music of the hammer along our wharves and the hum of busy industry will not be heard."[18] To answer this appeal, James Cheetham, hatter and coeditor of the *Republi-*

[16]Broadside, New York State Library, Albany.

[17]Paul L. Ford, ed., *The Writings of Thomas Jefferson* (New York, 1892–97), VII, 433–34.

[18]*New York Daily Advertiser*, Apr. 28, 1800.

THE

Strange and Wonderful

ACCOUNT

OF A

DUTCH HOG.

WHO RESIDES IN NEW-YORK.

COME Nathan, give a Penny Bill,
  To NAB or BIJAH Kitchell,
We'll ſend for 'Laſſes half a jill
  And make a mug of Switchell;

II.

For buſineſs now is at a ſtand,
  And caſh---there's no ſuch thing Sir,
So take your comrade by the hand,
  We'll drink about and ſing Sir.

III.

There is a man lives in our town,
  Whoſe tricks are now in vogue Sir,
And though his name I can't ſet down
  It ſounds ſomewhat like HOG Sir,

IV.

And all the Dutch Men great and ſmall!
  Who live beyond New-York Sir,
Or Pig, or Shcat, or Hog, do call
  A Coochey or a V-rck Sir,

V.

He is a Man of courage true,
  A Quixatonian Knight Sir,
But as his teeth are rather few,
  He'll neither bite nor fight Sir,

VI.

For once a certain Colonel White,
  With fierce intent to flog Sir,
Did chace around a Waggon quite
  This formidable Hog Sir.

VII.

He often ſits upon a bench,
  Much like unto a Judge Sir,
And makes the wretches boſom wrench
  To whom he owes a grudge Sir.

VIII.

But now he does a great offence,
  It is no thing to mock at,
He takes away the Cartmen's pence
  And puts them in his pocket.

IX.

We all are friends to Liberty,
  And he among the reſt Sir,
But then he would that ONLY HE,
  Should do as he thinks beſt Sir.

X.

He acts as tho' he fancies POWER
  Were made but for his uſe Sir,
And when it is—in luckleſs hour,
  He'd turn it to abuſe Sir.

XI.

For once two vulgar Ferrymen
  Some thought let freely ſlip Sir,
But ah! he ſent them to a Den,
  And made them feel the whip Sir.

XII.

This Hog, I vow, it is not fit
  That folks ſo well ſhould feed him,
It would be right that they ſhould let
  A CERTAIN Doctor bleed him.

XIII.

Or ſend him to his Pen ſo cloſe,
  'Twould be a funny joke Sir.
An iron ring upon his noſe,
  And on his neck a yoke Sir.

Courtesy of The New York State Library, Albany

can Watch-Tower, published a song in his paper which reminded workers that since the Jay Treaty negotiated by the Federalists with England, they had suffered a decline in employment which the election of Jefferson and his vice-presidential candidate, Aaron Burr, alone could remedy.

A SONG FOR HATTERS

"A New Song," by J.C.[19]

Before the bad English Treaty,
Which Jay with that nation has made
For work we need make no entreaty
All Jours were employed at their trade.

Philadelphia she then had a hundred
New York she had fifty and more
In the first scarce the half can be numbered
In the last there is hardly a score. . . .

And what has occasion'd this failing,
And caus'd us to fall at this rate
'Tis the English, whose arts are prevailing
With our Great rulers of state. . . .

When shortly in our constitution
A Republican party will sway
Let us all then throw in a petition
Our grievance to do away. . . .

That our party in Congress may now rule
Let each voter for liberty stir
And not be to England a base tool
When Jefferson aids us and Burr.[20]

The mechanics and laborers carried New York City for Jefferson, and the workers celebrated.

A NEW SONG

Rejoice, Columbia's sons rejoice,
And gratefully concur,
In praising your election choice,
Of Jefferson and Burr.

The federal jockies lose the field,
Tho' arm'd with yankey four,
With all their mettle forc'd to yield,
To Jefferson and Burr.

No more of slavery we dread,
To hear that odious slur;
To glorious Independence led,
By Jefferson and Burr.

In vain did feds to ev'ry art,
To ev'ry wile recur,
Our confidence they ne'er could part,
From Jefferson and Burr.

Soon had great titles swell'd the pride
Of many a lordly sir;
Had we not for redress relied,
On Jefferson and Burr.

Each federal cub now hangs his tail,
Like any whining cur,
Griv'd that his snarling can't prevail
'Gainst Jefferson and Burr.

Adams and Pinckney may retire,
We'll ne'er to keep them stir,
We have the men our hearts desire
In Jefferson and Burr.

Should foreign or domestic foe,
Henceforth our wrath incur,
For our defence, we'll let them know,
We've Jefferson and Burr.

Let those who love of freedom boast,
Now all without demur,
Clear off a bumper on my toast,
'Tis Jefferson and Burr.[21]

On many a July 4 during the Federalist administrations of Washington and Adams, the societies of carpenters, printers, cordwainers, coopers, and cabinetmakers had joined officially with the Democratic-Republican Society in the community to drink toasts to "the Fourth of July, may it ever prove a memento to the oppressed to rise and assert their rights."[22] Now that Jefferson was the third president of the United States, these workers' societies had additional reason to celebrate the Fourth of July, and they expressed this in their songs.

SONG

Sung on the 4th of July

Tune—"Jefferson and Liberty"

Fair Independence wakes the song,
Ye sons of Freedom join the lay,

19 James Cheetham.

20 *Republican Watch-Tower*, Feb. 21, 1801. Aaron Burr was the Republican vice-presidential candidate, but because each of the Republican electors in the electoral college voted for both Jefferson and Burr for the presidency, an electoral college tie resulted. Under the Constitution, the choice was to be made by the House of Representatives, and in the thirty-sixth ballot on February 17, 1801, Jefferson was elected president. Before the next election, the Twelfth Amendment to the Constitution, providing for separate balloting for president and vice-president, ruled out the danger that such a situation could arise again.

21 *Ibid.*, Dec. 31, 1800.

22 Eugene P. Link, *Democratic-Republican Societies, 1790–1800* (New York, 1942), p. 151.

The festal melody prolong,
And crown the anniversary day.

Sweet Independence we invoke,
Our voices raise in raptur'd strain,
All hail the day when first we broke
The British Tyrant's galling chain.

Fierce was the contest, long the toil;
Our friends their native fields bestrow,
'Till vict'ry deign'd at length to smile,
And turn'd the flight of the murd'rous foe.

Dear Independence we invok'd,
And shouting millions join'd the strain;
To hail the day when first we broke
The British Tyrant's galling chain.

Bright was the day but short the scene
When Liberty her lustre shed,
E'er Usurpation rear'd within,
Her fair insinuating head.

While Independence was the strain,
To foreign powers we partial bow'd;
Profusion shook the golden reign,
And fell Intollerance chain'd the crowd.

Exult ye patriots of the land,
Columbia's Genius towers once more,
To break each *Liliputian band*
She in her early slumbers wore.

Sweet Independence we invoke,
While Liberty refuses her throne,
And hail with soul-reviving hope,
The aera eighteen hundred one.

Disguise no more shall rule the State,
But Government with Light combine;
Fair Truth shall Confidence create,
And Interest with allegiance join.

True Independence we invoke,
The Independence of the Mind;
And yield Research her ample scope,
Thro' speech and writing unconfin'd.

Kind Peace with sage, impartial sway,
Shall guide our Councils far and nigh;
In frugal hands our Treasures lay,
And herds of Peculators fly.

Sweet Independence we invoke,
While Liberty resumes her throne,
And spurn our sordid fetters, broke
In eighteen hundred one.

Religion, free as air or wind,
Shall Scorn the foul support of Law;
Free Science elevate the mind,
And Virtue's mild allurements draw.

Sweet Independence, lend thy aid,
Our Arts and Tillage to refine;
Free Commerce, self-sustaining spread,
And ev'ry distant region join.

Sages rejoice in dawning hope,
That Ages down the stream of time,
A great millenial morn will ope
On ev'ry shore, on ev'ry clime.

Sweet Independence, thee we praise,
Thy bright career anew begun,
Thy peaceful victories that grace
The glorious eighteen hundred one.[23]

Not even the election of Jefferson, the advocate of the common man, guaranteed a democratic form of government. Hence an anti-Federalist song of 1801, often sung at gatherings of artisans and mechanics, emphasized limited tenure of office.

EVERY MAN HIS OWN POLITICIAN

Let every man of Adam's line
In social contact freely join
To extirpate monarchic power,
That kings may plague the earth no more.

As pow'r results from you alone,
Ne'er trust it on a single throne,
Kings oft betray their sacred trust,
And crush their subjects in the dust.

Nor yet confide in men of show,
Aristocrats reduce you low;
Nobles, at best, are fickle things,
And oft, far worse than cruel kings.

Nobles combine in secret fraud,
(Tho in pretence for public good)
To frame a law the most unjust,
And sink the people down to dust.

When laws are fram'd, the poor must lie,
Distrest beneath the nobles' eye;
Unpity'd there, to waste their breath,
In fruitless prayers 'till free'd by death.

A year is long enough to prove
A servant's wisdom, faith and love,
Release him from temptation then
And change the post to other men.

Now is the prime important hour
The people may improve their pow'r,
To stop aristocratic force,
And walk in reason's peaceful course.[24]

23*Republican Watch-Tower*, July 31, 1802.
24Broadside, American Antiquarian Society.

THE FIRST TRADE UNIONS

The mechanics' and artisans' societies which joined in such songs were no longer simply benevolent associations. Beginning with the 1790s skilled journeymen in several cities converted their mutual aid societies into trade unions that would conduct struggles for higher wages and shorter hours as well as assist members during periods of illness. The first organization of workers in the United States to maintain a permanent union was formed by the Philadelphia shoemakers. In 1791 the Federal Society of Journeymen Cordwainers of Philadelphia organized to protect themselves from scab labor, and this union continued to exist, with various branches, until 1806. In 1799 the society conducted the first strike by a permanent union. (Strikes before this had been spontaneous, and when they ceased, the group calling them went out of existence.) This strike against reduction in wages is also significant because it was the first sympathetic strike on record: the bootmakers turned out to help the shoemakers secure their demands. The society paid all of its members to picket the master shoemakers' shops. The strike lasted for about ten weeks but was lost. However, the twelve years' existence of the cordwainers' society was marked by a number of successful struggles for higher wages. Also noteworthy is the fact that the first trade union song in American labor history was written to recruit members for the Federal Society of Journeymen Cordwainers of Philadelphia.

ADDRESS TO THE JOURNEYMEN CORDWAINERS L. B. OF PHILADELPHIA

By John McIlvaine

Cordwainers! Arouse! The time has now come!
When our rights should be fully protected;
And every attempt to reduce any one
By all should be nobly rejected.

Fellow-Craft-men! Arouse! We united should be
And each man should be hailed as a brother,
Organized we should be in this hallowed cause,
To love and relieve one another.

Speak not of failure, in our attempt to maintain,
For our labor a fair compensation;
All that we want is assistance from you,
To have a permanent organization.

A commencement we've made, associations we have.
From one to thirteen inclusive,
Come join them my friends, and be not afraid,
Of them being in the least delusive.

Go join No. 1, and in it you'll find,
Men of courage and firmness, devoting
Their time and their money, in fact all they have
Your interest and mine they're promoting.

And join No. 2, if you wish to maintain,
For your labor a fair compensation,
You will find them at work for you and for me
Their success has far beat expectation.

If you join No. 3, you will find them aroused,
For much do they dread the oppression
They have been subject to in years gone by,
Go give them a friendly expression.

Join No. 4, defer not a day,
But go and with them unite,
Ah! give them assistance, for you they're at work,
And they'll ten times your trouble requite.

If you join No. 5, you'll find them awake,
Awake to the pledge they have taken:
Their hearts are all true, add yours to them too,
And by them you ne'er shall be forsaken.

Or join No. 6, if you wish to be
Raised from your present condition,
To rank with mechanics in wages and name,
And be able to keep that position.

Nos. 7, 8, and 9, if you with them join,
Your interest they have justly at heart,
Their motives you'll love, and with them you'll move.
And from them you ne'er will depart.

Come join No. 10, if you wish to find,
Men, whose hearts beat with love and devotion,
For the organization, to which they belong,
Come assist them to keep it in motion.

Or cross o'er to Jersey, if you be not afraid,
Of its native disease called the chills,
You will find men united their wages to raise,
On pump springs, welts, turns and heels.

Then join us my friends, and be not afraid,
That we will extort from our employers
Prices that will injure our fair city's trade,
Or frighten away from us buyers.[25]

The last two lines of the song refer to a common argument used by employers in their efforts to deprive workers of the right to combine in trade unions—that by forcing higher wages, the labor organizations would drive busi-

[25]Broadside, Library Company of Philadelphia.

ADDRESS TO THE
JOURNEYMEN CORDWAINERS
L. B. OF PHILADELPHIA.

BY JOHN McILVAINE.

Cordwainers! Arouse! The time has now come!
When our rights should be fully protected;
And every attempt to reduce any one
By all should be nobly rejected.

Fellow-Craft-men! Arouse! We united should be
And each man should be hailed as a brother,
Organized we should be in this hallowed cause,
To love and relieve one another.

Speak not of failure, in our attempt to maintain,
For our labor a fair compensation;
All that we want is assistance from you,
To have a permanent organization.

A commencement we've made, associations we have,
From one to thirteen inclusive,
Come join them my friends, and be not afraid,
Of them being in the least delusive.

Go join No. 1, and in it you'll find,
Men of courage and firmness, devoting
Their time and their money, in fact all they have
Your interest and mine they're promoting.

And join No 2, if you wish to maintain,
For your labor a fair compensation,
You will find them at work for you and for me,
Their success has far beat expectation.

If you join No. 3, you will find them aroused,
For much do they dread the oppression
They have been subject to in years gone by,
Go give them a friendly expression.

Join No. 4, defer not a day,
But go and with them unite,
Ah! give them assistance, for you they're at work,
And they'll ten times your trouble requite.

If you join No 5, you'll find them awake,
Awake to the pledge they have taken:
Their hearts are all true, add yours to them too,
And by them you ne'er shall be forsaken.

Or join No. 6, if you wish to be
Raised from your present condition,
To rank with mechanics in wages and name,
And be able to keep that position.

Nos. 7, 8, and 9, if you with them join,
Your interest they have justly at heart,
Their motives you'll love, and with them you'll move,
And from them you ne'er will depart.

Come join No. 10, if you wish to find,
Men, whose hearts beat with love and devotion,
For the organization, to which they belong,
Come assist them to keep it in motion.

Or cross o'er to Jersey, if you be not afraid,
Of its native disease called the chills,
You will find men united their wages to raise,
On pump springs, welts, turns and heels.

Then join us my friends, and be not afraid,
That we will extort from our employers
Prices that will injure our fair city's trade,
Or frighten away from us buyers.

Printed at Johnson's Cheap Card and Job Printing Office, No. 7 N. TenthSt., Phila

Courtesy of The Library Company of Philadelphia

ness out of the city. This argument was advanced against the Federal Society of Journeymen Cordwainers of Philadelphia in the first court cases in which the right of workers to combine in unions was tested. On November 1, 1805, a Philadelphia grand jury indicted eight of the society's members on charges of combining and of conspiring to raise wages. The indictment was based on the doctrine of conspiracy in English common law—the body of principles and rules of conduct which the courts developed from cases between individuals which were brought to the judges to settle—according to which any two or more men who plotted the harm of a third or of the public could be charged with conspiracy and legally punished.

The trial was of national importance because it became involved in the struggle between the Federalists and the Democrats over the former's control of the judiciary. The workers' resentment at this situation was reflected even before the trial of the cordwainers, in a lengthy song entitled "The Judiciary," the opening and concluding sections of which went:

The guardians of freedom,
Were lately (God speed 'em!)
Thrown into a terrible flutter,—
By numerous losses
And all the sad crosses,
Which Democracy's pupils could muster;
To cover the nation,
Against Innovation,
Each federal grand luminary,
Now boldly came forth,
From the south and the north,
In support of the Judiciary.

....

Such whining, such canting,
Such roaring and ranting,
Must meet with due estimation,
Whilst faction may strive,
To keep discord alive,
We'll trust the good sense of the nation,
May the men of our choice,
(Says the popular voice,)
At their posts be found ever unweary,
From time to time still,
As the people shall will,
New Model the Judiciary.[26]

In the Philadelphia cordwainers' case, the jury handed down a verdict of "guilty of a combination to raise wages," and the eight members of the society were each fined eight dollars. The decision served as a precedent for future verdicts in New York against the tailors and in Baltimore and Pittsburgh against the shoemakers. The workers were found guilty of conspiracy and given light fines. The moderate nature of the fines—a reflection of the influence of Jeffersonian opposition to the verdicts—could not obscure the fact that the employers were successful in hindering the development of the early trade unions, many of which found themselves outlawed by the courts.

That not all of the early unions were outlawed is indicated by the activities of these societies during the War of 1812. The Philadelphia Typographical Society appropriated a day's labor from each of its members to help build fortifications in that city and later voted to assist wives of members who were serving their country. David H. Reins, secretary of the New York Typographical Society, organized a company composed entirely of union printers. Five hundred members of the Journeymen Carpenters' Society worked on the fortifications of Fort Greene in Brooklyn for two weeks without pay, while members of the curriers', plumbers', cabinetmakers', and chairmakers' unions dug trenches to protect the city against an expected British invasion. On August 17, 1812, several hundred union workers from Paterson, New Jersey, came to help with the digging. Some 150 free Negroes joined in the work.

The defense of New York inspired one of the most popular songs of the war:

THE PATRIOTIC DIGGERS

To protect our rights
'Gainst your flints and triggers,
See on Brooklyn Heights
Our patriotic diggers;
Men of every age,
Color, rank, profession,
Ardently engage,
Labor in succession.

Pick-axe, shovel, spade,
Crow-bar, hoe and barrow,
Better not invade,
Yankees have the marrow!

Here the mason builds
Freedom's shrine of glory,

26*Republican Watch-Tower*, May 24, 1802.

While the painter gilds,
 The immortal story
Blacksmiths catch the flame,
 Grocers feel the spirit,
Printers share the fame,
 And record the merit.

Chorus:

Scholars leave their schools,
 With their patriotic teachers,
Farmers seize the tools,
 Headed by the preachers,
How they break the soil,
 Brewers, Butchers, Bakers,
Here the doctors toil,
 There the undertakers.

Chorus:

Plumbers, founders, dyers,
 Tinmen, turners, shavers,
Sweepers, clerks and criers,
 Jewellers, engravers,
Clothiers, drapers, players,
 Cartmen, hatters, tailors,
Gaugers, sealers, weighers,
 Carpenters and sailors!

Chorus:[27]

DEPRESSION OF 1819–22

The unions which survived adverse court decisions, blacklists, and unsuccessful strikes went under during the depression of 1819–22. Unemployment was general; twenty thousand workers in Philadelphia and a like number in New York City were without work. A printer in New York in 1820 recorded: "I had barely two dollars in my pocket when I got here with my family. We lived eight days without tea, sugar, or meat—on bread and butter only with cold water. It is pinching times."[28] The following song depicted the same desperate picture:

A LOAF OF BREAD

Duett. Air—"Robin Ruff"

JOHNNY GREEN:
 If I had but a small loaf of bread, Bobby Buff,
  If I had but a small loaf of bread,
 How happy I'd be, and we'd go and hab tea,
  If I had but a small loaf of bread, Bobby Buff!

BOBBY BUFF:
 I wish, from my soul, dat you had, Johnny Green,
  I wish, from my soul, dat you had;
 And you'd be on de square, and wid me would share,
  If you had but a small loaf of bread, Johnny Green.

Jonny GREEN:
 I scarcely can tell what I'd do, Bobby Buff;
  But I think that it runs in my head,
 I would break it in two, and give one half to you,
  If I had but a small loaf of bread, Bobby Buff.

Bobby BUFF:
 I think you're a brick to do that, Johnny Green;
  I think you're a brick to do that;
 For, if I fall away as I have every day,
  I'm certain I'll never grow fat, Johnny Green.

Johnny GREEN:
 There's a good time in store for us both, Bobby Buff,
  There's a good time in store for us both;
 To Blackwell's Island you know, we both, some day, will go;

Bobby BUFF:
  Then, we'll get our good bread for a year, Johnny Green.[29]

[27] Benjamin J. Lossing, *The Pictorial Field Book of the War of 1812* (New York, 1868), pp. 970–71.

[28] Samuel Rezneck, "The Depression of 1819–1822: A Social History," *American Historical Review*, XXXIX (Oct., 1933), 30–32.

[29] Broadside, Library Company of Philadelphia.

480

A LOAF OF BREAD.

DUETT. Air : ROBIN RUFF.

JOHNNY GREEN :
If I had but a small loaf of bread, Bobby Buff,
If I had but a small loaf of bread,
How happy I'd be, and we'd go and hab tea,
If I had but a small loaf of bread, Bobby Buff !

BOBBY BUFF :
I wish, from my soul, dat you had, Johnny Green,
I wish, from my soul, dat you had ;
And you'd be on de square, and wid me would share,
If you had but a small loaf of bread, Johnny Green.

JONNY GREEN :
I scarcely can tell what I'd do, Bobby Buff ;
But I think that it runs in my head,
I would break it in two, and give one half to you,
If I had but a small loaf of bread, Bobby Buff.

BOBBY BUFF :
I think you're a brick to do that, Johnny Green ;
I think you're a brick to do that ;
For, if I fall away as I have every day,
I'm certain I'll never grow fat, Johnny Green.

JOHNNY GREEN :
There's a good time in store for us both, Bobby Buff,
There's a good time in store for us both ;
To Blackwell's Island you know, we both,
some day, will go ;

BOBBY BUFF :
Then, we'll get our good bread for a year,
Johnny Green.

H. DE MARSAN, Publisher.
Songs, Ballads, toy books, paper dolls, small
playing cards, motto verses, &c.
38 & 60 Chatham St. N. Y.

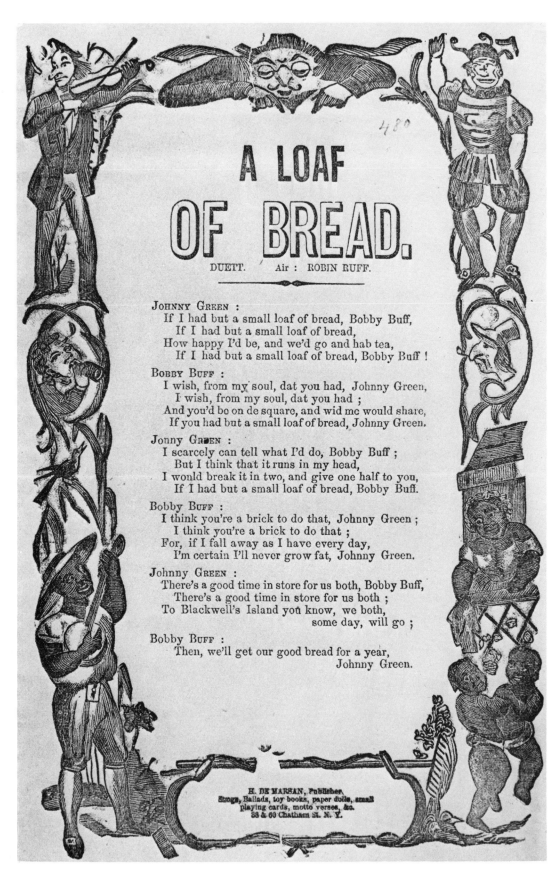

Courtesy of The Library Company of Philadelphia

2

The Era of Jacksonian Democracy 1823–40

REVIVAL OF TRADE UNIONISM

As early as 1823 signs of labor's awakening made themselves evident. In March, the printers of New Orleans formed a union, and soon workers in various trades in New York, Philadelphia, Baltimore, Charleston, Wilmington, and other cities were organizing, presenting their demands for increased wages and shorter hours, and threatening to strike if their terms were not met. In the spring of 1827 the Philadelphia carpenters struck for a ten-hour day. They were weary of working from sunup to sundown, which in the spring, summer, and early fall meant a sixteen-hour day. The strike was inspired in part by an anonymous pamphlet calling upon the workers to fight for sufficient leisure to attain the knowledge necessary to put the achievement of universal manhood suffrage to use. It specifically recommended a free press, libraries, reading rooms, and forums for workers. One result of this pamphlet was the formation in 1827 of the Mechanics' Library Company in Philadelphia, which published the weekly *Mechanics' Free Press*. It described itself as "a journal of practical and useful knowledge." This was the first labor paper in America of which there are any issues now in existence. It was soon followed by the organization in the same city and the same year of the Mechanics' Union of Trade Associations, the first city-wide federation of American workers. Its formation is considered by most labor historians as the emergence of the modern American labor movement.

Between 1833 and 1836, city centrals consisting of delegates from various craft unions were founded in many localities throughout the United States. By the end of the latter year, at least thirteen city centrals were in existence. They gave member unions financial aid during strikes, sometimes using the boycott, and even helped strikers in other cities.

Five trades—cordwainers, printers, combmakers, carpenters, and handloom weavers—set up national organizations between 1835 and 1836. In August, 1835, the first national labor federation came into being when delegates from city central unions of Boston, Philadelphia, Newark, and New York formed the National Trades' Unions.

FIRST LABOR PARTIES AND LABOR PRESS

Not only did workers during this period organize trade unions, city centrals, and a national labor federation—not only did they conduct and win militant strikes for higher wages and shorter hours (including the first general strike in American history, a successful strike in Philadelphia in 1835 for the ten-hour day)—but they also organized their own political parties. In 1829, a year after the Mechanics' Union of Trade Associations was formed in Philadelphia, the same city saw the appearance of the Working Men's party of Philadelphia, the first labor party in the United States. This movement spread westward to Pittsburgh, Lancaster, Carlisle, Harrisburg, Cincinnati, and other cities in Pennsylvania and Ohio. It went south to Wilmington, Delaware, and north to New York City, Newark, Trenton, Albany, Buffalo, Syracuse, Troy, Utica, Boston, Providence, Portland (Maine), and Burlington

(Vermont). All told, independent workers' political parties were organized in sixty-one cities and towns during the years 1828–34, and in communities where no independent parties were formed this movement stimulated the growth of mechanics' clubs which advocated legislation for the benefit of wage earners.

Along with the rise of trade unions and the workers' parties came the formation of labor papers. Almost fifty labor weeklies were published in those cities and towns during the years 1827–32. In the period from 1833 to 1836 still other labor papers were launched. Some city centrals started their own papers, and in 1835, the *National Laborer* was launched in Philadelphia by the National Society for the Diffusion of Useful Knowledge, to serve as a national labor organ. The following poem in the *National Trades' Union* of January 1, 1836, makes clear how much importance was attached to a strong press. The paper extended this spirited advice in its New Year's greetings to its patrons.

First then, *Mechanics*, you who labour hard,
Your free-born rights with watchful eye regard;
Let vain cabals your int'rests ne'er divide,
Act with Precaution, and with Truth decide.
Monopoly its brazen front still rears,
And seems yet stronger with advancing years;
A stubborn "Monster" which you *must* subdue,
Yours is the work to fight it hard and true;
No *"force of arms"* the contest will require,
Your safest bulwark is your *mental* fire.
Let not lukewarmness,—selfishness prevail,—
Nor petty strifes the general weal assail;
If for your wrongs you would obtain redress,
With heart and hand support an *honest Press.*
Mighty its influence, and supreme its pow'r,
Falsehood and Av'rice must before it cow'r;
Truth for its motto, Justice for its end,
Revere the *Press*, it is the *Poor Man's Friend.*
Your Leisure Hours to Wisdom dedicate,
For knowledge only can improve your state;
Men without mind are moulded into slaves,
And know no *rest* till shelter'd in their graves.
Should not Mechanics estimate their scale,
Despite the gibes and nonsense that prevail?
Who rear'd those palaces, the city's pride?
The very men that Folly's train deride.

Copies of most of these labor papers have disappeared,[1] but fairly complete files exist of the *Mechanics' Free Press* and the *National Laborer*, both published in Philadelphia, and the *Working Man's Advocate* and the *Man*, both published in New York City by printer and labor reformer George Henry Evans. In the four weekly pages of these papers, in a type often so small as to arouse wonder how they could actually be read, were texts of resolutions, reprints of articles and editorials from other labor papers, letters from mechanics, and a wide variety of material popularizing "working men's measures." These measures—denounced in conservative circles as "workeyism"—were the demands of the labor parties: establishment of a system of public education for the children of the poor as well as the rich; abolition of the compulsory militia system; abolition of imprisonment for debt; passage of mechanics' lien laws which would assure mechanics that they would get paid for their labor when their work was done; abolition of chartered monopolies, including the banking monopoly; elimination of convict labor competition; a more equitable system of taxation; and greater democracy in governmental machinery.

The "working men's measures" were advanced in the labor press by many types of educational material. A frequent medium was that of songs and ballads. Indeed, it is with the establishment of the first labor papers that labor songs made their appearance in large numbers, most of them written specifically for the labor press. A number of these songs reflected an early class consciousness.

SONG

By Minus

Apprentices and Journeymen,
Mechanics bond and free,
And all who dig the earth to live,
Come list a while to me:
My song will not detain you long,
So do not be alarmed,
And when you've read it to the end
You'll find yourselves unharm'd.—
I guess there are in these states
A million men or so,
Who swords and muskets too can use
If called upon to show
If foreign foes invade our shores
We'll fight—and fight for what?

[1] The circulation of these early labor papers was not recorded, though it is probable that each was only a few hundred. The *New York Courier and Enquirer*, with the largest circulation in the country, claimed 4,500 in 1833.

No wealth have we to save or lose,—
Ourselves are all we've got.
We'll fight for freedom and those rights
Which once our fathers gained,—
And while a freeman's heart shall beat,
Those rights shall be retained:
Yes, if across the treacherous main
A foe should find his way,
Columbian steel shall make him dear
For his adventure pay.
But Uncle Sam I guess can count
Some three-score ships of war,
And manned with men as brave as live
Beneath the solar star:
No ships of equal guns and men
That ride upon the main,
If with Columbia's barks they meet
A victory can gain.
By Britons this will be confessed,
And they should surely know,
For they have fought in many a clime,—
With every kind of foe.
They fought the Frenchman and the Dane,
The Spaniard and the Swede,
And many a gallant foe they found
But yet they did succeed;
But when they fought the foe that 'neath
Columbia's banner sailed,
'Twas then that British valor owned
An equal had been hailed
Then we have ships to guard the door,
And men to fight within;
And brave commanders living yet,
That in the wars have been,—
But while the stately oak defies
The tempest's fiercest blast,
Where'er a government is found
This truth will there endure;
Two classes are by all confess'd
The wealthy and the poor.
And here another truth I'll name
Before I further go:
The poor could live without the rich
As every man may know;
But none that labour for their bread,
Could by the rich be spared,
For 'tis to them they owe their wealth
As oft it's been declared,
But let the great ones of the land
Enjoy what wealth can give,
We envy not their luxuries
But wish all men to live.—
A truth it is both clear and plain
Which every one may know,
That always in the richest soil,
The rankest weeds do grow:
And thus it is in every land
Where most of labour's found,—
'Tis there that proud dictators rise
Like weeds in favouring ground,—
While every rising sun may see
Our daily work begun,
It is not every sun that sets
That sees our labour done,
Then we'll be careful while we toil
So look to the proceeds,
Nor be like others duped, nor let
Our labour nourish weeds.
This is a maxim we hold true,
Nor is it a vain conceit:
"The soil that's good enough for weeds
Is good enough for wheat."[2]

A NEW SONG

By J.

But if chang'd in demeanor we look for the brave,
'Mongst the poor rabble what is there to save,
This proud fallen country from ruin and shame,
They believed that divine right is only a name
But we the high born still look with surprise
At the fellows who tell such rascally lies;
They say that the *people*, the *vile herd*, the *crowd*,
Like ourselves have a right to bellow out loud;
And make their voice heard in the land of peace,
Let our children have learning, our comforts increase.
We have worked till we are tired, we now want some rest!
Let honest industry once on earth be blest;
And try if in fifty years from this time,
Mankind, will not say our cause was sublime.[3]

The New York General Trades' Union had its official organ, the *Union*, a daily newspaper, which was launched to answer the charges that trade unions advocated "acts of riot and violence," that the "leading members of trades' unions are foreigners," and that "personal aggrandizement is the main object of all the leaders—laziness and ease being characteristic of their whole lives."[4] The following songs appeared in the paper:

AN ORIGINAL SONG

In favor of

"TRADES' UNION,"

And unanimity in its supporters

Behold the "Trades' Union," a God on our side,
It buoys up our heart to be strong in the cause,

[2]*Mechanics' Free Press*, Dec. 5, 1829.

[3]Ibid., Nov. 13, 1830.

[4]Statements by the *Union*, reprinted in *National Laborer*, Apr. 9 and 30, 1836.

Shall we then *fail* our homes to provide?
Too long have we failed by oppressors' curst laws.
Awake to your rights, all ye "Scabs" of the last,
Knock off your shackles, and swear you'll be free;
Oppression's expiring, and soon will be past,
Employers must GIVE IN, for *never* shall we.

Ye mule-hearted screwers, unfeeling, purse-proud,
Are our ribs and our offspring less dear than your own?
Why then withhold what our wants claim aloud;
But your days, ye usurpers, will shortly be gone,
Awake to your rights, &c.

Days of *two-and-sixpence* that made our hearts bleed,
That robb'd us of comforts, we think of with pain;
'Tis firmness of "*Union*" that made you recede,
Nor shall av'rice or meanness recall you again.
Awake to your rights, &c.

There's an *empty subtile* one on the east side,
Who laughs at our wants, and "Trades' Union" defies,
Be *firm* my dear brothers, we'll pull down his pride,
His heart is as *black* as you'll find both his eyes.
Awake to your rights, &c.

A *father* and *son* and a vast many more,
Whose wealth has *increased* by the *rights* of the craft,
Are showing their meanness in keeping us poor,
But can't make us *knuckle*, we're not quite so *'saft,'*
Awake to your rights, &c.

Hail to the public, no murmurs we hear,
They scorn to close in with a savage's dream,
They know what we ask is but just and fair,
And reflects on the "bosses" dishonor and shame,
Awake to your rights, &c.

All hail to those "bosses" who first broke the ice,
They merit our praise and a flourishing trade,
And whilst the loaf's passing, are sure of a slice,
Of the sordid and haughty may they "go a-head,"
Awake to your rights, &c.

Then let unanimity bind us together,
As close as the hickory the forests sustain,
The storms of oppression we'll finally weather,
Be cheered by our labor, and blessed with our gain,
Awake to your rights, &c.[5]

FOR "THE UNION"

By Labor

Is there a heart that cannot sigh
For kindly feeling hearts distress'd?
Is there an eye that cannot weep
For toiling poverty oppress'd?—

Then curse the wretch—nor let him live,
Who bears that heart of mockery;
That tearless eye pluck out and give
To eagles' rav'nous progeny.

Ye spirits of our fathers dead!
From your high, blest abodes behold
Your last bequest extinguish'd—fled—
Your sons on slavery's lists enroll'd!

Shall chains and slavery prevail?
Or will you ward the impending blow?
Rise, fellow-men!—the host assail,
And crush the tyrant—crush the foe!

Stern justice bids you take the field;
Gird, gird the trusty armor on;
And mercy dictates, "never yield;
"Soon shall your glories be re-won."

Let mountain cliffs in thunder fall,
Let hell in fiercest battle rage;
Toilers! we call you—one and all—
In solemn conflict to engage.

Strike the loud drum—the trumpet's clang—
The tocsin sound from shore to shore,
'Till all shall hear the joyful twang,
And tyranny be found no more.

The *ballot-box* your weapon be;
Lose not a man his suff'rage there;
Your standard, bearing "LIBERTY,"
Raise high above your heads in air.

So shall your cause triumphant rise
Above the hopes of tyrant knave,
And working men at once despise
Alike the tyrant and the slave.

But UNION must your ranks pervade;
Without it, all your marshall'd band,
The sacred cause will but degrade,
And be but as "a rope of sand."[6]

Since the American Revolution was constantly in the minds of workers, it is not surprising that these labor songs celebrated the Fourth of July and the men who had led the struggle for independence. Thomas Paine occupied a special place among workingmen, particularly because of the constant attacks on his memory by the conservative press. A mechanic, in a letter to the *Working Man's Advocate* of February 6, 1830, wrote of the "shame it is to Americans, that they have never done that justice to his memory which he is so justly entitled to," and the labor paper published a number of songs which sought to remedy this situation.

[5] *Union*, May 24, 1836.
[6] Ibid., June 28, 1836.

ODE FOR THE FOURTH OF JULY

By Timothy

Come, rejoice and be gay,
On this glorious day,
And remember our father's decree;
When at Liberty's fame,
They kindled a flame,
And resolv'd that their sons should be free.

Let each musical voice,
In full chorus rejoice,
And join on this Jubilee Day—
We'll pledge them again,
And resolve to maintain
Our birthright which is—to live free.

Bring the tymbral and lyre,
Let's rekindle the fire,
That its blaze may all regions illume;
Let the trumpet of fame
Proclaim it again,
What these patriot sages have done.[7]

A SONG WRITTEN FOR THE FOURTH OF JULY 1828

Addressed to the Working Classes

By Yankee

When Freedom wav'd her signal high,
O'er this fav'rite chosen land—
"To arms! to arms!" was heard the cry
Throughout the faithful fearless band.

With patriotic fire they burn'd,
And 'rous'd to flame by freedom's breath,
They on their country's tyrants turn'd,
Resolved on *"Liberty or Death."*

Each heart was join'd to aid the cause
Of liberty and sacred right;
To give Columbia equal laws,
No longer yield to foreign might.

The God of justice view'd the strife,
And lent a force of freemen's blows;
While they, despising slavish life,
Rush'd fearless on their vet'ran foes.

They fought, they conquer'd, and then gain'd
Sweet liberty and high renown;
And shall their sons e'en now be chain'd,
And tremble at th' oppressor's frown!

Awake! ye humble men who toil,
Remember what our sires have done;
Remember this is freedom's soil—
Our fathers have the blessing won.

Shall we then bow to haughty pride,
Built on the labour of our hands!
Or shall we for ourselves provide,
And proudly spurn unjust demands!

The bright example of our sires,
Is still before our mental eyes;
Then may we feel those sacred fires,
Which bid them on their tyrants rise.

Freedom is ours—and shall we yield
To haughty speculator's claims!
Dare we not enter freedom's field?
Shall we still wear these humbling chains?

Come, let us rise in wisdom's might,
And firm united in the cause,
We'll boldly claim our sacred right,
Nor longer stand in doubtful pause.[8]

THE WORKING MEN

Here comes another song,
But the verses are not long,
Though I'll promise not to tax my friends with less than ten,
And I'm certain each mechanic
Will not be in a panic,
When I tell him that my song's about the Working Men.

First, Mechanics, one and all,
Think of him who built this Hall,
Which the voice of "seventy-six" has made resound again,
Who, ere Liberty had smil'd,
Made this Cradle for the child,
So we'll class him as a master, 'mongst the Working Men.

With courage and communion,
Let us rally round the Union;
As chickens seek the pinion of their parent hen;
To break, we should be shamed,
The bond our fathers framed,
When the "Declaration" issued from such Working Men.

When George brought in a bill
For claims on Bunker Hill,
Then Boston cross'd it out with a sharp steel pen,
And soon the job was done,
By Fayette and Washington,
For no work shop ever paralleled such Working Men.

But the King it is well known,
Who fills the British throne,
Was once a jolly sailor, with Tom, Jack and Ben,
At his skill we can't be scoffin,
For he sail'd with our Coffin,
And William was true blue among the Working Men.

When the French tri-color'd flag,

[7] *Mechanics' Free Press,* July 5, 1828.
[8] Ibid., July 5, 1828.

Made the tablecloth a rag;
A chance there was of Charley's changing color then,
"Tho' his King-ship's a first rate,
We will fight for freedom's freight,
And the Charter or the church-yard," cried the Working Men.

An excresence then grew great,
For the Church soon turned the State;
Preserve our body politic from such a wen;
If bigotry invents
Such scourging *implements*,
We'll not be made its *tools*, said the Working Men.

And as to *Don Miguel*,
They'll soon give him his gruel,
And victims sink no more within a despot's den;
'Gainst Ferdinand they'll rise,
And all his *Spanish flies*,
That have made so many blisters on the Working Men.

At home, we'll clap a claw
On the Jack o'lantern law,
That leads the honest debtor to a stagnant fen;
If for number *one* we strive,
Then good bye to number *five*,
"We'll not be so *re-warded*," says the Working Men.

Then we've vigilant committees,
Who perambulate our cities,
And who overlook a peacock, yet will shoot a wren,
And all their aim and end,
Is just to recommend
All work and no *play* to the Working Men.

I'm sure that there is no man,
That loves not lovely woman,
Whether dwelling in the city or mountain glen,
There's no one can forget her,
So I think we can't do better,
Than to toast the Wives and Sweet-hearts of the Working Men.

Now to this Association,
Make a generous libation,
And may our social compact be cemented when,
The wages of the good,
Shall be paid the brotherhood;
And life's labor shall be over with the Working Men.[9]

SONG

Written for the celebration of the
Birthday of Thomas Paine
By George R. McFarland
Air—"The Sun Flower"

Oh! believe not the slanders invention has framed
'Gainst the patriot honest and true,
But with highest respect let him ever be named,
And give honor where honor is due.
For 'twas he nerved the sense of our patriot sires
'Gainst oppression their rights to maintain,
And when freedom's brave sons lit her bright beacon fires
They were cheer'd by the counsels of PAINE.

When rebellion's foul stigma o'er shadowed the land,
And stain'd[10] every patriot name—
Ere America's chosen illustrious band
Independence had dared to proclaim—
Then his famed Common Sense, like a light from on high,
Illumin'd the darkness again,
And the thoughts of each freeman responded with joy,
To the words and the wisdom of PAINE.

Maintaining man's rights with vigorous mind,
Which tyrants essay'd to o'er throw.
The crowned oppressors together combin'd,
The friend of his race to lay low.
But, favor'd by fortune, he 'scaped from their toils,
To expose their deceptions again,
Freedom's fond hopes reviv'd when she saw her foes foil'd,
And rejoic'd in the safety of PAINE.

The idol of Priestcraft he next did assail,
And brought Reason's artillery to bear,
But the cry for "*revenge*" went abroad on the gale,
And her worshippers, rous'd by their fear,
From all points of the compass determin'd they ran,
Their vile object determin'd to gain.
To quench the fond hopes of regenerate man,
By crushing his champion, PAINE.

Say, shall we who reap all the rich fruits of his toils,
Join the foemen, his worth to deny?
Shall we wield his rich fame, as the conqueror's spoils,
And to rescue him basely deny?
No! while Freedom shall swell an American breast,
Or throb through a patriot's veins,
We will yield him a place with the honest and best,
And hallow the Birthday of PAINE.[11]

SONG

By Silas E. Steele
Air—"The Soldier's Dream"

When Science and Freedom, oppressed and amazed,
Lay 'neath the dark thralldom of proud tyranny,
Fair Nature revolted as on them she gazed,
And called forth a champion to bid them be *free*.

Then bless'd be the day!—ever may its return
See freemen thus joyfully hallow the hour

9Ibid., Oct. 16, 1830.
10The word is illegible; *stain'd* is my guess.
11*Working Man's Advocate*, Mar. 2, 1833.

When PAINE, the bold champion of freedom was born,
To crush superstition[12] and tyranny's power.

Like heaven's bright fire, in danger's dark hour,
From him burst the sage and the patriot flame
And the tyrants he robbed of their much abus'd power,
In vain may endeavor to tarnish his fame.

For e'er a heart beats to Liberty true,
Still bright as his virtues that honor shall be,
When Reason's keen arrow for Freedom he drew,
And planned the great course for the mind to be *free.*

He is gone! But each hour with joy we behold
For wisdom shine forth in the path which he trod;
And Reason's bright scroll, which his wisdom unroll'd
Still arm every heart against tyranny's rod.

Then brothers, rejoice! The bright hour is near
When dark superstition from earth shall be hurl'd
When heaven born Reason her altars shall rear
And the bright sun of truth shall illumine the world.[13]

The Working Men's party was honored in songs which urged mechanics and laborers to go to the polls and elect labor candidates. One song, in the form of an aristocrat's lament, indicated what would follow a victory for the labor party.

ARISTOCRATS' ELECTION SONG

Adapted to the air of "Go to the Devil and Shake Yourself"

By a Workey

Come, come to the polls, ye Aristocrats, Federals.
Nabobs, or Monarchists, no matter what,
Let's punish this fall, the vile Democrats, "levellers,"
"Ragged shirt Mobocrats, impudent State
Indolent epicures,
Holders of sinecures."

All those whom wealth allures, grasp at the prize!
If the Working Men's party,
My silk-stocking hearties,
Prevails at the polls, aristocracy dies!
Rejected from office, what then would become of us!
Gloomy and sad all our prospects would be,
If the "WORKIES" should give us, despite all our artifice,
A Pharoah-like duck in oblivion's dark sea,
It will then be too late
For nabobs to peculate.

Plunder and depradation ruin and rule;
Wealthy aristocrats
DOWN WITH MOBOCRATS,
Lies be our refuge and slander our tool.
On, on! and cry faction! disorder! distraction!
Cry "Mongrel," and "Ragged-shirt," "Workies," "base born";
With voice of detraction deride their extraction,
Cry "Poverty," "Poor-house," and treat them with scorn,
We'll ride then triumphant,
And each proud incumbent,
In office recumbent, (whom nought can abash)
May loll at his ease,
And do just as he please—
His polar-star INTEREST, *alias* CASH.[14]

Since the demand for public education was common to all of the Working Men's parties, it is not surprising that it should find expression in song.

HUZZA! HUZZA! FOREVER FOR THE LAND OF COAL MINES!

By Obed

Only look at her magnanimous School bill, one hundred thousand dolls. to be distributed, (when they can raise it,) among four hundred thousand children; or at twenty-five cents per annum for each scholar! Noble munificence!!!

Out upon you Pennsylvania
Lubber-land of sour-krout!
Long the world has call'd you zany,
Now you've proved it out and out.

Boast of all your roads and bridges,
Of your rail-ways and canals;
Of your fertile fields and hedges,
And your mountains full of coals.

But the road of education,
Is the way to honest fame,
This will elevate the nation,
And immortalize its name.

Surely Nature has been lavish,
To the noble State of Penn;
But her senators are knavish
To her honest working men.

Lawns may bloom, and cities flourish,
And your ships invade the sea;

12The reference is to Paine's *Age of Reason,* which attacked organized religion and became the bible of the Deists.

13*Working Man's Advocate,* Mar. 2, 1833.

14*Newark Chronicle,* reprinted in *Mechanics' Free Press,* Nov. 6, 1830.

Schools alone, the mind* can nourish,
That will save your liberty.[15]

*Public Mind.

While the Working Men's parties elected candidates, some of them, once in office, quickly forgot to press for the "working men's measures."

THE DEMAGOGUE'S SONG
For *Freedom*
"Doth Job serve God for nought?"

For freedom I'll bawl, and for freedom I'll write,
For freedom I'll swear, and for freedom I'll fight;
There's none that loves freedom so well as myself.
I love it (aside) for the sake of the *pelf.*

To the people I'll bow, to the people I'll kneel,
There's nought I regard like the pure public weal;
The will of the people I'll ever obey,
When that will—as it should—comes loaded with *pay.*

The tyrants I'll pull from their places on high,
Down, down with the tyrants! I'll shout and I'll cry;
From the poor people's shoulders I'll bid them begone,
And pull others off—so that I may get on.

Rotation in office! I'll shout and I'll bawl,
Rotation in office! through Senate and Hall,
Rotation in office! I'll constantly din,
Till I get others out—and get myself in.

The levelling doctrines I'll preach and I'll sing,
The levelling doctrines around me I'll fling;
Till the great ones are down, then, mark me I'll stop,
For when they're below me—Then I'll be *atop.*

But let me behold that all-glorious hour,
When I shall be lifted to places and to power,
Not a word about freedom more will I say—
A truce to the matter for once and for aye.

The ins and the outs are different quite,
The out, when he's in, has become a new wight;
Though once he did nothing but bawl, sing and shout,
The in can't remember the words of the *out.*[16]

The fact that some candidates of the Working Men's parties betrayed their trust is not surprising. Of the 100 candidates nominated by the Philadelphia Working Men's party, only ten were workingmen, while fifty-three were merchants or manufacturers. The situation was the same or even worse in the case of Working Men's parties outside of Philadelphia. This does not mean, however, that these parties did not represent workingmen or champion their causes. In its issue of September 12, 1829, the *Mechanics' Free Press* discussed the question of who was or was not a workman. In defining a workingman as "one engaged in productive labor," it implied clearly that employers, too, were included in the definition. Similarly, when a mechanic inquired in the April 3, 1830, issue of the *Working Man's Advocate* what a workingman was and what should be the attitude of a mechanic to non-mechanics or to former mechanics, George Henry Evans replied editorially that all useful workers, including farmers, were acceptable in the Working Men's party; that grocers, druggists, retail clerks, and general shipping merchants did useful work; that those who followed useless occupations included lawyers, brokers, and bankers "under the present banking system." When Thomas Skidmore, proponent of a program of dividing the landed estates, tried to draw the line somewhat vaguely between rich and poor, Evans insisted that it should be drawn "between the useful and the useless classes," for a man might have saved even $500 and still be useful and eligible for the Working Men's party.[17]

These statements were set forth, it must be remembered, at a time when an employer was often a master workman employing journeyman workmen and apprentices. At any rate, even though the Working Men's parties were not all they appeared to be, and even though they were all short-lived, they forced the older, established parties to incorporate into their programs demands of concern to working people. The abolition of imprisonment for debt, the enactment of mechanics' lien laws, the abolition of the compulsory militia, the adoption of more democratic methods for nominating candidates for office, and most important of all, the establishment of our public school system, free from the taint of charity—all this was achieved by the activities of an aroused and insistent wage-earning class armed with the ballot. Some credit, too, must be bestowed upon the composers of the labor songs, often anonymous, who contributed their talent to these activities.

15*Mechanics' Free Press,* Apr. 16, 1831.

16Ibid., Mar. 19, 1831.

17*Working Man's Advocate,* Apr. 24, 1830.

LABOR AND JACKSONIAN DEMOCRACY

The rebirth of trade unionism after the economic crisis of 1819–22 and the emergence of the first labor parties coincided with the rise of Jacksonian Democracy. The question of whether labor did or did not support Andrew Jackson has been one of the most disputed issues of early American labor history and is still a subject of controversy.[18] It is clear today that in some cities workers generally supported anti-Jackson candidates on a national level while supporting the principles of Jacksonian Democracy in local elections; in other cities, they were anti-Jackson in both local and national elections; and in still others, they supported Jackson and his party on both national and local levels. But when labor's attitude was expressed in song, there seems to have been only one point of view expressed, and that was pro-Jackson. In the contest between Jackson and South Carolina over nullification of the tariff of 1829, labor's support of Jackson was clear.

NULLIFICATION—A SONG
By Minus

Have ye heard of the nullification,
That makes such a fuss in the nation;
  The men of the South
  All declare with one mouth,
"Blood and thunder and nullification!"

Concerning the nullification
There's twenty-four states in the nation;
  And says Uncle Sam,
  "You're the same as I am,"
So pay for the support of the nation.

These lads for the nullification,
They're but half a state of the nation,
  All the rest gave their mite,
  And they thought it was right,
And all for the good of the nation.

Uproarious nullification!
It never will do for this nation;
  All black, white, or blue,
  Will most surely eschew
The rascally nullification.

Why surely this nullification
Would give ev'ry man in the nation,
  A round gun and dirk
  To cut throats like a Turk,
And fight about nullification.[19]

When Jackson ran for reelection in 1832, many workers were cool to him, feeling that he had so far shown no particular concern for labor. But when he vetoed the bill to recharter the Bank of the United States on July 10, 1832, he became the champion of American workers. Bray Hammond may argue, as he does in *Banks and Politics in America from the Revolution to the Civil War*, that workingmen were often influenced to oppose chartering new banks by political agents of existing banks who wished to avoid competition.[20] Other scholars have emphasized that labor opposition to rechartering the Bank of the United States was manipulated by agents for state banks. Nevertheless, the plain fact is that in the eyes of many workers, the bank represented an "oppressive monopoly," and Nicholas Biddle, its president, was regarded as a danger to American democracy. He was referred to in the labor press as "Emperor Biddle," "King Biddle," and "Autocrat Nicholas the First," and political supporters of the bank in Congress like Daniel Webster, Henry Clay, John C. Calhoun, and John Quincy Adams were labelled "King Biddle's Henchmen" and were condemned for betraying the principles of the American Revolution.

Anti-bank feeling in labor circles reached a climax in 1834 after the removal of the govern-

18For support of the thesis that the eastern laboring class formed one of the major components of Jacksonian Democracy and furnished many local leaders of that movement, see John R. Commons et al., *History of Labour in the United States*, 4 vols., (New York, 1918), I, 180–81, 459–62; and Arthur M. Schlesinger, Jr., *The Age of Jackson* (Boston, 1945), pp. 143, 205–13, 306–7, 344. For the controversy over this thesis, see William A. Sullivan, "Did Labor Support Andrew Jackson?" *Political Science Quarterly*, LXII (Dec., 1947), 569–80; Edward Pessen, "Did Labor Support Jackson?: The Boston Story," ibid., LXIV (June, 1949), 262–74; Robert T. Bower, "Note on 'Did Labor Support Jackson?: The Boston Story,' " ibid., LXV (Sept., 1950), 441–44; and Walter Huggins, *Jacksonian Democracy and the Working Class* (Stanford, 1960). The difficulty of reaching a clear conclusion is illustrated in the case of the Boston story. Edward Pessen, after examining election returns in Boston during the Jacksonian era, concludes that workingmen generally voted Whig rather than Democratic and that they either rejected or ignored so-called workingmen's candidates. But Robert T. Bower, working from the same sources, concludes that "Jackson and his political allies *did* get their support from working-class groups," and so did the workingmen's candidates (p. 444).

19*Mechanics' Free Press*, Nov. 13, 1830.

20Bray Hammond, *Banks and Politics in America from the Revolution to the Civil War* (Princeton, N.J., 1957), pp. 234–36.

ment deposits from the United States bank and the spell of hard times which followed. Workers believed that the economic crisis and mounting unemployment were engineered by Biddle and his supporters in an effort to force Jackson to surrender to the bank. When pro-bank employers resorted to economic intimidation, slashed wages, and discharged workers who refused to sign petitions demanding an end to Jackson's anti-bank policy, the trade unions rallied to the president's side and voiced their bitterness in song over the power of financial institutions and their allies to create hard times.

HARD TIMES

What's this dull town to me?
No cash is here!
Things that we us'd to see,
Now don't appear.
Where's all the *Plattsburgh* bills?
Silver dollars, cents and mills?
Oh! we must check our wills,
No cash is here.

What made the city shine?
Money was here.
What makes the lads repine?
No cash is here.
What makes the farmers sad,
Factors crazy, merchants mad?
Oh! times are very bad—
No cash is here.

Oh—curse upon the banks!
No credit's there.
They issue naught but blanks—
No cash is there.
Hard times! the men do cry,
Hard times! the women sigh,
Ruin and misery—
No cash is here.[21]

The struggle over the bank, which dominated the labor scene in 1834, produced the largest group of labor songs on a single issue up to that point in American history. Most of them appeared in two New York labor papers edited by George Henry Evans (the *Working Man's Advocate* and the *Man*), but they were reprinted in the labor press throughout the country and assumed national significance. Indeed, even the election for mayor in New York City in the spring of 1834, with which several of the songs dealt, was of national importance. This was the first popular election for mayor in the city, and the main issue in the campaign was the Bank of the United States, with Lawrence, the Democratic candidate, supporting Jackson, and Verplanck, the Whig candidate, supporting Biddle and the bank.[22] A victory for the Whigs would have represented a serious setback for Jackson. But the workers cast their votes for the Democratic candidate, and Lawrence became the first popularly elected mayor of New York. On April 12, 1834, the *Working Man's Advocate* broke the news of the "glorious triumph" with the headline "THE BANK DEFEATED."

Here are some of the songs which played a crucial role in rallying labor support behind Andrew Jackson in his battle with the Bank of the United States.

WAR BETWEEN DEMOCRACY AND ARISTOCRACY

A Song by Edward Earle, of Paterson

(Composed shortly after the formation of the General Trades' Union, in order to be sung not only by these brave heroes, who first formed that body in commemoration of their bold, fearless, and honorable opposition to the all-devouring Monster, Lordly Aristocracy, but by those who have since felt, as well as those who may hereafter feel, the necessity of enlisting in the good cause.)[23]

The monster was coming (we saw him appear)
To grasp all those rights which our forefathers won,
We marshall'd our small force, we fought without fear—
But still lives the foe and the warfare's not done.
Now let us stand firmly opposing his fire,
Until reinforcements be brought on the field;
Our cause being good, we have nothing to fear
Then cheer up, our foe must eventu'lly yield.

Yes! every city and hamlet around.
As soon as appriz'd of the dangerous foe,
Will gird on their armor, and fearlessly bound
To th' ballot box, where we'll strike the death blow.
Too long have we suffer'd in body and mind,
Harsh tortures and trammels in ev'ry degree;

21 *New England Songster* (Boston, 1845).

22 Cornelius W. Lawrence also gained labor support in the campaign because of his unequivocal endorsement of "equal universal education." He firmly asserted his belief that "the advantages of education should be thrown open to all classes" and declared that "the elevation of our national character depends more upon this than upon any other separate measure of public policy" (*Man*, Apr. 4, 1834).

23 The General Trades' Union of New York was organized as a city central labor body by the unions on August 14, 1833.

Too long have we suffer'd knave juntos combin'd
To feast on our labor voluptuously.

Too long we've been gull'd, and too long been deceiv'd;
The rich made our laws, and they bore on us hard,
The poor man be'ng thereby of justice bereav'd,
Met only contumely, contempt, disregard.
'Tis union can baffle the slave forging work,
And bring to the toil-worn worker fair play;
The gluttonous knights of the knife and the fork
Will have to surrender their ill gotten prey.

They'll strive to divide us by every intrigue
That they can in secret deceitfully scheme;
We'll show that we're not so unknowing and vague
As to be deceived any longer by them.
No weapons we'll use, nor for aught do we care
But knowledge and union to bring on the field;
For those are the keenest and those will we bear,
Whilst the *press* will inspire us and be our safe
shield.[24]

TENTH WARD BATTLE SONG

By One of the Tenth

Tune—March, "Ettrick and Teviotdale"

March! march, to the *Poll*, every Democrat,
Treason and Treachery threaten our border!
Vote 'gainst the Bank, and th' arrant Aristocrat!
Vote for your freedom! my gallant *Tenth Warder!*

Where is the Freeman can silently slumber,
While menaced our rights by a *Monied Marauder*,
March to the Polls! and show by your number,
They never can conquer a gallant *Tenth Warder.*

Shall we behold "the Flag of our Liberty,"
Struck in disgrace to "GENTILITY'S order,"
Up with the war cry! Be "*Lawrence and Victory!*"
The shout of the battle, my gallant *Tenth Warder!*

March! our Country and duty require us
To rescue our rights and restore us "good Order";
To be "*first in the field*" each heart is desirous—
To win a gay conquest, my gallant *Tenth Warder.*

Remember the fights of our fathers and Washington,
Virtuous Peace was each Victor's rewarder,
Remember the words of the sage "Thomas Jefferson":
"Down with the Bank," my gallant *Tenth Warder.*[25]

THE TAR'S ELECTION SONG

By Nep

Hurrah! my tar,
Born for the war,
Away let us go to the polls;
The lubbers shan't tell
That sailors they sell,
Tho' banks may buy landsmen in shoals.

Jackson's the man,
Choose him, we can,
For Sailors a patriot will back.
He's father of tars
Deep graven with scars,
And we are the SONS of old JACK.

Jacks-sons then up,
Leave unquaff'd the cup,
Verplancks sailors' rights will let slip;
LAWRENCE'S shout
Will serve this bout
True sailors *ne'er give up the ship.*[26]

A NEW SONG

To an old tune

Written by a Jeffersonian Cartman

Democrats, your country calls
To mark what *Feds* are doing;
To stem the *Tory Faction's* scheme
Of rule, or utter ruin!

Yankee doodle, smoke 'em out,
The *proud, the Banking faction;*
None but such as Hartford Feds
Oppose the poor and JACKSON.
Yankee doodle, doodle doo,
Yankee doodle dandy.

No more is *Harry* on our side,
And *Swarthy* there's no trusting;
Since *Biddle* with his dredging box
Gave many such a dusting.

Yankee doodle, *ease the screws,*
Quick in word, in action;
Our country's rights demand our votes
Identified with JACKSON.
Yankee doodle, &c.

The *ballot boxes* soon will show
The panic-making faction,
In spite of all the dog-*Star's* rage,
The poor are still for JACKSON.

Yankee doodle, how they quail!
Purchas'd presses falter;
Arnold quints at *Gibbet Isle,*
Dreading drop and halter!
Yankee doodle, &c.

MECHANICS, CARTMEN, LABORERS,
Must form a close connection;
And show the rich *Aristocrats*
Their power, at this election.

24 *Working Man's Advocate,* Mar. 15, 1834.
25 *Man,* Apr. 10, 1834.
26 Ibid.

JACKSON AND LIBERTY.

Tune—" *I've kissed and I've prattled with fifty fair maids.*"

I've seen all the heads of department and state,
And have studied them well, d'ye see,
And though some are call'd *cunning* and others call'd *great,*
Yet Jackson's the hero for me:
Bold Jackson's the man,
Let them say what they can,
Old Hickory's the hero for me.

While Johnny was lounging on crimson and down,
And stuffing both pockets with pelf,
Brave Andrew was pulling John Bull's colors down,
And paying his army himself:
In discharge of his duty,
Sav'd "Beauty and Booty,"
And paid the expenses himself.

While Johnny was gorging the fat of the land,
And bartering for *cod,* d'ye see,
Brave Jackson was feeding his patriot band
On nuts of the Hickory tree;—
The ground was his bed,
While the bold hero fed
On the nuts of the Hickory tree.

While Johnny made journeys, yet never stirr'd out,
At twenty-five dollars per day,
Bold Jackson o'er mountains and swamps took his route,
And mortgaged his land for his pay.
When Johnny had bought his commission of Clay,
And mounted the throne, d'ye see,
Brave Jackson, disgusted at rogues, turn'd away,
And sought his own Hickory tree.

But a voice from the south and a voice from the west,
From a people both *grateful* and free,
Have call'd the bold hero from slumber and rest,
To leave his lov'd Hickory tree;—
To exchange for a birth,
The most glorious on earth,
The shade of the Hickory tree.

Then let the loud clarion of glory and fame,
Proclaim from the lakes to the sea,
That laurels perennial encircle *his* name,
Who still loves the Hickory tree,—
While Adams and Clay,
Reluctant give way,
To the sage of the Hickory tree.

ORIGIN OF MILITARY INSTRUMENTS.—We owe the clarionet to the Germans of Nuremburgh, the horn to the Hanovarians, the bassoon and the drum to the Italians, the fife to the Swiss, the trumpet to the Moors of the Peninsula, the cymbals to the Asiatics, the long drum to the Turks, the keyed bugle to the English. The inventor of this last, was a man named Holiday, created in consequence of great changes in military music, and, above all, a necessity for a stronger bass than had before been in use. The gradual introduction of the serpent, bass horn, and ophicleide, in military bands, in assistance of the bassons and bass trombones, has now rendered wind instrument bands as nearly perfect in every respect as they can be imagined.

ANTICIPATING A WILL.—" Let a man do all the good he can in his life time." An old gentleman in the neighborhood of Honiton, having no family of his own, some short time since sent circulars to his nephews and nieces, thirty-six in number, to meet at his house on a given day. Before dinner he called them one by one into his private room, presented each with one hundred pounds, admonishing them all to be frugal and industrious, and live in harmony with each other. They then partook of an excellent dinner, after which his guests departed, thanking the donor for his great liberality, with merry hearts and cheerful countenances.—*English paper.*

The King of Prussia has issued an ordinance, declaring that all persons under accusation of crimes or offences, who may acknowledge their guilt before they are brought to trial, shall be sentenced to the *minimum* of the penalty only.

The Dardanelles are guarded by eleven forts, mounting 743 cannon. And these have been passed by a British fleet, with little comparative injury.

WANTED—A Carrier for this paper in Brooklyn, to commence to-morrow. mh26

COBBETT'S AMERICAN GARDENER—For sale at No. 6 Thames street. Price 50 cents. mh26

PARK THEATRE.

This Evening, (Mr. Hackett,) PAUL PRY, and the KENTUCKIAN. Nimrod Wildfire, Mr. Hackett.

MARINE INTELLIGENCE.

ARRIVED,

Ship Anson, O'Neill, from Charleston, 6 days.
Ship Elisha Dennison, Lane, Mobile, March 8, to E. D. Hurlbut & Co.
Barque Silas E. Burrows, Wilson, New Orleans, 14 days.
Brig Alcenus, Schofield, Ponce, P. R., 13 days.
Brig Elizabeth, Storey, of Salem, from Marseilles, Feb. 1.
Brig Pacific, Denison, Baltimore, to W. W. Todd.
Brig Halcyon, Truman, Charleston, to Scott, Shapter & Morrell.
Schr. Ajax, Pearce, Trinidad de Cuba, to Chastelain & Ponvert.
Schr. Intent, Higbie, of Huntington, from Ponce, PR.
Schr. Hornet, Pitts, Richmond, 6 days.
Schrs. Valiant, Booth, Philadelphia; Diana, Smith, do.
Schrs. Tantivy, from Richmond; Harriet, Pitts, do.
Schr. Enquirer, Mersey, Ocracocke, 8 days.
Schrs. Three Friends, Gibson, Rappahannock; Harriet, Gorm, do.; Adelaide & Jenny, Brown, do.

PASSENGERS.

By the Henri IV., sailed for Havre—Messrs. Phil. Kearney, Drake, Mills, and Geroux, of New York; E. Gerard, H. Geer, A. Lesparre, P. Blancq, of France; J. W. White, of England; L. G. Barbon, of Havana; Dr R. Blair, and G. Soulet, of New Orleans; and 10 in the steerage.

By the John Jay, sailed for Liverpool—Edmund Dexter and William L. Diston, of Cincinnati, Ohio; Augustus M. Merrin, of France; Robt. Blair, of Scotland; Hugh McLealand, and Mr. Church.

By the Elizabeth, from Marseilles—Mrs. Bellegrin and son, and Miss Lamberti.

☞ Advertisements 75c. a sq. 1st time, 25c. each time afterwards. ☜

THE PARADISE, within the reach of all men, without labor, by *powers of nature* and *machinery.* An Address to all intelligent men in two parts, by J. A. Etzler.

Toil and poverty will be no more among men;
Nature affords infinite powers and wealth;
Let us but observe and reason.
The wise examines before he judges;
The fool judges before he examines.

INDEX OF THE BOOK.

FIRST PART.

Introduction,	Flexible Stuff,
The power of wind,	Objects attainable in general,
The power of the tide,	Plan for the buildings of a community,
The power of the waves,	New state of human life,
Burning mirrors,	Occupations in the new state of things,
The power of steam,	The earth can nourish 1000 times more men than now exist,
General remarks on all these powers,	Pecuniary profit of the new means,
Perpetual motions,	Constitution of an association proposed,
Prospect and retrospect of the human condition in general,	General views on the subject,
System of machineries and establishments for the application of these powers,	Address to the Americans in particular.
Agriculture,	
Architecture,	

SECOND PART.

Proposals how to render the new means the most beneficial for the United States,	Comparative views on the condition of man at present and that attainable by the new means,
Formation of a new state,	In physical respects,
First period,	In moral respects,
Second period,	In intellectual respects,
Third period,	Conclusion of the second part,
Fourth period,	Petition to Congress on the subject,
Appeal of the Americans,	Letter to the President of the U. S.

This new original work shows in the clearest and most convincing manner that Nature is over rich in powers and means for human happiness, and is only waiting for an intelligent race, to make good use of them. Powers, hitherto idle, may henceforth do far more than 10,000 times the work of all the human race at present. A capacity of producing food and raiment, and all objects of human comforts and enjoyments, exceeding 1000 times all the actual wants of mankind, is in Nature. Consequently, nothing but slovenly adherence to customs—want of reflection—is the cause of the universal poverty and fear of poverty, and the concomitant evils and ignorance.

The book points out how to make use of those superabundant powers and means in Nature—to create a *Paradise, a new world,* within a few years, provided *attention* can be found among men. It proposes an association, similar to those for constructing canals, rail roads, etc., while in the same time it solicits the attention of the national government. The author offers, to that effect, every further communication required on the subject, gratis.

The objects of the book are too numerous to be here mentioned, too new and too brilliant to be understood, without perusing the book—it is an appeal to thinking minds, especially to those of the sciences of reason. No reader ever has found, nor ever will find, any material objection against the truths stated in this book, though the author eagerly challenges critics on the subject.

A universal revolution is now unavoidable throughout the whole human kind—a revolution from a universal state of poverty, ignorance, and barbarity, to universal superabundance, intelligence, and happiness.

AMERICANS! Are you to be the first or the last in this universal progress of reason? Time will soon show the answer. Read first the book, then reason!!

☞ Look to the proposed motto, and rank either with the *wise* or the *fools!!!*

☞ For sale, in New York, by C. Reinhold, No. 209 William street, between Frankfort and Duane streets; Philadelphia, by T. G. Wesselhoeft, No. 9 Broad street, between Second and Third and Arch and Race streets; G. Edler, No. 83 Race st., between Second and Third. Price one dollar. mh26

"THE MAN" is published daily at the office of the Working Man's Advocate, 6 Thames street.

Courtesy of General Research and Humanities Division, the New York Public Library, Astor, Lenox and Tilden Foundations

Yankee doodle, *down they go*,
By Democrats defeated;
The *Bone and Sinew* ne'er will be
By Biddle's Rag Mill cheated.
Yankee doodle, &c.

Our Mayor must be a Democrat,
True in word, in action;
Sir VERPLANCK* bows a Biddleeite,
But LAWRENCE is for JACKSON.

Yankee doodle, vote ARIGHT,
And get the poor protected;
'Tis money shavers cheat us all,
And DRONES must be rejected.
Yankee doodle, doodle doo,
Yankee doodle dandy.[27]

*Mr. Verplanck and family own 900 shares of United States Bank stock, therefore of necessity must be against the poor!!

JACKSON AND LIBERTY

Tune—"I've Kissed and I've Prattled with Fifty Fair Maids"

I've seen all the heads of department and state,
And have studied them well, d'ye see,
And though some are call'd *cunning* and others call'd *great*,
Yet Jackson's the hero for me:
Bold Jackson's the man,
Let them say what they can,
Old Hickory's the hero for me.

While Johnny was lounging on crimson and down,
And stuffing both pockets with pelf,
Brave Andrew was pulling John Bull's colors down,
And paying his army himself:
In discharge of his duty,
Sav'd "Beauty and Booty,"
And paid the expenses himself.

While Johnny was gorging the fat of the land,
And bartering for *cod*, d'ye see,
Brave Jackson was feeding his patriot band
On nuts of the Hickory tree;—
The ground was his bed,
While the bold hero fed
On the nuts of the Hickory tree.

While Johnny made journeys, yet never stirr'd out,
At twenty-five dollars per day,
Bold Jackson o'er mountains and swamps took his route,
And mortgaged his land for his pay.
When Johnny had bought his commission of Clay,
And mounted the throne, d'ye see,
Brave Jackson, disgusted at rogues, turn'd away,
And sought his own Hickory tree.

But a voice from the south and a voice from the west,
From a people both *grateful* and free,
Have call'd the bold hero from slumber and rest,
To leave his lov'd Hickory tree;—
To exchange for a birth,
The most glorious on earth,
The shade of the Hickory tree.

Then let the loud clarion of glory and fame,
Proclaim from the lakes to the sea,
That laurels perennial encircle *his* name,
Who still loves the Hickory tree,—
While Adams and Clay,
Reluctant give way,
To the sage of the Hickory tree.[28]

DADDY MACNEVEN'S SOMERSET

Air—"Bob and Joan"

O the devil's in the Bank!
How it sets the folks a raving;
It has play'd a pretty prank,
With William J. Macn——n,
He long was on the brink!
Unknowing which to favor,
Till the rattle of the *chink*
Decided him for ever.

O! Billy, love, adieu!
Are you gone, my honey?
When they *purchased* you,
They threw away their money.

The Bank was in a pout,
The Doctor, to console it,
Composed his "wheel about"—
We meant to say he stole it.
He filch'd the whining trash,
From Jeffrey and from Cobbett,
And then he clutch'd the cash!
And then began to fob it.

O! Billy, love, adieu!
Are you gone, my honey?
When they *purchased* you,
They threw away their money.

Poor Biddle—precious elf!
Believed, as true as fate is,
When Billy sold himself,
That we must follow gratis;
That such a "scribe divine"
Would set us all a voting,
Who couldn't write a line
Until he went a *quoting*.

O! Billy, love, adieu!
Wira sthrue, my honey,

27 *Working Man's Advocate*, Apr. 5, 1834.
28 *Man*, Apr. 5, 1834.

DADDY MACNEVEN'S SOMERSET.

Air—Bob and Joan.

O the devil's in the Bank!
How it sets the folks a raving;
It has play'd a pretty prank,
With William J. Macn——n,
He long was on the brink!
Unknowing which to favor,
Till the rattle of the *chink*
Decided him for ever.

O! Billy, love, adieu!
Are you gone, my honey?
When they *purchased* you,
They threw away their money.

The Bank was in a pout,
The Doctor, to console it,
Composed his "wheel about"—
We meant to say he stole it.
He filch'd the whining trash.
From Jeffrey and from Cobbett,
And then he clutch'd the cash!
And then began to fob it.

O! Billy, love, adieu!
Are you gone, my honey?
When they *purchased* you,
They threw away their money.

Poor Biddle—precious elf!
Believed, as true as fate is,
When Billy sold himself,
That we must follow gratis;
That such a "scribe divine"
Would set us all a voting,
Who couldn't write a line
Until he went a *quoting*.

O! Billy, love, adieu!
Wira sthrue, my honey,
When they *purchased* you,
They threw away their money.

He strove to do the State
Some service, but, beshrew it!
It wou'dn't take the bait,
Howe'er he brought it to it.
And wasn't Andy keen
To shun the Doctor's bolus,
Or now he hadn't been,
His body where his soul is.

O! Billy, love, adieu!
Wira sthrue, my honey,
When they *purchased* you
Threw away their money.

Long, long, O'Connell's fame
With envy made him frantic;
Some little brook the same
Might envy the Atlantic!
So when he found his mark
Unmated to his wishes
He fell, like any shark,
On Biddle's loaves and fishes.

O! Billy, love, adieu!
Are you gone, my honey?
When they *paid for* you,
They threw away their money.

You now may give your vote
To any bidder handy,
As soon as turn your coat,
Or take a cup of brandy.
But all your whine "wont draw,"
What Irishman so crude, as
To be the Kitten's paw,
Of any such a Judas?

O! Billy, love, adieu!
Wira sthrue, my honey,
When they *purchased* you,
They threw away their money.

Now Heaven protect the land
And Liberty and Jackson!
Whene'er he waves his hand,
He'll find us at his back soon;
But Billy James "*avic*"
We'll now hang up our fiddle.
And leave you to *Old Nick*,
Or worse—to Nicholas Biddle.

O! Billy, love, adieu!
Are you gone, my honey?
When they *purchased* you,
They threw away their money.

FREEMEN UP!

Freemen, up! the Foe advances,
Dire oppression heads his train!
High his golden banner dances,
Threat'ning manacle and chain;
Shall we see our Rights invaded?
Freemen up! arm! arm and out!
Arm! or see our sons degraded,
Rally to the Battle Shout!

Shall the sons of sacred sires—
Shall the noble and the free,
Yield their "altars and their fires"?
Yield—to threats and bribery?
Where's the heart that warms a freeman—
Where's the hand that dare be free?
Soldier! Citizen! or Seaman
Up! and strike for Liberty!

Up! your breast to Battle baring,
No coward courses fill your veins!
Be ours the arm, and ours the daring—
Ours to crush a Tyrant's chains!
Freeman up! the war-cry rages,
Ours be "Death or Victory!"
Strike! for home—for sires—and sages—
For LAWRENCE and for LIBERTY!

ONE OF THE TENTH.

MENTAL CHARACTER OF THE COBBLER.—Seated all day on a low seat, pressing obdurate last and leather against the epigastrium, dragging reluctant thread into hard and durable stitches, or hammering heels and toes with much monoton — the cobbler's mind, regardless of the proverb, wanders into regions metaphysical, political, and theological; and from men thus employed have sprung many founders of sects, religious reformers, gloomy politicians, "bards, sophists, statesmen," and other "unquiet things," including a countless host of hypocondriacs. The dark and pensive aspect of shoemakers in general is matter of common observation. It is but justice to them, however, to say, that their acquisition of knowledge, and their habits of reflection, are often such as to command admiration. The hypocondriacal cast of their minds is probably, in part, induced by the imperfect action of the stomach, liver, and intestines, in consequence of the position in which they sit at work.—*For. Quar. Review.*

THE ELECTION.—In a few days, the contest now waging, will terminate, and until it has terminated, we trust no democrat will relax his exertions. We are passing through an extraordinary struggle—such an one as has seldom been witnessed in this State, and as we hope never will again recur. Attempts are made by monied influence—the power of wealth, to control freemen.—What our opponents want in justice and truth, they have seemed determined to make up with force; and when they cannot convince, they have resolved to compel. *Workmen have been discharged—custom has been withdrawn—wages haue been withheld* from honest industry, because it would not submit to mental slavery. The doctrine has been that honest poverty must permit those whose pockets are better filled to think for them, to give them opinions, to manacle and fetter the immortal mind. It is thus that aristocracy forgets right, that wealth and power becomes corrupting, and, in the strife for ascendancy, their efforts to control, they would deprive merit if poor, honesty if humble, worth if in obscurity, of God's noblest attribute, an *independent* mind. If there is on earth a being so degraded as to be the tool of pampered and aspiring wealth, if he will permit himself to be influenced by threats and force, he is unworthy that freedom which was purchased with patriot's blood, and which freemen alone can appreciate. Such a man will be dragged np to the polls by the Bank gentry—and made to vote as they dictate.—*Hartford Times.*

PENNY TRASH.—Col. Webb, of the Courier & Enquirer,—alarmed at the prosperity of the penny papers,—is becoming very cross and ill-natured. In speaking of them he calls them "penny trash." But, Colonel, it is of no use. The public have been imposed upon with *ten dollar* trash long enough—and the citizens of New York, almost universally, have come to the conclusion that it is better to pay one cent a day for the same amount of reading matter, (exclusive of the advertisements,) than ten dollars a year for blank sheets. We are very sorry that our b siness encroaches on our neighbors of the mammoth sheets. But unless the large morning papers reduce their subscription price to $8 a year, some of them must go down!—*Sun.*

HORRIBLE BARBARITY.—Four men named Peter Connor, Jas. McGill, William Browne, and John Mc Ewen, went into the house of Stephen Henderson, corner of Stanton and Sheriff streets, on Friday night, and forced their way int o a back room, where there was a man named Israel Louis, both of whose eyes Connor "gouged" out of their sockets. Connor was immediately arrested, but unfortunately afterwards escaped. It is not known what motive induced him to commit so diabolical an act.—*Jour of Com.*

DEATHS.

April 6, Christian Hertell, butcher, aged 37.
At Baltimore, 4th inst; Alexander Brown, merchant.
Deaths in this city last week, 143. Consumption 27, Scarlet Fever 20.

MARINE INTELLIGENCE.

ARRIVED.

Packet ship Montreal, Champlin, 26 days from Liverpool.
Ship Virginian, Hewett, from Buenos Ayres.
Ship Lotus, Watts, of Hallowell, from Liverpool, March 16.
Ship Katherine Jackson, Fernald, from Liverpool, March 11.
British barque Britannia, M'Gill, from Liverpool, Feb. 5.
Brig Marcellus, Jennings, from Gibraltar, March 10, to G. Milne & Co.
Schr. John Richards, Eaton, from Roch lle, March 3, to B. Aymar & Co.

CLEARED.

Ships Thames, Griffin, London; Silas Richards, Nye, Liverpool; Sully, Forbes, Havre; Newark, Brewer, New Orleans. Georgian, Eldridge, Mobile—Sw. barque Louise, Aspling, Hamburg—Brigs Alber Henry, Stackpole, Guayama, P. R.; Athenian, Chapman, Carthagena; Olive Branch, Hart, Norfolk—Schooners Lydia, palachicola; Nestor, Washington, NC.

PASSENGERS.

By the Katherine Jackson, from Liverpool—Capt. S. T. Ball and 51 in the steerage.
By the Lotus, from Liverpool—117 in the steerage.
By the Marcellus, from Gibraltar—Francisco Pampilli.

WORKS ON THE CURRENCY.—For sal at the office of this paper—
Gouge's American Banking System, Price $1 20
Hale's "Useful Knowledge for the Producers," &c. 18¾
Roosevelt's "Mode of Protecting Domestic Industry," &c. 20
mh20

INSURANCE ON LETTERS.—Money sent by mail to any Post Office in the United States, or the British North American Provinces, will be insured by application to B. BATES, at the Post Office, N. York. mh29 tf

WANTED—Two or three more active Men, of good address, to take routes of "The Man" Apply immediately. mh17

"THE MAN" is published daily at the office of the Working Man's Advocate, 6 Thames street.

Courtesy of General Research and Humanities Division, The New York Public Library, Astor, Lenox and Tilden Foundations

When they *purchased* you,
They threw away their money.

He strove to do the State
Some service, but, beshrew it!
It wouldn't take the bait,
Howe'er he brought it to it.
And wasn't Andy keen
To shun the Doctor's bolus,
Or now he hadn't been,
His body where his soul is.

O! Billy, love, adieu!
Wira sthrue, my honey,
When they *purchased* you
Threw away their money.

Long, long, O'Connell's fame
With envy made him frantic;
Some little brook the same
Might envy the Atlantic!
So when he found his mark
Unmated to his wishes
He fell, like any shark
On Biddle's loaves and fishes.

O! Billy, love, adieu!
Are you gone, my honey!
When they *paid for* you,
They threw away their money.

You now may give your vote
To any bidder handy,
As soon as turn your coat,
Or take a cup of brandy.
But all your whine "wont draw,"
What Irishman so crude, as
To be the Kitten's paw,
Of any such a Judas?

O! Billy, love, adieu!
Wira sthrue, my honey,
When they *purchased* you,
They threw away their money.

Now Heaven protect the land
And Liberty and Jackson!
Whene'er he waves his hand,
He'll find us at his back soon;
But Billy James "*avic*"
We'll now hang up our fiddle.
And leave you to *Old Nick*,
Or worse—to Nicholas Biddle.

O! Billy, love, adieu!
Are you gone, my honey?
When they *purchased* you,
They threw away their money.[29]

BANK MELODIES—No. 1

Air—"John Anderson My Jo-John"

Nick Biddle, O! my auld Nick,
When we were first acquent,
The Bank had full five years to run,
The feels were freely lent;
But now the Bank is winding up,
The cash don't come so thick,
But blessings on your withered paw,
Nick Biddle, my auld Nick.

Nick Biddle, O, my auld Nick,
We've had our fun thegither,
Money and canty days, Nick,
We've spent wi' ane anither:
Now we maun totter down, Nick
But hand in hand we'll strick,
And growl thegither at the foot,
Nick Biddle, oh, my Nick.[30]

BANK MELODIES—No. 2

Air—"Fallen Is Thy Throne"

Fallen is thy throne, O Nicholas!
Silence is o'er thy Bank,
No more thy discounts tickle us,
Thy lawyers all are lank,
Where are the boys that hanker,
For notes approved and "done,"
Who vote for the old banker,
Wherever they're hard run.

Clay! thou did'st love Nick Biddle,
Once he was all thine own;
Thy harp, thy flute, thy fiddle,
Which thou did'st play upon;
Till Jackson came and blighted
Thy long-loved olive tree,
And the Banking House was lighted,
For other kings than thee.

Then sunk the son of Nicholas,
Then set his Evening Star,
And got into a pickle as
Bad as Duane's papa,[31]
When wrapped in wrath in wonder,
He frowned upon his son,
And lectured him like thunder
For what he had not done.[32]

29Ibid., Apr. 9, 1834.

30Ibid., Apr. 23, 1834.

31William John Duane was appointed secretary of the treasury by Jackson to withdraw the government deposits from the United States bank and place them with the state banks. When he refused to do so, he was removed from office by the president. Duane was the son of William Duane, editor of the *Philadelphia Aurora*.

32*Man*, Apr. 24, 1834.

"A GONE CASE"

Air—"Bruce's Address"

Have our fathers fought in vain?
Must the knee be bent again,
To oppression's lawless reign,
In servility?

Can a proud and monied knave,
Conquer freemen strong and brave,
Who could once their country save,
From a tyrant's grave?

Can a foul and soulless Bank,
Vanquish men who're bold and frank,
And forever turn the crank
Of our government?

No!—the spirit is there now,
Which laid cruel tyrants low,
From the unresisting blow
Of our noble sires.

The hirelings may spread false news,
And Nick Biddle "*turn the screws,*"
But the way the people choose,
They will surely go.

Major Jack may laugh and jest,
Davy Crockett "*grin his best,*"
To put Jackson to the test,
But it will not do.

Hick'ry roots are firm and stout—
Henry Clay may groan and pout,
But he cannot turn him out,
Or disgrace his name.

Base Calhoun may loudly howl,
Daniel Webster sternly scowl,
And the "*lesser lights*" may growl—
But 'twill be in vain.

Jackson's firm, undaunted yet,
(Altho' some their knives have whet,)
He can die without regret,
For his country's good.[33]

THE LULLABY PRESS

A Song adapted to the tune of "The Sailor's Lullaby"

Composed on reading the Report of the Committee appointed to investigate the affairs of the United States Bank.

By Edward Thompson, Philadelphia

Peaceful in yon House* reposing,
Bank men feared no dangers nigh;
And hireling presses, while so dozing,
Soothed them with their lullaby!
Lullaby, &c.

Are our Democrats arousing,
No dangers still these drones descry;
The base born press in wealth carousing,
Soothes them with its lullaby!
Lullaby, &c.

Behold proud Nick, and all his minions
In durance vile—and hear them cry
"Alas! and must we give up millions,
And hear no more sweet lullaby!"
Lullaby, &c.

Yes! off to Congress, Master Nicholas!
Thou with thy foul crew must hie;
Thy press hath brought thee to this pretty pass,
With its syren lullaby!
Lullaby, &c.

Prophetic this—thy reign is over,
That Bank oppressions are gone by;
Thy press-men, too, who lived in clover,
Shall hum no more sweet lullaby!
Lullaby, &c.

Too long hath this fraud existed,—
Aye, too long the cheat—the lie;
Nor could it be well resisted,
While spell-bound with its lullaby!
Lullaby, &c.

Then hail thou Patriot, Andrew Jackson,
Thy well earned praise we'll lift on high;
'Twas thou didst rout the hellish faction,
And still the syren lullaby!!!
Lullaby, mercy cry!
Lullaby, mercy cry!
The syren's dead, poor lullaby![34]

*The Bank in Chestnut street.

A SONG FOR THE BANK MEN

By Scrip, Philadelphia, June, 1834

Air—"The Kroos-Keen Lawn"

Let the farmer mind his soil,
And the artisan his toil,
And working men for labor give thanks;
We're favor'd more than they,
And are happy night and day,
With treasures we obtain through the banks.

Let the lawyer and the priest,
Enjoy their splendid feast,
And demagogues deceive by their pranks;
There's none can with us vie,
However they may try,
For our greatest blessings are the banks.

[33]Ibid., Apr. 29, 1834.
[34]Ibid., May 29, 1834.

The government directors,
Would be our base detectors,
We regard them as so many blanks;
We'll treat them as but flies
And call them Jackson spies,
Unworthy to be seen in the banks.

We've talked of blood and thunder
And made the people wonder
From our bounty what thousands have drank;
'Twas on Wellington's birthday,
We made a grand display,
And there fed the minions of the bank.

How great are all our glories!
We make good *Whigs of Tories;*
And people once so meagre and lank,
Have fatten'd by our care,
And enjoyed the best of fare,
And all through the kindness of the bank.

Now let us all be gay,
And huzza for Henry Clay!
And give Nulli McDuffie our thanks;[35]
There's Webster, god-like man,
Will do the most he can
To keep alive the mother of the banks.

But Jackson, that old Devil,
Has caus'd us all much evil,
In money getting projects and pranks.
Though we have tried to send him,
The people now defend him,
And will not let us shave them in our banks.

Now let us tune the fiddle,
To our gracious friend Nick Biddle,
Our paper money monarch *so frank;*
Should evils overtake him,
We never will forsake him,
Hurra! for King Biddle and the bank![36]

THE PRODUCERS' HYMN

Dedicated to the Working classes,
the Sons and Daughters of Industry

By the Poor Man's Poet

Air—"Chevy Chase"

"Man's inhumanity to man
Makes countless thousands mourn."—Burns

In hallow'd graves our fathers sleep,
Who fann'd up freedom's fire,
Until its flame illum'd the earth,
And dar'd despotic ire.

Nor is the holy glow extinct,
Columbia shall be free!
Defying native, foreign knaves,
To sap her liberty.

God spare the land from *Lawyer's* rule,
May industry proclaim;
From hirelings, mischief's busy tools
For dark or desp'rate game!

Yet we who labor are to blame,
More than the men we send
To make our laws; can bees expect
A drone to be their friend?

Shall we, in *Freedom's* cradle nurs'd,
Forsake her holy cause:
Fold up our arms, whilst money'd worms
Subvert the Nation's Laws?

Forbid it, shades of worthies pass'd
To death's unfathom'd deep;
That Labor should her children teach
To bow—to idlers creep.

Shall foreign catiff financiers,
Shall bankers through address
Direct the nation's destiny
And govern by finesse?

Not whilst that honor'd HERO rules;
The bold, unbending, brave,
Remnant of worth, of former times
Hath pow'r to guide and save!

Oh! is there one degenerate son
To shame a noble sire;
In whose cold bosom is extinct
The glow of freedom's fire?

Then rally round your President,
Ye hardy sons of toil;
Maintain your rights, the rights of Man,
Or perish on the soil!

'Tis needless now to call up names,
Examples from the grave;
The former and the latter war
Have prov'd the nation brave.

Wealth's abject spirit latent lay,
Courage and prudence blended;
Nor int'rest stay'd a noble act
The patriot once intended.

But now, alas! a change is seen
Throughout this fruitful land;
Rag Mills and Paper Monarchs rule,
And grind the working hand!

Then join the UNION, heart and hand,
Sustain your country's pride;

[35]George McDuffie, senator from South Carolina, favored nullification and was an enthusiastic supporter of the Bank of the United States. He broke with Jackson over the nullification and bank issues.

[36]*Man*, July 2, 1834.

Ye, who have conquer'd on the field,
And triumph'd on the tide.

The time is come, to stand prepar'd
Ere some foul deed is done;
A President may yet be bought,
A Senate NOW is won!

Like soldiers resting on their arms,
Producers must prepare,
Against the foes of Liberty,
Their country all their care.

Let men of thirty summers take,
And those of riper years,
The vow of honor—ne'er to quail,
To rich, dishonest peers.

Show faction our long muster roll,
Sign'd from the crimson vein;
With *Bunker Hill!* for countersign,
And watch-word, Trenton's Plain!

Call, call to mem'ry Washington,
Call Jefferson the sage;
Read, read the *Crisis, Common Sense,*
But blast the *Senate's rage!*

Ye, who have dealt the foeman out,
The sabre's mortal blow,
Have made the British warriors run,
Have brav'd the Indian's bow,

Arise! With freshness on the will,
Call up our father's ire,
Flourish the lance of Liberty!
And faction must expire.

And, if one coward spirit links,
Within a dastard frame;
Let him be call'd Apostate—Dog—
Skunk—Clay—or some base name!

May he be chas'd by honest curs,
By wolves with ceaseless yell,
And bay'd at by the canine race,
A purchas'd dog of hell.

Producers up! In bold relief,
Before your country stand!
If reason fails, then force alone
Must awe the PAPER BAND!

Then rally round your President,
Ye hardy sons of toil;
Maintain the laws, your legal rights,
Or, perish on the soil!

Adieu, yet watch like hungry hawks,
(When balanc'd on the wing,)
For *Traitors*—in your house of *Lords!*
With B, their Paper King!!

And should they dare you to the field,
With fife and rolling drum;
You'll hear the *Paper Demons* scream,
FLY! FLY! THE WORKIES COME![37]

SONG—THE EMIGRANT'S HOME!

Composed and sung by a Working Man,
on the Fourth of July, 1834

Air—"In the Downhill of Life!"

In Liberty's cause, I could yield up my life,
'Twas bondage that caused me to roam;
I have long left that land of *cursed faction* and strife,
To abide in this happier home—
Where sons of true freedom *here only exist,*
Tho' apostates are paid to mislead them;
Each Republican brave, nobly enters the list,
To support this *Great Standard of Freedom!*

Here, under the *Hickory Tree,** I enjoy
The solacing talk of my friends:
With few taxes to tease me, *no tithes* to destroy
The blessings which Providence sends,—
I'll bear in remembrance the kindness I've met,
For American souls say, "your welcome":
While pulse of my heart cannot ever forget
To uphold this *Great Standard of Freedom!*

Now in sweet peace and plenty I live every season,
Independence the creed of my mind;
My religion, not priestcraft; 'tis founded on reason,
To love God, and to prove true to mankind,
And freemen avow—that their motto will bear
Equal Rights, Equal Laws—and they'll heed them
As they spurn vile monopoly's arts,† that would dare
To prostrate this *great Standard of Freedom!*[38]

*The President of the U.S. is familiarly denominated "Old Hickory."
†United States Bank.

OUR COUNTRY'S GRATITUDE

By E. Thompson

Tune—"The Soldier's Gratitude"

Whate'er our fate in Freedom's cause,
Still will we perservere;
'Twould crime become were we to pause,
Bank Slavery so near.
Then let us join in Freedom's ranks
Until the foe's subdued,
Then may we claim our country's thanks,
Our Country's Gratitude.

The Bank rears up her hideous head,

37 Ibid., July 19, 1834.
38 Ibid., July 31, 1834.

The Bank our dreaded foe,
By her ten thousand hearts have bled,
In agonizing woe.
Then let us join, &c.

The outraged rights we hold so dear,
Demand Oppression's fall,
The widow's and the orphan's tear
Aloud for justice call,
Then let us join, &c.

Tune—"See, the Conquering Hero Comes"

Freemen once the pride of earth,
Shall we shame our noble birth?
Bank chains in gloomy silence wear,
And bend our heads in mute despair?

Hark! our fathers' spirits cry,
"Can our sons in bondage lie?
Do the rights we bled to gain
Our children view with cold disdain?"

No! ye spirits of our sires,
Freedom still Columbia fires;
Still our choral song shall be
Who would that live, and live not free?

Bankmen, 'tis in vain ye rave,
Freemen ye can ne'er enslave;
Ye can ne'er our bosoms awe,
Our sword is Truth, our shield is Law!

Dare not hope your threat of arms
Shake our breasts with dire alarms;
Tho' your thousands crowd the field,
Our native rights we ne'er will yield.

Bid your sabres gleam around.
And your cannon's thundering sound!
Sabres gleam and cannons roar,
But rouse Columbians' courage more!

See approach the long wish'd hour
Shall terminate your tyrant power:
Soon shall Justice hear our call,
And shouting millions hail your fall.

Tune—"Scots Wha' Ha wi Wallace Bled"

Patriots who to fame aspire,
Freemen who your rights desire,
Animate your hearts with fire
For glorious Liberty!

Bankmen with their pressmen blend
Meet and swear they will defend
And help each other to the end,
That we their slaves may be.

Who can now those Bankmen see
Assassinate fair Liberty,
And will not struggle to be free,
And aid *our* holy cause.

Now they have their standard shown
Throughout the Union be it known
That power is theirs, and theirs alone—
But we'll maintain the laws.

The Government, not wealth, that rules,
Not master Biddle and his tools,
Nor hireling presses, knaves or fools,
Nor Sprague, nor Harry Clay,

Nor Webster, Sergeant, or Calhoun:
Tho' fair in semblance as yon moon,
They speechify for monied boon
Bank paper buys their say.

These Banks too long have ruled the land,
Have too much pelf at their command,
Have bribed the editorial band
To raze fair Freedom's tree.

But now their race is nearly run,
Let us not the contest shun,
Nor make an end of every one,
This let us do or di'.[39]

BIDDLE, LET THE BANK ALONE

Air—"Barney, Let the Girls Alone"

The *Workies* lead me such a life,
The *Workies* lead me such a life,
I'm ripe for treason and for strife,
Unless they let me be.
For if I buy a Press or so,
Or Webb or Noah to make it go,
And Clay to preach *distress* and woe,
And pay as we agree,
It's *Biddle*, let the Bank alone,
Mr. Biddle, let the Bank alone,
Why can't you let the Bank alone,
That curse to Liberty?

Now there is something very extraordinary in all this. What's the difference, in a free country whether I buy a *Press*, a *Bank*, or a *Grist Mill?* it's a *pressing* and *grinding* business at any rate; and, if *"men and votes"* are sold *"like cattle in the market,"* I have a right to purchase either.—"it's a fair business transaction." But these *Jackson Democrats* must be bawling out

Mr. *Biddle*, let that Bank alone,
Mr. Biddle, let that Bank alone,
Why can't you let that Bank alone,
Before you're "up a tree"?

Bring your books and vouchers true,

39 *Working Man's Advocate*, Aug. 16, 1834.

Show your debts and credits too,
How many *bribed*—and tell us who,
And let the people see!
Biddle, you're a wicked boy,
To *Webster* kill and *Clay* destroy;
Old Nick will catch a slippery boy,
As—*Paddy caught the flea.*

Can any thing be more uncivil than to speak so disrespectfully of *dignitaries* and gentlemen of unbounded wealth and influence? Farmers, Mechanics, and Working Men have the impudence to call my "*Promises* to pay," mere *Rags*, and have no more sense than to prefer *Gold* and *Silver* to my pretty pictures. *Shame!* to let those noisy fellows loose upon the *Aristocracy* of the country—as if they had a right to say—

Mr. *Biddle*, let the Bank alone,
Mr. Biddle, let the Bank alone,
Why can't you let the Bank alone,
And leave the people free?

And so they vex me day and night,
Still I'd turn the screws so tight,
And make them *feel* my power and might,
But for *Old Hickory*.
He keeps me back, and thwarts my plan,
And blows me up—and so does VAN,[40]
And so does every honest man
From *Maine* to *Genesee.*

But that's not the worst of it, even those who fly from oppression in the old world, will now and then give me a dirk under the fifth rib, with—

Mr. *Biddle*, leave yon Bank alone,
We've seen *Old England* curs'd with one,
Oppressed with wrongs; give *Erin's* sons
One taste of Liberty![41]

A SONG FOR ALL GOOD MEN
By H.M.D.

Since Adam, at first on this earth was created,
Of manners and men a great deal is related;
But nature has never yet finished a job,
So mean in itself as that creature a Nob.
By nob we imply every thing that is knavish,
In nob we include every thing that is slavish,
In nob we can find every thing that is vile—
A treacherous, cowardly monster of guile.

Then shun with abhorrence the scums who annoy us,
And cold be the heart that would dare to destroy us;
The thief that goes boldly to plunder and rob
Is better by far than a dastardly nob.

How mean is the wretch who respects not his neighbor,
And steals from his brother the rights of his labor;
When tyrants oppress us by all that they can
We doubt of a nob—but we fear not a man;
For man is still noble, unflinching in trial—
As true in his course as the sun on its dial;
A nob is a villain, a cheat, and a knave,
Unworthy of aught but an infamous grave.

Then shun, &c.

Whate'er be our fate in this world of sorrow,
May hope cheer the bosom, nor fear for to-morrow;
May reason's pure light be forever in view,
And justice direct us in all that we do.
Let all round the standard of Unity rally,
Nor let it be said to be free we should dally!
Our foemen shall fall, or like fugitives fly—
Our watchword must ever be, "Conquer or die."

Then shun, &c.[42]

SONG
By a Reformed Wig

Who is 't edits the blanket sheet,
And garbles statements very neat,
At No. 56 Wall street?
James Double W.

Who attends Masonic Hall,
When the Wigs a meeting call,
With resolutions rather small?
James Double W.

Who sold himself to one Nick Biddle,
And said the Democrats he'd diddle,
Were he allowed to play first fiddle?
James Double W.

Who said—and said as all have thought—
The "Mammoth" was with danger fraught,
And "Men and votes like cattle bought"?
James Double W.

Who since has joined the same Bank faction,
And made for gold a wretched fraction,
Yet swore it was "a fair transaction"?
James Double W.

Who said aristocratic rights
Should supercede the poorer wights,
And calls mechanics "troglodytes"?
James Double W.

Who, when some emigrants contrived
To reach these shores, where Freedom thrived,
Announced them "*live stock*" just arrived?
James Double W.

40Martin Van Buren was elected vice-president with Jackson in 1832.

41*Working Man's Advocate*, Sept. 17, 1834.

42Ibid., Oct. 18, 1834.

Whose plighted faith and consequences,
His boasted knowledge—all pretence—
Was lately valued at *six pence?*
James Double W.

And who, to sum up all together,
Has changed with every change of weather,
A mocking bird, of Noah's feather?
James Double W.[43]

Some workingmen and trade union leaders supported the Whig party candidate, Henry Clay, in the presidential election of 1836, and still others dismissed all presidential candidates as second-rate men whose election would not aid workingmen. But the majority endorsed Martin Van Buren, the Democratic candidate, especially since his running mate, Colonel Richard M. Johnson of Kentucky, was the champion of a federal measure to abolish imprisonment for debt and a bitter foe of the Bank of the United States.

THE PRODUCER'S ELECTION HYMN,

Or an

Address to Poor Men

"I perceive in these modern Whigs, men wonderfully troubled with the itch of exaltation."—BENTON.
"Mr. Speaker, in these men I perceive the inceptive seed of a new nobility."—BURKE.

Arise! Arise! Sustain your rights,
Ye sons of labor rise!
Be wakeful, *to the ballot box,*
There, there your safety lies!
For the Bankers o'er the land
Are combined, to make a stand
Against your rights and Liberty!
They have plung'd you in distress;
Have suborned a *venal press,*
Which they bribe to induce your slav'ry!

Then to the polls like victors go,
Rushing like a river's flow,
Urg'd by wastes of melting snow.
Mark a Whig, and lo! a foe,
That would enslave you, work your woe;
Therefore support Van Buren!

Shall Bunker's Hill, and glory's war
Be blotted from our story?
Shall we forget *George Washington,*
And idolize a Tory?
Shall *Jefferson and Paine,*
Have driven pens in vain;
Shall we give up Democracy?
Shall the Bankers of the land,
Through their press and purchas'd band,
Make us crouch to a base Aristocracy?

Chorus:

Nature's nobles lived of yore—
They dared, they would be free!
Your sires, like men of Marathon,
Bled for your liberty!
Their spirits now are on high,
Are peering from the sky,
To behold yon prostrate faction:
Then as sons who do delight
In the holy cause to fight,
Arise, for decisive action!

Chorus:

The Paper Plague afflicts us all,
Its pains are past enduring;
Still, we have hope in Jackson's robe,
Whilst it wraps round VAN BUREN.
Then let the working class,
As a congregated mass,
Behold an insidious enemy:
For each *Banker* is a foe,
And his aim is for our woe—
He's the *canker-worm of liberty!*

Chorus:

Lo! murder, in demonian cloak,
Lifts his opprobrious hand,
And calls his Congress ruffians out,
A myrmidonian band!
And a widow weeps in Maine,
For a husband basely slain;
Yet, his death may his murderers rue,
For the poor will in their might
Arouse in native right,
And in vengeance, *will have their due!!!*

Then to the polls like victors go!
Rushing like a river's flow,
Urged by wastes of melting snow:
Mark a Whig, and lo, a foe!
That would enslave you, work your woe;
Therefore support Van Buren![44]

43*Man*, reprinted in *Working Man's Advocate*, Nov. 8, 1834. James Watson Webb, publisher of the *New York Courier and Enquirer*, was at first staunchly Jacksonian, but he deserted Jackson in 1832 on the United States bank issue and became a leading supporter of the Whig party.

44Broadside, Martin Van Buren Papers, Library of Congress.

THE PRODUCER'S ELECTION HYMN,

OR AN

Address to Poor Men.

"I perceive in these modern Whigs, men wonderfully tronbled with the itch of exaltation."—BENTON.
"Mr. Speaker, in these men I perceive the inceptive seed of a new nobility."—BURKE.

Arise! Arise! Sustain your rights,
Ye sons of labor rise!
Be wakeful, *to the ballot box*,
There, there your safety lies!
For the Bankers o'er the land
Are combined, to make a stand
'gainst your rights and Liberty!
They have plung'd you in distress;
Have suborned a *venal press*,
Which they bribe to induce your slav'ry!

CHORUS.

Then to the polls like victors go,
Rushing like a river's flow,
Urg'd by wastes of melting snow.
Mark a Whig, and lo! a foe,
That would enslave you, work your woe;
Therefore support Van Buren!

Shall Bunker's Hill, and glory's war
Be blotted from our story?
Shall we forget *George Washington*,
And idolize a Tory?
Shall *Jefferson and Paine*,
Have driven pens in vain;
Shall we give up Democracy?
Shall the Bankers of the land,
Through their press and purchas'd band,
Make us crouch to a base Aristocracy?
CHORUS.

Nature's nobles lived of yore—
They dared, they would be free!
Your sires, like men of Marathon,
Bled for your liberty!
Their spirits now on high,
Are peering from the sky,
To behold yon prostrate faction:
Then as sons who do delight
In the holy cause to fight,
Arise, for decisive action!
CHORUS.

The Paper Plague afflicts us all,
Its pains are past enduring;
Still, we have hope in Jackson's robe,
Whilst it wraps round VAN BUREN.
Then let the working class,
As a congregated mass,
Behold an insidious enemy:
For each *Banker* is a foe,
And his aim is for our woe—
He's the *canker-worm of liberty!*
CHORUS.

Lo! murder, in demonian cloak,
Lifts his opprobrious hand,
And calls his Congress ruffians out,
A myrmidonian band!
And a widow weeps in Maine,
For a husband basely slain;
Yet, his death may his murderers rue,
For the poor will in their might
Arouse in native right,
And in vengeance, *will have their due!!!*

CHORUS.

Then to the polls like victors go!
Rushing like a river's flow,
Urged by wastes of melting snow:
Mark a Whig, and lo, a foe!
That would enslave you, work your woe;
Therefore support Van Buren!

Courtesy of Library of Congress

LOCOFOCOS AND EQUAL RIGHTS

The labor vote for Van Buren did not signify that workers were satisfied with the Democratic party. On the contrary, a split had occurred a year before the presidential election over the bank question between labor elements and the party headed by Jackson. Labor leaders and rank-and-file workers were dismayed by Jackson's transfer in 1834 of $6 million of government deposits from the Bank of the United States to the "pet banks." As they saw it, this was merely transferring federal money from one monopoly to another. What they supported instead was a plan originally proposed by William Gouge, a Philadelphia editor and economist and a member in 1829 of a committee named by the Working Men's party in that city to draw up a report on the banking system. Under this proposal banks would become only institutions of deposit and exchange and would be deprived of the right to issue paper money. With hard money thereby becoming the circulating medium, workingmen would not be defrauded as they were when wages were paid in paper money.

In 1834 labor groups in the northeastern states proposed that Gouge's policy be incorporated into the Democratic platform. When this was rejected, they first sought to gain control of the party, and when this move was frustrated, they formed their own political organizations. In New York, where the conflict was most intense, the labor elements in 1835 formed the Locofoco,[45] or, more properly, the Equal Rights party, which gradually gained the balance of power in New York politics. It received considerable impetus from an 1836 court decision which found twenty-five members of the Union Society of Journeymen Tailors guilty of "conspiracy to injure trade, riot, assault and battery."

The Equal Rights movement, or locofocoism, as it was commonly called, was also influential in Pennsylvania, Massachusetts, and Rhode Island. In Rhode Island, it played an important part in Dorr's Rebellion, a movement which arose in the early 1840s for a more liberal constitution in the state and for the elimination of property qualifications for suffrage. Many workingmen marched in the great suffrage parades, carrying banners which proclaimed: "No taxation without representation"; "Suffrage—the inalienable Right of Man"; "Liberty or Revolution." Although Dorr's Rebellion was put down and Dorr himself served a year in prison in solitary confinement, the movement produced a liberal state constitution in May, 1843.

The Equal Rights movement gave birth to a group of labor songs which urged workingmen to treasure their right to vote and use it for labor's cause regardless of party attachments. They also stressed the theme of equal rights—anti-monopoly and true democracy—and, in the case of Dorr's Rebellion, expressed support for the cause of universal manhood suffrage.[46]

MY VOTE

The following song of a Working Man whose vote the Aristocracy had attempted to purchase by a bribe, breathes the sentiments and exhibits the treatment of multitudes in this town and other places.

They knew that I was poor,
  And they thought that I was base,
And would readily endure
  To be covered with disgrace;—
They judged me of their tribe,
  Who on dirty mammon dote,
So they offered me a bribe
  For my vote, boys, vote!
    Oh shame upon such critters,
      Who would my conscience buy!
    But shall I wear their fetters?
      Not I, indeed, not I!

My vote?—It is not mine
  To do with as I will;
To cast, like pearls to swine,
  To these wallowers in ill,
It is my country's due,
  And I'll give it while I can
To the honest and the true,
  Like a man, boys, man!
    Oh shame upon such critters,
      Who would my conscience buy!
    But shall I wear their fetters?
      Not I, indeed, not I!

[45]The name derived from the locofoco matches used by labor elements in New York to light candles at a meeting after the lights had been turned off by Tammany henchmen to prevent the nomination of labor candidates for state offices.

[46]This must be qualified by adding the word *white*. Dorr's movement actually favored removing the right of free blacks in Rhode Island to vote, a stand which caused black leaders like Frederick Douglass to condemn it and campaign in the state against the new constitution proposed by the Dorrites.

No, no, I'll hold my vote
As a treasure and a trust;
My dishonor none shall quote
When I'm mingled with the dust;
And my children, when I'm gone,
Shall be strengthened by the thought,
That their father was not one,
To be bought, boys, bought!
Oh shame upon such critters,
Who would my conscience buy!
But shall I wear their fetters?
Not I, indeed, not I![47]

SONG

Air—"Lonely Nan"—Dibden

Sweet are thy principles & Truth
Acknowledged here by sage and youth,
Sweet, O sweet—divine to scan;
Sweet, O sweet—divine to scan;
Sweet to teach fair Freedom's cause,
Impartial rights, and equal laws,
To uphold great nature's plan;
To uphold great nature's plan;
Sweet are thy smiles O Liberty!
When man aspires to be free;
When man aspires to be free;
Asserting Truth, and Rights of Man![48]

Mechanics all, and Workingmen,
By union—courage—and the pen,
Let's preserve in our just cause;
Let's preserve in our just cause;
The hallowed, holy, God-like theme!
Through ages yet to come—the same.
We know our rights, and them maintain;
We know our rights, and them maintain;
Happy by toil, those sweets to share,
With sweethearts, wives, and children dear;
With sweethearts, wives, and children dear;
That support the glorious Rights of Man!

The first to take the battle ground;
Americans—will still be found
To spurn oppression's combined plan;
To spurn oppression's combined plan;
Our rights; our liberties we'll guard;
Unwise opinions shall be marr'd.
Yes—perish every heart that's still
Yes—perish every heart that's still
The people's voice—the sovereign will,
That swells and throbs with Freedom's thrill;
That swells and throbs with Freedom's thrill;
Will Rally round the Rights of Man![49]

AWAKE! THE TORPOR OF THIS DREAM

Air—"Hail! Bacchus Hail!"

Awake! the torpor of this dream
This icy weight on Feeling's stream—
This dull, cold yielding to your foes
Invites and justifies their blows;

Not theirs such coward lethargy—
To prey, that will not fight nor flee,
Their swords will strike or cunning reach:—
Awake! let the past some wisdom teach.

Inactive still the fool reposes—
With the fierce foe the true heart loses:
Be yours the bold, the firm endeavor!—
Awaken! or be slaves for ever!

Your silence is your foemen's strength—
Come! beard them in the dens at length;
They wield the might of demon powers—
Prove that a holier might is ours!

Fling hence the toys of other days—
The anxious thirst for worthless praise!
Let these ne'er win the hearts again,
Whose throbs must burst Dishonor's chain!

Arise! and walk no more in night—
The dawn breaks on us free and bright;
But if ye'd have the brightness stay,
Make profit of its earliest ray![50]

THE SONS OF ART

By Thos. G. Spear

Tune—"Hail Columbia"

Hail! to Art's enlight'ning band!
Hail! ye sons of Freedom's land!
Who converse bold with all mankind,
And cheer the boundless realms of mind,—
'Tis yours to herald deeds renown'd,
And spread the thoughts of souls profound—
To bid the mists of Ign'rance fly,
And gladden Virtue's anxious eye,
With knowledge that was sent to fan
The love of Truth sublime in man.

Friends of light and Liberty,
Join'd in millions firm and free,
On the land, or on the waves,
Columbia's sons can ne'er be slaves.

Hail! ye heirs of patriots wise,
Blessed with Freedom's blood-bought prize,

47 *Newark Eagle,* reprinted in *Working Man's Advocate,* Oct. 24, 1835.

48 Thomas Paine's *Rights of Man,* with its defense of the French Revolution and of greater democracy in government, was widely read by American workers, and copies of the work, in cheaply printed editions, were to be found in the homes of many mechanics, artisans, and laborers.

49 *National Laborer,* July 2, 1836.

50 Ibid., July 9, 1836.

Who glory in that God-like band,
That first your country's greatness plann'd.
Still guard the rights ye proudly claim,
And hand them down through time the same;
And send them where a slavish fate,
On man's desponding ears may grate,
And through the world the torch relume,
That cheers his passage to the tomb.

Friends of light and Liberty, &c.

Sound the chorus to the skies,
While a nation's praises rise,
To hail the boon that Science found,
And will'd to earth's remotest bound—
That from the night of ages came
The last in birth, but first in fame,
And broke the long and cheerless gloom,
That clouded man's primeval doom,
And turn'd his thoughts from phantoms wild,
To scenes by peaceful arts beguil'd.

Friends of light and Liberty, &c.

Sons of Art! whose triumph claim,
Homage for your bloodless fame,—
Who wield the press or guide the plough,
With fearless eye, and cheerful brow,—
Whose quicken'd souls, and faithful hands,
The force of tyrant wrong withstands,—
As one in nation, name, and fate,
Together stem the storms of state—
Together shine—together stand—
A glorious and united band.

Friends of light and Liberty, &c.[51]

SUFFRAGE PLEDGE

Here on this sacred spot,
United heart and hand
We pledge to liberty,
A consecrated band.

Too long, alas! we've bow'd
Beneath a tyrant's laws;
The voice of justice cries—
Maintain your righteous cause.

Although our chosen guide
Is exiled from his home,
The day approaches near,
When he'll no longer roam.

That glorious morn will break,
When freedom's sun shall rise,
And roll in majesty
Through bright, unclouded skies.

The anthems of the free
On every breeze shall float,
And ransomed prisoners join
To swell the joyful note.

The aged and the young
Their thankful offerings bring,
And chant the requiem o'er
The usurped power of King.

Hail! happy day, thrice hail!
Farewell to "Martial law";
The conquering hero comes!
Hail! Thomas Wilson Dorr.[52]

THE FACTORY WORKERS

The factory system in America was established throughout New England after 1815 following the mechanization of all the processes of cotton-cloth manufactures by Francis C. Lowell, who had spent several years in England studying methods of textile manufacture. From New England it spread rapidly down into New York and Pennsylvania. While some men were employed, the majority of the workers in these early factories were children, boys and girls under twelve years of age, who earned from thirty-three to sixty-seven cents for a seventy-five-hour week, and the daughters of nearby farmers. The girls from the farms lived in crowded and badly ventilated company boarding houses. Their hours were long—from five in the morning to seven at night, and their wages averaged little more than two to three dollars a week. Moreover, fines were imposed even on these meager earnings for the least infraction of company rules.

A public appeal by the workers of Manayunk, a factory district near Philadelphia, vividly described conditions in the factories in 1833. Working thirteen hours a day in the summer, in foul air, so weakened the factory workers that they were barely able to work: "But nevertheless, work we must . . . or our families would soon be in a starving condition. . . . We cannot provide against sickness . . . for our present wants consume the little we receive, and when we are confined to bed any length of time, we are plunged into the deepest distress which often terminates in total ruin, poverty and pauperism. . . ." The Manayunk workers pointed out that in England the terrible condition of the children working in factories had been improved at least somewhat as a result of investigation.

51 Ibid., Jan. 14, 1837.

52 Broadside, Harris Collection, Brown University.

Here, however, nothing had been done for their children, who were "oppressed as much as those in the English factories." Children who had to enter the factories at an early age were "reared in total ignorance of the world, and the consequence . . . is the inculcation of immoral and often times vicious habits, which terminates in the disgrace of many . . . in the public prisons." If the factories worked reasonable hours at decent wages, the children could be placed in a public school, "but situated as they are, and reared in ignorance, they are made the tools of political as well as avaricious men, who lord over them as does the southern planter over his slaves." As far as the women were concerned, no allowance was made "on the part of the employers for their sex or age." Those grown to womanhood earned barely enough for their support. The appeal concluded with the sad observation that "it would be useless to point out in detail, all the injustices we suffer from an overbearing aristocracy."[53]

Since the early labor press appealed primarily to mechanics, it did not pay too much attention to factory conditions. An exception, however, was the *Man*, published by George Henry Evans in New York City. The paper carried reports on conditions in factories both in England and in this country as well as efforts on the part of factory workers to obtain improvements. The paper also featured songs, ballads, and verse which added substance to what was set forth in reports. The issue of June 21, 1834, featured on its front page a report entitled "The Factory System," along with a description of conditions in the factories "admirably expressed by an English poet":

The day was fair, the cannon roar'd,
Cold blew the bracing north,
And Preston's mills by thousands pour'd
Their little captives forth.

All in their best they paced the street,
All glad that they were free;
And sang a song with voices sweet—
They sang of liberty!

But from their lips the rose had fled,
Like "death in life" they smil'd;
And still as each passed by I said,
"Alas! is that a child?"

Flags waved, and men—a ghastly crew,
March'd with them side by side;
Where, hand in hand, and two by two,
They moved a living tide.

Thousands and thousands—oh—so white!
With eyes so glazed and dull!
Alas! it was indeed a sight
Too sadly beautiful!

And, oh, the pang their voices gave,
Refuses to depart!
"This is a wailing for the grave!"
I whispered to my heart.

It was as if where roses blush'd
A sudden, blasting gale,
O'er fields of bloom had rudely rush'd
And turned the roses pale.

It was as if in glen and grove,
The wild birds sadly sung;
And every linnet mourn'd its love,
And every thrush its young.

It was as if in dungeon gloom,
Where chain'd Despair reclined,
A sound came from the living tomb.
And hymn'd the passing wind.

And while they sang, and though they smil'd,
My soul groan'd heavily—
"Oh! who would wish to have a child;
A mother who would be!!"

The following two songs also appeared in the *Man*. The second is probably the most famous of all the ballads connected with the early factory workers. Originally entitled "The Factory Girl's Last Day," it was attributed by the November, 1883, *Cigar Maker's Official Journal* to a Mr. Sadler, a member of the committee of the House of Commons in England which in 1832 investigated conditions in the textile factories in connection with the demand for a ten-hour law.[54] The ballad, written after a witness before the committee described the incident, was "respectfully dedicated" by Sadler to the mill corporations. In the version published in the *Man*, the last eight lines were added by an anonymous American who was bitter over the fact that most abolitionists were indifferent to the plight of the "white slaves" while organizing opposition to

[53]John R. Commons et al., eds., *A Documentary History of American Industrial Society* (Cleveland, 1910), VI, 331–34.

[54]Michael Sadler was the leading champion in Parliament of the Ten-Hour Bill and chairman of the committee appointed to collect evidence on conditions in the factories.

black slavery. (In this connection, it should be noted that the appeal of the Manayunk workers compared the power of the employers and their agents to that of "the southern planter over his slaves.") The ballad was reprinted in the Fall River *Mechanic* of May 25, 1844, where it was preceded by an introductory comment describing it as a most effective portrayal of "the evils of the factory system," and though "it is poetry, it is not fiction, but, alas! too sad a reality." It appeared again in the *Voice of Industry*, a Boston labor paper, on December 11, 1845, preceded by a quotation from "Minutes of Evidence before a Committee of the House of Commons" in which the father of the ten-year-old factory girl described her death. On March 7, 1867, the *Boston Weekly Voice*, a post–Civil War labor paper, reprinted the ballad, introducing it as follows: "The testimony of female operatives, which we were privileged to hear Wednesday, before the Legislative Committee, makes the probability of such a scene as the following so striking as to give the deepest pathos to the lines.—Ed."

THE LITTLE FACTORY GIRL TO A MORE FORTUNATE PLAYMATE

I often think how once we used in summer fields to play,
And run about and breathe the air that made us glad and gay;
We used to gather buttercups, and chase the butterfly—
I loved to feel the light breeze lift my hair as it went by!

Do you still play in those bright fields? and are the flowers still there?
There are no fields where I live now—no flowers any where!
But day by day I go and turn a dull and tedious wheel,
You cannot think how sad, and tired, and faint I often feel.

I hurry home to snatch the meal my mother can supply,
Then back to hasten to the task—that not to hate I try,
At night my mother kisses me, when she has combed my hair,
And laid me in my little bed, but—I'm not happy there—

I dream about the factory, the fines that on us wait—
I start and ask my father if—I have not lain too late?
And once I heard him sob and say—"Oh better were a grave,
Than such a life as this for thee, thou little sinless slave!"

I wonder if I ever shall obtain a holiday?
Oh if I do, I'll go to you, and spend it all in play.
And then I'll bring some flowers, if you will give me some;
And at my work I'll think of them and holidays to come![55]

THE FACTORY GIRL

'Twas on a wintry morning,
The weather wet and wild,
Three hours before the dawning
The father raised his child,
Her daily morsel bringing,
The darksome room he paced,
And cried "The bell is ringing,
My hapless darling, haste!"

"Father, I'm up, but weary,
I scarce can reach the door,
And long the way, and dreary,
O carry me once more!
To help us we've no mother,
You've no employment nigh,
They killed my little brother,
Like him I'll work—and die!"

Her wasted form seem'd nothing,
The load was at his heart;
The sufferer he kept soothing,
Till at the mill they part.
The over-looker met her,
As to her frame she crept,
And with his thong he beat her,
And cursed her as she wept.

Alas! what hours of sorrow
Made up her latest day;
Those hours that brought no morrow,
Too slowly passed away;
It seem'd, as she grew weaker,
The threads the oft'ner broke,
The rapid wheels ran quicker,
And heavier fell the stroke.

The sun had long descended,
But night brought no repose,
Her day began and ended,
As cruel tyrants chose.
At length a little neighbor
Her half-penny she paid,
To take her last hour's labor,
While by her frame she laid.

At last the engine ceasing,
The captives homeward rush'd,
She thought her strength increasing—
'Twas hope her spirits flush'd;
She left, but oft she tarried,
She fell, and rose no more,

55 *Man*, May 13, 1834.

Till by her comrades carried,
She reached her father's door.

All night, with tortured feeling,
He watched his speechless child:
And close beside her kneeling,
She knew him not, nor smiled;
Again the factory ringing
Her last perceptions tried;
When from her straw bed springing,
"'Tis time!" she shrieked, and died.

That night a chariot passed her,
While on the ground she lay;
The daughters of her master
An evening visit pay[56]—
Their tender hearts were sighing,
As negroes' wrongs were told;
While the white slave was dying,
Who gained their father's gold![57]

A broadside issued in the 1830s reflected the feelings of the New England mill workers.[58] The "factory bell" refers to a regulation common in all mills which usually stated: "The bell to call the people to their work will be rung five minutes and tolled five minutes; at the last stroke, the entrance will be closed and a fee of 12½ cents exacted of anyone for whom it may be opened." Some factory workers complained that the employers "have been uniformly in the practice of deducting one quarter from each day's labor, when we were behind the time but five minutes."[59]

THE LOWELL FACTORY GIRL

When I set out for Lowell,
Some factory for to find,
I left my native country,
And all my friends behind.

Then sing hit-re-i-re-a-re-o
Then sing hit-re-i-re-a-re-o

But now I am in Lowell,
And summon'd by the bell,
I think less of the factory
Than of my native dell.

Refrain:

The factory bell begins to ring,
And we must all obey,
And to our old employment go,
Or else be turned away.

Refrain:

Come all ye weary factory girls,
I'll have you understand,
I'm going to leave the factory
And return to my native land.

Refrain:

No more I'll put my bonnet on
And hasten to the mill,
While all the girls are working hard,
Here I'll be lying still.

Refrain:

No more I'll lay my bobbins up,
No more I'll take them down;
No more I'll clean my dirty work,
For I'm going out of town.

Refrain:

No more I'll take my piece of soap,
No more I'll go to wash,
No more my overseer shall say,
"Your frames are stopped to doff."

Refrain:

Come all you little doffers
That work in the Spinning room;
Go wash your face and comb your hair,
Prepare to leave the room.

Refrain:

No more I'll oil my picker rods,
No more I'll brush my loom,
No more I'll scour my dirty floor
All in the Weaving room.

Refrain:

No more I'll draw these threads
All through the harness eye;
No more I'll say to my overseer,
Oh! dear me, I shall die.

Refrain:

[56]A later song popular among factory girls which contrasted the daughters of the poor and the rich went:
The poor working girl,
May heaven protect her,
She has such an awf'ly hard time;
The rich man's daughter goes haughtily by,
My God! do you wonder at crime!
(Carl Sandburg, *The American Songbag* [New York, 1927], p. 195.)

[57]*Man*, May 17, 1834.

[58]John Greenway also dates this song "around the 1830's" and points out that "the 'nine shilling' wage of which the singer complains coincides with the average weekly earnings of $2.25 paid to New England cotton-factory operatives in 1830" (*American Folksongs of Protest* [Philadelphia, 1953], p. 124).

[59]*Paterson Courier*, Aug. 12, 1835.

No more I'll get my overseer
To come and fix my loom,
No more I'll say to my overseer
Can't I stay out 'till noon?

Refrain:

Then since they've cut my wages down,
To nine shillings per week,
If I cannot better wages make,
Some other place I'll seek.

Refrain:

No more he'll find me reading,
No more he'll see me sew,
No more he'll come to me and say
"Such works I can't allow."

Refrain:

I do not like my overseer,
I do not mean to stay,
I mean to hire a Depot-boy
To carry me away.

Refrain:

The Dress-room girls, they needn't think
Because they higher go,
That they are better than the girls
That work in the rooms below.

Refrain:

The overseers they need not think,
Because they higher stand,
That they are better than the girls
That work at their command.

Refrain:

'Tis wonder how the men
Can such machinery make,
A thousand wheels together roll
Without the least mistake.

Refrain:

Now soon you'll see me married
To a handsome little man,
'Tis then I'll say to you factory girls,
Come and see me when you can.[60]

Although their conditions were among the worst any American workers knew, factory operatives did not play an important part in the labor movement of the 1830s. As the song indicates, most of them still had the freedom to return to the farm, and when conditions grew too intolerable, they left for home, cursing the factory owners who were trying to reduce them to the status of slaves and warning others to stay away from the "factory prisons." But while they did not form permanent unions, the factory girls conducted some of the most militant strikes of the thirties. When the wages at Lowell, Massachusetts, were cut 15 percent early in 1834, the girls held several protest meetings. A few days later, the leader of the movement was discharged. As she left the mill, she waved her bonnet in the air as a signal to the others who were watching from the windows. They struck, assembled about her, and—eight hundred strong—marched in a procession about the town. After listening to one of their leaders make a "flaming Mary Wollstonecraft speech on the rights of women and the inequities of the monied aristocracy,"[61] they announced their determination "to have their own way if they died for it." On the second day of the "turn-out," the strikers issued a proclamation entitled UNION IS POWER in which they called upon all "who imbibe the spirit of our patriotic ancestors" to support them by quitting work, by resolving, with those already on strike, not to "go back into the mills to work unless our wages are continued to us as they have been," and by pledging that none would "go back unless they receive us all as one." They appended to the proclamation the words of their strike song:

Let oppression shrug her shoulders,
And a haughty tyrant frown,
And little upstart Ignorance
In mockery look down.

Yet I value not the feeble threats
Of Tories in disguise,
While the flag of Independence
O'er our noble nation flies.[62]

Although twelve hundred girls responded and signed the pledge, the strike was broken. Many of the Lowell girls went home to the farms, but those who remained in the mills continued to struggle. When the factory owners cut wages another 12½ percent in 1836, the Lowell girls formed the Factory Girls Association and struck again. As they paraded in their strike demonstra-

[60]Broadside, Harris Collection, Brown University. Cf. "The Factory Girl's Come-All-Ye," pp. 69–70.

[61]Mary Wollstonecraft was a pioneer women's rights advocate in England.

[62]*Boston Evening Transcript*, reprinted in the *Man*, Feb. 20, 1834.

tion, fifteen hundred factory girls sang to the tune of "I Won't Be a Nun":

Oh! Isn't it a pity that such a pretty girl as I
Should be sent to the factory to pine away and die?
Oh! I cannot be a slave;
I will not be a slave,
For I'm so fond of liberty
That I cannot be a slave.[63]

The strike lasted a month. Evicted from the boarding houses and with no funds to sustain them, the girls were starved into submission. Once again, many quit the mills and returned home to the farms.

Other factory girls followed "the example of their pretty sisters at Lowell,"[64] and inspired by the militant women, weavers in the mill of R. H. Orth and Company in Steubenville, Ohio, struck in June, 1836, when the company refused to recognize their union. In an appeal to the public, the strikers asked other workers and sympathizers to join their demonstrations and learn their strike song, the words of which were appended to the appeal:

A STRIKE SONG
By the Society

Shall tyrants reign and rule us all?
Shall truth and reason cease to smile?
Ah, no! says Justice, they shall fail,
And Love and Union guard us all,
Truth and Justice hear our Call,
Defend our rights and guard us all!

Reward for toil by us is craved,
And Fortune has a scheme contrived:
Then why should Weavers be enslaved
And basely of their rights deprived?
Weavers, be firm, and never flee,
We have been bound but will be free!

By foreign yoke we're not oppress'd,
By evils laws we're not annoy'd,
Through war at home we're not distress'd,
Nor is our country's trade destroy'd,
Through drones and tyrants, we are poor,
We've suffer'd long, we'll bear no more.

Be firm and keep your point in view;
For one false step may lead astray
A noble club; but those are true
That's firm, but cowards soon give way.
Be firm, for Reason's on our side
And Justice will for us provide.[65]

PANIC OF 1837

We do not know the outcome of the Steubenville strike; but even if the Weavers' Society had gained recognition, it would not have survived long. The panic of 1837 dealt trade unionism a devastating blow. With one-third of the working class unemployed and most of the others working only part time, the trade unions of the 1830s found it impossible to keep their heads above water. One after another, local societies, city centrals, and the National Trades' Unions passed out of existence, taking with them the first labor newspapers.

THE MILL HAS SHUT DOWN

"The mill has shut down! Good God, shut down!"
Like the cry of flood or fire the cry
Runs swifter than lightning through the town.
"The mill has shut down! Good God, shut down!"
Men wring their hands and look at the sky;
Women fall fainting; like dead they lie.
At the very best they earned but bread,
With the mill shut down they'd better be dead.

Last year with patience a lessened wage
They helplessly took—better than none;
More children worked, at tenderer age—
Even their mite helped the lessened wage.
The babies were left at their home alone.
'Twas enough to break a heart of stone
To see how these people worked for bread!
With the mill shut down they'd better be dead!

"The mill has shut down! Good God, shut down!"
It has run at loss this many a day.
Far worse than flood or fire in the town
Will be famine, now the mill has shut down.
But to shut mills down is the only way,
When they run at a loss, the mill owners say.
God help the hands to whom it meant bread!
With the mill shut down they'd better be dead![66]

63*National Laborer,* Oct. 29, 1836; William Scoresby, *American Factories and Their Female Operatives* (Boston, 1845), p. 61.

64*Boston Evening Transcript,* Mar. 25, 1836.

65*National Laborer,* June 4, 1836.

66Broadside, Harris Collection, Brown University.

3
The Pre–Civil War Decades 1840–60

UTOPIAN REFORMS

The 1840s and 1850s saw a growth of utopian thought in the United States. For a time utopianism attracted workers who were suffering from the effects of the economic crisis which began in 1837. They also were becoming increasingly alarmed by the spread of the factory system and the accompanying "growing industrial feudalism." A song of the period published in the labor press expressed the widespread feeling in labor circles that there was something basically wrong with American society.

THERE MUST BE SOMETHING WRONG

When earth produces, free and fair,
The golden waving corn;
When fragrant fruits perfume the air,
And fleecy flocks are shorn;
While thousands move with aching head,
And sing this ceaseless song—
"We starve, we die, O, give us bread!"
There must be something wrong.

When wealth is wrought as seasons roll
From off the fruitful soil;
When luxury from pole to pole
Reaps fruit from human toil!
When from a thousand, one alone
In plenty rolls along,
The others only gnaw the bone,
There must be something wrong.

And when production never ends,
The earth is yielding ever;
A copious harvest oft begins,
But distribution—never!
When toiling millions work to fill
The wealthy coffers strong;
When hands are crushed that work and till
There must be something wrong.

When poor men's tables waste away
To barrenness and drought,
There must be something in the way,
That's worth the finding out;
With surfeits one great table bends,
While numbers move along;
While scarce a crust their board extends,
There must be something wrong.

Then let the law give equal right
To wealthy and to poor;
Let freedom crush the arm of might,
We ask for nothing more;
Until this system is begun,
The burden of our song
Must, and can be, only one—
There must be something wrong.[1]

An address in behalf of the workingmen of Charleston, Massachusetts, early in the forties reads: "Brethren, put these things together, and tell us, if the natural tendency in this country is not to reduce us, and that at no distant day, to the miserable conditions of the laboring classes of the old world? We stand on the declivity; we have already begun to descend! What is to save us?"[2]

The solution seemed to lie in the panaceas of the utopians: model communities, patterned after the ideas of Robert Owen of England and

[1] *Voice of Industry*, Feb. 12, 1847. This song was reprinted, without the last stanza, in *Truth*, September 1, 1883.

[2] *Boston Quarterly Review*, IV (Jan., 1841), 121.

Charles Fourier of France, land reform schemes, money reform, national workshops, cooperatives, labor-time banks, and social credit schemes. All were designed to establish a new social order which would abolish all types of slavery and oppression by restoring to the people control over the productive forces. This new social order, moreover, could be built overnight, for the plan was already formulated.

One of the schemes which influenced many Americans, including many of the leading intellectuals of the day and some sections of the working class, was associationism, or Fourierism. The first Fourierist "phalanx" in the United States, as the cooperative communities were called, was named the Sylvania Phalanx; it was launched in western Pennsylvania in 1843 by a group of mechanics who had formerly lived and worked in Albany and New York City. These workers had a song for their enterprise.

ASSOCIATION SONG

Tune—"Ole Dan Tucker"

O come where love makes labor light,
Where toil with pleasure we unite,
Where industry with a wisdom blends,
And bliss on social life attends.
O come with us we all are brothers,
Each one tries to bless the others.

The rusty chains you've worn so long,
Throw off, with all abuse and wrong;
Your hearts from social evil free,
Achieve a higher destiny.
O come with us, we all are brothers,
Each one tries to bless the others.

You dream and suffer day by day
While vampyres suck your life away—
An incubus upon your soul,
Its terrors all your thoughts control
O flee these ills and all the others
Be a band of social brothers.

Be simple gospel truth your guide;
As in its wisdom you confide,
Behold in each that treads the sod,
Your brother and a child of God.
O make yourselves a band of brothers,
Every one will help the others.

No strife nor discord do we sow,
Nor selfish competition know,
None enemies nor aliens call;
One is the interest of all.
O come with us, we all are brothers,
Each one tries to bless the others.

With us, life smoothly glides along,
In gentle current, like a song,
A sweet, glad melody it flows,
And joy and happiness bestows.
O come with us we all are brothers,
Each one tries to help the others.[3]

None of the model communities ever lasted very long. And no more successful were the producers' cooperatives, in which workers were to abolish the wage system by cooperatively producing goods and selling them, dividing the profits among themselves. But they did give rise to the following songs:

A COOPERATIVE SONG

The social brotherhood of man
Alone can bless the boon of birth;
And Nature in her generous plan,
Has taught us how to use the earth.

Hail! brothers, hail! in bark, or hut, or hall;
Hail! for each must live for all.

Why should a difference of birth,
Of creed, or country, men divide?
Behold the flowers of the earth,
Though various, blooming side by side.

Man, poor and feeble when alone—
The sport of every passing wind—
In war, in trade, in art has shown
He's all-resistless when combined.

If, then, when fears or interests plead,
Sustaining crowds together press,
Why should not social kindness lead
Mankind to join for happiness?[4]

In working-class circles, the greatest interest in utopian reforms centered around the movement led by group known as Agrarian or National Reformers, headed by George Henry Evans, formerly the editor of the *Working Man's Advocate* and the *Man*. In the 1840s, through his journals, the revived *Working Man's Advocate* and *Young America*, both published in New York City, Evans advanced the idea that land monopoly was the "king monopoly," the "cause of the greatest evils," and that the only way to solve the problems facing American workers was to restore their rights to ownership of the land.

3*Mechanic*, Nov. 16, 1844.

4*Bulletin of Sovereigns of Industry*, reprinted in *American Socialist*, May 25, 1876.

Not only would land reform free workers from dependence on capital by enabling them to settle as independent artisans and mechanics on the public lands, but as workers moved west, the employers would be forced to advance the wages of those who still remained in the East. Finally, when all had left for the West, nothing would remain in the cities except warehouses and shipyards for international commerce, while in the West, in rural republican townships, the mechanic would be a farmer-artisan, working part of the time on the land and part of the time making commodities with his own tools which he would exchange for goods produced by other farmer-artisans. Hence land reform would "undo the work of the Industrial Revolution" and restore economic independence to workers who were being crushed by machinery and other technological improvements.

The land reformers appealed to the workers to use their ballots to "vote yourself a farm." Workingmen throughout the North and West responded eagerly, joined the National Reform Association, organized ward clubs, and signed a pledge to vote for no man for any legislative office who would not agree in writing "to use all the influence of his station, if elected, to prevent all further traffic in the Public Lands of the States of the United States, and to cause them to be laid out in farms and lots for the full and exclusive use of actual settlers."[5] Some communities even witnessed the launching of independent workingmen's tickets to advance the principles of land reform along with other progressive reforms such as full right of suffrage, election of all officials by the people, direct taxation of property, and reform of the legal system.

The land reform movement played an important part in the ultimate enactment of the Homestead Act in 1862. It also gave birth to several labor songs.

THE AGRARIAN BALL

Tune—"Rosin the Beau"

Come all you true friends of the Nation,
Attend to humanity's call,
Come aid in your country's salvation,
And roll on th' Agrarian Ball.

Ye Democrats come to the rescue,
And keep on the glorious cause,
And millions hereafter will bless you,
With heart cheering song of applause.

Come Whigs bid adieu to hard cider,
And boldly step into the ranks,
To spread the proud banner still wider
Upset all the rascally banks.

And when we have form'd the blest union,
We'll firmly march on, one and all;
We'll shout when we meet in communion,
And roll on th' Agrarian Ball.

Th' Agrarian army's advancing,
The Monopoly of Land to destroy;
The glad eye of beauty is dancing,
Her heart's overflowing with joy.

How can you stand halting, while beauty
Is sweetly appealing to all,
Then come to the standard of duty,
And roll on th' Agrarian Ball.[6]

THE WORKING MEN'S LEAGUE

Tune—"Old Dan Tucker"

Come all you who are fond of singing,
Let us set a song a ringing;
Sound the chorus, strong and hearty,
And we'll make a jovial party,

Get out of the way you speculators,
You shall no longer be dictators.

Some love *Rents* and speculation,
Some with *Banks* would fill the nation;
In a lump we'll class the *critturs*,
And we'll catch them speculators.

Get out of the way, &c.

He who lives by labor only,
Ne'er shall find his friends lonely;
But his home a happy place is,
Blest with cheerful, smiling faces,

Get out of the way, &c.

Interest steals a man's good feelings,
He's a rogue in all his dealings;
Smirks and smiles until he's found you,
Then, O'crackey! how he's bound you.

Get out of the way, &c.

All who wish for homes to bless them,
All who wish the girls to kiss them,
Hark! while soberness is o'er us,
Here's a song, and this the chorus,

Get out of the way, &c.

Once we used to *beg to labor*,
Then to toil was thought a favor;

[5] *Young America*, Nov. 29, 1845, Mar. 6, 1847; *Working Man's Advocate*, Sept. 4 and Nov. 9, 1844, Jan. 25, 1845.

[6] *Working Man's Advocate*, May 18, 1844.

We'll have a home all smiling, sunny,
Without price and without money.

Get out of the way, &c.

Time was once when honest workers,
Were put upon a par with porkers,*
But now a new reform's beginning,
Selling land is now a sinning.

Get out of the way, &c.

See the Agrarian Ball a rolling,
Hark! the knell of Avarice tolling!
Roll the ball to every station,
In our own great Yankee nation.

Push along and keep it moving,
The People's cause is still improving.

Satan saw his trade was failing,
Heard no more the orphan's wailing;
Sent his imps about us yelling,
Don't stop! don't stop! but keep on selling!"

Get out of the way you old Land Seller,
You're a loafer, crafty *feller.*

True you once did *price* demand,
For what was Nature's gift, the *Land;*
Boast you may that you have done it,
Reform's on foot, and you can't come it.

Get out of the way, though have done it,
Reform's the word, and you can't come it.

Monopolists now just be a thinking,
No more at such great wrong be winking;
Come and own that you're mistaken,
Sign the Pledge, and save your bacon.

Push it along and keep it moving,
The People's cause is still improving.[7]

*"Swinish multitude."

A song in *Young America* for March 11, 1848, denounced the "land robber" who speculated in the public lands. "The earth is just as necessary to our subsistence as the air we breathe," protested the author, Martin Knapp, "and as much right have men to deal out the latter in quantities to suit the cash of the purchasers, as to deprive their fellows of the use of the former. The first eight lines of each of the following stanzas, contain the practical sentiments of the Land *Speculato alias Pirate.*"

SONG OF THE LAND PIRATE

Over earth's wide empire we have passed,
And girdled the land and sea,
The wealth of nations we have amassed,
For lords of the soil are we;
We have gathered the riches from every land,
Each soil our footsteps mark,
O'er the ocean deep, from the distant strand,
Comes home our bounding bark.
Thus sang the proud oppressor, but over land and seas
The voices of the millions spoiled, came swelling on the breeze.

We have bought their lands with the price of blood,
But money erased the stains,
We have driven from thence the humble good
To swell our earthly gains;
And the poor man's day we have turned to night,
And hushed his cheerful song,
For the time has come when might makes right,
And the weak must bend to the strong.
Thus sang the proud oppressor, but a voice in thunder told
The Robber, that the land was free and never should be sold.

The earth, the air, and the ocean blue,
And the showers that kiss the soil,
Were surely made for us wealthy few,
And not for the sons of toil;
'Tis theirs till life's long work is done,
To toil on the land and seas,
And ours to reap what they have won,
And live in splendor and ease.
Thus sang the proud oppressor, when lo upon his sight,
Uprose the mighty working men to vindicate their right.

Hurrah! hurrah! let the welkin ring,
With songs of wealth untold,
The praise of Mammon we'll chaunt and sing
And worship no god but gold;
To this let every thought be given,
For hireling priests devout,
Have made it the only way to heaven,
To shut the poor man out.
But here his song was ended, for in seeming vengeance hurled
All nature gave him back the lie and swept him from the world.

George Henry Evans argued that wage workers were worse off than Negro slaves, who, he contended, had the security of work and care during sickness and old age. Hence, to free the black slaves and reduce them to the status of wage slaves before land reform was accomplished, Evans insisted, would be a great disservice to the blacks, as they would exchange their

[7]Ibid., May 27, 1844, and Feb. 8, 1845.

"surety of support in sickness and old age" for poverty and unemployment.[8] This argument, so useful to the slave owners, found expression in song.

THE LABORER'S LAMENT

By Dreamer

Air—"Marble Halls"

O cruel—most cruel!—the laborer sigh'd,
The fate of the African slave.
Who crouches in silence his master beside,
From infancy down to his grave.
But tho' he is fetter'd, and forced to resign,
His right to the pleasures of earth,
The state of that captive is nobler than mine,
For want never visits his hearth.

'Tis not his to suffer the torture of mind,
That pains me at thought of my wife—
To see her tho' fainting still patient and kind—
Still facing the hardships of life.
For oft when her little ones ask her for bread,
She turns from their presence to weep—
Compell'd to refuse it, and send them to bed,
With hunger to haunt them in sleep.

But should my poor children misfortune outlive,
And enter unletter'd the world,
The sire of their being they ne'er can forgive,
But curses on him will be hurl'd—
And when in my sorrow and anguish of soul,
I brood o'er the evils I've sown,
The conflict of feeling is past my control,
And reason abandons her throne.[9]

Among the most popular of the songs of the land reform movement were those by Augustine Joseph Hickey Duganne, whom the *Voice of Industry* called "emphatically the poet of Labor."[10] Duganne's lyrics were published in a number of labor paper in the 1840s and were later included in *The Poetical Works of Augustine Duganne* (1855) and *Duganne's Poetical Works* (1865). Duganne, who believed that the poet must write for and in the interests of the working class, made his position clear in the following:

THE SONG OF TOIL

Let him who will, rehearse the song
Of gentle love and bright romance—
Let him who will, with tripping tongue,
Lead gleaming thoughts to fancy's dance;
But let me strike mine iron harp
As northern harps were struck of old—
And let its music, stern and sharp,
Arouse the free and bold!

My hands that iron harp shall sweep,
Till from each strike new strains recall;
And forth the sounding echoes leap,
To join the arousing Song of Toil;
Till men of thought their thoughts outspeak
And thoughts awake in kindred mind;
And stirring words shall arm the weak,
And fetters cease to bind!

And crashing soon, o'er soul and sense,
That glorious harp, whose iron strings
Are Labor's mighty instruments,
Shall shake the thrones of mortal kings:
And ring of axe, and anvil note,
And rush of plough through yielding soil,
And laboring engine's vocal throat,
Shall swell the Song of Toil![11]

Here are some of Duganne's poems which were especially popular among the agrarian reformers.

THE LANDLESS

The landless! the landless!
The wrestlers for a crust—
Behold to outer darkness
These wretched men are thrust.
I hear their sullen moanings;
Their curses low and deep;
And I see their bodies writhing
Like a maniac in his sleep!
Will no lightning rend their fetters?
Will no sunbeam pierce their eyes?—
In the name of truth and manhood,
Will they never—never rise?

The landless! the landless!
They have no household gods:
Their father's graves are trampled—
For strangers own their sods.
They have no home nor country—
No roof nor household hearth,—
Though all around them blossometh
The beautiful glad earth!
They fight a stranger's battles,
And they build a stranger's dome—
But the landless!—the landless!
God help them!—have no home![12]

8Ibid., Mar. 16, 1844.

9Ibid., Feb. 22, 1845.

10*Voice of Industry*, Dec. 3, 1847.

11Ibid., Nov. 12, 1847.

12Ibid., Aug. 20, 1845, reprinted in A. J. H. Duganne, *Duganne's Poetical Works* (New York, 1865), p. 144.

EPIGRAM

"God help me!" cried the Poor Man:
And the Rich Man said, "Amen!"
And the Poor Man died at the Rich Man's door:—
God *helped* the Poor Man then![13]

KEEP IT BEFORE THE PEOPLE

KEEP IT BEFORE THE PEOPLE—
That the earth was made for man!
That flowers were strewn,
And fruits were grown,
To bless and never to ban;
That sun and rain,
And corn and grain
Are yours and mine, my brother
Free gifts from heaven,
And freely given,
To one as well as another!

KEEP IT BEFORE THE PEOPLE—
That man is the image of God!
His limbs or soul
You may not control
With shackle, or shame, or rod!
We may not be sold,
For silver or gold.
Neither you nor I, my brother!
For freedom was given,
By God from heaven,
To one as well as another!

KEEP IT BEFORE THE PEOPLE—
That famine and crime and woe,
Forever abide,
Still side by side,
With luxury's dazzling show;
That Lazarus crawls
From Dives' halls,
And slaves at his gates, my brother!
Yet life was given
By God from heaven,
To one as well as another!

KEEP IT BEFORE THE PEOPLE—
That the laborer claims his meed:
The right of soil,
And the right to toil,
From spur and bridle freed;
The right to bear,
And the right to share,
With you and me, my brother!
What is given,
By God from heaven,
To one as well as another![14]

Duganne's pieces kept appearing in labor papers throughout the post–Civil War decades. As late as June 19, 1897, the *Birmingham Labor Advocate*, official journal of the Birmingham Trades Council and the United Mine Workers of America, published this interesting variant of "Keep It before the People."

KEEP IT BEFORE THE PEOPLE

Keep it before the people:
That the earth was made for man.
That the flowers were strewn,
And the fruits were grown
By the great Creator's hand;
That the sun and rain,
And the corn and grain
Are yours and mine, my brother—
Free gifts from heaven,
And as freely given
To one as well as another.

Keep it before the people:
That man is the image of God;
Whose limbs or soul
Ye may not control
With shackle or shame or rod—
We may not be sold
For silver or gold,
Neither you nor I, my brother—
For the land was given
Like the life from heaven,
To one as well as another.

Keep it before the people:
That famine, and crime, and woe,
Forever abide
Still side by side
With luxury's dazzling show;
That Lazarus crawls
From Dives' halls
And starves at his gate, my brother—
Yet the land was given
To man from heaven,
To one as well as another.

Keep it before the people:
That the laborer claims his need:
The right of all soil,
And the right to toil,
From spurs and bridle freed;
The right to bear,
And the right to share
With you and me, my brother,
Whatever is given
By God in heaven
To one as well as another.[15]

13 *Voice of Industry*, Jan. 21, 1848, reprinted in Duganne, *Duganne's Poetical Works*, p. 143.
14 *Voice of Industry*, Jan. 14, 1848.
15 *Birmingham Labor Advocate*, June 19, 1897.

LABOR PRESS OF THE FORTIES AND REVIVAL OF UNIONISM

The trade union movement revived slowly from the ravages of the crisis of 1837, but already in the early forties, mechanics' and laborers' associations were springing up in New England, to be followed by associations of the factory operatives. Labor papers, too, were reappearing in the cities of the region. These included the *Boston Laborer*, the *Lynn Awl and True Workingman*, the *Lowell Working Man's Advocate*, the *Voice of Industry* in Fitchburg and Lowell, and the *Mechanic* in Fall River. In 1842, a fortnightly periodical, the *Factory Girl*, saw the light of day in New Hampshire. Soon afterwards, the *Factory Girls' Album and Operatives' Advocate* began its career in Exeter, New Hampshire,[16] and the *Factory Journal and Laborers' Advocate* came into existence in Pawtucket, Rhode Island. The Pawtucket journal announced its birth in verse:

We come before the public with your sheet,
And trust their approbation we shall meet;
'Tis for the laboring class we would contend
Support their cause, their trampled rights defend.
Too long alas! like Israel's tribe of old,
They've felt the weight of power, sustained by gold;
The mind and body chained in servile state,
And made obedient to the haughty great.
How many thus in vice and ignorance kept,
Have met the grave, unhonored and unwept;
Then let us in the voice of Christian love
Exert our powers, their morals to improve.
Philanthropists, come forth, our work to sustain,
And then our labor shall not be in vain.[17]

The most widely read and influential labor paper of the forties was the *Voice of Industry*. It began publication on May 29, 1845, "by an Association of workingmen," under the editorship of William F. Young. In November it was combined with two other labor papers and moved to the textile factory city of Lowell. Here it was issued weekly by a publishing committee of three, consisting of Young, Sarah G. Bagley, and Joel Hatch. In its prospectus the journal described itself as the organ of the New England Workingmen's Association (of which more below) and stated its aims as "the abolition of Mental, Moral, and Physical Servitude, in all their complicated forms, and the interests of the Industrial Classes."[18] The paper devoted considerable space to the plight of the factory girls, even establishing a regular "Female Department, under the supervision of the Lowell Female Labor Reform Association . . . supported by contributions from the Operatives of this city and other manufacturing towns." In May, 1846, the paper's type and press were bought by the Lowell Female Labor Reform Association. For a time the association's president, Sarah G. Bagley, a former operative turned schoolteacher, was its editor-in-chief. After Miss Bagley left, another factory girl, Mehitabel Eastman, was coeditor and later managing editor until its demise.[19]

It is clear that one of the most important developments of the forties was the fact that for the first time, factory workers established fairly stable unions. As long as the majority of the factory girls came from nearby farms and their earnings in the mills were not their sole means of support, the appeals of trade unionists urging them to organize had little effect. But in the 1840s the situation was drastically altered. Gradually a permanent working class began to emerge in the factories. During the crisis of 1837, a good many farmers in New England lost their farms, and since many of the mill operatives could no longer return to the farms, they had to organize to improve the conditions under which they worked. Hence the 1840s saw the emergence of Female Labor Reform Associations of factory girls in Lowell and Fall River, Massachusetts, in Manchester and Dover, New Hampshire,

[16]Bertha Monica Stearns, "Early Factory Magazines in New England," *Journal of Economic and Business History*, II (Aug., 1930), 92–98, 702.

[17]*Factory Journal and Laborers' Advocate*, Apr. 14, 1843.

[18]The *Voice of Industry* changed its aims several times before it expired in the fall of 1848. Late in 1846 it became the organ of the New England Labor Reform League. In the summer of 1848 it ceased to be the organ of any particular body and, published in Boston, announced that it was "devoted to the Organization of Labor, Land Reform, Working Men's Protective Unions, Universal Freedom, Literature, and General Intelligence." For a short period in 1848 the paper's name was changed to the *New Era of Industry*.

[19]A number of the factory girls had previously written for the *Lowell Offering*, but when the editors refused to publish their articles on the need for shorter hours, higher wages, and better working conditions, the girls denounced the magazine as a company organ, which it was, and, in addition to setting up their own magazines and journals, contributed regularly to the *Voice of Industry*.

and in western Pennsylvania. The first and most important Female Labor Reform Association was that established in Lowell.

Before, during, and after ownership by the Lowell Female Labor Reform Association, the *Voice of Industry* featured poetry and songs and encouraged factory workers and mechanics to submit original compositions. One of the most significant signs of the period, it noted, was that poets like John Greenleaf Whittier, James Russell Lowell, William Cullen Bryant, and others were using their talents on behalf of the working class.[20] "Instead of standing aloof from the people, in the solitary sublimity of a fancied superiority, they mingle with the masses, sympathize with their joys and sorrows, and exult in the strong upheaving of the tide of humanity."[21] The *Voice of Industry* published several of Whittier's poems which appeared in book form in 1850 under the title *Songs of Labor and Other Poems.*[22] In its issue of April 3, 1846, the *Voice of Industry* featured the following by James Russell Lowell, written especially for the labor paper:[23]

SPEAK OUT

We will speak out. We will be heard,
  Though all the earth's systems crack;
We will not bate a single word,
  Nor take a letter back.

We speak the truth, and what care we
  For hissing and for scorn,
While some faint glimmerings we can see
  Of Freedom's coming morn?

Let liars fear, let cowards shrink,
  Let traitors turn away;
What we have dared to think,
  That dare we also say.

"These are heroic words; they are worthy of the poet from whose gifted pen they came; to them the true and brave soul says amen!" commented the labor paper.

While it supported the land reform movement, the *Voice of Industry* did not endorse the viewpoint of George Henry Evans and his followers that the black slaves were better off than white wage slaves in the North and in Europe and that priority should be given to ending wage slavery before combating chattel slavery. Rather, the labor paper took the position that both slaveries were evil and should be abolished together. "Needs it be attempted to decide whether Southern Slaves or the starving wage Slaves of Ireland are in the worse condition," it editorialized. "Suppose you could decide the question, would that abate the evil? Why man, instead of quarreling about which is the greater evil, let us be stirring ourselves to tip them both over into the Night of non-existence."[24] To hasten the abolition of black slavery, the *Voice of Industry*, almost alone among the labor papers of the forties, carried poems and ballads depicting the evils of the institution.[25]

WHAT IS IT TO BE A SLAVE

Hast thou ever asked thyself
  What is it to be a slave?

[20]For discussion of Whittier's and Bryant's support of trade unionism and workers' struggles, see Philip S. Foner, *History of the Labor Movement in the United States*, I (New York, 1947), 127, 155–56, 177.

[21]*Voice of Industry*, Apr. 3, 1846.

[22]The book contained "The Ship-Builders," "The Shoemakers," "The Drovers," "The Fishermen," "The Huskers," and "The Lumbermen." "The Shoemakers" was published in the *Voice of Industry*, August 25, 1845. Its opening lines went:

Ho! the workers of the old time styled
  The Gentle Craft of Leather!
Young brothers of the ancient guild,
  Stand forth once more together!
Call out again your long array,
  In the olden merry manner!
Once more, on gay St. Crispin's day,
  Fling out your blazoned banner!

It is interesting that although the words of Walt Whitman—more than any poet since Shakespeare—have been internationally set to music, none of them were used in the songs of American labor during the nineteenth century. However, Whitman's "Love of Comrades," with music by D.F., and his "Great City" appear in Edward Carpenter's *Chants of Labour* (London, 1891), pp. 56–57, 92–93.

[23]Lowell's poem "True Freedom," set to the "War Chant of the Druids" from Bellini's opera *Norma*, is included in Carpenter's *Chants of Labour* (p. 4); two lines went:

They are slaves who fear to speak
For the fallen and the weak.

[24]*Voice of Industry*, Feb. 25, 1848.

[25]Alone, too, among labor papers, the *Voice of Industry* emphasized the unity of all workers regardless of color. On December 31, 1847, it welcomed the publication of the *North Star* by Frederick Douglass, the fugitive slave and outstanding black abolitionist: "It gleams and flashes all over the light of genius. . . . Frederick Douglass is in every sense a gentleman, and his large acquaintance with men, individually and socially, as a slave and as a hunted fugitive in America and in England, fit him, as no other among us is fitted, to conduct an anti-slavery journal. We cordially welcome him to the labors, so recently entered upon ourselves, and earnestly wish the happiest success."

Bought and sold for sordid pelf,
  From the cradle to the grave!

'Tis to know the transient powers
  E'en of muscle, flesh and bone,
Cannot in thy happiest hours,
  Be considered as thine own:

But thy master's goods and chattels
  Lent to thee for little more
Than to fight his selfish battles
  For some bits of shining ore!

'Tis to learn thou hast a heart
  Beating in that bartered frame,
Of whose ownership—no part
  Thou can'st challenge—but in name.

For the curse of slavery crushes
  Out the life-blood from its core;
And expends its throbbing gushes
  But to swell another's store.

God's best gift from heaven above,
  Meant to make a heaven on earth,
Hallowing, humanizing love!
  With the ties which thence have birth;

These can never be his lot,
  Who, like brutes, are bought and sold;
Holding such—as having not
  On his own the spider's hold!

'Tis to feel, e'en worse than this,
  If aught worse than this can be,
Thou hast shrined, for bale or bliss,
  An immortal soul in thee!

But that this undying guest
  Sears thy body's degradation,
Until slavery's bonds, unblest,
  Check each kindling aspiration:

And what should have been thy light,
  Shining e'en beyond the grave,
Turns to darkness worse than night,
  Leaving thee a hopeless slave!

Such is Slavery. Couldst thou bear
  Its vile bondage. O! my brother,
How, then, canst thou, will thou dare
  To inflict it on another?[26]

NORTH AND SOUTH

By Mary

"For the wail of millions
Is sounding in our ears."

List ye that low and plaintive wail,
Borne on the southern balmy gale!
See Afric's wretched daugher weep,
Nor close her weary eyes to sleep.

Her wretched husband at her side,
Strives to assuage—her cares divide;
But cruel white, with lash appears,
Nor heeds his groans, nor minds her tears.

"Hie to your task—of darker hue,
What sympathetic chords have you?
Go, toil and sweat on yonder plain;
Ye were but made for white men's gain."

List ye again that plaintive moan!
It strikes the ear like childhood's tone;—
Ah, little one! thou weep'st in vain!
Thy mother toils on yonder plain.

Friends of freedom! heed the wail!
'Tis God's own cause,—we cannot fail!
His richest guerdon will be given,—
The joy of earth—the peace of heaven.

Remember, too, that wrong is here,
And give the north one pitying tear;
Oh! let the fruits of love go forth,
To free the South and bless the North![27]

The incidents alluded to in the following lines are strictly true; having been witnessed by a gentleman of veracity from the North.

THE SLAVE'S REVENGE

By Sarah W.

Lend, lend imagination wings,
While yonder sun in beauty wanes;—
Soar far away to southern clime,
Where souls in cruel bondage pine.

In yonder cabin kneels a form
That slavery's galling yoke hath worn;
In broken accents hear him cry,
"Must I in bondage always sigh?"

The morning dawned in beauty bright,
And chased away the darksome night;
But yet it brought no kind relief
To him whose soul was filled with grief.

The busy crowd the market throng,
And he whose prayer to heaven hath gone,
With heavy tread reached the stand
Where men are sold in Christian land.

His dark eyes flash in deep despair—
Yon little group—his all—stands there;—
Alas! deep anguish fills his heart;
With wife and children he must part.

The thought is mad'ning—worse than death—
Of loved ones, dear as life, bereft;—

26 *Voice of Industry*, Jan. 23, 1846.
27 Ibid., Feb. 13, 1846.

He crossed the stand with resolute air,
And whispered in the planter's ear.

"You own my wife, my children dear,"
And then he wip'd a briny tear;
"Me work for you by night, or day,
Oh! bid me off, good master, pray."

But soon advanced with haughty stride,
He who the Almighty's law defied;
The slave cast one dark, withering look,
All fear of man his soul forsook.

He raised his strong, athletic arm,
Then rose his voice in wild alarm—
"You cast my lot far far away;
Me never work for you a day."

Cease! cease these idle words, black slave!
No longer like a maniac rave;
The highest bid hath made you mine;
Henceforth you dwell in distant clime.

The bondman raised his eyes to heaven,
Then gazed on those whom God had given;
With frantic yell he leaped the stand,
Seized fast an axe—cut off his hand.

Then raised his bleeding arm to him
Who vainly thought the prize to win—
"Remember sir, again me say,
Me never work for you a day."[28]

The following brief definition appeared in the *Voice of Industry* of June 5, 1845: "Negro. A human being treated as a brute because he is black, by inhuman beings and greater brutes, who happen to be white. The Ethiopians paint the devil white; and they have much better reason for making him look like a European than we have for giving him an African complexion."

Nearly all labor papers of the 1840s bitterly opposed the war of aggression waged by the United States against Mexico. They viewed it as a war to expand slavery and land monopoly.[29] The following expressed labor opposition to the Mexican War in verse:

A GLORIOUS VICTORY

By J.W.R.

Make way for the victors! we've glory in store!
Our soldiers have massacred seven hundred more!
Wind shrilly, ye bugles! and scream all ye pipes!
We have not disgraced our broad banner of stripes;
True, true to the letter our army has been;
It has stripped the weak Mexicans once and again.
Hurra for our soldiers! hurra for our seamen!
Hurra for our nation of *Christians and Freemen!*

When we tread on a worm, and it bites at our feet,
We crush out its life;—and it surely is meet
That a band of uncivilized, barbarous knaves
Should not dare to insult our chivalrous braves.
What though they are ignorant, foolish and blind?
They've sought to harm us, and we'll pay them in kind.
Hurra for our soldiers! hurra for our seamen!
Hurra for our nation of *Christians and Freemen!*

When England endeavoured to force the Chinese
To take down her opium, and yield up their teas—
When we heard the loud noise of her cannon's red blast,
The nations with horror extreme stood aghast!
'Twas the cruelest wrong! oh, the poor Pagan souls![30]
But now 'tis Columbia's cannon that rolls.
Hurra for our soldiers! hurra for our seamen!
Hurra for our nation of *Christians and Freemen!*

To be sure we have stolen the best of their land,
And have peopled their realm with a cut-throat band,
And in flying to arms they but stood for the right;
But then the poor fools have no business to fight!
Tho' we took from their hands their ancestor's dower,
Our Creed knows no right but that born of Power.
Hurra for our soldiers! hurra for our seamen!
Hurra for our nation of *Christians and Freemen!*

Our people are frightened—the corners of streets
Thronged by terror-worn faces, are all that one meets;
And well may we tremble; the cloud, black and heavy,
That hangs o'er our heads, comes from Mexico's navy!
And in the bright realms of the Bravo's fair region,
List, list to the trampings of Mexico's legions.
Hurra for our soldiers! hurra for our seamen!
Hurra for our nation of *Christians and Freemen!*

Stand firm to your posts, oh ye warriors of might!
Do not suffer the freemen to put you to flight!
Repel them, and save us, our fortunes and lives,
Our rights and our children, our churches and wives!
Methinks I now witness their muskets' dread flashes;
Pray God our fair cities may not lay in ashes!*

28Ibid., June 18, 1847.

29New York workingmen voiced opposition to the Mexican War at a meeting in May, 1846, at which they branded the war as a scheme of the slave owners and their allies who lived "in such luxurious idleness on the products of the workingmen." At its 1846 convention the New England Workingmen's Association denounced "the foul disgrace" of extending the area of slavery and pledged that they would "not take up arms to sustain the Southern Slaveholder in robbing one-fifth of our countrymen of their labor" (*National Anti-Slavery Standard,* May 28, 1846). However, the *Champion of Labor,* a nativist paper published in New York City in 1847, supported the Mexican War.

30When the Chinese government prohibited opium imports, British traders induced the British government to wage two wars with China, as a result of which unrestricted opium trade was legalized in 1858.

Hurra for our soldiers! hurra for our seamen!
Hurra for our nation of *Christians and Freemen!*

The poets may sing in lyric and ballad,
Of Erin's thin cheeks, by hunger made pallid—
Of England's starved thousands, and India's slaves,
And the millions who slumber in China's red graves
But American bards hang their heads low with shame,
That their country now has such a dastardly name!
Still about for our soldiers! hurra for our seamen!
Hurra for our nation of *Christians and Freemen!*

Oh, brothers, boast on! pause ye not—still declare
That the Race's prosperity's always your prayer!
Proclaim to the world that you love all the nations,
When you're wronged and insulted you'll always have patience,
And yet when agrieved by a poor pagan horde,
Mow them down in your wrath with the musket and sword.
Hurra for our soldiers! hurra for our seamen!
Hurra for our nation of *Christians and Freemen!*[31]

*Gov. Shunk has issued a proclamation, urging the people of Pennsylvania to stand ready to defend their soil from Mexican aggression.

Both the *Mechanic* and the *Voice of Industry* published poems and songs expressing the pride of workers in their trades and their feeling that it was labor which was the important element in society.

MECHANIC'S SONG

All jovial Mechanics come join in my song,
And let the brisk chorus go bounding along;
Though some may be poor, and some rich there may be;
You all are contented, and happy, and free.

Ye *Tailors!* of ancient and noble renown,
Who clothe all the people in country and town;
Remember that Adam, your father and head,
Though the Lord of the world, was a trailor by trade.

Ye *Masons!* who work in stone, mortar and brick,
And lay the foundation deep, solid and thick;
Though hard be your labor, yet lasting your fame;
Both Egypt and *China* your wonders proclaim.

Ye *Smiths!* who forge tools for all traders here below,
You have nothing to fear while you smite and you blow;
All things you may conquer, so happy your lot,
If you're careful to *strike while your iron is hot.*

Ye *Shoemakers!* nobly from ages long past,
Have defended your rights with your awl to the last!
And *cobblers,* all merry, not only stop holes,
But work night and day for the good of our *soles.*

Ye *Cabinet Makers!* brave workers in wood,
As you work for the ladies your work must be good:
And *Joiners* and *Carpenters,* far off and near,
Stick close to your trades, and you've nothing to fear.

Ye *Hatters!* who oft, with hands not very fair,
Fix hats on a block for a blockhead to wear!
Though charity covers a sin now and then,
You cover the heads and the sins of all men.

Ye *Coach Makers!* must not by tax be controlled,
But ship off your coaches and fetch us home gold;
The role of your coach made Copernicus reel,
And fancy the world to turn round like a wheel.

Ye *Carders* and *Sippners,*[32] and *Weavers* attend,
And take the advice of "Poor Richard" your friend;
Stick close to your looms, and your wheels and your card,
And you never need fear of the times being hard.

Ye *Printers,* who give us our learning and news,
And impartially print, for *Turks, Christians,* and *Jews,*
Let your favorite toast ever sound in the streets—
"The *freedom of press,* and a volume in *sheets.*"

Ye *Coopers!* who rattle with *driver* and *adze*
And lecture each day upon hoops and on *heads,*
The famous old ballad of "*Love in a Tub,*"
You may sing to the tune of your bub a dub dub.

Ye *Ship Builders, Riggers* and *makers of sails!*
Already the fame of your labor prevails,
And still you shall see o'er the proud swelling tide,
The ships of our nation triumphantly ride!

Each *Tradesman* turn out, with his tool in his hand,
To cherish the *Arts,* and keep *Peace* through the land.
Each *'Prentice* and *Journeyman* join in my song
And let the brisk *Chorus* go bounding along![33]

THE PRINTER'S SONG

Print comrades, print; a noble task
  Is the one we gaily ply;
'Tis ours to tell to all who ask,
  The wonders of earth and sky!
We catch the thought all glowing warm,
  As it leaves the student's brain,
And place the stamp of enduring form
  On the Poet's airy strain.
    Then let us sing as we nimbly fling
      The slender letters round;
  A glorious thing is our laboring,
    Oh where may its like be found!

Print, comrades print; the fairest thought
  Ever lined in Painter's dream,

31 *Voice of Industry,* June 19, 1846.
32 Undoubtedly *Spinners.*
33 *Mechanic,* June 15, 1844.

The rarest form e'er sculptor wrought,
By the light of beauty's gleam,
Though lovely, may not match the power,
Which our proud art can claim;
That links the past with the present hour,
And its breath—the voice of fame.
Then let us sing as we nimbly fling
The slender letters round;
A glorious thing is our laboring,
Oh where can the like be found.

Print, comrades print; God hath ordained
That man by his toil should live;
Then spurn the charge that we disdained
The labor that God should give!
We envy not the sons of ease,
Nor the lord in princely hall,
But bow before the wise decrees
In kindness meant for all.
Then let us sing as we nimbly fling,
The slender letters round;
A glorious thing is our laboring,
Oh where may its like be found.[34]

THE MECHANIC

I am Nature's own nobleman, happy and free,
A peer of the realm might well envy me,
For the land of the eagle has given me birth,
And my sons are all free men that meet round my hearth.

Your cities now rising with beauty and might,
Whose palace like towers are fair to the sight,
My hands helped to build them, my strength lent its aid,
And by the sweat of my brow your proud cities are laid.

The ship that sweeps proudly o'er the far spreading sea,
Has been timbered and fashioned by the labor of me,
And the pure massive marble that strikes on the view,
Is chiseled and formed by the artisan too.

The smith as he hums o'er his anvil a glee,
He toils not for happiness or power—not he;
He dreads not lost office, he seeks none to gain—
And the smithy's a king in his own proud domain.

The bravest of men from mechanics have sprung,
And the sweetest of lays mechanics have sung,
And the proudest of hearts mechanics should wear,
When conscious of right in their bosom they bear.[35]

THOSE DIRTY MECHANICS

By H. G. Barrus

"These mechanics, oh dear! what a nuisance they are,"
Remarked Mr. Fop to Miss Flirt;
"In the boat or in the street they are sure to be there,
All covered with smut and with dirt.

"Why don't they all live on a street by themselves,
And associate there with each other?
I would not to one of them speak in the street,
No, not if that one were my brother."

"Tis surprising to me, my dear Mr. Fop,
And I think it should straight be put down,
That these dirty mechanics should dare to converse
With the aristocratic of town."

"Oh! had I the power my dear Mistress Flirt,
I'd soon set these fellows afloat;
I'd make them all walk in the middle of the street,
And cross in a separate boat."

"And out of our pews in the church, Mr. Fop,
I every mechanic would rouse;
And they should be seated in pews by themselves,
In the farthermost part of the house."

Pray stop your wild speech, Mr. Fop and Miss Flirt,
And make you no further ado;
Do you expect in the region of bliss you will find,
A place parted off there for you?

Then if for yourselves you have any respect,
Pray cease to traduce and deride;
For those whom you speak of and think of so light,
ARE AMERICA'S GLORY AND PRIDE.[36]

The *Champion of Labor*, a weekly published by an association of mechanics, appeared briefly in New York City in 1847 and sought primarily to halt immigration, which, it charged, was lowering the wage levels of American workers. Two songs in its pages trumpeted the virtues of a particular labor group and of mechanics in general:

FIREMAN'S SONG

Air—"Le Petit Tambour"

When the lurid flame at night,
Lights up the clear blue sky,
The fireman rouses in alarm,
And sees the danger nigh.
Now hear the heavy wheels,
That roll along the pave,
Turn out!—turn out! the firemen cry
The burning dwelling save.

Oh, the fireman's heart is free,
His motto is "to save";
We work without reward or fee,
Hurrah! the firemen brave!

[34] *Voice of Industry*, Nov. 28, 1845.
[35] Ibid., June 12, 1845.
[36] Ibid., Feb. 18, 1848.

Now the raging flame soars high,
The heavens look red and wild;
But hark! a mother's piercing cry,
Oh! save my darling child!
Now streams the water high,
While from the ladder raised,
Is heard the gallant fireman's cry,
The darling child is saved.

O, the fireman's heart, &c.

Quick moves the iron arm,
And rapid strikes the break,
The raging element to calm,
To quench the fiery flake.
But listen to the shout,
From noble firemen brave,—
"Our work is done—the fire is out,
We've conquered and we've saved."

O, the fireman's heart, &c.[37]

RISE IN YOUR NATIVE STRENGTH
By Joseph H. Butler

Rise in your native strength,
Mechanics of the land,
And dash the iron rule
From rude oppressor's hand!
By all the might of MIND,
Assume the place of man—
Heed not the scoff of those
Who scorn the artizan.

Ye sinews of a state,
Your nation's pride and boast,
Whose glory crowns her hills,
And guards your native coast,
You are her WEALTH IN PEACE,
Her vital breath ye are;
And, when the bolts of death are hurl'd,
Ye are her shield in war.

By the eternal sword,
To stern browed justice given
By freedom's holy self,
The might of wrong is riven!
Strong monuments arise,
In record of your praise,
Transmitting down your names,
To men of other days.

Proclaim to all the world,
Your usefulness and worth,
Speak out with trumpet tongue,
Ye mighty men of earth!
Was not the soil ye tread
Won by your father's blood?
Then on oppression's self
Roll back oppression's flood!

Seize with determined hand
The standard sheet of RIGHT,
And let not even death
Turn your resolves to flight,
By Him who gave to man
The soul's ethereal fire,
That glorious day is NOW,
Our motto, onward—HIGHER![38]

The following, also published in the *Champion of Labor*, struck a more moderate note:

LABOR SONG
By G. S. Stagg

Why stand ye idle at the door?
Hear ye not the furnace roar?
Go to work with might and main;
Though wearily,
Yet cheerily
Swing the hammer, drive the plane.

Honest toil is sure to thrive—
God help those who truly strive,
Whether by the hand or brain—
Though wearily,
Yet cheerily,
Swing the hammer, drive the plane.

See the man in yonder shop;
Not one moment doth he stop,
For his little ones he'd fain
Though wearily,
Yet cheerily,
Swing the hammer, drive the plane.

Hard at work, another pores
All night long at Learning's stores;
Say ye not his work is vain—
Though wearily,
Yet cheerily,
Swing the hammer, drive the plane.

Then up and work with heart so brave
'Tis heart and work will each one save.
Present want and future pain—
Though wearily,
Yet cheerily,
Swing the hammer, drive the plane.[39]

The reawakening of the labor movement after the panic of 1837 was mirrored in the songs and poems published in the *Mechanic* and the *Voice of Industry*.

37 *Champion of Labor*, July 24, 1847.
38 Ibid., July 3, 1847.
39 Ibid., May 15, 1847.

Come, come to the meeting,
Come one, and come all,
For true hearts are beating,
Responsive to the call;

From highland and valley—
From mountain and plain—
Come, come to the rally,
Our rights to regain.[40]

THE SUMMONS

By Amelia

Ye children of New England!
The summons is to you!
Come from the work-shop and the field,
With steadfast hearts and true.

Come fling your banner to the breeze,
For liberty and light;
Come, like the rolling of the seas—
The tempest in its might.

Aye, with a voice of thunder come;
And swear 'fore tyranny,
Thy vows are registered on high,
To perish or be free.

Hear ye the groans from foreign lands,
Ruled by despotic powers?
From Spain's bright shores, from Galia's strand,
And England's stately towers.

In costly splendid luxury,
Each royal board is spread;
While thousands in their streets may die
For lack of daily bread.

And turn to our own boasted clime,—
What scenes before us lie?
Aye, want and woe and care and crime,
Still greet the tearful eye.

'Tis mockery in the sight of God,
To say that land is blest
Where millions bow beneath the rod
Of tyranny oppressed.

For bread, where famished children cry,
And none their want supplies—
Where toiling thousands live and die
In ignorance and vice.

Then in the name of God come forth,
To battle with the foe;
Nor stay ye till your hands have laid
Each proud oppressor low.

Aye, come and blest, shalt then be,
By millions yet unborn,
Whom thou hast saved from misery,
From insult and from scorn.

Yet be thou strong—there yet remains
A promise sure to thee,
That God will break the oppressor's chains,
And set the prisoner free.

That righteousness and truth shall reign,
Through all the peopled earth,
And heaven repeat the exulting strain,
Which hailed creation's birth.[41]

THERE'S SPIRIT ABROAD

By M. C. Priest

"There's spirit abroad" on the face of the soil,
Ay! it lurks in the breast of the weary with toil,
It points to yon castle, feared proudly on high,
But it need not to tell that the tyrant is nigh;
He feels as he lends to the spade and the plough,
The strength of each sinew, the sweat of his brow,
That the harvest tho' golden, will yield him no part,
And he turns from the vision all stricken at heart.

There's spirit abroad in the miner's dark home,
Where no ray of the Sunbeam for ages hath come,
Those features grown pale by his poisonous trade,
By the lamp's lurid glare still more ghastly are made;
That spirit doth point to the gold by his side,
Which he mined while his loved ones have famished and
died;
He sees; 'tis the tyrant's—that glittering heap,
He feels—all in silence he turneth to weep.

There's a spirit abroad on the crest of the wave,
'Tis the home of the Sailors, the pall of his grave;
Winds lash, and waves roar, yet he fears not their strife
Yet for what—ay! for what doth he peril his tife[42];
Tho' the hold is deep laden, the decks are well stored,
Tho' of pearls and of germs[43] she beareth a hoard,
Yet he feels as he turns from each glittering store
That the sinews that win are forbidden to wear.

There's spirit abroad, where the swift shuttle flies
Where the lamp lends a light which the broad sun denies,
"Accursed be heart," grown so callous and cold,
That can barter the lives of our maidens for gold;
For the arm which doth boast of out-stretching to aid,
Is the same that is dark with the blood of betrayed;
And the stain is less deep in the hands of the 'Dyer,'
Than the guilt of that heart which defraudeth of hire.

There's a spirit abroad, wake! ye laboring bands,
Around Liberty's Altar, your hearts and hands;
Tho' light are its footsteps, more heavy they'll fall
Wake! laborers wake, and arouse to its call;

40*Mechanic*, Dec. 21, 1844.
41*Voice of Industry*, Nov. 7, 1845.
42Should be *life*.
43Should be *gems*.

'Tis the spirit of freedom, the spirit which led
Our forefathers forth o'er a field of the dead;
It call'd them through blood to the battle's dark fray,
O, say are their offspring more dastard than they?

'Tis the same spirit calls you, O! can ye refrain?
Tho' it calls you not now, to a field of the slain,
Yet the foe is as deadly—the conflict more deep,
Awake or forever in slavery sleep;
No clarion is sounding, no war-note is blown,
But a cry is abroad, wrung from misery's zone,
Will ye heed the deep summons, O! will you defend?
Dare ye stand against Might for the Right to contend.[44]

SONG FOR THE MILLION

By one of them

Up, brother, to your toil to-day,
Let fools the burden shirk;
Though idle men may snatch the pay,
Thank God, they leave the work.

Let purse proud, bloated sluggards preach
Of labor as a curse!
Their rotten health and morals teach
That idleness is worse.

Who labors, lives, though but a slave,
And reaping not the fruit;
His lazy lord, in manhood's grave,
Is but a wallowing brute.

Then ply the hoe and ply the plough
And ditch the drowsy hog;
And if it must be, why, allow
Your lords to play the hog.

Then ply the spindle, ply the horn,
Though tyrants take the cloth;
Your happy limbs they cannot doom
To feel the pains of sloth.

While life is left that can't destroy
Your blissful muscle-play;
That glorious spark, creative joy,
They cannot take away.[45]

DEMAND FOR PERSEVERANCE

Laborers, to the GREAT CAUSE plighted!
Firm of limb and high of soul!
Shall it e'er be said, united
We were forced to brook control?

What though broad petitions moulder,
In yonder Legislative Hall?
Let not hearts, or hopes grow colder—
Perseverance conquers all.

Trust ye not, O! trust ye never,
In the hearts, by gold enshrined;
Lift your own strong arm and sever
Galling chains ye would unbind.

Days and months may not restore us
Back the rights we boldly ask;
Yet while yon blue heaven is o'er us,
Shall we falter in our task?

What though strong hands droop around us—
Heart of iron feel dismay?
Yet while misery's cry surrounds us,
Let that urge us on our way.

Rude winds, so the poets tell us,
Firmer root the forest oak;
Then let adverse waves impel us
Onward in our glorious work.

Truth, your weapon, grasp defying,
Boldly standing in the fight—
Brave the tempest self-relying:—
ALLA and the Laborer's RIGHTS.[46]

TO THE WORKINGMEN

By D. Wilkins

Bring out your standard Workingmen,
And give its folds free air;
Now raise it to the loftiest peak,
And boldly nail it there.

Now lift on high each toil-worn hand—
Invoke each holy Fane;
And swear you'll never cease to strive
Till man his rights obtain.

Give work to every son of want,
Be hope no more defer'd,
And be the VOICE OF INDUSTRY
On every hill-top heard.

Be this our motto evermore
While Ocean rolls a wave,
That glorious Being we adore
Ne'er made nor own'd a slave.[47]

UNION IS STRENGTH

By Ivar

Tune—"Washing Day"

Unite! unite! for now's the time,
For workingmen to rally,
And echo forth the song sublime,
From hill-top, plain and valley;
To action! let the word go out!

44 *Voice of Industry*, Feb. 27, 1846.
45 Ibid., July 9, 1845.
46 Ibid., Apr. 10, 1846.
47 Ibid., May 29, 1845.

Nor longer slumber dumb!
But pierce the heavens with the shout,
We come! we come! we come!
And let your pealing anthem be,
And echo it loud abroad,
Too long we've bow'd the willing knee,
And kiss'd the oppressor's rod!
But now united, firm and true,
From plain and mountain home,
To claim our honest rights and due,
We come! we come! we come!
Unite! unite! united go
Firm to the moral fight—
Onward! onward! meet your foe!
And battle for the right!
To the rescue!—out—turn out!
HOPE is your guiding star!
And victory shall be your shout;
Hurrah! hurrah! hurrah![48]

THE VICTORY SONG

By E. G. A., Boston, Sept. 16, 1844

The workingmen now are awake and in motion
And onward they come like the waves of the ocean—
The tyrants will find to resist them is vain,
When FREEDOM'S the cause they are seeking to gain.

New England's brave sons have now sundered the bands
So long fastened on them by task-master's hands—
No longer shall *wealth* the criterion be
'Twixt master and servant, the bound and the free.

The mass of the people are rising in gladness
The Union of prosperity drives away sadness—
Hereafter themselves their own masters will be,
So loud ring to heaven the shouts of the free.

The *lords* of the land will now rule them no more,
Their days are all numbered, their power is o'er
They now must give way to the workingmen brave
Who strive from pale Hunger their children to save!

Their homes and their fires, although humble they be,
Will peaceful enjoyment and happiness see—
Gaunt poverty never will visit the cot
Where Industry reigns, content with its lot.[49]

THE WORKING MAN'S PROSPECT

Tune—"The Morning Light Is Breaking"

See! See! the day is dawning,
Bright, cloudless, and serene;
A brighter, fairer morning
Than mortals yet have seen.
A day of moral glory,
A day without a storm,
When all shall tell the story
Of Freedom and Reform.

When av'rice and oppression
Shall stay their grasping hand,
And warlike desolation
Shall mar no more the land:
When rules of good defeated,
The triumphing of crime;
Shall only be repeated
As scenes of olden time.

Ye Working-men of power,
Press onward to the fight;
Say, shall your spirits cower,
When pleading for the right!
Be firm and valiant-hearted,
Like warriors true and brave
And strive, with zeal undaunted,
Your Liberties to save.[50]

SONG

Air—"Scots Wha Ha'e we Wallace Bled"

By a Workingman

Sons of Patriotic Sires,
Fan afresh your latent fires,
Brave is he who now aspires
To the birthright of the free.

For their rights your fathers bled:
Has their noble courage fled?
Shall their sons again be made
Vassals at the tyrants' knee?

By the patent power of gold
Now, the oppressor dares to hold
Back your rights which ye have sold,
Yet ye may be—must be free!

Rise ye! rise in stern array,
To the combat haste away!—
Leave the recreant a pray[51]
To the fangs of tyranny.

Rouse! from your inglorious trance,
To the bloodless charge advance;
Seek in deep, calm tones at *once*,
Freedom's rights and equity.

See, O'erawed by force and arms
Where a pauper legion swarms,
Steep'd in want and wild alarms,
Hopeless griefs and misery.

48*Mechanic*, Oct. 12, 1844.

49*Boston Laborer*, reprinted in the *Mechanic*, Oct. 12, 1844.

50*Voice of Industry*, Nov. 7, 1845. The song was published earlier, in *Young America* of September 27, 1845, and appeared in the *Voice of Industry* of March 31, 1846, under the title "Fair Prospect."

51Probably *prey*.

That their fate may ne'er be ours,
Let us tax our utmost powers,
Till the cloud that o'er us lowers
Shall be scattered utterly.

Whilst we breathe God's common air,
Let us his free bounties share,
In propositions just and fair
This is life and liberty.[52]

Songs celebrating the Fourth of July emphasized the duty of workers to continue the struggle for the principles enunciated in the Declaration of Independence.

INDEPENDENCE DAY
Tune—"Yankee Doodle"

Again we hail the day's return,
That gave us independence,
And freedom's fires, that warmed our sires,
Still glow in their descendants.

Then let us sing till welkin ring,
When freedom's friends assemble,
And deal such blows upon her foes,
As made her foemen tremble.

This day we to each other pledge,
To fight for him who labors;
With truth we will our warfare wage,
And save our guns and sabres.

Then let us sing, &c.

While Justice is our aiming star,
And truth and Reason guide us—
No petty feuds our ranks shall mar,
Nor danger shall divide us.

Then let us sing, &c.

And while we have to cheer us on,
The smiles of female beauty,
We will not yield till victory's won
And we have done our duty.

Then let us sing, &c.

This day we do together meet,
To banish all repining,
Within a grove, with clams to eat,
To keep us from declining.

Then let us sing till welkin ring,
While smoking clams do greet us,
Saying, "here we are, all baked and rare,
Come hither, you may eat us."[53]

THE WORKING MEN'S FOURTH OF JULY ANTHEM
By R. E. H. Levering
Air—"Martyn"

Bone and sinew of the land,
Know your rights, and by them stand!
On this glorious day retrace
Deeds of your own working race!
We the nation's bulwark stand!
Freedom came by our right hand—
Guided by a WASHINGTON,
See the blessings we have won!

Mark the *Boston Harbor* scene!
Bold mechanics there could win—
They could scorn the British king
While the rich were cowering!
Glory in your glorious name,
Lighted by immortal fame—
First to crush the galling chain!
First to strike, and strike again.

Turn to storied Lexington—
See the "*Workies*" working on!
Farmers and mechanics there
Spill their blood, the cause to share!
Workies! let this day inspire
Your own breasts with their own fire—
Let the right o'er might prevail,
As we tell the workies' tale!

Freedom's Bird on Bunker's height
Saw them boldest in the fight—
First to deal the blows around,
Last to quit the bloody ground!
Working men of ev'ry grade,
Shout for courage thus displayed,
Feeling in another war
Ye could act these glories o'er.

Pass along through ev'ry fray,
Down to Yorktown's closing sway,—
Alpha and *Omega* still,
Freedom triumphs by their skill!
Workies of each noble art,
Let your lives those truths impart,
Showing still the hero true,
In each word and deed ye do!

Workies! see *your* flag displayed,
Stars and stripes which ye have made,—
Stars to light your onward path,
Stripes to show the workies' wrath!
By your arm it floated first,
Crushing tyranny accurst,—

52*Mechanic*, Aug. 31, 1844.
53Ibid., July 6, 1844.

By your strength it still shall wave,
As ye rise the land to save!

On your country's altar swear,
Still the nation's fame to rear,
Swear this matchless day shall see
Workies, like their fathers, free!
Raise the cry for quick "REFORM!"
Get it by the soul's right arm,
Win it by improving mind,
As the proud to bless ye bend!

Let this festal day have charm,
Ev'ry party feud disarm—
Joining still with heart and hand,
Save yourselves TO SAVE THE LAND!
Let Columbia show your might,
And on kings descends the blight,—
Let posterity proclaim
Workies' deeds and Workies' fame![54]

The *Awl*, published weekly by the Association of Cordwainers in Lynn, Massachusetts, reprinted some songs which appeared originally in the Fall River *Mechanic* and the *Voice of Industry*. But mainly its songs were written for the workers in the shoe industry, encouraging them to stand up and battle for decent conditions. They were directed to the journeymen or male shoeworkers, although in its editorial of January 4, 1845, the *Awl* urged the shoe binders, all of whom were women, to consider themselves included in the message contained in the songs and to make the paper their own: ". . . the Binder ought to unite with the Journeyman in carrying on the great work of reform. And it should be so conducted that they *may* unite or rather that they *can't help* uniting. The interests of the Awl and the Needle are one. They both point to the same thing. They are brother and sister and should work together in perfect harmony. . . . *We want all the Needles to take our paper.* It will then be not only an *Awl*, but a Paper of *Needles!* . . . Come forward then, sisters all, and show your devotion to so great a cause by helping to bear along on your shoulders the ark of its safety—*a free press.*"

CORDWAINERS' SONG

Tune—"My Bible Leads to Glory"

The cause of labor's gaining,
The cause of labor's gaining,
The cause of labor's gaining,
  Throughout the town of Lynn.
  Onward! onward! ye noble-hearted working men;
  Onward! onward! and victory is yours.

Arouse the working classes, &c.
Unite the free cordwainers, &c.
Let JUSTICE be our motto, &c.
Come, join us, all true hearted, &c.
Our prices are advancing, &c.
The WOMEN, too, are *rising*, &c.
New members daily join us, &c.
Our victory is certain, &c.
We'll *stitch* our SOLES still closer, &c.
Let all protect free labor, &c.
There'll soon be joy and gladness, &c.[55]

CORDWAINERS' RALLYING SONG

Tune—"Old Dan Tucker"

Band together Lynn cordwainers,
All as one, and you'll be gainers;
Ask for just and honest prices,
Fearless of your foes' devices.
  Stand for your rights! as true brothers,
  Each one try to help the others.

All who love the working classes,
Let them mingle with the masses;
Every one assist his neighbor,
In defence of honest labor.
  Freemen unite! altogether,
  To raise the price on shoes and leather.

Those who cry out "*home protection*,"
Keep your eye in Lynn direction;
Common (st.) bosses and *Broad* (st.) quakers,
Don't neglect your town shoemakers.
  Patronize Lynn! she has many,
  Whom you've never paid one penny.

Lynn has suffered to repletion,
Through a wicked competition;
Selling cheap, and paying orders,
Oft spreads ruin through our borders.
  Pay off in cash, all ye bosses!
  Credit less and make no losses.

All shoemakers round these borders,
Never take your pay in *orders*.
For depend, such frequent dealing,
Is a polished kind of stealing.
  Out of the way, all shinplasters!
  You no longer are our masters.

Bosses ne'er should be complainers
'Gainst the claims of GOOD cordwainers.
Men of *souls*, jours and employers,

[54] *New Era of Industry*, July 20, 1848.
[55] *Awl*, July 17, 1844.

Don't encourage *soul* destroyers.
Workmen unite, with your bosses!
And you'll each get rid of losses.

Learn a lesson, jours and bosses!
Here's the secret of your losses:
Paying *trash* for *botchy* jobbing,
And *trusting* those who live by *robbing.*
Finish your *shoes,* like true workmen!
Nor encourage careless shirkmen.

Working men, throughout the region!
Come let's form a mighty legion;
All true-hearted SOULS assisting,
Help us save the sons of Crispin.
Hammer away! till each neighbor
Gets the worth of honest labor.

WOMEN, too, must join our party,
We shall welcome them most hearty.
Sure our cause will be worth minding
When the WOMEN do the *binding.*
Women and men, join us hearty!
And we'll form one matchless party.

Now with EQUAL RIGHTS the motto,
WAX your *threads* as true *souls* ought to;
Through the *run-round* bosses *bristle,*
We'll rise a *peg,* and let them *whistle.*
Stick to the *last,* brave cordwainers!
In the *end* you'll *awl* be gainers.[56]

CORDWAINERS' SONG

Tune—"Cheer Up, My Lively Lass!"

By a Friend to the Cause

Oh, what does make the bosses sigh,
And sadly hang their heads so low?
The jours will not with them, comply,
But "striking" now is all the go.

Then cheer up, my lively lads,
In spite of opposition;
Then cheer up, my lively lads,
And better your condition.

The bosses think that we are weak,
And that our feeble hands are few;
In thunder tones we soon shall speak,
If they give not to us our due.

Then cheer up, my lively lads, &c.

"The laborer," we'll let them know,
"Is worthy of his hire";
And that we'll not be put down so,
But have what we require.

Then cheer up, my lively lads, &c.

Shin plasters, they have had their day;
To them we bid a last farewell;
And, bosses, when the jours you pay,
Fork o'er the "cash," or not at all.

Then cheer up, my lively lads, &c.[57]

NEW SONG TO AN OLD TUNE

Tune—"Lucy Long"

O, take your time, ye bosses!
Take your time, but don't be slow;
Just raise a bit your prices;
Our wages are too low!

'T is well known, Lynn mechanics
Are not behind the rest;
When you get up a panic,
You'll find them up and dressed!

O, take your time, &c.

O, "shoes wont sell at all at all,"
Is now the general cry;
And mittens, too, both great and small,
Are dull throughout July.

O, take your time, &c.

That shoes for summer wearing
Wont sell as heretofore,
All know—for this good reason,
The season for them's o'er.

O, take your time, &c.

Your tricks upon the workmen
Are getting rather stale;
Don't try to play the 'possum—
You'll only show your tail!

O, take your time, ye bosses!
Take your time, but don't be slow,
Pay cash, and better prices;
For "orders" will not go![58]

SONG

O, the shoe jours, they are rising,
O, the shoe jours, they are rising,
O, the shoe jours, they are rising,
In the old town of Lynn.
With a band of music,
With a band of music,
With a band of music,
We will sound it through the town.

You will see the jours a-coming, &c.
To the old Town Hall.

[56]Ibid., July 24, 1844.
[57]Ibid.
[58]Ibid.

With a band of music, &c.
We will sound it through the town.

O, the Broad-street bosses tremble, &c.
At the rise of the jours.
With a band of music, &c.
We will sound it through the town.

For we will not take their orders, &c.
In the old town of Lynn.
With a good, smart committee, &c.
We will sound it through the land.

O, the selfish men are worried, &c.
At the loss of their jours.
With a band of music, &c.
We will sound it through the town.

And such men shall still be worried,
By the shoe jours of Lynn.
With a band of music, &c.
We will sound it through the town.

For the jours will still keep rising, &c.
In the old town of Lynn.
With a band of music, &c.
We will sound it through the town.

Until we get our prices, &c.
Then we will be content.
With a band of music, &c.
We will sound it through the town.

For we must have our prices, &c.
In the old town of Lynn.
With a good smart committee, &c.
We will sound it through the land.[59]

A week later the *Awl* offered this variant:

SONG
By Crispin
Tune—"The Old Church Yard"

O, the shoe jours, they are rising,
O, the shoe jours, they are rising,
O, the shoe jours, they are rising,
Throughout America.
We're a band of brothers,
We're a band of brothers,
We're a band of brothers,
And we'll sound it through the land.

You will see the shoe jours moving, &c.,
In one grand mass.
We're a band of brothers, &c.,
And we'll sound it through the land.

O, the selfish bosses grumble, &c.,
At the rise of the jours.
We're a band of brothers, &c.,
And we'll sound it through the land.

For we'll not take their orders, &c.,
Throughout America.
We're a band of brothers, &c.,
And we'll sound it through the land.

And these men, they are worried, &c.,
By the old shoe jours.
We're a band of brothers, &c.,
And we'll sound it through the land.

And they still will be worried, &c.,
By those who wont be slaves.
We're a band of brothers, &c.,
And we'll sound it through the land.

For the jours will be marching, &c.,
Into the bosses' shops;
With a list of prices, &c.,
For we will have our rights.

Then we shall have our freedom, &c.,
Throughout America.
And a glorious jubilee,
We will have throughout the land.[60]

THE GRINNER'S LAMENT
Tune—"Dame Durden"

The bosses here have many forms
By which to oppress their men;
For they are beasts of many horns,
And ever thus have been.

For there's orders and trash,
Low wages, no cash,
And fraud of every hue;
Oh, are they not a tyrant crew
As ever a mortal knew?

The bosses, too, are very sly,
Deceivers from the first;
They'll crush you down until you die,
Then cry because you're crushed.

For there's orders and trash,
Low wages, no cash,
And fraud of every hue;
Oh, are they not a tyrant crew
As ever a mortal knew?

Oppressors all have had their day;
Their kingdom's crumbling fast;
Their *grinners* now are heard to say,
Our day of power is past.

59Ibid.
60Ibid., July 31, 1844.

For there's no orders nor trash,
But good wages and cash,
And all wear a healthy hue;
And now they are a happy crew,
And have given the devil his due.

The shout of our cordwainers now
Is heard on every hand;
No longer they to tyrants bow—
They've broke oppressions's band.

For there's no orders nor trash,
But good wages and cash,
And all wear a healthy hue;
And now they are a happy crew,
And have given the devil his due.[61]

CORDWAINERS' SONG

Come, brother craftsman, join the song,
And raise your voices high;
The prices we have had so long,
Reject and cast them by.

The panic's o'er; our trade revives;
Cordwainers! don't repine;
Our boss will raise our wages yet,
As they were in days lang syne.

Drive care and trouble from your breast,
Our day of toil is o'er;
No more to work at the low rate,
That we have done before.

The panic's o'er, &c.

Once more ye sons of St. Crispin,
Raise high each cheerful voice;
And from this joyous night begin
The shout, Rejoice! rejoice!

The panic's o'er, &c.

Our craft, you know, has been despised,
By fools of every grade;
Yet we can boast as noble men,
As any other trade.

The panic's o'er, &c.

The founder of great Babylon,
So says the Holy Writ,
Was first who made, from skins of beasts,
A covering for his feet.

The panic's o'er, &c.

And Crispin, too, our patron saint,
An eminent divine,
And hosts of other generous souls,
Have lived in days lang syne.

The panic's o'er, &c.[62]

TEN-HOUR MOVEMENT

In 1850, George Coolidge's *Joys of Toil* was published, with the opening line "The joys of Toil it is my bliss to sing."[63] That same year a Massachusetts paper published an even more effusive poem in honor of the women who worked in the factories fourteen to sixteen hours a day.

SONG OF THE FACTORY GIRLS

Oh, sing me the song of the Factory Girl!
So merry and glad and free!
The bloom in her cheeks, of health how it speaks,
Oh! a happy creature is she!
She tends the loom, she watches the spindle,
And cheerfully toileth away,
Amid the din of wheels, how her bright eyes kindle,
And her bosom is ever gay.

Oh, sing me the song of the Factory Girl!
Who no titled lord doth own,
Who with treasures more rare, is more free from care
Than a queen upon her throne!
She tends the loom, she watches the spindle,
And she parts her glossy hair,
I know by her smile, as her bright eyes kindle,
That a cheerful spirit is there.

Oh, sing me the song of the Factory Girl!
Link not her name with the Slave's;
She is brave and free, as the old elm tree
Which over her homestead waves.
She tends the loom, she watches the spindle,
And scorns the laugh and the sneer,
I know by her lip, and her bright eyes kindle,
That a free born spirit is here.

Oh, sing me the song of the Factory Girl!
Whose fabric doth clothe the world,
From the king and his peers to the jolly tars
With our flag o'er all seas unfurled.
From the California's seas, to the tainted breeze
Which sweeps the smokened rooms,
Where "God save the Queen" to cry are seen
The slaves of the British looms.[64]

Most workers in New England did not sing of the "bliss" of working long hours in the shops and factories but rather of the need for a shorter working day.

61Ibid.

62Ibid., Aug. 7, 1844.

63George Coolidge, *The Joys of Toil: A Poem* (Boston, 1850), p. 6.

64Vera Shlakman, *Economic History of a Factory Town* (Northampton, Mass., 1935), pp. 135–36, from the Chicopee, Mass., *Telegraph*, Mar. 6, 1850.

THE FACTORY BELL

Loud the morning bell is ringing,
Up, up sleepers, haste away;
Yonder sits the redbreast singing,
But to list we must not stay.

Not for us is morning breaking,
Though we with Aurora rise;
Not for us is Nature waking,
All her smiles through earth and skies.

Sisters, haste, the bell is tolling,
Soon will close the dreadful gate;
Then, alas! we must go strolling,
Through the counting-room, too late.

Now the sun is upward climbing,
And the breakfast hour has come;
Ding, dong ding, the bell is chiming,
Hasten, sisters, hasten home.

Quickly now we take our ration,
For the bell will babble soon;
Each must hurry to her station,
There to toil till weary noon.

Mid-day sun in heaven is shining,
Merrily now the clear bell rings,
And the grateful hour of dining,
To us weary sisters brings.

Now we give a welcome greeting,
To these viands cooked so well;
Horrors! oh! not half done eating—
Rattle, rattle goes the bell!

Sol behind the hills descended,
Upward throws his ruby light;
Ding dong ding,—our toil is ended,
Joyous bell, good night, good night.[65]

The New England workers had not shared the gains of the ten-hour movement of the twenties and thirties, and the vast majority of them—mechanics and factory workers alike—still labored twelve to fourteen hours a day. These workers joined forces in the 1840s in a struggle for the ten-hour day. The organization which spearheaded this demand was the New England Workingmen's Association, formed in the fall of 1844.

The association was largely the product of the mechanics of Fall River, Massachusetts. Early in 1844 these men organized a Mechanics' Association to further the ten-hour day and set up a publishing committee to print a four-page weekly, the *Mechanic*, "to advocate the cause of the oppressed Mechanic and Laborer in all its bearings." The issue of June 22, 1844, carried on its front page the text of the "Circular to the Mechanics of New England" issued by the Fall River association. It denounced the long hours of work required of the mechanic, laborer, and factory operative in New England, pointing out that "twelve to fourteen hours per day is more than the physical constitution of man can bear, generally speaking, and preserve a healthy state." To remedy this situation, as well as to prevent the New England mechanics and laborers from falling into the "disagreeable servile and degrading state of the English laborer," a summons was issued for a general convention of New England workingmen to be held in the fall of 1844.

To rally support for the convention and help organize associations among mechanics and factory operatives in favor of the ten-hour day, the Fall River Mechanics' Association sent out S. C. Hewitt, a mechanic, as a lecturer-organizer. Hewitt visited towns in Massachusetts, Connecticut, and Rhode Island, and succeeded in forming a number of associations among mechanics and factory workers which sent delegates to the founding convention of the New England Workingmen's Association in Boston, October 16, 1844. Hewitt's journal of his organizing tour includes the following entry for August 1, 1844:

> *Singing.* A great deal of enthusiasm was created at this meeting by connecting the singing of several songs adopted to the occasion with other performances. This struck me as a good idea, and affords others a hint, from which—if they take it, they may derive a great profit. When we observe the tremendous effect which was produced by *singing*, in the political campaign of 1840,[66] we should feel it a high privilege to make use of this means as a help in the furtherance of a better cause. Come on then, ye poets and give us some songs for our convention. We shall need them, and we will endeavor to make good use of them.[67]

Hewitt's advice was not lost upon the ten-hour movement. A key feature of the campaign

[65] *Factory Girl's Garland*, May 25, 1844.

[66] During the presidential campaign of 1840, the Whigs popularized their candidates, William Henry Harrison and John Tyler, with songs like "Tippecanoe and Tyler Too."

[67] Philip S. Foner, "Journal of an Early Labor Organizer," *Labor History*, X (Spring, 1969), 25–27; *Mechanic*, May 11, July 6, 20, and 27, Aug. 10 and 31, 1844.

was the petition crusade to persuade the legislatures of New England to enact ten-hour laws for employees of private concerns. (In 1840 the ten-hour day had been established for federal government employees by executive order of President Martin Van Buren, but the state legislatures alone had the power to institute the ten-hour system for workers in private establishments.) Petitions were sent to various towns by the New England Workingmen's Association for distribution by the mechanics' associations and female labor associations. After thousands of signatures were secured, the petitions were forwarded to the state legislatures. The petition crusade was furthered by the songs of the ten-hour movement.

SONG OF THE TEN HOUR WORKINGMAN
From Garrison's "Song of the Abolitionist"[68]
Air—"Auld Lang Syne"

I am a Ten hour workingman!
I glory in the name;
Though now by "all day" minions hissed,
And covered o'er with shame;
It is a spell of light and power—
The watchword of the free:—
Who spurns it in his trial-hour,
A craven soul is he.

I am a Ten hour workingman!
Then urge me not to pause:
For joyfully do I enlist
In FREEDOM'S sacred cause:
A nobler strife the world ne'er saw,
Th' enslaved to disenthral;
I am a soldier for the war,
Whatever may befall!

I am a Ten hour workingman,
Oppression's deadly foe;
In God's great strength will I resist,
And lay the monster low;
In God's great name do I demand,
To all be freedom given,
That peace and joy may fill the land,
And songs go up to heaven.

I am a Ten hour workingman!
No threats shall awe my soul,
No perils cause me to desist,
No bribes my acts control;
A freeman will I live and die,
In sunshine and in shade,
And raise my voice for liberty,
Of naught on earth afraid.[69]

THE TEN HOUR BANNER
Tune—"The Gospel Banner"

Now be the "*ten hour*" banner,
In every land unfurl'd;
And let the shout hosanna,
Re-echo through the world.
Till ev'ry isle and nation,
Till every tribe and tongue,
Receive the great salvation,
And join the happy throng.[70]

THE ALL DAY SYSTEM
By Ivar, Newport, R.I.
Air—"Eden of Love"

Oh, where is the heart with one sensitive feeling,
That does not recoil from oppression's deep thrall?
And feelingly weep when reflection comes stealing
Across the lone bosom, to fight and appall.
The mind cannot brood in its desolate sorrow,
O'er scenes to humanity's children confined,
But incensed, sends forth from its quiver the arrow,
To cripple the system that fetters the mind.
The old all day system, the ruinous system,
That fetters the body and crushes the mind.

Immersed in the dungeons of labor, excessive,
Where cruelty revels in barbarous glee,
And tyranny stalks in its vileness oppressive—
Go—look—and the woes of humanity see;
From the depths of the bosom, the picture revealing
Will cause the warm tear of affection to flow,
And induce every heart, to proclaim that has feeling,
'Gainst a system that filleth creation with woe.
The old all day system, the ruinous system,
That filleth creation with anguish and woe.

But rouse, ye mechanics! the day light is breaking,
That reveals good news to the wrong'd and oppress'd;
Humanity's sons from their slumber are waking,
To cheer and to gladden thy desolate breast;

68 Garrison's song went:
I am an Abolitionist,
I glory in the name
Though now by Slavery's minions hissed
And covered o'er with shame:
It is a spell of light and power
The watchword of the free:
Who spurns it in the trial-hour,
A craven soul is he!
(William Wells Brown, *The Anti-Slavery Harp* [Boston, 1848], pp. 3–4.)

69 *Mechanic*, May 4, 1844.

70 Ibid., June 8, 1844. In reporting a ten-hour meeting in Fall River, the *Mechanic* noted that at the end "the chorus struck up the soul stirring tune of 'The Gospel Banner' " (June 8, 1844).

The clouds are dispersing, the signs are all cheering,
Arouse, rouse yet to duty, mechanics once more,
On—onward to vict'ry, undaunted, nor fearing,
And tyranny will flee from Columbia's shore.
The old all day system, the ruinous system,
Affrighted will flee from Columbia's shore.

See—the ten hour banner is gallantly streaming,
A beacon of hope to the laborer's eye,
And the lightning of Truth and Justice is gleaming,
Athwart the dark gloom of the workingman's sky;
Soon—soon will the mists and the clouds that surround us,
By truth's burning glory be driven away,
And the hopes, and the fears that ultimately meet us,
Will in splendor, give place to meridian day.
Then gird on the armor—to action—to action,
And drive the old system forever away.[71]

SIX TO SIX

Tune—"Adam and Eve"

In days now gone the working men begun, sires,
To work with the sun, and keep on till he was done, sires,
The bosses were as bad as the overseers of blackees,
Because they wished the working men to be no more than lackies.
The niggers have their tasks, and when done they may spree it,
But the Jers they were asked to stick to work as long as they could see it.
The blackees they had friends of all varieties;
But workies made themselves their own abolition societies[72]
Oh dear! oh dear! why didn't they fix
The hours of labor from SIX to SIX.

Old Time, as on his swift wing, he ranges
Brings round about as many great changes.
Houses are built high, and church steeples higher,
And patent chests invented that get colder in the fire;
Pills are manufactured that cure all diseases;
Rocking chairs in which the sitter at his ease is;
Monied corporations, and institutions old, sires,
The people discover are not good as gold, sires,
As a notion new, the workies thought they'd fix,
The hours of labor from SIX to SIX.

By this the bosses were all made to stare, sires,
And to a man, each one did declare, sires,
The measure was violent—wicked—agrarian;
But they only said this 'cause the measure was a rare 'un,
Meetings were held in old Independence square, sires,
'Twas the second declaration that had been made there, sires,
And while the Bosses were coming to their senses,
Six to six was painted and chalked on all the fences!
O dear, oh dear, we had to fix,
The hours of labor from SIX to SIX.[73]

All over New England, factory operatives (mainly women) and mechanics (men) sang:

We will have the Ten Hour Bill—
That we will—that we will;
Else the land shall ne'er be still—
Never still—never still.[74]

The petition crusade for the ten-hour day, bolstered though it was by the power of songs, was unable to prevail against the greater power of corporation control over the state legislatures. Rather than continue under existing conditions, a number of the factory girls left the mills, some going west to teach school. The following song was learned by Mary E. Hindle in 1875, but it was probably current before 1850:

THE FACTORY GIRL'S COME-ALL-YE

Come all ye Lewiston fact'ry girls,
I want you to understand,
I'm a going to leave this factory,
And return to my native land.
Sing dum de wickety, dum de way.

No more will I take my Shaker and shawl
And hurry to the mill;
No more will I work so pesky hard
To earn a dollar bill.

No more will I take the towel and soap
To go to the sink and wash;
No more will the overseer say
"You're making a terrible splosh!"

No more will I take the comb and go
To the glass to comb my hair;
No more the overseer will say
"Oh! what are you doing there?"

No more I'll take my bobbins out,
No more I'll put them in,
No more the overseer will say
"You're weaving your cloth too thin!"

No more will I eat cold pudding,
No more will I eat hard bread,

71 Ibid., Sept. 7, 1844.

72 Here, as in "The Factory Girl," is labor's anger over the fact that the abolitionists showed no interest in the problems of white wage workers (see pp. 42–43).

73 Broadside, Harris Collection, Brown University.

74 *Factory Girls' Album and Operatives' Advocate*, Feb. 14, 1846.

No more will I eat those half-baked beans,
For I vow! They're killing me dead!

I'm going back to Boston town
And live on Tremont street;
And I want all you fact'ry girls
To come to my house and eat![75]

While many workers had not achieved the ten-hour day by the time of the Civil War, the ten-hour movement of the 1840s was responsible for a distinct reduction in the number of hours normally worked each week. By 1860 ten hours had become the standard working day for most skilled and unskilled laborers, and factory working time had also been reduced—from thirteen to eleven hours in Massachusetts and to ten and five-sixths hours in New Hampshire.

The 1850s witnessed the formation of strong local unions of skilled craftsmen in many cities which used the strike weapon to obtain higher wages and a shorter working day. On April 16, 1853, the *New York Herald* reported the formation of the Waiters' Protective Union in New York City. The meeting of eight hundred waiters in Grand Street Hall closed on the following interesting note:

> Addresses were also made by Mr. J. Reid and Mr. Hampton, after which the following song was sung by Mr. W. E. Topley, the audience joining in the chorus:

Waiters, all throughout the nation,
Why will you for ever be
Overburdened by oppression—
Overawed by tyranny?
Wait for the good time coming no longer;
Claim at once what is your due;
Toil no more like slaves, and hunger,
To support an idle few.

Be of good cheer, and do not fret,
A golden age is coming yet.

See your wives and children tender
Badly clothed and pine for bread,
While your bosses live in splendor,
And off dainty dishes fed.
If united, you are the stronger,
Why not to yourselves prove true?
Toil no more like slaves, and hunger,
To support an idle few.

Be of good cheer, &c.

At the conclusion of this song, the meeting adjourned.

Some eight or ten important national trade unions were organized in the period from 1853 to 1860. The National Union of Iron Molders (formed in 1860), under the leadership of William H. Sylvis, its national treasurer and later national president, was to become the model for all labor organizations in America with respect to effective methods of operation. However, the panic of 1857 and the following depression destroyed most of the local and national unions which had been organized during the preceding years.

SONGS OF TWO STRIKES

Once the panic of 1857 got under way, employers began to discharge workers wholesale and cut wages of those still employed. The workers resisted with unemployment demonstrations demanding public relief for those thrown out of work through no fault of their own. Employed workers fought back as best they could by strikes against wage reductions. Several strike songs of these struggles are in existence. The first strike, against a reduction in wages in the mills of Narragansett Bay, Rhode Island, probably occurred in 1858.

LINES ON THE REDUCTION OF PAY
Air—"Narragansett Bay"

Come all you operatives in this and other towns,
Now listen while I tell you how our pay has been cut down;
Some twenty-five per cent or more has been taken from the same.
If we remain submissive now they will try it o'er again.

Ring, ring the bell at the first grey streak of dawn,
Ring, ring the bell at half-past six in the morn;
Ring, ring the bell, ring, ring, ring, I say,
If we are not there at the given time, we shall get turned away.

I will tell you how these Companies divide their stolen spoils;
For the same the half-paid factory hand all day at labor toils;
They have to pay an Agent, a Super and a Clerk
The very best of wages, but, *do they do the work?*

Chorus, &c.

[75]Phillips Barry, "The Factory Girl's Come-All-Ye," *Bulletin of the Folk-Song Society of the Northeast,* II (1931), 12. Cf. "The Lowell Factory Girl," pp. 43–44.

Lines on the
Reduction of Pay.

AIR - - - NARRAGANSETT BAY.

Come all you operatives in this and other towns,
Now listen while I tell you how our pay has been cut down;
Some twenty-five per cent or more has been taken from the same,
If we remain submissive now they will try it o'er again.
CHORUS.—Ring, ring the bell at the first grey streak of dawn,
Ring, ring the bell at half-past six in the morn;
Ring, ring the bell, ring, ring, ring, I say,
If we are not there at the given time, we shall get turned away.

I will tell you how these Companies divide their stolen spoils;
For the same the half-paid factory hand all day at labor toils;
They have to pay an Agent, a Super and a Clerk
The very best of wages, but, *do they do the work?* Chorus, &c.

In all the past reductions did you ever hear them say,
To curtail our expenses we'll reduce our Super's pay;
But rather they'll advance it, knowing he will do his best
In case of an emergency to help to rob the rest. Chorus, &c.

Now what I wish to say is this, can that be just and right;
And against their foul oppression, we will like heroes fight.
I see you are well organized, and based upon this plan,
I am sure you will support it, or perish to a man. Chorus, &c.

I have worked in many places, am a Yankee through and through,
I think this is the meanest place of all I ever knew;
If God should require three just men it would be to their sorrow,
I think they would all perish, like Sodom and Gomorrah. Chorus, &c.

I see the Crescent weavers, God bless their noble souls,
Are the first among the strikers to have their names enrolled;
Next follows up the Granite help alike all made of steel,
And with the brave old Merchants' will perish but not yield. Chorus.

About one year ago or more, I cannot tell the date,
The market for their cloth was dull and in a dreadful state;
They thought they would improve it by running on short time,
And then a general cut down they thought would be sublime. Chorus.

That answered for that season, they were trying all our pluck.
They talked about the same at church, and of their glorious luck.
But now the time has come for them to steal from us some more,
But this is more than we can stand, starvation is at the door. Chorus.

Even the French-Canadiens, God knows can stand enough,
It's a pill that they can't swallow, nor be humbugged by such stuff.
Now is the time for us to nail our colors to the mast,
And swear we'll never haul them down while this oppression lasts.
Chorus, &c.

Courtesy of Brown University Library

In all the past reductions did you ever hear them say,
To curtail our expenses we'll reduce our Super's pay;
But rather they'll advance it, knowing he will do his best
In case of an emergency to help to rob the rest.

Chorus, &c.

Now what I wish to say is this, can that be just and right;
And against their foul oppression, we will like heroes fight.
I see you are well organized, and based upon this plan,
I am sure you will support it, or perish to a man.

Chorus, &c.

I have worked in many places, am a Yankee through and through,
I think this is the meanest place of all I ever knew;
If God should require three just men it would be to their sorrow,
I think they would all perish, like Sodom and Gomorrah.

Chorus, &c.

I see the Crescent weavers, God bless their noble souls,
Are the first among the strikers to have their names enrolled;
Next follows up the Granite help alike all made of steel,
And with the brave old Merchants' will perish but not yield.

Chorus:

About one year ago or more, I cannot tell the date,
The market for their cloth was dull and in a dreadful state;
They thought they would improve it by running on short time,
And then a general cut down they thought would be sublime.

Chorus:

That answered for that season, they were trying all our pluck.
They talked about the same at church, and of their glorious luck.
But now the time has come for them to steal from us some more,
But this is more than we can stand, starvation is at the door.

Chorus:

Even the French-Canadiens, God knows can stand enough,
It's a pill that they can't swallow, nor be humbugged by such stuff.
Now is the time for us to nail our colors to the mast,
And swear we'll never haul them down while this oppression lasts.

Chorus, etc.[76]

Songs of the second of the two strikes made their appearance during the great shoemakers' rebellion in New England. The strike started in Lynn and Natick, Massachusetts, on February 22, 1860, and spread rapidly throughout the state and into New Hampshire, Maine, and Connecticut, as shoeworkers rallied to resist further wage reductions and raise wages above subsistence levels. By the end of the month, shoeworkers' unions were organized in at least twenty-five New England towns, and close to twenty thousand shoeworkers were on strike. As the biggest strike in American history prior to the Civil War, it gained nationwide attention. Newspapers all over the country carried glaring headlines: "The Revolution in the North"; "The Rebellion among the Workmen of New England"; "The Shoemakers' Strike—Progress of the Social Revolution"; "Beginning of the Conflict between Capital and Labor."[77] It was in reference to the great shoe strike then in progress that Abraham Lincoln said at New Haven, March 6, 1860: "I am glad to see that a system of labor prevails in New England under which laborers can strike when they want to, where they are not obliged to labor whether you pay them or not. I like the system which lets a man quit when he wants to, and wish it might prevail everywhere. One of the reasons why I am opposed to slavery is just here. . . ."[78]

The women strikers in Lynn held their own strike meetings, did their own canvassing in Lynn and nearby towns to win support, and turned out in strength for the big street demonstrations, one of which was held in their honor. Escorted by a detachment of musket-bearing militia, eight hundred women strikers started at Lynn Common and marched in the falling snow for several hours past the central shops on Lynn's major thoroughfares. At the head of their procession they carried a banner with this inscription: AMERICAN LADIES WILL NOT BE SLAVES: GIVE US A FAIR COMPENSATION AND WE LABOUR CHEERFULLY.[79]

76Broadside, Harris Collection, Brown University.

77*New York Herald,* Feb. 25, Mar. 7, 1860; *Boston Traveller,* Feb. 26, Mar. 1, 1860.

78John G. Nicolay and John Hay, eds., *Complete Works of Abraham Lincoln* (New York, 1905), V, 247–50; Philip S. Foner, ed., *Abraham Lincoln* (New York, 1944), pp. 87–88.

79*Reporter,* Mar. 21, 1860.

The shoeworkers' strike lasted an entire month and resulted in a wage increase for the workers. While most employers would not sign agreements or recognize the unions formed during the strike, unions now existed in many towns which formerly had been unorganized.

THE SHOEMAKERS' SONG

Written for the strikers by Allen Peabody,
Wenham, Massachusetts
Tune—"Yankee Doodle"

Ye jours and snobs throughout the land,
'Tis time to be astir;
The Natick boys are all on hand,
And we must not demur.

Up and let us have a strike;
Fair prices we'll demand.
Firmly let us all unite,
Unite throughout the land.

This winter past, we've kept alive,
By toiling late at night.
With no encouragement to thrive—
Such unpaid toil ain't right.

Chorus:

Starvation looks us in the face,
We cannot work so low;
Such prices are a sore disgrace;
Our children ragged go.

Chorus:

Our children must attend the schools,
And we must pay our bills,
We must have means to buy our tools,
Gaunt stomachs must be filled.

Chorus:

We must have decent clothes to wear,
A place to get our rest.
Must not be burdened so with care,
And must go better dressed.

Chorus:

Are we not men of pluck and nerve?
Shall we supinely sit,
And starve—another's interest to serve,
No compensation get?

Chorus:

Shall we run constantly in debt,
And toil the while like slaves?
Old age may overtake us yet—
May yet fill pauper's graves.

Chorus:

Shall we saw wood with trembling hands,
With bowed and aged form?
Beg bread of those whom we've made grand,
When hoary age comes on?

Chorus:

'Twas union gained the glorious boon,
Our nation now enjoys;
Then let's awake and soon
Back up the glorious Natick boys.

Chorus:

Shame on the men, the stupid curs,
Who might speak if they would,
Who will not join the Union boys,
But whine, "'Twill do no good."

Chorus:

We are men like other men,
Must clothe and eat and sleep,
Have dignity and common sense,
And principles to keep.

Chorus:

The carpenters get up a strike
The masons do the same,
And we'll take hold with all our might,
And elevate our name.

Chorus:

'Twas union gained the glorious boon,
Our nation now enjoys;
Then let's awake and soon
Back up the glorious Natick boys.

Chorus:[80]

THE BAY STATE SHOEMAKERS' SONG

Take heed in time, you gentlemen
Of Haverhill and Lynn;
An awful fuss 'twixt you and us
May speedily begin.
Be warned, ye men of Marblehead,
And men of marble hearts,
If we but stand aloof, from you
Prosperity departs.

You feed upon us working-men,
And drink your cobblers too;
But we're rough men, so think again,
We're neither faint nor few.
It's true you haven't any souls,
And 'tis no use to beg,
But you shall know how long we'll go
Before we stir a peg.

[80]*New York Herald,* Feb. 29, 1860.

We know that you are full of wealth,
In purses and in lands,
But you can never get ahead
Without the aid of hands.
Against all thought of compromise
Our senses now are steeled,
And we will ne'er to shop repair,
Until our wrongs are healed.

Hunger and want may threaten us,
Grim woe and famine pale;
But be you sure we'll only stir
For cash upon the nail.
So on the anniversary
Of our Great Father's birth,[81]
You may allow how much the vow
Of "greasy jours" is worth.[82]

Alonzo Lewis, Lynn's leading man of letters, encouraged the strikers with this song, published in the Lynn *Reporter*, March 21, 1860:

CORDWAINERS SONG

Shoemakers of Lynn, be brave!
Renew your resolves again;
Sink not to the state of slave,
But stand for your rights like men!

Yes, we'll stand for our rights like men!

Resolve by your native soil,
Resolve by your fathers' graves,
You will live by your honest toil,
But never consent to be slaves!

No, never consent to be slaves!

The workman is worthy of his hire,
No tyrant shall hold us in thrall;
They may order their soldiers to fire,
But we'll stick to the hammer and awl!

Yes, we'll stick to the hammer and awl!

Better days will restore us our right,
The future shall shine o'er the past;
We shall triumph by justice and right,
For like men we'll hold onto the last!

Yes, like men we'll hold on to the last!

The peaceable people of Lynn
Need no rifles to keep them at peace;
By the right of our cause we shall win;
But no rum, and no outside police.

No rum, and no outside police.[83]

81The shoemakers' strike began on February 22, 1860, the birthday of George Washington.

82John B. Burrill Scrapbook, Lynn Historical Society, Lynn, Massachusetts (author unknown).

83I am indebted to Professor Paul Faler of the University of Massachusetts, Boston, for calling my attention to "The Bay State Shoemakers' Song" and "Cordwainers Song."

4

Foreign-Born and Black Workers

Throughout the forties and fifties, despite efforts of nativist propagandists to stir up antagonisms between native workingmen and immigrants, there was considerable unity and cooperation between the two sections of the working class. "The banner of the longshoremen's union [in New York City] was decorated with flags of France, Germany, the Netherlands, Sweden, Ireland, Denmark, Hungary, and Italy, bound together under the American flag and the word 'unity.' At the top of the banner was displayed the proud challenge: 'We know no distinction but that of merit.' "[1] Some unions conducted their meetings in several languages, but as the tide of immigration increased and more and more workers of specific nationality and language-group arrived, the unions tended to divide along linguistic or national lines. However, the separate unions were linked to the parent unions by mutual interest, and some adopted the same constitutions. Each nationality group had its own labor songs and ballads, many originating in the countries from which the workers emigrated, others emerging from experiences in the United States.

BRITISH INFLUENCE

British workers who immigrated to the United States in the pre–Civil War era brought their songs and ballads with them to this country. Some were adopted by American workers. American seamen, for example, sang a trade union song popular among northeast coast seamen in England:[2]

THE SEAMEN'S LOYAL STANDARD

Good people listen while I sing
A circumstance to mind I'll bring
The Sailors you know did begin,
    To form a loyal standard.
The Gentrey on them sadly frown'd
And wished their Standard to pull down,
But it's been try'd in London town
    And they still hold the Standard.

Your ballast heaving's laid aside;
You've nought but your own work to mind,
And on the sea your ships to guide,
    And think upon the Standard.
When you get to your Port I'm told,
No Coals shall you draw from the hold,
Poor men will be employ'd behold,
    Since you've begun the Standard.

And now my friends, I pray go on,
Be true and loyal every man,
And to your cause stand firm each one
    And still support the Standard
And may it stand for years to come,
In this and every sea-port town,
And children's children ever own.
    And still maintain the Standard.[3]

[1] Robert Ernst, *Immigrant Life in New York City, 1825–1863* (New York, 1949), p. 108.

[2] For the formation of the union, see D. J. Rowe, "A Trade Union of North-East Coast Seamen in 1825," *Economic History Review*, XXV (Feb., 1972), 78–98. For a good summary of the history of British labor songs, see John Miller, "Songs of the Labour Movement," in *The Luddites and Other Essays*, ed. Lionel M. Munby (London, 1971), pp. 115–42.

[3] *Voice of Industry*, Mar. 12, 1847.

The most popular British verse in the pre–Civil War labor press in the United States was Thomas Hood's "Song of the Shirt."[4] Appearing originally in the Christmas issue of *Punch* in 1843, it was an instant sensation. It was first reprinted in the United States in the Fall River *Mechanic* of December 7, 1844, and was widely published in an 1851 newspaper story concerned with efforts of women seamstresses in New York to form the Shirt Sewers Cooperative Union.

With fingers weary and worn,
With eyelids heavy and red,
A woman sat in unwomanly rags,
Plying her needle and thread:
Stitch! stitch! stitch!
In poverty, hunger, and dirt;
And still, with a voice of dolorous pitch,
She sang the "Song of the Shirt"!

Work! work! work!
While the cock is crowing aloof!
And work—work—work,
Till the stars shine through the roof!
It's oh! to be a slave
Along with the barbarous Turk,
Where woman has never a soul to save,
If this is Christian work!

Work—work—work!
Till the brain begins to swim;
Work—work—work!
Till the eyes are heavy and dim!
Seam, and gusset, and band,
Band, and gusset, and seam,
Till over the buttons I fall asleep,
And sew them on in my dreams!

Oh men, with sisters dear!
Oh men, with mothers and wives!
It is not linen you're wearing out,
But human creatures' lives!
Stitch—stitch—stitch!
In poverty, hunger, and dirt,
Sewing at once, with a double thread,
A shroud as well as a shirt!

But why do I talk of death,
That phantom of grisly bone?
I hardly fear his terrible shape,
It seems so like my own—
It seems so like my own,
Because of the fasts I keep:
Oh God! that bread should be so dear
And flesh and blood so cheap!

Work—work—work!
My labor never flags;
And what are its wages? A bed of straw,
A crust of bread, and rags;
A shattered roof, and this naked floor,
A table, a broken chair,
And a wall so blank, my shadow I thank
For sometimes falling there!

Work—work—work!
From weary chime to chime;
Work—work—work,
As prisoners work for crime!
Band, and gusset, and seam,
Seam, and gusset, and band,—
Till the heart is sick, and the brain benumbed,
As well as the weary hand!

Work—work—work,
In the dull December light;
And work—work—work,
When the weather is warm and bright;
While underneath the eaves
The brooding swallows cling,
As if to show me their sunny backs
And twit me with the spring.

Oh! but to breathe the breath
Of the cowslip and primrose sweet,
With the sky above my head,
And the grass beneath my feet;
For only one short hour
To feel as I used to feel,
Before I knew the woes of want,
And the walk that costs a meal!

Oh, but for one short hour!
A respite, however brief!—
No blessed leisure for love or hope,
But only time for grief!
A little weeping would ease my heart,
But in their briny bed
My tears must stop, for every drop
Hinders needle and thread!

With fingers weary and worn,
With eyelids heavy and red,
A woman sat in unwomanly rags,
Plying her needle and thread:
Stitch! stitch! stitch!
In poverty, hunger, and dirt;
And still, with a voice of dolorous pitch—
Would that its tone could reach the rich!—
She sang this "Song of the Shirt."

Next in popularity to "Song of the Shirt" among British verses was Ernest Jones's "A Song

[4]When Thomas Hood died in 1845, contributions were raised to erect a monument over his grave, and the American labor press helped raise funds. The monument reads: "He sang the Song of the Shirt."

of the Starving." Verses by Jones, a British barrister who became a Chartist leader and authored the celebrated *Chartist Songs* and "The Song of the 'Lower Classes' " (see pp. 102–4), continued to appear in the American labor press during and after the Civil War.

A SONG OF THE STARVING

By Ernest Jones

Now, hark ye on the highland,
Now, hark ye in the glen,
Throughout our fertile island,
The song of starving men:

There's honor for the waster
While money's in his span;
There's plenty for the master:
But there's nothing for the man.

There's wealth for building churches.
There's food for hound and steed,
But the country is a desert,
For the pauper in his need.

Now, hark ye in the cottage,
Now, hark ye in the mill,
The people have the power,
If they only had the will!

Let him still hug a fetter,
Who brooks to be a slave,
And calls the man a better
He knows to be a knave.

As long as ye will truckle,
So long will they oppress:
Hope not to win from others,
But from yourselves—redress.

Now, hark ye in the palace,
Now, hark ye in the hall,
Ye men of silent malice!
And ye men of bloody thrall!

Can ye face the judging nation,
Ye that feasted on their pain,
And made their desolations
The foundation of your gain?

Then down, each tarnished 'scutcheon!
And down, each blotted fame!
The million paupers dying
Cry shame upon you!—Shame!

Now, hark ye on the highland,
Now, hark ye in the glen:
Remember that ye struggle
With measures, not with men!

Ye need not crush the mighty,
But take away his might:
We ask not retribution,
We ask but for our right,

And he is not my brother
By whom a wrong is done;
Or visits on another
What HE would wish to shun.

Then, hark ye on the highland,
And hark ye in the glen,
Throughout our blessed island
The song of stricken men.

The shipwrecked sailor wending
To a haven of sure rest;
The wounded bird descending
On its lonely forest nest.

They feel no exultation,
On earth, or air or sea,
Like the gladness of a nation
That has striven, and is free.[5]

THE IRISH

Many Irish peasants came to American when their English landlords dispossessed them following the drop in the price of grain after the Napoleonic wars. But the greatest migration came after the potato famine of 1846. Over half the working class of Ireland emigrated to America to stave off starvation. They formed the largest national group among the 4,300,000 immigrants who arrived between 1840 and 1860.

Most of the Irish peasants came to this country as unskilled laborers, and they worked under murderous conditions on canals, turnpikes, and railroads. But thousands found no work at all for some years after they arrived; the notation "No Irish Need Apply" became a common feature of job advertisements of the pre–Civil War decade. The bitter reaction of the Irish to job discrimination spawned many songs.

NO IRISH NEED APPLY

I'm a decent boy just landed
From the town of Ballyfad;
I want a situation, yes,
And want it very bad.
I have seen employment advertised,
"It's just the thing," says I,
"But the dirty spalpeen ended with
" 'No Irish Need Apply.' "

[5] *Voice of Industry*, Jan. 14, 1848.

"Whoa," says I, "that's an insult,
But to get the place I'll try,"
So I went to see the blackguard
With his "No Irish Need Apply."
Some do count it a misfortune
To be christened Pat or Dan,
But to me it is an honor
To be born an Irishman.

I started out to find the house,
I got it mighty soon;
There I found the old chap seated,
He was reading the *Tribune*.
I told him what I came for,
When he in a rage did fly,
"No!" he says, "You are a Paddy,
And no Irish need apply."

Then I gets my dander rising
And I'd like to black his eye
To tell an Irish gentleman
"No Irish Need Apply."
Some do count it a misfortune
To be christened Pat or Dan,
But to me it is an honor
To be born an Irishman.

I couldn't stand it longer
So a hold of him I took,
And gave him such a welting
As he'd get at Donnybrook.
He hollered, "Milia murther,"
And to get away did try,
And swore he'd never write again
"No Irish Need Apply."

Well he made a big apology,
I told him then goodbye,
Saying, "When next you want a beating,
Write 'No Irish Need Apply.' "
Some do count it a misfortune
To be christened Pat or Dan,
But to me it is an honor
To be born an Irishman.[6]

The brutal conditions under which the unskilled Irish laborers were forced to work were depicted in their songs.

THE TARRIERS' SONG

Every morning at seven o'clock
There's twenty tarriers working at the rock.
And the boss comes along, and he says, "Kape still,
And come down heavy on the cast-iron drill."

And drill, ye tarriers, drill;
Drill, ye tarriers, drill!
It's work all day for the sugar in your tay,
Down behind the railway.
And drill ye tarriers, drill,
And blast! And fire!

Now our new foreman was Jean McCann,
By God, he was a blame mean man;
Last week a premature blast went off,
And a mile in the air went big Jim Goff.

Next time payday comes around
Jim Goff a dollar short was found;
When he asked, "What for?" Came this reply,
"Yer docked for the time you was up in the sky."[7]

PAT WORKS ON THE RAILWAY

In eighteen hundred and forty-one
I put me corduroy breeches on,
I put me corduroy breeches on,
To work upon the railway.

Fi-li-me-oo-re-oo-re-ay,
Fi-li-me-oo-re-oo-re-ay,
Fi-li-me-oo-re-oo-re-ay,
To work upon the railway.

In eighteen hundred and forty-two
I left the old world for the new;
Bad cess to the luck that brought me through,
To work upon the railway.

Our contractor's name it was Tom King,
He kept a store to rob the men;
A Yankee clerk with ink and pen
To cheat Pat on the railway.[8]

LEAVE HER, JOHNNY

I thought I heard the old man say,
"Leave her, Johnny, leave her!
You can go ashore and draw your pay.
It's time for us to leave her."

The winds were foul, the work was hard,
From Liverpool docks to the Brooklyn yard.

She shipped it green and made us curse,
The mate is a devil and the old man worse.

The winds were foul, the ship was slow,
The grub was bad, the wages low.

We'll sing, oh, may we never be
On a hungry bitch the like of she.[9]

6From Pete Seeger, who based his version on two songs from nineteenth-century songbooks in the Library of Congress, "No Irish Wanted Here" and "No Irish Need Apply."
7John Greenway, *American Folksongs of Protest* (Philadelphia, 1953), pp. 43–44.
8Ibid. pp. 42–43.
9Ibid., p. 233.

Most songs of the Irish immigrants, aside from "The Tarriers' Song," were not well known outside the Irish working class. But one song by an Irish immigrant did become very popular in the general labor movement. Mike Walsh, who was born near Cork, Ireland, and brought to America in his childhood, wrote the song in prison in 1845. He was then serving a sentence for libel arising from articles he wrote in his paper, the *Subterranean*, founded in 1843 in New York City, to rouse the working class against capitalists and politicians who exploited them. Walsh worked closely for a time with George Henry Evans on behalf of the land reform program, but Evans, finding Walsh's bitter and personal attacks on individuals an embarrassment to the cause, split with the Irish agitator. Walsh went on to build a political career as a demagogue, achieving notoriety for his attacks on abolitionists. He served three terms in the New York State Assembly and one in Congress, where he supported territorial expansion. He was defeated for reelection in 1854 and died penniless in 1859.

In publishing Walsh's song, the editor of the *Voice of Industry* wrote: "These lines strongly breathe their deep regard for the poor laborer which characterized his (Walsh's) speech while with us a few weeks since."[10]

Arise! degraded sons of toil!
Too long you've foully bent the knee,
To impious drones who claim the soil,
Which God for ALL created free:
If brave, and to ourselves but true,
I ask you what we cannot do?

A bitter destiny, alas!
Has ours been through the course of time;
A poor, despised, deluded class
In every age in every clime!
Of demagogues and wealthy knaves,
We're still the willing dupes and SLAVES!

The wealth which ingrate tyrants wield
To crush and starve us,—we create;
The blood we shed on flood and field,
Give greatness to the MISNAMED great:
But short would resign this favored few,
Were we but to each other true.[11]

The *Subterranean*, Mike Walsh's paper, carried poems and songs about Ireland. One voiced the feelings of the Irish emigrant to this country.

SONG OF THE EXILE
By A.D.A.

To all my kin I bade farewell,
And left my native land,
And methinks I see thee now
As when I left thy strand,
Isle of the ocean ne'er again,
I'll see thy sweet green shore,
Tho' exiled from my native land,
I'll love thee evermore.
I love, I love Columbia,
The free land of the earth—
Yet still I love sweet Ireland,
The place that gave me birth.

I think I see thee, Ireland,
In happy midnight dreams,
I think I see thy bright green halls,
Thy valleys, and thy streams—
And then ye glide away from me
When dawning morn draws nigh,
But leave thy memory on my heart
To draw from me a sigh.
I love, I love Columbia,
The free land of the earth—
Yet still I love sweet Ireland,
The place that gave me birth.[12]

While the *Subterranean* ceased publication in 1845, the *Irish American* appeared weekly from the 1840s to the 1880s. The songs and poems in this paper, however, dealt almost exclusively with the beauties and struggles of Ireland, and rarely did a theme related to labor appear in its pages. The following is one of these rare inclusions:

MIND—A LABOR CHANT
By John Savage

Ringers on the chiming anvil—
Tillers of the soil—
Men of nerve and sweated brows—
Men of truth and toil—
Levelers of primeval forests—
Craftsmen of the city;
Here's a chant—a labor chant.

[10] The song was sent to the *Voice of Industry* by a correspondent who wrote that he had visited Walsh in prison, where "I observed the following lines written in pencil on the walls of his prison, as an apostrophe to a poor dejected looking creature which he had skillfully sketched beside them. representing a poor laborer in search of employment."

[11] *Voice of Industry*, May 29, 1845. The song was also published in the *Subterranean* of June 28, 1845.

[12] *Subterranean*, Nov. 15, 1845.

Chorus now my ditty
Brothers, here's my hand and heart, too,
Ev'ry vein is for my kind—
What is wealth if it should part you
With its whisperings so golden;
As deceitful as 'tis olden
From the only god-found palace
Where, from Learning's crystal chalice
Draught ye mighty stoups of MIND.

Men of brawny bone and sinew,
Honest toil and craft—
Men whose homely brows are sun-dyed
Toiling on life's raft—
Down the wild sea of existence—
Truthful more than witty;
Here's a chant of sweet resistance.

Chorus now my ditty
Brothers, if you mean to lift your
Trusty heads among your kind.
Aid the giant Thought, to shift your
Lives upon the way of knowledge,
Learning's road is free of tollage—
And with shouts an hundred-hundred
Has the Age's spirit thundered—
Whoso ruleth?—Nought but mind!

Men whose only Mace and Sabre
Is the Scythe and Sledge—
Men whose corded sinews labor
At the wheel or wedge—
Men who love the earned prize.
Who scorn the rich man's pity,
Here's a chant—come chorus rise
And swell aloud my ditty!
Brothers, earth would be a dismal
Barren, wretched place designed
If it had not Nature's prismal
Sunlight, bright'ning, as it dallies;
O'er the hillside and the valleys—
But more darksome, soul-less carron
Is the heart whose vales lie barren,
Unlit by the Sun of MIND.[13]

THE GERMANS

A considerable number of immigrants in the forties and fifties came from Germany, and many contributed their experience in the labor and Socialist movements of their native land to the developing labor movement in the United States. This was particularly true of the group known as the "48ers," referring to the Germans who had fled during the reaction following the defeated revolution of 1848. Among them, the first to play an important role in the American labor scene was Wilhelm Weitling, who started a labor paper in New York City, *Die Republik der Arbeiter* ("republic of the workingmen"), and helped form the Central Committee of the United Trades, a central body of the German-American trade unionists, in the same city in April, 1850. Later that year, under Weitling's leadership, a national convention of German-American unions was held in Philadelphia which culminated in the formation of the General Workingmen's League.

Although Weitling had had some association with Karl Marx in Europe, he was not a Marxist. Instead, he advanced the idea of solving labor's problems through the adoption of labor exchange banks, by means of which a cooperative system of industry would come into being. Indifferent to trade unionism and the struggle for wages and hours, Weitling lost influence among the German-American workers, who turned in increasing numbers to the leadership of Joseph Weydemeyer, a Communist who had been in close contact with Marx and Engels in Europe before he migrated to the United States. In January, 1852, Weydemeyer started *Die Revolution* in New York, which was succeeded a year later by *Die Reform*. In these papers, Weydemeyer emphasized both the need for workers to struggle for immediate demands through trade unions and the importance of combining economic and political issues in the labor movement to improve immediate working conditions and educate the working class on the need for a new socialist society to replace capitalism. Late in 1852, to further these objectives, Weydemeyer took the lead in organizing the Proletarian League in New York, and, in 1853, the American Labor Union. The latter organization stressed the independent political organization of labor, the organization of the unorganized workers into trade unions, and the unity of all workers in the country, skilled and unskilled. Weydemeyer was also a force in the formation of the Communist Club in New York in October, 1857, whose constitution required all members to "recognize the complete equality of all men—no matter of what color or sex" and to "strive to abolish the bourgeois property system . . . and substitute for it a sensible system under which participation in the material and spiritual pleasures of the earth would be accessi-

[13] *Irish American*, Oct. 28, 1849.

ble to everyone and corresponding, as much as possible, to his needs."[14]

The German immigrants planted the seeds of scientific socialism in the United States. They also brought with them to this country the *Arbeiterlied* ("workers' song"), already a well-established feature of the German labor and Socialist movement, and they continued in this country their *Turnvereine* and *Gesangvereine*—their workers' athletic and cultural associations, their *Volksbunde.*

TABLE PRAYER (GRACE) OF THE
COMMUNISTS IN THE UNITED STATES

Melody—"Es soll uns der Naturgeist walten"
Or—"Wer nur den lieben Gott laesst walten"

Nature! you give us all we eat,
Not only to humans, but also the animals;
Not only the fish, but also the ant,
You maintain, feed and give them to drink.
And what is this magic strength
Which creates and makes all this?

It is the eternal quiet working
Which always, eternally goes on creating.
The spirit of creation works invisibly
In exercising his strength
It has no beginning and no end,
Many people starve in misery.

Creation spends with overflow,
A man takes away from another;
He hinders him in his pleasures,
And forces some to an early grave.
Nature remains the same always,
And man only acts unequally.

Even here in this land of freedom,
Where plenty is available;
Here is still no unified group
Which loves from the heart sincerely!
No matter where one looks around
There human rights are denied.

Much is preached about heaven,
As we wander down the path to hell;
Man is in a rummaging turmoil,
And often falls off the embankment into the river.
The rich take from the poor
Whatever they want from them.

The rich believe that they only love
The poor with their capital.
The poor believe: they are thieves
When everywhere they steal
Our own sweat and blood,
So brothers, up! be on your guard!

Take everything, land and property,
Then you'll have work enough for yourselves;
And untie these knots of error,
Then you'll all be rich yourselves;
Because only in you is all the strength
Which creates and produces everything.

Get rid of all speculators,
Who deal in millions of acres.
And for this you need no representatives
If you get yourselves together.
And everything that has strength stretches
Thus the shopkeeper's pass is blocked.

The sisters who have a belly,
They can also help the cause;
For woman's endowments are sweet,
I hope, they also wish that "free"
The hand that lies in many states,
You virgins help, victory will come.

The women who love goodness
Remain erect by the sides of their men,
And each virgin must make out of
Every young man what she can!
So that each and everyone says yes
And then the song can end.

For fourteen hundred million acres
Of virgin land is still waiting here;
For whom should it be saved???
Therefore verily say to it: "YES."
"160 acres should each
Receive for his prosperity."

Discuss it at each daily meal,
Now before the new elections;
And vote for those who say: PAY
NOTHING! And receive the full amount
From this free state's land;
Tell all your friends about this.

For almost half the population
Can be supported on so much land;*
The ships and many schooners
Remain manned in the ocean;

[14]"Statuten des Kommunisten-Klubs in New York," manuscript in Wisconsin State Historical Society, Labor Collection, Political Parties, Box 25. Weydemeyer and his associates paid considerable attention to the slavery question and stressed that the abolition of chattel slavery was a necessary precondition for the abolition of wage slavery. They thus differed from those in labor circles who urged concentration first on abolishing wage slavery and those who believed that the struggle against both slaveries was of equal importance and should be conducted simultaneously.

They bring in from Europe
Company to America.[15]

*8,750,000 population per 160 acres of 1,400,000,000.

The papers editied by Weitling and Weydemeyer featured labor songs. Some, as might be expected, were songs already familiar to the German-American workers in their native land, but others grew out of specific conditions and experiences in the United States. In the English translations below, no attempt has been made to reproduce the poetry of the original German.

For the Revolution of the 24th of February
THE LAST GENERAL MARCH
Tune—"Marseillaise"

Onward! Drummers, beat the reveille!
Ye faithful guards, blow your horns!
Your horns from Pest to Marseille
Your horns from Rome to Komorn!
Get on! Beat the marching tune for the holy war!
To march in Cologne, Paris and Vienna
To march in Warsaw and Berlin
To march to death and victory.

To arms! Man by man!
The holy war began!
March on! March on! death or victory!
To the last holy war!

Onward! You true veterans!
You chosen fighters for equality!
Onward, to join our red flags!
The eagle flees from our trident.
Everywhere shall freedom reign,
No longer in the narrow space of borders
Nor by the golden bridle of mammon
Shall she be further bound.

To arms! etc.

Onward! Let fly the holy flags!
The longed-for red of equality.
Yes, to die fighting for mankind
Is the most beautiful hero's death.
Such a struggle is our destiny,
And a hero's death awaits us,
With this holy red, in this fight
For freedom, equality and peace.

To arms! etc.[16]

WORKERS' SONG

The cock is crowing for the first time
And already our lamp is burning
And again our old torment begins
And the hammer falls down with a boom,
For wages, eternally uncertain
We toil without rest on this earth,
Perhaps tomorrow already comes misery—
What will happen in our old age?

Therefore stand together when in our circle
We drink to the salvation of the world
And don't lose the courage to act.
Therefore stand together with faith and fervor,
For the stars of our hope are shining.

With a hard soil and a false current
It is our lot to fight forever.
And the treasurers that are lying therein
It's we who bring them to light.
We extract the ore and the diamond
We sow for those who enjoy the fruits—
We poor lambs, what garments
The world is making of our hides!

Therefore stand together, etc.

Do we get the reward for our hard work,
At which our hands are busy without rest?
Where do the streams of our sweat go?
We are nothing but machines.
We build the cities for the rich
And all the splendor of this planet,
When the honey is gathered,
The bee is chased far away!

Therefore stand together, etc.

The pallid child of strangers
Drinks the pure milk of our women,
And when they have grown up
They are too proud to look at us.
The seignorial right of the old world
No longer frightens the village-bride
But still the gold of the match-maker
Victimizes the children of every hut.

Therefore stand together, etc.

Freezing, we must, under a roof
Where owls are screeching, thieves are crouching,
Pass mournfully the long night of our life.
And yet, our blood also is hot
And we partook, just like the rich,
Of the sun's blissful warmth
And the cool shades of our oak-trees.

15 *Der Volkstribune*, May 16, 1846. Trans. Lenore Veltfort.

16 *Die Republik der Arbeiter*, Feb., 1850. Trans. Lenore Veltfort. On February 24, 1848, a rising of the people of Paris drove Louis Philippe from the French throne and led to the proclamation of the Second Republic. The news of the revolution in France paved the way for the 1848 revolution in Germany.

Therefore stand together, etc.

However many times in beautiful rage
We have fertilized the fields with our blood
The old tyranny always rejuvenated
Itself through our martyrdom.
Share your blood, spare your strength
Love must achieve the highest reward.
The breeze that creates the new worlds
Soon will penetrate all the world!

Therefore stand together, etc.[17]

COMMON SENSE EXERCISES

Those were the days in Paris!
There for the Republic!
For the second time the people broke
The necks of royalty.
And scepter, throne and crown
Had to walk into the flames
And all stood as brothers,
One heart, one man together.

That was a victory, so great
As none before was gained;
That mean royalty
Of the money-bags was conquered.
The usurers begged for mercy
With wounded claws,
And for the first time labor let
Their flags victoriously wave.

O dawn of peoples' brotherhood!
Like lightning (goes) through the lands
A flashing through a thousand hearts,
Breaking the bonds of slavery—
Breaking the barriers which so long
Have separated and divided the people—
And freedom! ringing everywhere,
Equality, brotherly peace!

The rotten thrones were trembling
Our flayers already trembled
The princes and the whole crowd
Of goddamned sinners—
When the Samson of freedom
Lets himself be fooled by Delilah,
Puts in the lap of the bourgeoisie
His head, to be shorn.

And he lets the army of philistines
Trample down our green crops.
And where freedom barely won
It was betrayed again.
There, where first the holy sign
Of brotherhood and equality
Had won, it sank first into the dust,
Into ruins, blood and corpses.

O shame, O shame! but now comes
The hour of resurrection,
My ears are hearing across the ocean
News of the savage fight.
For everyone, for the terrible war
And the terrible victory is armed,
And all the scythes have been sharpened
For the bourgeois, princes and priests.

Now go down you ancient world
Go down to rot forever.
From slavery's might removes itself
The light of world-redemption.
For where it penetrates the hearts
It wakes up with its rays
The nations to form a "Familienbund"
The true, the social one.[18]

TURNER SONG

Come out, you Turners
To the bloody struggle,
To fight, to triumph,
To the merry dance.
The flags are flying,
The laurels are beckoning,

Young Turners
Joyously,
For battle or pleasure
Always ready.

Let them yell
We'll be glad!
Those miserable serfs,
They don't fight
For the good and the just,
We are not afraid!

Young Turners
Joyously,
For battle or pleasure
Always ready.

The sword, ha, it's swinging
In our strong fists,
And if we should die,
For freedom and light,
We shall live on forever,
We shall never die!

Young Turners
Joyously,
For battle or pleasure
Always ready.

And so, heigh-ho
Briskly, joyously and free

17 Ibid., Mar., 1850. Trans. Brewster Chamberlin.
18 Ibid., July, 1850. Trans. Brewster Chamberlin.

To the bloody struggle
To the merry fight!
We find our joy
In battle, not at home!

Young Turners
Joyously,
For battle or pleasure
Always ready.[19]

THE LITTLE COMMUNIST

I am a little Communist
And never need anything more
Than what I need to live
All else I give away to others.

I am a little Communist
Who loves his brothers
And all he calls his own
Gladly gives to others.

I am a little Communist
And don't have a mean heart
'Cause what's said for others
Gives me pain too.

I am a little Communist
And don't ask for money
Since our master Jesus Christ
Neither valued it.

I am a little Communist
And that I'm with love and faith
And some day as a good Christian shall
Join the workers' association.[20]

SONG OF A WORKING GIRL

A free translation from the English poem
by Miss Speridan Carrey

Working from the first glimmer of dawn
Until way into the dark night;
Working 'til our senses leave us,
'Til our eyesight fails us,
'Til in nebulous phantasies
Our minds move purposelessly;
Working, working all the time,
Working without any rest!

Working 'til the eyes are dead,
'Til red cheeks are pale,
'Til the good sun again,
Full of pity, sends its rays
Upon the tired lids
Which are bathed in tears;
Working for this scanty food (bread)
O! Have pity with such misery!

Look how robbers stole the proud
Force of youth, life's strength and sap.
What we have they stole
And of the gifts
Hanging on life's tree of joy
They hardly left the refuse,
And they sneer right into our faces:
"It's for us and not for you!"

Robbers whose god, money,
Keeps us down in misery,
Usurers who have grabbed our wages,
Daily made our fate worse,
Murderers you, feasting with the wealth (reveling in the
wealth)
Colored with our blood—
Tremble! tremble! The curse of the poor
Will weave your shroud![21]

WORDS OF THANKS
TO THE "GESANGVEREIN" OF THE WORKERS'
CONFEDERATION IN PHILADELPHIA

Wilmington, 1st of July, 1853

Workers! Singers! Brothers!
The songfest is over
The songs have died away;
Everyone returns now gladly
To the bungling and the toils of everyday.
Exchanged are the words of farewell,
The last echoes of the festival have passed;
But the flames of memory
Burn brightly together.

Thank you!

You have proven the federation's maxim
Which says to love your brother!
You have shown yourselves strong enough
To carry it out faithfully.
Those of you who parted, carried in their hearts
The noble joy of the past days;
And the flames of memory but
Burn brightly together.

Hail to you!

The Sängerbund already prepares—
They don't know forgetfulness—
To bring you joy in Wilmington
To the same extent.
And whoever calls himself a proletarian
Shall recognize as clearly as the sun:

[19] *Turn-Zeitung*, June 1, 1852. Trans. Lenore Veltfort.

[20] *Die Republik der Arbeiter*, Jan. 1, 1853. Trans. Rudi Bass. A partial rhymed translation by Patricia Grayson appears in Bruce Gordon Laurie, "The Working People of Philadelphia, 1827–1853" (Ph.D. thesis, University of Pittsburgh, 1971), p. 232.

[21] *Die Reform*, Apr. 23, 1853.

nen Interesse muß so gerügt werden — der Magen ist zuweilen ein gar armer, schwacher, bemitleidenswerther Schächer! — sondern die jesuitische Art und Weise, mit der sie beschönigt wird. Solche Winkelzüge!!! — Arbeiter, nehmt ein Exempel daran! — fallt nicht in die Schlingen der Rabulisten, welche eine Mücke mit einem Teleskop untersuchen, und sie für einen Elephanten ausgeben.

Stadt New-York.

Der Krystallpalast *rc.* Eine Blamage. Die ehernen Säulen stehen. Alles ist fertig. Und wie man die eisernen Dachstühle legen will, findet es sich, daß die Dachbedeckung zu kurz gegossen ist. Man hat versäumt, das bei dem Eisenguß stets vorkommende Einschwinden der Maße mitzuberechnen. Die ganzen Deckeisenbalken müssen umgegossen werden. Das war faul! Der praktische Yankee, und einen solchen Bock! — In Europa lebt man der Illusion, daß die Weltausstellung den 1. Mai eröffnet werde. Hier leben die Gastwirthe der süßen Täuschung, daß vom 1. Mai an Alles mit Gästen von Nah und Fern überschwemmt sein werde. Alles eitel! Die Europäer werden sich hüten, den Hotelbesitzern zu Gefallen 2 Monate ohne Zweck jene Mammuthbills zu bezahlen, die in den großen Hotels an der Tagesordnung sind. Vor Monat Juni ist an keine Eröffnung zu denken.

Ein anderer Baukohl ist neben dem Krystallpalast. Dort wird ein babylonischer Thurm gebaut, der mehrere hundert Fuß Höhe haben soll. Jetzt hat man gefunden, daß die Grundlage im Verhältniß der Höhe zu gering im Durchmesser ist, und der Boden nicht geeignet, eine solche Last zu tragen.

Wunderbar ist es, wie rings um den Krystallpalast weite Flächen sich wie durch Zaubergewalt mit Häusern bedecken — größtentheils Framhäuser, die an der Front der Straßen her, die Wüsten und die elenden Baracken dahinter dem Fremden verstecken. — Auch ein Sommer-Theater für 2000 Zuschauer wächst dort empor. — Jedenfalls wird es zweck-

und Florida **Weißmännerland** — auch **Großirland** (Irland it mikla), die von Iren bevölkert sei. Die alten Virginier also Abkömmlinge der Iren!! Ob sie diesen Stammbaum wohl anerkennen würden.

Ja, man hat nachgewiesen, daß die Einwohner von Grönland und Island erst von Virginien ausgekommen seien — und zwar irischen Stamms — weshalb sie den Namen **Westmänner** gehabt hätten. Doch diese ganzen irischen Geschichten sind unsicher, während das oben Mitgetheilte geschichtlich feststeht.

Diese erste Entdeckung Amerika's hat jedoch keine Erweiterung der Erdkenntniß geschaffen. Die Unkultur der Entdecker, die Kenntnißlosigkeit derselben und die Natur der gefundenen Gegenden lassen das nicht zu. Nur die Dichtung der Normänner wurde dadurch bereichert, nicht das Naturwissen. Obgleich reisende Isländer die Lehranstalten in Deutschland und Italien besuchten, verbreitete sich doch keine Nachricht des neuen Kontinents unter den Völkern von Mittel- und Südeuropa.

Ja in Island selbst scheint die Nachricht davon nicht einmal zu den Ohren des großen genuesischen Seefahrers gekommen zu sein. Columbus sagt in seiner jetzt seltenen Schrift „**über die fünf bewohnten Erdzonen**,“ daß er im Monat Februar 1447 Island besuchte, „wo damals das Meer nicht mit Eis bedeckt war, und das von vielen Kaufleuten aus Bristol besucht wurde.“

Hätte Columbus dort von dem gegenüberliegenden ausgedehnten Landstrich von Helluland, Markland oder von dem guten Weinland reden hören, und diese Nachricht mit seinen alten Projekten verbunden, so würde man ihm später in dem Prozeß über das Verdienst der ersten Entdeckung ganz sicher diese Reise nach Thyle (Thule, Island) vorgehalten haben, um ihn zu erniedrigen und sein Verdienst zu vernichten. Er würde alsdann nicht bei seiner ersten Entdeckungsreise von den kanarischen Inseln in südwestlicher Richtung gesteuert haben.

---

ten sich nun erklären, was sie zur Durchsetzung der Lohnerhebung zu thun gedächten.

„Die HH. **E. Kiesewetter, Siebenmann, Schneider, Winter, Boßnack, Betke, Schwalb, Hoffmann***) protestirten gegen diese Erklärung, und als die Versammlung darauf bestand, beantworteten sie die Frage: „ob sie sich mit den gefaßten Beschlüssen einverstanden und zur Durchführung bereit erklärten,“ — mit „Nein!“ — worauf sie unter lauten Mißfallensbezeugungen die Versammlung zu verlassen genöthigt wurden. Die übrigen Gehülfen vom „Demokraten“ erklärten sich unter großem Beifall **für** die gefaßten Beschlüsse. Es waren dies die HH. **Adler, Brehm u. Gunther.** — Ferner erwählte die Versammlung einen Präsidenten und einen Sekretär für die Exekutive und beauftragte dieselben, sowohl sämmtliche Buchdrucker der Union von den gethanen Schritten in Kenntniß zu setzen, damit diese Gleiches in's Leben rufen und ihre Lage nach Möglichkeit und Verhältnissen verbessern können, **als auch allen Arbeitern New-Yorks die höchst undemokratische Handlungsweise des Hrn. Wm. Schlüter mitzutheilen.** Zum Schluß wurde ein Komite von 5 Mitgliedern erwählt, um die Statuten des Vereins zu berathen und auszuarbeiten.“

Wir entnehmen diese Darstellung einem Anspruch der hiesigen Buchdruckergehülfen: „An die deutschen Buchdruckergehülfen in der Union,“ — der mit folgender Ansprache schließt:

„Collegen! Indem der unterzeichnete Vorstand sich der gegebenen Aufträge hiermit entledigt, fordert derselbe Euch auf, dahin zu wirken, daß in allen Städten der Union zur Wahrung unserer Interessen Aehnliches geschieht, wie in New-York. Nur dadurch, daß wir uns Alle zu **Einem** Zweck verbinden, ist es möglich, uns dauernd zu verbessern. Eine Hauptstütze zur Durchführung unserer und Eurer

*) Die beiden Letztern waren in der Versammlung nicht anwesend, schlossen sich aber den Erstern später an, und es hat sich so die Zahl der **Aushänge-Exemplare** bis auf **acht** vermehrt. Anm. d. Setz. d. „Ref.“

Lied einer Arbeiterin.*)

Nach dem Englischen der **Miß Speridan Carrey.**

Schaffen von des Frühroths Schein
In die finstre Nacht hinein;
Schaffen, daß der Sinn uns schwindet,
Daß das Augenlicht erblindet,
Daß in Nebelphantasien
Planlos die Gedanken ziehn;
Schaffen, schaffen immer zu,
Schaffen ohne Rast und Ruh! —

Schaffen bis das Auge todt,
Bis erbleicht der Wangen Roth,
Bis die liebe Sonne wieder
Auf die müden Augenlider —
In ein Thränenbad getränkt —
Mitleidvoll die Strahlen senkt;
Schaffen für dies kärglich Brod,
Ach! Erbarmen solcher Noth! —

Seht, die stolze Jugendkraft,
Seht, des Lebens Mark und Saft
Stahlen Diebe. Was wir haben
Stahlen sie, und von den Gaben
An des Lebens Freudenbaum
Ließen sie den Abfall kaum,
Höhnen uns in's Angesicht:
„Für uns ist es, für euch nicht!“ —

Räuber, deren Gott, das Geld
Uns im Elend niederhält, —
Wucherer, die den Lohn verkümmert,
Täglich unser Loos verschlimmert,
Mörder, die ihr schwelgt vom Gut,
Das gefärbt mit unserm Blut —
Zittert, zittert! Armenfluch,
Webt Euch Euer Leichentuch!

*) Man vergleiche oben die Nachrichten aus Cincinnati und New-York über die Lage der Näherinnen.

☞ Kürzlich hat **Wilhelm Loer** aus Ohio eine Vorlesung **über die Stellung der Farmer** zur sozialen Frage gehalten. Jedenfalls ein verdienstliches Unternehmen. Leider konnten wir der Vorlesung nicht beiwohnen.

☞ Die erste Lieferung von Thomas Paine's Werken ist uns zugekommen. Diese von Thomas in Philadelphia besorgte Volksausgabe des berühmten amerikanischen Volksmannes und Revolutionärs ist eben so wohlfeil wie schön ausgestattet. Sie ist ein neues erfreuliches Zeichen des zum rüstigen Leben aufstrebenden deutschen Buch- und Verlagshandels. Die lohnende Wirkung auf das deutsche Publikum wird nicht ausbleiben.

☞ Für **Franz Damian** aus Bruchsal (?) liegt ein Brief in der Office dieses Blattes.

Ein Herr, welcher sich in der deutschen Konversation zu vervollkommnen wünscht sucht Board bei einer deutschen Familie, welche außer ihm keine anderen Boarder aufnimmt. Die Nachbarschaft von Broadway, Crosby und Houston St. wird vorgezogen. Auskunft in der Expedition der Reform.

Broadway Post-Office.
Der Post-Steamer America
via LIVERPOOL.

Briefe und Zeitungen nach Bremen, Hamburg, Oldenburg, Preußen und allen andern Theilen Deutschlands und Frankreichs werden durch den obigen Steamer befördert und können bis Dienstag den 26. April 4 Uhr Nachmittags in der Broadway Post-Office, No. 422½ Broadway, vier Thüren von Canal Str., abgegeben werden. — Diese Office bleibt jeden Abend bis 9 Uhr offen.

Jas. G. Harriett.

Unfrankirte Briefe werden für 1 Cent nach irgend einem Theile der Ver. Staaten befördert.

Amerikanischer Arbeiter-Bund.
Versammlung des Central-Vereins

Sonntag d. 25. d. M., Vormittags 8½ Uhr präcis, im Lokale des Hrn. Straus, No. 15 Delancy Str.

Alle Arbeiter, welche der Sitzung beiwohnen wollen, sind eingeladen.

Mengler, Präs.

Aufruf
an die deutschredenden Schuh- & Stiefelmacher!

Laut des am 18. d. M. in der Schuhmacher-Massen-Versammlung gefaßten Beschlusses, sind alle deutschredenden Schuhmacher aufgefordert, sich zur Massen-Versammlung head quarters (Elizabethstr. cor. Grand-str.) präcis 7 Uhr Abends 25. April zahlreich einzufinden. Da der Sprachunterschied in den zwei vorhergegangenen Massen-Versammlungen die Uebersetzung von Englisch in Deutsch und Deutsch in Englisch nothwendig machte, wurde die Diskussion sehr erschwert, wie überhaupt sehr zeitraubend. Deshalb beschloß die Versammlung, daß die deutschen Arbeiter ihre eigenen Meeting halten sollen.

Eine allgemeine Schuhmacher-Arbeiter-Verbindung zur Erhebung und Aufrechterhaltung der Preise soll organisirt werden. Die deutschredenden werden unseren englischen Brüdern nicht nachstehen; sie werden ihnen die Bruderhand bieten, um gemeinschaftlich Das durchzusetzen, was uns vereinzelt unmöglich ist.

Darum auf! deutsche Schuhmacher! folgt dem Beispiel unserer englischredenden Bruder, beweist, daß Ihr in numerischer Zahl mit die Stärksten, nicht die Letzten sein könnt, Eure Hand zur Verbesserung der Arbeiterverhältnisse zu bieten.

NB. Es diene zur Nachricht, daß schon fünf Bosses eine Lohnerhöhung von 12 Procent bewilligt haben.

Das Komite.

Aufruf an sämmtliche Cigarrenarbeiter
in New-York, Williamsburg u. Brooklyn
zu einer großen Massen-Versammlung
nächsten Sonntag d. 24. April, Morgens 9 Uhr
in der Washington Hall, 101 Elizabeth nahe Grand St., früher Maghers Conzerthalle.

Jeder Cigarren-Arbeiter **ohne Unterschied** ist zu der obigen Versammlung auf das **Bestimmteste** eingeladen **pünktlich** zu erscheinen. Da bereits beschlossen: „daß eine allgemeine Cigarren Arbeiter Verbindung organisirt werden soll“, — so wird **sicher erwartet**, daß **kein** Cigarren Arbeiter zurück bleibt, — denn es gilt ja jedes Einzelnen eigenes Interesse zu verfechten, — darum auf Cigarren Arbeiter! zeigt Euch als **prinzipielle** Männer und die Welt wird sagen, daß Ihr in der jetzigen Arbeiter-Bewegung nicht die Letzten gewesen seid, die ihre Hand zur Verbesserung der Arbeiterverhältnisse dargeboten haben.

Im Auftrage des provisorischen Komite:

Ch. Glöckner, prov. Sekr. **Kauer**, prov. Präs.

Handschuhe	2	„	$1.
Hemdenkragen	1	„	
Hosenträger	2	„	$2.
Gravatten	1	„	$2-50.
Seidene Tücher	1	„	$2.
Leinene „	2	„	$2-50.
Neck ties	2	„	$1.
Seidene Unterwäsche	16	„	$1-50.
Baumwollene Taschentücher	1	„	$0-50.

sowie Knabenwäsche zu allen beliebigen Preisen, kurz und gut die Artikel seines Ladens sind zu zahlreich um sie alle anzuführen. Kommt und überzeugt Euch.

P. Koopman.

Vergeßt die No. 96 nicht.

H. Mommens
Frühlings-Mode.
45 Division Str.

Mommens empfiehlt dem geehrten deutschen Publikum sein reich assortirtes Lager von Herren- und Knaben-Hüten, Mützen in allen Sorten und beliebiger Façon, nach den neuesten Moden und elegant gearbeitet, die mit den im Broadway Etablissement in die Schranken treten. Es ist ihm sehr leicht dieselbe Arbeit zu liefern, indem er lange Zeit Werkführer des bekannten Genin im Broadway war, und früher in London und Paris in den besten und bekanntesten Etablissements angestellt gewesen, und ist daher befähigt, den Stoff auf die ökonomischte und vortheilhafteste Weise zuzuschneiden. Er wird keine Kosten scheuen und alles Mögliche aufwenden um sich die Gunst des Publikums zu erhalten, welche ihm seit er etablirt, so reichlich zu Theil geworden ist.

Er wünscht daß das geehrte Publikum seine Waare prüfe, und ist überzeugt, daß Jeder, welcher seine Hüte gesehen, den Store nicht verlassen wird, ohne gekauft zu haben.

H. Mommens fordert jede Konkurrenz bezüglich der Leichtigkeit, Dauerhaftigkeit und Qualität seiner Hüte in die Schranken.

Hüte auf Bestellung für $3 angefertigt.

Kinder-Hüte und Mützen in großer Auswahl werden um 25 pCt. billiger als in irgend einem andern Store verkauft.

Nicht zu vergessen: **No. 45 Division Str.**

Vom 1. May an wird das Geschäft nach **111** Nassau Str., nahe Ann Str., (früher Goleman's Laden), verlegt.

William Benett,
wohlfeiler Hemden-Store
und Herren-Wäsche aller möglichen Sorten,
No. 84 Chatham Str.,

zeigt hiermit dem deutschen Publikum ergebenst an, daß sein wohlassortirtes Lager durch neue Sendungen jetzt ganz vollständig ist, und daselbst gute Waaren zu äußerst billigen Preisen verkauft werden.

Hemden	von	6	Schill.	$2-50.
Unter-Hemden	„	4	„	$1.
Seidene Unter-Hemden	„	12	„	$3.
Unter-Hosen	„	4	„	$1.
Socken	„	1	„	$0-75.

Gravatten, eignen Fabrikats, in allen möglichen Sorten und Preisen; Taschentücher von Seide, Leinen und Baumwolle, Hemden-Kragen von 1 Sh. per Stück; Three ply-, Glace-, seidene, leinene, und baumwollene Handschuhe in allen Größen rc., die Artikel seines Lagers sind zu zahlreich, um sie alle zu nennen.

William Bennet ist überzeugt, daß die genannten Waaren, sowie die freundliche Bedienung und reelle Behandlung nichts zu wünschen übrig lassen.

Kommt und überzeugt Euch. Ein deutscher Clerk wird Alles aufbieten um seine Landsleute zu befriedigen.

Das ist der wohlfeilste Schuh- und Stiefel-Laden an Chatham Square, wo doch Alles am Billigsten verkauft wird.

$30,000 Werth in Stiefel u. Schuhen.
Bigelow & Gedney,

142 Chatham Square, gegenüber dem Nationaltheater, zeigen hiermit dem deutschen Publikum ergebenst an, daß sie stets die besten und wohlfeilsten Stiefel und Schuhe verkaufen; eine Konkurrenz mit ihnen ist rein unmöglich.

Stiefeln	von	$1-50	—	$2-50
„ feine kalbledrene	„	$3-00	—	$7-00
„ „ lackirte	„	$4-00	—	$7-00
Schuhe in allen Sorten	„	$1-00	—	$4-00
Damen-Schuhe	„	6 Sh.	—	$1-50
Kinder-Schuhe	„	3 „	—	$1-00

California and Australia Minen-Stiefeln zu allen Preisen und Größen.

Herren- und Damen-Gaiters in allen Sorten.

Kommt und Ihr werdet Alles so finden wie wir's sagen.

Vergesset nicht: **No. 142 Chatham Str.**

Die Frühlings-Mode für Herren-Hüte ist jetzt fertig, und Freeman hat keine Ausgaben gescheut um die elegantesten und schönsten Frühlingshüte zu verfertigen. Er hat seine eigne Fabrik und seine Hüte sind unter seiner Aufsicht vom besten Roh-Material fabrizirt, **dadurch sind 20 Prozent erspart**, und alle Opposition gegen ihn ist unmöglich. Er macht alle Sorten Hüte Castor-, Seiden-, Filz-, Hecker- und Kossuth-Hüte. Der Preis für seine Moleskin-Hüte ist $3, von der besten Qualität $3-50, die Hüte sind eben so gut als die $4-50 eines andern Stores; wir verkaufen einen feinen Hut für $2-50. Mützen aller Sorten von 50 Cts. bis $1. Hüte auf Bestellung werden in sehr kurzer Zeit pünktlich besorgt.

Man vergesse nicht die Nummer **90 Fulton Str.**, nahe Gold Str. **A. Freeman,**

Fabrikant und Händler in Hüten und Mützen im Großen und Kleinen.

Friedrich Michel,
Gasfitter und Messingarbeiter,
No. 301 Houston Str., nahe Avenue A,

empfiehlt sich zur Anfertigung von Gaseinrichtungen in Kirchen, Hotels, Stores und Privathäusern.

Georg Jacob,
Mulberry Str. No. 25,

Verfertiger von deutschen und französischen Schuhmacher-Werkzeugen, für deren Güte garantirt wird.

NB. Auch wird durch denselben Arbeit für Schuhmacher nachgewiesen.

Aeußerst wohlfeiler Verkauf
in dem als das größte und wohlfeilste in den Vereinigten Staaten bekannten
Carpet-Etablissement,
No. 99 Bowery, New-York,
von
HIRAM ANDERSON.

Acht große Verkaufs-Räume. — **Wholesale and Retail.**

Verkaufs-Raum No. 1.

enthält die größte, modernste und schönste Auswahl von Hare's berühmten englischen und amerikanischen Flur-Wachstuch-Teppichen nach der neuesten Mode, Seidenglanz, marmorirt, mit italienischer Fresco- und Arabesken-Malerei, wie sie in dieser Stadt ausgeboten wurden, von 2 Sh. 6 Cts. bis $1 die Yard, von 1 bis 8 Yard Breite.

Verkaufs-Raum No. 2.

Hier befinden sich 250 Stück der ausgewähltesten, schönsten und elegantesten Muster englischer und amerikanischer Ingrain-Teppiche zu unvergleichlich niedrigen Preisen, von 5 Sh. bis 6 Sh. 6 Cts. die Yard. Für unsere Stadtverkäufe angefertigt.

Verkaufs-Raum No. 3

enthält 300 Stück englischer und amerikanischer Imperial Three Ply Teppiche mit prächtigen Arabesken und gothischen Figuren, importirt und auf Bestellung gemacht; in keinem andern Etablissement der Vereinigten Staaten zu finden.

Verkauf-Raum No. 4

enthält 150 Stück feiner Ingrain-Teppiche mit neuen, brillanten Mustern und zu erstaunlich niedrigen Preisen 2, 2½, 3, 3½ und 4 Sh. die Yard.

Verkaufs-Raum No. 5

bietet eine wundervolle Auswahl englischer Druggets, 4 Yards weit. Ebenso 900 Yards Druggets, 1½, 2 und 3 Yards weit, zu 3, 3½, 4, 5 und 6 Sh. die Yard. Ebenso prächtige Mosaik- und Axminster Heerd-Teppiche, und 100 langhaarige zu 20 Sh.

Verkaufs-Raum No. 6

ist ganz angefüllt mit gestreiften und figurirten Treppen- und Garten-Carpets zu 2, 2½, 3 bis 6 Sh. per Yard. Ebenso englische Tapisserie-, Brüsseler und Sammet-Treppen-Carpets zu 7, 8, 9 und 10 Sh. per Yard.

Verkaufs-Raum No. 7.

Royal Sammet-, Axminster, Tapisserie- und Brüsseler Carpets, importirt von den berühmten englischen Fabriken von John Crossly u. Son und Henderson, ganz besonders für unseren städtischen Verkauf. Ebenso Mosaik-Carpet in einem Stück, 16 Fuß breit und 21 Fuß lang, und 1 Fuß 7 Zoll breit und 17 Fuß lang, $350 werth.

Verkaufs-Raum No. 8

enthält die Patent-Tapisserie-Ingrain-Carpets, welche in der Weltausstellung ausgestellt waren und jetzt wieder im New-Yorker Crystall-Palaste gehen. — Ebenso Fenster-Rouleaux zu 6, 8, 12, 16 und 20 Sh. das Paar; Tischdecken, plattirte und messingene Treppenstäbe, englische Schaaffelle, Areiaos und langhaarige Parlor-Thürmatten. — Ebenso weiße und bunte Matten, 4/4, 5/4 und 6/4 und Cocoa-Matten. All diese Waaren werden 20 Prozent wohlfeiler verkauft, als in irgend einem andern Etablissement der Vereinigten Staaten.

Hiram Anderson, 99 Bowery.

Courtesy of Tamiment Library, New York University

Recreation after hard work
Is prized with us very highly.

Greetings to you![22]

STAND UP!

European Song

By Harmuth Felseck

And what we hoped—that was betrayed,
And what they promised—that was lies,
And again it's the old misery
And again the daily bread is lacking.
We chew away at the lean horses,
The strong ones rest in court martial graves,
From the jails presses out a madman's cry,
And only the dead are still free.
All over the same old sound of chains,
All over the same old priests' confusion,
The same old lie, the same old fraud,
Which back then beat the world to ribbons.
It's the same old taxpaying,
It's the same old slavescrapping;
The same old torment, the same old pain
Crawls up to heaven everywhere.
They only tightened up the bonds,
And yoke and misery press us harder,
For all oaths new torment:—
So beat the hangman's servant to death!
Grab the scythe, grab the axes,
On to the stall of vengeance and ratchet
And crush the bones alive
Into many splinters small and fine!
They should not die like good people,
And not rot away in the sinner's bed;
—In self-inflicted agony of death
Let them decay and die forever!
God in heaven heard their sighs,
Even their devil will mock them,
And should a God hear them,
Then it's his own fault.
So stop complaining of the misery,
Stop the praying and the whining,
And arm yourselves in body and heart
And wreck to ruins everywhere.
To ruins altars and offices,
The churches and the temple's army,
And beat to splinters and mush
The whole black clergy!
Destroy the chains and the throne,
Smash the rod and the crown.
Rip up, rip open the crimson rabble,
Even if they're still in diapers!
No lengthy hesitation and no arrangements;
Destroy right now both root and branch:
That must be the man, who's promised jurisdiction,
That is the only thing that can bring salvation.—
Talk and complaining will not help,
Only iron will smash to ruins,
Only the rope will strangle,
Only the sound of swords can bring happiness.
Break the yoke, smash the chains,
Only the fist can save us,
Nothing will come from above,
You poor must hold court yourselves!
The fist, the strangling fist on the sword,
Because the three-headed god didn't hear us!
The day breaks, the seed is ripe!
What, are your limbs still stiff?
Wake up from sleep, this sleep of the dead,
Carry out the martyr's punishment!
Freshen up for a bloody act!
—There is and can be no other advice.
Freshen up for one last strangulation!
The last will stand forever:
"No eye cries anymore for bread,
No one dies anymore from hunger,
The clank of chains is heard no more,
Nowhere anymore the priests' confusion,
And end to all tyranny,
The brother-world, equal and free!"[23]

BLACK WORKERS

In 1860 there were four and a half million blacks in the United States. Of these, four million were slaves and a little over five hundred thousand were free blacks—two hundred seventy-four thousand in the South and two hundred thirty-four thousand in the North. Among the slaves were craftsmen and even factory workers, but they could not, of course, form trade unions or find a place in the existing organizations of American workers. Free blacks were also excluded from the trade unions, which remained lily white from the time the first unions were organized through the Civil War. Therefore, there were no labor songs of black workers before the Civil War which dealt with issues such as higher wages and shorter hours so common in the songs of white workers.

But there were slave songs. Many of these have vanished for the simple reason that few whites who heard slave songs took the trouble to record them. Charles Lyell described a boat trip which he took from Savannah to Darien in 1845: " . . . our black oarsmen made the woods echo to their song. One of them taking the lead,

[22]*Die Republik der Arbeiter,* July 16, 1853. Trans. Lenore Veltfort.

[23]*Die Reform,* Aug. 3, 1853. Trans. Brewster Chamberlin.

first improvised a verse, paying compliments to his master's family, and to a celebrated black beauty of the neighborhood, who was compared to the 'red bird.' The other five then joined in chorus, always repeating the same words. Occasionally they struck up a hymn, taught them by the Methodists, in which the most sacred subjects were handled with strange familiarity, and which, though nothing irreverent was meant, sounded oddly to our ears, and, when following a love ditty, almost profane."[24]

Lyell did not record any slave boatmen's songs. Two others about the same time did, however. In 1842, Bartholomew Rivers Carroll, Jr., published three songs of the Negro boatmen in *Chicora*, the Charleston magazine he edited.[25] He introduced the first song with this observation:

> Regularly and beautifully each oar is dipped into the seemingly glassy water, and as the canoe springs forward at the impulse, "Big-mouth Joe," the leading oarsman, announces his departure from the city with a song, in whose chorus every one joins—

Now we gwine leab Charlestown city,
Pull boys, pull!—
The gals we leab it is a pity,
Pull boys, pull!—
Mass Ralph,[26] 'e take a big strong toddy,
Pull boys, pull!—
Mass Ralph, e aint gwine let us noddy,
Pull boys, pull!—
The sun, 'e is up, da creeping,
Pull boys, pull!—
You Jim, you rascal, you's da sleeping,
Pull boys, pull!—

The voyage continued with "an improvisation of as pleasant melody as ever floated over the waters":

Mass Ralph, mass Ralph, 'e is a good man,
Oh ma Riley, oh!
Mass Ralph, mass Ralph, 'e sit at the boat starn,
Oh ma Riley, oh!
Mass Ralph, mass Ralph, him boat 'e can row,
Oh ma Riley, oh!
Come boys, come boys, pull, let me pull oh,
Oh ma Riley, oh!

During the voyage, if Joe perceived that one of the oarsmen perhaps lagged at his work, he at once struck up:

One time upon dis ribber,
Long time ago—
Mass Ralph 'e had a nigger,
Long time ago—
Da nigger had no merit,
Long time ago—
De nigger couldn't row wid sperrit,
Long time ago—
And now dere is in dis boat, ah,
A nigger dat I see—
Wha' is a good for nuthing shoat, ah,
Ha, ha, ha, he—
Da nigger's weak like water,
Ha, ha, ha, he—
'E can't row a half quarter,
Ha, ha, ha, he—
Cuss de nigger—cuss 'e libber,
Ha, ha, ha, he—
'E nebber shall come on dis ribber,
Ha, ha, ha, he—

Carroll commented: "The delinquent oarsman would sooner die than live under such a rebuke; and hence it is that few failures are ever met with in boat voyages of the kind." However, the editor of *Chicora* seemed not to realize that lagging on the job was part of what has been called "day-to-day resistance to slavery."[27]

The other person who documented an early slave boatman's song was Caroline Howard Gilman, Massachusetts-born wife of Samuel Gilman, pastor of the Unitarian church in Charleston. Mrs. Gilman described how Lewis, who was courting Cornelia, the slave owner's daughter, asked Juba, the head oarsman, to "sing us a song; the boys will help you," and how, after an appropriate delay, "Juba commenced a tune, the oarsmen striking in with full but untaught counter at the last word of every line":

Hi de good boat Neely?
She row bery fast, Miss Neely!

[24]Charles Lyell, *A Second Visit to the United States* (New York, 1849), I, 244–45.

[25]*Chicora*, I, 47 and 63 (Aug. 13 and 27, 1842), reprinted in Jay B. Hubbell, "Negro Boatmen's Songs," *Southern Folklore Quarterly*, XVIII (Dec., 1954), 244–45. See also Tristram Potter Coffin and Hennig Cohen, eds., *Folklore from the Working Folk of America* (New York, 1973), pp. 78–79.

[26]Carroll explained that "Master Ralph, or Uncle Ralph, is in charge of the boat crew."

[27]Raymond A. Bauer and Alice H. Bauer, "Day-to-Day Resistance to Slavery," *Journal of Negro History*, XXVII (Oct., 1942), 388–419. See also George P. Rawick, *The American Slave* (Westport, Conn., 1972), pp. 33–37.

An't no boat like a' Miss Neely,
Ho yoi'!
Who gawing to row wid Miss Neely?
Can't catch a' dis boat Neely—
Nobody show he face wid Neely,
Ho yoi'?

Mrs. Gilman noted that as Juba concluded this verse he paused; "a sly expression passed over his face; he put an additional quid of tobacco in his mouth, and went on":

Maybe Maus Lewis take de oar for Neely,
Bery handsome boat Miss Neely!
Maus Lewis nice captain for Neely,
Ho yoi'![28]

Most interesting are the songs which reflect the dissatisfaction of black workers under slavery and songs of struggle to end their bondage.[29] In the first category is "I Am Sold and Going to Georgia," which, according to the Reverend J. W. C. Pennington, himself a former slave and author of an early history of the Negro people,

> . . . is usually sung by the chained gangs of slaves who are on their way, being driven from Maryland, Virginia, and Kentucky, to the more southern state for sale. The last line of each verse is the chorus, and gives a most impressive effect when sung—as it often is—by 60 or 150 voices echoing the plaintive grief of their hearts. This last line is intended as an appeal to all who have it in their power to aid in bringing about the jubilee of emancipation.

O! When shall we poor souls be free?
When shall these slavery chains be broken?
I am sold and going to Georgia,
Will you go along with me?
I am sold and going to Georgia,
Go sound the jubilee.

I left my wife and children behind,
They'll never see my face again;
I am sold and going to Georgia,
Will you go along with me?
I am sold and going to Georgia,
Go sound the jubilee.

I am bound to yonder great rice swamp,
Where my poor bones will find a grave;
I am sold and going to Georgia,
Will you go along with me?
I am sold and going to Georgia,
Go sound the jubilee.

Farewell, my friends, I leave you all,
I am sold, but I have done no fault;
I am sold and going to Georgia,
Will you go along with me?
I am sold and going to Georgia,
Go sound the jubilee.[30]

A somewhat different version of this song is presented by William Wells Brown, a fugitive from slavery who became a noted abolitionist spokesman and the first black novelist and playwright in American history. In his *Narrative*, Brown wrote:

> The following song I have often heard the slaves sing, when about to be carried to the far south. It is said to have been composed by a slave.

See these poor souls from Africa
Transported to America;
We are stolen, and sold to Georgia,
Will you go along with me?
We are stolen, and sold to Georgia,
Come sound the jubilee!

See wives and husbands sold apart,
Their children's screams will break my heart;—
There's a better day a coming,
Will you go along with me?
There's a better day a coming,
Go sound the jubilee!

O, gracious Lord! when shall it be,
That we poor souls shall all be free;
Lord, break them slavery powers—
Will you go along with me?
Lord break them slavery powers,
Go sound the jubilee!

Dear Lord, dear Lord, when slavery'll cease,
Then we poor souls will have our peace;—
There's a better day a coming,

28 Caroline Howard Gilman, *Recollections of a Southern Matron* (New York, 1838), pp. 69–70, reprinted in Hennig Cohen, "Caroline Gilman and Negro Boatmen's Songs," *Southern Folklore Quarterly*, XIX (June, 1956), 116–17. Mrs. Gilman explained that—as with many plantation boats—"Neely" was named for a member of the family, in this case Cornelia.

29 Frederick Douglass was astonished on coming north from slavery in 1838 "to find persons who could speak of the singing among slaves as evidence of their contentment and happiness" (*Narrative of the Life of Frederick Douglass* [1845; reprinted, Cambridge, Mass., 1960], p. 38). Later, in his classic work *Souls of Black Folk* (New York, 1903), W. E. B. Du Bois wrote of the slave songs: "They are the music of an unhappy people, of the children of disappointment; they tell of death and suffering and unvoiced longing toward a truer world, of misty wanderings and hidden ways" (p. 161).

30 Library of Congress, Archive of American Folk Song, WPA Collection.

Will you go along with me?
There's a better day a coming,
Go sound the jubilee![31]

Another slave song on the same theme went:

SOLD OFF TO GEORGY

Farewell, fellow servants! (Oho! Oho!)
I'm gwine way to leabe you; (Oho! Oho!)
I'm gwine to leabe de ole county; (Oho! Oho!)
I'm sold off to Georgy! (Oho! Oho!)

Farewell, ole plantation, (Oho! Oho!)
Farewell, de ole quarter, (Oho! Oho!)
Un daddy, un mammy, (Oho! Oho!)
Un marster, un missus! (Oho! Oho!)

My dear wife un one chile, (Oho! Oho!)
My poor heart is breaking; (Oho! Oho!)
No more shall I see you, (Oho! Oho!)
Oh! no more foreber! (Oho! Oho!)[32]

The following song indicates the slave's well-developed understanding of the relation between the master and the black victims of oppression. Through such pieces, Frederick Douglass noted, "a sharp hit was given to the meanness of the slaveholders."

We raise de wheat,
Dey gib us de corn;
We bake de bread,
Dey gib us de cruss;
We sif de meal,
Dey gib us de huss;
We peal de meat,
Day gib us de skin,
An' dat's de way
Dey takes us in.
We skim de pot,
Dey gib us de liquor,
An' say dat's good enough for nigger.

Walk over—walk over!
Tom butter an' de fat,
Poor nigger, you can't get over dat.
Walk over![33]

Three major forms of resistance to slavery by blacks have been well documented: day-by-day resistance, flight, and insurrection. A song which voiced this attitude—and a century later was to be adopted by workers in the civil rights movement—went:

BEFORE I'D BE A SLAVE (OH, FREEDOM)

Before I'd be a slave, I'd be buried in my grave,
And go home to my Lord and be saved.

O, what preachin'! O, what preachin'!
O, what preachin' over me, over me!

O, what mourning, etc.
O, what singing, etc.
O, what shouting, etc.
O, weeping Mary, etc.
Doubting Thomas, etc.
O, what sighing, etc.
O, Freedom, etc.[34]

Slaves sometimes stopped work and fled to nearby swamps and forests, sending back word they would not willingly return until they were assured a redress of grievances. Tens of thousands of slaves, however, fled and never returned, most of them escaping to the North. Escape required tremendous courage and endurance, because the fugitive slave had to travel at night through hundreds of miles of hostile territory, hide in swamps and forests, and gradually make his way to freedom. Theodore Weld, a leading abolitionist, wrote of one slave who escaped to New York in 1838: "He had come 1,200 miles from the lower part of Alabama, traveling only at nights, feeding on roots and wild berries. He swam *every river* from Tuscaloosa (Ala.) to Pennsylvania."[35]

Many of the Negro slave songs deal in one form or another with the flight from slavery to freedom. Frederick Douglass, who escaped from slavery in Maryland in 1838 and went on to become perhaps the greatest figure in the abolitionist movement, attributed the first thought of escape to the following song:

RUN TO JESUS

Run to Jesus, shun the danger,
I don't expect to stay much longer here.

31William Wells Brown, *Narrative of William Wells Brown* (Boston, 1847), pp. 88–89.

32James Hungerford, *The Old Plantation and What I Gathered There in an Autumn Month [of 1832]* (New York, 1859), reprinted in Eileen Southern, *The Music of Black Americans* (New York, 1971), p. 176.

33Frederick Douglass, *Life and Times of Frederick Douglass* (1881; reprinted, New York, 1962). pp. 146–47.

34Southern, *Music of Black Americans*, pp. 238–39. See also William E. Barton, "Hymns of the Slave and the Freedman," in *Old Plantation Hymns* (Boston, New York, and London, 1899), p. 25.

35*Letters of Theodore Dwight Weld, Angelina Grimké Weld and Sarah Grimké*, ed. Gilbert H. Barnes and Dwight L. Dumond (New York, 1934), II, 22.

He will be dearest friend,
He will help us to the end,
I don't expect to stay much longer here.

Oh, I thought I heard them say,
There were lions in the way.
I don't expect to stay much longer here.

Many mansions there will be,
One for you and one for me.
I don't expect to stay much longer here.[36]

Many of the escape songs are associated with the Underground Railroad, the network of an unknown number of routes stretching northward from the upland country of North Carolina, Tennessee, Virginia, and Kentucky into Canada. W. H. Siebert estimates that there were twelve routes across Ohio alone and that by 1840 every northern state from Wisconsin and Illinois eastward was crossed by slaves on their way to Canada or into regions of the United States where they could be relatively safe from the kidnappers and agents of the planters.[37] While there is still a good deal of controversy over the hidden meaning in many of the slave songs, especially the spirituals,[38] there is little doubt that in the song "Follow the Drinking Gourd," for instance, the "gourd" stands for the Big Dipper—north.

A song well known to runaway slaves and often sung by a whole party of fugitives as they followed their conductor north was "I'm on My Way to Canada."

I'M ON MY WAY TO CANADA

Tune—"Oh, Susannah"

I'm on way to Canada,
That cold and dreary land;
The sad effects of slavery,
I can no longer stand.

I've served my master all my days,
Without a dime's reward;
And now I'm forced to run away,
To flee the lash abroad.

Farewell, old master, don't think hard of me,
I'm on my way to Canada, where all the slaves are free.

The hounds are baying on my track,
Old master comes behind,
Resolved that he will bring me back,
Before I cross the line;

I'm now embarked for yonder shore,
There a man's a man by law;
The iron horse will bear me o'er,
To shake the lion's paw.

Oh, righteous Father, will thou not pity me,
And aid me on to Canada, where all the slaves are free.

Oh, I heard Queen Victoria say,
That if we would forsake
Our native land of slavery,
And come across the lake;

36J. B. T. Marsh, *The Story of the Jubilee Singers* (Boston, 1880), p. 188. Douglass noted that the "air . . . had a double meaning. In the lips of some, it meant the expectation of a speedy summons to a world of spirits; but in the lips of *our* company, it simply meant, a speedy pilgrimage toward a free state, and deliverage from all the evils and dangers of slavery." He also pointed out: "A keen observer might had detected in our repeated singing of

'O Canaan, sweet Canaan,
I am bound for the land of Canaan,'

something more than a hope of reaching heaven. We meant to reach the *north*—and the north was our Canaan" (quoted in Southern, *Music of Black Americans*, pp. 129–30).

37William H. Siebert, *The Underground Railroad from Slavery to Freedom* (New York, 1898), pp. 184–86.

38Other controversial issues about Negro spirituals are: How much was the spiritual a carry-over of African expression; how much was it influenced by white spirituals; and how much did it express a desire for freedom on the part of the Negro in slavery? Eminent students of folklore have written on all sides of these questions. One scholar puts it this way: "There are two principal interpretations of the spirituals, the compensatory and the rebellious, the literalistic and the coded, the other-worldly and the this-worldly. Both are concerned with the plight of the slave and both promise freedom, the one via death ('Thank God I'm free at last' and 'I know de udder worl' is not like dis'), the other through physical escape ('Steal away to Jesus' or 'Git on board, little children') or rebellion ('Go down Moses' and 'Didn't my Lord deliver Daniel?')" (Leroy Moore, Jr., "The Spiritual: Soul of Black Religion," *American Quarterly*, XXIII [Dec., 1971], 673.) Lawrence W. Levine observes: "Over and over their [the slaves'] songs dwelt upon the spectacle of the Red Sea opening to allow the Hebrew slaves past before inundating the mighty armies of the Pharaoh. They lingered delightedly upon the image of little David humbling the great Goliath with a stone. . . . They told in endless variation the stories of the blind and humbled Samson bringing down the mansions of his conquerors; of the ridiculed Noah patiently building the ark which would deliver him from the doom of a mocking world; of the timid Jonah attaining freedom from his confinement through faith. The similarity of these tales to the situation of the slave was too clear for him not to see it; too clear for us to believe that the songs had no worldly content for the black man in bondage" ("Slave Songs and Slave Consciousness: An Exploration in Neglected Sources," in Lawrence W. Levine and Robert Middlekauf, eds., *The National Temper* [New York, 1972], pp. 205–6).

That she was standing on the shore,
With arms extended wide,
To give us all a peaceful home
Beyond the rolling tide

Farewell, old master, don't think hard of me,
I'm on my way to Canada, where all the slaves are free.[39]

One of the most sensational escapes via the Underground Railroad inspired the song "Escape from Slavery of Henry Box Brown." In 1848, a slave named Henry Brown, with the aid of a white Richmond carpenter, was shipped in an unmarked wooden box, three feet one inch long, two feet wide, and two feet six inches deep, from Richmond, Virginia,[40] to the Philadelphia office of the Vigilance Committee[41] by the Adams Express Company. When the box was opened in the committee's office, in the presence of William Still, its black secretary and author of the monumental *Underground Railroad*, Henry Brown stepped out and greeted the onlookers with "Good day, gentlemen." Taking on the middle name "Box," Brown traveled throughout the North and in England, describing his life as a slave and his remarkable escape and popularizing this song:

ESCAPE FROM SLAVERY OF HENRY BOX BROWN
Air—"Uncle Ned"

Here you see a man by the name of Henry Brown,
Ran away from the South to the North,
Which he would not have done but they stole all his rights,
But they'll never do the like again.
Brown laid down the shovel and the hoe,
Down in the box he did go,
No more Slave work for Henry Box Brown,
In the box by *Express* he did go.

Then the orders they were given and the cars they did start,
Roll along—Roll along—Roll along,
Down to the landing where the steamboat met,
To bear the baggage off to the North.
Brown laid down the shovel and the hoe,
Down in the box he did go,
No more Slave work for Henry Box Brown,
In the box by Express he did go.

When they packed the baggage on they turned him on his head,
There poor Brown liked to have died,
There were passengers on board who wished to set down,
And they turned the box down on its side.
Brown laid down the shovel and the hoe,
Down in the box he did go,
No more Slave work for Henry Box Brown,
In the box by Express he did go.

When he got to Philadelphia they said he was in port,
And down upon his head he did fall,
Then he heard his neck crack, and he thought he was dead,
But they never throwed him off any more.
Brown laid down the shovel and the hoe,
Down in the box he did go,
No more Slave work for Henry Box Brown,
In the box by Express he did go.

When he got to Philadelphia they said he was in port,
And Brown he began to feel glad,
And he was taken on the wagon and carried to the place,
And left "this side up with care."
Brown laid down the shovel and the hoe,
Down in the box he did go,
No more Slave work for Henry Box Brown,
In the box by Express he did go.

The friends gathered round and asked if all was right,
As down on the box they did rap,
Brown answered them saying "yes, all is right,"
And he was then set free from his pain.
Brown laid down the shovel and the hoe,
Down in the box he did go,
No more Slave work for Henry Box Brown,
In the box by the Express he did go.[42]

The highest form of slave resistance was the revolt. In his *American Negro Slave Revolts*, Herbert Aptheker, after defining a revolt as an uprising involving "a minimum of ten slaves" with "freedom as its object," concludes that there were 250 such revolts in the history of

[39]Reprinted in Earl Conrad, *Harriet Tubman* (Washington, D.C., 1943), pp. 81–82, from Sarah E. Bradford, *Scenes in the Life of Harriet Tubman* (Auburn, N.Y., 1869), pp. 32–33.

[40]Brown worked in a Richmond factory which made chewing tobacco and employed an all-black labor force of 150 laborers, 120 of whom were slaves.

[41]Vigilance Committees were organized in several northern cities to aid fugitive slaves in their adjustment to freedom, by helping them find refuge among free black families, by finding employment for those with special skills, and, if necessary, by assisting them on to Canada. The latter activity became especially important after the enactment of the Fugitive Slave Act of 1850. See Bradford, *Scenes in the Life of Harriet Tubman*, pp. 32–33.

[42]Broadside, American Antiquarian Society.

ESCAPE FROM SLAVERY

—OF—

HENRY BOX BROWN,

In a box 3 feet and 1 inch long, 2 feet wide, 2 feet and 6 inches high.

AIR—Uncle Ned.

I.

Here you see a man by the name of Henry Brown,
Ran away from the South to the North,
Which he would not have done but they stole all his rights,
But they 'll never do the like again.
Chorus—Brown laid down the shovel and the hoe,
Down in the box he did go,
No more Slave work for Henry Box Brown,
In the box by *Express* he did go.

II.

Then the orders they were given and the cars they did start,
Roll along—Roll along—Roll along,
Down to the landing where the steamboat met,
To bear the baggage off to the North.
Chorus—Brown laid down the shovel and the hoe,
Down in the box he did go,
No more Slave work for Henry Box Brown,
In the box by Express he did go.

III.

When they packed the baggage on they turned him on his head.
There poor Brown liked to have died,
There were passengers on board who wished to set down,
And they turned the box down on its side.
Chorus—Brown laid down the shovel and the hoe,
Down in the box he did go,
No more Slave work for Henry Box Brown,
In the box by Express he did go.

IV.

When they got to the cars they throwed the box off,
And down upon his head he did fall,
Then he heard his neck crack, and he thought he was dead,
But they never throwed him off any more.
Chorus—Brown laid down the shovel and the hoe,
Down in the box he did go,
No more Slave work for Henry Box Brown,
In the box by Express he did go.

V.

When he got to Philadelphia they said he was in port.
And Brown he began to feel glad,
And he was taken on the wagon and carried to the place,
And left "this side up with care."
Chorus—Brown laid down the shovel and the hoe,
Down in the box he did go,
No more Slave work for Henry Box Brown,
In the box by Express he did go.

VI.

The friends gathered round and asked if all was right,
As down on the box they did rap,
Brown answered them saying "yes, all is right,"
And he was then set free from his pain.
Chorus—Brown laid down the shovel and the hoe,
Down in the box he did go,
No more Slave work for Henry Box Brown,
In the box by the Express he did go.

Courtesy of American Antiquarian Society

American Negro slavery.[43] While Aptheker has been criticized for including conspiracies and alleged conspiracies in his calculation, his evidence establishes that there were many more American Negro slave revolts than was generally assumed before his work appeared in 1943. Two of these events, one a conspiracy which was exposed through informers and crushed before it could develop into an actual uprising, the other the greatest slave revolt in American history, are associated with songs.

A slave revolt leader in Spanish New Orleans during the 1750s is described in a song which was still being sung years later by Negroes in New Orleans.

THE DIRGE OF ST. MALO

Alas! young men, come, make lament
For poor St. Malo in distress!
They chased, they hunted him with dogs,
They fired at him with a gun,
. . . .
They hauled him from the cypress swamp—
His arms they tied behind his back,
They tied his hands in front of him;
They tied him to a horse's tail,
They dragged him up into the town.
Before those grand Cabildo men
They charged that he had made a plot
To cut the throats of all the whites.
They asked him who his comrades were;
Poor St. Malo said not a word!
The judge his sentence read to him,
And then they raised the gallows-tree.
They drew the horse—the cart moved off—
And left St. Malo hanging there.
The sun was up an hour high
When on the Levee he was hung;
They left his body swinging there,
For carrion crows to feed upon.[44]

In 1813 a secret organization of slaves in South Carolina was reported to have sung the following parody of "Hail, Columbia," written by a slave:

Hail! all hail! ye Afric clan!
Hail! ye oppressed, ye Afric band } Repeat
Who toil and sweat in slavery bound,
And when your health and strength are gone,
Are left to hunger and to mourn.
Let *independence* be your aim,
Ever mindful what 'tis worth,
Pledge your bodies for the prize,
Pile them even to the skies!

Firm, united let us be,
Resolved on death or liberty!
As a band of patriots joined,
Peace and plenty we shall find.

Look to heaven with manly trust,
And swear by Him that's always just } Repeat
That no white foe, with impious hand
Shall slave your wives and daughters more,
Or rob them of their virtue dear!
Be armed with valor firm and true,
Their hopes are fixed on Heaven and you,
That Truth and Justice will prevail.

Firm, united, etc.

Arise! arise! shake off your chains!
Your cause is just, so Heaven ordains; } Repeat
To you shall freedom be proclaimed!
Raise your arms and bare your breasts,
Almighty God will do the rest.
Blow the clarion's warlike blast;
Call every negro from his task;
Wrest the scourge from Buckra's hand,
And drive each tyrant from the land!

Firm, united, etc.[45]

This was also sung by Denmark Vesey and his coconspirators as they prepared for an insurrection in Charleston in 1822. Betrayed by informers, 131 Negroes and 4 whites were arrested. The whites, convicted of sympathy for the rebels, were fined and jailed. Of the Negroes, 37, including Denmark Vesey, were hanged, while the others were punished in various other ways.

Nat Turner organized and led the most important slave rebellion in this nation's history in August, 1831, in Southampton County, Virginia. The revolt was crushed, and the rebels were executed. On October 30, 1831, Nat Turner was captured; he was executed on November 11 in Jerusalem, Virginia. For years

43Herbert Aptheker, *American Negro Slave Revolts* (New York, 1943), p. 161.

44George W. Cable, "Creole Slave Songs," *Century Magazine*, XXXI (Apr., 1886), 814–15.

45Benjamin J. Lossing, who published this song in 1869, reported he had received it from an American scholar who collected it while engaged in research on the secret meetings of slaves during the War of 1812. Lossing wrote: "All along the coast, and far into the interior, secret organizations existed among negroes for united efforts to obtain their freedom; and in anticipation of the coming of the British army of liberation, they were prepared to rise in large numbers, at a given signal, and strike for freedom" (*The Pictorial Field Book of the War of 1812* [New York, 1868], p. 690).

thereafter, blacks sang of the leader of the great slave rebellion:

NAT TURNER

You mought be rich as cream,
And drive you a coach and four horse team;
But you can't keep the world from moving around,
And Nat Turner from the gaining ground.

You mought be reader and writer too,
And wiser than old Solomon the Jew;
But you can't keep the world from moving around,
And Nat Turner from the gaining ground.

And your name might be Caesar sure,
And got you cannon can shoot a mile or more;
But you can't keep the world from moving around,
And Nat Turner from the gaining ground.[46]

The execution of slave rebels did not dim the slaves' longing for freedom. In Georgetown, South Carolina, slaves were whipped for singing the following spiritual at the time of the election of Abraham Lincoln as president of the United States:

We'll fight for liberty,
We'll fight for liberty,
We'll fight for liberty,
Till the Lord shall call us home;
We'll soon be free,
Till the Lord shall call us home.[47]

"A pilgrim of God," Sojourner Truth believed she had been chosen to free her people from slavery. Her speeches, delivered in a bass voice which raised doubt in the minds of some concerning her sex, were so powerful and eloquent that she was one of the most effective anti-slavery orators of the 1850s. Escaping from bondage as Isabella, she renamed herself to symbolize her wanderings and her message. She presented this message in song as well as in speeches. An account of her lecture to an audience in New Lisbon, Ohio, on the evils of slavery reads in part:

> She sang the following original song at the close of the meeting:—

I am pleading for my people—
A poor, down-trodden race,
Who dwell in freedom's boasted land,
With no abiding place.

I am pleading that my people
May have their rights astored [restored];
For they have long been toiling,
And yet had no reward.

They are forced the crops to culture,
But not for them they yield,
Although both late and early
They labor in the field.

Whilst I bear upon my body
The scars of many a gash,
I am pleading for my people
Who groan beneath the lash.

I am pleading for the mothers
Who gaze in wild despair
Upon the hated auction-block,
And see their children there.

I feel for those in bondage—
Well may I feel for them;
I know how fiendish hearts can be
That sell their fellow-men.

Yet those oppressors steeped in guilt—
I still would have them live;
For I have learned of Jesus
To suffer and forgive.

I want no carnal weapons,
No enginery of death;
For I love not to hear the sound
Of war's tempestuous breath.

I do not ask you to engage
In death and bloody strife,
I do not dare insult my God
By asking for their life.

But while your kindest sympathies
To foreign lands do roam,
I would ask you to remember
Your own oppressed at home.

I plead with you to sympathize
With signs and groans and scars,
And note how base the tyranny
Beneath the stripes and stars.[48]

46Greenway, *American Folksongs of Protest,* pp. 92–93 (from the collection of Lawrence Gellert).

47Southern, *Music of Black Americans,* p. 236.

48*Narrative of Sojourner Truth* (Battle Creek, Mich., 1884), pp. 302–4.

5

The Civil War and Post-Civil War Era 1861–72

THE WAR AND SLAVERY

In the years before the Civil War, northern workers were divided in their attitude towards slavery. A number supported the abolitionists, while others were opposed to abolition. The latter were influenced by arguments that Negro labor would flood the North if emancipated, displacing white workers from their jobs or lowering standards by working for less. However, as the decade of the fifties advanced, a majority of northern workers supported the Republican party's stand in opposition to the further extension of slavery, and the labor vote in the North went, in the main, to Abraham Lincoln, the Republican presidential candidate in 1860. This did not mean that those who supported Lincoln were in favor of immediate abolition of slavery, although the German-American workers, under the leadership of Joseph Weydemeyer and other Marxists, did uphold this position while supporting Lincoln. Following Lincoln's election and the secession of southern states, labor leaders met in Philadelphia and came out in support of the Crittenden Compromise, which would have allowed slavery to expand indefinitely in the territories south of the line 36°30′.

Once the Civil War started, however, workers united in support of the Union. The trade unions, already weakened by the crisis of 1857 and the recession of the secession months, lost most of their remaining members as they left for service in the Union army. Some, like the German-American Communists and the New England workers, who had an anti-slavery tradition, fought to both save the Union and free the slaves. But most trade unionists joined the ranks to preserve the Union—or, as many put it, "for the maintenance of the flag of our country."

As the fighting and dying continued and it became clear that the only way to preserve the Union was to end slavery, Congress and President Lincoln moved towards that objective slowly but surely. The climax was the issuance on January 1, 1863, of Lincoln's Emancipation Proclamation. The proclamation declared all slaves free in states or parts of states still in rebellion against the government of the United States; it left slavery untouched in the border states (Kentucky, Missouri, Maryland, and Tennessee) and parts of states (like Louisiana) under Union army occupation. It greatly increased the flow of slaves from the slaveholding Confederacy into the ranks of the Union army, as hundreds of thousands of Negro slaves gained their freedom by following the increasingly victorious Union armies, which soon included one hundred eighty-six thousand Negro soldiers.

In their joy at being free, the Negroes sang jubilee songs:

MANY THOUSAND GONE

No more auction block for me,
No more, no more;
No more auction block for me,
Many thousand gone.

No more peck o' corn for me
No more, no more;
No more peck o' corn for me,
Many thousand gone.

No more driver's lash for me

No more, no more;
No more driver's lash for me,
Many thousand gone.

No more pint o' salt for me
No more, no more;
No more pint o' salt for me
Many thousand gone.

No more hundred lash for me
No more, no more;
No more hundred lash for me,
Many thousand gone.

No more mistress call for me
No more, no more;
No more mistress call for me,
Many thousand gone.

YOU ARE FREE

Mammy, don't you cook no more,
You are free, you are free!
Rooster, don't you crow no more,
You are free, you are free!
Old hen, don't you lay no more eggs,
You are free, you are free!

SLAVERY CHAIN

Tune—"Joshua Fit de Battle of Jericho"

Slav'ry chain done broke at last
Broke at last, broke at last,
Slavery chain done broke at last,
Goin' to stand up proud and free.

O mah Lord, how ah did suffer
In de dungeon and de chain
An' de days I went wit' head bowed down,
An' my broken flesh and pain,
But brethren. . . .

I done 'point a mighty captain
For to marshal all my hosts,
An' to bring my bleeding ones to me,
An' not one shall be lost,
For brethren. . . .

Now no more weary travelin'
Since mah brethren said to me,
"Dere's no more auction block for you,
For you too shall be free,"
For brethren. . . .[1]

From the outset of the war, the Copperheads, northern allies of the slave owners, most of whom were pro-southern and often even pro-slavery, sought to weaken labor support for the Union cause by launching a propaganda campaign to convince workers that the war was being fought against the interests of white labor and should be brought to a halt with slavery untouched. This propaganda intensified after the Emancipation Proclamation, January 1, 1863, and the Conscription Act, enacted later in 1863, which contained a clause making it legally possible to evade service by providing a substitute or paying a $300 commutation fee. The Copperheads took full advantage of the class nature of the Conscription Act. Handbills, circulated by the thousands in the summer of 1863 in the labor sections of New York and other cities, carried the words to "Song of the Conscripts," a typical excerpt from which went:

We're coming, Father Abraham, three hundred thousand more,
We leave our homes and firesides with bleeding hearts and sore
Since poverty has been our crime, we bow to thy decree;
We are the poor who have no wealth to purchase liberty.[2]

What would the workers fight for? the Copperheads asked. And they replied: "To enable 'abolition capitalists' to transport Negroes into northern cities in order to replace Irish workers who were striking for higher wages."[3] In truth, blacks were being used as strikebreakers. Fears of Negro economic competition and Copperhead propaganda combined to produce the summer, 1863, riots in New York City in which many Negroes were killed or seriously injured.

Despite all this, the evidence is plain that pro-Union sentiment was still the dominant one in labor circles. A song written in the fall of 1863 expressed this clearly.

A SONG FOR THE UNION

Tune—"Welsh Air"

Pottsville, November, 1863

Columbia! our country, to thee let us cling,
And stand for the Union; for God and the right—
Then glad songs of Freedom triumphant we'll sing,
And Despots and Tyrants shall quail at our might.

[1]Thomas Wentworth Higgenson, *Army Life in a Black Regiment* (Boston, 1882), pp. 242–43.

[2]*New York Copperhead*, July 18, 1863. The song was a bitter parody of the popular Civil War anti-slavery song "Three Hundred Thousand More," by James Sloan Gibbons (C. A. Browne, *The Story of Our National Ballads* [New York, 1919], p. 216).

[3]*New York Copperhead*, May 30, 1863.

Then liberty cherish—our country must flourish,
And Traitors shall perish, for Freedom we'll fight,
And the dark clouds of Treason we'll scatter away,
While the sunshine of Freedom assumes its bright sway.

Oh Freedom! thy blessings shall yet be enjoy'd,
And Washington's spirit infused thro' the land,
For Rebels and Traitors shall all be destroy'd,
And radiant with glory shall liberty stand.
Then liberty cherish—our country must flourish,
And traitors shall perish. At Freedom's command,
When her voice shall be heard, then Treason must flee,
And our Mountains they'll echo the shout of the Free.

When Liberty calls, o'er hill and o'er valley,
We'll rush to the summons; united we'll be;
The oppress'd to her standard nobly will rally,
And our flag shall wave proudly o'er land and o'er sea.
Then liberty cherish—our country must flourish,
And traitors shall perish. 'Tis Freedom's decree,
That we conquer vile Treason, the curse of our land,
And Freedom, with Plenty, shall go hand in hand.

Then let us be true to our country and laws;
Hold on to our Chief, who stands at the helm;
On Lincoln depend, for he's true to our cause;
May God give him strength our foes to o'erwhelm.
Then liberty cherish—our country must flourish,
And traitors shall perish, o'er Freedom's broad realm,
And Lincoln, the champion of Justice and Right,
Shall triumph o'er Treason—Secession's delight.[4]

The victory of the North in April, 1865, though saddened by the assassination of Abraham Lincoln, was celebrated in a labor song.

NATIONAL ANTHEM—GOD OF THE FREE

Tune—"Old Hundred"
By William Ross Wallace

God of the Free! upon Thy breath
Our Flag is still for Right unfurled,
As broad and brave as when its stars
First hit the darkness of the world.

For Duty still its folds shall stream,
For Honor all its glories burn,
Where Truth, Religion, Valor, guard
The patriot's sword and martyr's urn.

Though demons struck our Ruler down;
Though wrapt in wo, the Nation still
Shall march in its benignant path
With steadfast hope, unanswering will.

No tyrant's impious step is ours,
No lust of power on nations rolled—
Our Flag for *friends* a starry sky,
For *foes* a storm in every fold.

No slavery shall blast our clime,
But evermore on wave and sod
Only one master's shadow fall—
The golden shadow cast by God.

O thus we'll keep the Nation's life,
Nor fear the bolt by despots hurled;
The blood of all the world is here,
And they who strike us, strike the world!

God of the Right! the Ruler bless
Who guides our mourning Nation now;
Put Mercy's rainbow in his heart,
But storms of Justice on his brow.

Then, still rear high thine Oak, O North!
O South, wave answer with thy palm!
All in our Union's heritage
Together sing the Nation's psalm![5]

ADVANCE OF THE LABOR MOVEMENT

While more than 50 percent of the nation's working force was on the battlefield—the largest proportion of any economic group in American society—other workers remained at their jobs. By 1863 they were once again moving into unions, demanding higher wages to offset rising prices. Between December, 1863, and December, 1864, the number of local unions increased from 79 to 270. These locals joined together in local trades' assemblies or city central labor bodies, and some came together in national trade unions. Between 1850 and 1859, as we have noted, 6 national unions were formed; but during the next ten years, 21 new ones were created, with the largest upsurge during 1863–65. In 1866 the first important national labor federation in American history, the National Labor Union, was organized at a convention in Baltimore. During its six-year existence it dealt with many of the key issues facing labor: the question of whether white labor should join hands with black in basic self-interest and organize the blacks; the question of admitting women into the trade unions; the questions of producers' and consumers' cooperatives and of currency reform; and the most important labor issue at the time—the demand for an eight-hour day. These issues were also discussed in the labor

[4] *Miners' Journal,* Feb. 20, 1864.
[5] *Boston Daily Evening Voice,* June 16, 1865.

press, which emerged during and after the Civil War on an unprecedented scale, particularly in the three leading papers of this period: *Fincher's Trades' Review* of Philadelphia; the *Boston Daily Evening Voice*, and the Chicago *Workingman's Advocate*. Labor songs and ballads were written specially for these papers, and while they did not deal with all the issues mentioned above, they did concern themselves with the major ones. The songs of the eight-hour movement and those of the miners appear in later chapters. The following pages present representative songs on other aspects of the labor movement in the period 1861–72.

Quite a few songs upheld the cause of unionism, urging workers to join the unions of their trade and support the labor press.

APPEAL TO WORKINGMEN

"We will not accede to the price demanded by—a combination of men"—Resolution of the Master Printers of Boston & Vicinity

Rouse, Workingmen! will ye crouch down,
Beneath employers threatening frown?
Are ye not men?
Will ye submissive bow the neck
To yoke oppressive at their beck
Like goaded beasts?

Have ye not rights as well as they?
Are they to rule & ye obey,
Like abject slaves?
No! Justice, honor, manhood, all
That man ennobles sternly call
For union firm.

Yield but the right they now contest
Ye to the winds may fling the rest,
Nor hope to rise
But lower, deeper, baser sink,
Till robbed of e'en the right to think
As well as act.

Ye ask but justice, ask but right
These to obtain you must unite,
And firmly stand,
Unawed by threats, that weakness show,
And from no kindly impulse flow,
But greed for gain.
The noble souls, that think and feel
For others' wants, in woe and weal,
Ne'er stoop to wrest
From honest toil its hard-earned gain,
But help to fill instead of drain
Its scarcity purse.

Your price is fixed, your duty plain,
Your independence now maintain,
Nor flinch or cringe,
And labor will receive its due,
Though scorned by some, and paid by few
Its just reward
For labor is the world's true wealth,
The poor man's capital in health,
Which who employs
Must pay the usury that is just,
Not what he would, but what he must—
Its market worth.[6]

THE UNION'S RALLYING SONG

Dedicated to the Workingmen of America

By P. P. Higgins

Come, sing for the Cause that unites us to-night,
And God bless the men who are waging the fight,
With a will and a purpose unflinching and strong,
To conquer or die we are marching along.

Marching along, we are marching along;
For Justice & Right we are marching along.
There is fire in our souls, boys, and truth in our song,
To conquer or die we are marching along.

United together we come at all call
One brotherhood linked for the safety of all;
We have bowed to no storm, and have braved every shock,
True as flint to the steel, boys, and firm as a rock.

Marching along, &c.

They sought to allure us with bribes, but they failed;
They dared us with threats, and our hearts never quailed;
Like heroes we stood, & like Spartans we'll die,
Or be free as the woods from the sod to the sky.

Marching along, &c.

Then hurrah for the Union, & long may it stand,
The bulwark & shelter, the ark of our band.
To guard it, the life blood shall crimson our graves,
Ere we bend to the foe boys, or sue them as slaves!

Marching along, &c.[7]

LABOR SONG

By John Siney

Tune—"Marching through Georgia"

Start the music, brothers, we will sing a labor song,
Sing it with a vim that will speed our cause along.
Let it ring throughout the world, in chorus full and strong;
Yes, we are the members of the union.

Hurrah! Hurrah! Union makes us strong;
Hurrah! Hurrah! It helps our cause along;

[6] *Fincher's Trades' Review*, Dec. 12, 1863.
[7] Ibid., Mar. 12, 1864.

So we'll sing the chorus wherever we may throng
As we march onward in Union.

Take the pledge to Labor, boys; but after it is signed
Put your trust in Union, and work with heart and mind,
Opposing all oppression, leaving every fear behind,
While we are members of the Union.

Hurrah! Hurrah! etc.[8]

Welcome sisters, to our number,
Welcome to our heart and hand;
At our post we will not slumber,
Strong in union we shall stand.[9]

IN UNION'S MIGHT

By Ira Steward

Tune—"America"

Come, let our voices raise
In thankful songs of praise
For Union's might.
May we as brothers kind,
In Union strong combined,
United heart and mind,
Uphold the right.[10]

WORKMEN, AROUSE YE!

By M.M.

Workmen, arouse ye! gird your loins with the right;
Arouse to the battle, prepare for the fight;
Gird on your armor, old men and youth,
Take the good shield of honor, the sword of truth!

Arouse ye! arouse ye! the foe draweth nigh!
Arouse, to the battle, sound the rallying cry!
Be just and fear not—in Union there's power;
Soon Labor will triumph—God speed the hour!

Sound, sound the watchword, its echoes prolong;
Sound it for freedom, the death-knell of wrong,
Till from Berkshire's hills and the golden strand
The voice of freemen is heard through the land.

Light, light the camp-fires that the world may see
The banner of freedom on Liberty's tree!
Shout, shout for freedom! let the welkin ring
With our glorious motto "Labor conquers everything."

Arouse from your apathy ere it be too late;
Fling out your banner in the Old Bay State;
Strike with the ballot, the freeman's shield,
And slavery, North and South, its vantage shall yield![11]

SWELL OUR RANKS

An Appeal to Non-Union Men

Swell our ranks, ye sons of labor,
Why aloof from Union stand?
See our banner proudly floating
O'er the broad and fertile land.

Hour by hour your chains grow stronger,
Heedless stand ye looking on;
Is the love of home and freedom
From your souls forever gone?

Fast, oh! fast, you're sinking, brothers,
'Neath the iron hand of knaves—
God! is this fair land of freedom
To be doomed by self-made slaves?

Oh, ye old and peerless heroes!
Who did battle for us all,
In the days of Freedom's life-throes,
Look not earthward on our fall!

Look not on your servile offspring,
Who to brothers bend the knee,
Afraid to utter thoughts within them,
Or do battle with the free.

Is the sweat of God-like labor
Oozing for the pampered few?
Is the workhouse, in life's sunset,
All that falleth to its due?

Disunited we are nothing
But a straw before the blast;
But united we can grapple
With the spoiler till the last.

Rally round our standard, brothers—
Nothing else your rights can save;
Better 'neath the sod be sleeping,
Than be to fellow-mortal slave.

Come from golden California—
Come from forest-skirted Maine—
Come from ev'ry quarter, brothers,
Heralding great Labor's reign![12]

[8]*American Federationist*, VIII (Sept., 1901), following 397. John Siney was a leading figure in the Workingmen's Benevolent Association, a miners' union, but he wrote this as a general labor song. For an interesting and longer variant, see p. 154.

[9]*Fincher's Trades' Review*, Feb. 4, 1865. When eighteen working women were admitted to the Working Women's Union of New York City, organized by the sewing machine operators, the members formed a ring about them and sang this song.

[10]Elizabeth Balch, "Songs for Labor," *Survey*, XXXI (Jan. 3, 1914), 411. Ira Steward was the outstanding leader of the eight-hour movement in the post–Civil War era. This general labor song was adopted by the Machinists' and Blacksmiths' Union, of which Steward was a member.

[11]*Boston Daily Evening Voice*, Jan. 1, 1865.

[12]Ibid., Jan. 7, 1865.

ARISE! YE SONS OF LABOR!

By G.B.D.

Arise! ye sons of labor, rise!
In all your majesty and power;
For a tremendous conflict lies
Before you, and from dark'ning skies
Fates ominously lower.

See! haughty Capital doth stand
All ready for the coming fight;
A legion trained to his command,
Obey the waving of his hand
And clamor with delight.

And see! long suffering Labor tries,
With all her might and main,
To cast his fetters off and rise;—
She every nerve and sinew plies
Her ancient rights to gain.

And hark! she calls on you for aid;—
On you—each son of toil—
Her children all—to bare the blade
And sheathe it not till ye have made
Her haughty foe recoil.

Rise, then, ye sons of labor rise!
With armor girded for the fight,—
In one grand host resistless rise,
And fill the heavens with your cries
For Justice, Truth and Right.

Be firm—be resolute—be true!
With all your strength unite,
And roll your mighty columns through
The gap which Time hath made for you,—
God will sustain the right![13]

STRIKE!

By Rev. Ralph Hoyt

I've a liking for this "striking,"
"If we only do it well;
Firm, defiant, like a giant,
Strike—and make the effort tell!"

One another, working brother,
Let us freely now advise;
For reflection and correction
Help to make us great and wise.

Work and wages, say the sages,
Go forever hand in hand;
As the motion of the ocean,
The supply and the demand.

My advice is, strike for prices
Nobler far than sordid coin;
Strike with terror, sin and error,
And let man and master join.

Ever failing now prevailing
In the heart or in the head—
Make no clamor—take the hammer—
Drive it down—and strike it dead.

Much the chopping, lopping, popping,
Carpenter, we have to do,
Ere the plummet, from the summit,
Mark our moral fabric true.

Take the measure of false pleasure;
Try each action by the square;
Strike a chalk-line for your walk-line;
Strike to keep your footsteps there!

The foundation of creation
Lies in truth's unerring laws,
Man of mortar, there's no shorter
Way to base a righteous cause.

Every builder, painter, guilder,
Men of leather, men of clothes,
Each mechanic in a panic
With the way his labor goes.

Let him reason thus in season;
Strike the root of all his wrong;
Cease his quarrels, mend his morals,
And be happy, rich and strong.[14]

Songs of the period frequently asserted labor's prime role in society, emphasizing that whatever was worthwhile in it came from the toil of the working people, although the rewards of this labor went to the capitalists and monopolists.

THE DAY OF LABOR

By John Ross Dix

Ho, brothers, sing today a song—
A strain that for its burden
Shall heave, as trolls the lay along,
The toiling millions guerdon!
Let others warble beauty's praise,
Or wreathe with song the sabre;
United, we'll our voices raise
To chant the lay of labor.

The drops that bead the worker's brow
Are nobler far than laurels
That any victor chief can show,
Plucked from a nation's quarrels.
Some praise the minstrel when he sings;
I'd rather hear my neighbor,
Who on his smithy anvil rings
The melody of labor.

[13] Ibid., Nov. 24, 1865.
[14] Ibid., July 16, 1866.

The man who nobly toils for bread
On none needs dance attendance;
'Mid monarchs may he lift the head
Of honest independence.
The son of toiling ancestors,
He bears the burdens they bore;
And on his lot, though low, confers
The dignity of labor.

Then honor unto all who toil—
Strong man or gentle woman:
Amid the daily strife and moil
There's something superhuman!
To working duty lends a charm;
So join with me, good neighbor,
And sing on field, and forge, and farm,
The honor due to labor.[15]

SONG FOR WORKINGMEN'S UNIONS

By A. J. H. Duganne

Ho! brethren all! of manly craft!
Whose hands are cased in Labor's mall;
Who swing the sledge, and spring the shaft,
And fling the singing flail!
On sea or soil, where'er ye toil.
Brave hearts! I bid ye hail!
Awake! arise! uplift your eyes—
True friend and loyal neighbor!
There's never a man in Honor's van,
Who stands not there by Labor!

With Nimrod first, on Babel's plain,
A throne ye reared from desert mould;
Ye fired the forge of Tubal Cain,
And sailed with Jason bold!
And builded high, 'twixt earth and sky
The tombs of Pharoahs old!
With ringing peal of brass and steel,
More sweet than pipe or tabor,
Wherever ye go, the world shall know
That glory springs from Labor!

In thread and web of wondrous time
By you the world's great woof is wrought:
Your hammers beat, in tuneful chime,
To shape each ponderous thought
That leaps amain, from human brain,
With heavenly genius fraught!
The sledge weights down a monarch's crown,
The axe can cleave a sabre,
Or sever in twain a tyrant's chain
From off the limbs of Labor!

Ye delve the mine, and rend the hills,
And pile the marts with harvest grain;
Ye whirl the wheels of countless mills,
And curb the rolling main;
Each ill and ban ye turn from man,
Each good for him ye gain!
Uplift your song, ye toiling throng!
No need of pipe or tabor—
For iron has tongue, all lands among,
To sing the fame of Labor!

Sing, brothers, sing! with lofty hearts:
Your anthems lift, in proud acclaim;
Old Earth, through all her myriad marts,
Exalts the Toiler's name,
And lustrous charts of fadeless arts
Explore his deathless fame!
Sing, brothers, sing!—No chief nor king
Can curb ye down, with rod or sabre;
If out of your sleep, ye dare to leap,
And stand by glorious Labor![16]

THE WORKINGMEN

By C. B. Lincoln

Who raised those palaces of earth,
And deck'd their shrines with burnished gold?
Those lofty spires, who gave them birth,
Fashion, and form from marble cold;
And found for each exquisite gem
Its proper place? The Workingmen.

Who raised those pyramids on high,
And laid these deep foundations sure?
Who brought the lightning from the sky,
Subservient to his will and power?
And who the surging billows stem
And search these depths? The Workingmen.

Who raised the diamond from its bed,
That sparkles in a monarch's crown?
Who hath the light of science spread,
That breaks all superstition down?
Who measures heaven's boundless span?
The scientific workingman.

Who travelled through the forest wild,
Where savage tribes had only trod,
To preach the Gospel undefiled,
And bring the sinner home to God:
And thus reveal salvation's plan?
Who but the faithful workingman?

'Tis he that cultivates the soil,
And gives the teeming millions bread;
The hard, industrious hand of toil,
Has round us all our comforts spread,
Transformed the world—tho' fiends oppose—
"And made it blossom like the rose."

The workingman is lord of all;
You'll find him foremost everywhere—

[15]Ibid., Mar. 14, 1865.
[16]Ibid., June 15, 1865.

CHANTS OF LABOUR

No. 24. Song of the "Lower Classes."

Words by ERNEST JONES. Air—*My Old Friend John.*

We plow and sow, we're so ve - ry ve - ry low, That we
Air & Accompt. mf
delve in the dir - ty clay; Till we bless the plain with the
gold - en grain, And the vale with the fra - grant hay. Our
p
place we know, we're so ve - ry ve - ry low, 'Tis down at the land - lord's
feet :............ We're not too low the grain to grow, But too

CHANTS OF LABOUR

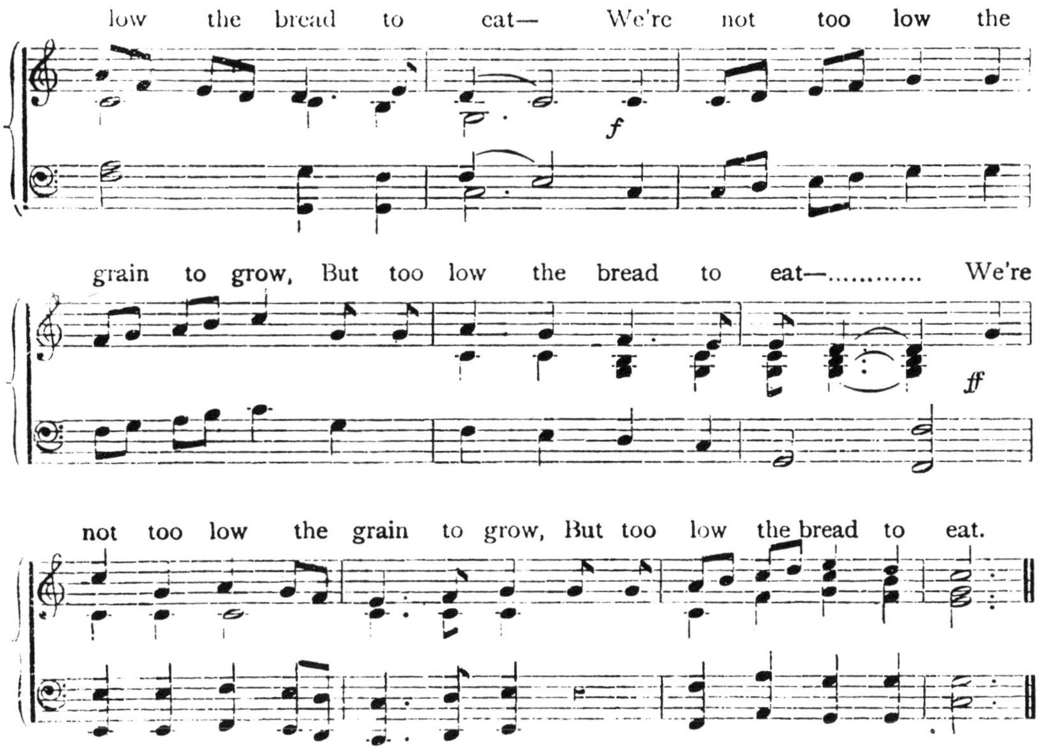
low the bread to eat— We're not too low the
grain to grow, But too low the bread to eat—........... We're
ff
not too low the grain to grow, But too low the bread to eat.

2\. Down, down we go, we're so very very low,
To the hell of the deep-sunk mines;
But we gather the proudest gems that glow,
When the brow of a despot shines;
And whene'er he lacks, upon our backs
Fresh loads he deigns to lay;
We're far too low to vote the tax, } *Repeat.*
But not too low to pay.

3\. We're low, we're low--mere rabble we know—
But at our plastic power,
The world at the lordling's feet will glow
Into palace and church and tower;
The prostrate fall in the rich man's hall,
And cringe at the rich man's door;
We're not too low to build the wall, } *Repeat.*
But too low to tread the floor.

4\. We're low, we're low—we're very very low—
Yet from our fingers glide
The silken flow and the robes that glow
Round the limbs of the sons of pride;
And what we get, and what we give,
We know, and we know our share;
We're not too low the cloth to weave, } *Repeat.*
But too low the cloth to wear.

From Edward Carpenter, *Chants of Labour*, 5th ed. (London, 1912), pp. 38–39.
Courtesy of Brown University Library.

The merchant's desk, the council hall,
The doctor's, the professor's chair.
The best of all creation's plan—
The faithful, honest workingman![17]

SONG OF THE UNENFRANCHISED

"We plow and sow, we're very, very low
That we delve in the dirty clay,
Till we bless the plain with golden grain,
And the vale with the fragrant hay.
Our place we know, we're so very low,
'Tis down at the landlord's feet;
We're not too low the grain to grow,
But too low the bread to eat.

Down, down, we go, we're so very, very low
To the hell of the deep sunk mines,
But we gather the proudest gems that glow
When the crown of a despot shines;
And whene'er he lacks, upon our backs
Fresh loads he deigns to lay;
We're far too low to vote the tax,
But not too low to pay.

We're low, we're low, mere rabble, we know,
But at our plastic power
The mould at the lordling's feet will grow
Into palace, church and tower.
Then prostrate fall in the rich man's hall,
And cringe at the rich man's door;
We're not too low to build the wall,
But too low to tread the floor.

We're low, we're low, we're very, very low,
Yet from our fingers glide
The silken flow, and the robes that glow
Round the limbs of the sons of pride.
And what we get, and what we give,
We know, and we know our share;
We're not too low the cloth to weave,
But too low the cloth to wear.

We're low, we're low, we're very, very low,
And yet when the trumpets ring,
The thrust of a poor man's arm will go
Thro' the heart of the proudest king.
We're low, we're low, our place we know,
We're only the rank and file;
We're not too low to fight the foe,
But too low to touch the spoil."[18]

LABOR IS HONOR

"Labor is Honor!" The Monarch Supreme
Made those bright sparkling stars, 'mid glory serene,
To show forth His power and His wisdom to plan,
And crown'd all His labor by making a man.

"Labor is Honor!" Go, learn from the bee
The lesson of wisdom—none wiser than she;
In summer's bright sunshine she lays up her store
Of sweetness from flowers which grow at your door.

"Labor is Honor!" No person e'er gains
Stores of great knowledge without labor and pains;
It strengthens our muscles, enlarges our brains,
And sends the warm blood coursing swift through our
veins.

"Labor is Honor!" Though fools may despise
To follow the course of the good and the wise;
There's health, wealth and virtue, and all good besides,
In Labor there's honor and glory and pride.[19]

A PSALM OF LABOR—FOR THE WORKINGMEN

By Erma Alice Browne

They may boast of their landed Autocrats
Till the hills are a cycle-old;
Of their Money Kings, in their gilded halls,
Of their "dividends," "stocks" and "gold"—
I sing of the labor-hardened hand,
And the heart of the Artisan bold.

For he whose arm is brawny and brown,
And rough with many a scar—
Who nurseth a spirit in his broad breast,
And a will to do and to dare,
Is noble and great, in his own good right,
As their goldenest nabobs are!

Aye! he that breaks with a sturdy force
The pride of the stubborn soil—
Who robbeth the hills, and the vales between,
With the fruits of his glorious toil,
Cometh a king from the harvest crowned
With the Seasons' generous spoil.

And he that tugs at the blazing forge,
And curbs with a cunning skill
The fiery strength of the molten ore,
Is Lord of an Iron Will!
And thrones may topple, and empires fall,
But he is a conqueror still!

17Ibid., Mar. 22, 1865. W. Barrett used the same theme in an almost identical piece, "The Working Men of England," which appeared in the *Bee-Hive*, the official organ of the London Trades Council and the leading British labor paper, in its issue of June 20, 1863.

18*Boston Daily Evening Voice*, Aug. 18, 1865. The song appeared in the *Labor Standard*, August 18, 1878, under the title "The Song of the 'Lower Classes,' " with authorship credited to Ernest Jones, "our deceased friend." It was reprinted in the Knights of Labor *Labor Reform Songster* (Philadelphia, 1892), with accompanying music. It also appeared, again with music, in Edward Carpenter's *Chants of Labour* (London, 1891, pp. 38–39).

19*Boston Daily Evening Voice*, Oct. 16, 1865.

And his name shall live for aye and aye,
In proverb toast and rhyme!
And his fame march on like an armed man,
Down the ringing aisles of Time!
From the Brazen Ages, lost in night,
Thro' the modern arts sublime!

Yea! Each rude Toiler, grappling well,
In the world's rugged fight,
That bares his right arm to the sun,
His broad breast to the light—
Strikes for a Grand Equality,
By Labor's might of Right.

Huzza! We crowd with our free-born blood,
The courts, the camps, the schools!
Huzza! We never bend the knee
To pampered knaves and fools!
We are Heirs of the Rights of Labor, and
Our monarch—SUFFRAGE—rules!

Sprung of the stalwart arm and heart,
Dowered with the subtle brain,
We stand erect in the light of God!
Spurning the broken chain
That fetters the strong men over the sea,
In the monopolists' gilded train!

Born in the purple and pomp of power,
Their Dynasties, old and new,
With the pale phantoms of Hunger and Strife
The paths of their conquests strew—
But a Prince of Plenty is a peer of their peers,
Born in the Red, White and Blue!

Huzza! For the land we are proud to own,
The best land under the sun!
Huzza! For the freedom and rights we'll own,
When the Money King's race is run!
Huzza! For the Empire that numbers its thrones,
Of its monarchs by millions—not one![20]

HONOR TO OUR WORKMEN

Whom shall we call our heroes,
To whom our praises sing?
The pampered child of fortune,
The titled lord or king,
They live on others' labor.
Take all and nothing give;
The noblest type of manhood
Are they who *work to live.*

Then honor to our workmen,
Our hardy sons of toil—
The heroes of the workshop,
And monarchs of the soil.

Who spans the earth with iron?
And rears the palace-dome?
Who creates for the rich man
The comforts of the home?
It is the honest toiler—
All honor to him, then!
The true wealth of the nation
Is in her *workingmen.*

Then honor, &c.

For many barren ages
Earth hid her treasures deep,
And all her giant-forces
Seemed found as in a sleep;
Then Labor's "anvil chorus"
Broke on the startled air,
And, lo! the earth in rapture
Laid all her treasures bare!

Then honor, &c.

'Tis toil that over nature
Gives man his proud control
And purifies and hallows
The temple of his soul.
It startles foul diseases,
With all their ghastly train;
Puts *iron* in the muscle,
And *crystal* in the brain!

Then honor, &c.

The Grand, Almighty Builder,
Who fashioned out the earth
Hath stamped His seal of honor
On labor from her birth.
In every angel-flower,
That blossoms from the sod
Behold the master touches—
The handiwork of God.

Then honor, &c.[21]

LABOR

There's a never-dying chorus
Breaking on the human ear,
In the busy town before us
Voices loud, and deep, and clear.
This is labor's endless ditty;
This is toil's prophetic voice,
Sounding through the town and city
Bidding human hearts rejoice.

Sweeter than the poet's singing
Is that anthem of the free;
Blither is the anvil's ringing
Than the song of bird or bee,
There's a glory in the rattle

20Ibid., Dec. 21, 1865.

21Ibid., Apr. 29, 1866, reprinted (with minor changes) in *National Workman*, Jan. 19, 1867.

Of the wheels 'mid factory gloom;
Richer than e'er snatched from battle
Are the trophies of the loom.

See the skillful mason raising
Gracefully yon towering pile;
Round the forge and furnace blazing
Stand the noble men of toil,
They are heroes of the people,
Who the wealth of nations raise;
Every dome, and spire, and steeple,
Rear their heads in labor's praise.

Glorious men of truth and labor,
Shepherds of the human fold,
That shall lay the brand and sabre
With the barbarous things of old.
Priests and prophets of creation,
Bloodless heroes in the fight,
Toilers for the world's salvation,
Messengers of peace and light.

Speed the plow and speed the harrow;
Peace and plenty send abroad;
Better far the spade and harrow
Than the cannon or the sword.
Each invention, each improvement,
Renders weak oppression's rod;
Every sigh and every movement
Brings us nearer truth and God.[22]

CAPITAL AND LABOR

By a Mechanic's Wife, Bridgeport, Connecticut
October 11th, 1866

"The autumn winds blow shrill and cold,
Bleak winter soon will come;
Heaven help the poor—protect the old—
And give us all a home."
Thus often does the rich man pray,
With solemn tone and word;
But, oh! how seldom does he say,
"I'll be thy agent, Lord.

"The needy that around me live
Shall have my daily care,
And from thy treasure lent, I'll give
To all who need a share,
And as this wealth is fast increased,
By laboring, needy men,
I will not grudgingly withhold
The profits due to them."

But, no! he has no goods to waste;
He has no time to spare;
So offering them to Heaven for help,
His conscience eased, he leaves them there
And turns his thoughts to earth again,
His factory or his farm,
And studies how to increase his wealth
By the laborer's sinewy arm.

And how to get from labor most,
And in return give least,
He cares not if his workmen starve,
If he can only feast.
And so he'll make their wages less,
Grind down with iron heel,
Until in poverty's distress
E'en manhood scarce they feel.
Men with God's impress in their soul,
His likeness in their brow,
Obeying Heaven's command to toil,
Most slaves before him bow,
Arouse ye laborers! Take a new
And nobler view of life;
Cast off these base, degrading chains,
Be manly in the strife;
Unite with brotherly accord,
In love, sincere and true,
Ah, standing firm, demand the rights
So long and justly due.

What are those rights? For every hour
Of toil, sufficient pay
To make your home less comfortless,
And keep grim Want away;
To lighten the too heavy load
We weary wives now bear;
To feed and clothe your little ones,
And have some time to spare
Neglected minds to cultivate,
To study and reflect,
And fit yourselves for usefulness,
Where duty may direct.

But struggle not for this alone,
For Principle contend;
Make Labor honored and revered,
Be this your aim and end,
And raise the humblest laborers,
At least to stand beside
The men, who live from off their toil,
In indolence and pride.[23]

A TOAST FOR LABOR

Here's to the man with horny hand
Who tugs the breathing bellows;
Where anvils ring, in every land,
He's loved by all good fellows.

And here's to him who goes afield,
And through the globe is plowing,

22 *Molders' International Journal*, Dec., 1866, p. 264.

23 *Coach Makers' International Journal*, reprinted in *Molders' International Journal*, Dec., 1866, p. 264.

Or with stout arm the axe doth wield,
While ancient oaks are bowing.

Here's to the delver in the mine,
The sailor on the ocean,
With those of every craft and line,
Who work with true devotion.

Our love for her who toils in gloom,
Where cranks and wheels are clanking;
Bereft is she of nature's bloom,
Yet God in patience thanking.

A curse for him who sneers at toil,
And shuns his share of labor,
The knave but robs his native soil,
While leaning on his neighbor.

Here may this truth be bought on earth,
Grow more and more in favor;
There is no wealth but owes its worth
To handicraft and labor.

Then pledge the founders of our wealth—
The builders of our nation;
We know their words, and now their health
Drink we with acclamation.[24]

In 1867 the Knights of Saint Crispin, a powerful shoemakers' organization, was founded in Milwaukee. By 1870 its fifty thousand members made it the largest labor organization in the country. The Crispins drew their strength from shoemakers all over the nation who were dismayed by swift technological changes in the shoe industry during the late sixties, in particular the introduction into shoe factories of the McKay pegging machine. But it also attracted workers because it favored development of a producers' cooperative system and independent political action. The Saint Crispins conducted a series of strikes in the shoe industry, principally as a result of the order's efforts to limit "green hands." The Boston labor paper *American Workman*, almost an official organ of the Knights of Saint Crispin, carried the following song by a member of the order:

ODE TO ST. CRISPIN

By Nonantum

Saint Crispin, indeed, is a very fine fellow;
He hammers all day, and at night he gets mellow
And if not religious, he works all the Sunday,
And takes compensation by keeping blue Monday.
Indeed, he's a saint, and a fine fellow, too;
And also a hero, with banner of blue.

He sings, and learns lessons, and always keep pegging;
He wrangles and tangles his strap, with his leg-in.
He asks you no favors, but often turns preacher;—
As cute as an Edwards, as palmy as Beecher!
Indeed, he's a saint, and a fine fellow, too;
And also a hero, with a banner of blue.

By punching and threading, he reaches the quorum.
Though keen and sarcastic, he speaks with decorum;
Though tramping, his ways are all lasting like leather;
And so the good saint keeps his knights altogether.
Indeed, he's a saint, etc.

By doubling and twisting, the Senate he reaches;
By tacks raises taxes—warm waxes at breaches
Oft made in the upper-fudge-soles of his faction,
And raises hard welts when they all get their packs on.
Indeed, he's a saint, etc.

By rasping and polish, he shines as a poet.
Ah! had I been knighted, my verses would show it:
This grace I'd forgotten, 'mid turnings and dodges,
Till I espied Har'rill among your good lodges,
Indeed, he's a saint, etc.

Now, honest St. Crispin, don't rise to hifalutin;
For St. Ego, too, may essay to high shooting:
And wood, flax, and leather must all yield to iron,
As your hammers prove, and as I yield to Byron.
Indeed, he's a saint, etc.

Now gentle St. Crispin, pray what are my honors?
I'd make your good paper float round like a Bonner's;—
But cannot be knighted, for unskilled in waxing,
My last, thread, and bristle would awl go for tacksing.
So here's for St. Crispin, a good fellow he—
May his tacks lessen taxes, and make our land free.

(The whole house)
And right our good vessel which founders at sea!
Its ballast is shifting, it drifts to the lea—
May tacks prick those taxers, whoever they be—
Those pirates that plundered our vessel, to free
The poor captives, enchained by their own vile decree.
Throw over the ballast—she lurches, you see.
The cook must go seaward, where wicked men flee.
Now, weigh the foul anchor—heave-o-hio-ho!
Now, straighten her jibs—let the spanker go free!
Mind her helm, captain, work; man her yards, boys, wi'
glee.
She trembles, she quivers, the breeze blows to sea.
To her awful grandeur, let kings bow the knee!
Praise God for her safety, let our song ever be.
His justice brings freedom, the world's jubilee.[25]

[24] *Boston Daily Evening Voice*, July 3, 1867.
[25] *American Workman*, Aug. 21, 1869.

THE FREEDMEN

Just as they had been divided over abolition before the war, so after the conflict and the abolition of slavery, white workers were split over the issue of full equality for the freedmen. Most workers supported the Reconstruction policy of President Andrew Johnson, under which former slaves in the South were being restored by black codes and other devices to a status not too different from slavery.[26] Most unions, too, continued to bar blacks from membership. However, the *Boston Daily Evening Voice* was a unique labor champion of black equality during this period, advocating Radical Reconstruction, under which the freedmen would become citizens and would be entitled to full civil rights and the rights of suffrage. The *Voice* also called upon the unions of white workers, in their own interest apart from principles of labor solidarity, to eliminate all barriers against black membership. It hailed the efforts of black workers to form their own unions and called for full unity between the organizations of black and white labor. These equalitarian sentiments were reflected in songs and ballads published in the *Voice*.

EQUAL RIGHTS FOR ALL

By George E. Davenport

Who would the rights of manhood claim
Should yield them unto others;
For in God's eyes we're all the same,
One common band of brothers.

What signifies our birth, our race,
Our pride, or lofty station?
Or e'en the color of our face,
All men, of every nation,

Thro' heaven's justice at their birth
Co-equal rights inherit
And none may claim superior worth,
Save by superior merit.

All alike, or poor, or rich,
Beneath the light of heaven,
One right possess in common which,
By God to them was given,

The right to freedom, justice, too,
To work out their salvation;
The right untrammeled to pursue
Their highest aspiration.

Let us yield unto others then
What we ourselves desire,
And aim to lift our fellow-men
In manhood's scales still higher.

No ban, or race, or creed, but free
As air is to mankind,
Let all the rights of manhood be
As a just God designed.[27]

UNCLE THAD. STEVENS

By Private Miles O'Reilly

Gnarled and tough from seventy winters,
A gritty, grizzly, bitter "Rad"—
Though our Union fall to splinters,
Here's to Pennsylvania Thad!

Brown his wig, but green his vigor,
Angry often, never sad—
Full of wit and prone to rigor,
Here's to Pennsylvania Thad!

Though lame his leg, his mind is rapid—
And all the House is hushed and glad,
When, to squelch some talker vapid—
Rises Pennsylvania Thad.

He's in candor a believer,
All may know the thought he had;
For no mealy-mouthed deceiver
Is our wrinkled Uncle Thad.

Into epithets he rushes;
All are "Traitors" or are "mad"—
All who dare to cross the wishes
Of our Pennsylvania Thad.

Thad, we like you; you are able—
And the biggest brick we have had
In our loud Congressional Babel
Is our Pennsylvania Thad.

Spite of age, he still is human,
And while to man he is not bad,
O dear, a good man to a woman—
The kindliest man is Uncle Thad!

Naked truth for him hath charms;
For the negroes like a "Rad,"
And for their rights to "be in arms,"
Nobly fought our Uncle Thad.

26The following lines reflect the disillusionment of the freedmen with the operation of emancipation under Johnsonian Reconstruction:

Nigger plow de cotton,
Nigger pick it out;
White man pockets money,
Nigger does without.

(John Greenway, *American Folksongs of Protest* [Philadelphia, 1953], p. 83.)

27*Boston Daily Evening Voice*, Mar. 21, 1866.

Go it, my old shoulder hitter!
  For though we think your logic bad,
You're just as brilliant as you're bitter—
  Here's to Pennsylvania Thad![28]

MACHINE VERSES
By J.S.A.

Who is he more than all the rest,
The loyal people all detest,
Who do the Copperheads love best,
  'Tis Andy.[29]

Who has removed brave
And shown as plain as mortal can,
How many tailors make a man,
  'Twas Andy.

Who once around the circle swung,
And wagged out West his rebel tongue,
Whose praise has Parson Nasby sung,
  'Twas Andy.

He is an eyesore to the brave,
He gives each crowd the "flag" to save,
He is the Moses of the slave,[30]
  Is Andy.

He always saves his hardest bits,
For loyal men, and gives them fits,
He'll "catch it" soon as Congress sits.
  Will Andy.

He's bound to have his little tod,
Till he is laid beneath the sod,
He always makes himself a "cod,"
  Does Andy.

In slavery's work he does not pause,
He mends the "breaches" in the laws,
He is a Judas to the cause,
  Is Andy.

At bragging he can beat the Dutch,
'Twill do for little boys and such,
But he cannot fool old Grant "not much,"
  Can Andy.[31]

THE CHINESE

Next to prejudice against blacks, the most extensive prejudice was against the Chinese. Anti-Chinese songs were already popular in California as early as 1855, shortly after the Chinese became numerous in the gold-mining areas, and were part of the vicious campaign to force them out of the mines by violence and restrictive legislation. Typical was "John Chinaman":

JOHN CHINAMAN

I thought you'd cut your queue off, John,
And don a Yankee coat,
And a collar high you'd raise, John,
Around your dusky throat.

I thought of rats and puppies, John,
You'd eaten your last fill,
But on such slimy "pot-pies,"
I'm told you dinner still.

Oh, John, I've been deceived in you,
In all your thieving clan,
For our gold is all you're after, John,
To get it as you can.[32]

During the Civil War, ten thousand Chinese laborers (and three thousand Irishmen) built the first transcontinental railroad, suffering numerous casualties amid the icy peaks and burning deserts. When the road was built, many who survived joined former miners in the cities of California and sought there to make a living. Again they encountered fierce opposition as "cheap" laborers who were driving out white workers. The following song illustrates how white workers, many of them Irish, reacted to this competition.

SINCE THE CHINESE RUINT THE THRADE

From me shanty down on Sixth Street,
  It's meself have jist kim down;
I've lived there this eighteen year—
  It's in phat they call Cork Town.
I'm on the way to the City Hall
  To get a little aid;
It's meself that has to ax it now
  Since the Chinese ruint the thrade.

28 Ibid., Sept. 3, 1866. Thaddeus Stevens, leader of the Radical Republicans in the House of Representatives, stood for a program of reconstruction which included full freedom for ex-slaves, including suffrage and even distribution of land among the freedmen.

29 "Andy" is, of course, Andrew Johnson.

30 At one time early in Reconstruction, Johnson had assured the ex-slaves that he would be their Moses to lead them out of bondage to full freedom. But he quickly forgot his pledge.

31 *Boston Daily Evening Voice*, Aug. 31, 1867.

32 *The California Songster* (San Francisco, 1855), reprinted in Cornel Lengyel, ed., *A San Francisco Songster, 1849–1939*, Works Progress Administration, History of Music Project, History of Music in San Francisco Series (San Francisco, 1939) II, 145. The song was revived by the Working Men's party; see p. 135.

For I kin wash an' iron a shirt,
An' I kin scrub a flure;
An' I kin starch a collar as stiff
As any Chineseman, I'm sure;
But there dhirty, pigtailed haythens,
An' ther prices they are paid
Have brought me to the state you see—
They've entirely ruint the thrade

I'm a widdy woman, I'd have ye know—
Poor Mike was kilt at work.
He got a fall from the City Hall,
For he was a mason's clerk,
An' me daughter Ellen is gone this year
Wid a Frinch bally troupe, ther jade,
So I find it hard to get along
Since the Chinese ruint the thrade.

It makes me wild, whin I'm on the street,
To see those haythens' signs:
Ah Sung, Ah Sing, Sam Lee, Ah Wing,
An' ther ilegatt sprid on ther lines.
If iver I get me hands on Ah Sing,
I'll make him Ah Sing indade—
On me clothesline I'll pin th' leather skin
Of the haythen that ruint the thrade.[33]

A strong movement arose to drive the Chinese out of all trades and occupations and prevent the further entrance of Chinese laborers into the United States. Most of the trade unions favored the complete exclusion of Chinese labor, although a few, notably the Colored National Labor Union, organized in 1869, made a distinction between normal Chinese immigration, which they insisted should not be interfered with, and coolie labor imported under contract, which they opposed. The more common view, however, favored the total exclusion of Chinese immigration on the ground that the Chinese would drive white workers out of jobs and cut wages. This view is expressed in the following song:

JOHN CHINAMAN

A Song by R. W. Hume

Oh, Sam! You vain and silly fool,
What have you gone and done?
To rouse that Eastern Goblyn Grim,
I'm sure it is no fun
Wherever you can put him now
I'm sure I cannot see,
Unless in Boston Bay so deep,
You ask him down to tea.

The servants in our palaces
Must now be smart and spry;
And keep their rooms all dusted clean—
And put their chignons by,
For Foo Choo has his eyes on them,
He knows what he's about,
He'll do their work at half the price—
Nor ask a Sunday out.

Now James, rub up your harness,
And brush your master's coats
Polish your band and buttons well,
And don't purloin the oats
Or Ho Sam Ling, in half a wink
Will turn you out to graze,
Where you'll have time enough to think
Upon your wicked ways.

Your sturdy tillers of the soil,
Prepare to leave full soon,
For when John Chinaman comes in
You'll find there is no room.
Like an Egyptian locust plague,
Or like an eastern blight,
He'll swarm you out of all your fields,
And seize them as his right.

Let the mechanic pack his traps,
And ready make to flit;
He cannot live on rats and mice,
And so he needs must quit.
Then, while he can with babes and wife,
Let him in peace retire,
Lest in the shadowed future near,
His children curse their sire.

At the full cost of bloody war,
We've garnered in a race,
One set of men of late we've freed,
Another takes his place.
Come friends, we'll have to leave this land
To nobles and to slaves,
For, if John Chinaman comes in,
For us—there's only graves.[34]

33 *The Poor Little Man and the Man in the Moon Is Looking, Love, Songster* (San Francisco, n.d.), p. 11.

34 *Workingman's Advocate,* Aug. 21, 1869. Anti-Chinese songs were also part of stage repertory in this period. Tony Pastor, for example, sang the following:

Now Coolie labor is the cry,
"Pat" must give way to Pagan "John,"
Whom Christian bosses, rich and sly,
Have anxiously the heart set on.
For he's a nice, cheap Chinaman,
Who ne'er turns Turk or "strikes" his work
For more pay, like the Irishman.

And won't he a fine Christian make?
The gentle, lamb-like Chinaman,
And for much toil small wages take,
The sweet, soft, yielding Chinaman?
The weak, tea-drinking Chinaman,

LABOR REFORM

During the years after the Civil War, the labor reform movement placed great emphasis on the need for independent political action by labor, to bring about the abolition of monopolies and the entire wage system by means of currency reform and producers' cooperatives. The movement also posed as the "emerging question of the day": Have the laboring men of the country any rights which capital is bound to respect?[35] Labor reform parties were organized in a number of states, and a National Labor Reform party arose in 1872. The movement was celebrated in song.

THE UPRISING OF LABOR

By I. G. Blanchard

Tune—"Star Spangled Banner"

Brave sires to the summons of Freedom upsprung,
Pouring forth loyal legions from hill and from valley;
Once again o'er the land is the war tocsin rung,
And the sons of those sires to a near contest rally,
In thunder and flame,
They spake Liberty's name,
And our right to defend her henceforth we proclaim,
Evermore the dear land of our fathers shall be
"The home of the brave and the land of the free!"

There's a moving of men—like the sea in its might—
The grand and resistless uprising of Labor!
The banners it carries are Justice and Right;
It arms not the musket; it draws not the sabre;
But the sound of its tread
O'er the graves of the dead
Shall startle the world and fill tyrants with dread;
For 'tis sworn that the land of the fathers shall be
"The home of the brave and the land of the free!"

In that land 'tis not meet that the earnings of toil!
Should gorge the god Mammon, the tyrant, the spoiler!
Every foot has a right to a piece of the soil,
And the product of toil is the need of the toiler.
The hands that disdain
Honest Industry's stain
Have no share in its honor, nor right to its gain;
And Worth over Wealth yet exalted shall be
In "the home of the brave and the land of the free!"

Stand up in your right, then, ye lords of the land!
The world's awaiting your wise proclamation—
That the worker no longer a menial shall stand;
The defrauder no more have respect in the nation.
Seers and prophets of old!
Lo, your visions unfold—
Tis LABOR doth usher the blest Age of Gold!
To the high mission true here we pledge to us be,
In "the home of the brave and the land of the free!"[36]

WHAT WE WANT—No. 1

By B. M. Lawrence, M.D.

When what we want comes uppermost,
Old wrong shall surely die;
Then love will conquer evil's host,
And all his power defy.
Then there shall be no starving poor,
Asking the rich to give;
Love will unlock the prison door,
For all shall truly live.

When what we want comes uppermost
Contentions all will cease,
The din of battle will be lost,
And nations live in peace.
Then spoilers will not lurk for pelf,
Wars will no longer wage,—
Man will not live alone for self,
In that fair golden age.

When what we want comes uppermost,
Bright angels from above,
Will fill the air—a mighty host—
With wisdom, light and love.
Then hypocrites with pious cant,
Will not pervert the word,
Nor pharisees, self-righteous, rant,
But all shall know the Lord.

When what we want comes uppermost,
The earth will then be free,
And all may have, devoid of cost,
Homes, light, and liberty.
The right to vote, the right to land,
The rights to life and love,
The right to work with willing hand,
All people will approve.

When what we want comes uppermost
Disease will disappear,
And Christians then may truly boast,
Of death they have no fear.
Then trees of Eden for mankind,
Will yield no poison food,
But fruits of knowledge for the mind,
Will all prove very good.

The unassuming, unpresuming,
Rice-consuming Chinaman.

(R. M. DeWitt, *The First She Would and Then She Wouldn't Songster* [New York, 1873], p. 42.)

35For a discussion of the labor reform movement, see David Montgomery, *Beyond Equality: Labor and the Radical Republicans, 1862–1872* (New York, 1967).

36*Boston Daily Evening Voice*, Jan. 20, 1866.

When what we want comes uppermost,
Rum will not rule the mind,
The foul tobacco will have lost
Its hold upon mankind;
Grand temples full of living light,
Our bodies will become,
The blest abode where spirits bright
Make heaven within their home.

When what we want comes uppermost,
Monopolies must fail;
Then capital will cease to boast,
And labor will prevail.
United true hearts strong and brave
Combined for human good,
Will then make wealth become the slave
OF ONE GRAND BROTHERHOOD.[37]

A somewhat different version was published in the Chicago *Workingman's Advocate* of May 23, 1868:

WHAT WE WANT

By B. M. Lawrence, M.D.

When what we want comes uppermost,
The old wrongs all must die;
Then love will conquer Evil's host
And all his powers defy.
Then there will be no marching poor,
Asking the rich to give,
Peace will unlock the prison door,
In plenty all shall live.

Rally all, together, united let us labor,
Now and forever, in life's great school;
Rally all, together, loving each our neighbor,
Now and forever, by the Golden Rule.

When what we want comes uppermost,
The earth will all be free;
Then each may have, devoid of cost,
Grand HOMES of industry.
The right to vote, the right to land,
The right to life and love
The right to work with willing hand,
All men will then approve.

Rally, &c.

When what we want comes uppermost,
Sex, race, and color too,
In points of law, will each be lost,
With neither Greek nor Jew,
Then woman will refuse to wear,
Death circling round the waist,
But men and women everywhere,
Will dress for health, with taste.

Rally, &c.

When what we want comes uppermost,
Rum will not rule mankind,
Then foul tobacco will have lost,
Its hold upon mankind.
Rare temples full of living light,
Our bodies will become,
The best abode where spirits bright,
Make heaven within their home.

Rally, &c.

When what we want comes uppermost,
Sick people will perceive,
The healing art has not been lost,
To those that do believe.
Then poison drinks and drugs, by man,
Will never more be made.
The laws of life, health and hygiene,
By all will be obeyed.

Rally, &c.

When what we want comes uppermost,
The angels from above,
Will fill each heart, a holy host,
With wisdom, truth and love.
The hypocrites with foemen cant,
Will not pervert the world,
Nor Pharisee's self righteous rant,
But all shall know the Lord.

Rally, &c.

When what we want comes uppermost,
Monopolies must fall.
Then capital will cease to boast,
And Labor will prevail.
United true hearts, strong and brave,
Combined for human good,
Will then make wealth become the slave,
OF ONE GRAND BROTHERHOOD.

Rally all, together, united let us labor,
Now and forever, in life's great school;
Rally all, together, loving each neighbor,
Now and forever, by the Golden Rule.[38]

HOPE FOR THE TOILING

By B. M. Lawrence

Air—"Tramp, Tramp, Tramp"

Daily at my task I work,
Thinking, brothers dear, of you.
How you toil in poverty from day to day,
And the tears of love will flow
Down my cheeks like drops of dew
While I try to cheer you on your weary way.

[37] Ibid., Jan. 29, 1867.
[38] *Workingman's Advocate*, May 23, 1868.

Hope, Hope, Hope,—the day is dawning!
Cheer up, brother, it will come,
When within your own "sweet home"
You shall sing a joyful song,
In the good time coming for the toiling poor.

Daily at my task I work,
Framing sonnets for the free,
In that grand NEW ERA coming bye and bye.
Though we look out on the sea
And no ship "comes in" yet we
Hear the car of human progress drawing nigh.

Faith, Faith, Faith, &c.

Daily at my task I work,
Thinking what reform has done—
How the sable bondmen have been all set free;
Yet the work so well begun,
Must continue to go on,
Till the toilers all have land with liberty.

Work, Work, Work, &c.

Daily at my task I work,
Singing what the angels say—
How the light is shining even at the door,—
Soon the darkness will give way,
Justice in the dawning day
Will give land and homes to all the toiling poor.

Sing, Sing, Sing,—the light is beaming;
Cheer up, brothers, while it comes;
Soon within your own sweet homes
You shall all sing joyful songs,—
When God gives His kingdom to the toiling
poor.[39]

WHAT WE WANT

By B. M. Lawrence, M.D.

Air—"John Brown"

We want to see reform go marching right along;
We want to see reform each day growing more strong.
Till the friends of freedom shall take the world by
storm,
And this shall be our song, Glory, &c.
Right soon will conquer wrong.

The army of old wrong has begun to decay
The army of old wrong soon will have to give way—
The people wanting right, have risen in their might,
To battle for the day, Glory, &c.
When justice shall have sway.

The true friends of freedom their banners have unfurled,
The true friends of freedom their colors have unrolled,
When justice takes command, the time will be at hand,
When right shall rule the world, Glory, &c.
With wrong to ruin hurled.

With wrong's army routed, the people will be free,
With wrong's army routed, old error's host will flee;
The homeless in the north, and the landless in the south,
Will gain their liberty, Glory, &c.
And banish tyranny.

With liberty for all, and wisdom from above—
With liberty for all, truth, purity and love,
Evils will all disappear, and heaven will be here.
With us it will prove, Glory, &c.
New light, new life and love.

Noble minded woman, full of inspiration—
Noble minded woman, will then find her mission,
To preach and practice truth, and teach the minds of
youth.
Will be her true position, Glory, &c.
She is the true physician.

To bring the reign of health for which the people pray
To bring the reign of health for which the people pray
To bring the reign of health, and all the world with
wealth.
Life's laws we must obey, Glory, &c.
Let reason point a way.

Sick people will then quit taking bitter pills,
Sick people will then quit multiplying ills,
With doses large and small, refusing nostrums all,
Nor paying doctors' bills, Glory, &c.
Nature's cure never kills.

When reason takes the rule, when reform gains the day,
When reason takes the rule, and all shall own her sway,
Long skirts will not be found a trailing in the ground.

(Chanted)
But women will be free,
From foreign fashions and perverse passions,
From foolish tastes for wasp-like waists,
From hoop and skirt to sweep the dirt,
Yes, free to go through mud and snow,
Or skait, or boat, to run or float,
Up stream or down, or through the town;
In nature's bowers, with buds and flowers,
In songs of praise her notes will raise,
And sing with glee most joyfully,
Glory, Glory, &c.,
Hurrah for liberty.

What we want now has come, we will then join and sing.
What we want has come, we'll make the welkin ring.
It is the jubilee, for woman now is free.
And freedom soon will ring, Glory, &c.
The reign of Love is king.[40]

39 *Boston Daily Evening Voice,* Jan. 17, 1867.
40 *Workingman's Advocate,* June 20, 1868.

SONG FOR WORKING VOTERS

Tune—"Tramp, Tramp, Tramp"

In the fields and shops we drudge, working on from day
to day.
Striving hard a home and comfort to command,
But our thoughts that often go, from our j—[41] and toil
away;
Thinking of the times and troubles in this land,
Work, work, work the poor are toiling,
Wanting because they cannot pay.
While the money lords and rich, faster than they ought
to do.
Still grow rich and strong and richer day by day.

If it was the wise design, some should have peculiar
rights,
While toilers suffer here, for want of work and pay;
Why did our fathers plan and fight, staking lives and
honor bright,
Keeping kings and lords from having their own way,
Fight, fight, fight was then in order
Tea-tax, they said, would not pay,
When the English lords and great, faster than they ought
to do,
Still grew rich and strong and meaner day by day.

Now we know by what they did, those brave toilers
good and free,
That for us they left some noble work to do,
Then let us up and act in time, for the cause we now can
see,
Is in our hands if we but dare be true.
Vote, vote, vote, let us go voting,
When we know that it will pay,
And ourselves and rights protect, from the rings and
haughty crew,
Why[42] still grow rich, and strong, and meaner night and
day.[43]

SONG FOR WHITE SLAVES

By Thos. Hubbard

Work! Work! Work!
With pick, and shovel, and axe!
To pay New England's protection,
Your own and the bondholder's tax.

Toil! Toil! Sweat!
Still harder each day than before,
It will go to keep thieves and bondholders up,
And the wolf away from your door.

Work! Work! Work!
From dawn to the dusk of day,
For your hopes are crushed with the weight of debt,
That the toil of your life won't pay.

You gave your son to the war,
The rich man loaned his gold
And the rich man's son is happy to-day,
And yours is under the mould.

You did not think—poor man—
You can scarce believe when you're told,
That the sum which the rich man loaned the war
Was the price for which you were sold.

Your son was as good as his,
And as dear, perhaps to you;
But yours died for his, and your daughter, now,
For his must wash and sew.

Nay, do not pause to think,
Nor sigh for your husband or wife,
For your moments are mortgaged to hopeless toil
The rest of your weary life.[44]

The following was probably the most popular song of the labor reform movement. It appears to have been sung originally by the Hutchinson Family, the traveling singers for the abolitionist movement, who, as natives of Lynn, Massachusetts, sang the song at meetings of shoeworkers to which they had been invited.[45] Published in the *American Workman* in 1869 as an anonymous song, it was reprinted in the December 8, 1877, issue of the *New York Socialist*, where it was attributed to Charles P. Shiras. A simpler version appeared again in the 1880s under the title "An Old Song."

THE POPULAR CREED

Dimes and dollars! dollars and dimes!
An empty pocket's the worst of crimes!
If a man is down, give him a thrust—
Trample the beggar in the dust.
Presumptuous poverty's quite appalling—
Knock him down, and kick him for falling!
If a man is up, oh, lift him higher,
Your soul's for sale, and he's the buyer—
Dimes and dollars! dollars and dimes!
An empty pocket's the worst of crimes!

I know a poor, but worthy youth,
Whose hopes are built on a maiden's truth;

41 Illegible.

42 Probably *Who.*

43 *Workingman's Advocate*, Sept. 10, 1870.

44 Ibid., Jan. 14, 1871.

45 Professor Paul Faler of the History Department, University of Massachusetts, Boston, who has made a study of the Lynn shoeworkers, observes in a letter to me (Nov. 25, 1973) that the Hutchinson Family was popular among the shoemakers of Lynn "because they were different than many abolitionists in that they attacked the injustices and inequalities of the emerging capitalist system. . . ."

But the maiden will break her vows with ease,
For a wooer cometh, whose claims are these:
A hollow heart and an empty head,
A face well tinged with the brandy red,
A soul well stained in villany's school—
And cash—sweet cash—he knoweth the rule:
Dimes and dollars! dollars and dimes!
An empty pocket's the worst of crimes!

I know a bold and honest man,
Who tries to live on the Christian plan,
But poor as he is, and poor will be,
A scorned and hated wretch is he;
At home he meeteth a starving wife,
Abroad he leadeth the leper's life—
They struggle against a fearful odds,
Who will not bow to the poeple's gods
Dimes and dollars! dollars and dimes!
An empty pocket's the worst of crimes!

So getteth ye wealth, no matter how!
"No questions asked" of the rich, I trow!
Steal by night and steal by day,
(Doing it all in a legal way)
Join the church, and never forsake her,
Learn to cant, and insult your Maker,
Be hypocrite, liar, knave, and fool,
But don't be poor!—remember the rule:
Dimes and dollars! Dollars and dimes!
An empty pocket's the worst of crimes![46]

AN OLD SONG

Dimes and dollars, dollars and dimes!
An empty pocket's the worst of crimes!
If a man is down, give him a thrust—
Trample the beggar into the dust!
Presumptuous poverty's quite appalling—
Knock him down and kick him while falling.
If a man is up, oh! raise him higher;
Your life's for sale and he is the buyer—
Dimes and dollars, dollars and dimes,
An empty pocket's the worst of crimes!

So get ye wealth, no matter how,
No questions asked by the rich I trow.
Steal by night and still by day,
But do it all in a legal way;
Join the church and never forsake her,
Learn to cant and insult your maker;
Be a hypocrite, liar, knave and fool!
But don't be poor, remember the rule;
Dimes and dollars, dollars and dimes,
An empty pocket's the worst of crimes![47]

TWO LABOR SONGWRITERS

B. M. Lawrence was an unusual labor reform songwriter in the sense that most composers of the period wrote only one or two songs. But at least two other men contributed groups of songs during these years: Robert W. Hume and Karl Reuber.

Robert W. Hume was the author of a series of "Labor Lyrics" published in the *Boston Daily Evening Voice* in late 1866 and early 1867. Here are three of the "Labor Lyrics"; the notes are by Hume himself.

Labor Lyrics—No. 4
THE FISHERMAN'S CHURCH
A Sermon

"Behold, the hire of the laborers who have reaped down your fields, which is of you kept back by fraud, crieth: and the cries of them which have reaped are entered into the ears of the Lord of Sabaoth." James, (the Fisherman), Chap. 3, v. 4.

When the friend of the poor
Stood on Palestine shore,
I'm certain with me you'll agree;
He stooped not to mate
With the wealthy or great
But he honored the men of the sea.

Oh, the Fisherman's Church,
Is a noble old Church!
Where they feather the lusty oar;
'Twill do us no wrong
If we all go along
And list to its teaching once more.

So we'll jump in the boat,
And away will we float
Again for to capture the prey;
And when all the fun
Is quite over and done,
We'll thus share the spoils of the day.

In true Fisherman's style
We'll divide the big pile
Laid out on the silvery beach;
Though only in song,
'Twill be well to look on,
For "just" is the lesson we teach.

Well parted in three
The good fish you may see,
In bright heaps as they shine on the sand;
Now Dick, turn your back,
And sing out in a crack,
Whose is this which I touch with my hand?

46*American Workman,* Aug. 21, 1869.
47*John Swinton's Paper,* Apr. 11, 1886.

"On a Fisherman's word,
We'll give that for the third
To pay for the net and the boat;
The first is well made,
And the other—old jade—
She's as lively a craft as doth float!"

As there's four hearty men,
We'll divide them again,
The two heaps that yet do remain;
So that Tom and young Nick,
And old Charley and Dick,
May each have his share of the gain.

Now like fishermen bold,
With our profits all told,
We'll home to our cottages all;
Not forgetting at night
To look up with delight
To Him who's the Giver of All.

Thus you factory boys,
If you'll stop the mill's noise
And listen to reason awhile?
Without charge or fee,
From these men of the sea,
May learn how to share your big pile.

Oh, the Fisherman's Church
Is a noble old Church!
Where they haul in the dripping seine;
If you visit it once,
You may call me a dunce,
If ever you quit it again![48]

Labor Lyrics—No. 8

MODERN HEROISM

Oh! Mother Massachusetts!
It surely can't be true,
That thus you treat your children,
Your youths and maidens too.
'Twas held you loved your little ones
And sent them all to school,
A place from which you've banished birch,
For higher moral rule.

'Twas thought you studied deeply
And learned from Horace Mann,
The limit of a lesson's time
In nature's early plan.
The half—and e'en the quarter—
Of one short passing hour,
Is deemed a period long enough
In kindergarten's bower.

But now your legislators,
(In their important work;)
Do gravely name ten hours per day
For youth's and women's work.

This measure is their mercy,
(Restricted, too, at that)
Oh! Mother Massachusetts,
Don't you feel very flat?

Right well to call them "victims,"
But wherefore not propose
To punish those who make them so,
As human nature's foes.
Cupidity and avarice,
Some look upon as crimes;
But, Mother, you are merciful
Where gold and silver shines.

Like pious old King David,
You've ventured on the sin,
To count your store of children,
And find it very slim.
Better, for us, it is so,
Than see them sweating still,
And grinding out their weary lives
Within a dismal mill.

But ere your sentence* you enforce,
On youth and Infancy,
You'd better go to Prussia
To learn your A, B, C.
Meantime your lack of babies,
(Falling from bad to worse,
Dear Mother Massachusetts;)
Looks very like a curse.

For surely all such little ones
Have a firm friend and true;
And truly those who injure them
Will suffer penance due.
Crimes against them committed,
Not lightly are forgiven;
Though "victims" they may be on earth,
They are "conquerors" in heaven.[49]

*Ten hours' toil per day. See verdict of the Commissioners.

Labor Lyrics—No. 9

HYMN

Come unto me, all ye that labor and are heavy laden, and I will give you rest. Matthew, chap. 11, ver. 28.

Forward, though the night be stormy,
And the path be straight and lone;
Onward, friends of man and labor,
Certain victory's our own.
Hoping, waiting,
Soon we'll hear truth's trumpet tone.

48 *Boston Daily Evening Voice,* Jan. 4, 1867.
49 Ibid., Mar. 5, 1867.

Courage, Toilers! What though Mammon
  Long has ruled with iron hand;
Wringing labor, health, and manhood,
  From the workers of the land?
    Morning dawning,
  Right shall in the end command.

Fear not, though affliction's furnace
  Spread its flames on every side;
Dross and ore are now commingled,
  'Tis by fire true metal's tried.
    Raging, blazing,
  That alone can them divide.

Courage, Sisters!—Faint and weary
  O'er your hopeless tasks forlorn;
Patient hold the path of virtue,
  Better want than guilt be borne.
    Watchful, cheerful!
  After darkness comes the morn.

Though our masses, broken, jarring,
  Many voiced, like Babel show;
Wisdom yet shall guide our counsels,
  Order out of chaos grow.
    Thinking, striving:
  Soon the better way we'll know.

Courage, children!—He who loves you
  Won't desert you in the war;
You, who know of life no morning,
  Early chained to Mammon's car.
    Listen, hearken!
  You can hear Him from afar.

What though, 'mid our proper columns,
  Sin and shame may still be found;
Though, unsanctified by sorrow,
  Error oft with us abound;
    Nathless, scathless,
  Righteousness shall yet be crowned.

Courage, Man! The shades are passing
  Of a long and weary night;
Soon the sun will gild the mountains,
  Soon the world rejoice in light;
    Beaming, gleaming,
  From his eastern portal bright.

And though wealth, and pride, and power,
  Seem to stand athwart our way:
Though the mighty head our foeman,
  Cheerily we'll join the fray.
    Onward, forward!
  Human rights will gain the day.

Yes!—The world shall shine in splendor
  Unknown yet, although revealed;
When we make our "Curse"* our Glory,
And our "Sorrow" is our Shield!
  Glorious future,
Then shall earth her increase yield![50]

*When Labor is honored in the heart as well as on the lip, and we accept our doom cheerfully, seeking not to avert (by ill constructed edicts) our proper individual share, thereof, our Curse—"In the sweat of thy face shalt thou eat bread"—will prove to be our Blessing.

In 1871 Karl Reuber of Pittsburgh, a polisher and repairer of pianos, organs, and furniture, published a booklet entitled *Hymns of Labor, Remodeled from Old Songs;* here are several of his songs.

SING THEM, SONGS OF LABOR!

Sing them, my brothers, sing them still,
  Those sweet, fresh Labor songs!
Oh, let these songs, with hearty will,
  Be heard from youthful tongues!
O, sing them at the early dawn,
  The rising morn to cheer;
And sing them 'round the evening hearth,
  When fires are blazing near.

Sing them when labor unions meet
  And your full voices raise
Your every evening melodies
  To noble Labor's praise.
So shall each unforgotten word,
  When distant far you roam,
Call back your heart which once is stirred,
  To Labor's blessed home.

Sing them, dear brothers: many friends
  These holy strains have sung—
From near and far have echoed them
  From many a brother's tongue.
Oh, sing them in a land like this,
  Where Labor's sons have roved;
Oh, brothers, sing these melodies,
  The songs of Labor loved.[51]

SONG OF LABOR

Friends of Freedom, swell the song
  Young and old the strain prolong:
Make the working army strong
  And on to victory.
Lift your banners, let them wave,
  Onward march a world to save!
Who will fill a pauper's grave,
  And bear his misery.

50 Ibid., Feb. 7, 1867.

51 Karl Reuber, *Hymns of Labor, Remodeled from Old Songs* (Pittsburgh, 1871), p. 2.

KARL REUBER,
POLISHER AND REPAIRER OF
PIANOS, ORGANS AND FURNITURE
PLEASE SEND ORDERS PER POSTAL CARD.
No. 4 Boston St. near Fifth Ave.
PITTSBURGH, PA.

HYMNS OF LABOR

REMODELED FROM OLD SONGS

BY

KARL REUBER.

PITTSBURGH.
BARROWS & OSBOURNE, PUBLISHERS.
No. 90 DIAMOND STREET.
OFFICE OF AMERICAN GLASS WORKER.

Courtesy of Labadie Collection, University of Michigan Library

Shrink not when the foe appears,
 Spurn the coward's guilty fears;
Hear the shrieks, behold the tears
 Of ruined families.
Raise the cry in every spot—
 All for Union—who will not?
Who would choose a traitor's lot,
 The worse of infamies.

Sisters, Brothers, hear us plead
 For your help we intercede;
See how many bosoms bleed,
 And heal them speedily.
Haste, O haste the happy day,
 When beneath its glorious ray,
Labor all the world shall sway
 And reign triumphantly.[52]

THE ARMY OF LABOR

The army of Labor is gath'ring its men
From hilltop and mountain, from valley and glen;
With Union forever, we are lusty and strong;
Then come join our army, and be marching along.

Marching along, we are marching along,
Come join our army and be marching along;
O Union will make us both valiant and strong,
Then come, join our army, and be marching along.

King Mammon's army is must'ring in might,
Then come to the rescue, come join the fight;
With *Right* on our banner, and love in our song,
We're sure now to win as we're marching along.

From mountain to lake, from gulf to the strand,
Our army is marching in strength through the land.
For Right and for Freedom we still will grow strong,
Then come join our army, and be marching along.[53]

WE'LL NOT GIVE UP OUR UNION

We'll not give up our *Union*,
 Great Labor's Right and Truth;
The blessed staff of hoary age,
 The guide of early youth,
The lamp which sheds a glorious light,
 O'er ev'ry dreamy road,
The voice which speaks a brother's love,
 Beneath the heaviest load.

We'll not give up our *Union*,
 Nor heed the crafty tongue,
That would this treasure take away;
 Ye wicked ones, begone!

For ye would fain condemn our minds
 To glooms of moral night,
But we defy your mortal power,
 Hurrah, for Labor's Right!

We'll not give up our *Union*,
 But could ye force away
That which is our life-blood dear,
 Yet hear us joyfully say:
The truth that we have learnt while young,
 Shall follow all our days,
And those engraven on our hearts,
 Ye never can erase.[54]

DARE TO BE A UNION MAN

Standing by a purpose true,
 Heeding Right's command;
Honor them the faithful few—
 All hail to Union's Band!

Dare to be a Union man;
 Dare to stand alone!
Dare to have a purpose firm;
 Dare to make it known!

Many workingmen are lost
 Daring not to stand,
Who for Right had been a host,
 By joining Union's band.

Chorus:

Hold the Labor banner high—
 On to vict'ry grand;
Mammon and his host defy,
 And shout for Union's band.

Chorus:[55]

52Ibid., pp. 6–7. Reuber's "Song of Labor" was "remodeled" for the *Carpenter* of March, 1885, where the tune was given as "Scots Wha Hai."

53Reuber, *Hymns of Labor*, p. 10.

54Ibid., p. 17, also published in the *Granite Cutters' Journal*, July, 1885.

55Reuber, *Hymns of Labor*, p. 20. Reuber continued to write songs and poems for the labor movement, some of which will be found below. As late as July 2, 1893, the *Labor Standard* published his poem of congratulations on the eighty-fourth birthday of "our venerable friend and co-worker in great labor's and humanity's cause, John F. Bray." Bray, author of *Labour's Wrongs and Labour's Remedy*, was so highly regarded in labor circles that the *National Labor Tribune*, which rarely carried poems or songs, reprinted Reuber's poetical tribute in its issue of July 9, 1893.

6

The Long Depression 1873–79

DEPRESSION SONGS

The economic crisis of 1873, like those of 1819, 1837, and 1857, destroyed most of the unions then in existence. When the banking house of Jay Cooke and Company failed on September 18, 1873, ushering in six long and terrible lean years, there were thirty national trade unions in existence. Only eight or nine remained alive for long. Those which went under simply lost many of their members who could no longer afford to pay even minimum dues because of the mounting unemployment. The rest was done by lockouts, blacklists, conspiracy charges, and "yellow dog contracts," in which workers were forced to swear they would never join a union.

By 1877 there were as many as three million unemployed. Two-fifths of those employed were working no more than six to seven months a year, and fewer than one-fifth were working regularly. The wages of those employed had been cut as much as 45 percent, often to little more than a dollar a day.

Labor songs and ballads not only pictured the misery of workers during the long depression, they also expressed the bitterness of the millions who were starving and their determination to alter these conditions. They appeared in the *Toiler*, published in New York, the *Workingman's Advocate* and the *Arbeiter-Zeitung*, published in Chicago, and the *Labor Standard*, published in Paterson, New Jersey, as the English organ of the American Socialist movement. The *Labor Standard*, edited by J. P. McDonnell, a Marxist and correspondent of Marx and Engels, came into existence following the formation of the Working Men's party of the United States in 1876 at a unity convention of Lassallean and Marxian Socialists. The paper mirrored the sufferings and struggles of the workers in the midst of the great depression and made effective use of songs in fulfilling this task. Since the depression was at its depths during the one hundredth anniversary celebration of the War for Independence, it is not suprising that three of the songs included below deal with this theme, from the standpoint of labor.

WORKERS' SONG

Melody—"Do You Hear the Mighty Sound?"
Written to be sung at the Workers' Festival,
Williamsburgh, February 15, 1873

Europe, the mighty, is trembling,
America, the proud, is shaking,
With its powers so long disunited,
A new people is rising;
We see it grow and unite itself,
Embracing tightly, full of love:
To live for the holy right of labor.

Where deep in the shaft of the earth
The man in the work shirt
Is struggling, where before the flaming forge
The heart and the face are aglow;
Everywhere resounds the oath
That everybody shall choose the password:
To live for the holy right of labor.

And where at the spindle with sorrow
Mother and child, oh, are suffering,
There now a brighter day is dawning,
There it whispers softly and quietly:
"O father, put an end to misery."

And now he begs the question—
Why fold your hands
To pray for the holy right of labor?

In the singe of the smoke of the factories,
Of the poverty that enrages the spirits,
We recognize a new people,
Hurrah, to whom the future belongs,
Which we bravely capture with the cry:
To win with the holy right of labor.[1]

A LABOR HYMN

By Phillip O'Neill

From beautiful Wyoming,
And from Lackawanna's vale,
The labor men are marching,
And determined to prevail.
Though the famine grip is pinching,
And the blood-hounds on their trail,
They will stand their ground unflinching,
Till justice turns the scale.

O, a glorious glad marching,
Is this marching of the free,
And a labor army chanting
The hymn of liberty.

O, see the sight entrancing,
Of these loyal men so true,
O, they are proudly marching
With human rights in view,
And the time is now approaching,
When the fight, though never new,
Must be waged, aye, unrelenting
Gainst the tyranny of the few.

O, a glorious glad marching,
Is this marching of the free,
And the myriad voters chanting,
The hymn of liberty.

O, the citizens are forming,
By river, lake and stream,
Their hearts in union beating
To the grandeur of the theme,
And they give a lurid warning
"'Tis the rocket signal gleam,"
Of the wrath that is awaiting,
As the people cease to dream.

O, the glorious glad marching,
Is the marching of the free,
And a hundred thousand chanting
The hymn of liberty.[2]

THIEVES AND STEALIN'

It makes me hoppin' mad to think
Of all the thieves and stealin'
Among the folks that live so high
And are so big of feelin';
With hands that do no sort o' work
Except to handle money,
And make it come so short o' count—
It sartin isn't funny.

But bless me!—can't they dress and swell,
In lofty style and splendor,
On stealin's that don't sartin make
Their conscience over tender?
When they can feel so high above
The smaller thieves and stealers,
Whose hen-roost stealin's wouldn't make
One of their plainest dinners.

Folks mostly now begin ter think
Sich loads o' silks and laces,
And jewels and grand carriages,
Means thieving in high places;
And lofty airs don't count for much
In honest people's feelin's,
Who have ter work for all the cash
They gobble up in stealin's.

They say that Washington is jist
A den of thieves together,
And they have plucked our eagle bird
Of every quill and feather,
And now they think to make it good
By taxin' us the greater,
When they had orter all be shot
Clean from the realms o' Natur.[3]

DEATH OR FREEDOM!

By Gerald Massey

Smitten stones will talk with fiery tongues,
And the worm, when trodden will turn;
But, Cowards, ye cringe to the cruellest wrongs,
And answer with never a spurn.
Then torture, O Tyrants, the spiritless-drove,
Columbia's Helots will bear;
There is no hell in their hatred no God in their love,
Nor shame in their dearth's despair.

For our Fathers are praying for Pauper-pay,
Our Mothers with Death's kiss are white;
Our Sons are the rich man's serfs by day,
And our Daughters his slaves by night.

The Tearless are drunk with our tears: have they driven
The God of the poor man mad?
For we weary of waiting the help of Heaven,
And the battle goes still with the bad.

1*Arbeiter-Zeitung*, Sept. 13, 1873. Trans. Rudi Bass.
2*Workingman's Advocate*, Jan. 10, 1874.
3*Industrial Age*, reprinted in *Woodhull & Claflin's Weekly*, June 27, 1874.

Oh! but death for death, and life for life,
It were better to take and give,
With hand to throat, and knife to knife,
Then die out as thousands live!

For our Fathers are praying for Pauper-pay,
Our Mothers with Death's kiss are white;
Our Sons are the rich man's serfs by day,
And our Daughters his slaves by night.

When the heart of one half the world does beat
Akin to the brave and the true,
And the tramp of Democracy's earthquake feet
Goes thrilling the wide world through,
We should not be living in darkness and dust,
And dying like slaves in the night;
But, big with the might of the inward "*must,*"
We should battle for Freedom and Right!

For our Fathers are praying for Pauper-pay,
Our Mothers with Death's kiss are white;
Our Sons are the rich man's serfs by day,
And our Daughters his slaves by night.[4]

THEN WHO ON EARTH'S TO BLAME?

By Benbow—Milwaukee

Bold Mariners who plow the sea,
And brave the dangers o'er
Desire to help all mankind free,
Yet seldom land ashore.
What hardships they thro' life endure
Who nobly brave the storm,
When age creeps in they, frail and poor,
Are looked upon with scorn.

Ah! badly off are those who spin,
But why should they complain,
For if they have the pow'r to win,
Why, who on earth's to blame?

Stout husbandmen who delve the soil
On casual employ,
From place to place must seek for toil,
No pleasure can enjoy.
The granaries filled to the brim,
With golden harvests reaped,
Are closed now, winter has set in
On labor want is heaped.

Chorus:

Skill'd artizans who make the wheel,
With lightning speed go round,
Are crush'd and trodden down at heel,
By speculators ground.
Yea! thousands now are wanting bread,
Who cannot earn a crust,
Oh! God those thousands must be fed,
Shall be employed, they must.

Chorus:

That needful grain heaped up in store,
By labor was brought in,
Yea! all the wealth you see galore,
Belong to labor's bin.
But crafty gamblers still lay claim
To all it does produce,
Oh! labor that must prove a stain,
To let them thus seduce.

Chorus:

Then organize ye one and all,
Speed on the golden time,
'Tis only waiting for your call,
To make this world sublime.
The State would a good parent be
To every working hand,
Without distinction hail all free,
Throughout this copious land.

How happy then mankind might live,
They need not then complain,
All would forget; all would forgive
All those who were to blame.[5]

A CENTENNIAL WAIL

By Robert W. Hume

(Read at the late Convention of a N.E. Labor League, at Rochester Hall, Boston)

I have a song to sing to you, to the tune of old John
Brown;
It sums the list of miseries which true hearts must put
down;
So listen, while I tell the woes that o'er our nation
frown
As we go marching on!

We had a farm unmortgaged, we held the same in fee,
On it we raised a billion to put down slavery;
But the money men they've fleeced us a couple more,
d'ye see,
And still go cheating on!

We fought to shield their property, but property
don't pay,
The man who did the battle's work, he must the cost
defray;
He's the money-holder's guardian, and the money-
holder's prey,
As he goes toiling on!

Our fathers left us freedom: broke superstition's
chain;
But some have done their level best to put it on again;

[4] *Toiler,* Aug. 1, 1874.
[5] *Labor Standard,* Nov. 25, 1876.

Alas! alas! 'tis only true; they shed their blood in
vain,
Though they went conquering on!

From North and South, and East and West, our
foreign friends have come,
Our "liberty of conscience" to them looks very glum,
As, bending to the dust before the ancient Sunday
drum,
They see us grinding on!

To save them from such insult, our prayers did not
avail,
The humbug of "our liberty" with them will ne'er
prevail;
While sucking Torquemadas they supervise our mail,
As we go slaving on!

You may talk about the rum-shops, and o'er them
raise a muse:
Our gambling dens are nasty, our churches perhaps
worse;
But our halls of legislation are the foulest spots for
us,
As they go stinking on.

Thus we from bad to worse advance. Oh, woe upon
our race!
To seek to serve the people now and gain a stateman's
place,
Is but to fill an office stained with crime and foul
disgrace,
As we go marching on!

Oh "Free and Independent" you rebelled against a
tax,
And burnt up old King George's stamps, and beat off
his attacks;
But now we're plastered everywhere, except upon our
backs,
As we go toiling on!

"Oh Liberty, thou jewel!" sings either Jones or
Brown:
But none of us can move about, or pass from town to
town,
But there's a double set of spies are paid to mark us
down,
As we go roving on!

Some mangy, briefless lawyer, he noses us around,
Then posts Commercial Agencies with all that he has
found;
And Y.M.C.A. ass's they rule us round and round
As we go moving on!

We dig gold for the Englishman, and keep it not on
hand,
Foreigners own our railroads, the railroads steal our
land;
And the "Free and Independent" hasn't anywhere to
stand,
So he goes wand'ring on!

To save them from such insult, our prayers did not
avail,
The humbug of "our liberty" with them will ne'er
prevail;
While sucking Torquemadas they supervise our mail,
As we go slaving on!

We've used up all our credit, and are chin-deep in
debt,
Our factories are closing up, our houses marked—"To
Let";
We've pawned our mines to Symm's hole, and deeper
cannot get,
So we go owing on!

Within their well-stored shops in rows our tradesmen
sit and grin
To see their money going out, and nothing coming in;
For none of us can make a trade, for none have got
the tin,
So we go wasting on!

Our villages and townships have all gone up the spout,
Our cities buried are in bonds, our States can't turn
about;
Our rates and taxes are so high that legislators doubt
They must stop taxing on!

Alas! Alas!—the bondholder, he truly rules us now,
For him we swing the hammer, for him we guide the
plow;
The "Free and Independent" has nothing left him
now
As he goes purseless on!

But surely from this fearful state we soon must be
released,
The goose that held the golden eggs is dying at the
feast;
For labor's arm is paralyzed, production's almost
ceased,
As we go staggering on!

There's many a subtle scheme proposed to cure the
working man,
Dethroning gold's by many thought to be the proper
plan;
The West and South against the East are looming up
quite grand
As we go toiling on!

If money be a tyrant, why, man has made it so;
It ought to be the people's slave, and not the people's
foe;
To conquer it the people's arm alone can strike the
blow
As they go fighting on!

Too heavy and too hard has been old Mammon's iron hand,
But Liberty, though crashed to earth, is rising in the land,
No spirit of the darksome pit can her from force withstand
As she goes carrying on!

With bloody tracks the soil is stained where her fair foot has trod;
The law securing interest has misery made a god!
Withdraw it, and at once we break the stern oppressor's rod,
And go triumphing on!

Annul it; and our nation will at once its strength renew,
For on that villany accursed by Gentile,* Turk and Jew
Stand all the shameless systems which rob men of their due
As they go working on!

Then shall we lay the usurer within his peaceful grave,
And the camel out of him, his priceless soul to save;
While o'er him we the Union Flag in holy rapture wave,
And go rejoicing on!

So, Sisters dear and Brothers, there's work for us to do,
To hasten on a happier time it is our duty true,
Then shall we leave a better world for all who follow too:
When we've done marching on.[6]

*Aristotle, Mohammed and Moses.

WORKINGMEN'S CENTENNIAL SONG

Our Country Born 100 Years Ago

By Frank Loring

God bless our noble Country, which
One hundred years ago,
First looked with infant-eyes upon
A *Tyrant's* overthrow:
It's patient parents long had bowed
Beneath Oppression's rod:
But now they threw their shackles off;
By the aid of mighty God.
And as their loud hozannas rose,
Nations were made to know
That peace smiled on our Country, born
One hundred years ago.

Then *Freedom's bright star* pointed,
Through battle's smoke and din,
To the *bow-of-peace* which God had set
To light our Nation in,
And, when the land was christened,
Freedom promised to defend
The rights of rich and poor alike,
Unto the Nation's end.
And our parent's loud hozannas rose,
And the world was made to know,
That peace smiled on the Country, born
One hundred years ago.

And shall *Freedom's* pledge be broken now?
Shall the rich for greed and gain,
Deny the workingmen their rights,
And thus end Freedom's reign?
No! rather let all Freemen rise
To strike those *tyrants* low,
Who dare *undo* what *Freedom* did
One hundred years ago.
Then *only* may hozannas rise,
And earth be made to know,
That peace smiles on our Country, born
One hundred years ago.

Remember then, ye rulers all!
That, when patriots wrythed beneath
A Despot's heel, bold *Henry* cried,
For "Liberty or Death!"
Then see to it, that you protect
The rights of all our Nation!
Lest workingmen, who raised you up,
Should hurl you from high station,
And send their loud hozannas up,
For *Tyrants* overthrow,
And thus bring peace to the Country, born
One hundred years ago.[7]

HO! WORKINGMEN!

A Ballad of the Hour

By John M'Intosh, Rochester, N.Y.

Written on Election day, November 7th, 1876

How will it be four years from this? A rooster in full feather, and with head upraised, will be shrieking in blazing capitals on the leading column of the *Labor Standard*—then a daily with four sheets—announcing a sweeping majority for the Workingmen's Candidates—Hurrah!

PART FIRST

Ho! workingmen of Yankeedom!
In 1776,
One hundred years ago today
Our sires were in a fix.

The bosses, from beyond the sea—
King George's blundering fools,
Resolved to bind the nation's shop;
With grinding despot rules.

[6] *Woodhull & Claflin's Weekly*, June 10, 1876.
[7] *Labor Standard*, Sept. 30, 1876.

What did the sires sit down and whine?
And like base hounds succumb?
Not they; but to a rendez-vous
They marched with fife and drum.

They left the shuttle in the loom,
The ploughshare in the field;
And each man swore this sturdy oath;
By God! WE SHALL NOT YIELD.

The land is ours from north to south,
From east to farthest west;
And my friends, this land shall hold
Against that king George's best,

A summons like a cry of fire
Shrieked in the throat of night;
Rung out through city, town and farm,
Up, neighbors, up and fight!

Come, join ye all a company,
And arm with sword and gun;
For by such weapons only can
Our victories be won.

They blest their children, kissed their wives,
And bravely marched they on;
Resolved nor wife nor child to see
Till victory was won.

And, still, sustained by that dread name
By which they stoutly swore,
They fought until the nation's shop
Was bossed by fools no more.

PART SECOND

Ho! workingmen of Yankeedom
In 1876!
The sons and fathers of this land
Once more are in a fix.

Our snobbish bosses have resolved
To play the role of knaves;
And would, by force of iron laws,
Make workmen scabs and slaves.

They seek our wages to reduce,
Their profits to increase;
And when we strike, they cry for help,
To crush us into peace,

Our Unions—manhood's brave resort;
Where virtue, worth and skill
Stand sentinel by freedom's shrine,
Stern duties to fulfill—

They ask us to abandon—all;
Or, scorning their behest,
Refuse all non-conformers work
North, south and east and west.

What the response to this demand?
This:—*While a tool we wield,*
Be ours the legend of our sires;
BY GOD, WE SHALL NOT YIELD!

Ho! agitate ye, one and all!
And haste the coming hour;
To pour the full tide of your will
In whelming ballot power.

Before our banded might, their force
Would crumble as the frost
Melts in the glory of the sun,
To be forever lost.

Up, up with dauntless firm resolve,
And vote for liberty;—
Trades Unionism only can
Make workmen truly free.[8]

THE WORKING CLASS

From the German, by E. Leidhold of London

Who toil from morn till night's dark hours
For pay which is so very slender
Although 't is they who bring the powers
The gold which makes their cruel splendors?
Who weave the silks and satins, worst
Of wretched rags about them clinging?
Who, though they suffer want accurs'd
Unto the rich are food still bringing?
The Working Class!
The Victim Mass'!
What ill does kill
The Working Class!!

Who must from morn's first shadows grey
Let anvil to the hammer ringing?
When sunset clasps the book of day
Whose burden still heavily's clinging?
Who does the rich man's chattels care
Though with dishonor repaid ever,
Who guards the wealth that he to share
Brotherly-wise may hope. Ah! never?
The Working Class!
The Victim Mass'!
What ill does kill
The Working Class!!

Who gives his poorer friend a hand
When he from work turn'd off may be?
Whose sole inheritance is the land
His father's tools and misery.
When wars his country desolate
Who then defends 'gainst foes distressing?
Not they, in sooth, who live in state,
But these made poor by wealth oppressing
The Working Class!

8Ibid., Nov. 18, 1876.

The Victim Mass'!
What ill does kill
The Working Class!![9]

STRUGGLES DURING THE LONG DEPRESSION

Although most unions were destroyed during the long depression, labor struggles did not cease. Unemployment demonstrations took place from coast to coast; strikes occurred in many industries, mostly to resist repeated wage cuts. One strike, in Saint Louis, was conducted by girls working in department stores, for the right to sit down during the day. Most of the strikes, though bitterly fought, ended in defeat. But a few succeeded, such as the victory of the iron and steel workers of Pittsburgh in 1875 against a wage cut.

The strike move culminated in the great railroad strike of 1877, which occurred after three successive wage cuts of 10 percent each. This first nationwide strike in American history began in July, 1877, on the Pennsylvania Railroad (whose president was Tom Scott) and spread from state to state and city to city, from West Virginia and Pennsylvania to Kentucky and Ohio, from New York to Chicago, from Saint Louis to San Francisco. In Saint Louis a general strike was proclaimed under the leadership of the Working Men's party of the United States, which also directed the strike in Chicago. By August 2, combined forces of police, militia, and federal troops had succeeded in crushing the strike everywhere. Scores of strikers were killed and many strike leaders were arrested.

The struggles of the depression years produced a number of labor songs.

THE VICTORY

By Mrs. S. A. Yates, Chicago, May 1, 1875

The Pittsburgh boys have won the fight,
Long may their victory last,
And may they never know again
The hardships of the past.

They have fought the battle bravely,
And the honor is their own,
Hundreds will reap the benefit
Of the fruitful seed they have sown.

But the war is not yet over,
For Troy is fighting still,
But the soldiers there are brave and firm,
Nor bend to tyrants' will.

Now every man and brother,
Should lend a helping hand,
And give a little from their store
To help that valiant band.

Soon the Unions will grow stronger,
And men will not be trampled down,
And soon the men that toil will be
The ones that wear the crown.[10]

GO WORK IN THE UNION

Go work in the Union, there's plenty to do,
The field is extensive, the labourers are few;
There is much to be done for the suffering poor,
For many are trying to punish them more.
Then join heart and hand in this laudable strife,
Great efforts are needed in the struggle for life;
The aged need helping, their strength is gone;
The children need feeding that they may grow strong.

Go work in the Union, go work in the Union, go
work in the Union, there's plenty to do.
Go work, go work, the field is extensive, the
labourers are few.

Go work in the Union, there's plenty to do,
The friends of the toilers are feeble and few,
And gigantic evils abound in the land,
Those who would uproot them united must stand,
But strife[11] to promote the best purpose of life—
To lift up the fallen, the lost to restore,
And banish grim want from the labourer's door.

Chorus:

Go work in the Union, go work while 'tis day,
Thy time, which is precious, will soon pass away,
And the battle deferred the fiercer will grow,
Then gird on your armour and fear not the foe.
Let all be true hearted and stand at their post,
Determined to conquer whatever the cost.
We the blessing of Union extended shall see,
Toil must be rewarded and labour made free.

Chorus:[12]

OH, LET THE GIRLS SIT DOWN

By J.R.S.

I tell you that 'tis very wrong.
It is cruel and not right,
To keep the girls upon their feet
From morning until night,

9Ibid., June 9, 1878.
10*National Labor Tribune,* May 8, 1875.
11Probably *strive.*
12*Cigar Maker's Official Journal,* Sept., 1876.

Their systems have not strength enough
Such great fatigue to bear—
Their faces will all freshness lose,
Ere long and paleness wear.

Then, let the girls sit down, I pray;
Oh, let the girls sit down;
Don't keep them on their feet all day—
Oh, let the girls sit down.

Behold how diligent they are,
And how surpassing neat;
And with what pleasant faces they
Each of your patrons greet;
They're so graceful in their actions, and
They're modest in their mien;
And that they truly ladies are
It's plainly to be seen.

Then let the girls sit down, etc.

When there's no one to wait upon,
No customer at hand,
I cannot see what earthly use
There is to make them stand.
Why do you not at such times give
(Oh, I don't heed your frown!)
The tired girls a little rest,
By letting them sit down?

Then, let the girls sit down, etc.

My neighbors and myself have met,
And talked the matter o'er;
And we've resolved, and firmly too,
To patronize no more
Those barbarous establishments
Not one of them in town—
That keep the girls upon their feet,
And let them ne'er sit down.

Then, let the girls sit down, etc.[13]

THE STRIKE

By Old Quiz

The newspapers attribute to Tom Scott the odium of saying: "*Ninety cents per day is sufficient to support any laborer's family!*" Now that would make for 7 days $6.30, and if the laborer had 4 children, as many of them have, and more, that would be $1.05 cents to support each one of them for a whole week. Tom would find himself anything but the father of a *Happy Family* had each one of them to live 7 days on $1.05. Tom's wife never went through the markets with a basket on her arm examining meat scraps, old, and tough; or vegetables that had been as long out of the ground as ever they were in it, trying to procure a meal. And when grubrations run short, to be compelled to carry Tom's good clothes and her own to the pawn shop to piece out until the end of the week. Old Quiz would like to keep two boarders, with power to make them partake of their own *generous bills of fare.* One of them would be King Tom of the Rail, and the other his chaplain, the "Nest-Hider of Plymouth Rock!"

Aye listen, ye millionaires, listen!
Tread light o'er your carpeted floors,
And see the red flames as they glisten,
And hear the wild shout of the boors,
Or slaves, as you've long tried to make them,
Hark! hark! that dread sound's drawing nigher.
Have you ventured at last to awake them
To spirits of vengeance and fire?
See! See! your grand palace cars blazing!
They light up the mountain, and glen,
And see maddened labor upraising,
To crush down the robbers of men!

There is fear on the faces of soldiers,
There is fire in the eyes of the poor,
There's wrath in the noble upholders,
Of those who have ceased to endure.
There is blood, warm blood on the bay'net,
There is death—icy death on the sword,
And hearts, whose last drop they would drain it,
Or labor must have its reward!
See up where the multitude's gazing,
Your millions fly in the red gleam
But not 'til we set it a-blazing,
Could we wake you from tyranny's dream!

List now to libidinous Beecher,
Who hym'd you his hypocrite song—
Your model high salaried preacher,
Who said: "*For a mere fancied wrong,*
The People"—The great starving people—
"*Should not step outside of the law!*"
This wretch 'neath a heaven-pointing steeple,
Would dare give such God-mocking jaw,
With lips smacking still of his amours,
He prates, and he preaches again;
Weaving sanctified prosaic glamours
To shield the base robbers of men!

There is force in the spade and the shovel,
When want digs necessity's grave;
There's life in the Palace and Hovel,
Which nature impartially gave;
One justice from neighbor, to neighbor;
What more can Theology plan?
All this, should the strong hand of labor,
Impress on the robbers of man!
Then accursed be the Lawyers and Preachers—
Conspirators none should endure!

[13] *Labor Standard,* Aug. 19, 1876.

Who sit in God's name as our teachers,
While robbing the laboring poor!

The monopolist-laughing hyena,
Can our poor puny efforts despise,
'Til we finish with this *nota bena*:—
That labor will now "*Organize!*"
The rich rogues together conspire,
In mockery of law and of peace;
But if we express our desire
We are clubbed by a brutal police!
Poor slaves who are sold by the hour,
Why crouch to the master that buys?
If you wish to meet power with power,
ORGANIZE! ORGANIZE! ORGANIZE![14]

THE STRIKE

By John M'Intosh

That's a fact that needs no arg'in',
It takes two to make a bargain.
Bosses, 'tis as well to know it,
Let the summer breezes blow it,
North and south and east and west.
First and last of facts the best!
One won't do;
Two, sir, two;
It takes two to make a bargain.

All opposing this is jargon,
It takes two to make a bargain,
Who doubts it is a foe to justice.
In that great fact all our trust is.
He who thinks *his* word should rule
Is a knave and eke a fool.
One won't do;
Two, sir, two;
It takes two to make a bargain.

What did labor by the war gain,
If one only makes the bargain,
And the workman must keep quiet,
Or be only heard in riot?
Bosses high and bosses low,
You must all be taught to know,
One won't do;
Two, sir, two;
It takes two to make a bargain.[15]

THE STRIKERS

By Pruning Knife, St. Louis

(Composed for the Cigarmakers Festival in aid of the New York Strike)

The Poets' muse and Minstrel's song,
With lofty rhymes and thrilling lay,
Through ages have cried down the wrong,
And strove to teach the better way.

Not deeds of men of great renown
Will be my theme to-night,
But honest labor trampled down,
Yet struggling for the right.

In stately mansions everywhere
The plenteous board is spread,
In labor's hovels coarsest fare,
They scarce can purchase bread.

For little labor some have wealth
Like Kings and fabled Knights of old—
While million toilers worked to death,
Scarce ever catch a glimpse of gold.

The sun in gorgeous splendor shines
And plenteous harvest bless the earth,
Yet man through Nature's bounteous mines
By selfishness has spread a dearth.

With empty purse and haggard care
Forced idlers tramp, a Nation's dread;
In midst of plenty everywhere
Compelled to beg for daily bread.

Our ——[16] bought with banker's gold
Are deaf to all our pressing need;
With reckless infamy they've sold
Our birthright for a mess of greed.

But craftiest knaves on mischief bent,
Ne'er failed to go a certain length
To kill themselves their avarice lent,
Their cunning overreached their strength.

And thus a people sorely pressed
Will rise to smite the tyrant's power,
Nor cease 'til every wrong's redressed
And tyranny to right shall cower.

From factory, mine, from shop and field,
Unite our interests all alike;
The cry is raised, no longer yield,
For homes and freedom we must strike.

Some say that strikes are ill advised,
At best we lose more than we gain
Yes, brothers, starve 'till they've devised
A way to forge a stronger chain.

They say we're free, the world is wide,
That none need suffer in this age;
And ever thus our wants deride,
If we're not suited with their wage.

Yes, free to tramp in search of toil,
But where to find it "that's the rub,"

14Ibid., Aug. 4, 1877.
15Ibid.
16Illegible.

Knaves hold the money and the soil,
It's hard to even earn our grub.

They preach contentment, yes they like
Obedience to their grinding will;
It's wrong dear sir, it's wrong to strike,
Of misery we must take our fill.

Some college Savant, Statesman wise
From classic odes and legal lore,
In time may something new devise,
You know! strikes are a dreadful bore.

The social body can't allow
The sons of toil to change our laws.
Preposterous! pshaw! I trow,
Some people always picking flaws.

"We'll see," excuse the homely phrase,
From out the workshop, field or mine
Another Moses, yet we'll raise
To usher in the better time.

The laws by monied rings are framed,
The ballot box for stuffing frauds;
And ——[17] a farce they say,
Society, but, painted bawds.

Through suffering, want and haggard care
One lesson we have learnt full well;
Give them the plenty, and our share,
For all they care may go to h——.

Such schooling for the last few years
Have wakened freemen into life,
Dispelled the coward's idle fears,
Resolved to conquer in the strife.

Thus ill paid labor roused at last
Against oppression's tyrant power,
Strike in the new, strike out the past,
And every Despot's standard lower.[18]

THE WORKINGMEN'S MARSEILLAISE

By a Workingman

Copyright 1877, by Charles Thomson

Ye sons of labor, Duty calling,
Uplift your standard to the sky;
Behold what tyranny enthralling.
Has raised its lawless head on high!
Shall throned brigands treason cherish,
And hireling hosts, a robber band,
Impoverish and blight the land,
While workingmen and women perish?

Arise ye freemen, strike!
Till sordid tyrants yield;
The ballot is the poor man's sword;
The law shall be his shield.

But see the blackening storm appearing,
As famished forms united rise;
Its hoarse, volcanic roar is nearing.
It is our fellow workmen's cries!
Then shall we stand, their wrongs lamenting,
And basely fold our arms, to rest.—
The heart that warms a freeman's breast,
Should fire with anger unrelenting!

Arise! etc.

With luxury and pride surrounded,
The vile, insensate despots dare,
Their thirst of power and gold unbounded,
Our living wages to impair,
Like beasts of burden would they load us—
Like gods, would bid their slaves adore—
But man is MAN—and who is more?
Then shall they longer lash and goad us?

Arise! etc.

But you, ye Titan bandits, tremble!
Since Justice now shall regnant stand;
And know,—for she shall not dissemble—
The day of vengeance is at hand,
Your base monopolies are crumbled;
Your selfish schemes to shreds are torn;
And ye shall be a jest and scorn,
In righteous indignation humbled!

Arise! etc.

Ye workingmen, in want bewailing,
The ruin gaming brokers cause;
Shall not their arts be unavailing—
Their frauds forbidden by the laws?
Must we to gamblers bend like cattle?—
In shame behind their banner rise,
To flaunt its triumph in our eyes,
And cowardly give up the battle?

Arise! etc.

Too long the traitor knaves conspiring,
Have scattered famine through the land;
Too long the nation's name bemiring,
While press and pulpit servile stand.
But Manhood's spirit is the leaven;
Its voice in silent ballots still,
Shall execute a freeman's will,
As lightning does the will of Heaven.

Then rise! ye freemen, strike!
The avenging bolt let fall!
March on! march on! to victory—
Down with the tyrants all![19]

17 Illegible.
18 *Labor Standard*, Feb. 3, 1877.
19 Ibid., Sept. 9, 1877.

The following song was based on the popular gospel song "Hold the Fort," which Philip Paul Bliss wrote after he heard Major Daniel Webster Whittle tell an 1870 Sunday school meeting in Rockford, Illinois, of General W. T. Sherman's message to beleaguered Union soldiers during his famous march to the sea: "Hold the fort, I am coming."[20]

WORKMAN'S HYMN

By Alfred Green

Tune—"Hold the Fort"

Look comrades, see the signal
Waving in the sky
Reinforcements now appearing
Liberty now is nigh.

Hold on friends, the time is coming
When workmen with one will
Shall claim the birth-right free from heaven
Just pay for their skill.

See the Oppressor's host advancing
Money leading on—
Workingmen around us falling
Courage almost gone.

Hold on friends, &c.

Freedom's glorious banner waving
Hear the bugle blow
In our manhood's name we'll triumph
Over every foe.

Hold on friends, &c.

Fierce and long the battle rages
But our help is near
Onward comes the mighty workman
Banish every fear.

Hold on friends, &c.[21]

The following song appears to have been inspired by the railroad strike of 1877. Henry Ward Beecher, referred to in the second verse, is the noted clergyman and orator who was a friend of the slave in the years before the Civil War but was notoriously anti-labor in the 1870s. During the long depression he commented: ". . . the man who cannot live on bread and water is not fit to live." Denis Kearney, the unscrupulous anti-Chinese demagogue, is discussed below (p. 135).

THE GENERAL STRIKE

Composed by Andrew A. Walls

The labors sensation spread fast over this nation,
While men in high station do just as they like;
They'll find out their mistake when it will be too late,
When they see the results of a general strike.
The butchers, the whalers, the tinkers, the tailors,
Mechanics and sailors will surely agree,
To strike and stand still, let the rich run the mill,
While I sing of the sights that I fancy we'll see.

We'll see Italians knocked sprawling,
Policemen help calling, capitol crawling from labors attack;
We'll see washwomen give blarney to the famed Denis Kearney,
For hanging the Chinamen up by the neck.

We'll see men and women run through the streets screamining
At the sight of each other all naked and bare;
We'll see Henry Ward Beecher the Plymouth Church preacher,
Giving up his fine robes for the fair sex to wear.
We will see men of fashion get into a passion,
At their coachmen and footmen doing just as they like;
You will see Kate O'Connor with a woman's rights banner,
Leading our working girls into the strike.

Chorus:

You will see Senator Astor get honest votes faster,
He fought for cheap fares for our poor sons of toil;
You will see Sammy Tilden fork up half a million,
Trying the Tammany movement to spoil.
We will see the cars stopped, up aloft and below,
The elevated won't run, nor the horses won't go,
The conductors and drivers will switch off the track,
And join with the rest in the general strike.

Chorus:

You'll see the butchers won't kill, nor the tailors won't sew,
The bakers they swear that they'll not mix the dough,
The sailors have kicked and will not go to sea,
What kind of a nation is this going to be?
They say the women won't marry, but this can't be true,
For to strike against wedlock is the last thing they'll do;
Just give one a chance with a man that she'll like,
And I'll bet you a dollar you won't see her strike.

Chorus:

But come let us see, with each other agree,
The sights of a strike I do not like to see;
Live and let live is the maxim for all,
As brave Morrissey said up in Tammany hall.
Let the rich and the poor always bear well in mind,

20See Paul J. Scheips, *Hold the Fort!*, Smithsonian Studies in History and Technology, no. 9 (Washington, D.C., 1971).

21*Labor Standard*, Aug. 26, 1877.

THE GENERAL STRIKE.

Composed by ANDREW A. WALLS.

The labors sensation spread fast over this nation,
While men in high station do just as they like;
They'll find out their mistake when it will be too late,
When they see the results of a general strike.
The butchers, the whalers, the tinkers, the tailors,
Mechanics and sailors will surely agree,
To strike and stand still, let the rich run the mill,
While I sing of the sights that I fancy we'll see.

CHORUS:—

We'll see Italians knocked sprawling,
Policemen help calling, capitol crawling from labors attack;
We'll see washwomen give blarney to the famed Denis Kearney,
For hanging the Chinamen up by the neck.

We'll see men and women run through the streets screaming
At the sight of each other all naked and bare;
We'll see Henry Ward Beecher the Plymouth Church preacher,
Giving up his fine robes for the fair sex to wear.
We will see men of fashion get into a passion,
At their coachmen and footmen doing just as they like;
You will see Kate O'Connor with a woman's rights banner,
Leading our working girls into the strike.—CHORUS.

You will see Senator Astor get honest votes faster,
He fought for cheap fares for our poor sons of toil;
You will see Sammy Tilden fork up half a million,
Trying the Tammany movement to spoil.
We will see the cars stopped, up aloft and below,
The elevated won't run, nor the horses won't go,
The conductors and drivers will switch off the track,
And join with the rest in the general strike.—CHORUS.

You'll see the butchers won't kill, nor the tailors won't sew,
The bakers they swear that they'll not mix the dough,
The sailors have kicked and will not go to sea,
What kind of a nation is this going to be?
They say the women won't marry, but this can't be true,
For to strike against wedlock is the last thing they'll do;
Just give one a chance with a man that she'll like,
And I'll bet you a dollar you won't see her strike.—CHORUS.

But come let us see, with each other agree,
The sights of a strike I do not like to see;
Live and let live is the maxim for all,
As brave Morrissey said up in Tammany hall.
Let the rich and the poor always bear well in mind,
The wealth of this world we must all leave behind;
We brought nothing here, we'll take nothing away,
The last strike is death, then we're under the clay.—CHORUS.

Courtesy of Brown University Library

The wealth of this world we must all leave behind;
We brought nothing here, we'll take nothing away,
The last strike is death, then we're under the clay.

Chorus:[22]

INTERNATIONAL LABOR UNION

The railroad strike of 1877 had wide repercussions, including the realization in labor circles that militancy was not enough and that strong unions were needed to make labor's demands effective. One attempt to meet this need was the International Labor Union, organized early in 1878 by Marxian Socialists and leaders of the eight-hour movement. The two groups united to create a union which would organize all unskilled workers and unite them with the trade unions of skilled workers, thus achieving nationwide labor solidarity regardless of sex, race, creed, color, or religion. The aim was to build a mass working-class organization which would lead the struggle for immediate demands—higher wages and shorter hours—and ultimately move on to industrial emancipation through abolition of the wage system. This program was reflected in a song published in the *Labor Standard* (Paterson, New Jersey), official organ of the International Labor Union. It, in turn, was modeled after the following abolitionist song made famous in the pre–Civil War era by the Hutchinsons, America's famous singing family:

GET OFF THE TRACK

Tune—"Old Dan Tucker"

Ho the car Emancipation,
Rides majestic thro' our Nation
Bearing on its train the story,
Liberty, a Nation's glory.

Roll it along, roll it along,
Roll it along through the Nation;
Roll it along through the Nation;
Freedom's Car, Emancipation.

Men of various predilections
Frightened, run in all directions,
Merchants, Editors, Physicians,
Lawyers, Priests, and Politicians.

Get out of the way, every station,
Clear the track, Emancipation.
Roll it along thro' the Nation,
Freedom's Car, Emancipation.[23]

The version used by the International Labor Union went:

THE WORKINGMAN'S TRAIN

By E. R. Place

Tune—"Old Dan Tucker"

Ho, the car Emancipation
Leaves to-day, Industrial Station,
Bearing on its train of treasures,
Labor's hopes in labor measures.

Get all aboard,
Get all aboard,
Get all aboard, leave your plunder,
Get off the track or you'll fall under.

Tracks of scheming politician
Are but railroads to perdition;
Civil Service not our freight, sir,
Banks and Tariffs let them wait, sir.

Get all aboard, &c.

Hark ye, Dives, Dick and Harry,
Come and view the freight we carry,
Blessings in all forms and guises,
Life, with all its joyful prizes.

Get all aboard, &c.

Leisure for the weary masses,
Work enough, no idle classes,
Time to think, sleep, rest or dance, sir,
Joy of living to enhance, sir.

Get all aboard, &c.

Wages now to needs uplifted,
Thoughts refined and wants well sifted,
Homes made shrines of sweet communion,
Circles knit in love's bright union.

Get all aboard, &c.

Want and crime and vice's blight, sir,
Vanish in the growing light, sir;
Woe of penury, curse of riches,
Cease to plow their miry ditches.

Get all aboard, &c.

Children happy, others' faces
Fresh and joyful as the graces;
Fathers, freed from slavery blightful,
Make the home spent hours delightful.

Get all aboard, &c.

Ho, the car Emancipation
Bears the seeds of all salvation;

22Broadside, Harris Collection, Brown University.

23William Wells Brown, *The Anti-Slavery Harp* (Boston, 1848), pp. 25–26. The cover of the 1844 sheet music for Jesse Hutchinson's "Get Off the Track!" is reproduced in David Tatham, *The Lure of the Striped Pig* (Barre, Mass., 1973), no. 29.

THE WORKINGMANS' TRAIN.

BY E. R. PLACE.

(Tune:—*Old Dan Tucker.*)

Ho, the car Emancipation
  Leaves, to-day, Industrial Station,
Bearing on its train of treasures
  Labor's hopes in labor measures.
    CHORUS:—Get all aboard,
      Get all aboard,
    Get all aboard, leave your plunder,
    Get off the track or you'll fall under.

Tracks of scheming politician
  Are but railroads to perdition;
Civil Service not our freight, sir,
  Banks and tariffs, let them wait, sir.
    CHO.—Get all aboard, &c.

Harkye, Dives, Dick and Harry,
  Come and view the freight we carry,
Blessings in all forms and guises,
  Life, with all its joyful prizes.
    CHO.—Get all aboard, &c.

Leisure for the weary masses,
  Work enough, no idle classes,
Time to think, sleep, rest or dance, sir,
  Joy of living to enhance, sir.
    CHO.—Get all aboard, &c.

Wages now to needs uplifted,
  Thoughts refined and wants well sifted,
Homes made shrines of sweet communion,
  Circles knit in love's bright union.
    CHO.—Get all aboard, &c.

Want and crime and vice's blight, sir,
  Vanish in the growing light, sir;
Woe of penury, curse of riches,
  Cease to plough their miry ditches.
    CHO.—Get all aboard, &c.

Children happy, mothers' faces
  Fresh and joyful as the graces;
Fathers, freed from slavery blightful,
  Make the home spent hours delightful.
    CHO.—Get all aboard, &c.

Ho, the car Emancipation
  Bears the seeds of all salvation;
Wise men hail it, fools impede it,
  Truth and Justice cry, "God speed it."
    CHO.—Get all aboard, &c.

A broadside variant of "The Workingman's Train." Courtesy of Brown University Library.

Wise men hail it, fool impede it,
Truth and Justice cry "God-speed it."

Get all aboard, &c.[24]

The International Labor Union lasted only five years, and throughout its existence it was dominated by textile workers. In the textile strike against the Adams Silk Company led by the ILU in Paterson, New Jersey, July, 1878, the following song was featured.

THE MARCH OF THE TOILERS

Air—"Marching through Georgia"

Shall we work for hunger pay, that's the question now,
Shall we yield our manhood, and to oppression bow,
Sell our toil for poverty, our lives to endless woe,
Send forth the cry that we shall not.

We'll fight, we'll fight, for justice and fair play,
We'll fight, we'll fight, nor care what despots say,
We'll make the cruel Adams' class stand back and clear the way,
We'll give them a taste of our Union.

He says our clothes are costly our stomachs too well fed,
That workingmen and women have no right to home or bed,
And offers them starvation and overwork instead,
This monster Shylock of New Jersey.

We'll fight, &c.

Too long we've been the victim of Adams and his class,
Too long we've borne the robber yoke imposed upon the mass,
But now we're free, we're up in arms, at length it's come to pass,
That we'll stand slavery no longer.

We'll fight, &c.

The Labor Union's our hope, our comfort and our joy,
Through it we can protect ourselves and cruel wrong destroy,
It aims at Shorter Hours and to give more men employ,
Send forth the cry of Labor Union.

We'll fight, &c.[25]

The depression years were hard ones for black laborers in the South. Forced into the status of sharecroppers under the domination of white landlords, they lived on a subsistence level, rarely earning enough at the end of a hard year's toil to provide even necessities for their wives and children, most of whom also worked in the fields. With the Hayes-Tilden agreement of 1877 sealing the complete end of Radical Reconstruction, conditions for the southern blacks grew even worse. In a desperate effort to rid themselves of peonage, violence, absence of educational facilities, widespread disfranchisement, and lynchings, about fifty thousand blacks began a great exodus from the South. Most of them—men, women, and children—headed for Kansas.

Exodus songs were a key feature of the movement, and copies of the songs, sold for ten cents, became a source of income for the campaign to leave the South. Here are two of these songs. The first mentions Benjamin "Pap" Singleton, an aged Negro who was a key organizer of the exodus. The second is a song of the black settlers of Nicodemus, one of the communities settled by the "exodusters" (as they were called).

THE LAND THAT GIVES BIRTH TO FREEDOM

We have held meetings to ourselves to see if we can't plan some way to live.
Marching along, yes, we are marching along.
To Kansas City we are bound.
We have Mr. Singleton for our president. He will go on before us and lead us through.
Marching along, et cetera.

For Tennessee is a hard slavery state, and we find no friends in that country.
Marching along, et cetera.
We want peaceful homes and quiet firesides; no one to disturb us or turn us out.
Marching along, et cetera.

NICODEMUS

Nicodemus was a slave of African birth,
And was bought for a bag full of gold,
He was reckoned a part of the salt of the earth,
But he died years ago, very old.

Good time coming, good time coming,
Long, long time on the way;
Run and tell Elijah to hurry up Pomp
To meet us under the cottonwood tree,
In the great Solomon Valley,
At the first break of day.[26]

24 *Labor Standard*, July 28, 1878. A broadside version is in the Harris Collection, Brown University.

25 *Labor Standard*, July 21, 1878.

26 Benjamin "Pap" Singleton's Scrapbook, Kansas Historical Society, reprinted in Arna Bontemps and Jack Conroy, *They Seek a City* (New York, 1945), p. 43.

ANTI-CHINESE POLITICAL ACTION

In view of the role of local, state, and national governments in crushing the railroad strike of 1877, it is not surprising that an important lesson learned by labor was that workers could place no reliance on either of the major political parties. Hence, independent political action by labor dominated the scene in the fall elections of 1877 and 1878. In California, workers joined Denis Kearney's Working Men's party to sing, in 1877:

When workingmen rule our grand country
And wipe out this political fraud:
We won't work for cruel corporations, I know,
For a dollar a day, without board.[27]

Kearney did not mean to include all workers in this crusade. On the contrary, while the song spoke of "cruel corporations" as the chief enemy of the workers, Kearney turned the anger of the workers from the corporations toward the Chinese and convinced many workers that their terrible conditions were due to the fact that Chinese were willing to work for wages on which it was impossible for American workers to exist. With his slogan "The Chinese Must Go," Kearney skyrocketed to temporary success, as his "Sandlotters" sang songs such as "John Chinaman"[28] and "Twelve Hundred More":

TWELVE HUNDRED MORE

O workingmen dear, and did you hear
The news that's goin' round?
Another China steamer
Has been landed here in town.
Today I read the papers,
And it grieved my heart full sore
To see upon the title page,
O, just "Twelve Hundred More!"

O, California's coming down,
As you can plainly see.
They are hiring all the Chinamen
And discharging you and me;
But strife will be in every town
Throughout the Pacific shore,
And the cry of old and young shall be,
"O, damn, 'Twelve Hundred More' "

They run their steamer in at night
Upon our lovely bay;
If 'twas a free and honest trade,
They'd land it in the day.
They come here by the hundreds—
The country is overrun—
And go to work at any price—
By them the labor's done.

If you meet a workman in the street
And look into his face,
You'll see the signs of sorrow there—
Oh, damn this long-tailed race!
And men today are languishing
Upon a prison floor,
Because they've been supplanted by
This vile "Twelve Hundred More!"

Twelve hundred honest laboring men
Thrown out of work today
By the landing of these Chinamen
In San Francisco Bay.
Twelve hundred pure and virtuous girls,
In the papers I have read,
Must barter away their virtue
To get a crust of bread.

This state of things can never last
In, this our golden land,
For soon you'll hear the avenging cry,
"Drive out the China man!"
And then we'll have the stirring times
We had in days of yore,
And the devil take those dirty words
They call "Twelve Hundred More!"[29]

With this kind of racist appeal, the Working Men's party in California won temporary success in 1878, but it soon disintegrated as a result of internal dissensions and petty squabbles. The movement had only one victory to its credit—that over the Chinese—as it helped bring about legislation in California to exclude the Chinese.[30]

GREENBACK-LABOR PARTY

Even before the railroad strike of 1877, there had been some labor support voiced for the Greenback movement and its demand for currency reform. This labor song, for example, championed Peter Cooper, the Greenback party's presidential candidate in 1876.

[27] *The California Songster* (San Franciso, 1855), reprinted in Cornel Lengyel, ed., *A San Francisco Songster, 1849–1939,* Works Progress Administration, History of Music Project, History of Music in San Francisco Series (San Francisco, 1939), II, 143.

[28] See p. 109.

[29] *The Blue and Gray Songster* (San Francisco, 1877), pp. 16–17.

[30] See Alexander Saxton, *The Indispensable Enemy* (Berkeley, 1971), pp. 138–39.

COOPER CAMPAIGN SONG

By Mrs. S. M. Smith

Air—"Hold the Fort"

Listen comrades! sore beleaguered,
In the toils we lie,
But above the din of battle,
Hear we not the cry?

"Hold the Fort, for we are coming—
Coming, millions strong,
Independents to the rescue,
Marching right along."

With a fearful odds against us,
Long we've stood at bay,
Now the tide of battle's turning,
Hear the shout to-day.

"Hold the Fort," &c.

See! at last our troops advancing,
As they nearer draw,
Reinforcements join our standard,
Hear their loud "Hurrah!"

"Hold the Fort," &c.

Veterans from the far Pacific,
New recruits from Maine,
Volunteers from every quarter,
Swell the loud refrain.

"Hold the Fort," &c.

Now the strong entrenchments, guarding
Robbery's designs,
One by one give way, and louder
Echoes down our lines.

"Hold the Fort," &c.

See! already our besiegers
From their shelter fly,
From the plunderer's doom, resounding
In the people's cry.

"Hold the Fort," &c.

——[31] crowned our veteran leader,
Now is almost here,
Loud the shouts of triumph mingle
With these words of cheer.

"Hold the Fort," &c.[32]

THE GREENBACK YANKEE MEDLEY

Air—"Cork Leg"

From my home in the hub of the old Bay State
My trip to New York pray just hear me relate.
The National Party right here let me mention
Asked me to sing at their great convention.
Right shall reign bye and bye
When the Nationals come into power,
Right will reign bye and bye
Then the gold-thieves will rob men no more.

To the grand Cooper hall by the tens and the scores
The people rushed in when they opened the doors,
Flags, torches and banners, quaint mottoes displaying,
While, marching with music all singing and playing.
Joyfully, joyfully shout the glad strain,
Soon we shall triumph, then greenbacks will reign.

The speakers soon came on the stage to discuss
The cause of hard times, and a most terrible fuss
They made about bonds, banks and money kings o'er us,
Then they joined in a song and this was the chorus—
Oh, that will be joyful, joyful, joyful, joyful,
Oh, that will be joyful, when gold shall reign no more.

Peter Cooper, the chairman, next arose and said,
Now the greenback and labor platform would be read.
Each speaker proclaimed that the hope of the nation
Was the Greenback and workingmen's organization.
Then let the people sing glory glory hallulujah,
glory glory hallulujah, glory glory hallulujah,
Down with the money king.[33]

During the railroad strike of 1877, unity was established between farmers and workers. A close relationship was built as farmers and small businessmen, hating the railroads and Wall Street, supplied strikers with food and even joined their demonstrations. In the fall of 1877, the two movements—workers' political parties and the Greenback parties—merged in Pennsylvania, Ohio, and New York, and the following year they put a national ticket in the field. In the fall elections of 1878 some one million votes were cast for Greenback-Labor candidates for Congress, fifteen of whom were elected—six from the East, six from the Midwest, and three from the South. The campaign led to the publication in 1878 of *The National Greenback Labor Songster* by Benjamin M. Lawrence, a physician, and a year later of the *United States Labor Greenback Song Book* by Mary Dana Shindler, a resident of Texas. Here are some of the songs of the Greenback-Labor movement.

POLL YOUR VOTE

Air—"Hold the Fort"

Greenback voters, take fresh courage,
Rouse and lead the way,

[31] Illegible.

[32] *Workingman's Advocate,* Oct. 14, 1876.

[33] Benjamin M. Lawrence, *The National Greenback Labor Songster* (New York, 1878), p. 43.

A HUNDRED THOUSAND AGENTS WANTED.

Millions of Copies of the

NATIONAL GREENBACK LABOR SONGSTER

Should be sold without delay

It is just the Book for the Times. It contains a choice variety of most appropriate Readings with **Original and Selected Music and Songs** set to popular tunes, all calculated to harmonize the conflicting elements pertaining to

A GREAT POLITICAL REVOLUTION,

while adding largely to the final triumph of **Justice for the Toiling Masses.** In order to aid in **The Overthrow of Giant Monopolies,** which are daily making **the Rich Richer and the Poor Poorer,** these songs have been written and published

They Must now be Sold Quickly.

To this end we propose, besides giving **the usual discount to Newsdealers and the trade generally,** to offer the most **Liberal Terms to Publishers of Greenback and Labor Papers, Workingmen's Clubs, Labor Lodges, and Leagues of all kinds.**

And also to active, enterprising

AGENTS, MEN AND WOMEN EVERYWHERE,

Who will engage to advertise, push the sales, or

CANVASS FOR THE SONGSTER.

Editors, Labor Leaders, Singers, and Speakers,

Please Send in your Orders at once.

For further particulars address,

D. M. BENNETT, Publisher,

141 Eighth St., New York.

PRICE TEN CENTS.

NATIONAL

GREENBACK

LABOR SONGSTER.

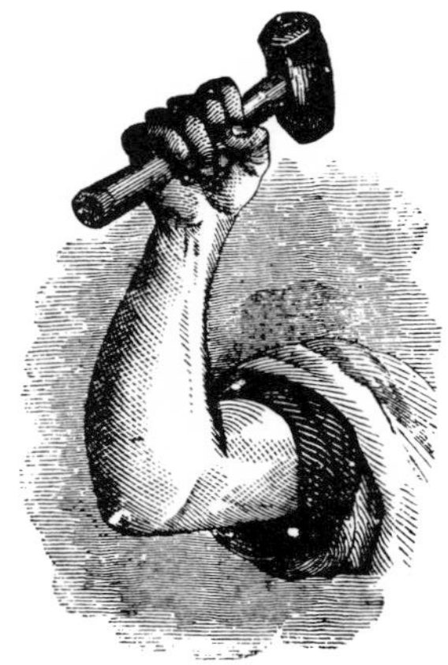

BY

B. M. LAWRENCE, M.D.

D. M. BENNETT,
LIBERAL AND SCIENTIFIC PUBLISHING HOUSE,
141 EIGHTH ST., NEW YORK.

Copyrighted, 1878, by D. M. Bennett.

Courtesy of Archie Green

Out of bondage into freedom,
Right will gain the day.

Poll your votes, boys, vote for true men,*
Greenbacks cannot fail;
Poll your votes, good times are coming,
Greenbacks shall prevail.

Hark, the Greenback boys are marching,
Victory now is nigh;
Short and fierce will be the conflict;
Old parties must die.

Chorus:

Business men are daily failing;
Tramps roam to and fro;
All the land is full of mourning,
Hear the wail of woe.

Chorus:

When the Greenback boys shall triumph,
Justice will ordain
To the homeless, poor and outcast,
Equal rights shall reign.

Chorus:

Onward then, ye hosts of true men;
Cheer, brave comrades, cheer;
By the help of God and woman,
Victory is near.

Chorus:[34]

*The name of a popular candidate may be substituted for "true men."

DOWN WITH THE MONEY KING

Air—"John Brown"

The Greenback labor boys, both with speeches and with song,
The Greenback labor boys now are marching right along;
The Greenback labor boys mean to put down fraud and wrong.

Let all the people sing, glory, glory, hallelujah,
Glory, glory, hallelujah, glory, glory, hallelujah,
Down with the Money King.

Though the bankers rule the press with their subsidy of gold,
Though the bankers rule the press it is time that they were told,
Though the bankers rule the press Greenback voters can't be sold.

Let all, &c.

Soon the old party frauds, please remember what we say,
Soon the old party frauds, sure as next election day,
Soon the old party frauds we are bound to wipe away.

Let all, &c.

The men who pay the taxes have got tired of the drones;
The men who pay the taxes hear too much about coupons;
The men who pay the taxes soon will smash the banks and bonds.

Let all, &c.

The business men are learning that contraction is a curse;
The business men are learning that resumption is still worse;
The business men are learning they want Greenbacks in their purse.

Let all, &c.

The workingmen's party know full well that they are right;
The workingmen's party have resolved they will unite;
The workingmen's party by their votes will show their might.

Let all, &c.

The ladies they are with us, in our platform they can trust;
The ladies they are with us, for we own their claims are just;
The ladies they are with us, we will conquer, boys, we must!

Let all, &c.[35]

WHAT WE WANT

Air—"Things I Don't Like to See"

What we want is reform, all the people well know,
And the road to reform is most easy to show;
Though the task may be great, yet the work will be done
When our faults we forsake and each reforms one.

A most excellent thing is reform for mankind,
'Tis the want of all *parties** and people we find,
Rally then for reform, but remember each one,
We must first reform self, then the work will be done.

We want preachers of truth, the old methods to mend,
Till religion and reason together shall blend.
To preach a good sermon may be easily done,
But practice your precepts, and each reform one.

Chorus:

We want lawyers to take our advice without fee,
Though with this opinion they may not all agree;
Let your plea be for peace,—strife and law always shun,
Then you and your clients will each reform one.

Chorus:

34Ibid., p. 6.
35Ibid., p. 13.

We want doctors to work for reform night and day,
And so do their patients, for indeed well they may;
But among the new schools, the reform has begun,
They practice a method that must reform one.

Chorus:

We want merchants who make such a splendid display
Of silk robes and ribbons, with dry goods rich and gay,
To pay proper wages for the work they get done,
If not they are robbers, till each reforms one.

Chorus:

We want workmen of every condition to know
That when labor unites it can soon overthrow
Every form of injustice found under the sun.
Combine then and conquer; let each reform one.

Chorus:

We want voters to send honest men to make laws,
And remember reform is the life of their cause.
Bondholders and bankers then will soon have the fun
Of earning their living when each reforms one.

Chorus:

We want dandies in kids, with a meerschaum or cane,
To forsake all such follies, as drinking champagne;
Many thousands the road down to ruin have run;
Then learn to love labor and each reform one.

Chorus:

We want, ladies, to lisp just one thought in your ear:
Be precisely the thing you take pains to appear;
For father and brother, for your husband or son,
Have a smile and a kind word, and each reform one.

Chorus:

We want speakers who talk to the people so true,
To hear one suggestion we shall offer for you:
While pointing out vices and habits to shun,
Live up to your teaching and each reform one.

Chorus:

We want, we, the people, our own matters to mind,
Each our own sins to see but to others be blind,
So when from our own eyes we have pulled out the beam,
The mote in our brother's much smaller will seem.

Chorus:

We want all the nations to enlist for reform,
Till the hungry are fed and the naked made warm;
Then we'll sing a new song, full of music and mirth,
How reforming ourselves has reformed the whole earth.

Chorus:[36]

*The word "parties" is changed in the chorus to each verse, substituting "lawyer," "doctor," etc., and the name of some well-known citizen may be used in place of "people," thus, " 'Tis the want of Lawyer Ben Butler," &c. [Benjamin F. Butler was the Greenback-Labor candidate for governor of Massachusetts. For more on Butler see below, pp. 257–60.—Ed.]

RALLY, BOYS, FOR GREENBACKS

Air—"Few Days"

The workingmen are growing strong
For Greenbacks, for Greenbacks;
They mean to right all forms of wrong,
And crush the money power.
The workingmen, a mighty band,
With ballots, free ballots,
Will drive oppression from the land
For ever, ever more.

Then rally, boys, hurrah for Greenbacks,
Greenbacks, Greenbacks;
Then rally, boys for the good old Greenbacks,
They must and shall prevail.

We want no class rule in this land
Of freemen, yes, freemen;
No money lords can longer stand,
When right obtains control.
Old party chains are breaking fast;
The voters, free voters,
Have formed a union, which shall last
Till ages cease to roll.

Chorus:

The workingmen are bound to rule;
Then paupers, rich paupers,
Will have to work in life's great school
And earn their daily bread;
Then justice, with her flag unfurled,
In triumph, grand triumph,
Shall reign supreme in all the world,
The starving millions fed.

Chorus:

Then, workingmen, be brave and free;
Take courage, true courage;
The Greenback cause, with harmony,
Will slay the money king.
Come one, come all, and join our band
For justice, sure justice,
Dealt out to all with even hand,
Let all the people sing, "Glory, Glory," &c.[37]

THE GREENBACK BOYS ARE WAKING

Air—"Webb"

The dawning light is breaking,
The dark night disappears,

36Ibid., pp. 16–17.
37Ibid., p. 25.

The Greenback boys are waking,
Let outcasts dry their tears.
Too long the wail of sorrow
Has sounded through the land,
Behold the coming morrow,
Good times are near at hand.

The bankers now are shaking,
They tremble in their shoes,
Bondholders, too, are quaking
Whene'er they read the news,
The money power is trying
To raise the cry "Commune!"[38]
They pay the press for lying,—
Greenbacks will change their tune.

Rouse up, rouse up, then, freemen,
The strife will not be long,
Let all the nations see, then,
The overthrow of wrong.
The Greenback cause prevailing,
Will speed o'er land and sea,
With love and peace unfailing
Through all Eternity.[39]

UP AND DO

By Mary Dana Shindler

Air—"Rousseau's Dream"

Up and do, ye working people!
Even while you waiting stand
For your hard-earned "bread and water"
Save, oh save this glorious land!
We will have no proud dictators,
Hardened by ill-gotten gain,
For we know our country can be
Rescued by her workingmen.

Brothers! do not feel elated
When you seem victorious—
Seem to carry all before you—
Armies have been conquer'd thus!
Brothers! there is always danger
Though its cause you may not see;
Only "vigilance eternal"
Is the price of liberty.

For your wives and for your children
Urge your holy crusade on;
Let their earnest voices cheer you,
Onward! 'till the victory's won!
Never for one weary moment
Lay your batter'd armor down,
'Till each honest workman's forehead
Sparkles with a victor's crown.

Oh, be earnest—Oh, be watchful!
Guard each outpost—guard it well!
While within your lines mean traitors
May be prowling—who will tell
Lies unnumbered to the people—
Heed them not, but onward go;
With clean hands clean platforms showing,
To be scann'd by friend or foe.

Working women! though the ballot
Is denied you, still you can
With kind Love's all potent weapons
Work beside your brother, man.
And when comes the joyful hour
Of your country's freedom, gained
By your country's working people,
Then will woman be unchained.

Free to vote beside her brothers,
Free to lay her loving heart
On her country's sacred altar,
Now defiled by trait'rous art.
Oh, my sisters! help your brothers,
Even while you waiting stand,
For your hard-earned bread and water,
Save, oh, save this glorious land![40]

IN THE ARMY

Words and Music by Mary Dana Shindler

We're in the Greenback army,
And there we mean to stay,
Till the rising sun of freedom
Has brought the perfect day.
We've borne too long all kinds of wrongs,
And now we must be free;
No longer slaves to wicked knaves,
We'll strike for liberty.

We're in the Greenback army,
And there we mean to stay,
Till the rising sun of Freedom
Has brought the perfect day.

[38]The established press frequently attacked the Greenback-Labor movement as dominated by the "red flag of Communism imported from Europe," especially from France, where the Paris Commune of 1871 sent chills through the respectable classes in this country as well as in Europe. In a pamphlet distributed by working-class Greenback clubs entitled *The Epistle of Nathan the Wise,* the Wise Man is asked, "What is Communism?" Finally, he answers: "Not to gather and keep in my stores fine bread and fine meats, wine and fruits, treasures of gold and silver, and precious stones of which I have not need, nor cunning garments made by work . . . when my brother fainteth for a crust. This is communism." Thereupon the people note this was what Jesus, Moses, and Confucius taught, and the Wise Man replies: "Trouble not your hearts for a word. It is humanity" (*Revelations: The Epistle of Nathan the Wise,* [n.p., 1878], p. 9).

[39]Lawrence, *National Greenback Labor Songster,* p. 27.

[40]Mary Dana Shindler, *United States Labor Greenback Song Book* (New Rochelle, N.Y., 1879) pp. 28–29.

We're in a noble army,
Our officers are men
Of honesty and courage,
All "wearing of the green."
The privates, too, their duty do,
And never will desert
Their banner green, as will be seen,
When the Shylocks all get hurt.

Chorus:

Oh, come, ye working people,
And join this mighty host
Of glorious reformers,
Let not a vote be lost!
When comes the hour to try your power,
Let each true man be seen,
With smiling faces in the right place,
Armed with a ballot green.

Chorus:

Sound, sound the Greenback war-cry,
Throughout the suff'ring land!
Wake up the slumb'ring millions
To deeds sublime and grand!
Turn not away, by night or day,
From this your high behest;
Good men and true, your duty do,
And leave to God the rest!

Chorus:[41]

WE ARE COMING
By Mary Dana Shindler
Air—"Sicilian Hymn"

We are coming! We are coming!
One united Greenback throng,
Not with guns and cannon booming,
But with valiant hearts and strong.
Hallelujah, hallelujah!
Shout aloud the battle song!

We are coming, we are coming!
We, the toilers of the land!
Like the sound of many waters
Is the gathering of our band;
Hallelujah, hallelujah!
Shout the battle cry so grand!

We are coming, we are coming!
Like a foaming, raging sea
Sweeping banks and bonds before it,
Awful shall the onset be;
Hallelujah, hallelujah!
Shout the song of victory!

We are coming, we are coming!
Soon to dry the widow's tears,
Soon to feed the starving millions,
Soon to quell the orphan's fears.
Hallelujah, hallelujah!
Shout the tidings through the spheres!

We are coming, we are coming!
Oh, ye working people all,
Hear ye not the gath'ring footsteps?
Will you heed your country's call?
Hallelujah, hallelujah!
Banks, and bonds, and gold must fall![42]

TRAMP, TRAMP, TRAMP!
By Mary Dana Shindler

Upon the western breeze,
And from the eastern seas,
The cheering cry of "Liberty" is heard;
The working people know
They must meet a deadly foe,
And "Liberty or Death" is now the word.

Tramp, tramp, tramp, the Greenback armies,
All bold and true are marching through the land;
At the polls to meet the foe, and they gather as they go,
The workingmen—a brave and honest band.

The bonds are to be paid,
Not with gold, as has been said,
But with legal-tender money—good as gold;
The banking fraud must end,
And the people's honest friend,
The Greenback—must her banner now unfold.

Tramp, tramp, etc.

The wicked railroad kings,
And the curst hard-money rings
Must be fought, and must be conquer'd in the strife.
Monopolists must learn
It is now the people's turn
To stop the cry—"Your money or your life!"

Tramp, tramp, etc.

With the ballot in each hand,
Will these soldiers take their stand,
And leave their votes within the ballot-box;
And a sturdy guard they'll mount;
Who will closely watch the count,
And keep their eye on many a cunning fox.

Tramp, tramp, etc.

God help the workingmen,
And strengthen heart and brain
To feel and labor for this holy cause;

[41]Ibid., p. 8.
[42]Ibid., p. 24.

Let them first elect their men
With honest votes, and then
They'll save the country through their honest laws.

Tramp, tramp, etc.[43]

TO THE TOILERS

By Mary Dana Shindler

Air—"Cheerful Companions"

O, workingmen all,
'Tis on you that we call,
In this hour of peril and gloom;
You must conquer or die,
'Tis on you we rely,
Your country to save from its doom.

Ye toilers, arise
For time rapidly flies,
And your enemies all are at work;
They have barrels of gold,
And resources untold,
And they know how to strike in the dark.

Oh, brothers, we know
You are crushed down so low
That of hope you are nearly bereft;
But your friends are alive,
And they'll manfully strive,
To strengthen what hope you have left.

Come up to their aid—
Let it never be said
That you left them to battle alone;
The fight is for you—
If you'll only be true
To yourselves, it will surely be won.

Be firm and be brave!
Tell each bondholding knave
That a workingman's soul is his own;
And that all HE is worth
Is to cumber the earth
Like a useless, detestable drone.

Be aggressive! be strong!
And it will not be long
Ere the workingman's woes shall be past;
But your sorrow and pain
Will have all been in vain
If you strike not for Freedom at last![44]

The Greenback-Labor coalition fell apart after 1878, when the farmers and small businessmen played down labor's demands and put all their stress on currency reform. By 1879, with industrial recovery under way, workers were turning their attention to rebuilding the unions shattered or weakened during the depression. They sought to recoup the losses they had suffered in reduced wages and longer hours of work. Before it vanished from the scene, the Greenback-Labor movement gave birth to a song which was to remain popular in labor and Socialist circles for the next several decades—"The Ninety and Nine," modeled on the famous Clephane-Sankey gospel hymn.

The labor words were written in 1876 by Mrs. S. M. Smith, wife of a farmer in Kewanee, Illinois, during the campaign for the Greenback party presidential candidate, Peter Cooper. In 1878 it was widely popularized by the Greenback-Labor party, and in 1880 the verses were read on the floor of the House of Representatives by E. H. Gillette, congressman from Iowa, in the course of a speech on the greenback question. They were printed, along with his remarks, in the *Congressional Record.* After the decline of the Greenback-Labor party, the song was popular among the Knights of Labor, where it was known as "Labor's Ninety and Nine." It was published with music in the Knights of Labor's *Labor Reform Songster* and in *The Alliance and Labor Songster*, issued by the Farmers' Alliance movement. In 1902 it appeared as "The Ninety and Nine" in *Socialist Songs with Music*, compiled by Charles H. Kerr, where it was attributed to Rose Elizabeth Smith. All told, it was probably the most widely reprinted song of the eighties and nineties.

THERE ARE NINETY AND NINE

There are ninety and nine that live and die
In want and hunger and cold,
That one may revel in luxury
And be lapped in its silken fold;
The ninety and nine in their hovels bare,
The one in a palace with riches rare.

They toil in the fields, the ninety and nine,
For the fruits of our mother earth;
They dig and delve in the dusty mine,
And bring her hidden treasures forth;
And the wealth released by their sturdy blows
To the hands of one forever flows.

From the sweat of their brows and desert blooms,
The forest before them falls,
Their labor has builded humble homes
And cities with lofty halls;

[43]Ibid., pp. 29–30.
[44]Ibid., pp. 4–5.

No. 29. Labor's Ninety and Nine.
Better sung as a Solo.
1. There are ninety and nine that live and die, In want and hunger and
2. They toil in the fields, the nine-ty and nine, For the fruits of our moth-er
3. By the sweat of their brows the desert blooms, And the forest before them
4. The night so drear-y, so dark, so long, At last shall the morning
cold, That one may revel in lux - u-ry, And be wrapped in its silk-en
earth; They dig and delve in the dusky mine, And bring its rich treasures
falls; Their labor has builded humble homes, And cit - ies with loft-y
bring; And over the land the Victor's song Of the ninety and nine shall
fold; The ninety and nine in their hovels bare, The one in his palace with
forth; But the wealth released by their sturdy blows, To the hands of the one for-
halls; But the one owns cities and homes and lands. While the ninety and nine have
ring, And ech - o a - far, from zone to zone, Rejoice, for la - bor shall
rich - es rare, The one in his palace with rich - es rare.
ev - er flows, To the hands of the one for - ev - er flows.
empty hands, While the ninety and nine have empty hands.
have its own, Re-joice, for la - bor shall have its own.

From Leopold Vincent, comp., *The Alliance and Labor Songster* (Winfield, Kans., 1891). Courtesy of Brown University Library.

And the one owns cities and homes and lands,
And the ninety and nine have empty hands.

Dear God! how long will their wrongs be dumb?
How long the hopeless strife
Ere the hearts that die and the souls benumbed
Shall quicken in new born life?
And the empty hands that toil from birth
Be clasped in a band that spans the earth?

Ere the night, so dreary and dark and long,
Shall that glorious morning bring,
When over the world the victor's song
Of the ninety and nine shall ring,
And echo afar from zone to zone,
"Rejoice, for labor shall have its own!"[45]

45Phillips Thompson, ed., *The Labor Reform Songster* (Philadelphia, 1892). There are several versions of the song. The one in Edward Carpenter's *Chants of Labour* (London, 1891, p. 11) follows the above closely; Carpenter got his text from the *Boston Globe*.

7

The Knights of Labor

THE NOBLE AND HOLY ORDER

In 1869 a small group of garment cutters in Philadelphia organized a new labor body called the Noble and Holy Order of the Knights of Labor. This was a period when unions were often smashed because their members became known to employers and were blacklisted. The Knights, therefore, made secrecy a key feature of the movement, and it continued as a secret organization until 1881. Another of its principles was labor solidarity. Uriah Stephens, founder of the order, maintained that since all workers had common interests, they should logically belong to a common society and be united by their bonds of "universal brotherhood."[1] This idea was put forth clearly in the great slogan of the Knights of Labor, "An injury to one is the concern of all."

In 1879, when Uriah Stephens resigned his position as Grand Master Workman to be replaced by Terence V. Powderly,[2] the order's membership was 20,151. Four years later it had grown to 51,914. Its meteoric rise during the next few years has hardly been paralleled in the history of the labor movement. Its growth resulted from successful boycotts and strikes, such as the strike on the Wabash and Jay Gould's Southwestern System in 1885, after which membership increased sevenfold within a year, from one hundred thousand in 1885 to seven hundred thousand in 1886. At its height, in 1886, the Knights of Labor united skilled and unskilled, men and women, North and South, black and white, native American and foreign born, workers of all religious and political opinions.[3]

"The fundamental principle of the Knights of Labor is *Education*," declared a leaflet issued by the order. It was a basic tenet of the Knights that workers would have to be educated before they could hope to assume the leadership in society which was their birthright. Since most of its members were "persons who, by circumstances not under their control, have been deprived of opportunities of knowledge as taught by schools,"[4] and since even those who had gone to school had not learned the truth of social, economic, and political issues, but only distorted, anti-labor, pro-capital interpretations, it was necessary for the order to establish its own educational program.

In the main, the educational activities of the order consisted of lectures given by prominent men and women in the organization as well as

1Terence V. Powderly, *Thirty Years of Labor, 1859–1889* (Columbus, O., 1889) p. 167.

2Many trade unions of this period had elaborate titles for their officers, but none carried the practice so far as the Knights of Labor. In addition to the Grand Master Workman, there was the Venerable Sage (or retiring president), the Worthy Foreman, the Unknown Knight, etc.

3The chief blot on the KL's record on the issue of labor solidarity concerned Chinese workers. Shortly after he became Grand Master Workman, Powderly ruled that Asians could not become members of the order and, furthermore, that they were unfit even to reside in the United States. The leaders of the order boasted that the organization had played an important role in securing passage of an anti-Chinese bill by Congress in 1882 providing for exclusion of the Chinese from this country.

4Leaflet attached to letter of James B. Davison to Powderly, Nov. 11, 1887, Terence V. Powderly Papers, Catholic University of America, Washington, D.C.

by friendly progressives on the outside. They also included the establishment of libraries and reading rooms. The Knights believed, too, that songs, ballads, and poems were important in educating workers on the key issues associated with the order, and the papers issued by the national organization and local assemblies throughout the country paid special attention to this form of education. In fact, no labor organization before the rise of the Industrial Workers of the World (IWW) in the opening decade of the twentieth century made songs and ballads so much a part of its activities as did the Noble and Holy Order of the Knights of Labor.[5]

GENERAL SONGS OF THE KNIGHTS OF LABOR

The following opening and closing odes were originally used by Local Assembly 1696, Ottumwa, Iowa. After the *Journal of United Labor*, the KL official organ, published them in March, 1881, with the notice that "other Locals may use them if so disposed," they were soon in general use throughout the order.

ODES FOR LOCALS

By M. A. Dalbey

OPENING ODE

Tune—"O That Will Be Joyful"

Once more within the sacred vail,
Our hearts in union sweet,
Let each one strive in peace to work—
No discord may we meet.
May social love prevail,
To give us harmony;
That right may triumph over wrong
When labor shall be free.

Oh that will be joyful, joyful, joyful,
Oh that will be joyful
When labor shall be free.

Oh may our minds be here inspired,
With wisdom from on high,
And justice, diligence and truth,
All evil may defy.
In labor's holy cause
May every action be,—
Each heart be filled with purpose strong,
For labor shall be free.

Oh that will be joyful, etc.

CLOSING ODE

Tune—"Marten"

We again are called to part,
And would now ourselves commend
Unto Him who knows each heart,
Who has ever been our friend.
He the poor will ever shield,
He the oppressed will surely free,
He the sword of justice wield,
Tyrants power destroyed shall be.

Though our evening's work is o'er
We our cause should ne'er forget;
We should labor more and more,
None should stop to rest him yet.
And when we shall meet again.
Strong to work may we be found,
Hoping soon to bring the day,
Labor's cause with victory crowned.[6]

Some local assemblies used the following opening and closing odes.

OPENING ODE FOR K. OF L.

By C. S. White, Halsted, Kan.

Knights of Labor, all fraternal,
Meet we here for mutual help;
Guarded each by truth and justice,
All our thoughts are not on self;
Needy brothers all around us,
Suffering from old Shylock's greed;
For the ones that hold the power
Rob us of our ev'ry need.

Hear the pleadings of the workers,
As they toil from day to day;
Let it be our aim and object
To drive the hungry wolf away;
Give protection to the workers,
Needy ones all o'er the land,
Extending to our toiling brothers,
Everywhere, a helping hand.[7]

CLOSING ODE

By Ellis

Air—"Auld Lang Syne"

Again we meet, again we part,
Again our work is done;

[5]In addition to the Knights of Labor songs in the present chapter, others are included in following chapters. See pp. 200–208, 235–51 passim, 267–82 passim.

[6]*Journal of United Labor*, Mar. 15, 1881.

[7]Leopold Vincent, comp., *The Alliance and Labor Songster* (Winfield, Kans., 1891).

No. 8. Opening Ode for K. of L.
C. S. WHITE, Halsted, Kan.
1. Knights of La - bor, all fra - ter - nal, Meet we here for mutual help;
2. Hear the pleadings of the work - ers, As they toil from day to day;
Fine.
Guard-ed each by truth and just-ice, All our thoughts are not on self;
D. S. For the ones that hold the pow - er Rob us of our ev - 'ry need.
Let it be our aim and ob - ject To drive the hungry wolf away;
D. S. Ex - tend - ing to our toiling brothers, Ev-ery-where, a help-ing hand.
D. S.
Need-y bro-thers all a-round us, Suf-fer-ing from old Shylock's greed;
Give pro - tec - tion to the work - ers, Need-y ones all o'er the land,
7

Courtesy of Brown University Library

Again we pledge each heart to heart
Until the victory's won.

Our cause is just, and win we must,
Our Union Label band
Will not forget when last we met
And clasped the honest hand.[8]

The following songs were adopted by all local assemblies at one time or another during the career of the Knights of Labor. They were usually sung at assembly meetings.

KNIGHTS OF LABOR

Composed and Sung by Budd Harris

I'll sing of an order that lately has done
Some wonderful things in our land,
Together they pull great battles have won,
A popular hard working band.
Their numbers are legion great strength they possess,
They strike good and strong for their rights,
From the North to the South from the East to the West,
God speed each Assembly of Knights.

Then conquer we must,
Our cause it is just,
What power the uplifted hand,
Let each Labor Knight
Be brave in the fight,
Remember united we stand.

They ask nothing wrong you can plainly see,
All that they demand is but fair,
A lesson they'll teach with me you'll agree,
To every purse-proud millionaire.
Fair wages they want, fair wages they'll get,
Good tempered they wage all their fights,
Success to the cause may the sun never set,
On each brave Assembly of Knights.

Then conquer we must, &c.

Then fight on undaunted, you brave working men,
Down the vampires who oppress the poor,
You use noble weapons, the tongue and the pen,
Successful you'll be I'm sure.
With hope for your watchword and truth for your shield,
Prosperity for your pathway lights,
Then let labor make proud capital yield,
God speed each Assembly of Knights.

Then conquer we must, &c.[9]

NOBLE KNIGHTS OF LABOR

Copyrighted and Music published by
Willis Woodward & Co., N.Y.

In the year of sixty-nine they commenced to fall in line,
The great Knights, the noble Knights of Labor,
Now in numbers mighty strong, gaining fast they march along,
The great Knights, the noble Knights of Labor.
They are men of brains and will, education, pluck and skill,
And in time they'll change the workman's situation,
East and West where'er we go, from the North to Mexico,
They're as thick as flies, and soon they'll rule the nation.

Oh, the great Knights, the noble Knights of Labor,
The true Knights, the honest Knights of Labor,
Like the good old Knights of old, they cannot be bought or sold
The great Knights, the noble Knights of Labor.

U. S. Stevens was the man this great order first began,
The great Knights, the noble Knights of Labor,
And he started what they say is the strongest band today,
The great Knights the noble Knight[s] of Labor.
Bless the mind that gave them birth, they're the finest men on earth,
And they're building up a mountain high of power,
Men with hearts and records each, men who practice what they preach,
And the men we need in Congress ev'ry hour.

Oh, the great Knights, the noble Knights of Labor,
The fine Knights, the gallant Knights of Labor,
'Till they treat our workmen fair, they will boycott ev'rywhere,
The great Knights the noble Knights of labor.

Every day that pass by,[10] they increase and multiply,
The great Knights, the noble Knights of Labor,
Let the millionaire reflect that their force cannot be check'd,
The great Knights, the noble Knights of Labor.
In the Senate when they sit, all the frauds will have to git,
Or they'll drive them from the country in a hurry,
Every dog has got his day, our mechanics want fair play,
And in union they will get it don't you worry.

Oh, the great Knights, the noble Knights of Labor,
The real Knights, the Monarch Knights of Labor,
They are heroes ev'ry one, but all scabs they hate and shun,
The great Knights, the noble Knights of Labor.[11]

8Elizabeth Balch, "Songs for Labor," *Survey*, XXXI (Jan. 3, 1914), 411.

9Printed card, American Antiquarian Society.

10Probably *passes by*.

11Printed card, American Antiquarian Society.

A. W. AUNER, SONG PUBLISHER & PRINTER,
Tenth and Race Sts., Philadelphia, Pa.

KNIGHTS OF LABOR

Composed and Sung by Budd Harris.

I'll sing of an order that lately has done
  Some wonderful things in our land,
Together they pull great battles have won,
  A popular hard working band.
Their numbers are legion great strength they possess,
  They strike good and strong for their rights,
From the North to the South from the East to the West,
  God speed each Assembly of Knights.

CHORUS.

Then conquer we must,
Our cause it is just,
  What power the uplifted hand,
Let each Labor Knight
Be brave in the fight,
  Remember united we stand.

They ask nothing wrong you can plainly see,
  All that they demand is but fair,
A lesson they'll teach with me you'll agree,
  To every purse-proud millionaire.
Fair wages they want, fair wages they'll get,
  Good tempered they wage all their fights,
Success to the cause may the sun never set,
  On each brave Assembly of Knights.
Then conquer we must, &c.

Then fight on uudaunted, you brave working men,
  Down the vampires who oppress the poor,
You use noble weapons, the tongue and the pen,
  Succesful you'll be I'm sure.
With hope for your watchword and truth for your shield,
  Prosperity for your pathway lights,
Then let labor make proud capital yield,
  God speed each Assembly of Knights.
Then conquer we must, &c.

A. W. AUNER'S
CARD AND JOB PRINTING ROOMS
Tenth and Race Sts., Philadelphia, Pa.

Courtesy of American Antiquarian Society

COME, BROTHERS, COME

By Red, Jr., Port Perry, Pa.

Come rally, noble Knights of Labor,
Come forth and prove your manliness;
No longer more, in spite your toiling,
Live in starvation and distress.

Come forth, ye men, and be true fathers,
Come grasp the sword of righteousness,
Come forth, ye women, be true mothers,
Help free your children from distress.

Come help us fight that noble battle,
That battle for humanity;
Come, sisters all, and come, O brothers,
And help to make all mankind free![12]

THE GOOD TIME COMING

By Charles Mackay

There's a good time coming, boys,
A good time coming;
We may not live to see the day,
But earth shall glisten in the ray
Of the good time coming.
Cannon balls may aid the truth,
But thought's a weapon stronger;
We'll win our battles by its aid;—
Wait a little longer.

There's a good time coming, boys,
A good time coming;
The pen shall supercede the sword,
And Right, not Might, shall be the lord
In the good time coming.
Worth, not birth, shall rule mankind,
And be acknowledged stronger;
The proper impulse has been given:—
Wait a little longer.

There's a good time coming, boys,
A good time coming.
War in all men's eyes shall be
A monster of iniquity
In the good time coming.
Nations shall not quarrel then,
To prove which is the stronger;
Nor slaughter men for glory's sake;—
Wait a little longer.

There's a good time coming, boys,
A good time coming,
Hated rivalries of creed
Shall not make their martyrs bleed
In the good time coming,
Religion shall be shorn of pride,
And flourish all the stronger;
And Charity shall trim her lamp;—
Wait a little longer.

There's a good time coming, boys,
A good time coming.
And a poor man's family
Shall not be his misery
In this good time coming.
Every child shall be a help
To make the right arm stronger;
The happier he the more he has;—
Wait a little longer.

There's a good time coming, boys,
A good time coming.
Little children shall not toil,
Under or above the soil,
In the good time coming;
But shall play in healthful fields
Till limbs and mind grow stronger;
And every one shall read and write;—
Wait a little longer.

There's a good time coming, boys,
A good time coming.
The people shall be temperate,
And shall love instead of hate,
In the good time coming.
They shall use, and not abuse,
And make all virtue stronger,
The reformation has begun;—
Wait a little longer.

There's a good time coming, boys,
A good time coming.
Let us aid it all we can,
Every woman, every man,
The good time coming.
Smallest helps, if rightly given,
Make the impulse stronger;
'Twill be strong enough one day;—
Wait a little longer.[13]

DEDICATION HYMN

By C. Fannie Allyn

Air—"Auld Lang Syne"

Our fathers crossed a pathless sea,
And sought a rock-bound shore,
To consecrate to liberty
Their lives forevermore.
And we, to keep that freedom bright,
Meet with our friends to-day,
To dedicate this hall to Right,
And Labor's noble sway.

Within these walls we know no creed,
No nation, sex or clan,
For "justice to all" we plead,

[12] *Alarm*, Feb. 21, 1885.
[13] *Knights of Labor*, Jan. 22, 1887.

Based on "the rights of man."
Here, honor is the royal robe
And highest rank on earth,
Our jewels, flashing round the glove,
Are faithfulness and worth.

We reverence the good and true,
Not broadcloth, silk or gold,
And all who pledge the same to do
We shield within our fold.
Oppression's iron hand shall find
The banner we've unfurled,
Frees from all tyranny mankind,
Assisting all the world.

Toil is the magic cornerstone
On which all wealth depends,
The keystone, holding strong and firm,
Each arch that upward tends
Then here's to Labor's holy name—
The mightiest own its thrall—
Within this hall we crown its fame,
The Earthly King of All.[14]

KNIGHTS OF LABOR SONG

By Francis M. Goodwin, M.W. L.A. 8378
Denmark, Lincoln Co., Kansas

Ye valiant Knights of Labor, rise,
Unfurl your banners to the skies
And go to work and organize,
Until the world is won.
See the lordly nabobs quake,
See the politicians shake,
Labor now is wide awake.
Justice will be done.

Though oppression's iron heel
Grinds us down and makes us feel
Poverty's accursed deal,
Yield not to despair.
Brighter days are yet in store,
Good old times will come once more,
Strive! the battle ne'er give o'er.
Victory we shall share.

Never mind the world's dread frown;
Though the press may run us down,
And preachers in their righteous (?) gown.
We never will retreat.
Because we know our cause is just;
With God to help us, win we must,
Monopoly must bite the dust.
Before our work's complete.

Then let us labor one and all
To spread the truth, at duty's call;
To organize, and then install
Our principles of right—
'Till justice shall be done anew
To all mankind, and not the few;
Till outraged labor gets her due.
And then we'll end the fight.[15]

ORGANIZE THE HOSTS OF LABOR

By Will H. Minnich

Organize the hosts of labor
In one common brotherhood,
He who drives the locomotive
And the one who turns the sod;
Those who dig the dusky diamonds,
And produce the shining gold.
Those in factory and in workshop,
Bring them to this shepherd's fold.

Bring the fireman and the brakeman,
And conductors, East and West;
Bring the switchmen and the Yardmen,
Section hands, and all the rest;
Bring them with the ironworker,
Sailor, soldier and the tramp;
Organize and school them fully
In the Knights of Labor camp.

Organize the Western ranchmen,
And the cow-boy of the plains;
Bring the herder and the hermit
And the student with his brains;
Bring them in and thus united,
Drill and school them in their rights,
Moving on in quiet prudence
Till we've gained the topmost heights.

Gain them through united effort,
Organize and drill with care
In the tactics of our Order
Knighthood teaches everywhere.
Moving on in one direction,
Labor's cause to guard and guide,
By the wise and wholesome council
Each assembly shall provide.[16]

AMERICA

New Version by Ralph E. Hoyt, Los Angeles, Cal.

Our Country, 'tis of thee,
Sweet land of knavery,
Of thee we sing!
Sweet land of Jobs and Rings,
And various crooked things—
Our social system brings
Full many a sting.

[14]*Labor Enquirer,* Feb. 26, 1887.
[15]*Journal of United Labor,* Apr. 16, 1887.
[16]Ibid., Aug. 2, 1888.

Our boodlers sometimes flee,
Far off to Cana-da,
To save their bacon.
But thousands more, we fear,
Will still continue here,
Each other's hearts to cheer—
With hopes unshaken.

Land of the great defaulter,
Of knaves who need the halter,
Where gold is king.
Land where fond hopes have died,
Where demagogues reside,
Monopolies preside,
And misery bring.

We love thy rocks and rills,
But not thy bitter ills—
And griefs that follow.
Thy boasts of "equal rights,"
Made through thy leading lights,
In rhetoric proud flights—
Are somewhat hollow.

Sweet Land, sweet Liberty,
Let Truth and Justice be
Allowed full sway.
When none shall toil in vain,
Monopoly cease to reign,
No heart be pierced with pain
By cruel wrong.

Land of true liberty,
We'll sound loud praise to thee,
In cheerful song.
Then will the oppressed arise,
The dawn salute all eyes,
Souls swell with glad surprise—
God speed the day![17]

MODERN MISSIONARY ZEAL

Anonymous

Tune—"Onward! Christian Soldiers"

Onward! Christian soldiers;
On to heathen lands!
Prayer book in your pockets,
Rifles in your hands.
Take the happy tidings
Where trade can be done;
Spread the peaceful gospel
With a Gatling gun.

Tell the wretched natives
Sinful are their hearts,
To turn heathen temples
Into spirit marts.
And if to your preaching
They will not succumb,
Substitute for sermons
Adulterated rum.

When the Ten Commandments
They quite understand,
You their chief must hocus
And annex their land.
And if they, misguided,
Call you to account,
Read them—in their language—
The Sermon on the Mount.

If, spite all your teaching,
Trouble still they give;
If, spite rum and measles,
Some of them still live;
Then, with purpose moral,
Spread false tales about,
Instigate a quarrel,
And let them fight it out.[18]

KNIGHTS OF LABOR

By W. J. Durham

Ho! Knights of Labor, one and all,
Be ready at the Master's call
To take your places here,
Each officer within his place,
And member, too, with smiling face,
The glorious cause to cheer.

Let us upon "the level" meet,
And "work" to make ourselves replete,
"Humanity" to bless,
"Obliterating" all that's wrong,
Forever from the "workman's" throng,
And ne'er forget "distress."

And "secrecy" remember well,
"Obedience," too, must ever dwell
Within our "circle" strong,
And "mutual assistance" give
That others may find work and live
And happiness prolong.

And when the "cover of the shield"
And "secret work" has been revealed,
May light from Heaven shine
To guide us in the paths of right,
Of truth and justice, and incite
True friendship to enshrine.

And when the "Master Workman's" call
To order from on high, may all
Obey without a fear
Each having done his earthly part,
As a true Knight to cheer the heart
At roll-call answer, "Here."[19]

17*Journal of the Knights of Labor,* July 3, 1890.
18Ibid., May 11, 1893.
19Ibid., July, 1898.

The leaders of the Knights of Labor, especially Terence V. Powderly, Grand Master Workman, were vigorously anti-Socialist and bitterly condemned radical forces in the order. Hence it is not surprising that the editor of the *Knights of Labor,* an official journal published in Chicago, took pains to introduce the song "The Red Flag" with the following cautionary note: "The originators of the red flag intended that it should be used as the symbol of the peace and brotherhood of mankind. The fact that its use has been sometimes abused does not alter its real significance any more than the use of the stars and stripes to float above an institution where 'liquid hell and distilled damnation' are dealt out to poor weak humanity. These verses express the sentiments of the author with a beauty and force which we are sure will be appreciated by our readers.—Ed."

THE RED FLAG

By John Thompson

"How do the heathen rage and imagine a vain thing."

Do you ask from whence I have come?
What means my blood red folds?
The color that conquers the gloam!
Ere the more of truth unrolls?
I come from my home in the sky,
Where the lightning strives for right!
In the voice of the Lord on high!
Midst gloom of the hireling's might.

I was first at the birth of light!
His sign in "the burning bush,"
Red! red! in the "pillar at night,"
And the glory of life is my flush.

I'm a sign on the workman's fold,
As I was on the 'Lintle' of yore,
And speak as the "prophets of old!"
Before the oppressor's door.
By the red shall "my people" be known
To the uttermost ends of the earth!
By the "blood of my Passover" shown
In the bond of God to the serf.

I was first, etc., etc.

From a darkness through blood to the right
Through Egypt's Red Sea to land,
I'm waved by the Lord in might!
As He leads his heroic band.
High above earth's madness I wave,
I laugh its ravings to scorn!
With princes and councils I'll pave
The path of the coming morn.

I was first, etc., etc.

On Liberty's cross is a stain,
Drawn forth by the archial spear;
I flush at the black of its shame!
Red! at the tyrant's white fear.
Oh! I tell you my face is fair
As the rainbow's reclining rings!
And my waft on the morning air
Like the rush of a thousand wings.

I was first, etc., etc.

Oh! Red in His "Let there be light!"
First chosen at birth of day,
His glory in Liberty's fight
In lighting the laborer's way.
Oh! the earth cries out to the sky!
And sky flashes back to the land
Awake! for my promise is nigh,
And "thy kingdom is at hand!"

I was first, etc., etc.[20]

As the title indicates, this song was to be sung once each year:

KNIGHTS OF LABOR NEW YEAR SONG

A glad New Year
With every cheer,
An arm that is strong, and a brain that is clear,
To every Knight!
But we watch for the dawn of the new New Year,
For the dawn of the hour, when the strength that is power,
Shall cause the grinding wheel to cease
And bruised Labor's hand release.
When the toil to be done, must cease with the sun.
Let your light shine forth, till the fight is won.
It shall come—it is near—aye! the sky is clear,
Then ho, for the dawn of the new New Year.

A bright New Year
With every cheer,
An arm that is strong, and a heart without fear,
To every Knight!
But we wait for the dawn of the new New Year,
For the dawn of the day, when the toilers shall say,
"We entreat no more the right to live,
But demand." Then shall the crushers give—
For the toil of a day—shall the worth repay
And the base of a new-old freedom we'll lay.
It shall come—it is near—aye! the sky is clear,
Then ho, for the dawn of the new New Year.

A New New Year
With every cheer,
An arm that is strong and a freedom that's dear
To every Knight!
When the cause of the one is the cause of all,

20*Knights of Labor,* Oct. 2, 1886.

When the power of the right shall usurp that of might,
And all men free and equal be
In a Knightly bond of unity.
When the wisdom of sage, the discretion of age,
And the skill of the toiler, shall form the fair page—
It shall come—it is near—aye! the sky is clear,
Then ho, for the dawn of the new New Year.[21]

One of the most popular songs of the Knights of Labor, sung in most assemblies and during many strikes conducted by members of the order, was "Storm the Fort, Ye Knights," sung to the tune of "Hold the Fort." The *Weekly Pelican*, a black New Orleans newspaper, reported on January 22, 1886, that an amateur quartet sang it as "Storming the Fort" at a meeting of a Negro assembly of the Knights of Labor in Louisiana.

STORM THE FORT, YE KNIGHTS

Tune—"Hold the Fort"

Toiling millions now are waking,
See them marching on;
All the tyrants now are shaking,
Ere their power is gone.

Storm the fort, ye Knights of Labor,
Battle for your cause;
Equal rights for every neighbor,
Down with tyrant laws!

Lazy drones steal all the honey
From hard labor's hives;
Banks control the nation's money
And destroy your lives.

Chorus:

Do not load the workman's shoulder
With an unjust debt;
Do not let the rich bondholder
Live by blood and sweat.

Chorus:

Why should those who fought for freedom
Wear old slavery's chains?
Workingmen will quickly break them
When they use their brains.

Chorus:[22]

SONGS OF VARIOUS ASSEMBLIES

The following songs from the Denver, Colorado, assemblies of the Knights of Labor were published in their official journal, the *Labor Enquirer*.

FLING TO THE BREEZE OUR BANNER

Air—"A Thousand Years"

Come, brothers, come, our country calls you;
Dare you your dearest rights maintain?
Let us dethrone presumptuous leaders,
Let Labor and true Brotherhood reign.

Fling to the breeze our glorious banner,
Fill up the ranks both young and old;
Stand by your friends, united freemen—
Freedom's grand host against the world.

Back to your dens, ye base-born traitors!
Down to your own degraded spheres;
Ye cannot crush the Labor Movement,
Though you should live a thousand years.

Chorus:[23]

LABOR FREE FOR ALL

Air—"Marching through Georgia"

Start the music, comrades, we'll sing a Labor song,
Sing it with a spirit that will speed the Cause along;
Let it ring throughout the world, in chorus full and strong,
Now we are fighting for Labor.

Hurrah, hurrah, Labor free for all;
Hurrah, hurrah, listen to the call;
Shout the joyful tidings, King Capital must fall.
Now we are fighting for Labor.

Take the pledge to Labor, friend, but after you have signed,
Put your trust in Liberty and fight with might and mind,
March against the enemy, leave every fear behind.
Now we are fighting for Labor.

Hurrah, hurrah, etc.

With justice as our standard we are bound to win the fight;
Raise the Labor Flag aloft and shout with all your might;
We strike for real Freedom, for Virtue, Truth and Right.
Now we are fighting for Labor.

Hurrah, hurrah, etc.[24]

21 *Journal of the Knights of Labor*, Dec. 31, 1896.

22 *John Swinton's Paper*, June 7, 1885, and *Labor Leaf*, Sept. 30, 1885.

23 *Labor Enquirer*, June 18, 1887.

24 Ibid., July 2, 1887. The song was picked up in Leopold Vincent's *Alliance and Labor Songster* as "Labor Free to All," with the tag line reading "Now we are marching for Labor." Other variations include "Sing it with a spirit that will move the cause along" (st. 1, l. 2), "Put your trust in liberty, and work with might and mind" (st. 2, l. 2), and "We strike for home and freedom, for virtue, truth and right" (st. 3, l. 3). For a quite different version of this text, see pp. 98–99.

THE FACTORY GIRL

By Charles Cheesewright

Air—"The Orphan Boy"

I am a poor little factory girl,
I toil from early morn till night;
My sisters and brothers must do the same
For us the factory is aught but bright,
My parents, they are seeking work,
But nothing can they find to do,—
Starvation stares us in the face
For us there's naught but want and woe!

In years gone by my father toiled,
And earned a decent livelihood,—
Machinery came to do his work;
My mother then helped all she could,
She struggled hard to make ends meet,
Though working almost night and day
Grim want still at our vitals gnawed,
Machinery marked us as its prey!

My poor, dear mother sank at last,
The factory lord heard not her moan,
But into wealth he still does coin
Our lives, our flesh, our blood, our bones.
I've heard folks say this land is free;
I think it is a hollow lie
To call it FREE, where some are doomed
To toil and starve in pain and die.[25]

THE CRADLE SONG OF THE POOR

By Adelaide Proctor

Hush I cannot bear to see thee
Stretch thy tiny hands in vain;
Dear, I have no bread to give thee;
Nothing, child, to ease thy pain!
When God sent thee first to bless me,
Proud and thankful, too, was I;
Now, my darling, I, thy mother,
Almost long to see thee die,
Sleep, my darling, thou art weary;
God is good, but life is dreary!

I have watched thy beauty fading,
And thy strength fail day by day;
Soon, I know will want and fever
Take thy little life away!
Famine makes thy father reckless,
Hope has left both him and me;
We could suffer all my baby,
Had we but a crust for thee!

Better thou should'st perish early,
Starve so soon, my darling one,
Than in helpless sin and sorrow
Vainly live as I have done!
Better that thy angel spirit
With my joy and peace were flown
Than thy heart grow cold and careless,
Reckless, helpless, like my own!

I am wasted, dear, with hunger,
And my brain is all opprest;
I have scarcely strength to press thee,
Wan and feeble, to my breast
Patience, baby, God will help us,
Death will come to thee and me.
He will take us to His heaven,
There no want or pain can be.

Such the plaint, both late and early,
Did we listen, we might hear;
Close behind us—but the thunder
Of a city dulls our ear.
Every heart, as God's bright angel,
Can bid one such sorrow cease;
God has glory when his children
Bring his poor ones joy and peace.
Listen! nearer while she sings,
Sounds the fluttering of wings.[26]

FATHER GANDER'S MELODIES

"Sing a song o' swindle
Safe full of stocks;
The man who tends the spindle
Going without socks!

"The loafer in his parlor
Counting up his gold;
The worker in his garret
Perishing from cold!

"See him in his mansion!
Man of might and means,
Who never knew the earning
Of one poor pot of beans!

"Yonder man is toiling
From dawn till dewy eve,
Two-thirds of his earnings
Go to fatten thieves!"[27]

The following, written for the San Francisco assemblies of the Knights of Labor, were published in *Truth*, their official organ.

THE LAND OF OUR FATHERS

By Mrs. Jacief

Air—"The Harp of Tara"

The land our fathers struggled for
Is cover'd now with shame,
They thought it worth a bloody war

[25] *Labor Enquirer*, July 16, 1887.
[26] Ibid.
[27] Ibid.

To keep a Freeman's name!
Alas! what is our country now,
Which erst was Freedom's home,
When we to Greed and Mammon bow,
Beneath a free sky's dome!

Rise! Freemen of Columbia, rise,
And break the galling chain,
Nor let your wives and children's sighs
Appeal to you in vain!
No more be minions bought and sold,
With scarce a right to live,
But realize "The Man's the gold,"
Not what he has to give![28]

COME BROTHERS ALL

By Mrs. Jacief

Air—"Royal Charlie"

Come Brothers all, attend the call,
Kill politics and party!
Oh come and join our noble throng,
With courage true and hearty.
Bring fathers and mothers, bring sisters and brothers,
To help resist oppression,
And swell our ranks till all shall see,
We truly mean Progression!
We mean to show till all shall know
That we have power of proving
That Labor's hand shall rule the land
And Labor's brain is moving!
No longer bow'd beneath a cloud that had no silver lining,
We mean as one to make a sun, to bless us with its shining.
So Brothers all, come heed the call, drop politics and party,
And quickly come and join our throng with hands and courage hearty.[29]

LABOR

Walldron Shear, K.L. 1760

San Francisco, Oct. 1882

Labor's noble! Labor's holy!
Type of the eternal cause;
Still achieving, surely, slowly;
Sub-creating without pause.

Labor for our wants or pleasures,
Climbs the mountain, tracks the plain;
Bridges oceans, grasps their treasures;
Fills the fields with golden grain.

Earth, to Labor owes its fullness,
Yielding but with toil and care;
Deserts that were realms of dullness,
Blossom now with verdure fair.

Give the rich their pomp and leisure,
All the joys that wealth can give;
Labor only knows true pleasure;
Earns alone the right to live.

Labor's noble! Labor's holy!
Let the loud hosannas ring:
Land and sea its subjects lowly;
'Tis the only earthly King![30]

A SONG

By Vindex

Air—"Scots Wha Hae wi' Wallace Bled"

Sons whose sires for freedom bled!
Whom Washington and others led!
Prepare to follow in their tread,
And strike for liberty!

Those Rights by them so dearly won
Have gone like snow in summer sun;
Shall we like cowardly serfs give in—
And welcome slavery?

Each day our hearts are filled with dread,
Our wives and children cry for bread—
Our masters give us stones instead
And mock our misery.

Up! "Spread the light" nor longer cower,
Go! Organize our mighty power
Resolve that tyrants shan't devour
The substance of the free!

Our sacred right—freedom of speech,
Is surely passing from our reach;
Great God—What can such lessons teach
But chains and slavery?

Loved land where Jefferson and Paine,
The rights of freedmen did proclaim,
We swear those rights we shall regain—
Our country must be free;

Shades of the great and martyred dead,
Whose blood in every age was shed;
We'll follow where you nobly led—
To death or liberty!

Columbia shouts the battle cry,
With heaving breast and flashing eye,
'Tis "Vox populi vox dei"
Then on to victory![31]

UNITY

Draw near, my weary laborers and listen to my song,

28*Truth*, Oct. 25, 1882.
29Ibid., Dec. 13, 1882.
30Ibid., Oct. 25, 1882.
31Ibid., Mar. 21, 1883.

And in truthful verses I will tell you what is
wrong;
'Tis true there is oppression, which for us means
slavery;
O yes, there is oppression, through our lack of
Unity.

If the oppress'd would join together, in a body
grand and great,
They could nurture human liberty in every land
and state;
They could wipe out all oppression, they could
banish tyranny,
If each would clasp a brother's hand and be in
Unity.

There is discontent among us, there's a war cry
in the air;
The decree in[32] almost written to banish the
millionaire.
For they're the oppressors of this land, and
cause our slavery,
And we can only break our chains by determined Unity.

We'll notify the millionaires when the battle cry
we call;
O yes, we'll notify 'em—with a potent rebel ball.
The money kings have goaded us, and we can
but mutiny;

And we'll abolish the last of them through our
blessed Unity.

We are in want and misery, for they have seized
our land;
Want and suffering are our lot, they dwell on
every hand,
But there must be a home for us, and all men
must be free.
Then, brothers, clasp your fellows' hand, resolved on Unity.[33]

The following were written for the New Haven, Connecticut, assemblies of the Knights of Labor and were published in the *Workmen's Advocate*, the official organ of the New Haven assemblies.

THE REIGN OF LABOR

By C. W. Beckett

Who is Labor, what is she,
That all our hearts proclaim her?
She shall reign and make us free,
Though fools and rogues would shame her,
Who so well our queen could be?

Is not Labor Beauty's foe,
Earth's fairness rudely soiling?
Nay, what loveliness should flow
From forced and gainless toiling?
Give her hope and ye shall know.

Then of Labor let us sing,
That she alone shall rule us,
Friendly knave and brutal king,
They did but rob and fool us.
Lo! their yokes from us we fling![34]

NURSERY RHYMES FOR THE POOR

There was a man in our town
And he was wondrous wise,
He stepped upon a piece of ground
And held it for a rise.

And when he saw the people come,
He said "It's very plain,
I must buy lots of land
To hold for further gain."

There was another man in town
Who was not wondrous wise,
He stepped into a wagon shop
And there his trade he plies.

And when the people swelled the town,
He saw it very plain,
That lots went up and wages down,
Yet did he not complain.

But overworked and bent and gray
He slaved with all his might,
And to his boys would always say
"Whatever is, is right!"[35]

LABOR'S CHORUS

By E. A. Bacon

Air—"Tramp, Tramp, Tramp"

In the labor ranks we stand!
Joining earnest heart and hand,
Seeking those who are in sorrow and distress;
Looking forward to the time,
When the bells of Freedom chime,
Ringing forth the peal of vict'ry and success.

Hail! all hail! O Knights of Labor!
For our cause is true and just;
We are bound to break the chain
That is forging links of pain—
In our strength and wisdom toiling millions
trust.

[32]This is certainly a misprint for *is*.

[33]*Truth*, Jan. 12, 1884.

[34]*Workmen's Advocate*, July 26, 1888. Although it is not indicated, the song was obviously to be sung to the tune of "Who Is Sylvia?"

[35]Ibid., June 20, 1886.

We are workers with a will,
We would in each mind instill
  Noble principles, to form of life a part,
Then the future years shall see
Labor's sons and daughters free,
  While a song of joy thrills ev'ry human heart.

Chorus:

Capital has had the rule,
Used the people as a tool,
  But the time is coming when this wrong shall cease;
For our army it is strong,
It is marching right along
  To the day of righteous settlement and peace.

Chorus:[36]

LABOR'S DEMAND

By Frank I. Fisher

I ask for mine!
No gracious boon do I demand
No largesse from wealth's mighty hand—
But what from earth's reluctant soil
I've won by patient, painful toil!
  By right divine
  I ask for mine!

I ask for mine!
I drove the plow in virgin soil,
My weary feet the furrow trod;
At last I gathered golden grain,
'Twas mine, hard-earned by toil and pain;
  The grain is mine—
  I ask for mine!

I ask for mine!
I carried rock from granite hill,
Laid stone on stone till giant mill
Transformed my grain to tempting food;
'Twas mine, hard earned by sweat and blood;
  The food is mine—
  I ask for mine!

I ask for mine!
I sheared the flock 'neath southern sun
I picked the cotton and I spun
All varied garments that men wear,
From coarsest jeans to satins fair;
  The raiment's mine
  I ask for mine!

I ask for mine!
In dangerous depths of fatal mine
Where light of sun doth never shine,
With pick and blast I gathered hoard
Of precious fuel God had stored;
  The coal is mine—
  I ask for mine!

I ask for mine!
The iron from earth's heart I brought,
With furnace heat the steel I wrought;
I hewed the timbers, laid the steel,
Great highways made for Traffic's wheel;
  The roads are mine—
  I ask for mine!

I ask for mine!
I felled the forest; by the streams
I smoothed and fashioned plank and beam,
All habitations built for men—
The palace grand and hovel-pen;
  The homes are mine—
  I ask for mine!

I ask for mine!
Keep thou thine own; by sweat of brain,
Or sweat of brawn, by toil or pain,
Whatever values thou hast wrought,
Belongs to thee—I ask for naught;
  Yes, keep thou thine—
  I ask for mine!

I ask for mine!
Still robbed by sly and subtle wrong,
Monopoly defiant, strong,
By trick of law, usurping right—
At last I'll conquer by the might
  Of right divine;
  I ask for mine![37]

The following song appeared in the *Labor Leaf*, the official publication of the Detroit assemblies of the Knights of Labor.

THE TOILERS OF MEN

By Patrick Carey

Air—"O'Donnell Aboo"

Swiftly the cause of the toiler is speeding,
  Onward and upward it shoots through the gloom;
On thro' the masts, where tired Labor lies bleeding,
  On thro' the forge and the swift clicking loom;
    On thro' the charnel mine,
    Over the iron line,
On thro' the city, the mountain, and glen
    Speeds the electric wave
    On in wild course to save
God's noblest handiwork, the toilers of men.

All honor to those who have tunneled the mountain,
  Also banded the earth with a girdle of steel;
They are life's heroes, their genius the fountain
  From whence flow the comforts the pampered now
    feel,
    On to their rescue, then,

[36]Ibid., June 27, 1886.
[37]Ibid., Mar. 10, 1888.

You that would dare be men,
Stand by the toiler with purse and with pen,
Theirs is the nation's fight,
Yours is their cause to right,
Freedom is staked on the toilers of men.

Ye who have read the great sermon of Thabor
Relax the fierce struggle, the Master is nigh,
The wealth you've acquired is the outcome of labor,
And wealth is but dross, at the soul's parting sigh,
Cease the fierce conflict, then,
Stewards of God and men;
Flaccid the muscle and aimless the life
Of the proud artisan,
God's noblest type of man
With gaunt hunger starving his children and wife.

The lilies of toil, Cohoes' fairest daughters,
Have buckled the armour of strife in their breast;
Fair as the maidens by Babylon's waters;
Honor their safeguard, and virtue their crest;
True when the order came,
Careless of love or blame;
Principle called; she ne'er wooed them again,
Braved they each scoff and jeer,
Braved they each threat and sneer,
To link their cause with the toilers of men.[38]

The Knights of Labor was an international labor federation, with assemblies in Canada, England, and even Australia. The following was written for the Canadian assemblies.

INDUSTRIAL EMANCIPATION

By George W. Goodwin, Picton, Ontario, Canada

Tune—"Battle Hymn of Union"

God has blessed this land, with plenty for many ages long,
He notes with sadness in His look—the world is going wrong!
He has born[39] with years of waiting, for His justice to be done;
E're he comes to claim His own.

The earth once teemed with blessings, now there are sighs instead of song!
Childhood's laughter has been banished, and men dread the days to come!
There is fear, in every household, and the father's against the son;
God's judgements now are come!

The toilers of our nation, dread to see tomorrow's sun;
For they see in contemplation—all the DUES that will be wrung
By Greed; which treads the wine-press, for the life-blood of the young,
God cannot sanction wrong!

Through hours, of tribulation, my soul has known her woe—
I think of Christ's temptations, and, they were great! I know—
Men should fish, to pay their taxes then; here, it once was so
That Liberty is gone!

We are tied up in the middle; and we are bound, both hands and feet,
The Tariffians played the fiddle, and, they gave us music sweet;
"Protecting Home Industries," they have left us "On the Street!"
Great Caesar! What's to come?

The rulers of our people are a mercenary throng;
Who scoop our mines and timber-lands, and do every form of wrong,
They restrain us by injunctions, and the "Old Coach Rolls Along"—
Heedless of what is to come!

Blow loudly on the bugle that sounds the Reveille;
Arise in marching order! Let us forward to the fray!
The hour of freedom is coming! See! The hosts are under way!
In God's name, marching on.

I sing the emancipation of the toilers of the world!
Their hour of triumph is coming, I can see their flag unfurled;
And Greed and Hate, and Tyranny in ruin shall be hurled!
When God fights for his own![40]

CONVENTION ODE

The general assembly, or national convention, of the Knights of Labor met annually, beginning in 1878, with delegates attending from district, national trades', and local assemblies. At the 1887 general assembly, the following "convention ode" aroused so much enthusiasm that, in response to hundreds of requests, the score of Tom O'Reilly's vocal and instrumental arrangement was published in the *Journal of United Labor.* The ode soon became a feature at every general assembly, which always "ceased its labor" at the close of the session with the singing of this song. Originally published under the title "A Labor Song" in the New York City *Socialist,*

38*Labor Leaf,* June 30, 1886.
39Should be *borne.*
40*Journal of the Knights of Labor,* Sept. 30, 1897.

The Journal of United Labor.

The Official Journal of the Order of the Knights of Labor of America.

VOL. VIII. PHILADELPHIA, OCTOBER 1, 1887. No. 13.

WATCHING.

I watch and wait for thee, love,
Through cold and dreary days;
I think of all thou art to me—
Thy tender, loving ways.

Then hasten to thy home, love,
Where waits a welcome true,
A heart whose every throb, love,
Beats warmly here for you.

I watch and wait for thee, love,
Oh! the bleak and weary day;
No glad light dawns in eastern skies,
When thou art far away.

Then hasten to thy home, love,
The world seems cold and drear,
Keen winter frosts chill summer flowers,
Because thou art not near.

Then hasten to thy home, love,
Where waits a welcome true,
And hearts by absence tried, love,
Beat warmly here for you.

—*Mrs. E. A. Bryant.*

WILL-O'-THE-WISP.

A TALE OF THE WAR.

BY "UNKNOWN."

CHAPTER III.

THE CAPTURE.

It was at the close of a gray winter's day, in the year 1863, when the war was at its fiercest between the North and the South, that a tall and slender man dressed in the dark blue uniform of the Northern soldier, burst from a clump of thick pines on the outskirts of the county town of Upper Marlboro', in Southern Maryland.

He ran hastily across a field and then to a paling inclosing a garden. Placing his hand on the top he leaped over and ran close to the fence in a stooping position. Reaching the kitchen door he at once entered without knocking. An old negro man was at that moment alone in the kitchen, who sprang to his feet and was about to leave as hastily as the rheumatism would allow on seeing the uniform of the Northern soldier. But a laughing voice stopped him as the panting soldier said:

"Uncle Jim, it is I—Will-o'-the-wisp!"

"So 'tis, bress God! But Mars Walter, chile, dis no place for ye; dee soldiers am all 'bout dee town, 'resting ebery body, and is a looking for ye, honey."

"I know that, Uncle Jim. I have been hunted from place to place for two days and nights. Last night I staid in the big oak in the woods with the soldiers right under the tree watching the road for me to pass and talking of me. To-day some false alarm took them away, and I slipped down, traveled by a roundabout route until it grew dark enough to come out. Now, see if any one is in the dining-room; I want to go in; I must see Mrs. Belt and Ella. Uncle Jim, tell them I am here; for I must know if there is any danger in my going in the house."

When Uncle Jim had carefully shut the kitchen door and crossed the yard to the Great House—as the white people's houses were called—Will-o'-the-wisp sat down by the fire and lit his pipe.

His enemies had named him thus, for they could liken him to nothing so much as the *ignis fatuus* seen in the Southern woods; for had they not chased him all over the Southern counties for the last three years? Had they not had him in their sight over and over, only to fail in making a capture? He had come and gone, being seen and disappeared, until he was known as the "Will-o'-the-wisp" by all the soldiers sent out to capture him. Even his friends had begun to call him the "Will-o'-the-wisp," half in fun and derision over the failure of the brag detective, Captain Bigfoot, sent especially from Washington to capture him. Large rewards were offered, and even posted up at the front door of his own family. Dead or alive he was to be captured and brought to Washington.

Will-o'-the-wisp was Captain Walter Bowie, in the famous guerillas of Colonel Mosby, also in the secret service of the Confederacy, but by the then government at Washington called a spy—and a dangerous one, too. He was just the man for such a service.

Splendid physical and mental powers; carefully raised and educated, an athlete in all the sports of the day, riding and leaping, climbing and boxing, he was as much master of the art of fencing as he was at the target, both with gun and pistol. He was full of gay humor, and had songs and stories at his ready tongue's end to guile away the time for friend or foe. Daring and intrepid to a fault, he courted adventure and laughed at danger—this time having been sent on a special secret and dangerous mission—in fact, to Washington to draw the plans of the fortifications, and pick up all the information he could. He was well fitted to do so, as he was a civil engineer, a fine mathematician, and a most excellent draughtsman.

He had remained in Washington and satisfactorily accomplished all he was sent to do, and had nearly reached the Potomac, where was his boat and safety, when he saw from the top of a high hill that his route was cut off by a large body of men.

He turned and galloped to a deep wood. Jumping from his beautiful dark bay horse, he had taken off the bridle and saddle, and hiding them in a clump of bushes, he turned and took the face of his horse in his hands and whispered in his ear, stroking him gently the while. The horse responded to his caresses by rubbing his nose against the face of his master.

"Now go, old fellow, until I whistle," he said out aloud.

And, as if in perfect understanding, the handsome but wearied horse disappeared in the deep thick woods.

Then it was that Captain Bowie made his way to the marshes that he knew so well. For, had he not often, as a boy, with his faithful negro guide, shot over them for miles for birds. And, then, in the last three years, he had traveled those marshes at night, even on horseback to the Potomac, and so escaped his foes, who watched and waited on the highway, believing the marshes to be impassable.

It was now the evening of the second day, and he had traveled far, and only tasted food once at a negro's quarter. He knew the soldiers by some means were close on his track. He had heard them all night in the woods near the town, speaking of him and his wonderful escapes, and saying they believed he was more than mortal man.

Now he was in the kitchen of Mrs. Belt, the mother of his sweetheart. He knew only ladies were at home. All the men had, at the beginning of the war, gone to Virginia. Would the soldiers trace him there? It was a chance. But he was this time completely surrounded. A large force—if he could judge—was out between the town and the river, and were waiting to intercept him. They had camped all along the line. He knew his capture meant death, but he smoked composedly, for the thought was not new to him.

A light step on the threshold and the door opened. A beautiful girl came in quickly and closed the door behind her.

Captain Bowie threw down the pipe and caught her to his heart.

"My Ella!" he whispered, as he kissed her again and again; for separation and danger made this pair very tender.

"Walter," she whispered back, "mamma sent me to say, do not leave the kitchen. The front of the house is surrounded by guards, and in the dining-room Captain Bigfoot has been all day. Somehow they have heard that I am your promised wife. This house will no longer be safe for you to come to."

Captain Bowie looked stern, and his dark blue eyes brightened with indignation.

"No harm must come to you, Ella, and your mother through me. Let me go, dear, the way I came, through the garden."

"You cannot, Walter; see"—pointing to the low window—"the soldiers are down by the fence. Wait until night."

A tap at the door, and then old Jim crept in. His face looked ashy with fear.

"Mars' Walter, Miss Anne say, do not stir. But I bring you something to eat in dis here basket."

And the old man fastened the door with a huge wooden bolt, set the basket upon the table, and at once closed the inside wooden shutters to the two windows.

Ella Belt, who was much agitated, tried to hide her fears; and, like all Southern women at that time, suppressed the aching womanly heart while they helped the brother and lover to do his duty.

She now at once took the things out of the basket, and, spreading a clean white cloth, arranged a nice repast. Then, as the tea-kettle boiled over the glowing coals in the wide open fire, Ella made Will-o'-the-Wisp a delicious cup of coffee.

He was watching her with love in his heart that brimmed the dark blue eyes with tears!

Uncle Jim was up in his room over the kitchen, kneeling on the floor close to the window, watching and praying!

The brave Confederate spy, in face of his danger, ate his supper and drank several cups of the coffee made for him by his darling.

At last Will-o'-the-Wisp rose from the table, and standing by the fire he drew Ella to his side:

"Now, dear, I must go."

"No, Walter; do not think of it yet."

"But this house and the great house will be searched, without doubt."

"Still you cannot leave this kitchen without being seen. Uncle Jim will tell us if anything new occurs."

"Ella, I am afraid that I am in a trap now that I cannot get out of. So I shall entrust you, dearest, with my papers. They must be got over the Potomac, no matter what happens."

While saying this Captain Bowie unfastened his pistol belt, and feeling along the lining soon found a slit, and drew out a flat paper encased in oil skin.

"This is the plan of the fortifications, and this other paper in it contains the knowledge they want in Richmond."

Ella took the papers, and thrusting them in her bosom, promised to get them safely to their destination, no matter what happened.

"If necessary, I will take them myself, dear Walter."

Before he could protest against such a course they heard Uncle Jim tumbling down the narrow stairs. They ran to meet him.

"Up here! dis a way, honey!"

And Captain Bowie bounded up the stairs, two steps at a time.

Ella unbolted the kitchen door; for, without a definite plan, she well knew that her lover could not escape from the kitchen; and that, if the soldiers were coming, it was better to have the door unbolted to avoid suspicion.

She stood irresolute for a few moments, then walked to the door and opened it. There stood a soldier with his musket. She attempted to pass, but he barred the door with his bayonet, and she stepped back and closed it. Then, seeing the remains of the supper on the table, she hastily cleared them away and sat down by the fire.

How her heart did beat with the terrible suspense and fear for her loved one!

Old Jim came down presently, and coming close to her, said:

"Miss Ella, I has hid Mars' Walter in the long box of feathers. Sure, dey cannot find him thar."

"But he will smother, Uncle Jim!"

"Oh! he has breathing place; don't you mind dat. I is now going out to Miss Anne."

"You cannot; a soldier is at the door."

"I taut so, honey. I see dem gwine disway. I will put some wood on dis here fire, den."

And old Jim was busy about the fire, when the door was roughly opened and a dozen or more soldiers came in, headed by Captain Bigfoot, the government detective before the war, and now captain of a troop of horse that was kept to scour Southern Maryland for spies and contraband goods. But Will-o'-the-Wisp had been his especial ambition for three years. He felt his whole future depended upon his capturing him.

They searched the kitchen and the closets; looked up the wide chimney, old Jim muttering:

"Who would be fool 'nuff to go up dar when so much fire an' smoke below?"

But he was not heeded at all. Up the stairs they went until the little room above was crowded. Old Jim's bed was punched on all sides with bayonets and his clothes thrown about, "jes for all de world as if Mars' Walter cud be in de pockets of dem." The box of feathers was reached and looked into, and even hands were pushed into them. As the box was deep and long, and well filled with the white feathers of geese—old Jim's perquisites—no one thought that a man could live at the bottom of the box. But a hole had been cut at the side next to the wall, and low down, the box emptied of feathers on an old quilt, while the Rebel spy, wrapping himself in a large white sheet, got in the box with his mouth close to the hole; and then old Jim covered him deep with the feathers and put the quilt under his bed.

It takes longer to write than it did to do.

The soldiers turned and left the room and the kitchen, and filed back to the house to have another search.

Ella was crouching by the chimney side as far back as she could get out of sight, and with her head in her hands prayed that he might not be found. Then, when she saw them go, and he was still safe, the tears burst from her overburdened heart in streams down her cheeks.

Old Jim clasped his hands and fell on his knees. "Praised be to God!" he whispered.

The stair door creaked and opened.

Will-o'-the-Wisp was in the kitchen.

"Now is my time!" he said. "They will return; I heard them say so. They have positive information this time I am here. I must run for it across the garden to the woods. Open the window, Uncle Jim."

Ella just clasped him around the neck and uttered not a word. It was too late. She saw the determination in his face.

Old Jim did, too. He opened the window and looked out. All was black as pitch.

Captain Bowie put Ella from him gently, went to the window, and leaped out some three or four feet right into the arms of a soldier. And then, before either could recover their balance, a dozen were around them, shouting and firing their pistols in the air to attract the attention of their Colonel, who was in the house.

For the men who had at last caught the "Will-o'-the-wisp" of Southern Maryland were not Captain Bigfoot's, but the men who had been sent to assist Captain Bigfoot—Colonel Hunter's command, and the Colonel was with them. But he was a gentleman and did not fancy the work, and had simply posted his men about, while Captain Bigfoot and his companions searched the premises. They were then at the barn, but hearing the shouts and shots, came running to the scene of action.

Captain Bowie had been seized by a dozen and disarmed, searched and carried into the house, into the dining-room.

Mrs. Belt and Ella, old Uncle Jim and several of the house servants stood in a frightened group.

Colonel Hunter gave his command to saddle up. Captain Bigfoot looked very crest-fallen, and tried to find out how the prisoner was at last caught, but Colonel Hunter would give him no satisfaction.

Captain Bowie remained calm, and even smiled once or twice to some question of Colonel Hunter's.

"We will at once start for Washington. Captain Bowie, are you ready?"

"I am, Colonel."

"Captain Bigfoot, you will remain in this neighborhood and keep order."

Captain Bigfoot did not dare reply; but he was choking with rage. He touched his hat, and, calling his men, withdrew.

Ella then, with her mother, went to Colonel Hunter and begged him to treat her lover with kindness on the way to Washington.

"I will, indeed, Miss Belt. He is an honorable soldier, and as such I regard him. He did me a great service once, and I shall repay it as far as is consistent with my honor."

Ella and her mother bid Captain Bowie a solemn good-bye, and so did the servants. All knew the importance of such an arrest. It meant death!

That night at twelve o'clock saw them in Washington City.

CHAPTER IV.

THE OLD CAPITOL.

Three days after the capture of Captain Bowie and his incarceration in the old Capitol prison, he had been brought before a court-martial and condemned to death.

It was now Monday, and on Friday of that week he was to die! "To be shot in the prison yard at eight in the morning"—so ran the report—"and as a rebel spy."

Well, it was what he had always known would be his fate if caught; it was the rule of war, and he had been captured with the uniform of his enemies on.

But how glad he was he had given his papers into safe hands.

He sat in a narrow room or cell at the end of a long corridor on the top floor of the old Capitol building, that had, since the war, been turned into a prison for the rebels. A small window was closed and barred; a straw pallet and one blanket was in the corner of the room, and he sat on the only stool the room contained, which, indeed, was the only furniture. He still wore the handsome dark-blue uniform, but the gilt buttons had all been cut off. His riding boots and spurs had been taken away, and he was in his stocking-feet, with the coat and vest hanging loosely open. His soldier cap was also missing. But he [illegible]

[Continued on page [illegible].]

THE SONG OF THE PROLETAIRE.

Dedicated to the Wage Workers of the World.

By Tom. O'Reilly.

Copyright, 1887, by TOM. O'REILLY.

NUMEROUS inquiries have been received at the General Secretary's Office asking to what melody the "Convention Ode" was sung at the Richmond Session of the General Assembly. Tom O'Reilly has just prepared and sent us an arrangement of the vocal and instrumental score, and we now present it to the thousands of readers of the JOURNAL OF UNITED LABOR.

Courtesy of Tamiment Library, New York University

May 6, 1876,[41] it was later reprinted by Elizabeth Balch in her article "Songs for Labor" with the title "If We Will, We Can Be Free."[42]

THE SONG OF THE PROLETAIRE
Dedicated to the Wage Workers of the World
By Tom. O'Reilly

Base oppressors! cease your slumbers,
Listen to a people's cry;
Hark? United, countless numbers,
Swell the peal of agony.
So from labor's sons and daughters,
In the depths of misery,
Like the sound of many waters
Comes the cry: "We will be free,"
Comes the cry: "We will be free,"
Comes the cry: "We will be free."

Tyrants *quail!* dawn is breaking,
Dawn of freedom's glorious day;
Mammon *on* his throne is quaking,
Iron bands are giving way.
Statecraft, kingcraft, black oppression
Can not bear our scrutiny,
For we've learned the startling lesson,
That if we will, we can be free,
That if we will, we can be free,
That if we will, we can be free.

By our own, our children's charta,
By the fire within our veins,
By each truth-attesting martyr,
By our tears, our groans and pains,
By our rights by nature given,
By the voice of liberty,
We proclaim before high Heaven,
That we will, we must be free,
That we must, we will be free,
That we must, we will be free.

Winds and waves, the tidings carry,
Electra, in your fiery car,
Winged with lightning, do not tarry,
Bear the news to lands afar.
Bid them sound the thrilling story,
Louder than the thunder's gleam,
That a people ripe for glory,
Are determined to be free,
Are determined to be free,
Are determined to be free.[43]

THE LABOR REFORM SONGSTER

In 1892 the Knights of Labor press published Phillips Thompson's *Labor Reform Songster.* Some of the songs were already in use by the order, while others were especially written for the official songbook. In the introduction to *The Labor Reform Songster*, A.W. Wright, editor of the *Journal of the Knights of Labor*, wrote:

> All movements which have had for their object the uplifting of humanity have been greatly helped by their poets. If it be true that the heart of a nation is dead when its songs are stilled, it is equally true that the vigor, the fervency of any great movement may be accurately measured by the earnestness of its poets and by the enthusiasm with which their songs are welcomed.
>
> It would not be easy to exaggerate the help such a book of songs as this may be to the industrial reform movement. . . . Armed with such songs, we can sing the new gospel of human brotherhood into the hearts of the people.

At the time this was written, the Knights of Labor were in decline as a result of the powerful employers' offensive, lockouts, lost strikes, anti-radicalism on the part of an inept leadership, and internal dissension. But the songs in *The Labor Reform Songster*, along with others already published in Knights of Labor journals throughout the country, remained alive in the waning years of the order, and many were to be sung by workers and their allies long after the Knights of Labor had vanished from the scene.

Except were otherwise indicated, all the following songs published in *The Labor Reform Songster* are by Phillips Thompson.

THE FACTORY SLAVE
Air—" 'Way Down upon the Swanee River"

Toiling amid the smoke and clamor
From morn till night,
Deafened by noise of wheel and hammer
Far from the glad sunlight.
Piling up store of wealth for others
While we grow poor,
Tell me, oh! suffering, toiling brothers,
How long shall this endure?

All my life is full of sorrow,
Welcome seems the grave;
Oh when will freedom's bright to-morrow
Dawn on the factory slave?

[41]The chief variations in the 1876 printing were "Listen to the workers' cry" (st. 1, l. 2), "The brutal bosses' black oppression" (st. 2, l. 5), and "Louder than the thunder's glee" (st. 4, l. 6); the last line of each stanza was not repeated as here.

[42]Balch, "Songs for Labor," p. 411.

[43]*Journal of United Labor*, Oct. 1, 1887.

Often in search of work we wander,
Hungry we pine;
While wealth we earn our masters squander,
Feasting in palace fine.
Hard to behold the pallid faces
Of wife and child,
Stifled in foul and loathsome places,
Thoughts fit to drive me wild.

All my life, etc.

Hard is the lot of honest labor,
Crushed and oppressed;
Where each is taught to rob his neighbor,
Greed steeling every breast.
Each has to freedom, air and earth right,
Such Heaven gave;
Rich men have robbed us of our birthright—
Landless, a man's a slave.

All my life, etc.[44]

THIRTY CENTS A DAY!

Air—"The Faded Coat of Blue".

In a dim-lighted chamber a dying maiden lay,
The tide of her pulses was ebbing fast away;
In the flush of her youth she was worn with toil and care,
And starvation showed its traces on the features once so fair.

No more the work-bell calls the weary one.
Rest, tired wage-slave, in your grave unknown;
Your feet will no more tread life's thorny, rugged way,
They have murdered you by inches upon thirty cents a day!

From earliest childhood she'd toiled to win her bread;
In hunger and rags, oft she wished that she were dead;
She knew naught of life's joys or the pleasures wealth can bring,
Or the glory of the woodland in the merry days of spring.

No more the work-bell, etc.

By the rich she was tempted to eat the bread of shame,
But her mother dear had taught her to value her good name;
Mid want and starvation she waved temptation by,
As she would not sell her honor she in poverty must die.

No more the work-bell, etc.

She cried in her fever: "I pray you let me go,
For my work is yet to finish, I cannot leave it so;
The foreman will curse me and dock my scanty pay,
I am starving amid plenty upon thirty cents a day!"

No more the work-bell, etc.

Too late, Christian ladies! You cannot save her now,
She breathes out her life—see the death-damp on her brow;
Full soon she'll be sleeping beneath the churchyard clay,
While you smile on those who killed her with thirty cents a day.

No more the work-bell, etc.[45]

LONG, LONG AGO

Where is the freedom which once we possessed,
Long, long ago, long, long ago?
Here in this glorious land of the West,
Long, long ago; long ago.
Where is the manhood that once was our pride?
Where is the promise on which we relied?
Was it for this that our ancestors died,
Long, long ago; long ago?

Once men stood equal and scorned to be slaves,
Long, long ago; long, long ago.
Hurling their tyrants to infamous graves,
Long, long ago; long ago.
Now we are trodden and spurned by the few,
Vassals and serfs to the plutocrat crew,
Fled is the spirit our ancestors knew,
Long, long ago; long ago.

Stealthy like wolves have the foul harpy band,
Long, long ago; long, long ago.
Reft us of liberty, money and land,
Long, long ago; long ago.
Land-thief and bond-thief have rushed to the spoil,
Fastened their clutch on our dear native soil,
Robbed us of even the freedom to toil,
Long, long ago; long ago.

Spirit of freedom! who once deigned to dower,
Long, long ago; long, long ago.
Heroes of old with invincible power,
Long, long ago; long ago.
Thrill every heart with the pulse of the free,
Rouse up the nation that yet we may be
Worthy of sires who were guided by thee,
Long, long ago; long ago.[46]

A MAN'S A MAN FOR A' THAT

By Robert Burns

Is there for honest poverty,
That hangs his head, and a' that?
The coward slave we pass him by,
We daur be puir for a' that,

[44]Phillips Thompson, ed., *The Labor Reform Songster* (Philadelphia, 1892).
[45]Ibid.
[46]Ibid.

For a' that, and a' that
Our toils obscure, and a' that;
The rank is but the guinea's stamp,
The man's the goud for a' that.

What though on hamely fare we dine,
Wear hodden-gray an' a' that,
Gie fools their silks and knaves their wine—
A man's a man for a' that,
For a' that and a' that,
Their tinsel show and a' that;
The honest man, though ne'er sae puir,
Is king o' men for a' that.

A king can make a belted knight,
A marquis, duke and a' that;
But an honest man's aboon his might,
Gude faith, he maunna fa' that!
For a' that and a' that,
Their dignities and a' that;
The pith o' sense and pride o' worth
Are higher ranks than a' that.

Then let us pray that come it may,
As come it will for a' that,
That sense and worth, o'er a' the earth,
May bear the gree and a' that.
For a' that and a' that—
It's comin' yet for a' that,
When man to man, the warld o'er,
Shall brithers be for a' that.[47]

UNION ALL ALONG THE LINE

Air—"Just before the Battle, Mother"

The crisis darkly looms before us,
Our chains are being tighter drawn,
The dollar rules the great Republic
And rights of men are laughed to scorn.

If our rights we would recover
We must at the polls combine,
Our only prospect for the future
Is union all along the line.

For long we've put our trust in parties
Whose promises are subtle snares,
They buy and sell the poor like cattle
To pander to the millionaires.

If our rights we would recover, etc.

Make a stand against oppression,
Nor at the feet of Mammon cower,
And let the ballot be our weapon
To make the tyrant feel our power.

If our rights we would recover, etc.

Do not heed the party shouters,
Striving ever to mislead;
Think rather of your wives and children,
The victims of the usurer's greed.

If our rights we would recover, etc.[48]

THE MEN OF AULD LANG SYNE

Air—"Auld Lang Syne"

Should old reformers be forgot
Whose names resplendent shine,
Who stood for right and faltered not
In the days of auld lang syne.

In auld lang syne, my dear,
In auld lang syne,
They lit the spark amid the dark,
In the days of auld lang syne.

Brave pioneers in freedom's cause,
With impulses divine,
Withstood the power of tyrants' laws
In the days of auld lang syne.

In auld lang syne, my dear, etc.

They lit the flame of reason's lamp
And bid its radiance shine,
No despot's wrath the zeal could damp
Of the men of auld lang syne.

In auld lang syne, my dear, etc.

In dungeon deep, on gallows tree,
In battle's foremost line,
They gave their lives for liberty
In the days of auld lang syne.

In auld lang syne, my dear, etc.

Then let the dust where heroes sleep
Be freedom's holiest shrine,
And green the memories will keep
Of the men of auld lang syne.

In auld lang syne, my dear, etc.[49]

STAND FOR THE RIGHT

Air—"Pull for the Shore, Sailor"

Hope for the future, toiler, help is at hand;
Hear ye the battle-cry that rings through the land!
Dark was your pathway, toiler, through the weary night,
Put your trust in union and stand for the right!

Stand for the right, toiler, stand for the right;
Out of the gloomy midnight into the light!
Each for the other striving giant wrongs to fight,
Throw away your selfish aims and stand for the right!

See how the vile oppressor thrives by your pain,
Singly your liberties you strive for in vain;

[47]Ibid. [48]Ibid. [49]Ibid.

Would ye regain your birthright? firmly unite;
Battle with monopoly and stand for the right!

Stand for the right, etc.

Think of your brothers, toiler, downcast and poor;
Help them to war against the ills they endure;
Joined in a common cause there's none can scorn your might,
Rally at the ballot-box and stand for the right!

Stand for the right, etc.

Wrongs done to humblest worker, robbed and oppressed,
Surely will soon or late recoil on the rest;
Union's your only safeguard, join to spread the light,
Banded in one brotherhood and stand for the right!

Stand for the right, etc.[50]

AWAKE! BE FREE!

By H. W. Fulson

Air—"America"

Our country, great and grand,
Is known in every land
As freedom's home.
Yet through man's greed and lust,
Through laws the most unjust,
And from the giant trust,
Great evils come.

Our liberties are gone,
Justice no more is done
To faithful toil.
But want and woeful need
From Mammon's reign proceed,
Which hurtful tumults breed
And freedom spoil.

How long shall we be slaves
And bow to sordid knaves
Who rob the poor?
Let every man awake
And freedom's weapon take,
The yoke of bondage break,
And serve no more.

Great God of Liberty!
Through truth that maketh free,
Make free the land.
Give us to see the light,
Lead us to follow right,
And show that right is might,
By Thine own hand.

Our country then shall be
A home for brave and free
And noble men.
No landlord then shall reign
To clutch the toiler's gain,
Our flag without a stain
Shall wave again.[51]

MARCH! MARCH! MARCH!

Air—"Tramp! Tramp! Tramp!"

In the crowded scenes of toil, in the workshop and the mine
There are those who sigh the weary hours away;
Not a single ray of hope on their wretched lot to shine,
Or the promise of a brighter, better day.

March! March! March! the ranks are forming,
Cheer up, friends, the time has come,
For the toilers of our land now begin to understand
Their just rights to comfort, liberty and home.

Where the earth is fresh and fair, in the seats of power and pride
Sit the favored few who live by labor's pains;
Not a wish is unfulfilled, not a luxury denied,
Though they scorn the toil of which they reap the gains.

March! March! March! etc.

Shall the many evermore be the vassals of the few,
And the landlord and the usurer rob the poor?
If your power you only felt, if your rights you only knew,
Not another day's oppression you'd endure.

March! March! March! etc.

So unite in all your strength and make ready for the fight,
Standing boldly by the cause with heart and hand,
To defy the tyrant foe who has robbed us of our right,
And assert a freeman's title to the land.

March! March! March! etc.[52]

THE MEN WHO WORK

By J. Richardson

Air—"Life on the Ocean Wave"

Hurrah for the men who work,
Whatever their trade may be;
Hurrah for the men who wield the pen,
For those who plow the sea;
And for those who earn their bread
By the sweat of an honest brow;
Hurrah for the men who dig and delve
And they who reap and sow!

Hurrah for the sturdy arm,
Hurrah for the steady will,
Hurrah for the worker's health and strength,

[50]Ibid. [51]Ibid. [52]Ibid.

Hurrah for the worker's skill!
Hurrah for the open heart,
Hurrah for the noble aim,
Hurrah for the loving, quiet home,
Hurrah for an honest name!

Hurrah for the men who strive,
Hurrah for the men who save,
Who sit not down and drink till they drown,
But struggle and breast the wave.
Hurrah for the men on the land
And they who are on the sea;
Hurrah for the men who are bold and brave,
The good, the true and the free![53]

THE GRAND LABOR CAUSE

Air—"Red, White, and Blue"

Oh union's the hope of the toiler,
A pledge of the freedom we crave,
A certain defense from the spoiler,
Who'd rob us from cradle to grave.
When workers stand shoulder to shoulder
And firmly insist on just laws,
Each heart will grow stronger and bolder
To fight for the grand labor cause!

Three cheers for the grand labor cause!
Three cheers for the grand labor cause!
Each heart will grow stronger and bolder
To fight for the grand labor cause!

When wealth seeks to rule through the nation
And crush down the landless and poor,
The ballot's our only salvation
From wrongs grown too great to endure.
A people united in spirit,
Who heed neither scorn nor applause,
Will reap the reward that they merit
In gaining the grand labor cause!

Three cheers, etc.

Then send round the watchword of union,
No more shall dissensions betray,
When banded in closest communion
We move on the tyrants' array.
Bright hopes for the future we'll cherish,
Free soil, equal rights and just laws,
Like a dog may the miscreant perish
Who's false to the grand labor cause!

Three cheers, etc.[54]

THE POWER OF THOUGHT

Air—"Comin' through the Rye"

Not by cannon nor by saber,
Not by flags unfurled,
Shall we win the rights of labor,
Shall we free the world.

Thought is stronger far than weapons,
Who shall stay its course?
It spreads in onward-circling waves
And ever gathers force.

Hopes may fail us, clouds may lower,
Comrades may betray,
Crushed beneath the heel of power
Justice lies to-day.
But every strong and radiant soul,
Whom once the truth makes free,
Shall send a deathless impulse forth
To all eternity.

Words of insight, sympathetic,
Flash from soul to soul,
Of the coming time prophetic,
Freedom's distant goal.
Kindling with one aspiration,
Hearts will feel their thrill,
And iron bands be ropes of sand
Before the people's will.

Right shall rule whene'er we will it,
All the rest is naught;
"Every bullet has its billet,"
So has every thought.
When the people wish for freedom,
None can say them nay,
'Tis slavery of the darkened mind
Alone which stops the way.[55]

MARCHING TO FREEDOM

Air—"Marching through Georgia"

Rouse, ye sons of labor all, and rally in your might!
In the Eastern heavens see the dawning of the light,
Fling our banner to the breeze, make ready for the fight,
Now we are marching to freedom.

Hurrah! Hurrah! we'll sound the jubilee!
Hurrah! Hurrah! the world shall yet be free!
Sweeping all before us like the billows of the sea,
As we go marching to freedom!

Long we sat disconsolate with hope of rescue fled,
Gloomy seemed our path before and dark the clouds overhead,
Now the shadows vanish and our doubts and fears are dead,
Now we are marching to freedom!

Hurrah! Hurrah! etc.

Frowning high before us see the money-despots' hold,
Built to shield the robbers with their piles of hoarded gold,
By the God above us! we'll no more be bought and sold!
Now we are marching to freedom!

53Ibid. 54Ibid. 55Ibid.

Hurrah! Hurrah! etc.

Sound aloud our battle-cry! press onward to the fray!
Right and might are on our side, no more we will delay,
Victory must crown the fight, the world is ours to-day,
Now we are marching to freedom!

Hurrah! Hurrah! etc.[56]

ONE MORE BATTLE TO FIGHT

Air—"One More River to Cross"

The car of progress rolls along,
One more battle to fight;
The voice of the people is growing strong,
One more battle to fight.

One more battle,
One more battle for freedom;
One more battle,
One more battle to fight.

Too long have the poor been bought and sold,
One more battle to fight;
And men bowed down to the shrine of gold,
One more battle to fight.

One more battle, etc.

Too long have the many like me and you,
One more battle to fight;
Enriched with our labor the wealthy few,
One more battle to fight.

One more battle, etc.

The signal sounds from shore to shore,
One more battle to fight;
To manhood rise! Be slaves no more!
One more battle to fight.

One more battle, etc.

We'll teach the world a wiser plan,
One more battle to fight;
When the little rag-baby becomes a man,
One more battle to fight.

One more battle, etc.

No more shall loafers own the soil,
One more battle to fight;
Nor bond-thieves fatten on poor men's toil,
One more battle to fight.

One more battle, etc.

Oppression shall perish and freedom reign,
One more battle to fight;
The people shall come to their own again,
One more battle to fight.

One more battle, etc.[57]

SPREAD THE LIGHT

Air—"Hold the Fort"

Fellow-toilers, pass the watchword!
Would you know your powers?
Spread the light! and we shall conquer,
Then the world is ours.

Spread the light! the world is waiting
For the cheering ray,
Fraught with promise of the glories
Of the coming day.

In the conflict of the ages,
In this thrilling time,
Knowledge is the road to freedom,
Ignorance is crime.

Spread the light, etc.

Wolves and vampires in the darkness
Prey on flesh and blood,
From the radiance of the sunlight
Flee the hellish brood.

Spread the light, etc.

Light alone can save the nations,
Long the spoilers' prey,
Bound and blinded in their prison
Waiting for the day.

Spread the light, etc.

Men who know their rights as freemen
Ne'er to tyrants cower,
Slaves will rise and burst their fetters
When they feel their power.

Spread the light, etc.[58]

IN THE REIGN OF JUSTICE

Air—"In the Sweet By and By"

There's a glorious future in store
When the toil-worn shall rise from the dust,
Then the poor shall be trampled no more
And mankind to each other be just.

In the sweet by and by,
When the spirit of justice shall reign,
By and by.
In the sweet by and by,
When the spirit of justice shall reign.

Then the world with new life shall be blessed,
Oppression shall vanish away,
None shall toil at another's behest
In the light of that glorious day.

56 Ibid. 57 Ibid. 58 Ibid.

In the sweet, etc.

In this weltering chaos of night,
Though the struggle be bitter and long,
Let us still turn our eyes to the light
And gain strength for the battle with wrong.

In the sweet, etc.

In the fullness of time it will come
And our labors the way will prepare,
Though our hearts may be cold in the tomb
Yet our spirits that rapture will share.

In the sweet, etc.[59]

[59]Ibid.

8

The Early American Federation of Labor

FORMATION OF THE AMERICAN FEDERATION OF LABOR

While the Knights of Labor attracted the support of hundreds of thousands of workers in the mid-eighties, an organization was emerging that was destined to outlive the Knights of Labor and practically monopolize the labor scene for half a century. This was the American Federation of Labor. Founded in 1881 as the Federation of Organized Trades and Labor Unions of the United States and Canada, it had its base among the skilled workers of the nation. It was organized along craft lines and sought to build strong and efficient ("businesslike") national unions financially able to carry on strikes, if necessary, and to secure increased wages, shorter hours, and improved working conditions. The early AFL occasionally mentioned the abolition of the wage system and the establishment of a new form of society as one of its objectives, since among its leaders were prominent Socialists like Adolph Strasser, Peter J. McGuire, and Samuel Gompers, who in those days considered himself a Marxist. It was therefore not strange to find the new national labor center adopting the following preamble to its constitution in 1886: "A struggle is going on in the nations of the world between the oppressors and the oppressed of all countries, a struggle between capital and labor, which must grow in intensity from year to year and work disastrous results to the toiling millions of all nations if not combined for mutual protection and benefit.[1] Accepting the class struggle as a focus for action and the strike as labor's most potent weapon, the new labor organization was to rally the nation's workers in many an important battle during its infant and early years. In these struggles, labor songs and ballads once again played their role.

SONGS OF THE NATIONAL AFL

While there are many conflicting views of the AFL, it is generally agreed that the federation did not pay much attention to labor songs. The Industrial Workers of the World (IWW), for example, considered this one of the major distinctions between itself and the AFL. "The A.F. of L. with its over two million members has no songs, no great poetry and prose," the *Industrial Worker*, official organ of the IWW, observed on May 27, 1916. "The I.W.W. has a vast wealth of both rising out of the toil and anguish of the disinherited. Only those who feel strongly and greatly broke into song. . . . Only great movements marking turning points in the history of humanity have produced great songs, appealing to the masses because they voice the inarticulate feelings and aspirations of the masses." Most students of folklore and labor history agree with this statement. Thus John Greenway writes: "The American Federation of Labor, a traditionally peaceful union, is virtually barren in songs which mark its path in the progress of

[1]American Federation of Labor, *Proceedings of the 1886 Convention* (Columbus, Ohio, 1886), pp. 10–11. This preamble was originally adopted by the Federation of Organized Trades and Labor Unions of the United States and Canada in 1881 and was reaffirmed at the 1886 convention, when the name of the organization was changed to the American Federation of Labor.

unionism; on the other hand, the Industrial Workers of the World—the Wobblies—whose active life was comparatively short but turbulent, have contributed many songs to the history of militant labor organization."[2]

The AFL's contribution to the literature of labor songs did not equal that of either the Knights of Labor or the IWW. But it is certainly an exaggeration to speak of the federation as "virtually barren in songs," especially if one considers the formative years of the organization, up to the turn of the twentieth century. In March, 1894, the *American Federationist* was launched as the official organ of the AFL. The second number contained a brief poem in tribute to the seamen's union, and the February, 1895, number featured a labor song.

LABOR CHANT
By Miriam Wheeler

Here, too, as in the old and outworn country,
Herded together, tier on tier, men live,
Though all around the great land, sweet and fertile,
Would give them liberty, for which they grieve.

Yet take heart, lads, unite,
Join your hands for the fight,
Scare away shades of night
With brotherhood and light.

Here, too, as in the sweat shops of foul Europe,
Labor works fettered for a mean reward;
While Capital, with army and policeman,
O'er its stolen treasure stand on guard.

Chorus:

Here, too, as o'er the seas in squalid England,
The homes are poor and dark, the rent is high,
While userers are squandering gains ill gotten,
And far from nature babes and mothers die.

Chorus:

Here, too, as far away in foggy England,
Labor is hoodwinked by a boodle press;
It does not sternly thrust aside its falsehood
And cry for justice, nothing more or less.

Chorus:

Here, too, as in the beating heart of England,
We hail the advent of a glorious dawn,
In the fearless, "love of comrades" brave and manly,
See the promise of a brighter day is born.

Chorus:[3]

Between 1895 and 1898 the *American Federationist* carried no songs, but the January, 1899, issue contained the words and music of the official American Federation of Labor song.

STICK TO YOUR UNION
Dedicated to American Federation of Labor
Words and Music by Thomas H. West

I'll now relate a story, it happened years ago,
And the words a noble father said, which all of
you should know
His son had quit the workshop, with others of
his trade.
They struck against injustice a cut the firm had
made.
His father old and feeble came to meet him at
the door,
And listened to the story that his son related
o'er.
About his shopmates' action and what the firm
had done,
The old man listened to it all and thus spoke to
his son:

Stick to your union lad, don't be a knave.
Show ev'ry tyrant that you won't be a slave.
Obey your aged father, God bless you now, my son,
Stick to your union till the strike is won.

The son was much affected, he grasped his
father's hand.
Said he we are united and justice we demand.
Don't be alarmed about us, we never shall return,
Until the firm restores to us the sum we justly
earn.
The union held a meeting that evening in their
hall,
Each member was determined the union should
not fall.
The old man to the platform by his son was
gently led,
Who 'mid great applause repeated, the words his
father said:

Chorus:

The strike was long and bitter, the men refused
to yield
No traitors were among them as time at length
revealed.
At last the firm relented, and sent for them one
day,

[2]John Greenway, *American Folksongs of Protest* (Philadelphia, 1953), p. 11.
[3]*American Federationist*, I (Feb., 1895), 281.

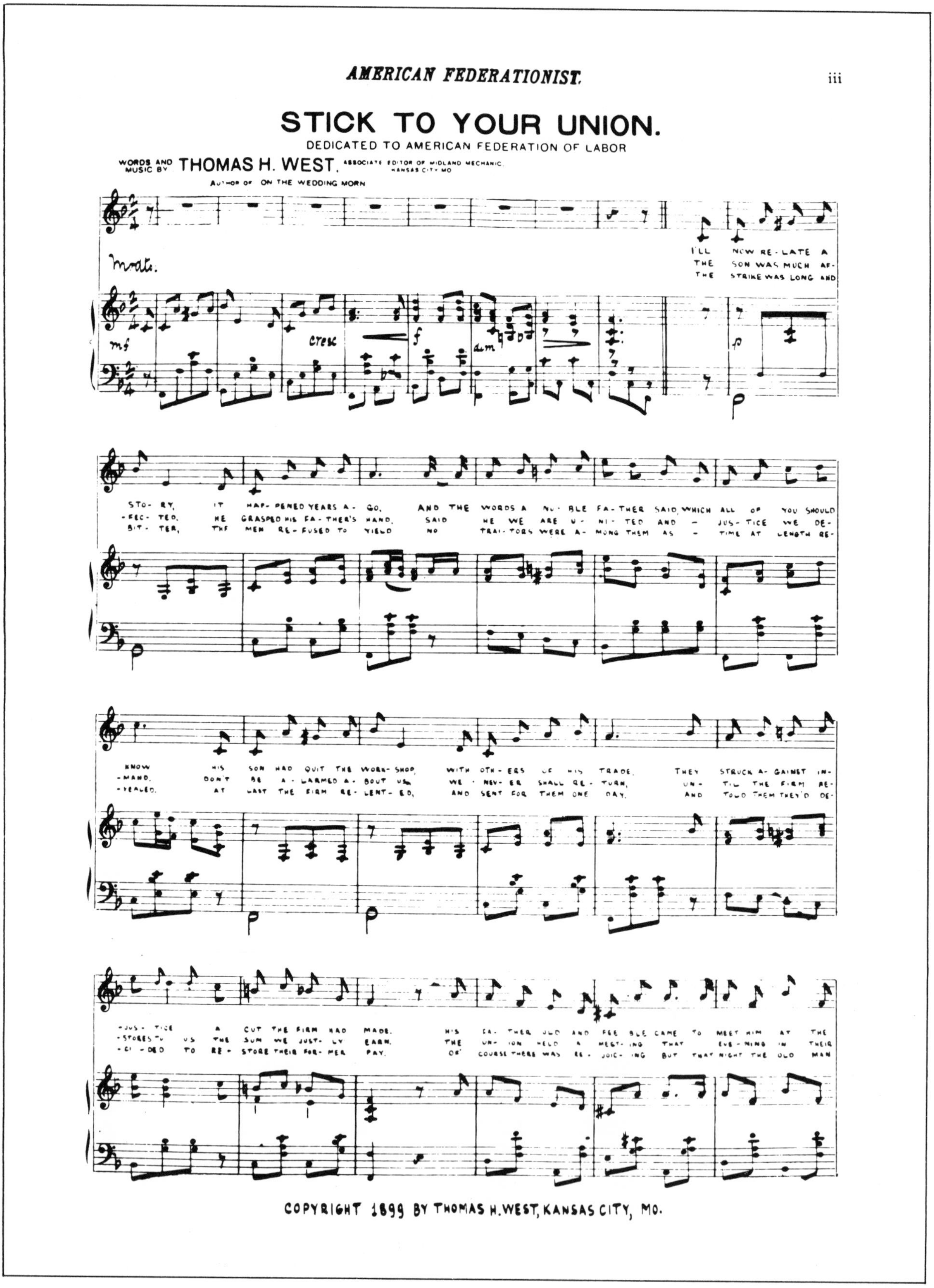
AMERICAN FEDERATIONIST.
iii
STICK TO YOUR UNION.
DEDICATED TO AMERICAN FEDERATION OF LABOR
WORDS AND MUSIC BY THOMAS H. WEST, ASSOCIATE EDITOR OF MIDLAND MECHANIC, KANSAS CITY MO
AUTHOR OF ON THE WEDDING MORN
Mod.to
mf
cresc
f
dim
p
I'LL NOW RE-LATE A STO- RY, IT HAP- PENED YEARS A- GO, AND THE WORDS A NO- BLE FA- THER SAID, WHICH ALL OF YOU SHOULD KNOW HIS SON HAD QUIT THE WORK- SHOP, WITH OTH- ERS OF HIS TRADE, THEY STRUCK A- GAINST IN- -JUS- TICE A CUT THE FIRM HAD MADE. HIS FA- THER OLD AND FEE- BLE CAME TO MEET HIM AT THE
THE SON WAS MUCH AF- -FEC- TED, HE GRASPED HIS FA- THER'S HAND, SAID HE WE ARE U- NI- TED AND - JUS- TICE WE DE- -MAND, DON'T BE A- LARMED A- BOUT US, WE NEV- ER SHALL RE- TURN, UN- TIL THE FIRM RE- -STORES TO US THE SUM WE JUST- LY EARN. THE UN- ION HELD A MEET- ING THAT EVE- NING IN THEIR
THE STRIKE WAS LONG AND BIT- TER, THE MEN RE- FUSED TO YIELD NO TRAI- TORS WERE A- MONG THEM AS - TIME AT LENGTH RE- -VEALED, AT LAST THE FIRM RE- LENT- ED, AND SENT FOR THEM ONE DAY, AND TOLD THEM THEY'D DE- -CI- DED TO RE- STORE THEIR FOR- MER PAY. OF COURSE THERE WAS RE- JOIC- ING BUT THAT NIGHT THE OLD MAN
COPYRIGHT 1899 BY THOMAS H. WEST, KANSAS CITY, MO.

Courtesy of Columbia University Library

And told them they'd decided to restore their
former pay.
Of course there was rejoicing but that night the
old man died,
Their joy was turned to sorrow for he was the
union's pride.
They marched to do him honor in silence to the
grave;
Now inscribed upon his monument, is this advice he gave:

Chorus:[4]

Thomas H. West was also the author of the popular AFL song "Don't Forget the Union Label," composed in the fall of 1900 and dedicated to the Women's International Label League. West announced that he hoped "its rendition will aid in creating a sentiment towards the demand for the union label,"[5] and since the union label was a major organizing weapon of the early AFL, the song became widely known in trade union circles.

DON'T FORGET THE UNION LABEL

Words & Music by Thomas H. West

Copyright 1901 by Thomas H. West, Kansas City, Mo.

Dedicated to the Woman's International
Union Label League

There's a precious little emblem thats familiar to you
all,
It's a tried and true protector, come what may,
And where labor is united in response to duty's call
There this brilliant little star lights up the way
For its mission is to bring about the brotherhood of
man,
There is nothing can your rights so well defend
So help it on with deed and word in ev'ry way you can
Don't forget the union label it's your friend.

It will make improved conditions better homes, a
better wage,
And your aid to its advancement you should lend
It will make your country better, It will brighten
history's page,
Don't forget the union label, it's your friend.

Though apparently so silent yet it speaks thro'out the
land,
For the noble cause it's striving to uphold,
And to free the sweat shop slaves the union label takes a
stand
From their wretchedness and miseries untold
It will educate the people to the evils that exist,
And success will crown its efforts in the end
Help it on it's noble mission it will win if you persist
Don't forget the union label it's your friend.

Chorus:[6]

The union label was popularized by another labor song:

TAKE UP THE UNION LABEL

Take up the Union Label,
Drive out the beastly breed
That keeps part of your earnings
To serve their selfish greed;
Go wait on all your merchants—
Upon the rich and great—
And say the working people
Intend to rule the state.

Take up the Union Label,
And thus do what you can
To lift the poor man's burden
With pure and simple plan;
Veil the threat of terror
That strikes so often bring,
By proving to your merchant
That "Label" now is king.

Take up the Union Label—
Our battles then will cease—
We'll fill the mouths of famine,
And burden change to ease.
The goal for which we're striving,
By Label methods sought,
Will soon relieve oppression
And bring all things to naught.

Take up the Union Label—
Resolve to be its friend;
It lifts the white man's burden;
To strikes 'twill put an end.
The Label is to toilers
A guide for what is true;
So raise its standard higher
In all you have to do.

Take up the Union Label—
Let no deceptive cry
Tempt you through selfish motives
To ignore it when you buy,
There's glory in its friendship,
There's honor, if you choose,
To those who make it duty
All labeled goods to use.

Take up the Union Label—
Ye should not stoop to less

[4]Ibid., V (Jan., 1899), following 230. A note in the original read: "In singing last Chorus, sing 'Stick to your Union 'till the FIGHT is won.' "

[5]*United Mine Workers' Journal*, Dec. 13, 1900.

[6]*Leather Workers' Journal*, IV (1920–21), 340–41.

To lift the poor man's burden
And ease his weariness.
The deeds you do are measured
The souls oppressed plead strong,
Then mark your course with Labels,
And thus avoid all wrong.[7]

On the back of a card published by the AFL announcing a speech by Samuel Gompers, federation president, at a Labor Day picnic, September 3, 1900,[8] were the words of "Labor's Marseillaise." The *American Federationist* of August, 1901, also carried the song, with the notice that the words and music were by Henry J. Sayers, composer of "Ta-ra-ra Boom-de-aye" and "Night Birds Cooing."

LABOR'S MARSEILLAISE

To be Sung at Scenic Park, Labor Day, Sept. 3, 1900

All are invited to join in the chorus.

'Tis no disgrace but virtue grand to earn one's bread,
So laborers, stand up erect!
Make Capital your rights respect!
Show tyrant greed you will not cringe, but fight instead,
God's holy word our just cause does inspire:
"The laborer is worthy of his hire."

Arouse, brave sons of toil,
'Tis time to do and dare!
All foes of honest labor,
We warn you to beware!
Beware! Hark to the swelling strain,
The world it will amaze;
Justice alone that mighty voice can still,
'Tis Labor's Marseillaise, alaise!

Created equal, Rich and Poor, God's children all;
We want our rights, not charity;
No heritage of poverty.
Freemen, oppressed by grasping might, to thee we call,
Unite! Unite! In union there is power;
Let union be your watchword of the hour.

Arouse, brave sons, etc.

No laws shall brand us with the badge of slavery;
We know our rights, we know our pow'rs;
Our battle cry: "8 Working Hours!"
We quarrel not with wealth nor rank, but knavery
That fills the world with wretchedness and woe,
And robs the Poor, that Rich may richer grow.

Arouse, brave sons, etc.

Another Labor Day song popular in the early AFL was published in the *Public*, a Chicago single-tax weekly, September 3, 1904. The reference in the second stanza to unity of labor regardless of race is unusual for the time.

LABOR DAY SONG

Air—American hymn, "Speed Our Republic"

By Mary M'Nabb Johnston

Flag of our Union, so proudly unfurled,
Float Labor's greeting to all the wide world;
From every nation the busy ones come,
Thrilling the air with the trumpet and drum,
Raising Toil's standard aloft in the sky;
Men, brave and loyal, by thousands are found
Marching in triumph on Freedom's fair ground,
Leaders of Labor whom gold cannot buy.

Hush for a moment the hum of the mill,
Let the strong hammer be idle and still;
Stop the great reaper on meadow and plain
While the air trembles with music's wild strain;
Let every list'ner the clear call obey;
This is the time when with one heart and voice
Men of all races clasp hands and rejoice—
Builders of nations, not dreamers are they.

World-honored craftsmen, your weapons of pow'r
Never gleamed brighter than in this great hour;
Never before was the burden you bear
Freighted as now with such deep, solemn care!
Weavers of life's wondrous fabric are you;
Clearly have nations their duty discerned,
Lessons are taught that can ne'er be unlearned—
Justice comes holding a guerdon for you.

Justice eternal! thy searchlight so strong,
Quenchless and deathless must find every wrong;
Sweep from our country the crimes we abhor;

7*Official Journal of the Amalgamated Meat Cutters and Butcher Workmen of North America*, Oct., 1901.

8The first Labor Day parade occurred in New York City on September 5, 1882, when twenty-five thousand workers, representing fifty-three unions, marched through Union Square. Labor Day was made a legal holiday in 1894 when President Grover Cleveland signed the measure passed by Congress. It has long been assumed that Peter J. McGuire, president of the Brotherhood of Carpenters and Joiners and AFL vice-president, was the "Father of Labor Day" and that it was he who sponsored the first Labor Day parade in 1882. However, in the Labor Day issues of the *Paterson* (N.J.) *Morning Call* for 1967 and 1968, Murray Zuckoff established that Matthew Maguire, a machinist from Paterson, was the real father of Labor Day and that it was Matthew Maguire and not Peter J. McGuire who had proposed the idea of a Labor Day parade at the May 8, 1882, meeting of the Central Labor Union of New York City. Among other facts, Zuckoff disclosed that when President Cleveland, who had originally honored Peter J. McGuire, learned that the credit belonged to Matthew Maguire, he sent the Paterson machinist a letter of apology and regret.

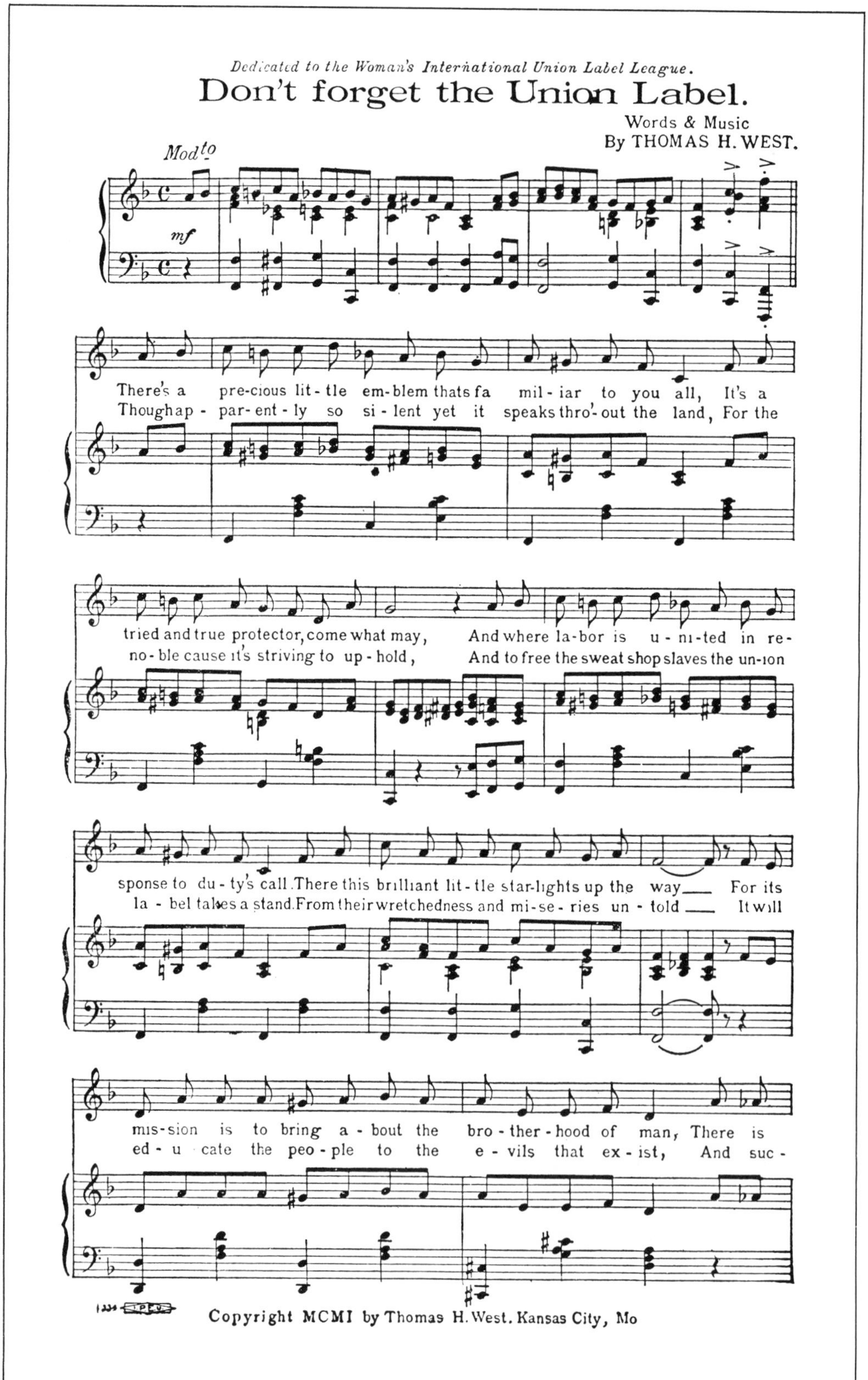
Dedicated to the Woman's International Union Label League.
Don't forget the Union Label.
Words & Music
By THOMAS H. WEST.
Mod^to
mf
There's a pre-cious lit-tle em-blem thats fa mil-iar to you all, It's a
Though ap-par-ent-ly so si-lent yet it speaks thro'-out the land, For the
tried and true protector, come what may, And where la-bor is u-ni-ted in re-
no-ble cause it's striving to up-hold, And to free the sweat shop slaves the un-ion
sponse to du-ty's call. There this brilliant lit-tle star-lights up the way___ For its
la-bel takes a stand. From their wretchedness and mi-se-ries un-told ___ It will
mis-sion is to bring a-bout the bro-ther-hood of man, There is
ed-u-cate the peo-ple to the e-vils that ex-ist, And suc-
Copyright MCMI by Thomas H. West. Kansas City, Mo

Courtesy of Economic and Public Affairs Division, The New York Public Library, Astor, Lenox and Tilden Foundations

WHERE ARE YOU GOING
THIS AFTERNOON?

...I am going to SCENIC PARK...
to hear

SAM GOMPERS

President of the Ameri an Federation of Labor, give an address to the VAST multitude. You are invited to join with us. Come and enjoy yourselves.

PROGRAM OF SPORTS.

1:30 p. m.—Fat Man's race: 100 yards (union men only). 1st prize, $2.00; 2nd, $1.00.

2 p. m.—Boys' race, under 12 years: 100 yards. 1st prize, $2.00; 2nd, $1.00.

2:15 p. m.—Young Ladies' race: 50 yards. 1st prize, $2.00, 2nd, $1.00.

2:30 p. m.—Bicycle race: one mile (union men only). 1st prize, $5.00; 2nd, $2.00; 3rd, years' subscription CITIZEN.

3 p. m.—Tug of War: 3 pulls (union men only). Between C. L. U. and B. T. C. $7.50 to winner, $2.50 to loser.

3:30 p. m.—Base Ball game between C. L. U. and B. T. C. $12 to winner, $6.00 to loser.

3:30 p. m.—Girls' race (under 15 years): 75 yards. 1st prize, $1.50; 2nd, $1.00.

3:45 p. m.—Race, open to all: 100 yards. 1st prize, $2.00, 2nd $1.00; 3rd, years' subscription CITIZEN.

4 p. m.—Married Ladies' race (wives of union men only): 1st prize, $2.00; 2nd, $1.00.

4:30 p. m.—Three-legged race (open to all): 500 yards. 1st prize, $3.00; 2nd, $2.00; 3rd, $1.00.

LABOR'S MARSEILLAISE

**TO BE SUNG AT SCENIC PARK,
LABOR DAY, SEPT. 3, 1900.**

All are invited to join in the chorus.

'Tis no disgrace but virtue grand to earn one's bread,
So laborers, stand up erect!
Make Capital your rights respect!
Show tyrant greed you will not cringe, but fight instead,
God's holy word our just cause does inspire:
"The laborer is w thy of his hire."

CHORUS—Arouse, brave sons of toil,
'Tis time to dó and dare!
All foes of honest labor,
We warn you to beware!
Beware! Hark to the swelling strain,
The world it will amaze;
Justice alone that mighty voice can still,
'Tis Labor's Marseillaise, alaise!

Created equal, Rich and Poor, God's children all;
We want our rights, not charity;
No heritage of poverty.
Freemen, oppressed by grasping might, to thee we call,
Unite! Unite! In union there is power;
Let union be your watchword of the hour.

CHORUS—Arouse, brave sons, etc.

No laws shall brand us with the badge of slavery;
We know our rights, we know our pow'rs;
Our battle cry: "8 Working Hours!"
We quarrel not with wealth nor rank, but knavery
That fills the world with wretchedness and woe,
And robs the Poor, that Rich may richer grow.

CHORUS—Arouse, brave sons, etc.

From Philip S. Foner collection

Cleanse from our banner the black stain of war;
Take slavery's fetter from childhood's frail hand;
Shatter in fragments the throne of misrule;
Send us true pilots in pulpit and school;
Give to the toilers a free, happy land.

The following song, written especially for the American Federation of Labor, was featured at many Labor Day celebrations during the late 1890s.

TO LABOR

By Charlotte Perkins Gilman

Tune—"My Maryland"

Shall you complain who feed the world?
Who clothe the world, who house the world?
Shall you complain who are the world,
Of what the world may do?

As from this hour you use your power,
The world must follow you.
As from this hour you use your power.
The world must follow you.

The world's life hangs on your right hand,
Your strong right hand, your skilled right hand,
You hold the whole world in your hand,
See to it what you do.

Or dark or light, or wrong or right,
The world is made by you,
Or dark or light, or wrong or right.
The world is made by you.

Then rise as you ne'er rose before
Nor hoped before, nor dared before;
And show as ne'er was shown before
The power that lies in you.

Stand all as one, till right is done,
Believe and dare and do;
Stand all as one, till right is done,
Believe and dare and do.[9]

At the 1901 convention of the American Federation of Labor, J. H. Maloney of Scranton, Pennsylvania, read a letter from the Union Publishing Company of Chicago which contained the text of a song "dedicated to Union Labor of America." The letter asked the federation's endorsement of the song, which was to be published by the company with "music in orchestra, brass band and piano."[10] This request was referred to the committee on resolutions, which recommended federation sponsorship of the song, and the sheet music was published in 1901 with a notice of the AFL's endorsement.

THE MARCH OF UNION LABOR

Dedicated to the Labor Unions of America

Arr. by Thos R. Confare

Words and Music by James C. Maloney

The march of union labor should be welcomed ev'ry-where,
From the humble little cottage to the door of the millionaire;
For the science of the universe is made by brain and brawn,
And the wisdom of the unions long ago began to dawn
Upon capital advancing and now in full command;
All we ask for is to show us a kind and generous hand;
For industries of this country demand of you the call,
The march of union labor should be welcomed by you all.

Oh, we'll march, march, march, over these roads of toil and strife,
Many are the hills we'll have to climb.
With capital in front these hills seem high and blunt
But we'll march, march, march all the time.
For the ladies of our land are now joining us hand in hand;
Stronger will they make our unions be.
So should ever our country call we'll see that the Stars and Strips don't fall,
Then the march of union labor will be welcomed by you all.

The march of union labor is progressing ev'ry day,
For the freedom of our country is helping us to smooth the way
So that capital and labor march together hand in hand,
Then there would be great rejoicing all over this glorious land.
And when life's march is ended we'll meet upon that shore,
Then let gratitude and blessing come out from every door,
For the progress of all nations demands this fitting call,
The march of union labor should be welcomed by you all.

Refrain:

SONGS OF AFL-AFFILIATED UNIONS

Quite a few unions affiliated with the AFL had at one time been associated with the Knights of Labor—in some cases they were connected simultaneously with the KL and the AFL—and

9Elizabeth Balch, "Songs for Labor," *Survey*, XXXI (Jan. 3, 1914), 412.

10American Federation of Labor, *Report of Proceedings of the 1901 Convention* (Washington, D.C., 1901), pp. 98–99.

they brought with them into the federation the labor songs they had learned while connected with the order. In addition, their official journals continued, as AFL organs, to feature labor songs. Presented below are songs from the journals of unions affiliated with the AFL—Cigar Makers, Carpenters (English and German branches), Granite Cutters, Bakers, Machinists, and the Sailors' Union of the Pacific.[11]

THE UNIONIST'S SONG

Air—"Marching through Georgia"

Gabriel, blow the clarion and sound the bugle-horn,
Make the starry welkin ring and tremble in the dawn,
Sound it to the nation, and proclaim it to the morn,
While we are joining the union!

Hurrah, hurrah,
We'll evermore be free!
Hurrah, hurrah,
Oh, sound the jubilee!
Our numbers they are swelling like the waves upon the sea,
While we are joining the union!

We're a band of workingmen, and gladly do we sing
Labor is our capital, the union is our king;
If we win the battle we must touch the central spring,
While we are joining the union!

Chorus:

We have built your cities and have garnered in your grain,
Sown the seeds of promise from the mountain to the main,
Your Shylocks[12] shall not rob us of our glory and our gain,
While we are joining the union!

Chorus:

In a joyful chorus let your voices all expand,
Sing it to the music of this great and mighty band,
Now swelling like a torrent and sweeping o'er the land,
While we are joining the union!

Hurrah, hurrah,
We'll ever more be free!
Hurrah, hurrah,
Oh, sound the jubilee!
Our numbers they are swelling like the waves upon the sea,
While we are joining the union![13]

SONG OF THE TOILERS

We build the homes of our masters,
Where always at ease they dwell,
And the sound of music greets them
'Midst the comfort they loved so well;
But we know that their ease is builded
On the hunger and pain we bear,
Their pleasure upon our toiling
Their hope upon our despair.

Then sing of the merry springtide,
Which is sweet to them indeed—
These wealthy whom we are clothing,
Whose little ones we feed;
But to us is the sun but a furnace,
The spring but a scorching hell,
The sky but a burning cauldron,
And life but a prison cell.

But the time will come when the beauties
Of earth shall be for all,
When none on his brother's slavehood
Shall base his freedom from thrall;
When the spring shall bring on gladness
And pleasure instead of pain—
To us who have toiled and sorrowed,
Nor tasted our toiling's gain.[14]

WHEN WORKINGMEN COMBINE

Tune—"Auld Lang Syne"

Shall song and music be forgot
When workingmen combine,
With love united may they not
Have power almost divine?

[11]Songs of the United Mine Workers of America, a leading affiliate of the AFL during this period, are presented in the next chapter.

[12]The frequent use of Shylocks in labor songs of the post–Civil war decades to represent money kings and Wall Street bankers was resented by Jewish workers, but in the songs it never reached such outright anti-Semitism as was indicated in reports of the Democratic convention of 1896, which nominated William Jennings Bryan for president, where the delegates screamed: "Down with gold! Down with the hook-nosed shylocks of Wall Street! Down with the Christ killing gold bugs" (*New York Sun*, Sept. 16, 1896; Edward Flower, "Anti-Semitism in the Free Silver and Populist Movement and the Election of 1896," M.A. thesis, Columbia University, 1952). For other discussions of anti-Semitism and the agrarian movements of the late nineteenth century, see Oscar Handlin, "American Views of the Jew at the Opening of the Twentieth Century," *Publications of the American Jewish Historical Society*, LX (June, 1951), 323–44; Richard Hofstadter, *The Age of Reform* (New York, 1956), pp. 77–81; John Higham, "Anti-Semitism in the Gilded Age: A Reinterpretation," *Mississippi Valley Historical Review*, XLIII (Mar., 1957), 559–78; Norman Pollack, "The Myth of Populist Anti-Semitism," *American Historical Review*, LXVIII (Oct., 1962), 76–80; Walter Nugent, *The Tolerant Populists* (Chicago, 1963).

[13]*Cigar Maker's Official Journal*, Apr. 15, 1882.

[14]*Carpenter*, Oct., 1889.

Shall those who raise the fruits and grain,
 Who feed and clothe the race,
Tramp through the land, and for their pains
 Starve, branded with disgrace?

Shall banks and railroad kings unite
 For base and selfish ends,
And those who labor for the right
 Prove false and not true friends?

Shall idle drones still live like kings
 On labor not their own,
While true men starve, and thieves and rings
 Reap—where they have not sown?

No! by the Powers Eternal, No!
 It must not longer be;
For the Union men are going to show
 That Workingmen are free.[15]

The song was later reprinted under the title "How the Workers Can Be Free" and attributed to William H. Foster. This version had some slight variations:

Shall song and music be forgot
 When workingmen combine?
With love united may they not
 Have power almost divine?
Shall idle drones still live like kings
 On Labor not their own?
Shall true men starve, while thieves and rings
 Reap where they have not sown?

No! by our cause eternal, NO!
 It shall not forever be;
And Union men will ere long show
 How the workers can be free.
No! by our cause eternal, NO!
 It shall not forever be;
And Union men will ere long show
 Now the workers can be free.[16]

HURRAH FOR THE NOBLE "CARPENTER!"
By Karl Reuber, Pittsburgh, Pa.
(Remodeled from an Old Song)

In the cause of Labor,
Working for success,
Learning wisdom's lesson,
Spread great Labor's Press!
Many, led by truth and love,
Chose in *Union* bold to move.

 To the cause of Labor
 Is the place for me,
 There in earnest service,
 Would I ever be,

In the cause of Labor,
Now—in ev'ry hour,
Loving hearts receiving
Help through Union's power—
Haste with joy to preach the word,
Let noble Labor's Press be heard!

 In the cause of Labor, etc.[17]

THE SONG OF THE WORKERS
Edward Willett

I sing the song of the workers, the men with the brawny
  arm,
Who give us our daily bread, and keep us from hunger's
  harm;
Who labor afar in the forest, who leave the fields with
  toil,
Who take no heed of the sunshine and mind not sweat or
  toil.

I sing the song of the workers, who harvest the golden
  grain,
And bind it and thresh it, and sift it, nor care for the
  sting and stain;
Who load it in creaking wagons and stoutly their oxen
  drive,
And bid them good-bye as they go, like the bees flying
  home to the hive.

I sing the song of the workers, the men who struggle and
  strain
Who give us their muscle and nerve, as they guard the
  loaded train;
Who give us their sinew and brain as they watch the
  poisoned steam,
And run the risk of their lives, as they pass the perilous
  stream.

I sing the song of the workers, the men who labor and
  strive,
Who handle for us the honey that comes to the human
  hive;
The patient and tireless worker, with muscles as tough as
  steel,
Who carry the heaviest burdens, and lift, and trundle and
  wheel.

I sing the song of the workers, demanding for every one
His just and rightful due for all the work he has done;
For all the work of the workers, no matter whom or
  where,
To each of the grand result his honest, proportionate
  share.[18]

15Ibid., Aug., 1885. The version which Benjamin M. Lawrence included in his *National Greenback Labor Songster* (New York, 1878), p. 19, had as its next-to-last line "The Greenback boys are bound to show."

16Balch, "Songs for Labor," p. 412.

17*Carpenter,* Sept., 1887.

18Ibid., Mar., 1894.

A LABOR SONG

By M.

From the busy mine and forge, from the mountain and the vale,
From the workers who have toiled thro' the years;
From the pent-up city toilers, from the dwellers in the dale,
Comes a song that shall triumph over fears.
Not alone, but united, in the country of their birth,
They are marching to the birthright of the free;
And the spoiler and the robber of the workers of the earth
Shall be numbered with the things that cease to be.

And the worn and weary mother, the ill-clad, starving child—
Those blots upon the freedom that we boast—
The worker who has hungered while another's wealth has piled,
All those who at our hands deserve the most;
They shall see the morning break thro' the misty clouds of tears,
They shall muster when the banner is unfurled,
And a brighter, better future shall be theirs throughout the years
When "the least of these" shall dominate the world.[19]

LET BROTHERLY LOVE CONTINUE

By A. R. Henderson, Union 19, Detroit, Mich.

There's a place in this world free from trouble and strife,
Which the wise strive their hardest to find,
Where the heart that encounters the sharp thorns of life,
Will meet nought that's harsh or unkind;
Where each tries his best to make joy for the rest,
In sunshine or shadow the same,
Where all who assemble in friendship's behest,
Are brothers in heart and in name.

Let brotherly love continue,
Let the flag of our craft be unfurl'd,
We'll join hand in hand,
While united we stand,
Is the way to get on in this world.

There's a pleasure in life, go wherever we may,
'Tis one of all pleasures the best,
To meet as we travel by night or by day,
One friend that's more true than the rest;
Whose heart beats responsive to friendship and love,
In faith, hope and charity's call,
Who blind to our follies is slow to reprove,
And friendly whate'er may befall.

Let brotherly love, etc.

Then let us my brothers through life's busy scene,
Should sadness or sorrow appear,
Be true to our promise as others have been
And strive this dark pathway to cheer;
Our stay is but short in this valley below,
On all sides we trouble might scan,
Let us help one another wherever we go,
And make hearts as light as we can.

Let brotherly love, etc.[20]

OPENING SONG

Brothers, let us give thanks
To our God, who loves us so much!
Let praise resound
For him who gives us all!
Let's raise our voices
To sing the hymn of thanksgiving!
He is our shelter in life—
His love is our defense.
Brother love unites us
Our aims are so pure
They make this love grow,—
Nothing can be more beautiful, more good,
Brother love we loudly praise
Always be your friend's brother!
When we get beyond the day
No foe of our Order shall we find.

CLOSING SONG

Father up there in the heavenly kingdom;
Receive today again our thanks,
Give strength always to our union of brothers,
So that brother for brother shall faithfully care.

Firmly we stand, firmly we stand,
For justice, for right,
For our brother wherever he may be.
For justice we stand firmly,
For justice, for right
For justice—
Real brothers, united and true.

We always trust your guidance,
You will show us the right path,
And prove our gratitude through our actions!

Chorus:

Now we depart, oh Lord, give your blessings,
To all the brothers in our union!
Stand by us at work and at rest!
And guide us to your heavenly land.

Chorus:[21]

19 Ibid., Aug., 1895.
20 Ibid., Dec., 1896.
21 *Der Carpenter*, Apr., 1889. Trans. Rudi Bass.

Let Brotherly Love Continue.

(SPECIALLY FOR THE CARPENTER.)

There's a place in this world free from troub le and strife, Which the
wise strive their hardest to find, Where the heart that en-count - ers the
sharp thorns of life, Will meet nought that's harsh or unkind; Where each tries his best to make joy for the rest, In
sun-shine or shad - ow the same, Where all who as-sem-ble in
rall.
friend-ship's be-hest, Are broth-ers in heart and in name.
CHORUS.
Let broth-er - ly love con - tin - ue, Let the flag of our craft be unfurl'd, We'll join hand in hand, While u - nit - ed we stand,
Is the way to get on in this world.

There's a pleasure in life, go wherever we may,
'Tis one of all pleasures the best,
To meet as we travel by night or by day,
One friend that's more true than the rest;
Whose heart beats responsive to friendship and love,
In faith, hope and charity's call,
Who blind to our follies is slow to reprove,
And friendly whate'er may befall.
Let brotherly love, etc.

Then let us my brothers through life's busy scene,
Should sadness or sorrow appear,
Be true to our promise as others have been
And strive this dark pathway to cheer,
Our stay is but short in this valley below,
On all sides we trouble might scan,
Let us help one another wherever we go,
And make hearts as light as we can.
Let brotherly love, etc.

A. R. HENDERSON, Union 19 Detroit, Mich.

Carving.

BY A. W. WOODS.

Carving is an art, and until it is mastered, better make no attempt at ornamentation in that line. Nothing sets off a gable so nicely as a well proportioned and handsomely executed piece of carving. On the other hand, nothing so detracts more than an ill-proportioned, poorly executed piece of work.

CENTER

FIG. 1.

It is not my intention to enter into relief carving, as that requires time and patience, as well as a liberal supply of artistic taste on the part of the learner; but to present some ideas as to scroll work that can be cut in with the gouge.

The scrolls should be bold, with graceful sweeping curves, avoiding sharp or irregular bends. The best way to lay out the design is to take a heavy piece of manilla paper, and with a piece of charcoal or chalk, sketch one-half of the general outlines of the design full size, then take a pencil and carefully go over the work, bringing out the smaller details and make such corrections as desired.

Now, take a sharp knife and make a stencil of the scroll.

This being done, we have an excellent pattern, and by placing it on the piece that we wish to carve and by tracing the stencil we have no superfluous lines to avoid in the cutting. By reversing the stencil we have the corresponding half as shown in Fig. 2. Fig. 1 shows one half of a design.

FIG. 2.

Bicycles and Lumber.

ABOUT 6,000,000 FEET OF HARD WOOD USED BY THE MANUFACTURERS OF WHEELS.

THE continuing and growing demand for bicycles has its effect upon the hardwood lumber trade. It is estimated that there will be produced in American factories this year nearly 800,000 bicycles. Practically all these are equipped with wood rims. Each rim requires two and one-half feet board measure, and allowing one-third for waste, that would mean a consumption of 6,000,000 feet, almost exclusively rock elm. This is for the rims alone, to say nothing of the guards and handle bars, but of the latter there is another story. The consumption of 6,000,000 feet or thereabouts of rock elm does not look very large in a business which is accustomed to deal with hundreds of millions, but when it is remembered that only about fifteen per cent. of hard maple is available for rim purposes, and that therefore 40,000,000 feet of one of the minor hardwoods must be handled over in order to obtain this material, the importance of the bicycle demand in this special way will be recognized.

It has had a marked effect upon the market for rock elm. It has increased the price of that portion of the stock from which the rims can be made, has increased the product and consequently has somewhat overburdened the market with lower grades and with nondescript grades; that is to say, this business has involved the picking over of the better part of the rock elm stock to such an extent that the remainder is damaged for the general market. It is a question whether the sometimes fancy prices secured for the bicycle stock have compensated for the injury done the remainder. Those who are interested in the manufacture and handling of rock elm should do some figuring in regard to this matter, and see if their prices have been properly adjusted as between the grades suitable for the different uses.

We spoke above of wooden handle bars: That is to be the next new thing in bicycles, according to authorities on the subject. Wood, principally hickory, perhaps a little ash, is to be used instead of steel tubing, not because of any decrease in weight, as that will remain about the same, but because of the superior elasticity of the wood, making the wheel easier to ride and less fatiguing to the hands and arms. Furthermore, it will be an advantage to the manufacturers, as bent tubing is a difficult article to manufacture, whereas hickory can be easily bent into any desired shape, and then, again, the new bars will be cheaper. There is no prospect of any less number of bicycles being manufactured in the near future than in the present or the past, and perhaps a million bicycles next year may be placed new upon the market. A considerable proportion of them, it is said, perhaps the majority, will have handle bars made of second growth hickory. That is another thing for the hardwood men to take note of.

But the consumption of lumber due to the bicycle trade does not stop with this. There is crating. What that amounts to no one seems to know; but about every bicycle sooner or later is invested with a crate of its own, and this requirement must mean a considerable increase in the consumption of coarse lumber; so though the bicycle is largely a thing of tubing, wire and forgings, it has some influence on the lumber trade, and what does not? The lumber trade is one which is in touch, in some way or other, with almost every branch of industry.—*Timberman.*

Organize! Build Up Your Union!

NOTHING is more important before the workers of this country and the bakers in particular, at the present hour than the work of organizing and solidifying the Unions of their calling.

Neither the gold or silver currency, mono or bimetallism, a protective or a tariff for revenue only, civil service or woman suffrage, neither the success or progress of the Populist, the Socialist or single taxer will do as much to rapidly improve the lot of the workers, than the plain, simple and unpoetic Trade Union in its efforts to promote the reforms in the shop, factory and mine, where the daily tragedy of labor is going on in spite of all the politicians and parties in the land.

The workingman who is unable to exact from his employer through organized effort a better wage and shorter work hours. A man who cannot assert his manhood in shop and home, the two elements nearest his life and his ambitions, can never think of successfully mastering the complicated machinery of political party management or of exercising a controlling influence over the powers of state.

Labor as at present constituted, may now and then, under particularly favorable conditions, exact from the forces of government some more or less valuable concessions, material advances it will not secure through that agency until its economic and its social influence has become vastly greater than it is to-day.

This desirable event, however, will not come through idle bluster, the passage of resolutions, the vituperation of the enemy, the formation of so-called progressive unions or any similar introduction of the methods of a Don Quixote into the modern labor movement. It can only be the result of hard and persistent work in the field of organization and education. Organization of the masses into their Local, their National and finally the great Confederated Union of American Labor, the A. F. of L., the education of the same vast host through the theoretical work of the labor press, the labor speaker, and the labor poet and novelist, and last but not least, through that very best and most successful of all teachers, experience and experiment in the field of practical endeavor.

All of these vast educational and active forces of reform slumber in the organization of labor on Trade Union lines.

It is therefore that we hesitate to follow the siren songs of the crank, the enthusiast and the political bunco steerer who would lead us out of the haven of security on to the high sea of a stormbound voyage that will wreck the great vessel that bears our hopes and aspirations.

It is therefore that we appeal now more fervently than ever to the workers to organize, to stand by their Unions, to extend their usefulness to study the economy of the labor movement and to stand firmly by their Trade Unions.—*The Bakers' Journal.*

THE shorter work day will give the toilers millions of hours of golden opportunities for physical, mental and moral improvement; these, with better homes, better lives, resulting from higher wages, giving an impetus to production and distribution, of industry and commerce, progress and human consideration for each, their rights, duties and happiness, it can receive in no other way.—*American Federationist.*

Courtesy of Tamiment Library, New York University

YOUNG WORKERS' SONG

Welcome to the Bund
To which you have been initiated today,
And of this sacred ceremony,
You must think at all times.

You have given your word—
Here in ours your brothers' hands!
Brother love shall be our shield,
United we are by the bonds of love.

Help the sick, he is poor—
Help your brother in need
Give the sick your compassion,
Stand by your brother unto death.[22]

PEACE SONG

By Karl Reuber, Pittsburg, Pa.

To all hearts, with power and gladness,
Comes a word of magic might;
Dries the tear and heals the sadness,
And with love doth all unite.

Peace! Oh, peace! with joy excelling,
Make in ev'ry heart thy dwelling;
Truth and justice shall prevail—
Freedom's happ'ness let us hail!

Nations in mad wrath contended,
Each arrayed in deadly strife;
Thanks, noble efforts! strife has ended,
Peace again returns to life.

Chorus:

Thee, their crown of life confessing,
All mankind thy praises tell,
Peace! the Christ's long promised blessing,
Truly, come and with us dwell.

Chorus:

Sisters, brothers, let us rejoice!
Onward to noble Brotherhood;
Ho, all unite with heart and voice,
Gladly singing pure and good.

Chorus:[23]

INDUSTRIAL FREEDOM

By S. M. Jones[24]

Tune—"Marching through Georgia"

Sing aloud the tidings that the race will yet be free,
Man to man the wide world o'er will surely brothers be;
Right to work, the right to live, let every one agree,
God freely gives to the people.

Hurrah, hurrah, the truth shall make us free!
Hurrah, hurrah, for dear humanity!
Right to work let all proclaim till men united be,
In God's free gift to the people.

Tell the story over to the young and to the old,
Liberty for every man is better far than gold;
In the sweat of labor eat thy daily bread, we're told,
As God's free gift to the people.

Chorus:

Shorter days for those who toil will make more work for all,
For a shorter workday then we'll sound a trumpet call,
And thus the fruit of labor on all alike will fall,
As God's free gift to the people.

Chorus:

Let us grant to every man the right to have a share
In the things that God has made as free as sun and air;
Let us have free land for all, then free work everywhere
God's gift will be to the people.

Chorus:

With justice done to every one then happy shall we be;
Poverty will disappear, the prisoners will be free;
The right to work, the right to live, the love of liberty—
All God's best gifts to the people.

Chorus:[25]

MAY HIT THE ROAD A WELT YOURSELF

By Brother George A. Roeth

When all the world is jolly, lad, and heart and pulse are gay,
And you're whistling at your banker, sorrow, trouble gang away;
When the lass you love the dearest seems the fairest of earth's queens,
And the future lies before you in a maze of roseate dreams;
When you eye the rest of mankind with that bold, defiant glance,
And you're ripe for fighting, singing, courting or a dance,

22Ibid. Trans Rudi Bass.

23*Granite Cutters' Journal*, Oct., 1898. This song was undoubtedly influenced by the war with Spain, which began in April, 1898, ostensibly to liberate Cuba, and continued with the war against the Filipino fighters for independence.

24Samuel M. "Golden Rule" Jones was the progressive, pro-labor mayor of Toledo, Ohio, who authored a number of songs in support of workers and their struggles.

25*Granite Cutters' Journal*, Apr., 1899. When this piece was printed in the September 7, 1899, issue of the *United Mine Workers' Journal*, without credit to Jones, it carried the title "God's Gift to the People" and the last line "All God's free gifts to the people."

Then some brother of misfortune asks your aid along the way,
Just help him out, for you may welt the road yourself some day.

You may hit the road a welt yourself some day,
So never turn your fellow-man away;
Misfortune lies in wait, it may catch you soon or late.
You may hit the road a welt yourself some day.

The time may come to you, my man—none can foretell the day—
When home and friends and those you love are far, oh, far away,
And there's not a job around you that's half level or half right,
Whilst your better and worst natures have a knock down, drag out fight;
When friends and coin and other things are, oh, so sadly few,
And you ask yourself the question, "What the devil shall I do?"
When box cars, barns and shining rails stretch thousand miles away,
You'll say, "My God! It's tough, for I must welt the road to-day."[26]

1900—THE BUGLES

By Brother George A. Roeth, the Granite Cutter Poet

Steady along the line, boys! Brush up there to the right!
Watch your centre; close your ranks; get ready for the fight.
Somewhere over in yonder meadow I hear the bugles play;
Up and down go the rollicking notes and this is what the bugles say:

Be true, men! For you, then, melodiously we'll play
The sweetest notes from the bugles' throats you've heard in many a day;
Now loud and clear—like the pibrock calling—We'll toss our notes to the breeze;
Then, tenderer than a lover's song, we'll lute soft lays ease.

Men of the West, what say you to the bugles' ringing notes?
What say you, men of the East, to the music of their throats?
Shall the bugles' notes sob for you in defeat and despair?
Or shall they rise triumphantly upon the morning air?

If you, men, are true; then, oh, far across the seas
To the toilers of the olden world we'll wing upon the breeze
The story of your truth and your manhood, the light of new-born day;
The beacon that gilds the rose that heights which beckon along the way.[27]

THE FUTURE "AMERICA"

By H. C. Dodge

My country 'tis of thee
Land of lost Liberty,
Of thee we sing,
Land which the millionaires,
Who govern our affairs,
Own for themselves and heirs—
Hail to thy king.

Land once of noble braves
But now of wretched slaves—
Alas! too late
We saw sweet Freedom die,
From letting bribers high
Our unprized suffrage buy!
And mourn thy fate.

Land where the wealthy few
Can make the many do
Their royal will,
And tax for selfish greed
Thy toilers till they bleed,
And those not yet weak-kneed
Crash down and kill.

Land where a rogue is raised
On high and loudly praised
For worst of crimes
Of which the end, must be
A hell of cruelty,
As proved by history
Of ancient times.

My country, 'tis of thee,
Betrayed by bribery,
Of thee we sing.
We might have saved thee long
Had we, when proud and strong,
Put down the cursed wrong
That makes a king.[28]

BALLAD OF THE SHOP GIRL

By Ernest McGaffey

"The wolf of poverty follows me on
Through the dingy streets of town;
So close beside that his shaggy hide
Might almost brush my gown;
And after him thrust, the wolves of lust
Come, eager to drag me down.

26 *Granite Cutters' Journal*, May, 1899.

27 Ibid., June, 1899.

28 *Bakers' Journal*, Mar. 23, 1889. Two years later the song reappeared, without author credit, in Leopold Vincent, comp., *The Alliance and Labor Songster* (Winfield, Kans., 1891); there, line 6 of stanza 2 reads "Our unpriced suffrage buy," and the last line of stanza 3 reads "Crush down and kill."

No. 2. The Future America.
1. My coun - try, 'tis of Thee, Land of lost Lib - er - ty,
2. Land once of no - ble braves, But now of wretch - ed slaves.
3. Land where the wealth - y few Can make the ma - ny do
4. Land where a rogue is raised On high, and loud - ly praised
5. My coun - try, 'tis of Thee, Be - trayed by brib - er - y,
Of Thee we sing. Land which the Mill - ion-aires, Who gov - ern
A - las! too late! We saw sweet Free - dom die, From let - ting
Their roy - al will, And tax for sel - fish greed The toil - ers
For worst of crimes; Of which the end must be A hell of
Of Thee we sing. We might have saved Thee long Had we, when
our af-fairs, Own for them-selves and heirs, Hail, to thy King.
brib - ers, high, Our unpriced suff - rage buy, And mourn thy fate.
till they bleed; And those not yet weak-kneed, Crush down and kill.
cru - el - ty, As proved by his - to - ry Of an-cient times.
proud and strong, Put down the curs - ed wrong That makes a king.

From Leopold Vincent, comp., *The Alliance and Labor Songster* (Winfield, Kans., 1891). Courtesy of Brown University Library.

"And the body and soul have a scanty dole
From the pittance that I earn;
And cold as the breath of the wind of death
Are the lessons that I learn;
With a pitfall dug for my weary feet
And a trap at every turn.

"And ever a tempter is near at hand
To lure with a Judas-kiss;
And lead me away, if be led I may,
To the depths of that black abyss,
Where, in serpent guise, old memories rise
And over the fallen hiss."

* * *

"And the Christ that the Bible teaches of
For only men did die;
Or he also would heed in this dreadful need
My bitter, despairing cry;
And the creeds alway for the heathen pray
And the Christians pass me by.

"And many and fast the days whirl past
While early I work and late;
And around my path for the aftermath
The basllisk[29] watchers wait;
And civilization bids me choose
The grave or a harlot's fate."

* * *

"And I dread the light of to-morrow's dawn
And the weight of future years;
My life is blurred by a hope deferred
And my heart is numb with fears;
And my hands that rise to the sullen skies
Are wet with a woman's tears.

"Alone I walk where the specters stalk
In the roar of the mighty town.
Oh! God, for a Knight to aid my flight,
Of high and of pure renown;
Is there never a man to lift me up
Where myriads drag me down?"[30]

Songs of Labor

THE FACTORY GIRL

By J. A. Phillips

She wasn't the least bit pretty,
And only the least bit gay,
And she walked with a firm, elastic tread,
In a business kind of way;

Her dress was of coarse, brown woolen,
Plainly but neatly made,
Trimmed with some common ribbon,
And a hat with a broken feather,
And a shawl of modest plaid.

Her face was worn and weary,
And traced with lines of care,
As her nut brown tresses blew aside
In the keen December air;
Yet she was not old, scarcely twenty,
And her form was full and sleek,
But her heavy eye and tired step
Seemed of wearisome toil to speak
She worked as a common factory girl
For two dollars and a half a week.

Ten hours a day of labor,
In a close, ill-lighted room,
Machinery's buzz for music,
Waste gas for sweet perfume;
Hot, stifling vapors in summer,
Chill drafts on a winter's day,
No pause for rest or pleasure
On pain of being sent away;
So ran her civilized serfdom—
FOUR CENTS an hour the pay!

"A fair day's work," say the masters,
And "a fair day's pay" say the men;
There's a strike—a raise in wages,
What effect on the poor girl then?
A harder struggle than ever
The honest path to keep,
And to sink a little lower—
Some humbler home to seek,
For rates are higher—her wages
Two dollars and a half per week.

A man gets thrice the money—
But then a "man's a man,
And a woman surely can't expect
To earn as much as he can."
Of his hire the laborer's worthy,
Be the laborer who it may;
If a woman do a man's full work.
She should have a man's full pay,
Not to be left to starve—or sin
On forty cents a day.

Two dollars and a half to live on,
Or starve on, if you will,
Two dollars and a half to dress on,
And a hungry mouth to fill;
Two dollars and a half to lodge on
In some wretched hole or den,
Where crowds are huddled together—
Girls and women and men;
If she sins to escape her bondage
Is there room for wonder then?[31]

29Should be *basilisk.*

30*Bakers' Journal,* May 31, 1900.

31*Machinists' Monthly Journal,* Sept., 1895, p. 346.

THE DAWN OF A NEW DAY

By Ella Wheeler Wilcox

All hail the dawn of a new day breaking,
When a strong armed nation shall take away
The weary burdens from backs that are aching
With maximum labor and minimum pay;
When no man is honored who hoards his millions,
When no man feasts on another's toil,
And all poor suffering, striving billions
Shall share the riches of sun and soil.

There is gold for all in earth's broad bosom,
There is food for all in the land's great store,
Enough is provided if rightly divided;
Let each man take what he needs—no more.
Shame on the miser with unused riches,
Who robs the toiler to swell his hoard,
Who beats down the wages of the digger of ditches,
And steals the bread from the poor man's board.

Shame on the owner of mines, whose cruel
And selfish measures have brought him wealth,
While the ragged wretches who dig his fuel
Are robbed of comfort and hope and health,
Shame on the ruler who rides in his carriage
Bought with the labor of half-paid men—
Men who are shut out of home and marriage,
And are herded like sheep in a hovel pen.

Let the clarion voice of the nation wake him
To broader vision and fairer play,
Or let the hand of a just law shake him
Till his ill-gained dollars shall roll away,
Let no man dwell under a mountain of plunder,
Let no man suffer with want or cold;
We want right living, not mere alms-giving,
We want just dividing of labor and gold.[32]

THE SAILOR'S FAREWELL TO THE SEA

By T. Wells

Ye sing us the song of the wide, rolling sea,
Or the heroes whose fame on it rang;
Ye sing us the song that would lure us again—
'Tis the song that the Siren sang.

Come, tell us what sentiment speaks in the Flag
That in Liberty's conquests we bore,
Ah! its stars and stripes are but symbols to mark
A freedom that ends on the shore.

And was it for this that we gave up our blood
At the young nation's earliest call—
That your sons on the land should forever be free,
And your sons on the sea be thrall?

Lord, give us the voice of the loud sounding gale,
And the sting of the lightning's fierce flame,
For a sign that the heroes of Ocean still live
And share in the seaman's black shame.

So, call us away to the drylands afar,
From the sound of the wild moaning wave,
And let the sea court the poor spiritless one
Who is fit for the badge of a slave.

No more may the sound of the ocean's deep roar
Inspire us with Freedom's proud thrill,
Nor her voice lure the brave to her treacherous breast—
And the song of the Siren be still.[33]

THE LOG OF THE LOST

By Thomas H. Mathias

A thousand miles to east, a thousand miles to west,
A thousand miles to north and south, out on the ocean's breast!
I ain't no navigator, but as near as I can tell
That's about our ship's position in the latitoode of hell!

Three months ago we set our kites, and with a spankin' breeze
We left the Hook behind us as we scattered o'er the seas
With bran' new pots and pannikins from Split-Nose Dunn's bazaar,
And gum boots out o' Baxter street we got from Paddy Marr.

We cut a purty figger when all hands wuz mustered aft
To hear the "riot act" read out beneath the mainsail's draught,
An' we wuz given to understand that if we'd civil be
No other ship flew buntin' that would be as good as we.

Yes. 'twuz the same old story; we had heard it lots before;
For ships, you know, is always good a week or two off shore.
But when we got well round the Horn, 'bout 30° from the line.
Of eighteen men that left the Hook we only boasted nine!

First, Brock and Scot, one dirty night went out to furl the jibs.
When a sheet-block struck poor Brock a whack that stove the beggar's ribs;
And Scot tried hard to grab him as beneath the boom he fell—
When he, too, missed the foot-rope and went head-long in the swell.

No use o' shoutin' 'gainst the wind when its unearthly sound
Just shrieked a requiem over the beneath our forefoot drowned.
They lost the number of their mess, but not much better we,

32 *Coast Seamen's Journal,* Oct. 28, 1896.
33 Ibid., July 7, 1897.

As later on the scurvy took away another three.

An' growlin' seemed to do no good, the grub wuz not aboard
To give the sick men nourishment, no matter how we roared;
'Twuz sartin some one wuz to blame for grub a-bein' scarce,
Or else the Act o' Congress is a damned an' blasted farce!

Then discontent began to reign when health and strength wuz gone,
An' no one gave a tinker's if the voyage it wuz done,
For there wuz we, short-handed, an' to get around the Horn
Wuz the most one-sided argument I'd known sence I wuz born.

We got a taste in misty south that rattled up our bones,
An' four more hands that left the Hook was sent to Davy Jones;
Too weak to grab a bucket, an' too sick to skin a sail,
They damned the hooker as they fell, and falling cleared the rail!

An' when the storms had done their worst, a purty sight wuz we—
A big two-thousand tonner founderin' round upon the sea
An' such of us as now is left, the horrid tale to tell,
'ill not dispute there's Heaven after having lived in Hell![34]

[34]Ibid., Mar. 14, 1900.

9
The Miners

COAL-MINING CONDITIONS

Deep beneath the firm set earth
Where volcanoes have their birth,
Where, engraved on leaves of stone,
Are pictured ages past and gone;
Far from God's own blessed light,
There the miner toils in night!
Tenant of the depths below,
Working with the pick and crow.

Not for him the painted mead,
Sacrificed to serve man's need;
Not for him the sweet perfume,
Of flowers in this spring-tide bloom;
From life's early morn a slave,
Earth to him a living grave.

First, on father tending well,
Next, a youthful sentinel;
Careful, watching day by day
Close to keep his guarded way;
When his lamp with fitful blaze,
Tells of "choke-damp" in the ways;
Or when flickering it proclaims
Gas is oozing from the veins;
To be diligent on guard,
And, with care, keep watch and ward!
Tracer next, a human soul
Harnessed to a car of coal;
Last, a miner bold and brave
Kin to Christ, but mammon's slave!

Look upon him as he stands
Picking coal with grimy hands,
Think, in all this world of strife,
Not for him the joys of life. . . .

Thus did Robert W. Hume describe the life of the coal miner in his poem "The Miner," frequently published in the labor press of the sixties, seventies, and eighties.[1]

The tyranny of the corporations in American industrial society was felt by every worker, but it is doubtful any felt it as much as the coal miners. Their wages had fallen drastically after the Civil War, and the downward trend continued. Then there was the "truck system," which forced them to buy at company stores where they were charged exorbitant prices for shoddy goods. Excessive rents for company houses and high rates for the oil and powder they were compelled to buy from the operators added to their discontent. Worst of all were the abominable conditions under which the miner worked. Knee deep in water, his head and body drenched by seepage, his vision obscured by thick clouds of powder smoke and coal dust, the miner toiled in the most dangerous occupation in the nation, constantly risking bodily injury or death.

When a miner left in the morning dark for the mine, neither he nor his wife nor his children knew if they would ever see him again. In

[1] There are two versions of Hume's poem. The first, originally published in the *Boston Daily Evening Voice* of January 12, 1867, has the same first eight lines as appear above but continues differently. The version above was published in *Truth* (San Francisco) of February 14, 1883, preceded by the comment: "The problem presented to the present age, is not by means of a barbaric money system to provide ways and means by which schemers can live on the labors of others, while themselves leading a life of uselessness, but to improve the condition of the useful workers who contribute their labor to the requirements of modern civilization. The following poem treats of the care that society owes to a most important class of such workers. . . ." Both versions of Hume's poem were headed: "Am I my brother's keeper? Genesis, Chap. 4, Ver. 9."

Schuylkill County, Pennsylvania, alone, 566 miners were killed and 1,655 seriously injured over a seven-year period; in a single year, 1871, 112 miners of that county were killed and 339 badly injured. Robert W. Hume's "Labor Lyrics—No. 6" dealt with one such accident.

Labor Lyrics—No. 6
By Robert W. Hume
ONE DAWSON

"Yea, though I walk through the valley of the shadow of death, I will fear no evil; for thou art with me; thy rod and thy staff they comfort me."—Psalm 23:ver. 4.

'Twas at Barnsley—Wednesday morn;
Fated never to return,

Never more to see the sky,
Hundreds left their homes to die.

Down into the pit they went,
On their daily labors bent;

But, ere few short hours had passed,
Flashed the fatal lightning blast;

Then deep beneath the groaning ground
Was heard the rushing thunder sound.

And, rolling from the blasted pit,
A murky flag waved over it.

Ah! then were heard fell shrieks of woe,
For those brave hearts entombed below;

And mothers, wives and fathers strain,
The entrance of the pit, to gain.

But the black and pitchy stith*
Forbids them e'en to gaze beneath;

And in that hot and fetid air
None yet to face the danger dare;

Though soon a volunteering band
Round the pit's mouth sadly stand;

Down they go—away! away!
From the sight of men—and day.

Twice they strive—but twice in vain,
The fire damp drives them back again.

Nought of pity do they move,
Jeered with taunts by those above;

Utter misery and woe
E'en to friends no mercy show.

Now seven more of note and mark
Dive beneath the treacherous dark.

Hark! again—the shafts resound
And thunder shakes that trembling ground;

The smoky flag again does wave
In triumph o'er those heroes brave.

Behold their friends with horror dumb;
(There's not a cry to cheer the gloom;)

Still hanging round the seething pit,
But none so bold to enter it;

Until one Dawson treads alone,
The fearful path the rest have gone.

None to cheer him in his deed,
None to help him in his need;

Dove of Hope to those beneath,
Pilot in the Gulf of Death!

Mercy's last and only stay,
Aid him, angels, on his way!

In vain. Again the fearful roar
Proclaims the miner's toils are o'er.

Then far resounds the fearful cry
Of deep and hopeless agony.

And one by one—the young—or grey,
By danger daunted, turn away;

With downcast eyes and brows of gloom,
Nor dare descend to Dawson's tomb.

For that black pit henceforth is meant
To stand for Dawson's monument.

But far its most enduring part,
Its inscript on each miner's heart.

And, long beside the cottage-fire,
To prattling child the aged sire,

Shall oft, with awe and wonder tell,
How Dawson dared, and where he fell.

Farewell, brave heart! You cannot die—
Fate could not kill such bravery.

Your dauntless courage, and your faith,
And constancy have conquered death!

And your bold deed with praise will rise
'Till virtue fades—and valor dies![2]

*Stith—A miner's term for thick smoke.

A writer noted in the *New York Herald* of June 22, 1877: "No part of the world ever presented so favorable an opportunity as the coal regions for the rich to oppress the poor workingman. In many instances the opportunity was not neglected. The rapacity, extortion and

[2]*Boston Daily Evening Voice*, Jan. 14, 1867.

CHANTS OF LABOUR

No. 25. Song of the Miners.

Words by W. H. UTLEY. Air—*Husarenlied.*

We dig and delve in the dark-some mine, With a flick-'ring can-dle
Air & Accompt.
near;......... We delve and dig 'mid the dust and grime, In the
long black gal-ler-ies drear. And a-bove in the air in his
car-riage and pair The proud lord rolls a-long;......... He
spends our gold, for our strength is sold To him thro' in-jus-tice and

CHANTS OF LABOUR

wrong— To him thro' in - jus - tice and wrong.

2.

We toil and moil while o'er naked limbs
  The water trickles and glides;
We moil and toil till our life nought seems
  Save a woe that on earth long abides.
And above heaven rings, as the blithe lark sings,
  But our children moan and weep,
For the rich man takes what each miner makes
  In the pit so dark and deep—
  In the pit so dark and deep.

3.

We hew and hammer, each stroke of the pick
  Makes fuel for furnace and hearth;
We hammer and hew that iron made quick
  May run to the ends of the earth.
And our brothers in toil who delve in the soil,
  Or work 'mid the factory's roar,
Like us are all bound to toil the year round,
  While the rich cry ever for more—
  While the rich cry ever for more.

4.

But we live and we love, and our tyrants shall learn
  We are men with passions and might;
We love and we live, and our rough hearts yearn
  For the day that shall follow our night:
When we'll live joyous lives with our children and wives,
  No longer debased by our toil,
When each man shall take what each man shall make
  In the pit, the mill, or the soil—
  In the pit, the mill, or the soil.

Courtesy of Brown University Library

refusal to pay the laborer his just wages are still remembered . . . [and] still exist. Any attempt on the part of the workers to ameliorate their conditions was at all hazards immediately crushed. Those who took a prominent part in such movements . . . were 'marked,' 'black-listed.' "

EARLY SONGS AND BALLADS OF THE COAL MINERS

In their struggles to change the feudal conditions under which they were forced to work and live, coal miners made regular use of songs and ballads, producing the largest number of these forms of expression of any labor group in this country. Five nationalities—the Welsh, English, German, Irish, and Scots—composed the anthracite industry's laboring force. The Welsh and German immigrants who came to the mines of America in the forties and fifties brought with them a rich musical tradition. The most popular song of the British miners (also sung in the United States) went:

SONG OF THE MINERS

Words by W. H. Utley
Air—"Husarenlied"

We dig and delve in the darksome mine,
With a flick'ring candle near;
We delve and dig 'mid the dust and grime,
In the long black galleries drear.
And above in the air in his carriage and pair
The proud lord rolls along;
He spends our gold, for our strength is sold
To him thro' injustice and wrong—
To him thro' injustice and wrong.

We toil and moil while o'er naked limbs
The water trickles and glides;
We moil and toil till our life nought seems
Save a woe that on earth long abides.
And above heaven rings, as the blithe lark sings,
But our children moan and weep,
For the rich man takes what each miner makes
In the pit so dark and deep—
In the pit so dark and deep.

We hew and hammer, each stroke of the pick
Makes fuel for furnace and hearth;
We hammer and hew that iron made quick
May run to the ends of the earth.
And our brothers in toil who delve in the soil,
Or work 'mid the factory's roar,
Like us are all bound to toil the year round,
While the rich cry ever for more—
While the rich cry ever for more.

But we live and we love, and our tyrants shall learn
We are men with passions and might;
We love and we live, and our rough hearts yearn
For the day that shall follow our night:
When we'll live joyous lives with our children and wives,
No longer debased by our toil,
When each man shall take what each man shall make
In the pit, the mill, or the soil—
In the pit, the mill, or the soil.[3]

The thousands of Irish who fled famine and British oppression and found their way to Schuylkill County in the post–Civil War years had nothing comparable to the musical traditions of the Welsh and German miners. But they developed a song tradition as they worked in water up to their knees, fearful that at any moment the rotting timbers would crack under the weight of sliding tons of falling coal, or as they relaxed in the miserable little company-owned shacks in which they and their families were forced to live.

Much of the repertoire of the coal miners has been carefully collected and studied by the late George C. Korson and published in his books *Songs and Ballads of the Anthracite Miner*, *Minstrels of the Mine Patch*, and *Coal Dust on the Fiddle*. Many of the songs and ballads Korson collected as he made the rounds of the coal fields in the 1930s and 1940s dealt with the hard times and disasters which were an integral part of the miners' lives and with the repeated—often unsuccessful—efforts to organize and improve their living standards and working conditions. He also found tunes and humorous ditties, which, though not protest songs, were just as vital a part of the musical tradition of the miners. The present chapter, however, reproduces only those songs and ballads which relate directly to the conditions under which the miners worked and lived and to the efforts to change them through unionization and strikes.

The history of unionism among coal miners in the United States began in 1849 when an English miner, John Bates, who had been active in the British Chartist movement, formed the first American miners' union in Schuylkill County. The Bates union held its first and last strike in

[3]Edward Carpenter, *Chants of Labour* (London, 1891), pp. 40–41.

1849 and was dead by the middle of 1850. In 1861 the American Miners' Association, an industrial union which included all who worked in the mines, was founded by Daniel Weaver, also a former Chartist, who stressed the need for unity of all national groups within the union. The constitution of the American Miners' Association was headed by a poem which was put to music and sung by the union membership:

Step by step, the longest march
Can be won, can be won,
Single stones will form an arch,
One by one, one by one.

And by union, what we will
Can be accomplished still,
Drops of water turn a mill,
Singly none, singly none.[4]

The first real miners' song in this country of which we have record was published in the Saint Louis *Miner and Artisan* on January 5, 1865, and was reprinted, by popular request, in the *Boston Daily Evening Voice* of Febraury 7, 1866, and in the Chicago *Workingman's Advocate* of August 5, 1871. The *Workingman's Advocate* noted: "The song was adapted to a well known Welsh air, and is frequently sung at miners' meetings and celebrations." Then followed a historical note which explained that the third and fourth stanzas of the song had special references "to actual occurrences which actually took place in the winter of 1863 and 1864, on the northern spur of the Alleghanies, in Pennsylvania, which occurrences were one of the results of power given unscrupulous men by the legislature of that State, by an infamous 'Ten-days eviction Bill.' " The bill empowered the owners of houses to evict tenants after ten days' notice, should the tenants "refuse or neglect to perform such labor, or render such services" provided for in the agreement under which the houses had been rented. The *Workingman's Advocate*'s note continued:

> After the Governor's sanction had been obtained to the above bill, and while the keen winter's winds still careened over the area, the people in the mines were evicted. The people thus summarily evicted, had, some of them, held tenure of their humble homes for a long series of years, under the old "Landlord and Tenant law" of Pennsylvania which law had no reference, whatever, to the "performance of labor or service under the agreement," and they were ejected, simply and solely because they refused to sign such an agreement as would bring them within the purview more completely, of this infamous law, after having been first locked out from their employment, for the space of nearly three months time.

A LABOR SONG

Written for the *Miner and Artisan* by the Editor

Why should the toilers look sad in this land—
This land of the brave and the free?
Divided, they fall, but united they stand,
Then, let UNION their watchword still be.
Arouse! unite!

For Union your watchword should be!
Ye, who delve in the mine—
Ye, who sweat at the forge—
Or who plough up the stubborn lea.

O, where are the hopes we have cherished so long?
Shall we quench them in idle despair?
No, no! we'll revive them again, in a song,
And its chorus shall ring on the air,
Shout and sing!

For Union our watchword must be!
And the anvil shall ring
In response to our song,
And the furnace shall light on the Free.

Let truth, like the sun, o'er yon mountains career!
And break the dark spell that now binds,
Those Cyclopean slaves, with the shackles of fear,
Of exposure to bleak northern winds,
Hard and cold!

Is the grave of poor Watty's dear wife!
Where the infant just born,
And its mother forlorn,
Mid the bleak winds, once struggled for life!

Indignation shall dry up the source of our tears,
But memory shall store up the wrongs,
We have borne in the past, and this story for years,
Shall be the sad theme of our songs.
Hard and cold!

Is the grave of poor Watty's young bride,
But harder the hearts,
The emotions as cold,
As the tyrant's by whose will she died.

Let the hills and the valleys resound with the song,
Of myriads of brave men and free—
Only cowards and slaves to their masters belong—
Independence and union for me!
Arouse! unite!

4Edward A. Wieck, *The American Miners' Association* (New York, 1940), p. 217.

Let Union the watchword still be!
Ye, who delve in the mine—
Ye, who sweat at the forge,
Or who plough up the stubborn lea.

THE WORKINGMEN'S BENEVOLENT ASSOCIATION

By the time the next important mining song appeared, the American Miners' Association had already vanished. It was replaced in July, 1868, by the Workingmen's Benevolent Association of Saint Clair, which became a general union for all anthracite miners in Pennsylvania eight months later. The union grew slowly at first, but almost six months after it was formed, a terrible tragedy occurred in the mines which caused miners to flock into the union. On September 6, 1869, at Avondale, a breaker above a shaft caught fire and brought suffocation and death to 110 men and boys. The Avondale disaster gave rise to a ballad which was all too familiar to miners.

THE AVONDALE MINE DISASTER

Good Christians all, both great and small,
I pray you lend an ear,
And listen with attention while
The truth I will declare;
When you hear this lamentation,
'Twill cause you to weep and wail,
About the suffocation
In the mines of Avondale.

On the sixth day of September,
Eighteen sixty-nine,
Those miners all then got a call
To go work in the mine;
But little did they think that [day]
That death would soon prevail
Before they would return again from
The mines of Avondale.

The women and their children,
Their hearts were filled with joy
To see their men go to their work
Likewise every boy;
But a dismal sight in broad daylight,
Soon made them turn pale,
When they saw the breaker burning
O'er the mines of Avondale.

From here and there and everywhere,
They gathered in a crowd,
Some tearing off their clothes and hair,
And crying out aloud—
"Get out our husbands and our sons,
Death he's going to steal
Their lives away without delay
In the mines of Avondale."

But all in vain, there was no hope
One single soul to save,
For there is no second outlet
From the subterranean cave.
No pen can write the awful fright
And horror that prevailed,
Among those dying victims,
In the mines of Avondale.

A consultation then was held.
'Twas asked who'd volunteer
For to go down this dismal shaft
To seek their comrades dear;
Two Welshmen brave, without dismay,
And courage without fail,
Went down the shaft, without delay,
In the mines of Avondale.

When at the bottom they arrived,
And thought to make their way,
One of them died for want of air,
While the other in great dismay,
He gave a sign to hoist him up,
To tell the dreadful tale,
That all were lost forever
In the mines of Avondale.

Every effort then took place
To send down some fresh air;
The men that next went down again
They took of them good care;
And traversed through the chambers,
And this time did not fail
In finding those dead bodies
In the mines of Avondale.

Sixty-seven was the number
That in a heap were found.
It seemed that they were bewailing
Their fate underneath the ground;
They found the father with his son
Clasped in his arms so pale.
It was a heart-rending scene
In the mines of Avondale.

Now to conclude, and make an end,
Their number I'll pen down—
A hundred and ten of brave strong men
Were smothered underground;
They're in their graves till the last day,
Their widows may bewail,
And the orphans' cries they rend the skies
All around through Avondale![5]

[5]George Korson, ed., *Pennsylvania Songs and Legends* (Philadelphia, 1949), pp. 386–88 (from the singing of John J. Quinn).

As the bodies were brought up one by one from the stricken mine, John Siney, head of the Workingmen's Benevolent Association, stood upon a wagon and said to the weeping miners: "Men, if you must die with your boots on, die for your families, your homes, your country, but do not longer consent to die like rats in a trap for those who have no more interest in you than in the pick you dig with."[6] He appealed to the miners to join the union, and thousands did so on that day. By the end of 1869, the WBA had thirty thousand members, about 85 percent of the workers in the anthracite mines, and the mine owners were forced to sign an agreement which recognized the union as the bargaining agent for the miners and provided for a sliding scale of wages based on the prevailing price of coal, with a minimum below which wages could not fall.

But as the price of coal plunged downward, so did the miners' wages, which were slashed in some instances by almost 50 percent. Then when the union resisted wage cuts below the minimum stipulated in the contract, Franklin B. Gowen, head of the Philadelphia and Reading Railroad and the combine of coal companies in Pennsylvania, determined to smash the union. One device used by the operators was to distribute songs and ballads among the miners to persuade them to abandon the Workingmen's Benevolent Association.[7] In the following broadside, written in Irish dialect and circulated in the mines in 1871, the mine operators' determination to crush the union was expressed in plain language:

W.B.A.

Go back to yer work, me broth of a boy,
An' shtop all yer strikes an' yer fuss.
Or divil a wun will get any employ,
An' ye'll soon all be shtarvin' or wuss.

It's d——d little minin' yer doin' at all;
There's others work betther nor you.
Yer fit but for ditchin' out in the canawl,
Or workin' wid some railroad crew.

If minin' don't suit yez, why go till the Wist,
Or anywhere's out of the way;
'Twouldn't grieve uz at all if yez all were at rist
'Neath the sod of yer bog in the say.

So shtart or be off—(we're wanting no such)
An' lit those min who want to work, be:
We've miners enough, both English and Dutch,[8]
An' in your place we'll get the Chinee.[9]

This device was not successful, but the operators were not discouraged. Having learned from the Pinkerton undercover agent in the WBA that the union was riddled with internal dissension and could not sustain a prolonged lockout, the Reading closed its mines in November, 1874. The other coal companies followed suit or were forced by Gowen to do so, since they were unable to market the coal on the transportation companies he controlled. By December 1, most mine workers were either idle or working part time.

Gowen and his allies now played their trump cards. The operators announced a 15 to 20 percent reduction in contract rates and a 10 percent reduction in wages, and they withdrew the base minimum. The aim was to provoke the union into a strike during which the operators hoped to destroy the organization.

THE LONG STRIKE OF 1875 AND ITS AFTERMATH

The Workingmen's Benevolent Association responded with a strike. While the miners had little money, their spirit was magnificent, as expressed in a song written during the bitter struggle.

THE LONG STRIKE

Come all you jolly colliers, wherever you may
be,
I pray you will attention give and listen unto
me,
I have a doleful tale, and to relate it I will
strive—
About the great suspension in eighteen seventy-
five.

In eighteen hundred and seventy-five, our
masters did conspire
To keep men, women, and children without
either food or fire.

[6] Edward Pinkowski, *John Siney, the Miners' Martyr* (Philadelphia, 1963), p. 76.

[7] The use of songs by employers to turn workers against unions did not originate with the mine operators. In the 1840s textile manufacturers in New England employed men to write songs in favor of the factory system and to sing the praises of the contented factory workers who did not need female labor reform associations to protect them. See, for instance, "Song of the Factory Girls," p. 66.

[8] The "Dutch" were the Germans.

[9] George Korson, *Minstrels of the Mine Patch* (1938; reprinted, Hatboro, Pa., 1964), p. 221. The complete text appears on pp. 220–21.

They tho't to starve us to submit with hunger
and with cold,
But the miners did not fear them, but stood out
brave and bold.

Now two long months are nearly o'er—that no
one can deny,
And for to stand another month we are willing
for to try,
Our wages shall not be reduced, tho' poverty do
reign,
We'll have seventy-four basis, boys, before we'll
work again.

And when we get the basis boys, we'll work again with
joy,
We'll never mind those blacklegs named peddlers or
decoys,
May the world all frown upon them, for such traitors
they have been!
And may each miner think of them whene'er we do
begin.

So come all you jolly colliers, that appreciate good
times,
And never mind them blacklegs I have mentioned in my
rhyme,
They are a disgrace unto their race, wherever they may
be—
Traitors to their fellow miners, likewise society.[10]

Unfortunately, spirit was not enough to win out against the power of the coal operators. The union's treasury was small, and its appeals for aid brought little response in a period when so many workers were unemployed. When the local merchants refused to extend further credit, the near-starving miners sought vainly to negotiate. This failed, and the miners were forced to return to work on the operators' terms. With the WBA now dead, the miners lamented:

AFTER THE LONG STRIKE

Well, we've been beaten, beaten all to smash,
And now, sir, we've begun to feel the lash,
As wielded by a gigantic corporation,
Which runs the commonwealth and ruins the nation.
Our "Union" lamp, friend John, no longer shineth:
It's gone up where the gentle woodbine twineth;
A great man demonstrated beyond a doubt
The miners would better fare without
Any such thing; trade unions were a curse
Upon God's fair creation, nothing worse.
It died, because the miners did neglect it;
And he declares they shall not resurrect it.
And thus the matter stands. We do not dare
To look a boss in the face and whisper "Bah,"
Unless we wish to join the mighty train
Of miners wandering o'er the earth like Cain.
And, should you wish to start upon a tramp,
O'er hillock, mountain, valley, plain and swamp,
Or travel as the pilgrim of John Bunyan,
One talismanic word will do it, "Union."
Just murmur that, and all the laws of state
Or Congress will not save you from your fate.
They'll drive you out, forfeit your goods, degrade you,
Just as the British did in old Acadia.

Our wages, John, grow beautifully less,
And, if they keep on growing thus, I guess
We'll have to put on magnifying specs,
To see the little figures on our checks.
The sliding scale which once some comfort sent us
Is now declared to be non compos mentis.
To curse it dreadfully we are incited,
Because, somehow, it works so darned one-sided,
It suffers from a bad disease, "decline,"
And pines away right down to twenty-nine.
It's nothing strange to find on seeing the docket
We've worked a month and still are out of pocket.
It makes a man feel dirty cheap, you bet,
To work a month and then come out in debt.
And now, friend John, in fewer words I'll state
What I've been trying to communicate:
Lest anything herein you misconstrue,
In Anglo-Saxon plain I'll say to you—
If in exchange for the labor of a day
You wish to have an honest fair day's pay;
If you do wish to have just rights among
Those of freedom of action, speech and tongue,
If you do wish to have a fair supply
Of wholesome food, be buried when you die
With decent rites—by this I mean at least
Sufficient to distinguish man from beast,
Stay where you are, or, if you must go hence,
Go East, go North, go South, no consequence.
Take any one direction; you'll be blest
Sooner with what you seek than coming West.
In short, if you wish to enjoy God's bounty,
Go anywhere except to Schuylkill County.[11]

With the union destroyed, wage cut followed wage cut, and working conditions grew worse and worse. The miners voiced their complaints in bitter songs, one of which was originally in German:

SONG OF THE PENNSYLVANIA MINERS

The anvil rings, the hearth steams,
The wheel turns, the rod stamps,

[10]George Korson, *Songs and Ballads of the Anthracite Miner* (New York, 1927), pp. 161–62 (from William Forgay).

[11]Korson, *Minstrels of the Mine Patch*, pp. 225–26 (from an 1878 Pottsville, Pa., paper).

We give it life.
We hammer, softly, blow by blow.
The miner's lamp is our day.
Surrounded by grave's darkness
We bring up
The coal
From deep shafts,
From eternal night.
Good luck!

Commerce races from land to land,
Weaves its golden band around the world,
While we in fear of death
Deep underground,
Pale of face, sore the knee,
Lend it its wings.
We bring up
The coal
From deep shafts,
From eternal night.
Good luck!

A little child stands near the fireplace,
Freezing, it stretches out its little hands—
And deep in the bowels of the earth
We give battle to the power of elements
To warm the little child.
We bring up
The coal
From deep shafts,
From eternal night.
Good luck!

While you enjoy the beauty of summer,
How heavy becomes here the breathing,
How it presses on all pores.
For God's sake! Watch out for the lamp.
Didn't you see that blue light?
Away, away, we're lost.
Coal damp.
We bring up
The coal
From deep shafts,
From eternal night.
Good luck!

Already our fate is decided,
Two thousand feet deep in the earth,
Hundreds are buried
Who also received the heart in the breast
For happiness and sadness and love of life from God.
We bring up
The coal
From deep shafts,
From eternal night.
Good luck!

At home wife and child are hungry,
Daily we have to gamble our bodies
For our masters.
The masters are God on earth.
And all the poor miner gets for his complaints
Are mean disdain and ridicule.
We bring up
The coal
From deep shafts,
From eternal night.
Good luck!

Let sledge and iron rest,
Let the masters do it all.
The masters who have no regard for blood and sweat
Let them take with their soft hands
The rough ride up and down,
And let them suffer in the shaft.
We bring up
The coal
From deep shafts,
From eternal night.
Good luck![12]

TWO CENT COAL

Tune—"The Jam on Gerry's Rocks"

Oh, the bosses' tricks of '76
They met with some success,
Until the hand of God came down
And made them do with less.
They robbed the honest miner lad
And drunk his flowin' bowl
Through poverty we are compelled
To dig them two cent coal.

But the river* it bein' frozen—
Of course, the poor might starve;
What did those tyrant bosses say?
"It's just what they deserve."
But God who always aids the just,
All things He does control,
He broke the ice and He sent it down
And sunk their two-cent coal.

Their tipples, too, fled from our view,
And down the river went.
They seemed to cry as they passed by:
"You tyrants, now repent!
For while you rob the miner lad,
Remember, you've a soul,
For your soul is sinkin' deeper
Than the ice sunk your two-cent coal."

It's to conclude and finish,
Let us help our fellow man,
And if our brother's in distress
Assist him if you can,
To keep the wolf off from his door,
And shelter him from the cold,

12*Arbeiter-Zeitung*, Mar. 13, 1875. Trans. Rudi Bass.

That he never again shall commit the crime
Of diggin' two-cent coal.[13]

*The Monongahela.

THE HARD WORKING MINER

By Patrick J. "Giant" O'Neill

Air—"I'm a Man You Don't Meet Every Day"

I'm a hard working miner, you can see by my
hands,
Although I am friendly and free.
A dollar a day is a very small pay
For a man with a large family.
I didn't come here, boys, to boast or to brag,
But just for to tell you my troubles,
I work day and night and the world I must fight
And load coal with my pick and my shovel.

I work in the mines where the sun never
shines
Nor daylight does ever appear;
With me lamp blazing red on the top of
my head
And in danger I never know fear.

Just think of the poor man who works in the
mines
With the mules and the rats underground;
Where the smoke is so thick you can cut it with
a stick,
And can weigh it on scales by the pound.
My face it is black from the dust of the coal,
Though my heart it is open and free;
I would share my last loaf with the man that's in
want,
Though I earn it hard you can see.

Now, my kind friends, I will bid you good-bye;
I cannot stay here any longer,
I'll pick up my pack, throw it o'er my back,
And I think I will make my road shorter,
I have a wife and small family at home in the
house,
And to meet me I'm sure they'll be glad,
They will stand at the door when I'm on my
way home,
And they'll say to their mama, "here's
dad."[14]

THE OLD MINER'S REFRAIN

I'm getting old and feeble and I cannot work no
more,
I have laid my rusty mining tools away;
For forty years and over I have toiled about the
mines,
But now I'm getting feeble, old and gray.
I started in the breaker and went back to it
again,
But now my work is finished for all time;
The only place that's left me is the alm's-house
for a home,
Where I'm going to lay this weary head of
mine.

Where are the boys that worked with me in the
breakers long ago?
Many of them now have gone to rest;
Their cares of life are over and they've left this
world of woe,
And their spirits now are roaming with the
blest.

In the chutes I graduated instead of going to
school—
Remember, friends, my parents they were
poor;
When a boy left the cradle it was always made a
rule
To try and keep starvation from the door.
At eight years of age to the breaker I first went
To learn the occupation of a slave;
I certainly was delighted, and on picking slate
was bent—
My ambition it was noble, strong, and brave.

Where are the boys that worked with me in the
breakers long ago?
Many of them now have gone to rest;
Their cares of life are over and they've left this
world of woe;
And their spirits now are roaming with the
blest.

At eleven years of age I bought myself a lamp—
The boss he sent me down the mine to trap;
I stood in there in water, in powder smoke and
damp;
My leisure hours I spent in killing rats.
One day I got promoted to what they called a
patcher,
Or a lackey for the man that drives the team:
I carried sprags and spreaders and had to fix the
latch—
I was going through my exercise, it seems.

I next became a driver, and thought myself a
man;
The boss he raised my pay as I advanced.
In going through the gangway with the mules at
my command,
I was prouder than the President of France.

13George Korson, *Coal Dust on the Fiddle* (1943; reprinted, Hatboro, Pa., 1965), pp. 403–4 (from the singing of David Morrison, who heard the song in 1878).

14Korson, *Songs and Ballads of the Anthracite Miner*, pp. 77–78 (from the singing of Patrick O'Neill).

But now my pride is weakened and I am weakened too;
I tremble till I'm scarcely fit to stand.
If I were taught book learning instead of driving teams,
Today, kind friends, I'd be a richer man.

I next became a miner and laborer combined,
For to earn my daily bread beneath the ground
I performed the acts of labor which came in a miner's line—
For to get my cars and load them I was bound.
But now I can work no more, my cares of life are run;
I am waiting for the signal at the door
When the angels they will whisper, "Dear old miner, you must come,
And we'll row you to the bright celestial shore."[15]

DOWN IN A COAL MINE

I am a jovial collier lad, as blithe as blithe can be,
And let the times be good or bad, they're all the same to me;
There's little of this world I know and care less for its ways,
And where the Dog Star never glows, I wear away the days.

Down in a coal mine, underneath the ground,
Where a gleam of sunshine never can be found;
Digging dusky diamonds all the year around,
Away down in a coal mine, underneath the ground.

My hands are horny, hard, and black from working in the vein,
Like the clothes upon my back my speech is rough and plain;
And if I stumble with my tongue I've one excuse to say,
It's not the collier's heart that's bad, it's his head that goes astray.

Down in a coal mine, underneath the ground,
Where a gleam of sunshine never can be found;
Digging dusky diamonds all the year around,
Away down in a coal mine, underneath the ground.

At every shift, be it soon or late, I haste my bread to earn,
And anxiously my kindred wait and watch for my return;
For death that levels all alike, whate'er their rank may be,
Amid the fire and damp may strike and fling his darts at me.

How little do the great ones care who sit at home secure,
What hidden dangers colliers dare, what hardships they endure;
The very fires their mansions boast, to cheer themselves and wives,
Mayhap were kindled at the cost of jovial colliers' lives.

Then cheer up, lads, and make ye much of every joy ye can;
But let your mirth be always such as best becomes a man;
However fortune turns about we'll still be jovial souls,
For what would America be without the lads that look for coals?[16]

THE PLIGHT OF A MINER'S WIDOW

Kind ladies and kind gentlemen, come lend a helping hand,
For I am a poor widow as you will understand;
My husband, he the best of men, was killed while in a mine,
Leaving me and my two children in this lonely world behind.

Oh, when he lived no care I knew, for all was happiness,
With him to look to for support and my children to caress;
I little thought that morning when we parted at the door
That I my loving husband would see alive no more.

He has gone up to a better world, his dangerous work is o'er,
Whilst we must struggle on below, he cannot help us more;
Yet one fond hope I cherish, and shall until I die
I will meet my loving husband in a better world on high.

We have a little house and lot, and on it there's a debt,
Which I must pay this coming fall, or out we'll have to get;

[15]Korson, *Pennsylvania Songs and Legends*, pp. 378–79 (from the singing of Daniel Walsh).

[16]Ibid., pp. 373–74 (from the singing of Morgan Jones; originally an 1872 stage song). See also Korson's *Songs and Ballads of the Anthracite Miner*, pp. 122–25, and his *Black Rock* (Baltimore, 1960), pp. 65–66.

So I wrote these little verses, and took this little
plan,
To try and save my children's home—I'll do the
best I can.

My little boy is five years old, my little girl is
three,
So they cannot help me much, as you can
plainly see;
I want to pay the mortgage, and cancel out the
debt,
And then my children's living I can make out to
get.

Now in these little verses my case I've strived to
state,
My story's one of sorrow and hard for to relate;
But when I think of him who's gone and my
little children dear,
I cry sometimes, and then nerve up and onward
persevere.

And now my little children—a suffering can it
be?
No one but them is left me, no one to pity me!
Five cents you'll never miss, but sure to have the
more,
Help the widow and orphan, and heaven will
bless your store.

Now, kind ladies and kind gentlemen, buy my
little rhyme—
In passing through life's journey you'll not miss
half a dime;
In writing up these verses poverty is my
defence—
One of these little rhymes of mine will cost you
but five cents.[17]

Some miners did more than bewail their sad fate in songs and ballads. Under the leadership of the Ancient Order of Hibernians, formed by a group of young Irish miners, they began to fight back, determined to restore miners' wages and rebuild their union. It was this renewed struggle which produced the story of a series of crimes, including murder and arson, committed by a secret society called the Molly Maguires. Today it is generally conceded that there was no society in America calling itself the Molly Maguires; that the name was tagged to the Ancient Order of Hibernians by the operators and their allies in the press in order to crush any organization in the mining industry; and that the Pinkerton agency hired by Franklin B. Gowen to ferret out the so-called criminals actually committed many of the crimes. In any case, as a result of evidence furnished by James McParlan, a Pinkerton spy who had wormed himself into the ranks of the miners, twenty-one miners were condemned to death after a biased trial and executed. Hugh McGeehan, one of the executed miners, is said to have composed the following as he awaited trial in 1876:

Just think, James McKenna, the detective, has gained
himself a name,
And in the detective agency has risen to great fame.
He said he came amongst our people in November
'seventy-three
Which leaves many's the wife and babe to mourn and
curse his memory.[18]

KNIGHTS OF LABOR

With the destruction of the Ancient Order of Hibernians so soon after the death of the Workingmen's Benevolent Association, the miners appeared powerless. But not for long. After 1876 the Knights of Labor began moving into mining regions and attracted many miners. The universal membership of the order was well suited to the mining industry, which had long been organized along industrial lines, and its early secrecy permitted the miners to continue in the labor movement in spite of the blacklists that were set up after the defeat of the long strike of 1875. National District Assembly 135 was established as the center for miners, and it became one of the most important national trades' assemblies of the Knights of Labor. It had its own song, which every miner in the order knew and sang. Published in the *United Mine Workers' Journal* of October 8, 1891, under the title "The Miners' Bewail and Expected Triumph," to the tune of "Three Cheers for the Red, White, and Blue," it was better known under the title "Our Brave Little Band: A Knights of Labor Ballad," to be sung to the tune of "Columbia, the Gem of the Ocean."

THE MINERS' BEWAIL AND EXPECTED TRIUMPH

Tune—"Three Cheers for the Red, White, and Blue"

Let's awake from our long, silent slumber,
And no more in deep sorrow repine,

[17] Korson, *Black Rock*, p. 388 (a broadside "composed and written by Mrs. Clara Austin whose husband was killed in a coal mine in 1881").

[18] From "Hugh McGeehan" in Korson, *Minstrels of the Mine Patch*, p. 264. James McKenna was the name McParlan assumed as a spy among the miners.

For the day star of hope in its splendor
Is beginning, my brother to shine;
When the chains of old heathen oppression
With its links ever galling to bear,
By the true Knight of Labor oblation
One by one into fragments we'll tear.

Three cheers for our brave little band.
Three cheers for our brave little band!
A just recompense for our labor
Is all the poor miners demand.

Let me sing with a joy in the morning,
Chant aloud in a musical "lay,"
At noon tide and evening rejoicing
To hail the approach of the day,
When freedom the boast of our nation
Will crown every true son of toil
And despots to labor's oblation
Be stamped the refuse of the soil.

Chorus:

From the mine—life of bitter experience
These lines are indited as such,
To tell the world wide our grievance,
The heart of stern justice to touch,
But cautions to touch the chord lightly
For fear of some moneied rebuke
By those standing high and politely
As lords, or some old English Duke.

Chorus:

In the dark dismal cell we are mining,
The air often pregnant with damp,
Not a ray from the sun brightly shining
But the small glim'ring light of the lamp.
And the "gas" from its torch when igniting
Spreads carnage and death as it goes
All means of escape blockading
Poor miners oft buried below.

Chorus:

And to tighten the bands of oppression,
Dishonest unhumanly mean,
Near a third of the coal we are mining
Passes down with a smash through a screen.
Like the rest it is sold in the market,
The masters receiving the pay,
Not a cent for the miner, please mark it,
We're only their tools, by the way.

Chorus:

In the weight we are cunningly cheated,
The monitors, conscience, they lack
And again as a rule we're defeated
With a "five hundred" dock for the slack.
And if from the grate of our feeling
Our grievance found spatting about
A voice from the "boss" comes appealing,
"I want you to bring your tools out."

Chorus:

"As discord you seem to be brewing,
I judge by the way you have spoke,
It's 'we' bear in mind has the ruling,
All here must submit to 'my' yoke."
And on the great day of our nation,
That blessed old "Fourth of July,"
These tyrants are first at their station,
"Hurrah" for sweet freedom to cry.

Chorus:

We want a fair price for our labor,
Our pay at the end of each week
To do and act with our neighbor
As right as we know, so to speak.
Our dear wives and children maintaining
From what honest labor may bring,
Put an end to their tears of complaining,
All join in the chorus and sing:

Chorus:

We've sought a redress from the able
And "law" making force of our land,
Which too oft has been read as a fable
Or something they'd not understand.
While the man with his thousands is favored,
The rich making richer each day,
And the "poor" who so willingly labored
Curtailed or reduced in his pay.

Chorus:

But the day of deliverance is dawning
For the "light," as an omen we see.
Denoting the joy of the morning
When miners from serfdom are free.
Never more to bow down to oppression
Which so often has made us feel sad,
Beholding the day of salvation,
Let's lift up our hearts and be glad.

Three cheers for our brave little band.
Three cheers for our brave little band!
By the united true Knights of Labor,
Oppression must cease in our land.

The mine operators were no more ready to accept unionism under the Knights of Labor than they had been willing to accept it under the WBA. In the general employers' offensive of 1887–88, they set out to destroy the miners' unions affiliated with the order. Militant union miners were dismissed, and when the union answered with a strike in the anthracite region of Pennsylvania, the employers locked out all members of the Knights of Labor. They imported "blacklegs" (scabs) and hired Pinkerton detectives to guard them from the enraged miners. In a battle with the Pinkertons, several miners were killed. When the miners still held fast, the operators evicted them from the company houses and denied them credit at company stores. Although faced with starvation, the strikers continued to fight back. Their songs expressed both their hatred of "blacklegs" and Pinkertons and their determination to win.

THE PENNSYLVANIA MINER

By Phillips Thompson

Come, listen, fellow-workingmen, my story, I'll relate,
How workers in the coal-mines fare in Pennsylvania
State;
Come, hear a sad survivor, from beside his childrens'
graves,
And learn how free Americans are treated now as slaves.

They robbed us of our pay,
They starved us day by day,
They shot us down on the hillside brown,
And swore our lives away.

For years we toiled on patiently—they cut our wages
down;
We struck—they sent the Pinkertons to drive us from the
town;
We held a meeting near the mine, some hasty words were
said,
A volley from the Pinkertons laid half-a-dozen dead.

They robbed us, etc.

I had a little family, the youngest scarce could creep;
Next night the hireling ruffian band aroused us out of
sleep;
They battered in our cabin door—we pleaded all in vain—
They turned my wife and children out to perish in the
rain.

They robbed us, etc.

They died of cold and famine there beneath the open
sky,
While pitying neighbors stood around, but all as poor as
I;
You never saw such misery—God grant you never may—
The sight is branded on my soul until my dying day.

They robbed us, etc.

Half-crazed I wandered round the spot, and just beyond
the town
I met a dastard Pinkerton and struck the villain down;
My brain was frenzied with the thought of children,
friends and wife
I set my heel upon his throat and trampled out his life.

They robbed us, etc.

And now I roam an outlawed man, no house or friends
have I,
For if the law can track me down I shall be doomed to
die;
But very little should I care what may become of me,
If all the land would rise and swear such things no more
shall be.

They robbed us, etc.[19]

THE KNIGHTS OF LABOR STRIKE

We're brave and gallant miner boys
That work in underground,
For courage and good nature
None like us can be found.
We work both late and early,
And get but little pay
To support our wives and children,
In free Americ-a.

Here's to the Knights of Labor,
That brave and gallant band,
That Corbon and old Swigard
Is trying to disband.
But stick and hang brave union men,
We'll make them rue the day
They thought to break the K. of L.
In free Americ-a.

If Satan took the blacklegs,
I'm sure 'twould be no sin,
What peace and happiness 'twould be
For us workingmen.
Eight hours we'd have for labor,
Eight hours we'd have for play,
Eight hours we'd have for sleeping,
In free Americ-a.

Corbon, Cox and Swigard,
What will you have to say
When you meet our master
Upon the Judgment Day?
With a frown He will confront you,
And show you the other way,
Saying, you have straved my children,
In free Americ-a.

They're trying to run the Keystone,*
Assisted by Adam Knapp,
Bill Davis at the bottom,
And Bill Raudy at the top.
But stick and hang, brave union men!
We'll show them Yankee play,

19Phillips Thompson, ed., *The Labor Reform Songster* (Philadelphia, 1892).

No. 3. THE PENNSYLVANIA MINER.

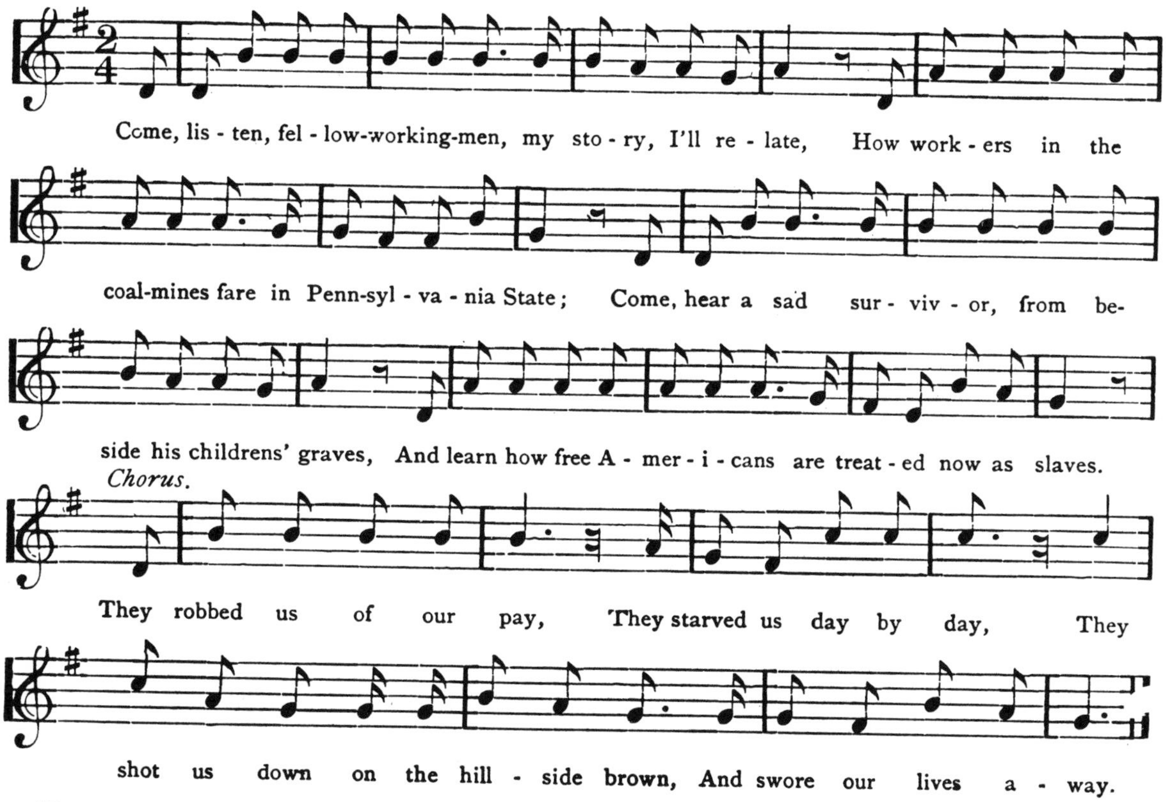
Come, lis - ten, fel - low-working-men, my sto - ry, I'll re - late, How work - ers in the
coal-mines fare in Penn-syl - va - nia State; Come, hear a sad sur - viv - or, from beside his childrens' graves, And learn how free A - mer - i - cans are treat - ed now as slaves.
Chorus.
They robbed us of our pay, They starved us day by day, They
shot us down on the hill - side brown, And swore our lives a - way.

For years we toiled on patiently—they cut our wages down;
We struck—they sent the Pinkertons to drive us from the town;
We held a meeting near the mine, some hasty words were said,
A volley from the Pinkertons laid half-a-dozen dead.

CHORUS.—They robbed us, etc.

I had a little family, the youngest scarce could creep;
Next night the hireling ruffian band aroused us out of sleep;
They battered in our cabin door—we pleaded all in vain—
They turned my wife and children out to perish in the rain.

CHORUS.—They robbed us, etc.

Courtesy of Brown University Library

And drive them off to blazes
In free Americ-a.

When this strike is at an end,
And we have gained the day,
We'll drink a health to our miner boys,
Both near and far away;
And our brothers on the railroad
In free Americ-a.[20]

*A colliery near Ashland.

The miners, determined to hold out until victory no matter how long the battle lasted, sang:

In looking o'er the papers now,
A funny thing appears,
Where Eckley Coxe and Padee say
They'll stand for twenty years,
If God should call us miners off,
We'll have children then alive,
Who will follow in our footsteps
Keep the strike for thirty-five.[21]

But starvation again won out, and the strike was lost. The rejoicing of the operators was cynically depicted in a labor song.

THE COAL BARON'S HYMN

Oh! let them strike as much as they like,
To us 'tis a perfect boon,
For if they don't stop, the price must drop
They can't go out too soon
Though they starve by bits in the inky pits,
Though their children cry for bread,
The end of the game must be the same,
King Capital keeps ahead.

Good pay? Absurd! Upon my word!
What more can the men require?
You speak of the poor—what they endure,
Deprived of their bit of fire.
If we who control the price of coal
Reduce it at this time of year,
Our dividends, my Christian friends,
Would rapidly disappear!

I am willing to add that the work is bad,
And dangerous to face,
But whenever one stops, and reels, and drops,
There's another to take his place.
"Supply and demand," throughout the land,
By that we will stand or fall,
Our business is coals, but bodies and souls
Are none of our business at all.[22]

A somewhat different version, attributed to J. L. Frank, was published in 1895 with accompanying music:

Let them strike as much as they like,
To us 'tis a perfect boon;
Merrily high the prices fly,
On monopoly's big balloon,
Tho' they starve by bits in the inky pits,
Tho' their children cry for bread,
The end of the game must be the same,
King Capital keeps ahead.

The end of the game, must be the same,
King Capital keeps ahead.

Good pay? absurd! Upon my word,
What more can the men require?
You speak of the poor—what they endure,
Deprived of their bit of fire,
If we who control the price of coal,
Reduced at this time of year,
Our dividends, my worthy friends,
Would rapidly disappear.

Our dividends, my worthy friends,
Would rapidly disappear.

I'm willing to add, Their work is bad,
And dangerous, too, to face;
But when one stops, and reels and drops,
There's another to take his place.
Supply and demand, throughout the land,
By that we will stand or fall,
We're dealing in coals, but bodies and souls,
Are not in our line at all

We're dealing in coals, but bodies and souls
Are not in our line at all.[23]

Knights of Labor miners were more successful in the Coal Creek Rebellion, the great struggle in eastern Tennessee in 1891–92 against convict labor.[24] It was a revolt against the vicious system under which the state rented convicts to private businessmen. Since 1889, convicts in Tennessee had been contracted out to the Tennessee Coal, Iron & Railroad Company, which owned and controlled nearly all the mines in

[20] Korson, *Songs and Ballads of the Anthracite Miner*, pp. 173–74, from John Hory, the composer. Some twenty years after they were written, the first and third stanzas turned up in the *United Mine Workers Journal*, without author credit (see p. 234).

[21] Harold W. Aurand, "The Anthracite Strike of 1887–88," *Pennsylvania History*, XXXV (Apr., 1968), 176.

[22] *Craftsman*, reprinted in *Workmen's Advocate*, Apr. 7, 1888.

[23] George Howard Gibson, *Armageddon* (Lincoln, Nebr., and London, 1895), pp. 14–15.

[24] For a history of this rebellion and the songs which commemorate it see Archie Green, *Only a Miner* (Urbana, Ill., 1972), pp. 155–93.

eastern Tennessee. (The same company operated mines in Alabama with convicts, most of whom were blacks arrested on any pretext so that the state might supply the company with cheap labor and profit from the payment received for the convict laborers.) Determined to eliminate the use of convict labor in Tennessee to break strikes, the union miners in Coal Creek rounded up the convicts and sent them out of the community. When Governor Buchanan came to the aid of the coal operators by sending in the state militia, the union miners again rounded up the convicts and sent them away. A third attempt to introduce convicts was also successfully resisted by the miners.

Three songs came out of the Coal Creek Rebellion:

BUDDY WON'T YOU ROLL DOWN THE LINE

Way back yonder in Tennessee,
They leased the convicts out.
They worked them in the coal mines
Against free labor stout.
Free labor rebelled against it;
To win it took some time.
But while the lease was in effect,
They made 'em rise and shine.

Oh, Buddy, won't you roll down the line?
Buddy, won't you roll down the line?
Yonder come my darling, coming down the line.
Buddy, won't you roll down the line?
Buddy, won't you roll down the line?
Yonder come my darling, coming down the line.

Every Monday morning
They've got 'em out on time.
Marched them down to Lone Rock,
Said to look into that hole;
March you down to Lone Rock,
Said to look into that mine;
Very last word the captain say:
"You better get your coal."

Chorus:

The beans they are half done,
The bread is not so well;
The meat it is burnt up
And the coffee's black as heck!
But when you get your task done,
You're glad to come at all.
For anything you'd get to eat
It'd taste good, done or raw.

Chorus:

The bank boss is a hard man,
A man you all know well;
And if you don't get your task done
He's gonna give you—hallelujah!
Carry you to the stockade,
That's on the floor you'll fall,
Very next time they call on you
You'll bet you'll have your coal.

Chorus:[25]

COAL CREEK TROUBLE

My song is founded on the truth
In poverty we stand
How hard the millionaire will crush
Upon the laboring man
The miner toiling under ground
To earn his daily bread
To clothe his wife and children
And see that they are fed.

Some are from Kentucky
The place known as my birth
True and honest hearted men
As ever trod the earth.
The governor sent the convicts here
And works them in the bank
The captain and the soldiers
Are laying by in rank.

Although the mines are guarded
The miners true and fair
Mean to deal out justice
A living they declare
The corruption of Buchanan
Brought the convicts here
Just to please the rich man
And take the miners share.[26]

THE COAL CREEK REBELLION

The miner's toiling underground,
To earn his daily bread,
To clothe his wife and children,
And see that they are fed.

Old Buchanan and his militia,
A-layin' by in ranks,
Just to hold the convicts,
And work them in the banks.*

[25] Ibid., pp. 216–17 (from the singing of Uncle Dave Macon, Brunswick 292).

[26] Kentucky folksongs collected through the Federal Music Project, Works Progress Administration, Library of Congress. The first stanza appears, with music, in *Folk Songs from East Kentucky*, Federal Music Project, WPA (ca. 1939).

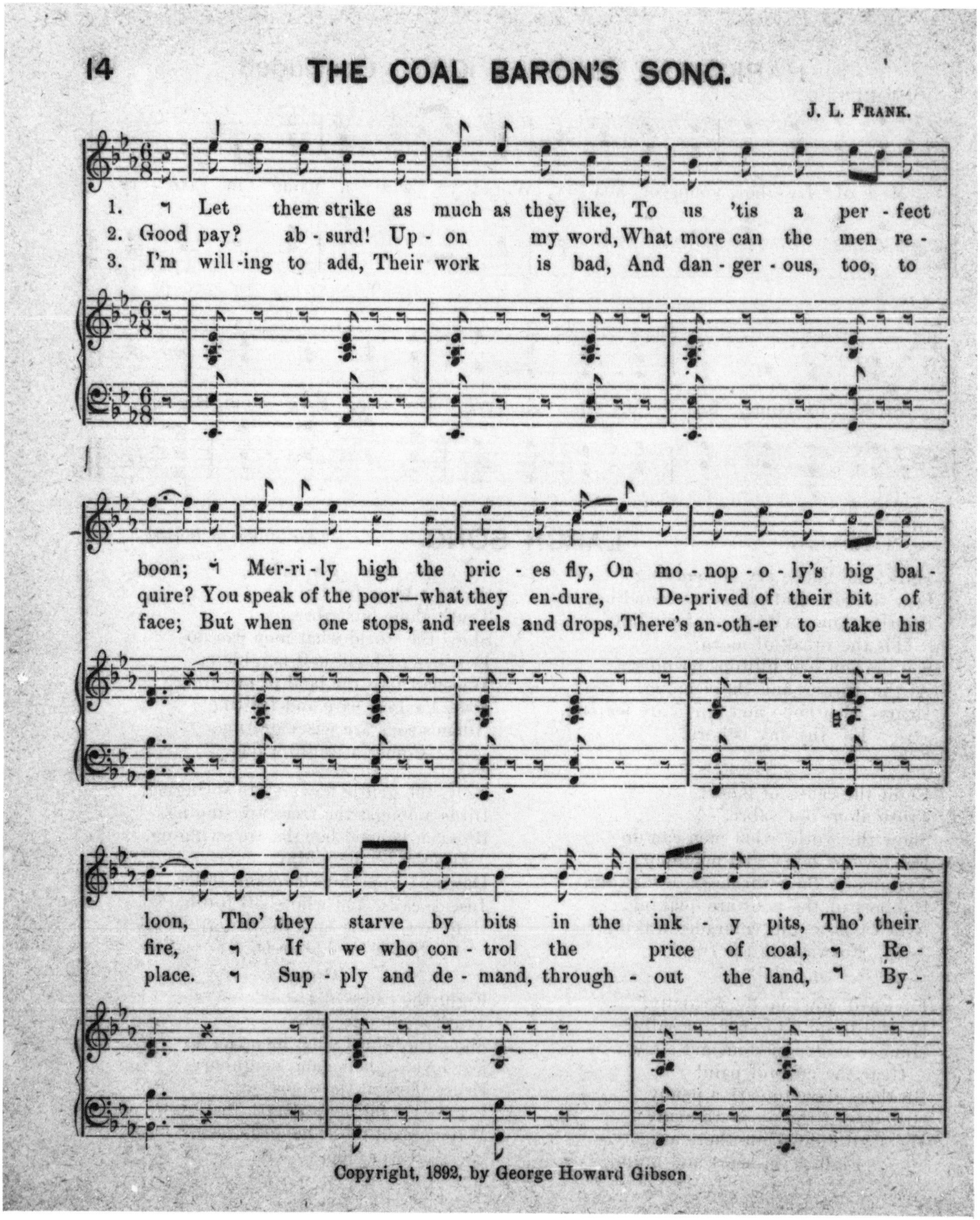
14 THE COAL BARON'S SONG.
J. L. Frank.
1. Let them strike as much as they like, To us 'tis a per - fect
2. Good pay? ab - surd! Up - on my word, What more can the men re -
3. I'm will - ing to add, Their work is bad, And dan - ger - ous, too, to
boon; Mer-ri - ly high the pric - es fly, On mo - nop - o - ly's big bal -
quire? You speak of the poor—what they en - dure, De-prived of their bit of
face; But when one stops, and reels and drops, There's an-oth-er to take his
loon, Tho' they starve by bits in the ink - y pits, Tho' their
fire, If we who con - trol the price of coal, Re -
place. Sup - ply and de - mand, through - out the land, By -
Copyright, 1892, by George Howard Gibson.

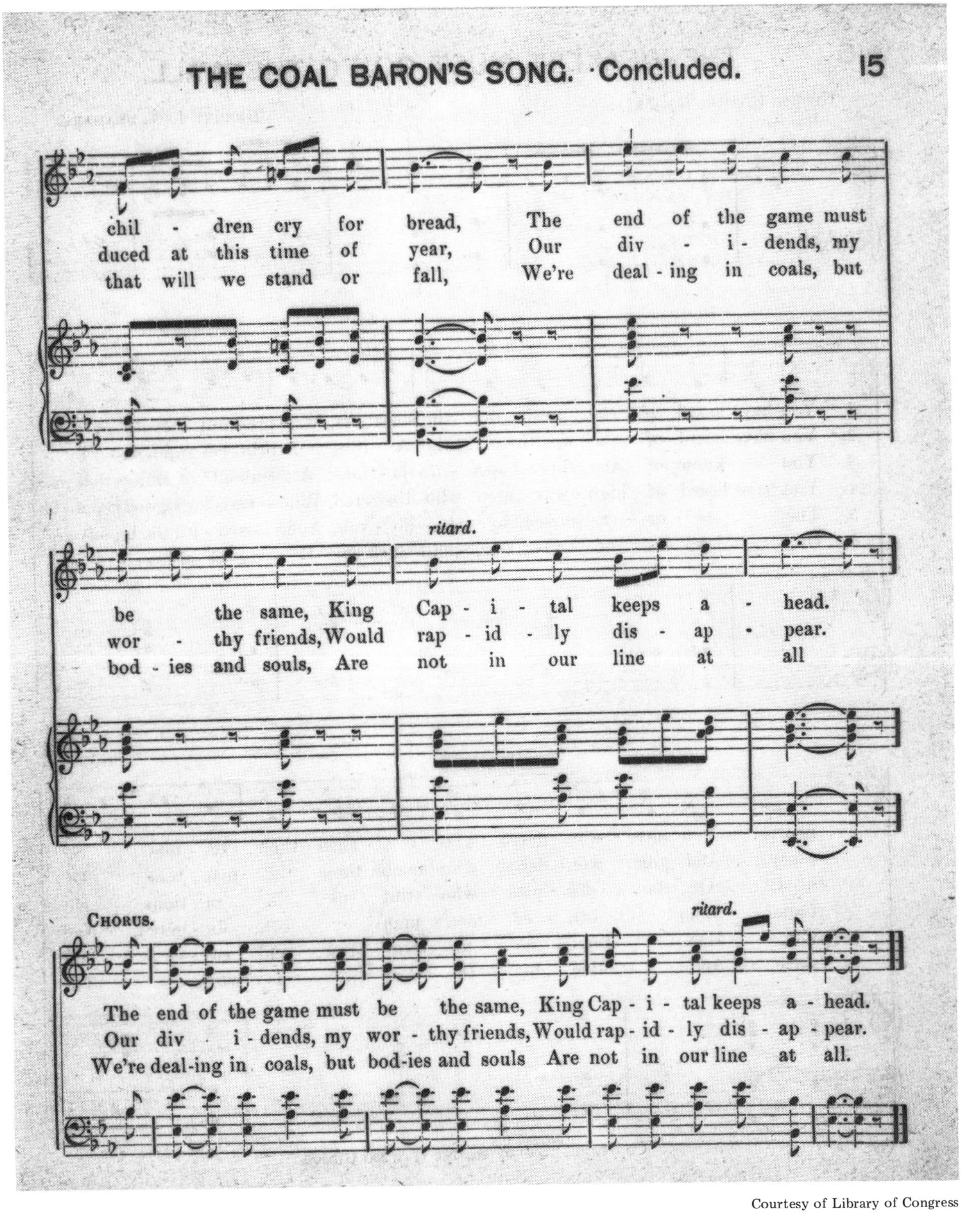
THE COAL BARON'S SONG. ·Concluded.
15
chil - dren cry for bread, The end of the game must
duced at this time of year, Our div - i - dends, my
that will we stand or fall, We're deal - ing in coals, but
ritard.
be the same, King Cap - i - tal keeps a - head.
wor - thy friends, Would rap - id - ly dis - ap - pear.
bod - ies and souls, Are not in our line at all
CHORUS.
ritard.
The end of the game must be the same, King Cap - i - tal keeps a - head.
Our div i - dends, my wor - thy friends, Would rap - id - ly dis - ap - pear.
We're deal-ing in coals, but bod-ies and souls Are not in our line at all.

Courtesy of Library of Congress

They know it's no law
  To work them only in the pen,
To keep them off the public works,
  To rob the laboring man.[27]

*Mines.

UNITED MINE WORKERS OF AMERICA

The Coal Creek Rebellion ended when most of the companies agreed to stop importing convict labor. The agreement was signed with committees representing the miners, but the committees were no longer from the Knights of Labor. Instead, they came from the United Mine Workers of America, for the miners had switched to that organization during the final stage of the Coal Creek Rebellion. The United Mine Workers had been formed at a convention at Columbus, Ohio, in January, 1890, and eventually all of the KL miners went over to the new organization. From its inception, the *United Mine Workers' Journal*, the new union's official organ, carried songs. Here is one of the early UMW songs.

GOD BLESS OUR UNION

By G. Parker, Nowerytown, Pennsylvania

Come you of America
  And listen to my song,
It's about our union principle
  And the scab that does us wrong;
We have fought a union battle
  For our wives and children dear.
To establish freedom in our midst,
  And pave our way right clear.

    Then three cheers for John McBride,
      Our president so grand;[28]
    For the leading part that he did take
      In this our native land.

He has done his level best
  The working class to serve,
And to gain for them the bread of life
  And make the big bugs swerve.
There is full and plenty in this land
  To serve us one and all;
But the big bug has the capital
  And the miner none at all.

Chorus:

The time is close at hand, boys,
  When all men will combine,
And the miner will be recognized
  And in the senate shine.
In future mind your vote, boys,
  And look at laws when made.
And always look at truth and fact,
  And keep the upward grade.

Chorus:

The sun that shines upon the rich
  The same sun shines on the poor.
And when labor rules our capital
  We'll keep hunger from our door.
So, now, let's build our funds up, boys,
  And make the oak to bend.
And let our legislatures see,
  Our friends we mean to send.[29]

The strike of 1897 has been called "the spontaneous uprising of an enslaved people."[30] It was the first successful strike conducted by the United Mine Workers as a national organization. Over two hundred thousand men in the mines in Pennsylvania, Virginia, West Virginia, and Ohio went out on July 4, 1897, paralyzing about 70 percent of the soft coal production in the United States. For twelve weeks the miners stood firm, heeding the advice of this song:

MINER'S LIFEGUARD

Miner's life is like a sailor's
  'Board a ship to cross the wave;
Every day his life's in danger,
  Still he ventures being brave.
Watch the rocks, they're falling daily,
  Careless miners always fail;
Keep your hand upon the dollar
  And your eyes upon the scales.

    Union miners, stand together,
      Heed no operators' tale;
    Keep your hand upon the dollar
      And your eyes upon the scales.

Soon this trouble will be ended,
  Union men will have their rights,
After many years of bondage,
  Digging days and digging nights.
Then by honest weight we labor,
  Union workers never fail;
Keep your hands upon the dollar
  And your eyes upon the scales.

Chorus:

27 Korson, *Coal Dust on the Fiddle*, p. 370 (from the singing of "Old Charlie").

28 John McBride, formerly president of the Ohio State Miners' Union, was elected president of the United Mine Workers for one term in 1894.

29 *United Mine Workers' Journal*, June 28, 1894.

30 *American Federationist*, IV (Oct., 1897), 188.

Let no union man be weakened
By newspapers' false reports;
Be like sailors on the ocean,
Trusting in their safe lifeboats.
Let your lifeboat be Jehovah
Those who trust Him never fail.
Keep your hand upon the dollar
And your eyes upon the scales.

Chorus:

You've been docked and docked, my boys,
You've been loading two for one;
What have you to show for working
Since this mining has begun?
Overalls, and cans for rockers,
In your shanties sleep on rails.
Keep your hand upon the dollar
And your eyes upon the scales.

Chorus:

In conclusion, bear in memory,
Keep the password in your mind;
God provides for every nation,
When in union they combine.
Stand like men and linked together,
Victory for you will prevail,
Keep your hand upon the dollar
And your eyes upon the scales.

Chorus:[31]

STAND OUT, YE MINERS

By Flora P. Ford, a miner's wife

Stand out, stand out, ye miners,
Let wife and children beg;
Please don't go to the mines
And be called a scab, blackleg.

Stand out, stand out, ye miners,
You'll win the day at last;
You will not have to suffer
As you have in the past.

Stand out, stand out, ye miners,
The victory shall be yours;
This awful conflict must soon end,
And peace surround your doors.

Stand out, stand out, ye miners,
Your families will be fed;
After this strike is over
They will not cry for bread.

Stand out, stand out, ye miners,
The victory's almost won;
You miners have our sympathy
Till the victory is won.

Stand out, stand out, ye miners,
And hold your own today;
Don't listen to the tyrants
No matter what they say.

Stand out, stand out, ye miners,
And wave the banners high;
The flag under which we're marching
We must wave until we die.

The royal banner given
To set this country free;
Oh! do not let the tyrants
Take it from you and me.

But let us still march forward
With victory in our hand;
May we never let the tyrants
Make us slaves in our land.[32]

The strike ended on September 4, 1897, with a resounding victory for the miners. At a meeting in Chicago on January 18, 1898, the coal operators and the UMW signed the first national agreement any important industry had reached with its employees. The victory stimulated the growth of the UMW. In April, 1897, there were only ten thousand members in the union; by April, 1900, the membership had grown to one hundred seventeen thousand. Of these, about 20 percent were blacks, representing the highest percentage of black membership in any union of the period.

One of the objects of the UMW was "to unite in one organization, regardless of creed, color, or nationality all workmen employed in and around coal mines." The UMW constitution contained a clause which stated: "No member in good standing who holds a transfer card shall be debarred or hindered from obtaining work on account of race, creed or nationality."[33] Apart from the fact that it was impossible to separate workers in the mines into craft unions and exclude one part of the miners—as was the case with most of the unions affiliated with the AFL—the presence of a large black membership in the UMW was due, first, to the tradition of labor solidarity which the miners brought with

[31] *United Mine Workers' Journal,* Sept. 30, 1897.

[32] Ibid. British miners expressed the same sentiments in a song produced during the miners' lockout of 1893; see "Miners' Lock-Out" (sung to the tune of "Marble Arch") in Raymond Challinem, *The Lancashire and Cheshire Miners* (Newcastle upon Tyne, 1972), facing p. 256.

[33] Frank Julian Warne, *History of the United Mine Workers of America* (New York, 1905), p. 35.

them when they moved from the Knights of Labor into the United Mine Workers, and, second, to bitter experience, which had taught most white miners that unless the blacks were organized, they would be used as strikebreakers. This lesson was driven home time and again during the seventies and eighties and again in the miners' strikes of 1894 in Alabama and of 1898 in Virden and Pana, Illinois. In the latter strike, the coal operators sent agents to Alabama who hired a thousand Negroes to come north and work in the struck mines. Some blacks quit when they reached Illinois and learned they were brought north to break a strike, but most were prevented from leaving by Pinkerton and other private detective guards hired by the operators for this purpose. On October 12, 1898, a bloody skirmish occurred in Virden as strikers fought the hired gunmen protecting the strikebreakers; fourteen persons were killed and fifty wounded.

The opposition to Negro strikebreaking in the UMW produced a number of songs. However, these were resented by the black membership of the union because of the use of racist expressions and the failure to indicate that black union miners also opposed Negro strikebreaking.

THE MAIDEN'S PRAYER

I saw a little maiden
Upon a Miners' knee,
Asking for a bit of bread
And this is what she said:

What will become of Alabama, Pa
If things go on this way?
There are hundreds of the colored men
Scabbing every day.

I hear there's a man in Birmingham,
Or not very far away,
Who's trying mighty hard to make
A Negro Eden pay.

* * * * *

And then there is the grand jury—
They did not treat us right;
They called us cutthroats in the day
And chicken thieves at night.

O, miners, stick, I beg you stick!
For ours' is a noble fight.
And the Lord of hosts will help us
As long as we're in the right.

And do not burn the bridges, boys
Nor wreck a railroad train,
For everything bad that's done
The miners get the blame.

So now, fellow workingmen,
I hope you will keep still:
You might do harm to some innocent man
Who bears us no ill will.[34]

ON THE BANKS OF THE RAILROAD

To the tune of "On the Banks of the Wabash"

Away down in our homes in Alabama,
Us coons we were contented to stay,
'Till Mr. Lukins[35] come and told us what he would give us
If we would come with him to Virden far away.
When we arrived in Virden Sunday morning
We found that things were not what Lukins say,
The miners were all lined up along the railroad
And you bet us coons was glad to get away.

The moon is shining brightly along the railroad,
And the miners are situated there to stay.
The candle lights are gleaming in the stockade;
Mr. Lukins thinks he's having things his way.
He told us the miners were all in Cuba,
And there wasn't only eight men there to stay;
He didn't tell us what a pen he'd put us into,
When he got us down to Virden far away.
Then good-by to Mr. Lukins, we are bound for
Alabama there to stay;
If Mr. Lukins ever comes to Alabama
We will show him what us coons will do that day.[36]

THE VIRDEN MARTYRS

'Twas down at Virden where bold Lukins,
To break our union vowed.
But shoulder to shoulder stood our miners
Before his convict crowd.

"We'll fill the shaft with negro convicts,"
The sordid Lukins said.
"You shall not!" said our union miners,
"Our children must have bread."

"Send us soldiers," was the message
To our Governor sent.
"You must protect rich operators,"
Was what the message meant.

34Robert David Ward and William Warren Rogers, *Labor Revolt in Alabama* (University, Ala., 1965), pp. 98–99.

35Lukins was manager of the company which imported scab labor from Alabama. For a discussion of the Pana and Virden battles, see Philip S. Foner, *Organized Labor and the Black Worker, 1619–1973* (New York, 1974), pp. 78–80.

36*United Mine Workers' Journal*, Oct. 13, 1898.

"I will not use our state militia
To land your convict crew,"
Said 'Honest John', "but life and land
I will protect 'tis true."

The night was cold and dark and dreary,
The rain in torrents fell;
And there they watch those toil-worn brothers,
Thinking neither of shot or shell.

"Stand firm, brothers! there's the signal:
Onward comes the train,
Laden down with convict labor,
Turn them back again."

There they stood, our noble brothers,
Shot from tower and train
By those swarthy dark-skinned convicts,
Brought there for owners' gain.

There they fell, our martyred brothers
Oh, God, that it would be!
Martyred to the sacred cause
Of labor, unity.

Then hail our union! miners, brothers,
United let us stand.
Shall their blood be shed in vain,
This noble martyred band?

Hand in hand then let us be
For our union grand.
United we shall have success,
Divided we cannot stand.[37]

In 1899 John Mitchell succeeded Michael D. Ratchford as president of the United Mine Workers, and in the eyes of many miners, especially the recent immigrants from Slovakia, Hungary, Poland, and Romania, the UMW came to be known as "John Mitchell's union." The Slavs were organized in the UMW along with the Irish, and their enthusiasm for the union was expressed in the song "Me Johnny Mitchell Man."

ME JOHNNY MITCHELL MAN

By Con Carbon

Tune—"Underneath Your Window"
or "Say You Love Me, Sue"

Now you know Mike Sokolosky—
Dat man my brudder.
Last night him come to my shanty,
Un me tellin': "What you cummin' fer"?
Him tellin' 'bout tomorra dark night,
Every miner all, big un shmall
Goin' fer on shtrike.
Un him say t' me: "Joe, me tellin' you
Don't be 'fraid or shcared fer nottin', never, never do."
"Don't be shcabby feller," him tellin' me again.
I'm say, "No sir! Mike, me out o' sight—
Me Johnny Mitchell man."

Me no 'fraid fer nottin',
Me dey never shcare.
Sure me shtrike tomorra night,
Dat's de business, I don't care.
Right a-here me tellin' you—
Me no shcabby feller,
Good union citizen—
Johnny Mitchell man.

Now me belong t' union, me good citizen.
For seven year, me livin' here
In dis beeg America.
Me workin' in de Prospect,
Workin' Dorrance shaft, Conyngham, Nottingham*—
Every place like dat.
Workin' in de gangway, workin' in de breast,
Labor every day, me never get a rest.
Me got plenty money, nine hundred, maybe ten,
So shtrike kin come, like son of a gun—
Me Johnny Mitchell man.[38]

*Collieries in and around Wilkes-Barre.

ON JOHNNY MITCHELL'S TRAIN

I'm an honest union laborin' man,
And I'll have you understand.
I'll tell you just the reason why,
I left the mining land.
It was Baer and Morgan done it,
And for it they'll repent,
For we don't intend to work a tap,
Till we get the ten per cent.

There's no use for Mr. Durkin,
In the coal mine to be workin';
We were a little shaky,
But no longer we're in pain.
So what's the use o' kickin',
When the top and bottom's stickin'?
I'll pack me grip and make a trip
On Johnny Mitchell's train.

I struck a place called Coatesville,
A flourishin' iron town,
Where politics were very strong,
And candidates goin' round.
I was invited to a party,
He says, "Phat are you doin', Dan?"

37Ibid., Dec. 29, 1898, reprinted in Korson, *Coal Dust on the Fiddle*, pp. 380–81.

38Korson, *Songs and Ballads of the Anthracite Miner*, pp. 180–81.

I says, "I'll tell you plumb and plain,
I'm a Johnny Mitchell Man."

When I landed in New York City,
I a friend of course did meet,
I axed him if he would show me
The place they call Wall Street.
I met several operators,
Assembled in a mob,
Along with Morgan's prisident,
I think they called him Schwab.

The small operators they were pl'adin',
And they wanted to give in,
And recognize the union—
But Baer said that's too thin.
So it broke up in a wrangle,
Put Baer nearly insane,
Then I took a side-door Pullman car
On Johnny Mitchell's train.

So I'll bid ye all adieu now,
Let ye bid me the same,
The strike is nearly over,
And with joy I'm near insane.
Here's health unto the union,
Which is very strong they say,
Likewise to the conductor
On Johnny Mitchell's train.[39]

John Mitchell's prestige soared as UMW membership rose dramatically after 1897. It reached a high point at the end of the century, when the union forced the coal companies, under the financial control of J. P. Morgan, to sign a new agreement. Miners of many nationalities joined to sing this parody of the popular tune of the day "Just Break the News to Mother."

BREAK THE NEWS TO MORGAN
Air—"Break the News to Mother"
By Henry Carey

When monopolists were trying to satisfy their greed,
The miners they were struggling their families to feed,
When a call from brave John Mitchell: "Come boys,
Your tools throw down and drive those slavery days away."
"We will," the miners shouted. "We'll shake them off or die,
Shake them off but stay united;
It is an honest cause, we cannot fail,
And some day we'll have the abolition of the sliding scale."

Just break the news to Morgan, that great official organ,
And tell him we want ten percent of increase in our pay.
Just say we are united and that our wrongs must be righted,
And with those unjust company stores of course we will do away.

From that great and glorious Mitchell, our national president,
To all the corporations an invitation went,
To attend a joint convention to be held in Hazelton
And there our grievances arbitrate.
But when they ignored his message, he said: "I'll call a strike
And have our wrongs adjusted in that way."
We struck and were successful, so then a scale was formed,
Agreeable unto the first of May.

It came from J. P. Morgan, that great official organ.
He said, "I'll give you ten percent of increase in your pay."
He saw we were united, that our wrongs must be righted,
And now for brave John Mitchell, we will give three cheers, hooray.[40]

Miners' conventions were marked by singing. Not all the songs, however, grew out of the miners' struggles or even the labor movement. The *Birmingham Labor Advocate* of June 30, 1900, reported on a district convention of the UMW in Birmingham, Alabama, at which black and white miners met and sang together:

Delegate Scott sang "The Honest Workingman" in fine voice. Some of the delegates joined in the chorus:

"It's a glorious union,
Deny it who can.
That defends the rights
Of a workingman."

Mr. Fairley then called for a song from one of the colored brethren.

Charles Farley, colored, ascended the rostrum and sang "We are Marching to Canaan." It had the old-time camp-meeting lilt and the colored delegates crooned the lines and broke into the chorus:

"Who is there among us,
The true and the tried,
Who'll stand by his fellows,
Who's on the Lord's side."

Delegate Jack Orr responded to the call of the

39Korson, *Pennsylvania Songs and Legends*, pp. 396–98 (from the singing of Jerry Byrne).

40Korson, *Minstrels of the Mine Patch*, p. 233.

convention with "Silver Bells of Memory." The convention took up the refrain with gusto.

There was a storm of calls for "Bill Fairley," to sing a song. "I'm never bluffed," he said with a smile. "I hope the reporters will not take down my song." He sang "Give Me Back My Heart."

Delegate Hopper sang "That Pack of Cards," a serio-comic recitation, with considerable dramatic effect.

Loud calls were made for a song by Vice President Brooks, who begged off. Ed Flynn, chairman of the scale committee, also asked to be excused.

J. T. Allen, a colored delegate, sang in a powerful voice "I am a Child of the King."

WESTERN METAL MINERS

While eastern coal miners were building their union and waging their strikes in the 1890s, western hard-rock miners were engaged in similar activities. A common bond of oppression linked the eastern coal miners and the western metal miners. By 1890 the great majority of western miners were dependent for their livelihood upon corporations dominated by absentee owners. Gone were the independent miners of the early "rushes" into the mine fields. In their place were strictly wage earners working for corporate organizations under a whole new set of restrictions and regulations and piling up profits for absentee owners in what, along with coal mining, was the most dangerous of America's major industries. William D. "Big Bill" Haywood, the militant leader of the western miners, wrote in his description of a typical mining town: "Human life is the cheapest by-product of this great copper camp."[41]

In May, 1893, after a successful strike in Coeur d'Alene, Idaho, marked by armed clashes between Pinkertons and strikers, then by the use of the National Guard and finally the United States Army, the metal miners organized the Western Federation of Miners. The WFM rapidly became the most militant union in the United States, and its struggles against the powerful mining corporations, including the Standard Oil trust, which controlled many of the mines, are legends in American labor history. Unfortunately, the western metal miners had no one like George Korson, who collected the songs and ballads of the coal miners.[42] However, the *Miners' Magazine*, the official organ of the Western Federation of Miners, did carry a few songs and ballads in the issues of March, April, and July, 1900.

WESTERN FEDERATION OF MINERS

By John F. McDonnell, Virginia City, Nevada

The miners have a Federation, the grandest ever known,
And it gives emancipation to slaves the rich men own.
Her name is heralded with joy throughout the western
 land,
And though the "rich combine" arroy, her deeds of
 fame expand.

In the horn of plenty's legion her choicest gifts are
 strewn,
And her name in every region on labor's hearts are hewn.
Her march is in the sunlight ray of intellect and fame;
Her every act just means fair play, and justice guides her
 name.

'Twas on old "Bull Hill's" towering crest, she waged her
 foremost fight,
There capital entrenched its best, was forced to onward
 flight
On Leadville's rocky mountain brow the miners' fight
 was gained,
And since the Federation's prav the heights of fame
 attained.

On Coe'ur d'Alene's eternal hills her power sublime is
 known,
And o'er her vales and crystal rills she rules upon her
 throne.
No martial law, nor tyrant hand her onward march can
 check;
Her mandates reign throughout the land, her sons are all
 on deck.

And when she gave the world her laws, and call'd her
 sons to arms
She met the people's glad applause and filled the earth
 with charms;
And like an eagle in her nest upon the mountain's brow,
She holds her place, Queen of the West, while knaves
 before her bow.

41 William D. Haywood, *Bill Haywood's Book* (New York, 1929), p. 83.

42 A collection of twenty-five songs which emerged during the second decade of the twentieth century, *New Songs for Butte Mining Camp*, was published in Butte, ca. 1920; the late John Neuhaus gave a copy to folklorist Archie Green, in whose library it now exists. Some of these songs are also published in S. Page Stegner, "Protest Songs from the Butte Mines," *Western Folklore*, XXVII (July, 1967), 157–67, and in Wayland D. Hand et al., "Songs of the Butte Miner," ibid., IX (Jan., 1950), 1–49.

"Old Steunenberg" now hides his head in dark oblivion's
gloom.[43]
His aspiration are all dead, he met a traitor's doom;
And "Duty Hughey" in his den, shall long regret the day
That he was chief of the "Bull Pen," or ever there held
sway.

"Old Sinclair" and her godless gang have hid their heads
in shame.
The tocsins have given a last clang, oblivion hides each
name.
While Corcoran's name, on deathless wing, shall ever live
sublime;
Unborn millions his praise shall sing, adorn the years of
Time.

Tyrants at her banner tremble, as to victory she moves
on,
When her toiling sons assemble, liberty's fight is won.
Down the great waters of old Time, her stately boat still
flies.
Her deeds shall ever soar sublime, her glories touch the
skies.[44]

A GREAT COUNTRY

A Patriotic Song by an American
with a Chorus by his Conscience

By A. La Sims

There is no land like ours, no people like her sons;
There's wealth, there's plenty everywhere, and swift our
warm blood runs,
Our tables groan with luxuries, and welcome is our
guest—

Conscience:
Though, truth to tell, you always treat the richest ones
the best.

Our senators keep open house, and dine in regal state,
They feast the lions when they come, the wealthy and
the great.
With lavish hand on foreigners, we squander heaps of
gold—

Conscience:
And leave your poor in agony to perish in the cold.

Our universities we cannot count, since legion is their
name,
The largesse of our wealthy men, is trumpeted to fame;
Our hospitals are noble piles, where skills with kindness
vie—

Conscience:
While every day we read about some poor left to die.

Here justice is not bought or sold; here innocence we
guard—
No paid official, as abroad, on prisoners is hard.
No monchard plots to ruin men, no victims justice
claims—

Conscience:
Don't mention Parsons, Spies and Lingg—they might be
awkward names.[45]

Here suff'ring finds a ready friend to answer its appeal;
Here every woman has a heart for women's woes to feel.
Here people meet to guard the rights of nigger and of
Turk—

Conscience:
Here children toil twelve hours a day and die from
overwork![46]

ONLY A MAN IN OVERALLS

By Frank Aley, Member of Globe Miners' Union No. 69
Western Federation of Miners, Globe, Arizona

Only a man in overalls, lay him anywhere—
Send for the company doctor—we have no time to spare;
Only a little misfire, only a miner crushed,
Put another one on, for from dark till dawn
The smelter must be rushed.

Only another widow under another's roof,
Only another victim beneath the iron hoof,
Only a batch of orphans, and thus the drama ends,
Just let them go, with their anguish and woe,
So we make our dividends.

Only a man in overalls—a very good man, as a rule—
But a man with us is rated as a farmer rates a mule;
One is as good as the other, but the long-eared slave's the
best,
He's a little rougher, decidedly tougher,
And doesn't need half the rest.

Only a man in overalls, bury him anywhere—
The burleigh is boring, the furnace is roaring—
We have no time to spare;
Let the tears of the widow fall on his worthless clay,
To h——l with the orphan, to h——l with the man,
To h——l with the judgment day.[47]

Frank Aley's "Only a Man in Overalls" is related to the popular song of the western metal miners, "Hard-Working Miner."[48]

43Frank Steunenberg, governor of Idaho, fought the Western Federation of Miners during the Coeur d'Alene struggles, drove its members out of the mines, and sent one of its officers to prison.

44*Miners' Magazine*, Mar., 1900, pp. 11–12.

45Parsons, Spies, and Lingg were three of the eight men involved in the Haymarket tragedy. See pp. 227–31.

46*Miners' Magazine*, Apr., 1900, p. 16.

47Ibid., July, 1900, p. 16.

48For a history of this song see Green, *Only a Miner*, pp. 63–111.

HARD-WORKING MINER

To the hard-working miner whose dangers are great,
So many while mining have met their sad fate,
While doing their duty as miners all do,
Shut out from daylight, and their loving ones, too.

Only a miner killed in the ground,
Only a miner, and one more is gone,
Killed by an accident, no one can tell,
His mining is over—poor miner, farewell.

He leaves his dear wife, and his little ones, too,
To earn them a living as all miners do,
And while he is working for those that he loved,
He met a sad fate from a boulder above.

Though comrades were near him, so quick was the call,
The message of death, the miner did fall,
Though comrades were near him, no one could say,
Now the poor fellow rests in his grave.

Only a miner killed in the ground,
Only a miner, and one more is gone,
Killed by an accident, no one can tell,
His mining is over—poor miner, farewell.[49]

49Duncan Emrich, "Songs of the Western Miners," *California Folklore Quarterly*, I (July, 1942), 222–23.

10

The Eight-Hour Day and the Haymarket Affair

Apart from political action, no single issue in nineteenth-century labor history produced as many songs and ballads as did the movement for a shorter working day. Some songs, as we have already seen, came out of the ten-hour movement of the 1840s. But it was the campaign for the eight-hour day which produced the largest number.

IRA STEWARD

Although some unions had raised the demand for an eight-hour day before and during the Civil War, the movement began in earnest when the war was over. During this period, it was led by Ira Steward of the Machinists' and Blacksmiths' Union (the "father of the eight-hour day"), and it received wide support from all national and local unions and the National Labor Union.

Ira Steward's eight-hour philosophy was based on the idea that labor's demands were small because long hours gave the workers little chance to realize that they needed more. If hours were reduced, the leisure time would create new desires, and in order to satisfy them, wages would have to move upward. Instead of resulting in lower wages, therefore, as was commonly charged by employers, the eight-hour day would actually bring higher wages. Steward even popularized a little couplet written by his wife, Mary B. Steward, which assured workers:

Whether you work by the piece or work by the day,
Decreasing the hours, increases the pay.[1]

Steward's strategy was to secure the eight-hour day through legislation. To further this goal, he organized a network of eight-hour leagues which mobilized workers during elections to apply pressure on candidates and obtain their pledge to further eight-hour legislation once elected. The crusade to gain the eight-hour day through the ballot box made rapid headway and was advanced by the "Rallying Song of the Eight-Hour League," sung at meetings of hundreds of leagues. It was published on December 22, 1865, in the *Boston Daily Evening Voice*, which described it as the "prize labor song."

RALLYING SONG OF THE EIGHT-HOUR LEAGUE

Hail, brothers!—we are coming!—we will rally in our might,
We are coming from our workshops, our phalanx to unite;
We leave our clanking engines, we will let the forge grow cold,
While we gather 'round our standard, and Labor's cause uphold.

Rally, brothers! rally, brothers! rally while we may!
Rally to the standard, boys—we work eight hours a day!

The joyful hour is coming, 'tis the dawn before the day,
When the masses quit their toiling and demand their honest sway;
Eight earnest hours for Labor, eight in rest we pass away,
But the other eight for progress, brothers, we may claim today!

Chorus:

[1] Ira Steward, *Poverty* (Boston, n.d.), preface; *Labor Standard*, Mar. 3, 1877.

We gather at the watchword, and we clasp each brother's
hand,
As with our hearts united, in the cause of Truth we
stand;
And our League shall still around us its cheering hopes
entwine—
The beacon of our safety, as we rally round its shrine.

Chorus:

We quit the noisy anvil, and we lay aside the plane—
Let worthy toil be honored while our rights we shall
maintain;
Let every earnest worker, then, our high behest obey,
To gather 'round our standard, and to work eight hours
a day!

Chorus:

EIGHT-HOUR SONGS OF THE SIXTIES

In the summer of 1865, *Fincher's Trades' Review* of Philadelphia launched a contest for songs dealing with the demand for the eight-hour day. In the issue of August 12, 1865, Jonathan C. Fincher, the editor, announced that he was publishing the first song received but was not entirely satisfied with the product: "We insert the lines sent by our correspondent in the hope that they may elicit some 'Eight-hour lyrics' worthy of the mighty reform which has inspired them. They are decidedly rough and their author must try to do better.—ED." The editor was not easily satisfied, for on August 26, 1865, he printed a song with this comment: "The above is an improvement on the last upon the same subject, but we hope our contributors can do still better.—Ed. Rev." Then on September 9, 1865, he printed a song entitled "The Eight-Hour Law," but advised: "The above is given more in order to keep the eye of the reader upon the subject than for its merits. . . . Try again, there is ample room for a creditable poem without tredding on former efforts.—ED." Evidently the first product which completely satisfied the editor was the following, published in *Fincher's Trades' Review* of September 23, 1865.

EIGHT-HOUR LYRICS

Air—"My Country 'tis of Thee"

Ye noble sons of toil,
Who ne'er from work recoil,
Take up the lay;

Loud let the anthem's roar
Resume from shore to shore,
Till Time shall be no more.
Eight Hours a Day.

Hark! hark! The cry comes on
From where the setting sun
Declines the day;

O'er every hill and vale
Is borne upon the gale,
The glorious motto hail,
Eight Hours a Day.

Once more then let the sound
O'er all the earth redound
For e'er and aye.

Shout, shout the noble strain,
Until from the land and main
Is heard the loud refrain,
Eight Hours a Day.

One other eight-hour song appeared in *Fincher's Trades' Review* before the weekly expired. The editor remarked: "The above is the composition of Mr. Charles Haynes, of Chicago, who has the misfortune to be blind. It is, without exception, the best yet received, and will soon become popular." His estimate had some substance, for the song was reprinted in the *Workingman's Advocate* of March 7, 1868.

EIGHT-HOUR SONG

Tune—"Tramp, Tramp, Tramp the Boys"

Let us gather once again,
Let us strike with might and main,
We must overcome the proud without delay;
Let the laboring men unite,
For each one must have his right,
And the law be made for work, Eight Hours a day.

Hear your leader's voices call you,
Hasten quickly on your way;
We must rally for the fight,
Stand for justice and for right,
Till the law for work be made 8 hours a day.

Now the lowly must be raised,
And the haughty made to feel
That oppression can no longer be endured;
If we stand as firm as steel,
Then the foe shall surely yield,
And the evils that we suffer will be cured.

Chorus:

Forward boys and fill the ranks,
Press the foe in front and flanks,
We must fight until the victory is won;

If we crush the tyrant's might,
We shall then emerge from night,
Let us work until our glorious task is done.

Chorus:

Put each shoulder to the wheel,
Crush the foeman neath your heel;
Let each laboring man be steady in the fight—
We must break the tyrant's power,
Now's the glorious day and hour,
If we strike we'll surely win the cause of right.

Chorus:[2]

Other labor papers continued publishing eight-hour songs after *Fincher's Trades' Review* disappeared, especially the *Boston Daily Evening Voice.*

HURRAH FOR OUR BOYS IN BLUE
Song and Chorus by R.B.D.

Hurrah! Hurrah! Hurrah for our boys in blue!
They'd never forsake us, They always were true,
Hurrah! hurrah! hurrah!

Hurrah! hurrah! Hurrah for our boys in blue!
Eight hours for us, and bounty for you,[3]
Hurrah! hurrah! hurrah!

Hurrah! Hurrah! Hurrah for our boys in blue!
They fought 'neath the shade of the damp Southern glade,
Hurrah! hurrah! hurrah!

Chorus:

Hurrah! Hurrah! Hurrah for our boys in blue!
They fought for me, they fought for you,
Hurrah! hurrah! hurrah!

Chorus:

Hurrah! Hurrah! Hurrah for our boys in blue!
With hand joined in hand Our rights we'll demand,
Hurrah! hurrah! hurrah!

Chorus:

Hurrah! Hurrah! Hurrah for our boys in blue!
With God on our side In his strength we'll abide,
Hurrah! hurrah! hurrah!

Chorus:[4]

EIGHT-HOUR SONG
By C. N. Brown
Air—"Tramp! Tramp! the Prisoner's Hope"

We have toiled for others' gains, and have robbed both purse and brains,
But we know the course is neither just nor right;
Now the people of the land for their rights have made a stand,
And the sons of toil will prove they're men of might.

Eight Hours, boys, proclaim the watchword,
Hilltops echo with the sound;
Won't the miser yield his "tin" and the jubilee begin—
Wealth and knowledge with the workmen shall abound.

We have labored to defend, and we labor to extend,
Every glorious institution of our land;
This we do with willing heart, but we ask to share a part
In fruits which are produced by labor's hand.

Chorus:

While the workingman in the field has made the boasted rebel yield,
Speculation has been stuffing out his jowls,
But the war abroad is done and we're now commenced at home,
And we'll show our valor shortly at the polls.

Chorus:

Shoddy men have made their pile, and the greasy rogue *struck ile!*
Still the workman has been trudging on his way;
But because he has been mute, judge him not to be a brute,
For he *thinks* as much as other people *say.*

Chorus:

Though oppression we deplore, workingmen do not ignore,
Rights and profits which to capital belong;
But if wealth begins to rule, counting workingmen his mule,
Then the more he *drives* the more "he won't go 'long."

Chorus:

Now ye workingmen unite, and be valiant for the right,
Equal rights shall then prevail throughout the land;
Here, in freedom's happy bower, bloated wealth has lost its power,
For the law is in the working people's hand.[5]

[2] *Fincher's Trades' Review,* Nov. 18, 1865.
[3] Veterans of the Union army were urging Congress to enact legislation granting pensions and land-grant bounties for those who fought against the Confederacy.
[4] *Boston Daily Evening Voice,* Feb. 2, 1866.
[5] Ibid., Feb. 19, 1866.

Labor Lyrics—No. 11

By Robert W. Hume

"To Our Brethren in Illinois"

A CAROL

On the passage of the Eight-Hour Law by the Legislature of Illinois which is an acknowledgement of that State of the Justice of the demand.

Ye Men of Illinois,
With steadfast heart and true,
Your brethren of the East
Their greeting send to you.
You've nobly earned our praise,
There's no denying that,—
So, like fair-dealing men,
We pass to you—the hat.

Some merit, too, is due
Unto the lazy folk
You send upstairs to prate,
Because they've eased your yoke,
The day has not arrived,
Though opening fair and bright,
When workingmen alone
Will judge on labor's right.

Although the bill that's passed
Stands rickety and lame,
Let's hope 'twill find its feet
When next you try again.
For surely there are none
(To truth and justice dead)
Amongst you to betray
The men who raised your bread.*

The tiller of the soil
Must never be forgot,
The hardy farmer's boy
With us has part and lot,
We'll take his horny hand
And lift him on high,—
When laborers unite,
They can their foes defy.†

We are not idle here,
We have a State in tow;
It is that famous place
Where wooden nutmegs grow.
Dead issues are forgot
Before "our time of day";
And, ballot in his hand,
The workman hews his way.

God speed him to the polls.
If, with a loyal heart
To all who live by toil,
He plays his chosen part.
But unto you, Brave Boys,
Fair Freedom's Pioneers!
We hail you with your thanks,
And send you hearty cheers.[6]

*Sec. 2 "This Act . . . shall not in any sense be held to apply to farm labor."

†It will be remembered, that when the strike of the Caulkers and Ship-Carpenters took place, fears were openly expressed, at a meeting of the bosses, that in it the mechanical and agricultural laborers will become united. Let us remember the old Roman maxim, and "learn from the enemy."

DECLINE AND REVIVAL OF THE EIGHT-HOUR MOVEMENT

The struggle for the eight-hour day made rapid headway during the mid-sixties. Several states passed eight-hour laws; by the end of 1868, six states and several cities had adopted such legislation. Congress passed a law on June 25, 1868, providing an eight-hour day for laborers, mechanics, and all other workmen in federal employ. But after 1868, the movement declined. For one thing, the national law proved to be defective. Wages of federal workers were reduced as the shorter workday was put into effect, and the government took the position that the eight-hour law did not affect contractors on government jobs. The state laws, too, were emasculated by the insertion of nullifying clauses. Thus the Illinois law was to be effective only where there was "no special contract to the contrary." After the passage of these laws employers informed their workers that only those who signed contracts agreeing to work longer hours could hold their jobs. Finally, with the onset of the panic of 1873, even the eight-hour day gained by workers through strikes was swept away.

The Boston Eight-Hour League, headed by Ira Steward, stayed alive, however, and met in annual conventions where the delegates sang the song written for the league in 1871 by Edward R. Place of Cambridge, Massachusetts, known as "the labor poet."[7]

[6] *Boston Weekly Voice*, Apr. 4, 1867.

[7] *Socialist* (New York), June 17, 1876. When Place died (Nov. 7, 1881), the *Labor Standard* carried a tribute to him as "the Eight Hour poet and philosopher," pointing out that he "was a book-binder by trade, and followed his trade as long as his health would permit" (Nov. 19, 1881).

SONG OF THE BOSTON EIGHT HOUR LEAGUE

By Edward R. Place

Says now, warm-dissenting brother,
"Absurd the cry, Less Hours,
These are the things excel all other:
Banking, finance and interest talking,
Landlords their unearned fortunes raking;
While legal wrong the land devours,
Cease the vain cry, *Less Hours.*"

And still we sing with trebled voices,
Less hours! less hours! less hours!
Betwixt two things our only choice is:
Affirm this justice, and obtain it,
Or, asking feebly, never gain it,
Dividing schemes build Babel towers,
Join the *one* cry—EIGHT HOURS!

Wake! sons of toil; Up! power-crushed daughter;
Your own are all the hours.
Rescue from Mammon's cruel slaughter
Heav'n's gift of gifts,—arouse to action!
Be Truth your sword, not murd'rous faction.
Onward in column! mass your powers!
For Justice, and Eight Hours![8]

Late in the depression years, the eight-hour movement revived. This time the *Labor Standard* (published in Paterson, New Jersey, by J. P. McDonnell) spearheaded the drive. The first eight-hour song to appear in the *Labor Standard* was published early in 1877.

EIGHT HOURS A DAY

A Labor Song

By John M'Intosh

Eight hours a day, fellows, not a breath over it
Put your foot down upon that with a will;
Resolute, confident, every one go for it;
Toiler in workshop, in office, or mill.
Up with our banner, all cheery and hearty men;
Motto still Equity, Justice, Fair play!
Loyal to Honor, to Right and the Party, men,
Shout our great battle cry, EIGHT HOURS A DAY!

Eight hours a day, fellows,
Justice, fair play, fellows,
Never say nay, fellows,
Eight hours a day!

Not with the bullet and carnage of shot and shell
Seek we with bloodshed to bolster our cause;
Come we with ballots, alone for each vote to tell
Just legislators, to alter our laws,
Up with our banner, then, cheery and hearty, men!
Motto still Equity, Justice, Fair play;
Loyal to Honor, to Right and the Party, men,
Shout our great battle cry, EIGHT HOURS A DAY!

Eight hours a day, fellows,
Justice, fair play, fellows,
Never say nay, fellows,
Eight hours a day!

Shoulder to shoulder, all firmly unified men;
Union with union cemented as one;
Welded in honor till labor be righted, men,
Onward, still on, till the battle be won.
Up with our banner, all cheery and hearty, men;
Motto still equity, Justice, Fair Play;
Loyal to honor, to right and the party, men,
Shout our great battle cry, Eight hours a day!

Eight hours a day, fellows,
Justice, fair play, fellows,
Never say nay, fellows,
Eight hours a day![9]

In 1878, when the *Labor Standard* became the official organ of the International Labor Union, formed by leaders of the eight-hour movement (including Ira Steward) and the Marxian Socialists, it began to devote even more space to eight-hour songs, such as these popular pieces by Edward R. Place. The first was published in the *Labor Standard* of May 19, 1878; the second appeared in the issue of June 16, 1878, and was also printed as a broadside (a copy of which is in the Harris Collection, Brown University).

A SONG OF EIGHT HOURS

By E. R. Place of Mass.

Tune—"Marching through Georgia"

Lo, a vision of dismay, a lurid glimpse of doom,
Bursts from out the shadow of a world-enshrouding gloom;
Murmurs of the soul are heard as from a sounding tomb.
Ring through the world the grand chorus!

Eight hours! eight hours! shall bring the jubilee;

[8]In a letter to the *Labor Standard* a few weeks after Place's death, Ira Steward noted that the song was written and published by Place "in 1871, after its delivery to the league." But the only version I have found is the one Steward submitted to the *Labor Standard* in this letter. He hailed Place as "the poet of the Boston Eight Hour League" and added: "Better poetry may be written by Longfellow or Tennyson; but the topic most worthy a poet, was chosen by Edward R. Place. For the laborers cause, includes, all causes" (Dec. 17, 1881).

[9]Ibid., Apr. 28, 1877, reprinted in Detroit *Socialist*, Mar. 23, 1878.

Eight hours! eight hours! shall set the people free;
Less for daily drudging counts the more for you and me.
Ring through the world the grand chorus!

Through the Ages hath the soul made haughty rulers quake;
Evermore at last the soul some rightful claim doth take;
Evermore the fight will on, and wrong's dominion shake.
Ring through the world the grand chorus!

Eight hours! &c.

What disturbs the tyrant's rest, and smites his heart with fear?
'Tis the rising, rousing shout, "We'll seize the boon that's near;
Shorter hours of wearing toil! Toll out with lofty cheer,"
Ring through the world the grand chorus!

Eight hours! &c.

Bands of gold by Mammon welded hold oppression's power;
Time it has to plot new ways to rob the people's dower;
Well enough it knows the pith and value of an hour.
Ring through the world the grand chorus!

Eight hours! &c.

See the scribblers trim and lie; the slaves of slaves are they,
Selling, as base Judas did the truthful Christ for pay.
Happy were the people would they go Iscariot's way.
Ring through the world the grand chorus!

Eight hours! &c.

Are we still an ignorant crowd, or still the placeman's tools,
Spite of all the church's grace and boasted Common Schools?
Know we of a famous charm shall wise men make of fools,
Ring through the world the grand chorus!

Eight hours! &c.

Shoulder against shoulder, brothers, union each with all,
Union of all hearts and hands, our armor and our wall;
Backward reels the servile host that potent gold may call.
Ring through the world the grand chorus!

Eight hours! &c.

Better than your "stateman's" wit, the common sense of things;—
Stir the soil, Oxhusbandman, or naught the harvest brings;
Stir the mind with quick'ning thought, and, lo, all nature sings.
Ring through the world the grand chorus!

Eight hours! &c.

Stronger leaps the toiler's pulse, a light is in the eye,
While he hears the watchman call the morn of Freedom nigh;
Hope revives, the soul awakes, and greets the bright'ning sky.
Ring through the world the grand chorus!

Eight hours! &c.

Simple, as all truest things, the mandate of the hour:
Plenty, and a home for all—the watchword and
Now behold the haughty front of old oppression cower,
Ring through the world the grand chorus!

Eight hours! &c.

JAMES BROWN

By E. R. Place

Tune—"John Brown's Body"

James Brown's body toils along the rocky road,
James Brown's body bends beneath a crushing load,
James Brown's body feels the point of hunger's goad,
His soul cries out for help.

Come, O bearer of Glad Tidings,
Bringing joy from out her hidings,
Come, O bearer of Glad Tidings,
O come, O come, Eight Hours!

James Brown's wife is worn and pale with many cares,
James Brown's wife so weak can scarce get up the stairs,
James Brown's wife is dying 'neath the load she bears,
Her soul cries out for help.

Refrain:

James Brown's children go a-shivering in the cold,
James Brown's children young, with work are growing old,
James Brown's lambs are torn by wolves outside the fold,
O, save, O, save, the lambs!

Refrain:

James Brown feels oppression's iron within his breast,
James Brown broods and ponders, he is not at rest.
James Brown swears he will with wrong and power contest,
His own right arm shall help.

Refrain:

James Brown may sometime become a desp'rate man,
James Brown may sometime go join the tramper's clan,
James Brown then may say, "I'll do the worst I can."
O, blame not him alone.

Refrain:

EIGHT HOURS.
Words by I. G. BLANCHARD.
Music by Rev. JESSE H. JONES.
1. We mean to make things o - ver, we are tired of toil for naught,
2. The beasts that graze the hill - side, and the birds that wan - der free,
3. The voice of God with - in us is.... call - ing us to stand
4.. Ye deem they're fee - ble voi - ces that are raised in La - bor's cause?
5. From fac - tor - ies and workshops, in... long and wea - ry lines,
9. Hur - rah, hur - rah, for La - bor! for it shall a - rise in might;
With but bare enough to live up - on, and never an hour for thought;
In the life that God has met - ed have a bet - ter lot than we.
E - - rect, as is be - com - ing to the work of his right hand;
But be - think ye of the tor - rent, and the wild tor - na - do's laws!
From all the sweltering forg - es, and from out the sun - less mines,
It has filled the world with plen - ty, it shall fill the world with light!
We want to feel the sun - shine, and we want to smell the flowers,
Oh! hands and hearts are wea - ry, and homes are heavy with dole;
Should he, to whom the Mak - er his glo - rious im - age gave,
We say not Toil's up - ris - ing in ter - ror's shape will come,
Wher - ev - er toil is wast - ing the force of life to live,
Hur - rah, hur - rah, for La - bor! it is mustering all its powers,

We are sure that God has will'd it, and we mean to have eight hours.
If our life's to be filled with drudgery, what need of a hu - man soul!
The meanest of his creatures crouch, a bread and but - ter slave!
Yet the world were wise to lis - ten to the mon - i - to - ry hum.
There the bent and battered arm - ies come to claim what God doth give,
And shall march a - long to vic - tor - y with the ban - ner of Eight Hours!
We're sum - mon - ing our for - ces from the ship - yard, shop and mill,
Shout, shout the lus - ty ral - ly from ship - yard, shop and mill,
Let the shout ring down the val - leys and ech - o from ev - 'ry hill,
Soon, soon the deep-toned ral - ly shall all the na - tions thrill,
And the bla - zon on their ban - ner doth with hope the na - tions fill,
Shout, shout the echo - ing ral - ly till all the wel - kin thrill,
CHORUS.
Eight hours for work, eight hours for rest, eight hours for what we will!
Eight hours for work, eight hours for rest, eight hours for what we will!
Courtesy of Tamiment Library, New York University

James Brown hears the call, his soul is up in arms,
James Brown grasps the shield, his soul with ardor warms,
James Brown marches forth to fight the thickening harms,
Now dauntless, strong and free.

Refrain:

OFFICIAL EIGHT-HOUR SONG

The most popular of all the eight-hour songs was published in the *Labor Standard* of July 21, 1878. Indeed, it may well have been the most popular labor song before the appearance of "Solidarity Forever." Originally appearing as a poem by I. G. Blanchard in the *Workingman's Advocate* of August 18, 1866, it was set to music by the Reverend Jesse H. Jones and was published in the *Labor Standard* with the music.

EIGHT HOURS

Words by I. G. Blanchard—Music by Rev. Jesse H. Jones

We mean to make things over, we are tired of toil for naught,
With but bare enough to live upon, and never an hour for thought;
We want to feel the sunshine, and we want to smell the flowers,
We are sure that God has will'd it, and we mean to have eight hours.
We're summoning our forces from the shipyard, shop and mill,

Eight hours for work, eight hours for rest, eight hours for what we will!
Eight hours for work, eight hours for rest, eight hours for what we will!

The beasts that graze the hillside, and the birds that wander free,
In the life that God has meted have a better lot than we.
Oh! hands and hearts are weary, and homes are heavy with dole;
If our life's to be filled with drudgery, what need of a human soul!
Shout, shout the lusty rally from shipyard, shop and mill,

Chorus:

The voice of God within us is calling us to stand
Erect, as is becoming to the work of his right hand,
Should he, to whom the Maker his glorious image gave,
The meanest of his creatures crouch, a bread and butter slave!
Let the shout ring down the valleys and echo from ev'ry hill,

Chorus:

Ye deem they're feeble voices that are raised in Labor's cause?
But bethink ye of the torrent, and the wild tornado's laws!
We say not Toil's uprising in terror's shape will come,
Yet the world were wise to listen to the monitory hum,
Soon, soon the deep-toned rally shall all the nations thrill,

Chorus:

From factories and workshops, in long and weary lines,
From all the sweltering forges, and from out the sunless mines,
Wherever toil is wasting the force of life to live,
There the bent and battered armies come to claim what God doth give,
And the blazon on their banner doth with hope the nations fill,

Chorus:

Hurrah, hurrah, for Labor! for it shall arise in might;
It has filled the world with plenty, it shall fill the world with light;
Hurrah, hurrah, for Labor! it is mustering all its powers,
And shall march along to victory with the banner of Eight Hours!
Shout, shout the echoing rally till all the welkin thrill,

Chorus:

The song rapidly became the official song of the eight-hour movement. An account of the ninth convention of the Boston Eight Hour League in May, 1878, carried the following note: "The Evening Session was opened with the Eight Hour song, words by I. G. Blanchard, music by Jesse H. Jones. Mr. Ira Steward was then introduced as the man whose thoughts would yet revolutionize the political economy of to-day."[10]

MAY DAY AND THE HAYMARKET AFFAIR

By 1886 hundreds of thousands of workers were joining together to carry out the resolution adopted by the Federation of Organized Trades and Labor Unions of the United States and Canada (predecessor of the American Federation of Labor) at its 1884 convention: "... that eight hours shall constitute a legal day's labor from and after May 1, 1886, and that we recommend to labor organizations throughout this dis-

[10] *Labor Standard*, June 9, 1878.

trict that they so direct their laws as to conform to the resolution by the time named."[11] Although workers during the 1886 upsurge for the eight-hour day mainly sang the Blanchard-Jones song, others were also written for the occasion.

EIGHT HOURS THE WORK DAY

By Karl Revere

(Remodeled from an old song)

Look to the Union only,
Brother in the fight;
When the trouble thickens
Keep the spirits bright;
Though the foes be many,
Though thy strength be small,
Look to the Union only—
She shall conquer all.

Look to the Union only,
Mid the toil and fray,
Soon will come more leisure
With eight hours work a day,
Overwork has dangers,
All thy woes it bore;
Look to Union only—
Trust her evermore!

When amid the music
Of the victory's feast,
All will sing her praises,
Thine shall not be least;
Look to Union only
When by wrong oppressed;
Brothers who have suffered,
Come to her and rest.[12]

AN EIGHT HOUR SONG

Air—"Hold the Fort"

Ho! my brothers! see the danger,
Gath'ring fast and dread;
Mammon's legions are preparing,
Stealthily they tread.

Hold your ground, for they are coming,
Up our breast-work throw;
Rally for EIGHT HOURS, Oh, brothers;
Hurl we back the foe!

Rise! Oh, people! chains are forging!
Power and pride conspire;
Children slayers, home despoilers,
Crime promoters dire.

Hold your ground, etc.

Who are plotters? Who are traitors,—
Foes of God and Man?—
They who grind and plunder labor,
Grasping all they can.

Hold your ground, etc.

Creep they onward, undermining
Freedom's proudest tower,
Stealing from the people ever,
Sapping hope and power.

Hold your ground, etc.

Bolder still grows Mammon's challenge,
Baser grows his arts;
For he sees the people rising,
Courage in their hearts.

Hold your ground, the battle's coming.

Freedom calls out, "Oh, my children,
Help me, or I fall."
Shall we back the lofty answer:
All join—"March we at thy call!"

Hold your ground, the battle's coming.

Shall the people live or perish?
We the answer give;
Ho, my brothers, lift your voices;
All join—"Live the people—live!"

Hold your ground, the battle's coming.[13]

About three hundred fifty thousand workers in 11,562 establishments throughout the country went out on strike May 1, 1886, for the eight-hour day.[14] The following song explains better than dozens of resolutions why they struck.

11 Federation of Organized Trades and Labor Unions, *Proceedings of the 1884 Convention* (Chicago, 1884), pp. 8, 10–14.

12 *Labor Leaf*, Jan. 20, 1886.

13 *Carpenter*, Mar., 1886. Curiously, the January, 1887, issue of the *Carpenter* carried a variant of this song, entitled "Hold Your Ground," the chorus of which exhorted, "Rally for NINE HOURS, O brothers." Other alternate readings include "Bolder grows his arts" (st. 5, l. 2), "Freedom calls us: 'O my children' " (st. 6, l. 1), and "Shout we back the lofty answer" (st. 6, l. 3).

14 These workers included members of the Knights of Labor as well as the Federation of Organized Trades and Labor Unions of the United States and Canada. The KL workers went out in defiance of attempts by Terence V. Powderly to torpedo the eight-hour movement. On March 13, 1886, he issued a secret circular denying that the order favored an eight-hour strike on May 1. But most Knights ignored the directive. They showed their solidarity with the movement by wearing "eight-hour shoes," footwear manufactured in establishments which had already granted the shorter workday, smoking "eight-hour tobacco," and, of course, singing the song "Eight Hours," shouting over and over again the line "Eight hours for work, eight hours for rest, eight hours for what we will!"

THE STRIKERS' STORY

I've got a baby ten months old,
Till I went out on strike
I swear I never had a chance
To see what she was like.

At any rate, it's solid fact—
And doubtless will surprise
You—that till now I never knew
The color of her eyes.

All day and half-way through the night
The company would keep
Me, and, when I was home, the kid,
Of course, was fast asleep.

'Twas seldom, even, that I got
A good look at her ma;
And baby, bless her little heart,
She never saw her pa.

Folks say there's compensation for
Most every ill in her life:
The strike gave me time to get
Acquainted with my wife.

And she has introduced me to
The kind. I tell you what
I just began to realize
The blessings I have got.

For them I'll freeze in Winter's cold
Or broil in Summer's sun:
For them I'll stand in rain or hail,
Though, tisn't such great fun.

But working all the time, that is
A little bit too rough:
And wife and I and baby think
Eight steady hours enough.[15]

A similar story appears in the Yiddish-language ballad by Morris Rosenfeld:

MY LITTLE BOY

I have a little boy at home,
A pretty little son;
I think sometimes the world is mine
In him, my only one.

But seldom, seldom do I see
My child in heaven's light;
I find him always fast asleep
I see him but at night.

'Ere dawn my labor drives me forth;
'Tis night when I am free;
A stranger am I to my child;
And stranger my child to me.

I am grieved and full of pain.
Bitterly I think:
When my child awakes again,
He'll find me gone once more.[16]

In Chicago, scene of the most aggressive effort to win the eight-hour day, the Social Revolutionaries—anarchist leaders of the International Working People's Association (the so-called Black International)[17] —threw themselves wholeheartedly into the movement and were largely responsible for the tremendous drive in that city for a shorter working day. The *Alarm*, the English organ of the Chicago Social Revolutionaries edited by Albert R. Parsons, was an early supporter of the eight-hour movement, although, as the following song it published indicates, it mixed the anarchist doctrine of force with the struggle to improve working conditions immediately.

A LABOR SONG

By Brutus

Come! sing me a song! that's ringing and clear,
I weary of hearing your idle lays,
Strong and ripe as the corn in the ear;
Under the sun of the autumn days.
Sing out, sing out
With a virile shout,
Let it be strong, and sharp as a sabre,
To hell with the crews
Who'd give us the blues.
Let's ring out a curse on the foes of labor.

Come! sing me a song! that's sterling and strong,
No more of your mamby pamby verses,

[15]*Workmen's Advocate*, Mar. 19, 1887.

[16]Morris Rosenfeld, *Poems of Morris Rosenfeld*, ed. and trans. Aaron Kramer (New York, 1955), p. 34. See also Ruth Rubin, "Yiddish Folksongs," *New York Folklore Quarterly*, II (Winter, 1946), 18–19. A more complete version, entitled "My Little Son," appears in *The Teardrop Millionaire and Other Poems by Morris Rosenfeld*, selected and trans. Aaron Kramer (New York, 1955), pp. 16–17.

[17]The IWPA was formed at a congress of American anarchists held in Pittsburgh, October, 1883. The convention was dominated by Johann Most, the German anarchist leader who had migrated to the United States, and its manifesto emphasized Most's indifference to immediate demands, stressing, instead, one remedy for the evils of capitalism—force. In Chicago, however, men like Albert R. Parsons, August Spies, Michael Schwab, Sam Fielden, and others rejected Most's position and adopted an anarcho-syndicalist approach, working with the trade unions for higher wages and the eight-hour day. Parsons became recording secretary of the Chicago Eight-Hour League.

Let dynamite down with the thing that is wrong,
No blessing be given to evil—but curses.
Act out, act out,
While your voices shout,
Iniquity to hell we'll leave her,
Into hell be he crammed,
With his "public be damned,"
Who pays a dollar a day for labor.

Come sing me a song! that tells me of hope,
Of all the past and the future advances,
Which will make of this earth a heaven, nor grope
After things unreal; with fantastic prances,
Shout, then, shout!
'Till the states ring out,
Against the fornicating preachers,
Who pray, and say
That a dollar a day,
And bread and water's enough—the Beechers.

Come! sing me a song! that tells me of hate
And scorn for wrong where'er it be lurking,
Of death to the loafer, the thief the same fate,
Who'd live off the fruits of his neighbor's working,
Send out! send out!
An electric shout
And shock, my every honest neighbor,
That shall powder the bones
And stifle the drones
Which "toil not nor spin" in the hive of Labor.[18]

About forty thousand workers went on strike for the eight-hour day in Chicago, and more than forty-five thousand were granted a shorter working day without striking. "Every railroad in the city was crippled, all the freight houses were closed and barred, and most of the industries in Chicago were paralyzed," a contemporary paper reported about the May 1 demonstration in the Windy City. A Chicago paper commented, "No smoke curled up from the tall chimneys of the factories and mills, and things had assumed a Sabbath-like appearance."[19]

On May 4, 1886, a protest meeting was called in Chicago's Haymarket Square by the Social Revolutionaries to condemn police brutality against workers at the McCormick Harvester factory who were on strike for the eight-hour day and a two-dollar daily wage. Toward the end of this peaceful meeting, a bomb was thrown by an unknown person, and its explosion killed one policeman instantly, wounded five others so severely that they died later, and inflicted less serious wounds on some fifty people. The Haymarket tragedy offered employers an excellent opportunity to kill the eight-hour day by associating the movement with anarchism. Newspaper headlines equated "bomb-throwers" with the eight-hour agitation.

After a series of police raids on the homes of workers, eight men were charged and brought to trial: Albert R. Parsons, August Spies, Samuel J. Fielden, Eugene Schwab, Adolph Fischer, George Engel, Louis Lingg, and Oscar Neebe. These men were all anarchists. They were also responsible for the fact that on May 1, 1886, Chicago had made a great contribution to the struggle for the eight-hour day, and the employers were anxious to have them removed from the scene. Many workers, while condemning anarchism, rallied to the defense of the men in the firm conviction that they were being persecuted not for their anarchist beliefs but for their militancy in the eight-hour movement.

The eight men were found guilty after a travesty of a trial in which they were accused not of having thrown the bomb at the Haymarket meeting, rather of having said or written things which might cause someone to throw a bomb. Seven of the defendants were sentenced to be hanged, and the eighth, Oscar Neebe, was sentenced to fifteen years' imprisonment.

The convicted men were called upon to speak before sentence was pronounced. Albert R. Parsons began his lengthy speech with a poem which was soon set to music and popularized in the campaign to save the condemned men from execution. After reading it, Parsons declared: "That poem epitomizes the aspirations, the hope, the need of the working classes, not alone of America, but of the civilized world."

FREEDOM

By Albert R. Parsons

Toil and pray! Thy world cries cold;
Speed thy prayer, for time is gold;
At thy door Need's subtle tread;
Pray in haste! for time is bread.

And thou plow'st and thou hew'st,
And thou rivet'st and sewest,
And thou harvestest in vain;
Speak! O, man; what is thy gain?

Fly'st the shuttle day and night,
Heav'st the ores of earth to light,

[18] *Alarm*, Jan. 24, 1885.

[19] *Bradstreet's*, May 8 and 15, 1886; *Chicago Daily Tribune*, May 2 and 3, 1886.

Fill'st with treasures plenty's horn—
Brim'st it o'er with wine and corn.

But who hath thy meal prepared,
Festive garments with thee shared;
And where is thy cheerful hearth,
Thy good shield in battle dearth?

Thy creations round thee see—
All they work, but naught for thee!
Yea, of all the chains alone
Thy hand forged, these are thine own.

Chains that round the body cling,
Chains that lame the spirit's wing,
Chains that infants' feet, indeed,
Clog! O, workman! Lo! Thy meed.

What ye rear and bring to light,
Profits by the idle wight,
What ye weave of diverse hue,
'Tis a curse—your only due.

What ye build, no room insures,
Not a sheltering roof to yours,
And by haughty ones are trod—
Ye, who toil their feet hath shod.

Human bees! Has nature's thrift
Given thee naught but honey's gift?
See! the drones are on the wing,
Have you lost the will to sting?

Man of labor, up, arise!
Know the might that in thee lies,
Wheel and shaft are set at rest
At thy powerful arm's behest.

Thine oppressor's hand recoils,
When thou, weary of thy toils,
Shun'st thy plough; thy task begun
When thou speak'st: Enough is done!

Break this two-fold yoke in twain;
Break thy want's enslaving chain;
Break thy slavery's want and dread;
Bread is freedom, freedom bread.[20]

Appeals to the Illinois and United States supreme courts failed, and the seven men were scheduled to be hanged on November 11, 1887. As the execution day neared, the defense movement grew in intensity and transcended national boundaries. Workers in the United States, England, France, Holland, Russia, Italy, and Spain protested the impending executions, and they were joined by prominent labor leaders, such as Samuel Gompers, AFL president, and Frank Ferrell, Negro leader of the Knights of Labor, and by intellectuals like William D. Howells, Robert G. Ingersoll, William Morris, and George Bernard Shaw. The defense movement also had a song:

A SHOUT OF PROTEST

By Arthur Cheesewright, Denver, Colorado

In Chicago stand convicted
Seven of nature's noblest men,
Jailed because they have predicted
What was truth and clear to them;
Giving to the rich a warning
That their end is drawing near,
Telling of a coming dawning
Of a future bright and clear.

Let us save our noble brothers!
Raise your voices loud and high!
Noble men who lived for others,
Cannot, will not, must not die!

Foully tried by judge and jury,
Victims of rich scoundrels' hate,
Devilish capitalistic fury
Would for such reserve the fate
Of Jesus Christ and other martyrs;
Bloody-minded tyrants they,
Wolves, hyenas, murdering Tartars
Worse than any beast of prey.

Shout aloud, STOP this foul murder!
Let it ring throughout the land!
Tell the brutal Judge Magruder
That we will no longer stand
Foul injustice to our brothers—
Making liberty a lie—
Noble men who STARVED for others
Cannot, will not, must not die![21]

The defense movement did have some effect. Governor Oglesby of Illinois commuted the sentence of Fielden and Schwab to life imprisonment.[22] Louis Lingg committed suicide in prison (or was murdered by police guards). But Parsons, Spies, Engel, and Fischer were hanged on November 11, 1887. The following song, written after the execution, provided its own introductory explanation.

[20] *Life of Albert R. Parsons* (Chicago, 1903), pp. 128–29.

[21] *Labor Enquirer*, Oct. 19, 1887.

[22] On June 26, 1893, John Peter Altgeld, the fearless, progressive governor of Illinois, pardoned the imprisoned men; his message stated that they were completely innocent and that they and the executed men had been the victims of hysteria, packed juries, and a biased judge.

THE PRICE OF FREEDOM

Air—"Annie Laurie"

("At midnight preceding the morning of his execution Albert R. Parsons' voice rang out clear and proud through the corridors of the jail as he sang in distinct tones the beautiful ballad, 'Annie Laurie.' " The following was prompted by reading the above item in the daily papers.)

The night is dark about me;
I hear the midnight bell;
Before another midnight
It will ring my funeral knell,
It will ring my funeral knell,
Oh! the hours are speeding by
When to buy the toilers' freedom
I shall pay the price and die.

To-night my babes are crouching
By their weeping mother's side,
For this country's sake the father
Leaves his children and his bride,
Leaves his children and his bride,
When men for succor cry,
Then to buy the toilers' freedom
I shall pay the price and die.

Pent in a dismal dungeon,
Forbidden to be free,
A slave in chains and prison,
O, what were life to me?
O, what were life to me?
Speak out, my heart, reply,
That to buy the toilers' freedom
I will pay the price and die.

What greater love hath mortal
For one whom he holds dear,
Than for his sake to gladly
Meet death without a fear!
Meet death without a fear—
Yes, such a love have I,
And to buy the toilers' freedom
I pay the price and die.

The night will soon be over;
For me 'twill be the last;
And the night of wrong, my country,
From thee shall soon have passed,
From thee shall soon have passed,
I see the star on high,
So to buy the toiler's freedom
I will pay the price and die.

Weep not above my ashes,
This is no hour for tears,
Let every man stand ready
When he the bugle hears,
When he the bugle hears,
Let every man reply:
We to buy the toilers' freedom
Will pay the price and die.[23]

As the deputy adjusted a mask in front of August Spies's face before pulling the noose, the condemned man spoke a single sentence: "There will come a time when our silence will be more powerful than the voices you strangle today." These words inspired a song, written originally in German.

THE DAY WILL COME!

A November 11th Song

By Martin Drescher

The day will come! our silence will become
More powerful than our speeches.
So you spoke and courageous, unconfused,
You gave your body over to the hangman,
And brave like you, your small band climbed
Down with you into the dark regions.
The day will come! Your proud hope was
Theirs: The spirit of light must be victorious!

The day will come! For the human race you
Fell in the heavy struggle;
In this struggle, which since time immemorial
Has always drunk the heart's blood of the best,
In this battle, in which the oppressed of all lands
Strike out against tyranny—
The day will come when the slave breathes free,
—You carried the banner out before him.

The day will come! Your shadows go
Through the earth and unceasingly recruit fighters;
All over where the low huts stand,
Where suffering and pain and hunger are the
Companions of oppressed children, there you
Intervene to throw a spark into their hearts.
The day will come! This you whisper and teach
The working people to sharpen their weapons for the struggle.[24]

Bitterness and anger over the execution of the four labor martyrs was voiced in resolutions adopted by many trade unions in this country and abroad. It also found expression in the following songs.

HYMN

By Arthur Cheesewright

Bitter and sad is the strain I sing,
And my heart is filled with sorrow,

23*Labor Enquirer*, Dec. 17, 1887, reprinted in *Workmen's Advocate*, Dec. 24, 1887.

24Pierre Ramus, *Der Justizmord von Chicago* (Vienna, 1922), iv. Trans. Brewster Chamberlin.

For what can the dismal future bring
But a dark and dreary morrow.
Five of the bravest ever born
Have been slain spite all our pleading,
And the thinking men of the nation mourn,
And their hearts are torn and bleeding.

Dead are the heroes who fought for right,
And their wives and their children are weeping;
For them 'tis a dark and bitter night,
For their loved ones are silently sleeping,
Brave and true, for the poor they fought,
For the cause of humanity filled them,
And the brotherhood of man they taught,
And for this they have foully killed them.

Nobly they stood when they heard their fate;
Not born in such brave men to falter,
But they stood like the old martyrs great,
And like them they were paid with a halter;
Hanged by an ignorant people's howl,
For the rich and the prejudiced tried them,
'Twas a dastardly crime; 'twas a murder foul
Yet in dying these brave men defied them.[25]

WHO WERE THEY?

By David Edelshtadt, Cincinnati, O., September 23, 1889

They would not sleep in shame, like all the rest,
Nor could they either slaves or swindlers be.
They spoke the free and open truth. Till death
They fought for human rights and liberty.

They carried in their breasts the scarlet flame
Of Truth, sweet radiance that freedom casts.
They bid us speak in Truth's unsullied name,
And summoned us to man's unfinished tasks.

They never gave consent to those decrees
Which only blind the people, and enslave.
They ripped apart the laws of tyranny,
To laws of nature recognition gave.

They broke a window through in mankind's hated
Prison-house of black obscurity,
And freely let the sunlight permeate
The pallid world of human slavery.

Usurpers paled and tyrants shook in fright;
The slave was waking, tearing at his chain,
Had understood at last his human right,
"Liberty or Death!" his fierce refrain.

But when the cruel, man-devouring class
Had barely heard the Truth thus spoken free,
It seized its bloodstained knife in deadly grasp
And plunged into this monstrous butchery.

Oh brothers! They have killed our champions, who
Were leading us through strife to victory.
Oh baseness vile! how brilliantly have you
Prevailed, in this, the nineteenth century!

How powerless the people stood, and mute—
So like a child! Not one bold hand to thwart
The rope, to stop the tyrant's hangman-brute!
Oh masses! Where your reason? Where your heart?

In Waldheim now,[26] man's freedom-thinkers rest.
And still are heard, from that eternal site,
The savage hangman's roaring epithets,
Which rouse the world of slaves to freedom's fight.

They ask no hymns of praise, no monument
Of marble, bloodied by the slave's own hand,
Their sole request is man's enlightenment,
The fight for human rights their one demand.

Unite, oh people! Learn your strength! Awake!—
And heed the wish that echoes from their graves.
Throw off your yoke! And crush the vicious snakes
Which poisoned you and turned you into slaves![27]

THE ELEVENTH OF NOVEMBER, 1887

By Chas. Diether

For the fourth time the day has come around
It reminds hesitatingly and full of shyness;
The sun itself as if conscious of the shame,
Surrounds its presence with mourning wreaths;
And, usually blooming lovely like the roses,
Aurora's cheeks glow angry red.

Because today is the day—Columbia—
That you, standing else the guardian of freedom,
Erected a second Golgotha,
Baptized in blood your pure hands.
The cowardly murder is an eternal disgrace!
Curse! Threefold curse! to you and your land.

To the voice of truth you turn a deaf ear
And trample justice with your feet.
A cry of anger is forced from their breast
Loud rumbling with resentment they stand ready for revenge.
Woe to you Columbia—siren—
You hypocrite-woman, honorless, shameless whore.

Your starry path—that in proud flight
Luminous, was a symbol of freedom,
That magic-like carried hope into the heart,
That lay bloody in the bands of slavery—

25*Labor Enquirer*, Nov. 19, 1887.

26Following a funeral procession through the streets of Chicago in which thousands of workers marched, the Haymarket martyrs were buried in Waldheim cemetery.

27Originally published in Yiddish in *Der Gesezlicher Mord in Chicago fun 11 November 1887*, ed. Roman Lewis (New York, 1889), and translated by Max Rosenfeld in *Jewish Life*, IX (Nov., 1954), 12.

Does the vanished splendor cherish mourning,
Your wounded-winged eagle cultivate quiet?

For today you sew it as your emblem on
The gallows—a sign worthy of you—
And you even dance, in reeling steps,
The cancan—for you an appropriate round—
The masks fell!—your characteristics are naked!
A portrait of murder-lust, money-greed, cruelty, lies.

It was a holiday for you—Columbia—
The blood of the victims still drips on your garments;
And cold and motionless, that's how you stood there,
As your hangman's hand strangled "five."
Five voices you wanted to silence,
But instead of "five," "many thousands" ring out.

And Waldheim's voice calls out loud and louder,
Already the slaves are breaking their chains!
Soon it will thunder and lightning out of the dark grave,
The structure of tyranny will fall in ruins.
And laughing friendly the avenging angel welcomes
And lisps: "Parsons, Spies, Lingg, Fischer, Engel."[28]

RENEWED STRUGGLE FOR THE EIGHT-HOUR DAY

In his speech to the court, August Spies charged that he and his comrades were condemned for their leadership in the struggle for the eight-hour day. He predicted that capitalists who believed they could destroy the movement by killing them would soon discover their mistake. "Here you will tread upon a spark, but there and there, behind you and in front of you and everywhere, flames blaze up. It is a subterranean fire. You cannot put it out."[29]

Spies was correct. The Haymarket tragedy and the general employers' counteroffensive after May 4, 1886, slowed but did not end the struggle for a shorter workday. At its 1888 convention, the AFL decided that organized labor should concentrate all its efforts on inaugurating the eight-hour workday on May 1, 1890. In March, 1890, after polling all the affiliated unions to see whether they wished to be selected to make this demand, the AFL executive council selected the United Brotherhood of Carpenters and Joiners to lead the way. They were to be followed by the United Mine Workers whenever that union's executive board should decide to take the step. The miners were scheduled to make their demand on May 1, 1892, but deciding that conditions did not warrant their acting, they called it off.

In 1890 the carpenters and joiners led the movement for the eight-hour day. The union reported that it had won the eight-hour day for 46,197 workers in 137 cities and that nearly thirty thousand had reduced their hours from ten to nine.[30] Two of the songs featured during the 1890 movement follow.

THE EIGHT-HOUR DAY

A Campaign Song by T. C. Walsh, Local 63, New York

A glorious dawn o'er the land is breaking,
And from the sleep of serfdom waking;
See the sons of toil arise.
Hearken to the song they're singing,
Through the welkin gladly winging,
Joy unto the weary bringing,
On, still on, it flies.

"Let scabs and cowards
Do what they may,
Eight hours, eight hours,
Shall be our day."

Aloft our banner courts the sky,
The glorious day of freedom's nigh,
From toiling long and late;
"Eight hours" shall be our working day,
"Eight hours" to sleep fatigue away,
"Eight hours" to seek in wisdom's ray,
Improvement of our state.

"Let scabs and cowards
Do what they may,
Eight hours, eight hours,
Shall be our day."

Accursed be him who leaves us now,
Let slavery's brand be on his brow;
Let honest men him shun,
Let the viper crawl and creep
Within himself a hell fire deep
His conscience be, may he ever reap
Of evils many a one.

"Let scabs and cowards
Do what they may—
Eight hours, eight hours,
Shall be our day."[31]

[28] *Der Anarchist*, Nov. 14, 1891. Trans. Brewster Chamberlin.

[29] *Famous Speeches of the Eight Chicago Anarchists in Court* (Chicago, 1910), pp. 20–24.

[30] As a result mainly of the eight-hour-day agitation the average working week was reduced from 60 hours in 1880 to 58.4 hours in 1890 and the average working day from 10.3 to 10 hours.

[31] *Carpenter*, Apr., 1890.

THE TOILER'S NATIONAL ANTHEM

"Eight Hours a Working Day"

Composed by M. J. Heany

To be sung to the music of "Tramp, Tramp, Tramp, the Boys are Marching"

Toiling brothers, why contend
Till our youthful days are spent
And the vigor of young manhood pass away
We, the stalwart sons of trade
From our course will not be swayed
Till eight hours constitute a working day.

Eight hours a day sing we loudly,
Eight hours a day for toilers all,
Whether in the mills or mines
Or wherever trades combine
For eight hours a day we'll stand or fall.

We are no braggart mob
Organized to kill and rob,
But honest toilers working for our pay,
Arrayed in all our might
To protect our sacred right
And make eight hours a lawful working day.

Eight hours a day, etc.

The bosses are unwise
If trade unions they despise
For unity will ever hold the sway
What are they but a few
When compared with millions true,
Who will make eight hours a lawful working day.

Eight hours a day, etc.

Old slavery days are gone
Better times are marching on
And the toilers are already in the fray,
We scorn to retreat
Till the bosses we defeat
And make eight hours a lawful working day.

Eight hours a day, etc.

We'll have eight hours to rest,
Oh! how long we've been oppressed
We'll have eight hours to work and eight to play,
We'll have eight dollars, too.
Every cent before we're through
When eight hours constitute a working day.

Eight hours a day, etc.

When election day comes on,
Act with wisdom every one,
In bold defiant language proudly say,
I will vote for men that're true
Who will labor's cause pursue
Till eight hours constitute a working day.

Eight hours a day, etc.

When toilers all unite
And aid with all our might
Labor's cause without delay,
To succeed we're fully bent,
And we'll never rest content
Till eight hours constitute a working day.

Eight hours a day, etc.[32]

After 1891, the AFL left the task of achieving the eight-hour day to the individual unions. In 1895 Samuel Gompers, AFL president, proposed that the federation select another union to strike for the eight-hour day on May 1, 1896, but nothing came of this proposal. However, the *American Federationist* published the following song in its issue of July, 1896.

HIP! HIP! FOR EIGHT HOURS

By Edward O'Donnell

What tramp is that shaking our land in its sphere,
From the vain Massachusetts to 'Frisco's far plain;
And the lords of industry, why pause they in fear
While straining each neck to the swelling refrain?

As fierce as the tempest, as fixed as the pole,
Despising obstruction and mocking earth's powers,
The toilers, oppressed long in body and soul,
In thunder tones take up the cry for eight hours.

No vandals or pirates are we, by our troth!
But the ploughers of oceans, the builders of lands,
Whose limbs become weary, whose hearts teem with wrath,
Through the unequal contest which science demands.

Improvement and progress belongs to the whole,
Their blessings are curses when claimed by a few,
For the workers grow lean on starvation's grim dole,
And manhood is dead once you force it to sue.

We've labored in silence, dear knows, long enough,
While want 'round our homes threw a chill, painful air,
And at times we checked protest—content with the rough—
'Till greed, drunk with power, bade us die in despair.

The ring of the anvil should cease to vibrate,
The ploughshare permitted to rust in the soil,

32 Ibid., July 15, 1890.

Until man wins from science a share in his fate—
More leisure, less hours in the o'er straining toil.

As fierce as the tempest, as fixed as the pole,
Despising obstruction and mocking earth's powers,
The toilers, oppressed long in body and soul,
United, re-echo the cry for eight hours.

On May 1, 1898, the United Mine Workers launched their drive for an eight-hour day, and during that year the *United Mine Workers' Journal* published what are probably the last of the eight-hour songs.[33]

HAIL TO THE EIGHT-HOUR DAY
By Scott, Wellston, Ohio
Air—"The Lea Rig"

Ye miner lads, come gather round,
And listen to my roundelay;
Ye lads who labor underground,
Where never shines the light of day,
We fought and won a gallant fight,
Threw our enslaving chains away;
United labor's peerless might,
Brought shorter hours and longer day.

Then make the welkin loud resound,
Triumphant came we from the fray;
Unfurl our flag, let mirth abound,
And joyfully hail the eight-hour day.

From Eastern hill to Western plain,
United labor's signal ran,
From sunny South to northern Maine,
Came forth the brotherhood of man.
Mark well the patriotic tide.
Can nobler, braver hearts be found
Than those who crushed the tyrant's pride—
The lads who labor underground?

Chorus:

Ye labor friends from every craft,
Who helped the miners' cause along,
With grateful hearts we fondly waft
Returning thanks in simple song.
Oh, soon may reason's sway enfold
The homes of labor far and near;
For right we fought and will uphold
Our rights with every coming year.

Chorus:

No Eolian harp on Grecian isle,
Awoke of old such grand refrain;
In bygone age no minstrel wile
Attuned the lyre to sweeter strain.
From mountain peak to sheltered vale,
Let maid and miner lad be gay,
Proclaim with joy o'er hill and dale,
United labor gained the day.

Chorus:[34]

DIVIDE THE DAY
Written by Mayor S. M. Jones of Toledo

Divide up the day! divide up the day!
If you're willing to help brother men on the way.
The plan is simple that none can gainsay.
All that is needed is to split up the day.
Divide up the day and it soon will be found
That there's plenty of food to reach all around;
When father has work, there'll be no lack of bread,
Nor innocent children go hungry to bed.

Divide up the day, then divide up the day,
If you're willing to help brother men,
To help brother men on the way.
The plan is so simple that none can gainsay.

Divide up the day, divide up the day!
In more ways than one 'tis a plan that will pay.
Then all who desire will have work for their hand,
And the problem is solved that darkens our land.
With millions of idle in fruitful employ,
The home of the workers will echo with joy;
Then want and distress will flee far away,
We can bring it about just by splitting the day.

All that is needed. Yes, all that is needed
Is split up the day.

'Tis eight hours for work and eight hours for play,
With eight hours for rest make the true eight hour day.
'Twas our father above that gave us this plan.
Then let us be fair with our own brother man.
Don't make him a pauper, a tramp or a shirk.
Just give him a chance at a part of your work;
No question of wages will stand in the way,
He'll be saved from this fate if we split up the day.

Chorus:[35]

33This does not mean that songs for the shorter workday ceased to be written and sung, but many dealt with demands for the ten-hour and nine-hour day, and were mainly songs of the twentieth century. One, however, which arose in the 1890s in Czarist Russia, was carried to the United States, where it was sung by needle-trades workers in New York City in the struggle for the ten-hour day; see "This Is How the Tailor Sews" in Rubin, "Yiddish Folksongs," pp. 18–19.

34*United Mine Workers' Journal*, Apr. 21, 1898. At least part of this song carried over into the present century; in *Black Land* (Evanston, 1941), George Korson cites a variant of the chorus as a rousing and memorable marching song (p. 8).

35*United Mine Workers' Journal*, Sept. 1, 1898.

THE EIGHT HOUR DAY

We're brave and gallant miner boys who work underground.
For courage and good nature no finer can be found.
We work both late and early, and get but little pay
To support our wives and children in free Amerikay.
If Satan took the black legs, I'm sure 'twould be no sin;
What peace and happiness 'twould be for us poor working men.
Eight hours we'd have for working, eight hours we'd have for play,
Eight hours we'd have for sleeping in free Amerikay.[36]

[36]Ibid., Oct. 1, 1898. For a fuller text see pp. 202–4.

11

Boycotts, Strikes, and Unemployment Demonstrations 1880–1900

"There are too many millionaires and too many paupers," declared the *Hartford Courant* in 1883.[1] A song published in *John Swinton's Paper*, the outstanding labor paper of the period,[2] expressed the same viewpoint, calling upon workers to fight to change this situation:

Men! the millionaires are reigning,
While your backs are sorely aching,
Men! those grabocrats are draining
Of your life blood while ye're making,
Ye the stalwarts of the land.
Men! will ye much longer suffer,
Ruled by money despots grinding?
Or will ye, who may command,
By the power of labor's band,
Change and break the robber band?[3]

BOYCOTTS

The "power of labor's band" in the eighties and nineties was exercised through boycotts, strikes, unemployment demonstrations, and independent political action, and in all four areas songs and ballads played an important part.

By 1885 boycotts were being levied against hotels, theaters, excursion steamers, newspapers, manufacturers, meat-packers, coal-mining companies, and dealers in hats, cigars, clothing, carpets, drygoods, shoes, stoves, and many other items. Most of these boycotts were launched by the Knights of Labor. In practically every case there was also a secondary boycott, with the person or firm disregarding the boycott being boycotted in turn. A good example is illustrated in a song associated with the boycott of the New York *Tribune* conducted by Typographical Union No. 6, with the aid of the Knights of Labor. The union was publishing its own paper, the *Boycotter*, to present its side of the controversy and to appeal for workers' support:

STAND BY US

By J. E. D.

If Labor would exert her power
With a scientific aim,
She would win in a single hour
Battles that are fought in vain.
If she would know that to destroy
Was easier than to make, she'd soon
Join with us in a constant cry:
Boycott the cruel "rat" *Tribune!*

If she would learn what boycott meant,
And practice it with thorough zeal,

[1] *Hartford Courant*, reprinted in *John Swinton's Paper*, Dec. 30, 1883.

[2] On October 14, 1883, John Swinton resigned from his lucrative post as managing editor of the *New York Sun* to start his four-page weekly, *John Swinton's Paper*. "My objects in starting it," he declared, "were to raise the social question, and to induce the working people to bring their interests in politics." The paper's statement of principles, carried in the first issue, were: "1—Boldly upholding the Rights of Man in the American Way. 2—Battling against the accumulated wrongs of society and industry. 3—Striving for the organization and interests of workingmen, and giving the news of the Trades and the Unions. 4—Warning the American people against the treasonable and crushing schemes of Millionaires, Monopolists, and Plutocracy" (*John Swinton's Paper*, June 1, 1884). From this first issue until August 21, 1887, when the last number was published, *John Swinton's Paper* frequently published songs and ballads to help battle for these objectives.

[3] *John Swinton's Paper*, Dec. 23, 1883.

Tyrants would she make repent
Who now crush her beneath their heel;
For boycott is a sacred word,
Bringing Labor's foes to ruin—
More potent than the pen or sword—
'Twill yet destroy the "rat" *Tribune.*"

Then join us, brothers, in our fight;
Feed not the asp that did us sting;
Our case is one of Right 'gainst Might—
The shackled slave against his king.
The day is ours if you will grant
The favor asked in earnest tune:
Only obey the sacred chant:
Buy not—boycott the "rat" *Tribune!*

It has been said a bee can sting
A bull, and he'll scarce feel it,
But if a thousand to him cling
You'll find that he will "heel it."
And it is thus we mean to beat
A Croesus with the picayune;
If you'll withhold them, 'twill defeat
Our monstrous foe, the "rat" *Tribune.*

Then vow with us to take a stand—
A solemn and unflinching one—
Against this organ contraband
That even now is near undone.
Buy not of those who patronize,
Who thus defer its certain doom,
And boycott those who advertise
Their business in the "rat" *Tribune.*[4]

More than a score of newspapers were being boycotted in 1885–86, many because they refused to hire union printers, others because of their anti-labor views. Appeals to boycott these "rat sheets" included songs:

BOYCOTT THEM

By Peter Peppercorn

Being the soliloquy of an old printer on rats, rat supporters and rat sheets, and may be whistled, where singing is forbidden, to the tune of "Who Would Be a Scab?"

A typo stood by his case,
With pensive look upon his face;
No cash nor credit could he trace,
Though both he prized—
And this (of some one in some place)
Soliloquized:

"Is there a Union man so dead,
Who never thought and scratched his head,
And then, in profane language said,
To fire! Odd rot them,
With scabby rats, they steal my bread—
Vile sneaks, boycott them!

Although not really worth their snivel,
Like Satan, they are doing evil,
Unprincipled, unskilled, uncivil—
A scurvy lot,
In fact, the modern printer devil—
All such boycott.

No matter where you chance to meet—
Upon news stand or in the street—
A 'pauper labor set-up' sheet,
Don't fail to spot it,
Put out by renegade 'dead beat,'
Keep mum, boycott it.

Moreover, you who justice prize,
Unite, and act without disguise,
Shun all saloons, and stores likewise,
In memory dot them,
If they rat papers patronize,
Pass on, boycott them.

More on the subject might be said,
But never mind, just go ahead;
Dissension is the thing to dread."
Bid that adieu,
And boycott all of every grade
That boycott you.[5]

YE GENTLE BOY-CAT

A Jolly Boycat Song

By Pat of Molingar

Sing to the air of "Wearing of the Green"

Says Fritz to Pat, d'ye hear all that
Loud talk that's going 'roun"?
The *Morning News* is now refused
By honest men in town.
You ask them why—they all reply
They know what they're about—
It's run by rats, but old boycat's
Agoing to clean them out.

Then keep the ball a rolling, boys,
The iron strike while hot;
Aim heavy blows at all your foes,
Your watchword be Boycott!
The enemies of Labor all your patronage refuse,
And read the WORKMEN'S ADVOCATE.
Boycott the *Morning News.*

Not long ago, as you all know,
It flew its colors high,
It was a friend to workingmen,
It loudly then did cry.

[4] *Boycotter*, Apr. 4, 1885.
[5] *Workmen's Advocate*, July 25, 1885.

YE GENTLE BOY-CAT.

A JOLLY BOYCAT SONG.

BY PAT OF MOLINGAR.

Sung to the air of "Wearing of the Green."

Says Fritz to Pat, d'ye hear all that
Loud talk that's going 'round?
The *Morning News* is now refused
By honest men in town.
You ask them why — they all reply
They know what they're about
It's run by rats, but old boycat's
A-going to clean them out.

Chorus.
Then keep the ball a-rolling, boys,
The iron strike while hot,
And heavy blows at all your foes,
Your watchword be Boycott!
To friends of Labor all your patronage return
And read the WORKMEN'S ADVOCATE
Boycott the *Morning News*.

Not long ago, as you all know
It flew its colors high
It was a friend to workingmen,
It loudly then did cry.
For greed of gold it first grew cold,
And then it swung around
But workingmen who built it up
Can also pull it down.

Chorus.

Its circulation grew immense,
Ten thousand, so they say,
Until the Printers' Union scale
They did refuse to pay.
Then in its garret it got rats,
And a boycat just as well,
Supported by staunch Union men
And gallant K. of L.

Chorus.

This boycat very lively is
And jumps all 'round the State,
At least he's been reported so
By one "walking delegate."
In Branford and in Meriden
He's done some lively work,
And now all through the Valley he
Is working like a Turk.

Chorus.

To throw cold water on a rat
That's drowning, seems a shame,
But if the rat jumps in a well
He's no one else to blame.
The squealing of the mourning rats
Our boycat will amuse,
While we attend the funeral
Of the late *Morning News*.

Chorus.

Boycat *News Requiescat*.

"Only fifty subscribers lost!"

"M" stands for missing "ad."

What's dat ar cat? I hears long-tail rats a-squealing.

Brother Fowler: Scratch a man on the back nowadays and you will find a boycotter.

The *Morning News* begins to realize that a hornet when it backs up against a man will push more than a horse can draw. "A word to the wise is sufficient." *Anonymous Postal Card.*

The boycotted Derby Silver Co.'s goods are distinguishable by a trade mark, consisting of an anchor with a crown underneath, in most cases placed on the bottom of the goods.

He that taketh from the poor giveth to the Lord seems to be the "new version" adopted by the devout and erudite proprietors of the *News*, one of whom, Prof. Simeon E. Baldwin, is credited with donating one or two thousand dollars to the Y. M. C. A.

It is reported that the notorious firm of Bolton & Neely are the only dealers in this city who sell or keep the boycotted Derby Silver Co.'s silver plated ware. This is to be expected. Over two hundred K. of L. are out of work on account of the avarice of the Derby Silver Co., and their brothers and sisters in New Haven will take the hint and act accordingly.

A. S. Blackman, the Grand street druggist, says he is not and never has been a subscriber for the *News*. But he does not understand the philosophy of boycotting. A little reflection will enable him to see that when the wages of workmen are cut down, druggists as well as other dealers suffer. "An injury to one is the concern of all." Therefore we trust that he will assist the union printers and help to keep up wages by discouraging those who would cut them down.

The *News* editorially says, "That the boycott is an attempt to commit a great wrong for which there is no existing provocation whatever." Well, then, the great body of Knights of Labor must be fools or idiots; they certainly do not, according to the big-brained (?) editor of the *News*, know what they are doing. What is the *News* howling about, is it hurt? Who hurt the poor thing? I think the thing is dying hard; what do you think? I think boycott it until it kicks the kettle. The *News* should have talked arbitration fifteen months ago on "business principles," and then there would not have been a boycott on "business principles." Can't arbitrate where there are rats—they might bite—then hydrophobia—then a trip to Europe. The boycat is attending to the rats.

And again, the rat squeals editorially, "The assertion that the *Morning News* is unfriendly to the workingmen is equally unfounded, as all our readers know. Certainly, some "interested" person has been lying again. Yes, Knights, it is "unfounded," all of K. of L. men have been imposed upon; isn't it too bad to have some "interested person" among us "unfounding" things. Brother Knights, the *News* is the best friend you ever had; the rat sheet always reported workmen's meetings in fair style, and telegraphed the same to New York dailies, and would have been doing the same thing now, only some "interested person" got the *News* reporters all "unfounded," and you ought to know what is going to happen when everything is "unfounded" by "interested persons." And still arbitration can't be did because it is "unfounded" by some "interested person."

COMMUNICATIONS.

To the Workmen's Advocate:

There seems to be a good deal of contrariety of opinion about the age at which children may be permitted to leave school and go to work. At the present time it is entirely in the hands and at the discretion of their parents. We never hear of any law to the contrary being enforced. Still the public admit that it is a proper subject for State regulation and supervision.

But the question is, what would be a proper age at which children may take their place in the labor mart and commence the fierce competitive struggle for existence?

If we have any regard for their healthy, robust physical development, for intellectual attainments that shall qualify them to understand and appreciate the varied phenomena of nature and of human existence and to creditably discharge the multifarious duties of life, an education that does not meet these requirements is a fraud, then sixteen years is as low a limit as the public ought to accept or as the exigencies of the case demand. Gov. Harrison would not allow children to be sent to work under ten, but would allow them to be sent to work, during school vacations, between the ages of ten and twelve. Now, as the Summer vacation is the longest, and the one of which parents would be most likely to avail themselves, lasting for nine weeks, and commencing the latter end of June, and as the heat, in our cotton and woolen mills and match and other manufactories where juvenile labor is largely employed, would be hotter than sheol during that period, registering over one hundred degrees of heat, I maintain that that nine weeks of labor by children of that tender age would not only be an act of intolerable cruelty but a drain upon their vitality, that not one in a thousand can endure without sapping the foundations of health, life and longevity. Has the Governor any children of his own?

Pass a school house when children of that age are being dismissed for the day. Observe their buoyancy of motion, their hilarity of feeling, the rosy flush of health upon their cheeks; then pass a labor bastile when the same class come surging out from their labors. Observe the pallor upon their cheeks, the weary, languid lassitude of feeling, the sluggishness of motion, and then invoke if you can the enactment of a code of laws that shall damn their young lives to such a degraded, suicidal employment. But who are the parties and what are the interests that demand that hecatombs of human victims shall be annually sacrificed to this moloch of gain? It is the mere matter of the saving of the fraction of a cent in the manufacture of a yard of woolen or cotton cloth. Away with such a heartless, murderous system. There is plenty of unemployed mature labor in the country amply qualified to endure dust, grease and heat of a factory without having recourse to these helpless victims. Their labor would cost a little more, but shall that consideration be weighed in the balance against the material welfare, the moral and intellectual training and physical development of the helpless, unprotected class whose case we have been considering? Would legislation work any less practical results for having a little humanity infused into it? Of all the generous aspirations of our nature there is none, in a moral sense, but must be held subordinate to a devotion to the interest of humanity and a desire to alleviate human suffering.

"No radiant pearl that crested fortune wears,
No gem that sparkling hangs from beauty's ears,
Not the bright stars that night's blue arch adorn,
No rising suns that gild the vernal morn,
Shine with such lustre"

G. M.

To the Workmen's Advocate:

In reference to the remarks of "G. A. M.," I would like to say a few words. He says it makes no difference whether the president of the St. Aloysious Society is a laboring man or not, so long as he is a temperance man. Probably it would make no difference to him if the president of the society was a dishonest man, as long as he lived up to the principles of temperance. But I question whether the members of the society would be content to have a dishonest man as its official head. Is there anything more detrimental to a man's character for honesty than to be able to say that he cannot be trusted by his fellow workers? For that is the exact position in which the president of the St. Aloysius Society stands to-day. There is an old adage which says "If a man plays you false in one thing keep your eyes open for him in everything else he undertakes." I would advise the older members to bring this matter up at their next meeting and settle it, so that when we give our excursion this year we will have an honorable man for president, instead of a miserable, contemptible, sneaking, Judas-like "rat" printer. For if we do not, the society can rest assured that Organized Labor will "boycott" us in as thorough a manner as it is now doing for the squealing *News*.

ALOYSIUS.

To the Workmen's Advocate:

I was shown a copy of the *News* in which they claim that the K. of L. are being misled by a few men, who, for personal motives, are endeavoring to prevent them from settling their troubles with Organized Labor. Now I have perfect faith in those who have this matter in charge, as I am assured they are acting for the benefit of us all. It is not alone the fact that the *News* has broken faith with its compositors in the past; but the stand this paper has at all times taken against Labor. The different instances can not be enumerated here, suffice to say, they are numerous and are treasured up in the memory of those who strive to advance the welfare of their fellow-workmen. The K. of L. do not take a stand against anyone, unless justified. I for one would not be in favor of any compromise short of the conditions imposed by the committee. Let the word be: Up, Knights, and at them!

K. of L.

Meetings.

AMERICAN SECTION, S. L. P.—Regular meeting on the Second Sunday evening in each month.

CIGARMAKERS' PROG. UNION NO. 2.—Regular meeting the third Friday in each month, 8 P. M., at Trades' Council Hall.

EQUAL RIGHTS DEBATING CLUB.—Debate this (Sunday) afternoon, at 2 o'clock, at Good Samaritan Hall, 817 Chapel street.

JOURNEYMEN TAILORS' UNION.—Regular Meetings at Trades Council Hall on the second and fourth Mondays in each month, at 8 o'clock p. m.

NEDERDEUTSCHE PROPAGANDA CLUB meets first and third Thursday in each month at 86 Crown street.

SECTION NEW HAVEN, S. L. P.—The regular meetings of this Section are held at Trades Council Hall on the first Monday in each month at 8 o'clock p. m.

TRADES COUNCIL. Regular meetings on the first and third Sundays in each month, at 2 o'clock in the afternoon. All unions should be represented.

Advertisements.

HANGING LAMPS!
A LARGE VARIETY, AND CHEAP.
LAMPS AND LAMP GOODS
AT
P. J. CARROLL'S,
254 State Street, New Haven.

P. J. KELLY & CO.
CARPETS AND OILCLOTHS.
FURNITURE! FURNITURE!
821 AND 823 GRAND STREET.
LARGE STOCK!
LOW PRICES!
EASY TERMS!

UNION MADE HATS.
KILBOURN & CO.
816 CHAPEL STREET,
SOLE AGENTS FOR NEW HAVEN.

JOHN NORMAN,
PRACTICAL HATTER
Superior Workmanship Guaranteed
Special and Prompt Attention given to
REPAIRING.
792 Chapel St., Room 10, New Haven.

HATS
"THE CO-OPERATIVE HAT"
AT OSBORN'S
Fine Goods AT LOW PRICES 91 CHURCH ST.

ONE DOLLAR SAVED
Is two earned. You can save your hard earned money by buying your
CROCKERY, GLASS, LAMPS,
TINWARE, WOODENWARE, &c.
OF
FRANK M. HALL 30 Church Street.

C. P. BUTLER,
Wholesale and Retail Dealer in
FISH, OYSTERS AND CLAMS
Sea Food of All Kinds.
TERMS CASH. CONNECTED BY TELEPHONE
93 BROADWAY.

FISH AND OYSTERS
OF ALL KINDS.
PRICES TO SUIT.
Please give us a call and be convinced.
A. K. BROWN, 744 Grand Street.

Advertisements.

S. H. BARNES,
DEALER IN
Choice Beef, Mutton, Lamb,
ETC., ETC.
GAME IN THEIR SEASON.
STALL NO. 1, CITY MARKET.
Come and see me and we will do you good.
S. H. BARNES.

CASPER KIPP,
DEALER IN ALL KINDS OF
Groceries and Provisions,
Cor. Dixwell Av. and Henry St.

ELM CITY
CASH GROCERY
74 & 76 Congress Ave.,
Cor. Hill Street, NEW HAVEN, CT.
DIRECTIONS
Where to get satisfaction in price and quality of goods in the Grocery line.
We do not aim to sell the cheapest goods, but to sell the best staple goods at the lowest prices. An assortment of Fresh, Salt and Smoked Meats constantly on hand. Pure Spices, fine Teas and Coffees. We call particular attention to our Flour, Butter and Canned Goods. The following complete line—Canned Succotash, Sweet Corn, Lima Beans and Peas, 9 cents per can, $1.00 per doz.
J. H. KEARNEY.

Good Wages for the Workman means Prosperity for the Merchant.

M. J. SARSFIELD.
FIRST-CLASS
GROCERY
AND
MEAT MARKET
Cor. Farren Avenue and Meadow St.,
ANNEX.

For a Stylish Cut of the Hair or a First-class Shave, call on
HENRY FLENTJE,
889 Grand Street, - Near State Street.
Special attention given to
CHILDREN'S HAIR-CUTTING.
Depot for Sale of WORKMEN'S ADVOCATE

THE OLD TROY LAUNDRY.
12 Gregson-St., rear P. O.
The BEST WORK with the LEAST WEAR and TEAR to the goods. Good Work guaranteed.
M. CURLEY, Prop.

CHARLES KLEINER,
LAWYER
Notary Public. Justice of the Peace.
ROOM 22, WHITE'S BUILDING,
69 Church St., New Haven, Conn.
OFFICE OPEN EVENINGS

B. SHONINGER & CO.,
MANUFACTURERS OF
PIANOS AND ORGANS, General State Agents for the Renowned Weber, Emerson and Wheelock Pianos.
Being manufacturers we are enabled to offer instruments at lower prices, for Cash, or on easy monthly payments than any other house and would respectfully solicit a call before purchasing. Warerooms, 801 Chapel St.

All the leading makes of American, English and French Writing, Combined, Copying and Extra Copying
INK, MUCILAGE,
Underwood's World famed CARBON PAPER and RIBBONS for type writers and caligraphs, and patent COPYABLE PRINTING INK.
are sold by
MATTHEWS, the INK MAN,
100 Crown Street, bet. Church and Orange Sts.

Courtesy of Tamiment Library, New York University

For greed of gold if first grew cold,
And then it swung around,
But workingmen who built it up
Can also pull it down.

Chorus:

It's circulation grew immense—
Ten thousand, so they say;
Until the Printers' Union scale
They did refuse to pay;
Then in its garret it got rats,
And a boycat just as well,
Supported by staunch Union men
And gallant K. of L.

Chorus:

This boycat very lively is
And jumps all 'round the State,
At least he's been reported so
By our "walking delegate,"
In Branford and in Meriden
He's done some lively work,
And now all through the Valley he
Is working like a Turk.

Chorus:

To throw cold water on a rat
That's drowning seems a shame,
But if the rat jumps in a well
He's no one else to blame.
The squealing of the mourning rats
Our boycat will amuse,
While we attend the funeral
Of the late *Morning News*.

Chorus:[6]

Boycotts were also used to continue the struggle against employers after strikes had failed. When workers in the Armour & Company stockyards were defeated in their efforts to prevent the company from forcing them to leave the Knights of Labor, they urged workers throughout the country to boycott Armour:

BOYCOTT ARMOUR

The aged year was dying fast,
As through Chicago's streets there passed,
A walking delegate carrying high,
A banner with this new war cry:
"Boycott Armour!"

In the town of Lake he saw the light
Of pallid famine, that ne'er grew bright;
Around him special shadows shone
And from his lips escaped a groan:
"Boycott Armour!"

"Boycott the tyrant's Kansas branch!
"Boycott the monarch's western ranch!
"Boycott his goods on land and sea,
"Let all from Armour boycotted be!
"Boycott Armour!"

"Let the Milwaukee general store
"Perish from earth forevermore!
Let all his corners, schemes and steals
Sink in the hell the book reveals!
"Boycott Armour!"

"When rotting ships and sweltering cars,
"Attest the downfall of his stars,
"When he has learnt to suffer and to die
Then! Then alone will cease the cry,
"Boycott Armour!"[7]

STRIKES

Although the Knights of Labor leadership frowned upon strikes, the order's growth was marked by walkouts of assembly members throughout the country. One of the earliest strikes by the Knights involved freight handlers at railroad company piers in New York City, June, 1882. During the strike the workers paraded and sang, especially this ballad written for them and published as a broadside.

THE FREIGHT HANDLERS' STRIKE

Composed by Andrew A. Walls

Tune—"Rambling Rake of Poverty"

It was at Cooper's Institute, Jack Burke and I chanced to meet;
It's years since last we parted, leaving school on Hudson Street.
He introduced me to his friends, the Doyles, the O's, the Macs,
And the subject of the evening was about the railroad strike.

We're on the strike and we won't go back,
Our claims are just and right;
Trade unions and the public press
Will help us with all their might.

There's Field, Jay Gould, and Vanderbilt,[8] their millions they did save
By paying starvation wages and working men like slaves;

[6]Ibid., Jan. 31, 1886.

[7]*Labor Enquirer*, Mar. 26, 1887.

[8]Cyrus W. Field, William R. Vanderbilt, and Jay Gould were three of the leading heads of railroad corporations in the seventies and eighties.

They hum round honest labor as the bee does the flower,
And suck the sweetness of your toil for 17 cents an hour.

Refrain:

They advertised in English, French, Irish, and Dutch,
They got a sample of all nations to work in place of us;
They marched them to the depot and told them not to fear,
And to shake their courage up in them, they gave them lager beer.

Refrain:

The lager beer and sandwiches with them did not agree;
In place of handling merchandise they all got on the spree.
The Russian Jews soon spread the news about their jolly times,
And all the bums from Baxter Street rushed for the railroad lines.

Refrain:

The Italians made themselves at home and soon began to call
For William H., the railroad king, to pass the beer along;
Jay Gould was making sandwiches and Field began to cry
Because he couldn't snatch the man that blew up his English spy.

Refrain:

Those mean monopolizers had the cheek to take the stand
And ask to get protection from the honest working man
Who tries to sell his labor in a manly upright way,
And will not handle railroad freight for less than two a day.

Refrain:

Does the devil makes those fools believe that they are smart and clever—
Does he tell them wealth will bring them health and make them live for ever;
Does he lead them from their gambling dens and to some shady bower,
To make them fix a workman's pay at 17 cents an hour?[9]

The freight handlers' strike lasted three weeks but was broken by the importation of scab labor. Freight handlers' president Jeremiah Murphy told a meeting of the union's executive council how the strikers planned to counter the use of scabs: " . . . we propose to boycott them. We shall have circulars containing their names printed and distributed over the city, and sent home to Ireland, too. We will march 1,000 men in front of their houses and let the people know who the boycotted men are. We shall not speak to them on the street, and you will see that this system of boycotting will go much further than using personal violence. We shall not harm them; they needn't fear that."[10] But it did not go far enough to win the strike, and after the battle was called off on August 7, 1882, many of the strikers, Irish-Americans, sang a doleful song in which they complained of the technique used by the employers to break their strike.

THE POOR MAN'S FAMILY

I am a roving Irishman,
I sailed from Greenland's shore.
To drive hungry wolves away
From the poor old lands-man's door.

Oh give us pay for ev'ry day,
That's all we ask of thee.
For it's right that we're out upon a strike
For the poor man's family.

The rich man's home by the cheery fire,
And their horses swift and strong:
If a poor man should ask for a crust,
They'd tell him that he's wrong.

Refrain:

"You take your ribbons in your hand
And you go and plow for me,
You can die or live, I'll have nothing to give
For the poor man's family!"

Refrain:

They'll bring their Italians over here,
And the Negroes from the South,
Thinking they can do our work,
Take the bread from a poor man's mouth.

Refrain:

And the American children, they must starve?
And that we'll not agree:
To be put down like a worm in the ground,
For to starve a family.

Refrain:[11]

A different version of the same song was

[9] Broadside, Harris Collection, Brown University.
[10] *New York Times*, July 2, 1882.
[11] *Irish World and Industrial Liberator*, Aug. 15, 1882.

The Freight Handler's Strike.

COMPOSED BY ANDREW A. WALLS.

AIR—Rambling Rake of Poverty.

1. It was at Cooper's Institnte, Jack Burke I chanced to meet,
It 's years since last we parted, leaving school on Hudson Street;
He introduced me to his friends, the Doyles, the O.'s, the Macs,
And the subject of the evening was about the Rail Road Strike.

CHORUS.

We're on the strike and we wont go back, our claims are just and right,
Trade unions and the publio Press will help us all their might.

2. There 's Field, Jay Gould and Vanderbilt their millions they did save
By paying starvation wages and working their men like slaves;
They hum round honest labor as the bee does round the flower,
And suck the substance of your toil for seventeen cents an hour.

CHORUS.—

3. They advertised in English, French, Irish and Dutch,
They got a sample of all nations to work in place of us;
They marched them to the depot and told them not to fear,
And to shake the courage up in them they gave them lager beer.

CHORUS.—

4. The lager beer and sandwiches with them did not agree,
In place of handling merchandize they all got on the spree;
The Russian Jews soon spread the news about their jolly times,
And all the bums from Baxter Street rushed for the rail road lines.

CHORUS.

5. The Italians made themselves at home and soon began to call
For William H., the rail road king, to pass the beer along;
Jay Gould was making sandwiches and Field began to cry,
Because he couldn't snatch the man that blew up his English spy.

CHORUS.—

6. Those mean monopolizers had the cheek to take the stand,
And ask to get protection from the honest working man;
Who tries to sell his labor in a manly upright way,
And will not handle rail road freight for less than 2 a day.

CHORUS.—

7. Does the devil make those fools believe that they are smart and clever—
Does he tell them wealth will bring them health and make them live for ever;
Does he lead them from their gambling dens unto some shady bower,
To make them fix a workman's pay at seventeen cents an hour.

CHORUS.—

THE COLUMBIAN BOOK AND NEWS COMPANY,

C. W. SIMPSON, Manager,

No. 69 Centre Street, New York City.

A broadside variant of "The Freight Handlers' Strike." Courtesy of Brown University Library.

issued as a broadside during a strike of longshoremen in New York in the early eighties.

LONGSHOREMAN'S STRIKE

I am a decent laboring man who works along the shore
To keep the hungry wolf away from the poor longshoreman's door;
I work all day in the broiling sun on ships that come from sea,
From broad daylight till late at night for the poor man's family.

Give us good pay for every day,
That's all we ask of you;
Our cause is right, we're out on strike,
For the poor man's family.

The rich man's gilded carriages with horses swift and strong;
If a poor man asks for a bite to eat they'll tell him he is wrong.
Go take your shovel in your hand and come and work for me,
But die or live, they've nothing to give to the poor man's family.

They bring over their 'talians, and Naygurs from the South,
Thinking they can do the work, take beans from out our mouth,
The poor man's children they must starve, but we will not agree,
To be put down like a worm in the ground and starve our families.[12]

In January, 1885, the Knights of Labor shoeworkers in Haverhill, Massachusetts, went on strike after the employers informed them that no members of the order would be allowed to work in their shops. This strike ended in victory and recognition of the Knights of Labor assembly. The victory was aided by the spirit of the strikers.

THE BOOT MAKERS' GREAT STRIKE
Composed by Messrs Carey and Duggan,
for the benefit of the strikers

Air—"Poor Old Dad"

Kind friends, if you will listen now, a story I'll relate,
It's of a little notice that was posted up of late
In every boot and shoe shop in our quiet little town,
The Knights refuse to go to work until 'twas taken down.
The contents of that little note I'm sure you all know well,
Its object was to break the grand and noble K. of L
But while they stand their ground like men I'm sure they'll win the day.
They'll go to work as true Knights should and for a fair day's pay.

We'll stand our ground like noble men, I'm sure we're not afraid,
The bosses they will need us yet, the boots they must be made,
Although they may get "rats" and bums Skowhegan "scabs," as well,
I'm sure they'll never break the grand and noble K. of L.

It was in midwinter's chilling blast our papers bore the news,
"Make individual contracts or your situation lose,"
To this the Knights both one and all replied "We'll not submit,
So bravely to the shops they marched and quickly took their kits.
Two thousand strong they marched along true workingmen were they,
All striking for a principle and for a fair day's pay,
We'll win this battle in the end, for time alone will tell,
That victory crowns the efforts of the noble K. of L.

We'll stand our ground, etc.

So now, kind friends, take my advice, from Spencer stay away,
For if you help that noble band they'll help you all some day,
I'm sure that every honest man will say our cause is just,
In spite of all the "rats" and "scabs" we'll win, for win we must.
Although there's traitors in our ranks their number's very small,
We'll have their little "photographs a-hanging in our hall,
We'll keep the vows we've taken and we'll stick out for our rights,
We're not afraid to tell the world we're members of the Knights.

We'll stand our ground, etc.[13]

Two of the greatest strikes in American labor history occurred in the 1890s: the Homestead strike and the Pullman strike. Songs were featured in both.

In 1892 workers at the Carnegie, Phipps & Company's Homestead plant were organized in-

[12]Broadside, Harris Collection, Brown University.

[13]Ibid. The broadside carried the following caution: "All persons are forbidden using this song without permission from the composers, D. T. Carey and J. P. Duggan."

LONGSHOREMEN'S STRIKE;

OR THE

POOR MAN'S FAMILY.

OH! I am a simple laboring man,
I work along the shore,
To keep the hungry wolves away
From the poor longshoreman's door;
I toil all day in the broiling sun,
On the ships that come from sea,
From broad daylight till late at night,
For a poor man's family.

CHORUS

Give us fair pay for every day
Is what we ask of ye;
Our cause is right,
We are out on a strike
For a poor man's family.

Oh! the rich ones gilded carriages,
And horses swift and strong,
Whin a poor man asks for a bite to eat
They tell him he is wrong;
Go take your shovel in your hand,
Go out and work for me;
Die or live they have nothing to give
To a poor man's family.

They bring over their Italians
And Chinamen from the South,
Thinking they can do our work,
Take the bread from out our mouths;
The white man's children they must starve,
Sure we will not agree
To be put down like a worm in the ground,
And starve our family.

ARTHUR SAINT CLAIR SMITH,
CENTENNIAL SONG PUBLISHER,
No. 16 FAYETTE STREET,
(Between 9th and 10th. Below Arch.)
PHILADELPHIA.

A broadside variant of "Longshoreman's Strike." Courtesy of Brown University Library.

to six lodges of the Amalgamated Association of Iron and Steel Workers, affiliated with the American Federation of Labor. However, only eight hundred of the working force of twenty-five hundred were members of the union. In keeping with the craft union concept of the Amalgamated, they were mostly skilled workers in the rolling mills and puddling furnaces. The union members were operating under an agreement signed by the company and the union in 1889. When the contract expired in 1892, Henry Clay Frick, the notorious anti-union manager of the company, told the union that unless a new agreement on the company's terms was reached in twenty-nine days, the company would cease dealing with the union. Frick acted with the consent of Andrew Carnegie, the millionaire owner of the company. When the ultimatum period expired, the Homestead workers were promptly locked out. The union responded with a strike, and the non-union steelworkers, convinced that their future, too, was at stake, joined the battle. The steelworkers' determination to win was expressed in the following song:

THE HOMESTEAD STRIKE
As Sung by the National Trio

Now, boys, we are out on strike, you can help us if you like,
But you need not till I tell you what it's about.
They want to lower our wages, we think it is not right;
So for union's cause I want you all to shout.

We will sing the union's praise while our voices we can raise,
With noble Mr. Garland at our head,[14]
Hugh O'Donnell's good, that's true, we give him all the praise;[15]
We can't go wrong when by such men we're led.

The struggle may be long, there's no one yet can say,
But we'll take it as it comes for a little while;
We will fight both night and day, for we're bound to win the day,
And down this great steel king in grandest style.

Now let us all stand firm and take things very cool,
Then, you bet, we're sure to win this little strike;
But if men don't mind and start and act a fool,
That's sure to cause no end of care and strife.

My advice to you is this, let us work with a cool head,
And try and do the best thing in our power;
We'll have the good will of all, which will bring us back our bread,
And drive the demon Hunger from our door.

Let us unite with heart and hand and spread the news through this broad land,
We'll not give in until the company yield,
And fight with might and main and travel hand in hand
To win this strike or die upon the field.[16]

Even before the lockout and strike, Frick erected barbed-wire fences around the plant and hired three hundred Pinkertons to serve as company guards. A song described this conversion of the steel plant into an armed fortress:

THE FORT THAT FRICK BUILT

Twixt Homestead and Munhall
If you'll believe my word at all
Where once a steel works noisy roar
A thousand blessings did pour
There stands today with great pretense
Enclosed within a whitewashed fence
A wondrous change of great import
The mills transformed into a fort.[17]

The Pinkertons were assembled at a point on the Ohio River below Pittsburgh on the night of July 5. They were armed with Winchester rifles, placed aboard two barges, and towed up the Monongahela river to Homestead. Despite all efforts at secrecy, the strikers learned of the movement of the flotilla even before the barges had left Pittsburgh. They met the Pinkertons in the mill yards and warned them to turn back. When the Pinkertons moved to land, a battle broke out; a dozen men on each side were killed, and scores were wounded. But the Pinkertons were driven off.

The battle aroused the entire nation, and William W. Delaney, a prominent New York songwriter, reacted so angrily to the use of Pinkertons that he composed a song about it. However, since the commercial press was praising the Pinkertons and denouncing the strikers, Delaney took care to ascribe his song simply to "Willie Wildwave."

[14]M. M. Garland was president of the Amalgamated Association of Iron and Steel Workers.

[15]Hugh O'Donnell was head of an advisory committee of fifty members elected to handle all aspects of the strike.

[16]*The Homestead Strike Songster*, extra ed. (New York, n.d.).

[17]Printed card (1892), AFL Archives, Washington, D.C., reprinted in Philip S. Foner, *History of the Labor Movement in the United States*, II (New York, 1955), 207.

FATHER WAS KILLED BY THE PINKERTON MEN

'Twas in a Pennsylvania town not very long ago
Men struck against reduction of their pay
Their millionaire employer with philanthropic show
Had closed the works till starved they would obey
They fought for home and right to live where they had
toiled so long
But ere the sun had set some were laid low
There're hearts now sadly grieving by that sad and bitter
wrong
God help them for it was a cruel blow.

God help them tonight in their hour of affliction
Praying for him whom they'll ne'er see again
Hear the orphans tell their sad story
"Father was killed by the Pinkerton men."

Ye prating politicians, who boast protection creed,
Go to Homestead and stop the orphans' cry.
Protection for the rich man ye pander to his greed,
His workmen they are cattle and may die.
The freedom of the city in Scotland far away
'Tis presented to the millionaire suave,
But here in Free America with protection in full sway
His workmen get the freedom of the grave.

Chorus:[18]

Workers wrote their own songs in tribute to the strikers who had fallen in the battle against the Pinkertons.[19] The second one given below was by Michael McGovern, the "Puddler Poet."

THE HOMESTEAD STRIKE

We are asking one another as we pass the time of day,
Why workingmen resort to arms to get their proper pay,
And why our labor unions they must not be recognized,
Whilst the actions of a syndicate must not be criticized.
Now the troubles down at Homestead were brought
about this way.
When a grasping corporation had the audacity to say:
"You must all renounce your union and forswear your
liberty
And we will give you a chance to live and die in slavery."

Now the man that fights for honor, none can blame
him,
May luck attend wherever he may roam,
And no son of his will ever live to shame him,
Whilst liberty and honor rule our home.

Now this sturdy band of workingmen started out at the
break of day,
Determination in their faces which plainly meant to say:
"No one can come and take our homes for which we
have toiled so long,
No one can come and take our places—no, here's where
we belong!"

A woman with a rifle saw her husband in the crowd,
She handed him the weapon and they cheered her long
and loud.
He kissed her and said, "Mary, you go home till we're
through."
She answered, "No, if you must fight, my place is here
with you."

When a lot of bum detectives came without authority,
Like thieves at night when decent men were sleeping
peacefully—
Can you wonder why all honest hearts with indignation
burn,
And why the slimy worm that trods the earth when trod
upon will turn?
When they locked out men at Homestead so they were
face to face
With a lot of bum detectives and they knew it was their
place
To protect their homes and families, and this was neatly
done,
And the public will reward them for the victories they
won.[20]

THE HOMESTEAD STRUGGLE OR "FORT FRICK'S" DEFENDERS

Hurrah for the light of Truth and Right!
Whose rays our cause illumine;
Which shows the way how toilers may
Unite and all be true men:
Which wakes the slave to a sense of brave
Pursuits, and truly renders
To timid men the power to win,
Like "Fortress Frick's" Defenders.

Hurrah for the cause which to it draws
Of Freedom's minds the purest!
Whose love of truth and right forsooth
Affects its foes the surest;
Whose couraged defied the thugs who tried
To come as peace offenders.
With the "Little Bill," to Homestead mill—
Hurrah for the bold Defenders!

Hurrah for the men who were ready, when
Aroused through Frick's defiance,

[18] Sigmund Spaeth, *Weep Some More, My Lady* (Garden City, N.Y., 1927), pp. 235–36.

[19] An eight-foot stone shaft stands today at a street intersection in Homestead and carries this inscription: "Erected by the members of the Steel Workers Organization Committee Local Unions, in memory of the Iron and Steel workers who were killed in Homestead, Pa., on July 6, 1892, while striking against the Carnegie Steel Company in defense of their American rights."

[20] George Korson, *Coal Dust on the Fiddle* (1943; reprinted, Hatboro, Pa., 1965), pp. 405–6 (from the singing of Peter Haser).

To man the breach and nobly teach
The grist of self-reliance!
That Vulcan's sons 'gainst Pinkertons
Were steel compared to cinders;
Hurrah for such men, and hurrah again
For "Fortress Frick's" Defenders!

Hurrah for the bright redeeming light
Which guides the cause of Labor,
And union men who, with tongue and pen,
Fear not the gun or sabre:
Who'll wage the fight till despot might,
Like the Pinkertons, surrenders.
Hurrah! true Sumter heroes are
Our brave "Fort Frick" Defenders![21]

The steel strike spread to other mills, and soon over eight thousand workers were involved. Labor throughout the land expressed its sympathy for the strikers in resolutions and contributions. But Carnegie and Frick were determined to crush the Amalgamated, and, on November 20, 1892, its treasury empty, the union called off the strike. The defeat practically ended the career of the Amalgamated Association of Iron and Steel Workers; after 1892, unionism was virtually eliminated in the Pittsburgh area mills.

On June 20, 1893, the American Railway Union was born in Chicago, with Eugene V. Debs as president. It was a new kind of union, an industrial union which united all railroad workers—all, that is, except blacks—into one organization instead of dividing them into separate crafts. The success of the American Railway Union was almost instantaneous, and when the Great Northern surrendered in the spring of 1894 and recognized the union after an eighteen-day strike, the ARU's reputation was made. Railroad workers flocked to join, and at its second convention the ARU boasted one hundred fifty thousand members.

Among the railway men who joined the ARU in the spring of 1894 were the employees of the Pullman Palace Car Company. These workers had sought to end some of the abuses they were forced to endure in the "model town" of Pullman, Illinois—especially the reduction in their wages of as much as 40 percent, while no reduction was made in the high rents they paid for company houses. However, they were bluntly refused, and some members of the committee who had tried to negotiate with the company were discharged. Pullman workers walked off the job, and when the Pullman Company rejected Debs's offer to arbitrate, the American Railway Union began a sympathetic boycott of the company's cars on June 26, 1894. When the General Managers' Association, representing the railroad corporations, rallied to support the Pullman company, the walkout developed into a general strike on the railroads, and by July 4, more than one hundred fifty thousand men were on strike.

The Pullman strike, or the "Debs Rebellion," as it was named by the newspapers, was broken by a powerful alliance of anti-labor forces: the use of strikebreakers and the United States Army, federal injunctions issued by the courts, the imprisonment of strike leaders, and an extremely hostile press. Most important of all were the strikebreaking activities of the federal troops sent by President Grover Cleveland over the objections of Illinois governor John Peter Altgeld. Cleveland's action prompted this bitter song:

THE PULLMAN STRIKE
By Willie Wildwave
Air—"The Widow's Plea for Her Son"
Copyright, 1894, by William W. Delaney

Near the city of Chicago, where riot holds full sway,
The workingmen of Pullman are battling for fair play;
But the Boss he would not listen to the workingmen's appeal,
And scorned their mute advances, no sympathy did feel.
The railroad men refused to move even a single car,
Till suddenly from Washington they heard the White House Czar
Proclaim them all law breakers, and then in mournful tone
To their countrymen they sent their cry with sad and dismal moan:

Remember we are workmen, and we want honest pay,
And gentlemen, remember, we work hard day by day;
Let Pullman remember, too, no matter where he roams,
We built up his capital, and we're pleading for our homes!

The troops are ordered from the East and from the Western shore,
The firebrands of anarchy are brought to every door;
Honest workmen repudiate the work of thugs and tramps,

[21]Michael McGovern, *Labor Lyrics and Other Poems* (Youngstown, Ohio, 1899), pp. 30–31.

And think it is an outrage to be reckoned with those
scamps.
Arbitration was what they asked, but the Boss he quick
refused,
"Your fight is with the railroads," was the answer they
perused;
But Pullman will regret the day he gave this harsh reply,
And workingmen throughout the land will heed our
pleading cry:[22]

Arrested and convicted of contempt of court because he refused to abide by a federal injunction, Eugene V. Debs spent six months in prison. At a mass meeting in New York City's Cooper Union Hall, workers voiced their support of the Pullman strikers and their leader, Debs:

They hanged and quartered John Ball,[23] but Feudalism
Passed Away.
They hanged John Brown, but Chattel Slavery Passed
Away.
They arrested Eug. Debs, and May Kill Him, But Wage
Slavery Will Pass Away.
Such Souls Go Marching On.[24]

The American Railway Union never recovered from the disastrous defeat it suffered in the Pullman strike. Its leaders were in jail, and its members, as the following song indicates, were blacklisted out of whatever jobs they could obtain.

A.R.U.

Been on the hummer since ninety-four,
Last job I had was on the Lake Shore,
Lost my office in the A.R.U.
And I won't get it back till nineteen-two
And I'm still on the hog train flagging my meals,
Ridin' the brake beams close to the wheels.[25]

In January, 1895, the motormen on the Brooklyn trolleys, organized in the Knights of Labor, went on strike to raise their wages from two dollars for a fourteen-hour day to two dollars and a quarter for a twelve-hour day. The company gave them the "Pullman" treatment, calling in scabs, state troopers, and local police to break the strike. This was the last important strike called by the Knights of Labor, and it produced a moving song.

BROOKLYN TROLLILEE

Of the trolley strike I now will sing that's caused so
much ado.
And try to show both sides of the facts and story true.
Now, we'll first take the monopolist, with all his cars
and cash,
Who'll stand no arbitration, but declares the Knights
he'll smash;
The next we'll take the poor man, working 14 hours
they say;
Who asks only honest wages, two dollars and a quarter a
day.
Judge for yourself—is that too much the rich man to
them pay
The men who run our trolley cars 14 hours a day?

They have pleasure, they have comfort, every luxury
of this life.
A home that's grand, wealth at command, children
and a wife.
They never give a thought at all for the poor man or
his strife.
But strive to pile their riches up—I ask you is that
right?

They have used the bluff "protection," for more soldiers
they have called;
The want of men, not protection, is the reason that
they've crawled.
The police on steady duty they have kept them night
and day,
While the poor man who is fighting right for their protection pay.
What causes fights and riots? No, it is not the motor
man;
It's hoodlums, toughs and loafers I'm sure you understand
And while I earn my living from the poor man just as
they.
I hope tonight they'll win their fight—two dollars and a
quarter a day.

Chorus:[26]

A sympathetic ballad about a strike was published in the *Springfield Republican* of August 31, 1899.

WHEN THE STRIKE WAS ON
By Adrian Templeton Gorham

The streets were choked with a motley crowd
That swayed like a wind-blown tree,

22 Broadside, Harris Collection, Brown University.

23 John Ball (1338–81) was a revolutionary English priest and a supporter of the Wat Tyler Rebellion, for which he was hanged. He was memorialized in William Morris's *A Dream of John Ball* (London, 1888).

24 *New York Times*, July 13, 1894.

25 Carl Sandburg, *The American Songbag* (New York, 1927), p. 191.

26 *New York World*, Jan. 28, 1895.

And curses were vented, fierce and loud,
On the grasping monopoly.
There were slaves who toiled from the break of morn
Till the sun's last ray was gone.—
Pale men with overalls grimed and torn,
For the journeymen's strike was on.

There were shoeless women, with unkempt hair,
Who knew neither hope nor rest;
Poor wrecks of the ghetto, with shoulders bare,
And little ones at the breast.
There were children from whose staring eyes
The joy of young life was gone,
And sad lips parted with poverty's sighs,
For the journeymen's strike was on.

"Bread, bread," their petition, "money for bread,
And the rent of our hovel homes,—
The dreary abodes where we make our bed,
And the blessed light never comes!
You have coined your gold from our flesh and blood,—
Wrung wealth from sinew and bone,"
But stern and relentless the masters stood
When the journeymen's strike was on.

"Away! away!" cried the lords of wealth,
"No parleying now with you!
We are not in this business for our health,
And the syndicate claims its due.
Be off to your tasks and your servile path
Ere the hope of employ is gone!"
Then the pale-faced mob grew paler with wrath,
When the journeymen's strike was on.

A missile was thrown,—a weapon flashed,
And the roundsmen's clubs were swung;
The image of God was mauled and mashed
As the people were backward flung.
Poor beggars! they strove with the idol, Gold,
And under its wheels were cast;
The "scabs" came down like the plagues of old,
And the strike was "off" at last.

THE SCAB

The widespread use of scabs to break strikes in the eighties and nineties produced a whole literature of anti-scab songs and poems. This theme was symbolized in the concluding verse of John Smith's "The Scab's Death," published in the *Carpenter* of June, 1883:

And when the golden gate he reached,
He read this legend, bold and grim;
No scab or rat from earth below,
Among the blest shall enter in.[27]

Here is an example of an anti-scab song of the period.

THE SCAB'S LAMENT

I am an anti-unionist
A low-lived-go-between
A blackleg in the first degree,
Such is my languid spleen.
I'll own it breaks my aching heart,
And almost drives me mad,
To hear the folks while passing by
Call me a noted scab.

Had I kept on the common path
My fellow-workmen tread,
And not used foul and cowardly means
To earn my daily bread,
I would not need a police guard
To escort me in a cab;
Nor would the boys yell "rats" at me
Had I not been a scab.

Even Anarchists and socialists
Will battle for the right,
But no earthly good was ever done
By workmen of my type.
They're always ready to step in
And make things worse than bad,
For matter will accumulate
When covered by a scab.

An outcast from humanity,
I wander through the street,
A foe to all my fellow-men
And slurred by those I meet;
I'm a Judas to the world at large,
My dismal fate is sad,
I'm branded with the countersigns
Of blackleg, rat and scab.[28]

The most popular anti-scab song of the late nineteenth century was "After the Strike." The version published in the *United Mine Workers' Journal*, May 24, 1894, carried the notice that it was by Joseph A. Hemer, Corning, Ohio. The line "Why do shopmates call you a scab?" is changed to "Why do miners call you a scab?" Similarly, "After the shops have opened" is changed to "After the mines have opened," and "That's why my shopmates call me a scab"

[27]Joe Hill's famous song "Casey Jones, the Union Scab," has a scab entering heaven, but he is finally exiled to hell. So hated were scabs that a factory official complained in December, 1884, that when the company tried to board out the strikebreakers, "not a boarding house would recluse them. Even the restaurant keeper at the depot refused to supply them with food" (*John Swinton's Paper*, Dec. 21, 1884).

[28]Scrapbook of Newspaper Clippings Relating to Strikes, 1886–87, New York Public Library.

becomes "That's why the miners call me a scab."

AFTER THE STRIKE
Air—"After the Ball"

Once a pretty maiden climbed an old man's knee
Asked for a story—"Papa tell me,
Why are you lonely, why are you sad,
Why do your shopmates call you a scab?"
I had friends, pet, long, long years ago,
How I lost them you soon shall know;
I'll tell it all, pet, tell all my shame;
I was a scab, pet, I was to blame."

After the strike is over,
After the men have won,
After the shops have opened,
After the notice is down;
Many the heart is aching,
Though the hope seems bright
That many a scab will vanish
After the strike.

Brave men were fighting, standing side by side,
Fighting for justice, fighting with pride,
I then was with them—with them heart and soul,
But when the test came, I left them in the cold,
I thought it best, pet, best to turn a scab;
Best to return, pet, to the job I had,
That's why I'm lonely, that's why I'm sad,
That's why my shopmates call me a scab.

Chorus:

Many years have passed, pet, since I won that name,
And in song and story they have told my shame,
I have tried to tell them, tried to explain,
But they will not listen, pleading is in vain;
Everywhere I wander, everywhere I roam,
The story of my shame is sure to find my home,
I'd give my life, pet, I'd give my all,
If I had not turned traitor, or scabbed at all.

Chorus:[29]

Michael McGovern, the "Puddler Poet," composed the following after he read of the persecution of a worker who had denounced a scab. He explained in his introductory note the nature of the punishment.

BLACKLISTED

Lines on an *impartial* Judge who refused a member of a labor association his naturalization papers, though brought up from childhood in the court's vicinity and of unimpeachable character. His offense, being convicted of shouting "bah" at blacksheep, was the only item against him. The learned judge, while lecturing him on his abhorrent crime, said this country needed better human material than he to become parents of our future presidents and upholders of the nation's honor.

"Young man, this most impartial court
Has come unto the just conclusion
That such ingredients as you
Are hurtful to our nation's fusion.
Tho' living here since childhood's days,
And otherwise of good character,
One act of yours compels this court
To class you as a malefactor.

"You've forfeited through this one crime
The right to be, in our opinion,
A citizen of this free land,
Where liberty claims sole dominion;
Where giant wealth by law can tread
Our states and cities unresisted,
And you, by crossing *once* its path,
Are held before this court *blacklisted.*

"A firm may follow its pursuits,
And men may labor unrestricted,
But you who dared intimidate
Stand on our court records convicted.
You went on 'strike,' and shouted 'bah'
At him who took your situation;
Accordingly we must refuse
Your claim for naturalization.

"The offspring of a man like *you*,
Who 'gainst our institutions budges
A whispering 'bah,' should ne'er become
Our future presidents and *judges.*
Away! your crime outweighs your worth;
Our wealthy firms must be respected;
So this *impartial* court decrees
Your citizenship claim rejected."[30]

Almost as despicable as the scab in the eyes of union men was the non-union worker who received all the benefits of the struggles waged by organized labor for better conditions but refused to contribute his share to the victories and the maintenance of achievements.

THE NON-UNION CHORUS
By the late William Willen

We're on the outs with union men,
Although we like their plan.
We'd like to have our wages raised
By any union clan;

[29] *Carpenter*, Jan., 1894.
[30] McGovern, *Labor Lyrics*, p. 31.

But still no sacrifice we'll make—
No stock we'll risk to lose—
We always take the benefits,
Though we never pay the dues.

They say we're mean, unmanly men,
But why they call us such
We cannot tell, for we have done
No crime the law can touch.
Our only fault exists in that
"Diplomacy" we use
In taking all the benefits,
Though we never pay the dues.

We know that those we're working for
Will keep our wages down,
Unless they feel uncertain,
Whether labor union frown;
But what they'll give to union men
To us they won't refuse,
So, while we get the benefits
We need not pay the dues.

And then there is our employers,
We always try to please.
Although they frown at union men
We always feel at ease.
They know the kind of men they want,
To tell them all the news,
Are those who get the benefits
But never pay the dues.

When asked to join our answer is,
We think, quite 'propriate,
"There's men in that there lodge with whom
We will not 'sociate."
"We do not like your leaders,"
Or with any other ruse,
We try to get the benefits
Though we never pay the dues.

We boast in this great land of ours
That every man is free
To act the part which he thinks best
Will suit him, therefore we
Prefer to see our fellows fight,
While we hold different views,
And then we take the benefits
Though we never pay the dues.

When strike's the question and we're asked
Whether we will or won't
We tell the men we want to strike;
Then tell the boss we don't.
So if the strike is lost, we're safe
If won we hail the news
With joy, and take the benefits
Though we never pay the dues.

And so it is from day to day,
Still in the same old rut,—
We always eat the kernel,
Though we never crack the nut.
Our motto proud has been
The same which now we use;
"Take all the benefits you can,
But never pay the dues."[31]

THE ECONOMIC CRISIS OF 1893–97

The Pullman and Brooklyn trolley strikes took place in the midst of the most severe economic crisis the nation had yet experienced. It began on May 4, 1893, when the National Cordage Company failed, and by the end of the year, more than sixteen thousand business firms were bankrupt; thousands of shops and factories were shut down; more thousands worked only part time, and at least three million out of a total labor force of five million were unemployed. As want and hunger intensified among the working people, their songs expressed their bitterness and anger.

LABOR IN WANT

By E. H. Belden (Merlinde Steins), Horton, Mich.
(National Anthem)

Can you give any reason how it comes about
That my children are dyin' for bread,
When I've worked all my life and am nearly played out,
Trying' hard to get somethin' ahead?
There is some folks I know of that hain't done a tap,
And they ride in their carriage and four,
And have got so much wealth they don't know where they're at,
While the toilers are ragged and poor.

Too proud to beg, too honest to steal,
I know what it is to be wantin' a meal;
When I ask for work they call me a tramp,
Or say I'm a shappy genteel.

When they foreclosed the mortgage and took the old home,
It was sad to lay mother away;
And I couldn't keep from thinkin' of what would become
Of poor Bessie and Bennie and May.
For I'm gettin' old now and my work's nearly done,
Upon whom will my darlin's depend?
Without clothin' or food, without friends or a home.
Will the millionaires care for them then?

Chorus:

31 *United Mine Workers' Journal,* May 17, 1894.

There is something wrong somewhere as things are right now,
Thousands are out of shelter and bread,
While the wealth they've created is taken somehow
By the trusts and the shylocks instead.
Nature's done her part well and the toilers their share
To make the world happy and gay,
Had the laws been preserved that our fathers prepared
There's but few would be wantin' to-day.

Chorus:

They have burned up our greenbacks to make gold go up,
As would buy twice as much as before;
They are tryin' hard now to knock silver clean out,
So our debts will be twice as much more,
Had the works of our fathers and Lincoln's remained
Shylock's greed would have never had birth,
And the nation would live as at first it was framed
Until freedom encircled the earth.

Chorus:

It will be equal rights or else slav'ry and serfs,
It is hard tellin' which way 'twill go;
For the gold-bugs are fig'rin' to fence in the earth,
And to own us both body and soul.
But we'll have rights for all and give priv'leges to none,
Or we'll march, like our fathers, in blood,
And beneath the same flag we will work, pray and vote
For our homes and our children and God.

Chorus:[32]

DAN RAGG

By Robert E. Rich, Portsmouth, N.H.

Air—"Bonnie Dundee"

My name it is Ragg, sir! Dan Ragg, if you please;
My eyes have grown dim and I'm weak in the knees;
'Tis three score and ten since the year of my birth,
And I'm now limping down to my rest in the earth.

Then fill up my cup and fill up my can,
With a flagon from Lethe for weary old Dan;
For fifty long years, under sorrow and care,
I have breakfasted, dined and supped with Despair.

And the pathway is darker and rougher each day!
The pulse beating weaker and joints giving way,
For when work is over there's little to eat,
And little to wear in the pitiless street.

I have mined the bright coal for the sharper and drone,
And have warmed every hearth in the land, but my own
I have toiled on the railway, in meadow and mill
And have gutted the marts and the other man's till.

I have toiled till I fainted for great millionaires,
And got, when disabled, their plasters and prayers;
O they sigh when no longer I add to their hoard,
And send me a ticket to Barmecide's board.

In the shape of a tract or pet treaties on rent,
With the dictum of Malthus to make me content;
But they smile and ignore while I add to their swag,
Till election reminds them of Master Dan Ragg!

See the houses I've built by the rivers and seas,
And filled them with rarest appointments of ease;
While in some filthy alley they forced me to hive,
And rear my poor children next door to a dive.

The good things all pass through the hands of old Dan,
But they stick when they come to the craftier man,
Who places Ed Atkinson's bust in a niche
For telling the Raggs they are growing so rich!

For Ned says 'tis poverty makes me a boor,
And the drinking of beer that keeps me so poor,
And it brings all the dissolute Raggs to the ditch,
While champagne and brandy ennoble the rich.

Now see my wife there—some call her a hag!
A lady she would be, were she not a Ragg!
But Want stole the gentleness out of her face,
That once was so winning with maidenly grace.

So, since we must stagger neath poverty's knout,
Old Dan and his kidney don't die with the gout;
And why should so much be expected of Raggs
While his master so often goes off with his Jags?[33]

POVERTY AND WEALTH

By Maurice Enright

Air—"The Pretty Girl Milking Her Cow"

How empty our freedom, oft vaunted,
How hollow our liberty fair,
When thousands by hunger are haunted
And driven by want to despair;
Where riches and wealth in abundance
Accumulate day after day,
And hoarders enjoy their redundance
While manhood is left to decay.

If wealth, which is hoarded so often
Could lengthen life's fast-fleeting hours,
Or the last dying moments could soften,
Why, then, we might worship its powers;
But, no, this bright gold, so alluring,
The darkness of death can't illume,
Though life we may give to procuring,
Its worth is all lost in the tomb.

The workman is often insulted
By seekers of alms in his name,

32 *Journal of the Knights of Labor,* Nov. 2, 1893.
33 *Coming Nation,* Feb. 17, 1894.

Would surely, if he were consulted,
His scorn for such begging proclaim;
Why mingle the proud name of labor
With charity, alms and the rest,
For health, strength and brains ask no favor,
They are of God's blessings the best.

The toilers, the pride of our nation,
As mendicants ne'er will appeal,
But as part of God's noblest creation,
A right to His bounty they feel;
To work is their highest ambition,
And live independent and free,
Content with their humble position,
If a prospect of labor they see.

In this fair land which plenty still blesses,
No misery e'er would appear,
Would all to refrain from excesses
And be to each other sincere;
And practice like generous brothers
The "Golden Rule," simple and true,
Just always to "do unto others
As you would they should do unto you."[34]

HYMN FOR THE UNFORTUNATE

By C. H. Murray

Though labor my not be supplied
To anxious crowds that throng the street,
And natural rights may be denied
And Justice driven from her seat,
Shrink not from what such sorrows bring,
"Simply to the cross we cling."

If not yet on this fertile earth
Has come the reign for which He prayed,
If men in hunger mourn their birth
While thieves in purple are arrayed,
We should shout and gladly sing,
"Simply to the cross we cling."

If trusts and combines tax our food
While 'neath the yoke we toil and sweat,
Contending with conditions rude,
Should we express the least regret?
Let the nabobs have full swing,
"Simply to the cross we cling."

If we are ninny-headed fools
That cannot feel the present wrong,
Some party's willing servile tools
That see not where our rights belong,—
Why should we question anything?
"Simply to the cross we cling."

We hear the helpless children cry,—
From woman's lips come pleas for bread;
The living envy those that die
And wish that they were with the dead,
From this they claim sweet blessings spring,
If "simply to the cross we cling."

For happiness why should we strive,
The world is for a favored few
Who by unjust exactions thrive
And gather what is not their due,
While we feel their scorpion sting,
"Simply to the cross we cling."

The hypocrite that wealth employs
To preach forbearance to its scheme,
Is pregnant with religious noise
To make woes other than they seem,
" 'Tis but Heaven's sweet chastening,"
If "simply to the cross we cling."[35]

AMERICA—1895

By O. J. Graham

Tune—"America"

Our country 'tis for thee,
Land where once all were free,
We take our stand.
We once had liberty,
Peace and propserity;
Now, want and misery
All through our land.

Silver demonetized,
Business all paralyzed,
By a thieving clan,
Bankers and railroad pools,
Brokers and money tools,
Protection tariff fools
Robbing Uncle Sam.

Tramps line our public way,
Men starving every day,
How just, how grand,
Laws made by plutocrats,
And mugwump democrats,
All owned by autocrats
From a foreign land.

Something must soon be done,
Hard times grind every one
Down to hard pan.
People are all in debt,
Money they cannot get,
Mortgages not paid yet
Will take their land.

You should not vote away
Your right to have your say,
Hark, now, hear me,
You should not cringe and crawl

[34] *Journal of the Knights of Labor*, Feb. 22, 1894.
[35] *Coming Nation*, May 26, 1894.

To men with cheek and gall,
Demand for each and all
Perfect liberty![36]

THE POOR WHITE SLAVE

Anon.

Tune—"Old Black Joe"

Down where the coal mine lifts its ugly shaft,
There stands a hut, beside a narrow lane,
List to the strains the summer breezes waft—
From out the open window comes
This sad refrain—

"I'm starving, I'm starving,
And I'll fill a pauper's grave,
No one but God now cares for me,
A poor white slave."

Loved ones have gone—a darling child and wife—
Dead for the want of care that money brings,
Left here alone the miner gasps for life,
No ear but God's to listen while
He faintly sings—

"I'm starving, I'm starving,
And I'll fill a pauper's grave,
No one but God now cares for me,
A poor white slave."

Long years he toiled—a pittance was his pay,
Still growing less, till hope at last had flown,
Sickness and hunger now bear him away
Away to Him who pitying hears
His last faint moan:

"I'm starving, I'm starving,
And I'll fill a pauper's grave,
No one but God now cares for me,
A poor white slave."

O Christ of Love, who once Thyself was poor!
Where are the ones who falsely bear Thy name?
No brother man to seek this cottage door,
No one to hear this last appeal
Or heed its claim:

"I'm starving, I'm starving,
And I'll fill a pauper's grave,
No one but God now cares for me,
A poor white slave."

God speed the day when want shall be no more,
When none shall feel the grip of Hunger's hand,
Soon may this wail of living death be o'er
Now heard in hut and hovel through
Our suffering land,

"I'm starving, I'm starving,
And I'll fill a pauper's grave,
No one but God now cares for me,
A poor white slave."[37]

Armies of unemployed roamed the country, "tramping on and on—in search of work in far-off places." The commercial press called them tramps, but a song of the period, a forerunner of Joe Hill's famous "Preacher and the Slave," told a different story.

A TRAMP'S THOUGHTS

As he sits on the church steps and hears the choir singing the hymn: "I Have Heard of a Beautiful City"

By Jane Keep

I have read of beautiful cities,
Far off in the land of the blest;
But in the only city I know of
The weary get no rest.

I have heard of beautiful mansions,
Far up in the azure sky;
But the only mansions I know of
Are not for you and I.

I have listened to beautiful stories
Of times that are "going to be,"
But the only times I know of
Are bad for you and me.

I have heard of beautiful countries
Way off in the Land of the Dead;
But in the only countries I know of
The poor and the hungry lack bread.

I have heard of beautiful garments
To be worn by the Fighters of Sin;
But the only garments I know of
In winter are terribly thin.

I have heard of beautiful visions
Far off in the Land to Be,
But the only visions I ever knew
Could never be real for me.

I have heard of beautiful banquets,
In the land of the Bye and bye;
But the only banquet I ever had
Was a piece of damaged pie.

I am tired of hearing of beautiful things
In the Land Beyond the Grave
One thing I know for certainty
That here I am a slave.[38]

[36] *Labor Journal*, reprinted in *Coming Nation*, May 11, 1895.

[37] *Appeal to Reason*, Aug. 28, 1897.

[38] *People*, reprinted in *Appeal to Reason*, Jan. 25, 1896.

COXEY'S ARMY

Unemployment demonstrations became the order of the day. One of the most famous, led by General Jacob S. Coxey of Massillon, Ohio, was known as "Coxey's army." Coxey formulated a plan to put the unemployed to work on public projects financed by the issuance of greenbacks. The march began Easter Sunday, 1894, and reached Washington on May 1, with five hundred in line. But the police prevented the unemployed marchers from presenting Coxey's plan for the relief of the jobless to Congress. Coxey and other leaders were quickly arrested for the trivial offense of stepping on the grass, and the demonstrators were dispersed. Before Coxey's army passed into history, however, it had produced a number of labor songs. The first of the songs below was written by an anonymous member of the AFL Central Labor Council of Richmond, Indiana, which printed and distributed copies for the price of "one loaf of bread to feed Coxey's Army."

MARCHING WITH COXEY

Tune—"Marching through Georgia"

We are marching to the Capital, three hundred thousand
 strong,
With live petitions in our boots to urge our cause along,
And when we kick our congressmen, they'll feel there's
 something wrong.
As we go marching with Coxey.

Hurrah! hurrah! for the unemployed's appeal!
Hurrah! hurrah! for the marching commonweal!
Drive the lobbies from the senate,
Stop the trust and combine steal
For we are marching with Coxey.

We are not tramps nor vagabonds that's shirking honest
 toil,
But miners, clerks, skilled artizans, and tillers of the soil
Now forced to beg our brother worms to give us leave to
 toil,
While we are marching with Coxey.

Chorus:[39]

AFTER THE COMMONWEAL MARCH IS OVER

By Carl Browne

Tune—"After the Ball Is Over"

After the march is over
After the first of May
After these bills are passed, child
Then we will have fair play.
Many a heart will be happy
As to their homes we'll away
For we will have no interest on bonds
After the first of May.[40]

COXEY ARMY!

By Willie Wildwave

Air—"Marching through Georgia"

Copyright, 1894, by William W. Delaney

Bring the good old bugle, boys, we want to tell in song
The Coxey army's marching from the town of Massillon,
Soon they'll meet old Grover,[41] a good four million
 strong,
Marching in the Coxey Army!

Hurrah! hurrah! we want the jubilee!
Hurrah! hurrah! hard workingmen are we!
We only want a chance to live in this land of the free,
Marching in the Coxey Army!

Coxey is our leader, from the State of Ohio,
When we get to Washington, he'll let legislators know
That we are all workingmen, and not tramps "on the
 go,"
Marching in the Coxey Army!

Yes, we have Union men—men who fought in sixty-one,
Who faced ev'ry danger 'neath the broiling Southern sun,
Out of work, they're marching on to Washington—
Marching in the Coxey Army!

Bring the good old bugle, boys, let all join in the song,
We'll let the politicians know, they've tried our patience
 long,
We cry for honest labor, four million people strong,
Marching in the Coxey Army![42]

ON TO WASHINGTON

Tune—"John Brown's Body"

We're headed straight for Washington with leaders brave
 and true,
The foremost men, the mighty men, who fight the Wall
 Street crew;
They lead the People's Army forth, injustice to undo,
And truth goes marching on.

Glory, glory, hallelujah!
Glory, glory, hallelujah!
Glory, glory, hallelujah!
And truth goes marching on.[43]

39Printed copy in American Federation of Labor correspondence, AFL Archives, Washington, D.C.

40*Post* (Pittsburgh), Mar. 26, 1894, reprinted in Donald L. McMurry, *Coxey's Army* (Boston, 1929), p. 66n.

41President Grover Cleveland.

42Broadside, Harris Collection, Brown University.

43Ibid.

THE NATIONAL GRASS PLOT

Tune—"Star Spangled Banner"

O say, can you see, by the dawn's early light,
That grass plot so dear to the hearts of us all?
Is it green yet and fair, in well-nurtured plight,
Unpolluted by the Coxeyites' hated foot-fall?
Midst the yells of police, and swish of clubs through the
air,
We could hardly tell if our grass was still there.
But the green growing grass doth in triumph yet wave,
And the gallant police with their buttons of brass
Will sure make the Coxeyites keep off the grass.[44]

COXEY'S ON THE GRASS!

Oh I've been down to Washington, That city of renown,
I was there the morning that Coxey struck the town,
It was fun to see the plutocrats and hear the gold bugs
squeal,
As they march'd along three hundred strong the Coxey
Commonweal;
Says Tom Read to John Sherman, will you kindly kneel
and pray,
Says Dan the Great, I'll irrigate, will you join me Bro.
Quay?
Says Mister Vest, I'm going West, Good-bye says Tommy
Platt,
While Oats of Alabama murmured, I wonder where I'm
at?[45]

Then arise, Columbia, wake up Uncle Sam!
Order out your army, call out ev'ry man,
Load up your gatling guns, trouble's come at last,
Plutocracy is terrified, (Spoken) Why? Cause Coxey's
on the grass![46]

A strike described in verse by a working-class wife of the 1880s reveals that adherents of women's liberation raised issues in the late nineteenth century which are still with us. "I[nternational] L[abor] O[rganization] Bids Men Aid Working Wives" ran the headline of a front-page article in the *New York Times* of January 6, 1975.

A STRIKE

Once upon an evening dreary
As I pondered, sad and weary,
O'er the basket with the mending from the wash
the day before.
As I thought of countless stitches
To be placed in little breeches,
Rose my heart rebellious in me, as it oft had
done before.
At the fate that did condemn me, when my
daily task was o'er,
To that basket evermore.

John, with not a sign or motion,
Read no thought of the commotion
Which within me rankled sore.
"He," thought I, "when day is ended,
Has no stockings to be mended,
Has no babies to be tended,
He can sit and read and snore!
He can sit and read and rest him;
Must I work thus evermore?"
And my heart rebellious answered,
"Nevermore; no, nevermore."

For though I am but a woman,
Every nerve within is human,
Aching, throbbing, overworked,
Mind and body sick and sore,
I will strike. When day is ended,
Though the stockings are not mended,
Though my course can't be defended,
Safe behind the closet door
Goes the basket with the mending, and I'll
haunted be no more.
In the daylight shall be crowded all the work
that I will do.
When the evening lamps are lighted, I will read
the papers, too.[47]

[44]Ibid.

[45]Thomas B. Reed was the Republican Speaker of the House and a strong advocate of the repeal of the Sherman Silver Purchase Act. John Sherman was the Republican senator from Ohio, secretary of the treasury under President Hayes, and author of the Sherman Silver Purchase Act, which was repealed on August 26, 1893. Matthew S. Quay was the Republican senator from Pennsylvania; George Graham Vest, U.S. Senator from Missouri; Thomas C. Platt, Republican senator from New York. William Calvin Oates, member of Congress from Alabama, supported President Grover Cleveland in opposing free silver.

[46]*Coxey Good Roads and Non-Interest Bond Library*, (Jan., 1898).

[47]*Labor Leader*, Sept. 7, 1889.

12

Labor Parties, Labor–Farmers' Alliance Coalition, and Labor-Populism 1880–97

ANTI-MONOPOLY

During the opening years of the eighties, most workers concentrated on economic activities, on rebuilding the unions shattered during the long depression of the seventies, and on boycotts and strikes for higher wages, shorter hours, and union recognition. But there were some, like John Swinton, who insisted that workers could not afford to ignore the ballot box, since capital was creating powerful monopolies which kept increasing their domination over American society. By 1879 the Standard Oil Trust controlled 95 percent of the oil-refining business, and with its remarkable success, the trust became the most popular type of combination in American industry. In 1884, the American Cotton Oil Trust was formed, followed a year later by the National Linseed Oil Trust. In 1887 came the Distillers' and Cattle Feeders' Company (Whiskey Trust), the Sugar Refining Company (Sugar Trust), the National Lead Trust, the Cordage Trust, and others. Said President Grover Cleveland in a message to Congress on December 3, 1888: "As we view the achievements of aggregated capital, we discover the existence of trusts, combinations and monopolies, while the citizen is struggling far in the rear or is trampled to death beneath an iron heel. Corporations, which should be carefully restrained creatures of the law and servants of the people, are fast becoming the people's masters."[1]

Two songs of the period noted this development:

WHY COAL GOES UP

By Mrs. Frances A. Bingham

Why does the price of coal go up
At the "combination's" sign?
It darkens this winter the poor man's hearth,
As if by a title divine.

Does it mean more pay for those who dig
All day in the reeking mine?
Truly the hearts must be warm and big,
Of the Godly men who combine.

Does it safety mean from the poison damp,
From the gasping death of flame;
From a living grave, with its smothered lamp,
From a tomb without a name?

To give the collier a chance to hold
His little one by the hand?
And to see the birds of a waking world,
In the beauty of Spring expand?

To make his bread and his home so sure,
That its daily wearying care,
He need not carry to darken still more
The shaft's long perilous stair?

If it means all this, then we concede
All Christians had better combine
To "put up coal" and thrill with light
The cold and pitiless mine.

And we are glad to pay extra toll
For each precious jetty ton,
To give these toilers, grim and sad,
The bath of God's free sun.

[1]U.S., Congress, House, 53rd Cong., 2d sess., 1888, *Miscellaneous Documents*, 210, pt. 8.

"It is not for them that coal goes up,"
Please tell me who 'tis for then,
That it "jumps" to the tune of one hundred cents
At the word of these pious men?

We know that thousands of little feet
Are scarred and blue with cold;
That women's fingers grow all too stiff,
The needle of life to hold.

There's many a home that is fetid with death
For the want of bright, generous fires;
And hearts grow hard with revengeful thought
When starved of common desires.

'Tis God that hath piled the wondrous wealth
In acres of goodly mine—
Yes, they style themselves the lords of the coal,
These freebooters who combine.

But coal goes up, and wages go down,
And still do the gamblers play
In their palaces and white-winged yachts
Forgetting their Judgment Day!

They can buy the smiles of women fair,
Their ease, their horses, their wine—
Do we need to ask why coal goes up?
Why these church-going men combine?[2]

THE SONG OF THE TRUST

Where a chimney is smoking, where a miner is crouching,
Where there's boiling, forging, racking and stretching,
Where coal or pit-salt is dug up,
Where gin is brewed, or beer or champagne—
There with great cheer(s)
The Trust is, too,
Which pockets the profits for itself.

Where they adulterate food and water the wine,
Where they meddle and dabble and thrash and fish,
Where they build and plaster, weave or cudgel,
Where they fish for codfish or oysters,
Right away like a smart man
Comes the man of the Trust
Who does the mixing of the cards for the company.

Sugar, salt and poison, printing-paper and writing,
Rags, pumps, lye, slops, rum,
Ropes, velvet, bastiste, false birdshit,
Everything he makes into stocks.
All property
Is taken by the company,
Then he makes prices for the public.

Yes, the Trusts nowadays are smart people,
They hatch chickens even from rotten eggs,
Make money from sweat, raise the prices,
Slaughter millions with great cheer.
If the working-man complains
What do they care?
All the more they'll do their swindling!

And their new move was a smart trick:
They even have the president!
He was nominated and the Trusts' money
Gave him the post without much trouble.
That for our benefit
The devil may get them,
The Postman wishes, 'cause he hates them.[3]

Since neither the Republicans nor the Democrats were doing anything to curb this development, a third-party movement arose in the early eighties, the Anti-Monopoly party. It made itself felt first on the state level. Here is a song written for the Anti-Monopoly party of California in 1882:

ANTI-MONOPOLY WAR SONG

By R. J. Harrison

Lo! the car of Juggernaut,
Lo! the ruin it hath wrought,
As it moves o'er hill and dale
Riding on its iron rail,
Will you let the idol grim
Tear ye, brothers limb from limb?
And your breath of Freedom choke
With its clouds of poisoned smoke.

No! then onward to the fray
Hurl the monster from your way,
Let your cry of battle be
Death to all Monopoly!

Merchants! crushed beneath the weight
Of your contract-laden freight—
Fettered by each tyrant line
Of the craven bond you sign,
Farmers, ye who sow the plain
With its wealth of precious grain,
Yet must see your fruit of toil
Be the Rail-Roads robber-spoil,

Onward! onward to the fray!
Hurl the monster from your way,
Let your cry of battle be
Ruin to Monopoly!

Citizens of all degrees,
Victims of vile subsidies—
Ye, who basest burdens bear
Of unjust unlawful fare,
Cast the loads from off your backs,
Tear the tyrants from his tracks—

[2]*Workmen's Advocate,* Mar. 19, 1887.

[3]*Gross New Yorker Arbeiter-Zeitung,* May, 1889. Trans. Lenore Veltfort.

Let elections glorious morn
Show your moving might of scorn

Onward! onward to the fray
Hurl the monster from your way,
Let your cry of battle be
Ruin to Monopoly!

Cast your votes for honest men,
Trust no wily tongue or pen—
Should the rail-road hireling dare
Offer smile and promise fair,
Tell him you have had enough
Of the Engine's poison puff
And send him to oblivion's vale
Riding on his Master's rail—

Onward! onward to the fray,
Hurl the monster from your way,
Let your cry of battle be
Ruin to Monopoly![4]

In 1884 the People's party, a combination of the Anti-Monopoly and Greenback-Labor parties, nominated Benjamin F. Butler for president and called upon labor to rally behind him. Butler was maligned as the "beast of New Orleans," ostensibly because of his notorious "woman order,"[5] but actually because as a Union army general he had stood up for the rights of blacks in that city. He had long championed labor's rights; had been a leading advocate before the Civil War of the ten-hour day; and had been elected congressman in 1878 and governor of Massachusetts in 1882 largely with labor support. It is not surprising, therefore, that the People's party campaign was endorsed by a number of labor papers, especially *John Swinton's Paper*, and that several labor songs emerged during the 1884 presidential campaign in behalf of Butler's candidacy.

PEOPLE'S PARTY SONG

What portentous sounds are these,
That are borne upon the breeze?
What means this agitation deep and grand?
Whence comes this discontent?
Why are parties torn and rent
That before in solid phalanx used to stand?

Hark! See the people are advancing,
In solid columns to the fight;
We will let the bosses see
We're determined to be free,
And for bullets we'll use ballots in the fight.

Let the demagogue and knave
Storm and bluster, fret and rave,
And assail with filth our leader's honored name.
All that malice can devise
Of scurrility and lies,
Only adds a brighter luster to his fame.

Refrain:

Then arise, ye workingmen,
In support of gallant Ben
Who is trying to unravel right from wrong.
Don't be lured by party pride,
Tell the bosses, "Stand Aside!"
And swell up your ranks at least three million strong.

Refrain:[6]

THE WORKINGMEN'S ARMY
Tune—"March through Georgia"

When rebel shot and rebel shell burst open Sumter's wall,
When honest Abraham Lincoln's voice aroused the people all,
General Butler was the first who answered Lincoln's call,
To lead on the great Union army.

Hurrah! hurrah, hurrah for liberty!
Hurrah, hurrah, we workingmen are free!
We've burst the bonds of party like those of slavery,
And joined the great workingmen's army.

And there's now another army, fighting for another cause.
Striving to get fair and just and equitable laws;
And Butler, tried and true, is now again, as then he was,
Commanding the workingmen's army.

Refrain:

He'll push aside from power and place, with strong, avenging hand,
The sordid politician who would desecrate the land;
He'll burst the rings, and make this nation pure and free and grand,
With his brave, fearless, workingmen's army.

Refrain:[7]

[4]Sheet music, Library of Congress, Music Division.

[5]Butler's Order No. 28, issued to counter the unpleasant treatment of Union troops by the women of New Orleans, read that "when any female shall, by word, or gesture, or movement, insult or show contempt for any officer or soldier of the United States, shall be regarded and liable to be treated as a woman of the town plying her avocation."

[6]Broadside, Harris Collection, Brown University.

[7]Ibid.

ANTI-MONOPOLY WAR SONG.
Tempo di Marcia.
Lo! the car of Jugg - er - naut, Lo! the ruin it hath wrought,
As it moves o'er hill and dale Rid-ing on its ir - on rail,
Will you let the i - - dol grim Tear ye, brothers limb from limb!
And your breath of Freedom choke With its clouds of poi - soned smoke.
Copyrighted A.D. 1882 by R.J. HARRISON.

2.

Merchants! crushed beneath the weight
Of your contract–laden freight–
Fettered by each tyrant line
Of the craven bond you sign,
Farmers, ye who sow the plain
With its wealth of precious grain,
Yet must see your fruit of toil
Be the Rail-Roads robber–spoil,
CHORUS. Onward! onward to the fray!
Hurl the monster from your way,
Let your cry of battle be
Ruin to Monopoly!

3.

Citizens of all degrees,
Victims of vile subsidies–
Ye, who basest burdens bear
Of unjust unlawful fare,
Cast the loads from off your backs,
Tear the tyrants from his tracks–
Let elections glorious morn
Show your moving might of scorn
CHO: Onward! onward to the fray
Hurl the monster from your way,
Let your cry of battle be
Ruin to Monopoly!

4.

Cast your votes for honest men,
Trust no wily tongue or pen–
Should the rail - road hireling dare
Offer smile and promise fair,
Tell him you have had enough
Of the Engine's poison puff
And send him to oblivion's vale
Riding on his Master's Rail–
CHO: Onward! onward to the fray,
Hurl the monster from your way,
Let your cry of battle be
Ruin to Monopoly!

Courtesy of Library of Congress

SONG

By T. R.

Air—"O Susannah, Don't You Cry for Me"

I dreamt a dream the other night,
When everything was still;
I dreamt I saw Ben Butler boys,
Upon the White House hill.
The White House door was open wide
The porter with a grin
Just made a bow and stepped aside
And Benjamin walked in.

O Blaine and Cleveland[8]
Why did you ever try?
You might have known the workingmen
Would send you up sky high.

Monopolists look green and blue.
Landgrabbers claims were sold;
The speculators bursted up,
Their corners wouldn't hold.
The frauds turned pale and skipped away,
To England or to France,
They know that Ben would make them pay
The piper for the dance.

O Blaine, etc.

The toilers flung their hats on high
And shouted loud and long;
Three cheers for Benny Butler boys,
For he will right our wrong.
Three cheers for Benny Butler boys,
For he is bold and true;
He'll give fair play to the many boys,
And not enrich the few.

O Blaine, etc.[9]

WE ARE COMING

By T.R.

"We are coming!" "We are coming!" cry the people.
And they come;
Not with sound of brazen trumpets, or of fife and rolling
drum.
Or decked out with flaring colors, like the clowns in
masquerade.
For the children's admiration in a foolish street parade.

"We are coming!" Some are farmers, and they feel the
burdens grow;
Their lands are mortgaged heavy, their pocket bocks are
low;
Some are miners, and the darkness of the night is in each
soul.
For their little children suffer out there by the hills of
coal.
Some are masons; some are blacksmiths—men of
handicraft and skill
Many work at dredging labor, others with the sledge and
drill;
Some are printers, some are painters, some are living by
the pen;
But each of them's a toiler, each and all are workingmen.

"We are coming!" "We are coming!" We have patiently
endured
It is time the ills we suffer by the ballot should be cured.
Both the hack-ridden parties have been long enough
afloat;
So for Benjamin F. Butler we will cast a vote.[10]

INDEPENDENT POLITICAL ACTION OF 1886

Most trade unions, however, refused to support Butler, and despite the vigorous efforts of *John Swinton's Paper*, he polled only eighteen thousand votes in New York State. Moreover, from November, 1884, to the middle of 1886, the dominant trend in the labor movement was away from political action, largely because trade unions began to feel that labor could secure more through boycotts and strikes than through legislation. But the employers' offensive and the reign of terror following the Haymarket affair, the lockouts and blacklists, the increasing use of Pinkertons and scabs, the widespread police brutality against strikers and the use of the courts against boycotters convinced most workers that it was necessary to move ahead politically if labor's economic gains were to be protected. Some now argued that the ballot box was the only answer to labor's problems.

THE BALLOT

By Jack Plane

Ho, horny hands!
Come on in bands,
With votes between your fingers;
On to the polls,
March up in shoals!
Shame on the man who lingers!
Taboo each name
Old parties claim,
And all within their border,
Dead beats and bums,
And such like chums,

[8]Grover Cleveland and James G. Blaine were the candidates respectively of the Democratic and Republican parties. Cleveland was elected president in 1884.

[9]*John Swinton's Paper*, Sept. 14, 1884.

[10]Ibid., Oct. 5, 1884.

The rogues of "Law and Order";
A rascal shout
That's playing out—
A bomb they kept for you was,
We'll break their laws
In freedom's cause,
By legislating new ones,
Leave bombs to thugs,
And shots to plugs,
With ballots spend your fury;
When boycotts fail
To hit the nail,
We'll taboo judge and jury,
Old party votes
We leave to bloats,
And such like low attendance.
The ballot box
Not bombs or rocks
Is freemen's best dependence.[11]

A real upsurge of independent political action by labor occurred in the fall of 1886. Labor ran candidates for Congress in Maine, Connecticut, New York, New Jersey, Pennsylvania, Ohio, Kentucky, Michigan, Illinois, Wisconsin, Arkansas, Kansas, and Washington. It entered independent candidates for the legislatures of many states and for municipal posts in a score of cities. In the fall of 1886 in New York City, the workers, led by the trade unions, came close to winning the mayoralty election.

The candidate of the Independent Labor party of New York and Vicinity was Henry George, whose book *Progress and Poverty*, first published in 1879 and widely read by workers, made the "single tax" popular. George suggested that the inequalities of wealth from which modern society suffered could be eradicated by the imposition of a single tax on land values. Several songs of the period commented on the inequalities of land ownership.

MARY HAD A LITTLE LOT

By Mary C. Hudson

Mary had a little lot,
The soil was very poor;
But still she kept it all the same
And struggled to get more.

She kept the lot until one day
The people settled down;
And where the wilderness had been
Grew up a thriving town.

Then Mary rented out her lot
(She would not sell, you know)—
And waited patiently about;
For prices still to grow.

They grew, as population came,
And Mary raised the rent;
With common food and raiment now
She could not be content.

She built her up a mansion fine;
Had bric-a-brac galore—
And every time the prices rose,
She raised the rent some more.

"What makes the lot keep Mary so?"
The starving people cry—
"Why, Mary keeps the lot, you know,"
The wealthy would reply.

"And so each one of you might be—
Wealthy, refined, and wise—
If you had only hogged some land
And held it for the rise."[12]

THE LAND SONG

Air—"Marching through Georgia"

Sound a blast for Freedom, boys, and send it far and
wide!
March along to victory, for God is on our side!
While the voice of Nature thunders o'er the rising tide—
"God made the Land for the People!"

The Land! the Land! 'twas God who gave the Land!
The Land! the Land! the ground on which we
stand!
Why should we be beggars, with the ballot in our
hand?
"God gave the Land to the People!"

Hark! the shout is swelling from the East and from the
West:
Why should we beg work and let the Landlords take the
best?
Make them pay their taxes for the Land—we'll risk the
rest;
The Land was meant for the People!

The Land! the Land! 'twas God who gave the Land!
The Land! the Land! the ground on which we
stand!
Why should we be beggars, with the ballot in our
hand?
"God gave the Land to the People!"

The banner has been raised on high to face the battle
din:
The Army now is marching on the struggle to begin.

11*John Swinton's Paper*, reprinted in *Workmen's Advocate*, Oct. 3, 1886.

12*Standard*, reprinted in *Labor Enquirer*, Mar. 10, 1888.

We'll never cease our efforts till the victory we win,
And the Land is free for the People!

The Land! the Land! 'twas God who gave the Land!
The Land! the Land! the ground on which we stand!
Why should we be beggars, with the ballot in our hand?
"God gave the Land to the People!"

Clear the way for liberty! the land must all be free!
True men will not falter in the fight, though stern it be,
Till the flag we love so well shall wave from sea to sea,
O'er land that's free for the People.

The Land! the Land! 'twas God who gave the Land!
The Land! the Land! the ground on which we stand!
Why should we be beggars, with the ballot in our hand?
"God gave the Land to the People!"[13]

Although *Progress and Poverty* was popular in labor circles, the workers who supported Henry George for mayor of New York in 1886 did not do so because of their belief in the single tax. Rather, they rallied behind him as the standard-bearer of a labor party whose platform, along with the demand for the single tax, called for more democracy in government, the end of "officious intermeddling of the police with peaceful assemblage,"[14] enforcement of sanitary inspection of buildings, abolition of contract labor in public works, granting of equal pay for equal work without distinction of sex in public employment, and municipal ownership and operation of the means of transportation. The workers' enthusiasm for the labor party, which made the 1886 campaign one of the liveliest in New York history, was reflected in two songs written for the campaign. The first was sung to the tune of "Hold the Fort."

HENRY GEORGE CAMPAIGN SONG

Ho! ye workmen, see the campaign
Now is raging high
For we now are all united
Victory is nigh!

Hold New York for George is Coming
Loud his praises sing!
We will cast our votes together
For our labor king!

See the workmen now advancing
George is leading on!
Politicians now are falling
They will soon be gone!

Hold New York etc.

Fierce and long the campaign rages
But our help is near
Onward comes the labor hero,
Cheer, ye workmen, cheer!

Hold New York etc.[15]

A CAMPAIGN SONG

We march, we march to victory
And George is our rallying cry
In vain, our foes
Will our march oppose
The Right can never die.

We come from our homes and workshops,
And we cry with a voice sublime,
Oh thieves and knaves,
Who would keep us slaves,
We will have a reckoning time!

Chorus:

We are not dumb beasts to be driven!
We are men, and we will be free!
And hand in hand,
We will take our stand
For George and our Liberty.

Chorus:

Oh fools, who thought that safely,
You could barter our rights for gold!
Who laughing said,
"At so much *per head*
Votes can be bought and sold."

Chorus:

There are rights which you cannot alter,
And one is our right to be free,
A lawyer's pen
Cannot swindle men
Of the right of liberty.

Chorus:

Our fathers fought for freedom,
Shall we be less brave than they?
And what *they* won,
When the fight was done,
Shall we let slip away?

Chorus:

Oh, *each* of us must labor,
There are votes that we must gain,

13 *The Single Tax* (Chicago, 1887).
14 *John Swinton's Paper*, Oct. 3, 1886.
15 *New York World*, Oct. 6, 1886.

GEORGE-McGLYNN, ANTI-POVERTY

LAND AND LABOR SONGS,

A Choice Collection of One Hundred and Thirty Popular, New and Original Compositions, with Radical Words, to Favorite Old Familiar Tunes, also about Eighty New Pieces of Music, arranged for

Quartets and Solos, with Ringing Choruses,

ALL DESIGNED FOR

Land and Labor Lectures, Anti-Poverty Societies, George-McGlynn New Cross Crusade Meetings, Knights of Labor Assemblies, Trade Union Associations, and all Orders or Lodges intended to improve the

Physical, Moral, Social and Spiritual Condition of Mankind,

ESPECIALLY PREPARED FOR

32

THE UNITED LABOR PARTY CAMPAIGNS,

Also for Amusements, the Home Circle, and to Cheer and Encourage Every Friend of

JUSTICE, PEACE AND PROGRESS.

LIBRARY OF CONGRESS, COPYRIGHT
AUG 31 1887
18125
CITY OF WASHINGTON

By B. M. LAWRENCE, M. D.,

AUTHOR OF CELESTIAL SONNETS, THE NATIONAL LABOR SONGSTER, TEMPERANCE AND PROGRESSIVE SONGS, ETC., ETC.

COPYRIGHTED BY B. M. LAWRENCE, M. D.

1887.

Philadelphia
J. M. Armstrong & Co

Courtesy of Library of Congress

And gold is strong
And defends the wrong—
We have but voice and brain.

Chorus:

But the cause in which we labor,
Is Justice against Sin
If you and I
To our utmost try,
The Right is sure to win.

Chorus:[16]

ELECTIONS OF 1887

In the elections of 1887, Henry George ran for state office in New York on the United Labor ticket. He gained labor support, but his split with the Socialists and his insistence on making the single tax the major issue of his campaign weakened the independent political movement he headed. Benjamin M. Lawrence, the physician who in 1878 had compiled *The National Greenback Labor Songster*, published a book for this campaign, *George-McGlynn, Anti-Poverty Land and Labor Songs . . . Especially Prepared for the United Labor Party Campaigns.*[17] (Father Edward J. McGlynn was president of the Anti-Poverty Society which George and his disciples established. He had been excommunicated from the Catholic church because of his support of the single tax.) Lawrence announced in his preface that "these Land and Labor Songs have been hastily written during spare moments while engaged in professional duties. They are intended to foster the belief that POVERTY CAN AND MUST BE ABOLISHED." Private ownership of land was "the great cause of poverty," and only Henry George's program offered a "rational remedy for crime or poverty"; the author believed the songs would help in the crusade Henry George and the Reverend Dr. McGlynn were leading for "industrial freedom." Many of the songs had previously appeared in *The National Greenback Labor Songster;* here are two which were specifically geared to the 1887 campaign.

EIGHT AND SIXTY THOUSAND

"Five of you shall chase a hundred, and a hundred of you shall put ten thousand to flight."—Lev. 26:8

Words by B. M. Lawrence—Music by G. J. Webb

The light of truth is shining,
  The darkness dies away,
Sad hearts have ceas'd repining,
  They see the dawning day.
From mountain, hill, and valley,
  We hear the glad refrain,
The "New Cross Crusade" rally
  Will break the tyrant's chain!

Hear labor's trumpets sounding,
  The notes of triumph ring,
Each Knight, with high hopes bounding,
  The joyful strain will sing.
Let tyrants all take warning,
  Monopolies must fail;
Behold the day is dawning,
  The right must soon prevail.

Old error, with his legions
  Of fraud and crime and wrong,
Shall migrate to those regions
  Where rogues and thieves belong;
Then ever upward, onward,
  The truth moves swift as light,
With justice for your standard
  Will come the rule of right.

Full eight and sixty thousand
  Have broke all party ties,
Soon millions more will rouse and
  Give greed a new surprise;
The people want no fooling,
  Land-lords must now disgorge,
The courts of heaven are ruling,
  All hail MCGLYNN and GEORGE![18]

LABOR, LAND, AND FREEMEN

By B. M. Lawrence

Tune—"Battle-Cry of Freedom"

Yes, we'll rally round the polls, boys,
  We'll rally once again,
Fighting for labor, land and freemen
  We'll rally from the workshops,
From valley, hill and plain,
  Voting for labor, land and freemen.

With freeland forever, hurrah, boys, (or men)
    hurrah,
  Down with the slave trade in land
Yes, we'll rally round the polls, boys,
  We'll rally once again,
Voting for labor, land and freemen.

We are thinking of the fall of
  Our brothers gone before,

[16] *John Swinton's Paper*, Oct. 24, 1886.

[17] The book was more popularly titled *Land and Labor Songs.*

[18] Benjamin M. Lawrence, *Land and Labor Songs* (Philadelphia, 1887), p. 3.

Fighting for labor, land and freemen;
They who fell to free the slaves leave
Three hundred thousand more,
Voting for labor, land and freemen.

Chorus:

We will welcome to our ranks, boys
The loyal, true and brave,
Fighting for labor, land and freemen;
And although it may seem strange, boys,
This nation we shall save,
Voting for labor, land and freemen.

Chorus:

We are coming to the polls, boys,
From workshop, farm and forge
Fighting for labor, land, and freemen;
And our soldiers they are brave, boys,
Led by McGlynn and George,
Voting for labor, land and freemen.

Chorus:[19]

LABOR'S YANKEE DOODLE
Tune—"Yankee Doodle"

We, toilers, have made up our minds
To have a revolution,
And make the "fighting dollar" soon
A standing institution.

Yankee Doodle, Banks and Bonds,
Yankee Doodle Dandy,
Bounce the banks and burn the bonds,
Yankee Doodle Dandy.

We'll make the Greenback crisp and new,
A lasting, legal tender,
For Labor and Bondholders, too,
And Gold-bugs shall not hinder.

And when our debts shall all be paid
In lawful greenback money,
Our country—Labor's promised land—
Shall flow with milk and honey.

Let honest homespun take the lead
Till Truth is resurrected,
And wealth gives place to honest worth
And Labor is respected.

For Labor's Party is in the field
For Labor's elevation;
We must put workers to the front
To rule the State and Nation.[20]

The Chicago supporters of Henry George sang this song:

RALLY SONG

The morning light is breaking,
The nation is awaking;
For Henry George is raking
In the presidential making,

So now you are awakened
To the needs of rally making;
Come join me in our labors
For right and justice making.

Oh, tillers of the soil
And cullers of the flowers,
Remember ye who toil
Must in God's land have powers.

Then, Hurrah! for Henry George,
For he'll redeem the land,
Call me early, mother dear,
So I may be on hand
In time to vote for Uncle George.[21]

A labor party ticket in the Chicago fall election of 1887 had the following song.

A CAMPAIGN SONG
By J. W. Jackson
Air—"Hold the Fort"

Say, boys, did you hear the thunder?
Look out for a storm!
See the boodlers of both parties
Filled with the dire alarm.

Brace up, boys, the foe is coming—
Gird your armor on;
Stand your ground and be undaunted,
Every mother's son.

Now the fight is in the ballot,
For the right of a wrong;
'Tis for you which way to use it,
For the weak or strong.

Chorus:

Where's the man who'd be a traitor
To a cause that's good,
And with shackles chain his brother,
Where's the man that would.

Chorus:

There's none among this noble army
Who would stoop so low,

19Ibid., p. 121.
20J. D. Talmadge, *Labor Songs Dedicated to the Knights of Labor* (Chicago, 1888), p. 25.
21*Labor Enquirer*, May 7, 1887.

We will ever fight for right,
Wherever we may go.

Chorus:

Laws are framed for poor men only;
Others for the rich
Known by mysterious long names—
We know which is which.

Chorus:

Our laurels rest upon our wisdom—
May our objects be
Freedom from despotic thraldom,
And forever free.

Chorus:[22]

MARCH OF UNITED LABOR
Words by George Campbell
Tune—"Marching through Georgia"

Come forth, ye toiling millions, and join our worthy band,
As on we pass to victory to free our native land.
Our glorious cause we will defend and equal rights demand.
While we go marching to victory.

Hurrah! Hurrah! a shout of joyful glee!
Hurrah! Hurrah! We bring the jubilee!
The farms and labor shall unite and sweep from sea to sea,
While we go marching to vict'ry.

The lords of mammon tremble when they hear our joyous shout,
As on we press to victory and put them all to rout.
The trusts and pools and money-kings—we'll turn the rascals out.
While we go marching to vict'ry.

The toiling millions can't unite; that's what the bankers tell.
But hark! the tramp of millions and their chorus anthem swell,
They shout for home and country, and monoplies' death knell,
While they go marching to vict'ry.

We'll raise our fathers' banner, boys, and spread it out on high,
Beneath these sacred stars and stripes, monopolies shall die.
We have the ballot in our hands, all traitors we'll defy.
While we go marching to vict'ry.

Our weapon is the ballot and our word is "Right About!"
All hail the power in Union, boys, we'll give the word a shout;
The hand is writing on the wall: go cast the devils out!
While we go marching to vict'ry.[23]

All the local and state labor parties suffered serious setbacks in the fall elections of 1887, and most of them disappeared, the victims of internal dissensions. Independent political action appeared to be a thing of the past for labor, especially since the American Federation of Labor, under the leadership of Samuel Gompers, frowned upon such practice and placed major emphasis on economic activities and on working within the existing major parties. But in the local campaigns of 1890, the Farmers' Alliance movement and the Knights of Labor united to launch independent tickets.

LABOR AND THE FARMERS' ALLIANCE MOVEMENT

The Farmers' Alliance movement grew out of farmers' discontent over steadily declining prices for farm products, high prices for everything the farmers had to buy in a highly monopolized market, excessive railroad rates, usurious interest rates on loans and mortgages, loss of farms through foreclosure of mortgages, and a rapid increase in farm tenancy. The Alliances came into existence in the mid-eighties.[24] They called for more currency, silver coinage, easier freight rates, government loans on crops, and government ownership and operation of the railroads. The movement grew rapidly in farm areas, and an official estimate in 1891 placed the total membership of the Farmers' Alliances—the National Farmers' and Industrial Union (or Southern Alliance), the National Farmers' Alliance (or Northern Alliance), and the Colored Farmers' National Alliance and Cooperative Union—at between three and four and a quarter million members.[25] As the movement grew, the alliances

22Ibid., reprinted in *Workmen's Advocate*, Sept. 24, 1887.

23Collection of Professor Richard Stephenson, University of Kansas. The song was also included in Leopold Vincent, comp., *The Alliance and Labor Songster* (Winfield, Kans., 1891).

24The Farmers' Alliance was founded about 1875 in Texas. It really became a major force in 1886, when it swept through the whole South, establishing thousands of suballiances at the community level.

25In 1891 the Colored Farmers' National Alliance and Cooperative Union had 1,250,000 members and insisted that the farmers' fight and the laborors' fight were one and the same. Meanwhile, *John Swinton's Paper* stressed the same point, publishing songs sympathetic to the farmers in revolt. In 1885, for instance, "The Battle Song" exulted:

The agrarian cause is glorious,
And still is gaining ground;
'Tis spreading, all victorious,
To earth's remotest bounds. [26]

However, it was not until the 1890s that a labor–Farmers' Alliance coalition emerged. In the election of 1890, labor demands were incorporated into the platforms of the Alliance–Knights of Labor parties—enforcement of laws establishing the eight-hour day, opposition to the use of Pinkertons in labor disputes and to the use of convict labor—and labor representatives were nominated for office. Outstanding successes were recorded in Nebraska, Kansas, and Colorado; in the last-named state, the Alliance-KL coalition boasted that all elected officers were members of the Knights of Labor.[27]

Out of the labor–Farmers' Alliance coalition emerged a whole series of songs. During the 1880s, a group of songwriters was busy preparing songs for the Farmers' Alliance, paraphrasing such old and stirring favorites as "Johnny Comes Marching Home," "Good-bye, My Lover, Good-bye," "The Girl I Left behind Me," "John Brown's Body," and "Bring Back My Bonnie to Me."[28] After the coalition of the Farmers' Alliance and the Knights of Labor proved to be both a reality and a success at the ballot box, the Alliance songwriters turned their attention to the common problems of farmers and workers and the need for joint action against their common enemies—the corporations, trusts, railroads, and financial monopolists.

CALL TO ARMS

Come join the Alliance, to battle we go;
Labor united will conquer the foe,
Defending the rights and opposing the wrong
The Farmers' Alliance is marching along.

Marching along, we're marching along,
Labor united, be valiant and strong;
The people will triumph and right every wrong,
The Farmers' Alliance is marching along.
Come join our reform, and enter the field.
The numbers are ours, the power we wield.
Our armor is bright and our weapons are strong,
The Farmers' Alliance is marching along.

Come into our ranks, the foe must be driven,
Our motto: "To justice the world shall be given."
Though foes may surround us, we'll press through the throng,
The Farmers' Alliance is marching along.

Come fall into line, the foe we defy,
With truth for our weapon we'll fight till we die,
We'll lift up our voices in cheers and in song,
The Farmers' Alliance is marching along.[29]

WHAT'S WRONG
By W. E. R. Hoping

Oh what is the matter? Oh tell me what's wrong,
That the farmers and workingmen can't get along,
Though the harvest is great that we get in the fall,
When the spring rolls around we have nothing at all.

Rouse, sons of freedom: Something's not right;
Drive out the darkness, let in the light.
There is over-production it has often been said,
Where in parts of our land they are calling for bread.
If it's overproduction, and that is conceded,
Why not enjoy it 'till there is more needed?

But the cry comes rolling up over our land,
Give us money in volume to meet the demand;
We must have money to exchange production,
Pay mortgage and debts, or we go to destruction.

What's wrong, that our government favors a faction
Who work for themselves and cause a contraction?
The interest we pay to these great financiers
Will ruin us all in a very few years.

When money is issued on real estate,
And the interest is low, say one per cent rate;

state organizations in twelve states. However, relations between black and white farmers deteriorated in the next few years, due to racist influences among the whites; white farmers, often employers of Negro labor, refused to grant the blacks decent wages and living conditions.

26 *John Swinton's Paper*, Dec. 27, 1885.

27 Alliance men elected forty-five congressmen and three senators in the South pledged to support their demands; they secured control of eight state legislatures. In the West, several independent third parties of different names, set up by Alliance men, elected eight congressmen and two senators.

28 These were sung at camp meetings where thousands of farmers gathered, and glee clubs formed to sing them competed for honors at Farmers' Alliance meetings and conventions.

29 Federal Writers' Project, *More Farmers' Alliance Songs of the 1890's*, Nebraska Folklore Pamphlets, no. 20 (Lincoln, 1939), pp. 1–2.

Won't money be plenty and prices be high?
And we'll pay all our debts "in the sweet by and by."

The board of trade and the great corporations—
Who live on our earnings, and ruin all nations—
We must break their shackles, for slaves we'll not be
But we'll say to the world "our country is free!"[30]

Eighteen hundred and ninety-one saw the publication of *The Alliance and Labor Songster*, compiled by Leopold Vincent; and a year later came the Knights of Labor–sponsored *Labor Reform Songster*, edited by Phillips Thompson. The songs in both collections were sung at Alliance and Knights of Labor meetings; indeed, in his preface to *The Alliance and Labor Songster*, Vincent made the point that since the Alliance movement and its songs had gained "endorsement by the official bodies of several great Labor organizations," the book's usefulness for workers as well as farmers made its appearance especially important. Likewise, in his introduction to *The Labor Reform Songster*, A. W. Wright, editor of the *Journal of the Knights of Labor*, predicted that the songs in that collection would be sung "in Assembly rooms, in Alliance meetings, at meetings of Unions and at public gatherings. . . ." Here are some of the songs in the two collections which were sung by both workers and farmers.

RING THE BELLS OF FREEDOM

Ring the bells of freedom! there is joy today
For a band that's battling for the right.
See the people meet them out upon the way,
Welcoming their weary, wand'ring feet.

Glory! Glory! how the people shout!
Glory! Glory! how the drums peal out!
'Tis the ransomed labor like a mighty sea,
Pealing forth the anthems of the free.

Ring the bells of freedom! there is joy today
For the vict'ry of each noble Knight,
Yes a slave is rescued from the birds of prey,
And the lab'rer's hold the ransomed seat.

Chorus:

Ring the bells of freedom! there is joy today.
Sisters swell the grand triumphant strain,
Tell the joyful tidings, bear it far away;
Welcome all the true Knights of today.

Chorus:[31]

A NEW NATIONAL ANTHEM

By Thomas Nicol

Tune—"The Future America"

My country, 'tis of thee,
Once land of liberty,
Of thee I sing.
Land of the Millionaire;
Farmers with pockets bare;
Caused by the cursed snare—
The Money Ring.

My native country, thee,
Thou wert so pure and free;
Long, long ago.
Yet still I love thy rills,
But hate thy usury mills,
That fill the bankers' tills
Till they overflow.

So when my country, thee,
Which sould be noble, free,
I'll love thee still;
I'll love thy Greenback men,
Who strive with tongue and pen,
For liberty again,
With right good will.

And then my country, thee,
Thou wilt again be free;
And Freedom's tower.
Stand by your fireside then,
And show that you are men,
Whom they can't fool again,
And crush their power.[32]

TO THE POLLS

To the polls! to the polls! ye are thus serving God;
Let us follow the path that our fathers have trod;
With the light of their counsel our strength to renew,
Let us do with our might what our hands find to do.

Voting on, (voting on,) voting on, (voting on,)
Voting on, (voting on,) voting on, (voting on,)
Let us work, and watch, let us vote, and trust,
And labor till the vict'ry comes.

To the polls! to the polls! let the hungry be fed;
To the banner of life let the weary be led;
In our ballot and banner our glory shall fall.
While we herald the tidings *the people are free.*

Chorus:

30 Federal Writers' Project, *Farmers' Alliance Songs of the 1890's*, Nebraska Folklore Pamphlets, no. 18 (Lincoln, 1938), p. 11.
31 Vincent, *Alliance and Labor Songster.*
32 Ibid.

To the polls! to the polls! there is labor for all,
For the kingdom of rapine and error shall fall,
And the rights of the people exalted shall be,
In the loud-swelling chorus *the people are free.*

Chorus:

To the polls! to the polls! we will rally again;
We will free our dear homes from the bondman and chain;
Then the home of the faithful our dwelling shall be,
And we'll shout with the ransomed *the people are free.*

Chorus:[33]

STORM THE FORT

By B.J.K.

Oh, my brother, see the children,
Crying in the street,
Hunger's ravages revealing—
Weary, half-clad feet.

Storm the fort at the election,
Hear the leaders cry;
Send the laboring men to congress,
With our votes, we'll try.

See the mortgaged, burdened farmer
Tremble 'neath his load.
Hear the mother's cry of anguish,
Families sent abroad.

Chorus:

Fierce and long may be the struggle,
But our cause is dear.
Soon the labrers ranks will double,
Cheer, then brother cheer.

Chorus:

Soon our banner will be waving
Up and down the street;
The labring men have won the battle
Victory's complete.

Chorus:[34]

OUR BATTLE SONG

Tune—"Storm the Fort"

Hark! the bugle note is sounding
Over all the land;
See! the people forth are rushing,
Oh! the charge is grand.

Storm the forts, ye Knights of Labor,
'Tis a glorious fight;
Brawn and brain against injustice—
God defend the right!

How the mighty host advances,
Alliance leads the van;
The Knights do rally by the thousands.
On the labor plan.

Strong intrenched behind their millions,
Sit the money kings;
Salary grabbers, thieves and traitors
Join them in their rings.

Vile injustice fills their coffers
With their blood bought gold;
And the might of their oppression
Ruins young and old.

Who will dare to shun the conflict!
Who would be a slave?
Better die within the trenches,
Forward, then, be brave![35]

STAR SPANGLED BANNER

Oh, say do you see, by the daylight's broad glare,
That blot that arises to tarnish our glory?
'Tis the blot of oppression to all kinds of toil—
The greed of the Shylock, the same, same old story;
Rouse, ye people today; do not longer delay;
Too long we have loitered, make haste now, we pray,
Or the Star Spangled Banner no longer will wave
O'er the "Land of the Free" but the Home of the Slave. } repeat

When Treason's foul breath swept across our fair land,
How quickly responded the laboring classes;
We owe them today for their brave fearless stand.
Oh, where had we been were it not for their masses?
Now they're taxed for everything, while the rich men hear the ring
Of their money as it jingles in their coffer's wide brim;
Oh! do something quickly to put down these knaves,
Or our land is not free, nor the Home of the Brave. } repeat

Farmers, stand to your rights; the time has now come
When we must take the lead in the oncoming battle.
By the right of your suffrage put good men and true
To lead us to vict'ry and give the death rattle
To all future efforts to grind workmen down
To worse than the slave, or acknowledge a crown,
Let our Star Spangled Banner once more proudly wave
O'er a "Land of the Free" made by men that are brave.[36] } repeat

[33]Ibid. [34]Ibid.
[35]Ibid. [36]Ibid.

THE RIGHT WILL PREVAIL

Tune—"Labor's 'By-and-By' "

When the Workingmen's cause shall prevail
Then the class-rule of rich men shall cease,
And the true friends of Labor will hail
With a shout the glad era of peace.

Right will reign by-and-by,
When the Workingmen come into power;
Right will reign, by-and-by,
Then the gold thieves shall rule men no more.

Whatsoever men sow they must reap;
Since the rich to the whirlwind have sown,
More just laws they must now learn to keep.
Then what Workingmen earn they will own.

Right, ordains that old parties must die
And make way for the growth of Reform;
Truth and wisdom proclaim from on high
That the triumph of Labor must come.

Chorus:

Right on earth, evermore then shall reign,
And the angels will sing once again;
While the Workingmen join the refrain,
"Peace on earth and good will unto men."

Chorus:[37]

SHOUTING THE BATTLE-CRY OF LABOR

P. of L. Opening Ode

Tune—"Battle Cry of Freedom"

Written for the *Farmer's Voice* by
A. A. Smith, Belle River

We are marshalled for a conflict, with the enemies of toil,
Shouting the battle-cry of labor.
Mankind will hail our progress as we plow the fertile soil,
Shouting the battle-cry of labor.

Down with the trust pools, crown labor king,
Farmers, mechanics and toilers may sing,
For the Carpenter of Nazareth a jubilee will bring,
Shouting the battle-cry of labor.

We are weary of the "cornering" of grain by boards of trade,
Shouting the battle-cry of labor.
Why should they double tribute take on corn our labor made,
Shouting the battle-cry of labor.

Chorus:

The railroad combination takes the crop to pay the freight,
Shouting the battle cry of labor.
Monopolistic capital has captured every state,
Shouting the battle cry of labor.

Chorus:

We've borne the burden many years, we're ready for the fight,
Shouting the battle-cry of labor,
Let counter combination now protect the toilers' right,
Shouting the battle-cry of labor.

Chorus:

We seek a dispensation which will give a just reward,
Shouting the battle-cry of labor.
And we base our expectations on the righteousness of God,
Shouting the battle-cry of labor.

Chorus:[38]

THE ORPHAN SONG

Tune—"The Orphan"

By Miss Winnie Johnson

"No home; no home," said the little girl,
As she stood at the rich man's door.
As she tremblingly stood on the polished step,
And leaned on the marble wall.

Her clothes were thin, and her feet were bare,
And the snow had covered her head,
"Oh! give me a home and something to wear—
A home and a piece of bread.

"My father, also, I never knew,"
And the tears dimmed her eyes so bright,
"While my mother sleeps in a new-made grave,
'Tis an orphan that begs to-night."

The night was dark, and the snow fell fast
And the rich man shut his door.
With a frown on his brow, he scornfully said:
"No home, no bread, for the poor.

"I must freeze," she said, "upon this step,
As she strove to cover her feet
With her old tattered dress, all covered with snow,
Yes, covered with snow and sleet.

The rich man slept on his velvet couch,
And dreamed of his silver and gold,
While this little girl lay on a bed of snow
And murmured, "so cold, so cold."

When morning dawned, this little girl
Still lay at the rich man's door,

37 Ibid. The song had earlier appeared in Benjamin M. Lawrence, *The National Greenback Labor Songster* (New York, 1878), p. 3, with *Nationals* rather than *Workingmen* in the chorus and the final verse.

38 Vincent, *Alliance and Labor Songster.*

But her soul had fled to that land above.
Where there's room enough for the poor.[39]

THE MARCH OF LABOR

By Isaac Jameson, Newton, Kas.

Come and see the Sons of Labor rising in their might and main;
Come and join in the procession, come and follow in the train,
Let us haste the day Monopoly shall cease his tyrant reign,
As we go marching on.

Come, ye brave, from ev'ry nation;
All who're looking for salvation;
Come and join in the procession,
As we go marching on.

I have seen them 'round the watchfires of ten thousand circling camps;
I have seen them climbing mountains; I have seen them crossing swamps.
We may read their righteous sentence by the great electric lamps,
As we go marching on.

Chorus:

I have read that righteous judgment, and 'twas stamped with God's great seal;
"As ye deal with my poor children, so with you shall justice deal."
Let the hero, born of woman, crush the tyrant with his heel,
As we go marching on.

Chorus:

They have sounded forth the trumpet that shall never call retreat;
They are sifting out the brave and true before the judgment seat.
Oh, be swift, brave hearts, to answer, and be jubilant our feet,
As we go marching on.

Chorus:

Look ye now, the day is breaking, e'en the gloaming now I see,
Shining forth in a bright halo that transfigures you and me.
Let us put forth ev'ry effort, all humanity is free,
As we go marching on.[40]

THERE COMES A RECKONING DAY

Air—"Susannah, Don't You Cry"

I had a dream the other night when every thing was still;
I dreamt I saw the lab'ring men all going down the hill;
Their clothes were rags their feet were bare, a tear was in their eye;
Said I, my friend, what grieves you so, and causes you to cry?

O, bondholders, take pity, now, we pray.
We're out of food and out of clothes—
There comes a reckoning day.

We have to work to earn our bread, and our children cry for food;
Have scarce a place to lay our heads, complaining does no good;
We hate to beg, we will not steal, pray tell us what to do;
We cannot starve—what shall we do?—we leave the case to you.

Our greenbacks 're gone, you've made us poor, reduced us all to slaves;
You took our means, you took our homes, you've treated us as knaves.
We fought your battles, saved your homes, took greenbacks as our pay,
Now, when we ask for work or bread, you boldly answer, nay.

Bring in your bonds and get the cash the same you gave to us;
'Twas greenbacks then, 'tis greenbacks now; we'll end this little muss.
We must have money through the land, and business lively, too;
We'll feed the hungry, clothe the poor, with work for all to do.

You own the bonds but pay no tax, for justice now we cry.
You bought with greenbacks, now ask for gold; pray tell us how and why?
Who promised you to pay in gold? the people now inquire,
We'll keep our contract, you keep yours, as honest men admire.[41]

LABOR'S HARVEST HOME

Air—"Jesus, We Thy Lambs Would Be"

By Phillips Thompson

Rouse the sleepers through the land,
Harvest time is now at hand,
Fields are white with ripened grain,
And plenty smiles on hill and plain.

39Ibid. A variant of this song appeared in the 1902 Alabama edition of *The Sacred Harp;* see the discussion and additional texts in H. M. Belden, *Ballads and Songs Collected by the Missouri Folk-Lore Society,* 2d ed. (1955; reprinted, Columbia, Mo., 1973), pp. 277–78.

40Vincent, *Alliance and Labor Songster.*

41Ibid.

When the reaping time shall come
And labor shout the harvest home,
When the reaping time shall come
And labor shout the harvest home.

Those whose toil has given birth
To the products of the earth
Claim the right the fruit to keep,
Nor where they sowed let others reap.

When the reaping time shall come, etc.

Ye who bar the reapers' way,
Is it sword or sickle—say?
Ere the famished throng can pass
Must they mow you down like grass?

When the reaping time shall come, etc.

Down with the idler, robber, knave!
Freedom for the toiling slave!
Nevermore shall stealth or sloth
Enjoy the field's luxuriant growth.

When the reaping time shall come, etc.

Fruit of bitter, toilsome years,
Sown in struggle, pain and tears,
We shall garner when the world
Sees from its place oppression hurled.

When the reaping time shall come, etc.[42]

THE POOR VOTER ON ELECTION DAY

Air—"Partant pour la Syrie"

By John G. Whittier

The proudest now is but my peer,
The highest not more high;
Today, of all the weary year,
A king of men am I;
Today alike are great and small,
The nameless and unknown,
My palace is the people's hall,
The ballot box my throne,
My palace is the people's hall,
The ballot box my throne.

Who serves to-day upon the list
Beside the served shall stand;
Alike the brown and wrinkled fist,
The glove and dainty hand!
The rich is level with the poor,
The weak is strong to-day;
And sleekest broadcloth counts no more
Than homespun frock of gray. } repeat

To-day let pomp and vain pretense
My stubborn right abide;
I set a plain man's common sense
Against a pedant's pride.
To-day shall simple manhood try
The strength of gold and land;
The wide world has not wealth to buy
The power in my right hand! } repeat

While there's a grief to seek redress
Or balance to adjust,
Where weighs our living manhood less
Than Mammon's vilest dust.
While there's a right to need my vote,
A wrong to sweep away,
Up! clouted knee and ragged coat!
A man's a man to-day! } repeat[43]

WHEN LABOR HAS COME TO ITS OWN

Air—"When Johnny Comes Marching Home"

By Phillips Thompson

When labor has come to its own again,
Hurrah! Hurrah!
We'll live in a real Republic then,
Hurrah! Hurrah!
Then none shall rule by wealth or birth,
And each shall have his share of earth,
For we'll all be free when labor has come to its own.

The millionaires will hunt their holes,
Hurrah! Hurrah!
And drop their cash to save their souls,
Hurrah! Hurrah!
For we'll clear out Wall Street's robber den,
And burn each bond and mortgage then,
For we'll all be free when labor has come to its own.

We'll pile them up so that all may see,
Hurrah! Hurrah!
As high as the Statue of Liberty,
Hurrah! Hurrah!
And we'll make Jay Gould the torch apply,
To flare the light over sea and sky,
That shall tell the world that labor has come to its own.

Then all must ply some useful trade,
Hurrah! Hurrah!
And none their rights will dare invade,
Hurrah! Hurrah!
And those who honest toil would shirk,
Shall have no bread if they will not work,
We'll have no more drones when labor has come to its own.

Grim poverty will be unknown,
Hurrah! Hurrah!
And plenty through the land be strown,
Hurrah! Hurrah!

42Phillips Thompson, ed., *The Labor Reform Songster* (Philadelphia, 1892).
43Ibid.

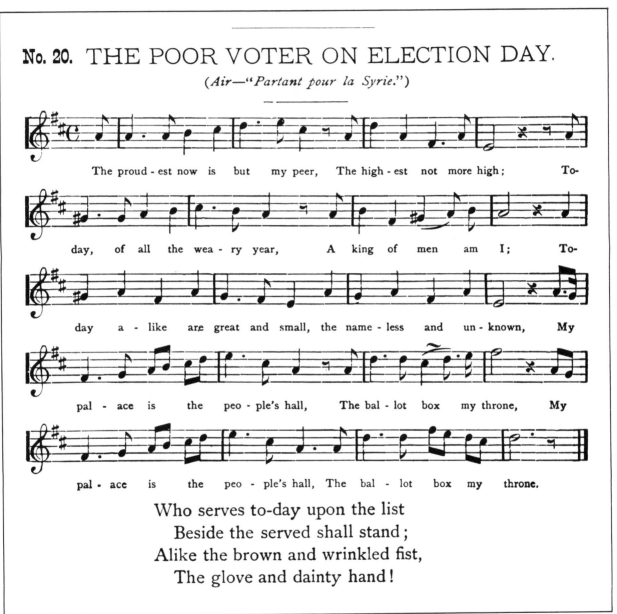

No. 20. THE POOR VOTER ON ELECTION DAY.

(Air—"Partant pour la Syrie.")

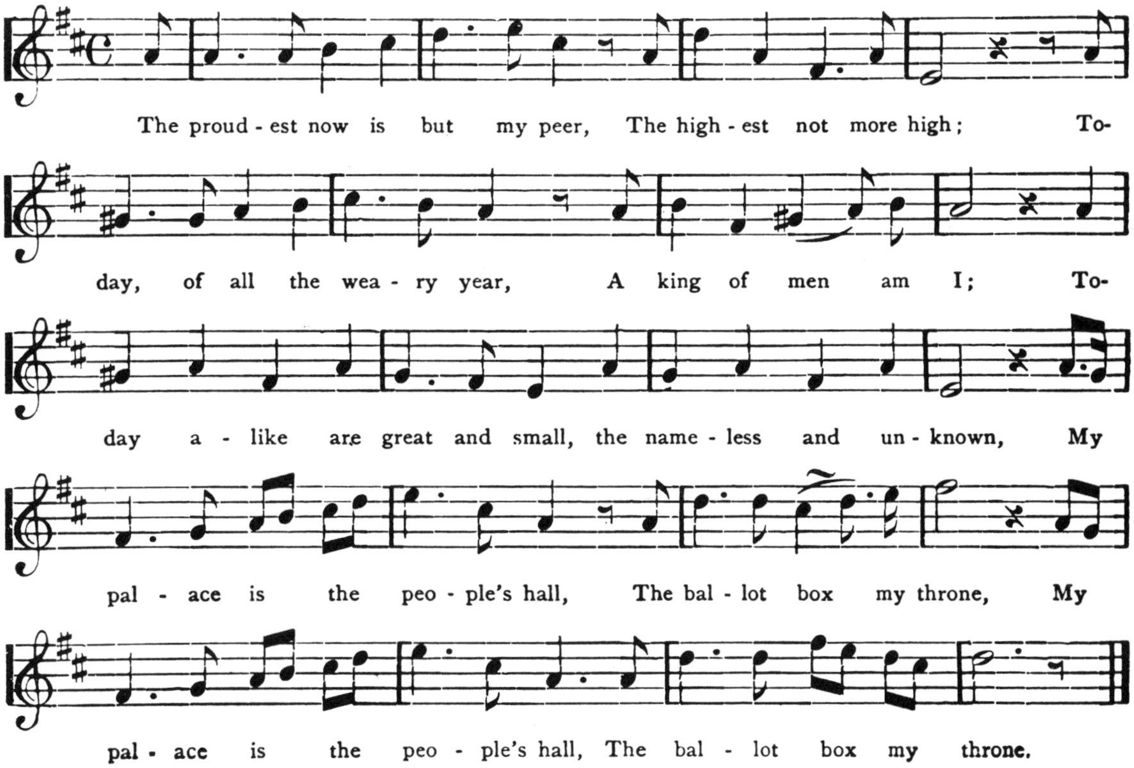
The proud - est now is but my peer, The high - est not more high; To-
day, of all the wea - ry year, A king of men am I; To-
day a - like are great and small, the name - less and un - known, My
pal - ace is the peo - ple's hall, The bal - lot box my throne, My
pal - ace is the peo - ple's hall, The bal - lot box my throne.

Who serves to-day upon the list
  Beside the served shall stand;
Alike the brown and wrinkled fist,
  The glove and dainty hand!

Courtesy of Brown University Library

Then, farmers and laborers, all combine
And bring the stragglers into line,
Let us haste the day when labor shall come to its own.[44]

ROUSE AND RALLY

By Phillips Thompson

Our patriot sires in days of old
Threw off the Briton's sway
Americans were free and bold;
Where are their sons today?
Our wrongs are greater thousand fold
Than were our fathers' then;
Then rouse, and rally, by hill and valley,
And claim our rights as men. } repeat

Despotic power, oppressive laws,
Our fathers brave defied,
And baffled in their country's cause
The lion in his pride.
And shall we cower before the wolf,
The usurer in his den?
No! Rouse and rally, by hill and valley,
And claim your rights as men. } repeat

The money-kings now rule the land
While men of freedom dream,
They crush the poor with iron hand
And boast their power supreme.
But liberty will yet revive
To bless the land again,
So rouse and rally, by hill and valley,
And claim your rights as men. } repeat

The broad and fertile plains which stretch
Their leagues of golden grain
Enrich some greedy, thievish wretch
Who profits by our pain.
Let each true heart resent the wrong
With voice and vote and pen,
And rouse and rally, by hill and valley,
And claim your rights as men. } repeat[45]

In 1895 George Howard Gibson published a work bearing the impressive title *Armageddon: The Songs of the World's Workers Who Go Forth to Battle with the Kings and Captains and Mighty Men.* After describing the rapid growth of monopoly in the United States and predicting that corporate wealth would hasten the approach of "the final battle between all right and might, need and greed, truth and error"—"the Armageddon conflict foreshown by ancient and modern seers"—Gibson announced that he was sending out "this volume of songs to help in the work of awakening, inspiring, and uniting at the ballot box the great industrial army, the wealth-producing millions, who alone have the right to wealth, but who now must beg for work and divide their product with those members of the ruling class who control labor and exchange." The songs had been prepared for use "in every worker's home and especially for the social and public meetings of Farmers Alliances and other farm bodies, the American Federation of Labor, Trades Union, the United Mine Workers, the K. of L. Assemblies, the A.R.U. Industrial Legions or People Party clubs, S.L.P. meetings, Single Tax clubs, Nationalist clubs, and all political rallies and gatherings in the interest of organized and unorganized workers."[46] Actually, many of these songs were already familiar to the groups for which they were intended, having appeared in *The Labor Reform Songster*, *The Alliance and Labor Songster*, or as broadsides connected with the Pullman strike and Coxey's army. However, a few were written by Gibson himself, such as the following:

THE MONEY POWER ARRAIGNED

Words by George Howard Gibson—Music by J. L. Frank

The bankers and brokers by breed
Are gold bugs and governed by greed;
They haughtily fasten and feed
On the sweat and the blood of the workers
As shirkers, they fasten and feed
On the sweat and the blood of the workers.

They crawled thro' congressional halls
When war thundered hard at the walls,
And while we were facing the balls
They enacted new laws for the shirkers—
The workers, while stopping the balls,
Were enslav'd by a scheme of the shirkers.

They gathered the gold they could get,
Then, holding it, plung'd us in debt,
And prices of ev'rything set,
By a law that controll'd legal tenders—
They gathered our wealth and our debt
While they sold us their gold legal tenders.

By crippling the greenbacks we made,
They injured our credit in trade

[44] Ibid.

[45] Ibid.

[46] Gibson also prepared the songs for "the use of similar bodies in England, including the Independent Labor Party, now under the splendid management of Keir Hardie, M.P., Tom Mann, and others." *Armageddon* was published simultaneously in Lincoln, Nebraska, and in London.

With ourselves, and our honor bewray'd,
But it gave them a grasp on our money—
The nation they foully betray'd
When they gained the control of our money.

They bought up our bonds with our bills,
Sent in with an order that kills,
The bills that were dragged to their tills,—
And for these got new notes they could lend us—
Got money *and* bonds for their bills—
And so national paper they lend us.

We pay for a credit our own,
Our debts and our labor they loan;
So gold has extended its throne,
Till we owe it about thirty billions—
With only scant millions its own
It has dragged us in debt THIRTY BILLIONS.

Curse on you, ye usurers bold,
Corrupted with blood is your gold;
You're worse than Barabbas of old,
With your scheme of oppression and plunder—
You sweat, starve and kill with your gold
And your legalized system of plunder.

You ride in your pride with the high,
Upheld by the toilers who sigh;
And weak ones competing must die,
Trampled down by the classes who plunder—
You heed not the millions who cry,
And you trample on all who are under.[47]

THE BATTLE HYMN OF FREEDOM
By George Howard Gibson
Arranged from a French air

Ye sons of liberty, defenders
Of Freedom, and deathless Right,
Again the Lord of Sabaoth tenders
"A sword," a sword, and bids you fight!
Behold the poor and hear their cries!
Behold the poor and hear their cries!
Shall tyrants drag them bound in fetters
Of cursed law which keeps them slaves,
And even grudge them land for graves?
Shall workers be perpetual debtors?

Unite, unite, ye just!
The sword of truth draw forth!
Advance, advance with mighty tread,
From west and south and north!
Advance, advance with mighty tread,
From west and south and north.

Here, here where Liberty first lightened,
And freedom spoken shook the world,
Where hope for all the humble brightened,
And mightiest kings were backward hurled,
Lo here, where equal rights are pledged,
Lo here, where equal rights are pledged!
Are kings with all their brood of curses!
In this broad land by blood made free,
Dependent millions bend the knee
And plead with tears for sov'reign mercies!

Unite, unite, &c.

With titles flaunted in our faces
They trample down the peoples' will!
They crowd the millions from their places,
And call on hireling hordes to kill.
Above the earth they sit enthron'd!
Above the earth they sit enthron'd!
And sweep their realm with hunger scourges!
They drive the poor from nature's stores.
For greater gain they lock the doors,
And dare the crowd that round them surges!

Unite, unite, &c.

They claim the ways which commerce uses,
As bold highwaymen robbing all;
They hold exchange, and each refuses
Its use till all before them fall!
The people now are ruled by gold!
The people now are ruled by gold!
But shall we here be made the minions
Of kings, on freedom's sacred soil,
And yield them wealth by slavish toil,
Content to wear their galling pinions!

Unite, unite, &c.

Once more, once more are heroes waking,
As dawns a righteous day foretold.
And marching forth, their cry is shaking
The hideous shapes of evils old;
By all for all our laws shall be!
By all for all our laws shall be!
The forming hosts of honest labor
Shall give to each his place, his part,
With equal worth in every mart,
And neighbor live at peace with neighbor!

Unite, unite, &c.[48]

LABOR-POPULISM

Farmer and labor representatives, the latter mainly delegates from the Knights of Labor, met at Cincinnati in May, 1891, to launch the People's, or Populist party. While the Populist platform stressed farmers' demands, such as free coinage of silver, abolition of national banks, and regulation of railroads, the planks also in-

47Gibson, *Armageddon*, pp. 102–3.
48Ibid., pp. 120–22.

cluded demands designed to appeal to labor: a graduated income tax; direct election of president, vice-president, and senators; direct legislation through the initiative and referendum, based on the system operating in Switzerland; universal suffrage; and an eight-hour day. The platform was reaffirmed at a convention of the Populist party in Saint Louis in February, 1892. Nearly two-thirds of the 860 delegates were representatives of farmers' organizations. Still, 29 percent came from labor organizations: the KL, with eighty-two delegates, and organizations affiliated with the AFL—the International Association of Machinsts, the Paper Hangers' National Union, the International Wireworkers' Union, the United Mine Workers, as well as the central labor bodies of Saint Louis and Springfield, Missouri; Kansas City, Kansas; and Memphis, Tennessee.

In the spring and summer of 1892, farmer-labor unity on the economic front stimulated labor support for the People's party. Farmers' Alliance and Populist groups and leaders endorsed KL and AFL boycotts, urged the adoption of an eight-hour day in all factories, shops, and mines, and voiced widespread sympathy for and support of the steelworkers during the Homestead strike. Labor responded to such support by endorsing the People's party in a number of cities and towns, and Populist clubs were established by trade unions in Cleveland, Toledo, Columbus, Akron, San Francisco, Los Angeles, and Sacramento. Nor did the membership of these clubs come only from the declining Knights of Labor. Many were from AFL affiliates, even though the top leadership of the American Federation of Labor, especially Samuel Gompers, looked with disfavor on any ties with the Populist movement, charging that it was made up largely of employing farmers whose interests clashed with those of agricultural laborers and workers in general.

The coolness of the AFL leadership toward the Populist party weakened labor support for the Populist presidential candidate in the election of 1892, James B. Weaver. But the onset of the 1893 depression, the ignominious arrest of General Jacob Coxey for walking on the Capitol grass,[49] the breaking of the Pullman strike through the use of federal injunctions and United States troops, and the imprisonment of the strike leaders changed the situation dramatically, and labor support for populism soared. Even the farmers' demand for free silver as a means of reviving industry by increasing the demand for goods in agricultural regions began to appeal to many unemployed workers. Labor-Populist alliances emerged on a large scale, beginning in Illinois in 1894 and spreading to Massachusetts, New York, Ohio, Indiana, Minnesota, Wisconsin, Montana, Texas, and California. State federations of labor and city central labor bodies affiliated with the AFL endorsed the People's party at their conventions. In short, as Chester McArthur Destler and Norman Pollack have made clear, populism, though primarily agrarian, especially after the economic crisis of 1893 got under way, received significant support from industrial labor.[50]

Many of the songs in *The Alliance and Labor Songster* and *The Labor Reform Songster* were carried over into labor-populism after 1891. But new songs were also being composed, such as the variety given here.

THE PEOPLE'S RALLY CRY

Tune—"Battle Cry of Freedom"

We will rally round the flag, boys, we'll rally till we gain
For every workingman his freedom;
We will rally from the workshop, from city, hill, and plain,
To give the workingman his freedom.

Our Union, forever! Press on, boys, press on!
We'll down with the money, and up with the man;
While we rally round the flag, boys, and rally till we gain
For every workingman his freedom.

We are joining hands to conquer the wrongs that gall us sore,

[49]Populists voiced the farmers' support of Coxey's army of unemployed workers in "Song of the Times," which went in part:

They may sneer at General Coxey
And may call his plan unwise,
May style him a fanatic,
And his followers despise;
Yet Coxey's cause is righteous
And above the wrong 'twill rise—
The Lord has spoken it.

(Roger L. Welsch, *Treasury of Nebraska Pioneer Folklore* [Lincoln, Nebr., 1966], pp. 72–73.)

[50]See Chester McArthur Destler, *American Radicalism, 1865–1901* (New London, Conn., 1946), Norman Pollack, *The Populist Response to Industrial America* (Cambridge, Mass., 1962), and the chapters "Labor and Early Populism" and "The Rise of Labor-Populism" in my own *History of the Labor Movement in the United States*, II (New York, 1955), 300–326.

That all may work and live in freedom;
And we'll fill the Union up with a million votes or more
To give the workingman his freedom.

We will welcome to our numbers all who are true and brave,
Who'll give to toil the fullest freedom;
Right to all that's earned by labor, t'unchain the wages slave
And raise him up to manhood's freedom.

So we're forming everywhere—North and South, and East and West
To give the slave of wage his freedom;
And we'll hurl the Idol GOLD from the land we love the best
And give to every soul his freedom.[51]

THE INDEPENDENT MAN

By Mrs. J. T. Kellie

Tune—"The Girl I Left behind Me"

I was a party man one time,
The party would not mind me—
That's all for which I have to thank
The party's left behind me.

An older, sadder, poorer man
Sure every year did find me—
That's all for which I have to thank
The party left behind me.[52]

LEAVING THE PARTY

By Theo. P. Stelle

Tune—"I's Gwine Back to Dixie"

I've worked for my old party,
I've toiled for many an hour,
I used to say we'd have good times
Whenever we got in power;
But now I've been taught better,
They've but increased the fetter,
They've broken every promise,
And I will go.

I'm going to leave the party,
I'll stay with it no longer,
I'll help the money power to overthrow,
I'll join the People's party,
Support it true and hearty,
It labors for the people,
And I will, too.

Old party politicians
Are faithless, drunk or sober;
It took them nearly thirty years
To learn the war is over.
They rave about the tariff,
But little do they care if
They only get the offices,
High or low.

They both submit to Wall street,
And do just as they plan it.
And then aver they had no hand
In bringing on a panic.
No cash in circulation,
And still they tell the nation
The law which made the money
Must be no more.

They work so well together,
We're going now to leave them.
There's nothing the old parties have
That ever can retrieve them.
The court house rings control them,
Their party leaders sold them,
They're rotten to the very core.
We'll let them go.[53]

THE ONLY ROAD TO FREEDOM

By George Howard Gibson, Lincoln, Neb.

We may organize in "brotherhoods" and talk our time away,
We may theorize forever and yet dependent stay,
We may "resolute" 'gainst robbery and do whate'er we like,
For capital is stronger than the very strongest strike.
The money power is safe enough while workers still divide
And vote against each other—they who should be side by side;
The rich will be defended by the soldier and the laws
Till the workers get together and vote for labor's cause.

O workers, weary workers, who bear the rubs and knocks,
The only road to freedom runs past the ballot-box.

The kings of transportation each takes a robber's toll,
They stand between consumers and labor's wage control;
The gold monopolizers curst usury demand,
And millions drawn from labor enrich the lords of land.
But all this legal robbery at toil's behest should be
Itself outlawed forever—the people may be free,
We all must vote together for equal birthrights lost,
For money, land and commerce secured to us at cost.

O workers, weary workers, who bear the rubs and knocks,
The only road to freedom runs past the ballot-box.

51John Greenway, *American Folksongs of Protest* (Philadelphia, 1953), p. 61.

52Federal Writers' Project, *Farmers' Alliance Songs of the 1890's*, p. 11.

53Gibson, *Armageddon*, pp. 136–37.

The men who spend in luxury what others' toil has
earned
Should stand exposed for what they are, and be as robbers spurned;
The universal law of God that each shall sweat for bread,
In justice on our statute books, should fill the dudes
with dread.
The useless butterflies who cost their sisters lives of
shame
Should be considered vastly worse and wear the vilest
name;
But those whose lives should give them rank as lowest of
the race
Will proudly reign as kings and queens till labor claims
its place.

O workers, weary workers, who bear the rubs and
knocks,
The only road to freedom runs past the ballot-box.[54]

CIRCUMSTANCES ALTER CASES

By A. D. Cridge

We're Communists and Socialists
And dynamiters, too;
We're slaves of walking delegates[55]
Who tell us what to do,
There's nothing we should kick about,
We've all got "cheek" sublime;
But we're "bone and sinew of the land,"
About
Election
Time.

We're howlers of calamity,
We're crazy flat fools,
We're lawless scum and foreign scruff,
And "stubborner nor mules."
They threaten us with Gatling guns
And in our "hair to climb";
But we're "thinking toilers of the land,"
About
Election
Time.

We're wild-eyed hayseeds, lazy shirks,
Alliance traitors, knaves;
We're looters of the vaults of wealth,
And our speaker always "raves";
We're a danger to the country
And Republic all the time;
But we're "honest, sturdy farmers,"
About
Election
Time.

We're everything that's vile and mean,
For twice three hundred days;
Nihilists, thugs and Pinkertons
Are urged on us to blaze,
If we but demand justice,
As against a gilded crime;
But we're "valiant hosts of labor,"
About
Election
Time.

They tell us of protection,
And the glory of a tax;
The right of honest capital
To ride upon our backs;
Our comfort and prosperity
(Though we haven't got a dime),
And to once more save the party,
About
Election
Time.

They tax us, and they drive us,
And mock us in our woe;
They tell us we're responsible,
Though they know it isn't so;
And we stand right up and take it,
While the "bloats" their pockets line,
Oh, we're several million darndest fools,
About
Election
Time.[56]

VOTE HIM OUT

By F. Scrimshaw

There's a demon in the land;
Vote him out!
Dealing death on every hand;
Vote him out!
In his train come famine slow,
Ruin, blight and bloody woe,
And the nation's overthrow;
Vote him out!

Fierce and pitiless is he;
Vote him out!
Capital monopoly;
Vote him out!
Naught for conscience careth he,
Justice, truth or honesty;
Either he must rule or we;
Vote him out!

Labor Samsons! 'Tis your hour;
Vote him out!

54 *Journal of the Knights of Labor*, Nov. 3, 1892.

55 The term *walking delegates* was applied to union organizers whom the commercial press accused of coercing workers to join unions by unscrupulous tactics.

56 *Journal of the Knights of Labor*, May 4, 1893.

Rise and use your dreaded power;
Vote him out!
Fear not this Philistine's frown;
Spoil him of his stolen crown;
Tear his lordly temple down;
Vote him out!

He for naught of reason cares;
Vote him out!
Naught but VOTES will touch his fears;
Vote him out!
Vote and break this demon's chain;
Vote your long-lost rights to gain;
Vote your MANHOOD back again;
Vote him out![57]

WE'LL OWN THE EARTH

Parody on a Gospel Song

Let us corner up the sunbeams
Lying all around our path,
Get a trust on wheat and roses,
Give the poor the thorns and chaff.
Let us find our chiefest pleasure
Hoarding bounties of to-day,
So the poor shall have scant measure
And two ounces have to pay.

Then give us bonded money,
Then give us bonded money,
Then give us bonded money,
And we'll own it by and by.

Yes, we'll reservoir the rivers,
And we'll levy on the lakes,
And we'll lay a tripling poll tax
On each poor man who partakes;
We'll brand the number on him
That he'll carry through his life,
We'll apprentice all his children
Get a mortgage on his wife.

We will capture e'en the wind-god,
And confine him in a cave,
And then through our patent process,
We the atmosphere will save,
Thus we'll squeeze our little brother
When he tries his lungs to fill,
Put a meter on his windpipe
And present our little bill.

We will syndicate the starlights
And monopolize the moon,
Claim a royalty on rest days
A proprietary noon,
For right of way through ocean's spray
We'll charge past what it's worth,
We'll drive our stakes around the lakes—
In fact, we'll own the earth.[58]

ANCIENT NURSERY BALLAD

(As sung by John Bull and the latter day American tories)

By A. B. Snell

Sing a song of bribery,
Pockets full of boodle;
The easiest and best way
To conquer Yankee Doodle.

With Grover in the white house
To kill all legislation,
The people may inaugurate
To save the yankee nation.

While Sherman in the senate
Our servant of finances,
With many a shrewd and wily trick,
Our glory much enhances.

In vain the patriot loudly calls
And scores the people roundly,
They only grant "you are a crank"
And go on sleeping soundly.

Their lands, their homes and liberties
Are passing from them plainly,
And when they wake a view to take
They'll cuss themselves quite vainly.

Then sing a song of Grover
A bottle full of rye,
And all the noble tories
Who toted off the "pie."[59]

CAMPAIGN SONG

Air—"Rally round the Flag, Boys"

The works have all shut down, boys, the wolf is at the door.
So we'll vote the people's ticket now and ever,
There'll be better times ahead, boys and brighter days in store.
If we vote the people's ticket now and ever.

So down with corporations, corners and combines,
That toilers may enjoy the wealth of meadows, mills and mines.
Then rally 'round the ballot-box and join us heart and hand,
We'll vote the people's ticket now and ever.

The workingmen shall no more feed the greedy bulls and bears,
If they'll vote the people's ticket now and ever,
Their honest hands will toil no more for dandy millionaires,
If they'll vote the people's ticket now and ever.

57Ibid., Sept. 28, 1893.
58*Coming Nation*, Feb. 3, 1894.
59Ibid., Feb. 10, 1894.

Let Grover tend the baby, 'tis all he'll have to do,
If we vote the people's ticket now and ever,
For we'll run the ship of state with the people's chosen crew,
If we vote the people's ticket now and ever.

Break off old party ties, seek our platform just and true,
And vote the people's ticket now and ever,
Then the working man shall have what his toil-worn hand has earned,
If he'll vote the people's ticket now and ever.[60]

BANG! BANG! BANG!

Air—"Tramp, Tramp, Tramp"

Come, ye toilers of the land,
Join the people's party band,
With its principles of honest work and pay;
Have no fear of money powers,
For the conquering ballot's ours—
We will meet them at the polls election day.

Bang! bang! bang! the workmen's anvil,
Gee! who! bright! the farmers say;
Horny handed sons of toil
Make the politicians boil
When they meet them at the polls election day.

Men are sick of court house rings,
Boodle gangs and slurs and flings
At the sturdy toiler's hopes and aims so grand,
We will show them that we're right,
By the power of our might,
For our ballots must prevail throughout the land.

Gamblers live in luxury,
Shylocks claim their usury,
Legal sharks, the tools of base monopoly,
Idlers, raising not a hand,
Claim the best in all the land,
But we'll change it when we gain the victory.

Come, ye farmers from the hills,
Come, ye toilers from the mills,
Join your hearts and hands in our united band,
Pledged to down monopoly,
Pledged to make the toiler free
From the selfish grasping tyrants of the land.[61]

YANKEE BOODLE

By C. A. Sheffield

Air—"Yankee Doodle"

Once on a time old Grover C.
Sent forth a great big bellow
To stop the use of white mon-ee
And coin alone the yellow.
So congress gathered at his beck
And loud and long debated,
Till silver got it "in the neck,"
And Shylock's thirst was sated
Yankee Boodle did the job—
Boodle there was handy,
Old Grover handled well his mob,
Congress was a dandy.

But still the panic moved along
And got its deadly work in,
Each plutocrat was waxing strong
While congress kept on shirkin',
Old Grover vetoed seigniorage,
Against the people's wishin'
And having nothing more to do
The old cuss went a fishin',
Boodlers soon will lose their job,
Though boodle now is handy,
Old Grover cannot rule his mob,
Ain't these times a dandy!

O how they feared the "Commonweal,"
A guilty conscience pricked them,
Just think how awful they would feel
If General Coxey licked them!
Perhaps for once a good big scare
Might stir them up for action,
And tide us through this desert bare
Until next fall's election.
Boodlers soon will lose their job,
Though boodle now is handy,
Old Grover cannot rule his mob—
Ain't these times a dandy![62]

DON'T TAX THE MILLIONAIRE

Anonymous

Tax the land, tax the water,
Tax the sunbeams, tax the air
Tax the earth, tax perdition,
But don't tax the millionaire!

Tax the crops, tax the trees,
Tax common people everywhere,
Tax the schoolhouse, tax the churches,
But don't tax the millionaire!

Tax the moonbeams, tax the stars,
Tax the planets where they are
Tax the widow, tax the orphan,
But don't tax the millionaire!

Tax the living, tax the dead,
Tax the clothing, tax the hair,
Tax the coffin, tax the gravestone,
But don't tax the millionaire!

Tax the preacher, tax the teacher,

60 Ibid., Feb. 24, 1894.
61 Ibid.
62 Ibid., May 12, 1894.

Tax the saints though few and rare,
Tax ambition, tax hope of heaven,
But don't tax the millionaire.[63]

COMIN' THRO' THE RYE

By C. A. Sheffield

If a Jacob meet an Esau,
Starving in the street,
If he offered soup to Esau,
Why not Esau eat?
Every freeman has a stomach—
Soup is quite a treat—
Make haste to sell your birthright, Esau,
Jacob would not cheat!

If a brother meet a brother,
Struggling hard for bread,
If a brother starve a brother,
Need there tears be shed?
Every man for self must battle—
Drag his neighbor down—
Such gospel sweet, with soup to eat!
So gulp without a frown.

If a banker meet a "crank" or
Any other writer.
If the "crank" write up his bank
And terribly indict her,
Every plute his mouth will shoot
To house him in the asylum.
This "lunatic"—he makes them sick
The truth is bound to rile 'em.

If a party meet a party
Fighting spoils to share—
If a party beat a party,
Need a party care?
Every pluty knows his duty
Whichever one may win.
Each party goes where boodle flows
And calmly scoops it in.

If a party shock two parties
Next election day,
If a party knock two parties
Down the "broad—braodway,"
Every worn and wretched toiler
Now by greed oppressed
Shall then arise and seize his prize—
His birthright repossessed.[64]

THE CAUCUS

By Uncle Ben Clark

Tune—"Nellie Bly"

You and I
Shut our eye,
When the caucus meets,
And never question whether they
Are honest men or cheats.

Hi! voters—ho! voters,
Listen unto me.
I'll show to you—I'll prove to you,
Some things you ought to see.

The lobbyist
With his fist
Full of rich men's cash,
Well knows the man on whom he can
With money "make a mash."

Hi! voters—ho! voters
Listen unto me,
The man who pays the biggest price
The candidate will be.

Then we fools
Are his tools,
And vote for him because
He's put upon the ticket—so
We let him make our laws.

Hi! voters—ho! voters
Listen now to me,
And vote the poor man's ticket where
You know there is no fee.[65]

DEDICATED TO OLD PARTY VOTERS

By Gamaliel

Tune—"Bright Jewels"

Ragged voter, ragged voter,
Come see your redeemer,
A bright dollar, a gold dollar,
Behind the banker's bars.
It can buy you, it can sell you,
It has power to enslave you.
It will give you starvation,
While you worship its power.

Foolish voter, senseless voter,
Bow down to your idol,
It is yellow, it is metal,
And is made out of gold.
Old John Sherman and Cleveland,
Took occasion to tell you,
That you needed a redeemer,
Before you was old.

You believed them, you believed them,
And voted their tickets,
They deceived you, and enslaved you,

63Ibid.

64*Railway Times,* reprinted in *United Mine Workers' Journal,* July 26, 1895.

65*Journal of the Knights of Labor,* Jan. 23, 1896.

You are now in their power.
They are planning and scheming,
To get all your earnings,
While you worship your idol,
The yellow gold dollar.

Will you quit it? Will you quit it?
And be true to your family,
That is crying, that is hungry,
And starving for bread,
There's a duty before you,
That is calling for action,
Will you listen and hasten,
Right thoughts in your head?[66]

THE SWISS REFERENDUM

By B. M. Lawrence, M.D., Indianapolis, Ind.
Air—"O! Susannah!"

Fair morning comes, behold the dawn,
Of Direct Legislation;
Dark, fearful days will soon be gone,
All hail, co-operation!
Great wrongs abound with shame we own;
But, voters, we must end them;
By Switzerland the way is shown,—
They call it Referendum.

O! come, brothers,
Unite and vote with me,
Let Gold bugs know
Bond lords must go,
The people shall be free.

When any city, town or state
Feels need of reformation,
They will have power to formulate
And force new legislation,
When laws are made, if good vote yes
If not, at once amend them.
The plan is practiced by the Swiss,—
They call it Referendum.

Chorus:

With this reform the voter will
Give all laws close inspection,
No trust can form a tariff bill,
For free trade or protection,
Then politicians will not try
To purchase votes, to send them
As tools for rings;—gold cannot buy,
Nor bribe the Referendum.

Chorus:

The people then will have full sway,
And coin each precious metal;
Gold bond-bank rule will pass away,
Free voters then will settle
Taxation and a host of things,
Outlaw saloons and end them,
Break up the railroad trusts and rings,
All with the referendum.

Chorus:

The great monopolies will fall,
With soulless corporations,
The friends of labor will prevail,
And we shall lead all nations,
The outcast poor in every land,
Will feel our flag befriend them,
For over "old glory" grand
Shall wave the Referendum.

Chorus:

With this reform the people can
Retain the veto power,
Frame laws to voice the rights of man
And make rich "combines" cower,
Then voters come, resolve to break
Old party ties and end them,
Vote for your wives and children's sake,—
Demand the Referendum.

Chorus:

Take courage friends, and work today
To banish want and sorrow,
The morning dawns, a golden ray
Shall light the coming morrow,
Old wrongs must die, new truths shall live,
With strong arms to defend them,
But equal rights we cannot have,
Without the Referendum.

Chorus:[67]

ELECTION OF 1896 AND DECLINE OF LABOR-POPULISM

In 1895 a sharp split emerged in the Populist movement between the wealthier farmers and the millionaire silver interests on one hand and the labor-populist forces on the other. The former wanted to use the third party primarily to secure passage of a law for the free coinage of silver, while the latter wished to see all the positive labor planks of the People's party continued, not just free silver. By the fall of 1895, this conflict was well on the way to wrecking the labor-Populist alliance. The finishing touches came at the 1896 Populist convention in Saint Louis, where the labor-Populist groups failed in their efforts to nominate Eugene V. Debs as the

66 *Appeal to Reason*, May 23, 1896.
67 *Coming Nation*, Mar. 28, 1896.

presidential candidate of the People's party on a broad platform; the Populist leadership went on to achieve convention endorsement of William Jennings Bryan, the Democratic presidential candidate on a platform which emphasized free coinage of silver. The Saint Louis convention, marking the fusion of populism with the Democratic party, sounded the death knell for the People's party. Although it lingered on after 1896, it was never again a vital political force.

Although the cause which Bryan championed in 1896 was essentially that of the farmers and the middle class, organized labor, with few exceptions, supported the Democratic-Populist presidential candidate over the Republican candidate, William McKinley. In part this was due to the growing belief in labor circles that increasing the volume of currency in circulation through the unlimited coinage of silver at the ratio of 16 to 1 would help revive business and end unemployment. It was also influenced by the fact that, as the campaign advanced, Bryan spoke out vigorously against government by injunction. Labor also reacted to the hysterical nature of conservative attacks on Bryan. Eugene V. Debs expressed the views of many in the labor movement when he declared that "the triumph of Mr. Bryan and free silver would blunt the fangs of the money power."[68] Labor songs popular during the presidential campaign of 1896 voiced the same sentiment.

FREE SILVER

Laboring men please attend
While I relate my history
Money it is very scarce
Let's try and solve the mystery.

The question we will argue now
Has caused a great sensation
It interests both old and young
The welfare of our nation.

The farmer is the corner stone
Though he is cruelly treated
Bryan is the poor man's friend
He wrongly was defeated.

You know our nation owes a debt
'Tis true and I will say it
The bonds they issued calls for gold
And silver will not pay it.

You rascals in your easy chairs
Your crime you are concealing
We are sure to cut your salaries down
On you it's fastly stealing.

A few more years you'll hold the reins
Before our next great battle
We'll arise, defend free silver's cause
Regain our precious metal.[69]

GOLD BUGS GO DOWN BEFORE BRYAN

A rousing Free-Silver song
Air—"Marching through Georgia"

Bring the silver bugle, boys,
We'll sing another song,
Sing it with a spirit that
Will move the world along.
Sing it as they sung it in
The anti–gold bug throng
At St. Louis and Chicago.

Hurrah! hurrah! 16 to 1 shall be!
Hurrah! hurrah! the money of the free!
From Canada to gulf, east and west, from sea to sea,
Gold bugs go down before Bryan.

How the gold bugs whined and yelled,
When plainly it appeared;
Farmers and all laborers
Were not at all "afeared,"
Though John Bull and Cleveland and
McKinley growled and sneered
At St. Louis and Chicago.

Chorus:

Noble men from north and south
Did weep with joyful tears,
To see the patriotism that
They had not seen for years,
And that the people could not help
From breaking forth in cheers,
At St. Louis and Chicago.

Chorus:

Americans want honest rule,
Fair dealing they do crave,
But never shall a freeman here
Be England's bonded slave;
Thus declared, with emphasis,
The people in conclave
At St. Louis and Chicago.

Chorus:

68*Railway Times,* Jan. 1, 1897.

69Kentucky folksongs collected through the Federal Music Project, Works Progress Administration, Library of Congress. The first two verses appear, with music, in *Folk Songs from East Kentucky,* Federal Music Project, WPA (ca. 1939).

From *Folk Songs from East Kentucky*, Federal Music Project, WPA (ca. 1939). Courtesy of Library of Congress.

We will make a thoroughfare
For Progress—make it well;
Break these gold bug shackles off,
We'll end old shylock's spell;
And if John Bull don't like it, he
Can go right straight to h——ll,
While we go onward to glory.

Chorus:[70]

Many organized workers supported Bryan, but others were persuaded to vote for McKinley because of the press predictions that his victory would guarantee a restoration of prosperity. Still others were intimidated to vote for the Republican candidate by employers' threats to shut down their plants in the event of a Democratic-Populist victory. When the returns were in, McKinley had received 7,035,638 votes; Bryan, 6,467,946.

McKinley's election was a bitter disappointment to many workers. The depression continued after his victory, producing the following song.

FAR, FAR AWAY

A New Song by J. R. Sovereign,
Grand Master Workman, Knights of Labor

Where, Oh where! has confidence gone?
Far, far away.
'Twas promised in chunks by the ton,
Far, far away.
Elect me, 'twill come—was McKinley's cry—
Mark Hanna swore it was no lie;
Now Wall street points us up to the sky,
Far, far away.

Where, Oh where! did prosperity go?
Far, far away.
Is the thing we would all like to know,
Far, far away.
The banks they are bursting by the score,
Wages are lower than ever before,
And prosperity is on the other shore—
Far, far away.

Where, Oh where! can we find the gold?
Far, far away.
'Twould makes us all rich, we are told—
Far, far away.
They said it would come and start the mill,
Hard times and poverty it would kill.
But it never came closer than Wall street's till,
Far, far away.

Where, Oh where! can those jobs be found?
Far, far away.
That labor was to get if the money was sound—
Far, far away.
About those jobs they told us a lie—
The only job is McKinley pie—
For now they are winking the other eye,
Far, far away.

In nineteen hundred where will they be?
Far, far away.
From outraged people they'll have to flee,
Far, far away.
With Wall street promises we'll not be caught;
The voters with Bryan will cast their lot
And send gold-bugs where the climate is hot,
Far, far away.[71]

By mid-1897, however, the depression was over, and with the return of prosperity the third-party movement which began as the Farmers' Alliance and later merged into the Populist party and gave birth to labor-populism passed into political oblivion. Yet the labor-Populist alliance left its mark upon American life. Measure after measure advocated by the labor-Populist alliance was to be included in the platform of one or the other of the major political parties and was destined to be enacted into law: the eight-hour day, the institution of more adequate mine and factory inspection in industrial areas and other specific labor legislation, direct election of United States senators, the initiative and referendum, the Australian ballot, and municipal ownership of public utilities. Finally, labor-populism and the labor—Farmers' Alliance coalition which preceded it left a treasury of protest songs that were sung at many meetings of workers and farmers after the disappearance of the movements which had given them birth.

70 *Journal of the Knights of Labor,* Oct. 22, 1896.

71 Ibid., Jan. 14, 1896, reprinted in the *Railway Times,* Feb. 1, 1897.

13
Socialism

GROWTH AND COMPOSITION OF THE SOCIALIST MOVEMENT

Many of the songs sung at trade union meetings and rallies from the seventies through the nineties were also sung at meetings of Socialist groups. Socialists were among the most active workers in the formation of trade unions. In addition, a number of labor paper editors were Socialists, and quite a few of the papers functioned as organs both of KL local assemblies and of local Socialist parties. Even workers who were not members of a Socialist group were influenced by conditions in the United States during the seventies and eighties to turn an attentive ear to the Socialist concept that the people should own and operate the means of production for their own benefit rather than for private profit. Richard T. Ely noted in 1886 that the "more modern trades-unionist, while working along old lines, is . . . looking forward to something far more radical."[1] This view was confirmed by Edward and Eleanor Marx Aveling, son-in-law and daughter of Karl Marx, who reported in *The Working-Class Movement in America* that in their fifteen-week tour of this country in 1886 they had discovered a "vast body of unconscious working-class Socialists."[2]

During this period the promise of American life lured many immigrants from Europe. No doubt many shared the exultation which Norwegians expressed in the folksong "Oleana":

I'm off to Oleana, I'm turning from my doorway,
No chains for me, I'll say good-by to slavery in Norway.
Oh, Oleana!

They give you land for nothing in jolly Oleana,
And grain comes leaping from the ground in floods of golden manna.
Oh, Oleana!

The grain it does the threshing, it pours into the sack, Sir,
And so you take a quiet nap a-stretching on your back, Sir,
Oh, Oleana![3]

The disillusionment experienced by many immigrant workers helped turn them into "unconscious working-class Socialists." In the late nineteenth century, the introductory note in *Survey* makes clear, the following song was popular among Italian workers in this country.

Nothing work, nothing work,
Bad time is this;
Nothing work, nothing work,
How lean is my face.

Nothing job, nothing job,
I come back to Italy;
Nothing job, nothing job,
Adieu, land northerly.

[1]Richard T. Ely, *The Labor Movement in America* (New York, 1886), p. 357. Samuel Gompers made this same point in his letter of January 9, 1891, to Frederick Engels, in which he expressed his great admiration for the ideas of Karl Marx and Engels (see Philip S. Foner, "Samuel Gompers to Frederick Engels: A Letter," *Labor History*, II [Spring, 1970], 207–11).

[2]Edward Aveling and Eleanor Marx Aveling, *The Working-Class Movement in America* (London, 1891), p. 139.

[3]Halvdan Koht, *The American Spirit in Europe* (Philadelphia, 1949), p. 76.

Nothing job, nothing job,
My fatherland I want;
Nothing job, nothing job,
Oh, my land so pleasant.

Nothing job, nothing job,
This sky now is dark;
Nothing job, nothing job,
From coal I am all black.

Nothing job, nothing job,
O! sweet sky of my Italy
Nothing job, nothing job,
How cold is this country.

Nothing job, nothing job,
Here is not my mother;
Nothing job, nothing job,
Here is not my lover.

Nothing job, nothing job,
Oh, divine beauty of Naples;
Nothing job, nothing job,
Oh, the enchantment of Venice.

Nothing job, nothing job,
Oh, warm climate of Sicily;
Nothing job, nothing job,
All is nice in Italy.

Land, sky, cities, flowers,
Seas, women, and their loves;
I go prompt to Italy,
Land of sun and beauty.

Nothing job, nothing job,
I return to Italy;
Comrades, laborers, good-by;
Adieu, land of "Fourth of July."[4]

A Slovakian coal miner lamented:

THE LONELY MINER OF WILKES-BARRE

While my wife is in the old country,
I am in America seeking work;
In the mines of Wilkes-Barre I found it—
And, dear Lord God, help me!

Each morning I am hoisted down
Four cars per shift to load;
Three hundred times an hour I look about me
Lest a fall of coal or rock kill me.

And at the eleventh hour,
My miner leaves for home;
Now there's none but me in the mine—
I am alone, dear Lord God, except for thee.

O God, help me finish my work,
And safely return home
To my dear wife and children—
My heart is so sad—hear my plea![5]

A Slovakian steelworker wrote the following song after he saw a friend killed under an ingot buggy. He sang it for his friend's widow, who arrived in America shortly after the accident.

I LIE IN THE AMERICAN LAND

Ah, my God, what's in America?
Very many people are going over there.
I will also go, for I am still young;
God, the Lord, grant me good luck there.

I'll return if I don't get killed
But you wait for news from me.
When you hear from me
Put everything in order,
Mount a raven-black horse,
And come to me, dear soul of mine.

But when she came to McKeesport,
She did not find her husband alive;
Only his blood did she find
And over it bitterly she cried.

"Ah, my husband, what did you do,
Orphaned these children of ours?"
"To these orphans of mine, my wife, say
That I lie in America.
Tell them, wife of mine, not to wait for me,
For I lie in the American land."[6]

Even more bitter was this piece published in the *Amerikanische Arbeiterzeitung:*

THE JOURNEY TO AMERICA

After in my dear Germany
I've toiled so long in vain
I'm going to America
Where they've chased me away.

That is the republic with greatest freedom
For fraud, for robbery and murder;
And every born scoundrel so far
Has become a cabinet minister.

So I suppose for an honest man
There also is a place;

[4]"Song of an Italian Workman," *Survey*, XXI (Dec. 26, 1908), 492–93.

[5]George Korson, ed., *Pennsylvania Songs and Legends* (Philadelphia, 1949), p. 376 (translated from the Slovakian version sung by Mary Rusin in 1947, recorded by Jacob A. Evanson).

[6]Jacob A. Evanson, "Folk Songs of an Industrial City," in Korson, *Pennsylvania Songs and Legends,* p. 43 (transcribed from the singing of Andrew Kovaly by Jacob A. Evanson in 1947).

And the ordinary people who govern there
Are also striving for progress.

It won't be as it is here at home
Where speech and press are forbidden.
There you can tell all you wish,
As long as it's only fictional stories.

They say the born Americans
Are very fine people indeed.
They say their statesmen are really great,
Although, all in all, not quite right in the head.

This latter fault does after all
Not really mean very much,
For in order to win, all you need to do
Is to beat your opponent's hide.

They say that in "free" America
Justice is in full bloom;
What a pity that it's administered always
Only by money-bags!

They say the Constitution was made
According to concepts of justice;
And since it is the Best of All,
Has been thought up by the biggest swindlers.

All right, I am going and very soon
I shall be in New York
And I shall to the "free" people there
Proclaim some blessed Freedom.[7]

The conditions confronting many immigrant workers once they began their daily toil in the Promised Land were poignantly set forth in a Yiddish song:

THE SWEATSHOP
By Morris Rosenfeld

The machines in the shop, so wildly they roar
That oft I forget in their roar that I am—
In the terrible tumult I'm buried,
The me is all gone, a machine I become.
I work, work, work on unceasing;
'Tis toil, toil, toil unending.
Why? For whom? I know not, I ask not.
A machine? How can it e'er fashion a thought?

No room for feelings, for thought or for reason,
All bitter and bloody the work kills the noblest,
The best, the most beautiful, the richest, the deepest.
The highest in life is crushed to the earth
On fly the seconds, the minutes, the hours,
The nights like the days flee swiftly as sails;
I drive the machine as though I would catch them,
Unavailing I chase them, unceasing I speed.

The clock in the workshop is never at rest;
Ever pointing and ticking and waking together.
Its ticking and waking had meaning, they told me.
And reason was in it, they said to me then;
And still something as though a dream, I remember;
Life, sense, and the something the clock wakens in me—
What it is, I forget; ask me not!
I know not, I know not, I am a machine!

And then, at times, the clock I hear,
Its pointing, its language, I understand different;
Its unrest (pendulum) pushes me onward;
"Work more, more, much more."
In its sound the angry words of the boss,
In its two hands his gloomy face I see.
The clock, I shudder—it seems to drive and cry:
"Machine," and shriek out, "sew, sew."[8]

Edward Bellamy's *Looking Backward*, published in January, 1888, at the height of the intense industrial conflict of the decade, gave impetus to the growing interest in a new social system. Hundreds of thousands read this utopian account of a cooperative commonwealth in the United States in the year 2000. Overnight, Nationalist groups, seeking "to nationalize the functions of production and distribution," sprang up everywhere, linked loosely through correspondence and lecture exchange, recruiting their membership mainly from the urban middle class.

Although the short-lived Nationalist movement had little in common with scientific socialism, and Bellamy himself went to great pains to point out that he was no Marxist, it did contribute to the growth of the Socialist movement in this country. Not a few Nationalists moved into the Socialist Labor party—in too many cases taking with them much more of Bellamy's utopianism and his emphasis on gradual evolu-

[7] *Amerikanische Arbeiterzeitung*, June 5, 1886. Trans. Rudi Bass.

[8] *Coast Seamen's Journal*, June 22, 1898; the translator is not indicated. A different rendition, entitled "In the Factory," appears in Morris Rosenfeld, *Songs of Labor, and Other Poems*, trans. Rose Pastor Stokes and Helena Frank (Boston, 1914), pp. 7–8. Still another version, translated by Aaron Kramer, may be found in *Morris Rosenfeld*, ed. Itche Goldberg and Max Rosenfeld (New York, 1964), pp. 26–28; here it carries the title "The Sweatshop."

The author of "The Sewing Machine," published in the *Workingman's Advocate*, August 23, 1873, humorously compared his wife to the machine, pointing out the advantages of the former. The poem included these lines:

Mine is not one of those stupid affairs
That stands in the corner with what-nots and chairs, . . .
None of your patent machines for me,
Unless Dame Nature's the patentee!

tionary reforms than they did of Marxism. For a number of years, *Looking Backward* continued to constitute the first introduction many Americans had to socialism.

While anarchism attracted workers in the seventies and early eighties, it declined rapidly after the Haymarket affair. Most of those who believed in a socialist society were organized in the Socialist Labor party, founded in 1877. Its members were active in the formation and growth of important national trade unions, local unions, and city central labor organizations, and they played an important role in the rise of the Knights of Labor as well as the American Federation of Labor. The SLP led workers' struggles which won important gains in higher wages, shorter hours, and better working conditions.

However, the influence of the Socialist Labor party was limited by its almost exclusively immigrant composition—mainly Germans, with a scattering of Jews, Poles, Bohemians, and Italians. "The Socialist Labor Party of the 'eighties," observes Justus Ebert, "was a German party and its official language was German. The American element was largely incidental."[9] There were SLP papers, like the *Workmen's Advocate* in New Haven and the *Labor Enquirer* in Denver, which reached an English-speaking audience in the eighties, but the party's main papers were still published only in German. Thus, while the German-language Socialist press published songs and ballads, they were known only by workers who knew German. English-speaking workers obtained such Socialist pieces as they knew primarily from the *Labor Standard*, the *Workmen's Advocate*, and the *Labor Enquirer*. In San Francisco, *Truth*, published by Burnette G. Haskell, leader of an independent Socialist movement in the Far West and the Rocky Mountain region, did carry Socialist songs along with songs of the Knights of Labor local assemblies.

James H. White of Chicago was a Socialist lecturer in the 1880s who combined talks on socialism with a variety of entertainment. One of his songs, "Battle of the Viaduct," dealing with a struggle between Socialist workers in Chicago and the police, was a regular feature of his "entertainment." Unfortunately, no copy of the song is known to exist. In a letter to Phillip Van Patten, secretary of the Socialist Labor party, January 19, 1881, White wrote that his method "of agitating for Socialism" by combining songs with recitations and lectures was winning converts as well as more than covering his expenses. "A great meney of the working class small farmers as well as other take up with the idea of 'Socialism' when they understand it rightly."[10]

In the 1890s the English-language Socialist press increased in both numbers and influence. For one thing, Daniel De Leon, a brilliant writer and a man of broad culture, moved into the Socialist Labor party from the Nationalist movement and rapidly became the most prominent figure in the party. As editor of the *People*, the party's organ, he antagonized many trade union Socialists by his indifference to immediate demands and his penchant for forming dual unions. He urged Socialists to leave the existing labor organizations and join only those unions which he founded and which were dedicated to achieving socialism. However, despite his faults, De Leon did much to lift the Socialist Labor party out of the narrow confines of the German-speaking element. Under De Leon's editorship, the weekly and daily *People* published Socialist organs, devoting more space then to workers. While quite a few were songs of the English Socialist movement, many were written especially for the *People* by American Socialists.

On January 1, 1897, Eugene V. Debs officially announced that he had resigned from the People's party and had joined the Socialist movement. At about the same time, Julius A. Wayland, editor of the *Coming Nation* and the *Appeal to Reason*, both of which had carried songs friendly to socialism along with those especially geared to labor-populism, broke with populism and turned these papers into official Socialist organs, devoting more space then to Socialist songs and ballads. De Leon, Debs, and Wayland did not see eye to eye on many issues related to socialism; De Leon, for example, had only contempt for Debs's belief that socialism could be achieved by organizing thousands of

[9]Justus Ebert, *American Industrial Evolution* (New York, 1907), p. 66.

[10]Socialist Labor Party Papers, Box 6, Folder 6, State Historical Society of Wisconsin. With his letter White included the "bill" he distributed in advance of his appearance. It was headed "Sense and Nonsense!" and announced that J. H. White of Chicago "will give an Entertainment for THINKERS and all those who like Pleasure, Consisting of LABOR, TEMPERANCE, Comic & Sentimental Impersonations, Recitations and Songs." At the bottom of another of his handbills, White printed this notice: "AFTER ENTERTAINMENT WILL ORGANIZE AN ASSEMBLY OF THE KNIGHTS OF LABOR."

SENSE

—AND—

NONSENSE!

J. H.

WHITE,

—OF—

CHICAGO,

Will give an Entertainment for

THINKERS

And all those who like Pleasure, Consisting of

LABOR, TEMPERANCE,

Comic & Sentimental

Impersonations,

Recitations and Songs.

——AT——

PROGRAMME.

Think of your Head in the Morning (original)....................Song
Applying for Divorce....................Recitation
The condition of society that the terrible socialists want to inaugurate. Having become informed of their awful intentions by joining them, I will expose them for the benefit of humanity....................Speech
Streets of Baltimore....................Recitation
The Drunkard and his Dog....................Recitation
Old Black Slavery way....................Song
Sam Jones and the Devil....................Recitation
Peoples' Advents coming....................Recitation
Modern Orator (original)....................Impersonation
Rum's Maniac....................Impersonation
Grand Father Sam....................Song
Money Less Man....................Recitation
Yea are Many, They are few....................Recitation
Mary's Lamb (original)....................Recitation
Suppressing the Press (original)....................Impersonation
Characters: Henpecked Husband, The Capitalist, Yankee Farmer
Widow Green....................Recitation
Battle of the Viaduct....................Song
Slavery of Wages Labor....................Recitation

Admission 10 Cents.

SUN PRINT, GENESEO, ILL.

Courtesy of Socialist Labor Party Papers in the State Historical Society of Wisconsin

Fredonia Louisa Co Iowa
Jan 19- 1881

Comrade Van Patten,

Sir, Enclosed please find three dollors, for Pamphlets. If you have all the tracks send $1,00 worth of them, sepical number of each, $1,00 in John Ehrmann pamphlet, 1,00 the Nove Dec & Jan numbers of our monthley, the rest in good ould father Douai "Better times". If you have onley four of the diferant kind of tracks, send them, or onley yours on the 'Paris Commune' send 25 cts worth & the rest of the money divid eayaly for "Better times" & Ehrmann if you have not any tracks send all in the two them to James H White ~~Mt~~ Mt Pleasant Henry Co Iowa send on receipt of this as

~~of this~~ as I Shal be thes the first of Next week.

I send you one of my bills, since the election I have been giving Entertainments moast of the time. You can see from bill that I am Showing up "Socialism" for the benefit of "humanity" in doing so I give a good "Socialistic" Speech of one hours length, which takes the natives by surprise, than I ring in a lot of Socialisms in my recitation & especially in the "Suppressing of the Press" when I get through the Ent which last two hours, Farmers will say to me "Why! I thought that Socialism ment divide up" Such Ideas are all right".

I give the Ent moastly in small towns & School Houses it is nearly five months since

I left Chicag, Since then I have
lectired & given Ent in ten cont
in Ills, and in this Co, in Iowa
I expect to work South aways
than west to Addams Co, so
that I can see the workings
of the Icurians a French community. By my plan of agitat-
-ing for socialism I more than
make my expenses. A great meney of the working class small
farmers as well as other ~~text~~ take
up with the idea of "socialism"
when they understand it rightly.
I would start sections as you
suggested but in the farming
districts enough cannot be got
to gether like in large towns.
So I will try and do all I can
to spread the "truth" by "agitatin"
& ~~through~~ by our tracts & Pamphlets
knowing that our cause must yet
"prevail" because it just. I remain
yours for the truth James H White

Courtesy of Socialist Labor Party Papers in the State Historical Society of Wisconsin

workers into a cooperative that would set up factories in basic industries, control them, and return the profits to laborers. Nevertheless, all three men helped base the Socialist movement in the United States more firmly on the native American population. By publishing Socialist songs and ballads, the *People*, the *Coming Nation*, and the *Appeal to Reason* continued a tradition already well established in the Socialist press. Especially after the demise of the *Labor Standard*, the *Workmen's Advocate*, the *Labor Enquirer*, and *Truth*, they were able to bring such songs to the attention of large groups of English-speaking workers.

On July 29, 1901, at a unity convention in Indianapolis, the Socialist party of the United States was formed by all elements in the Socialist Labor party, except those who supported De Leon, and by Eugene V. Debs and his followers in the Social Democratic party. One of the first acts of the Socialist party designated the cooperative publishing firm of Charles H. Kerr in Chicago as the Socialist publishing organization. Among its earliest publications was the reissue of Charles H. Kerr's compilation *Socialist Songs*, originally published in January, 1900, as number 11 of the Pocket Library of Socialism. The preface of an enlarged version, published under the new title *Socialist Songs with Music* (1901), noted:

> This book is a first attempt at bringing together a collection of Socialist Songs with music for the use of American Socialists. This will explain many of the most serious defects that will doubtless appear in it, and it will also explain the fact that we have had to borrow more than half our songs from our English comrades, . . . [several] from the admirable book entitled 'Chants of Labor,' compiled by Edward Carpenter and published by Swan, Sonnenschein & Co. of London. The remainder are drawn from various sources, only a few being original. We American Socialists are only beginning to sing.[11]

Actually, Kerr seems to have been unaware of the existence of Socialist songs in the German-language press in this country as well as those published in the *Labor Standard*, the *Workmen's Advocate*, the *Labor Enquirer*, and *Truth*, all of which were "original." Moreover, he overlooked the songs published in the *Coming Nation*, the *Appeal to Reason*, and the *People*. (The failure to mention the *People* is not surprising, since De Leon was anathema to the founders of the Socialist party.) As the songs and ballads in this chapter reveal, American Socialists were already singing years before 1901, when *Socialist Songs with Music* was published.

THE SEVENTIES

THE TIME HAS COME

Dedicated to Wages-Slaves

By William Benton

The time has come to stand erect,
In noble, manly self respect;
To see the bright sun overhead,
To feel the ground beneath our tread,
Unled by priests, uncursed by creeds,
Our manhood proving by our deeds.

The time has come to break the yoke,
Whatever cost the needed stroke;
To set the toiling millions free,
Whatever price their liberty—
Better a few should die, than all
Be held in worse than deadly thrall.

The time has come for men to find
Their statute-book within the mind;
To read its laws, and cease to pore
The musty tomes of ages o'er;
Truth's golden rays its pages illume;
Her fires your legal scrolls consume.

The time has come to preach the soul;
No meager shred, the manly whole;
Let agitation come! who fears?
We need a flood; the filth of years
Has gathered round us! Roll, then, on—
What cannot stand had best be gone![12]

Section 12 of the International Workingmen's Association (the First International) in New York City was organized in the summer of 1871 by a group of radical reformers led by Victoria Woodhull and Tennessee Claflin, two ardent woman suffragists and preachers of free love. The two sisters published a radical feminist newspaper, *Woodhull & Claflin's Weekly*, which offered news of the First International and trade unionism along with articles dealing with prostitution, venereal disease, abortion, and female sexuality. Attention was paid to socialism and communism; the *Weekly* not only published interviews with Karl Marx but was the first Ameri-

[11] Charles H. Kerr, *Socialist Songs with Music* (Chicago, 1901), publisher's note.

[12] *Labor Reformer*, reprinted in *Woodhull & Claflin's Weekly*, Nov. 29, 1873.

can periodical to publish the *Communist Manifesto.* Occasionally, too, the *Weekly* printed songs combining socialism with free love, such as the following:

A SONG OF
"THE IMPENDING REVOLUTION"
By D.D. L.

Men of Labor, wherefore toil?
All the products of the soil
Adds to wealth obtained by spoil,
And wicked knavery.
Must you ever thus remain,
Bowed beneath oppression's chain
Wearing on your souls the stain
Of abject slavery?

Are ye then so slow to learn,
That the profits you may earn
Ne'er to your advantage turn,
Nor pleasures borrow.
You have seen your babes denied
E'en the bread for which they cried,
When they famished, sank and died,
In bitter sorrow.

You have felt the rich man's hand
Grasp from you the nation's land,
Leaving naught on which to stand,
Without his pleasure.
Ye have toiled and added care
To a burden hard to bear,
While enough he has to spare
Of hardest treasure.

Treasure earned by you alone,
Though no cent of it you own,
Nor a moment's pleasure known,
But sad despairing.
Long subdued by craven fears,
Ye have toileth with empty tears
Through the sad and bitter years,
And none were caring.

Oft have ye most vainly thought
Justice could at law be sought,
Though our judges all are bought
By golden dower.
Law is like a bubble burst
To the poor by want accurst,
For the rich are even first
In legal power.

Oft have ye most vainly plead
That the Church, by Jesus led,
Might upon you blessings shed
And tender feeling.
But the clergy shrank aghast,
Bidding you repent and fast,
For your lot in life was cast
By God's own dealing.

Law and Gospel stand arrayed
Side by side, and have betrayed
Human rights for which you prayed
In accents tearful.
Can ye wait for actions worse,
When all the law is in the purse,
And the clergy breath a curse
Of a future fearful?

Dally not to meekly rue,
Ye are many, they are few,
Strike the blow for ages due
To careless pleasure.
Rise en masse in sturdy might
With your hearts prepared to fight
In a strife for human right,
And equal measures.

Let your souls with ardor burn,
Firm resolved to overturn
All that pilfers what you earn
By legal stealing.
Drive the varlets out of sight
Who by farce of "legal right"
Make your lives a wretched blight,
No hope revealing.

With such purpose firm and true,
Ye may make the married few
Shrink, dismayed from public view,
And sink forever.
Only so shall equal right
Ever triumph over might,
Or your souls see freedom's light
Or bonds shall ever sever.[13]

Several thousand German workers fled to the United States to escape the reaction in Germany following the Franco-Prussian War of 1870. Among them were former members of the *Allgemeiner Deutscher Arbeiter-Verein* (General German Workers' Association), founded in Leipzig, in May, 1863, with Ferdinand Lassalle as its president. These workers joined the American branch of the association, organized in New York City on October 6, 1865, by a small group of disciples of Ferdinand Lassalle and some members of the Marxist Communist Club. At their meetings they sang the famous song of the General German Workers' Association, written by Georg Herwegh, which closed with these verses:

13*Woodhull & Claflin's Weekly*, Feb. 24, 1872.

Men of labour, now arisen—
Use your strength to break your prison!
You can stop the wheels at will
When you rule that they be still.

All the tyrants twitch with fear
When they see their end is near,
When your hands lay down the plough,
And you cry: the time is now!

Break the bond that yokes the free!
Break the dread of slavery!
Break the slavery of dread!
Bread is freedom, freedom bread![14]

Once in this country, the German workers, who had been Socialists in their own land, joined the German-Americans already in the United States in Socialist organizations. Among the most popular of the Socialist movement songs of the 1870s were the following:

BE UNITED, UNITED, UNITED!
By M.K.
Melody—"Up, Brothers, Let Us Throng"

Watch out! The storm clouds are threatening!
Build yourselves a shielding roof
Before the lightning strikes blindingly,
Before the thunder hits you.
Up you proletarians all,
Who battle and struggle singly.
Only your unity will ever conquer the enemy.

Whether you gather far from the sunlight,
Deep in the shafts of the earth, the ore,
Whether, with sad face,
You spin wool at the loom,
Whether you stride in the heat of the sun,
Behind the plow.
Whether you sail through the waves
Across the wide ocean.

You all call yourselves brothers,
The same suffering oppresses you.
And the same mark of Cain
Burns on everybody's forehead.
Yes, it is the same pain that
The world puts upon you.
And in all of your hearts stirs
The same anger.

Up, therefore, and do not
Hesitate any longer.
Give each other the brother's hand,
From a bond of defense
And attack against your oppressors
In the battle for your rights.
Let every proletarian hasten,
That a small, stalwart band no longer fight alone.

Where the red flag is flying
There alone is your place.
If you stand fast together
Victory is certain under it.
What you all want to achieve
Believe me it will be easy if you are united
What seems impossible to you
You will then achieve as in play.

You can create a better world
For the happiness of all people.
But you all must stick together
None shall cowardly retreat.
Yes, the dawn of a new time is breaking
But don't ever forget this:
You must be united, united, united.[15]

THE HYMN OF THE PROLETARIAT
By Johann Most, translated from the German
Melody—"Andreas Hoffer"

Who hammers brass and stone?
Who raiseth from the mine?
Who weaveth cloth and silk?
Who tilleth wheat and vine?
Who worketh for the rich to feed,
Yet lives himself in sorest need?—
It is the men who toil, the Proletariat.

Who strives from earliest morn?
Who toils till latest night?
Who brings to OTHERS wealth,
Ease, luxury, and might?
Who turns alone the world's great wheel,
Yet has no right in common weal!—
It is the men who toil, the Proletariat.

Who is from aye a slave
To all the tyrant brood?
Who oft for them must fight?
Oft sacrifice his blood?—
O fool! hast thou not yet perceived,
'Tis THOU that ever art deceived!
Awake, ye men who labor! Up, Proletariat!

Together join your powers!
And swear to banner red!
For Freedom boldly fight!
So win ye better bread!
Then quicken ye the despot's fall,
Bring peace unto the nations all,
To battle, ye who labor! Up, Proletariat!

In YOUR hands lie the means;
Work but with UNITY,

[14]English translation in Heinrich Gemkow, *Karl Marx* (Dresden, 1968), p. 238.
[15]*Sozial Demokrat*, May 28, 1874. Trans. Rudi Bass.

Hold ye but firm together
Then ye will soon be FREE,
With quick-march forward to the fight,
Though scorn the foe in grape-shot might!
Then win, ye men who labor! Win, Proletariat![16]

Even though they had left Germany, the German-American Socialists continued to respond to events in that country. No event stirred them more than the anti-Socialist law, sponsored by Prince Otto von Bismarck, which was passed by the Reichstag on October 19, 1878. The law gave the government authority to suppress all independent labor organizations, all political and economic associations of the Socialists, all their newspapers, periodicals, and printing presses. Socialist meetings were forbidden; the police were empowered to expel "socialist agitators"; and states could declare a state of emergency anywhere in the country for a one-year period.

The anti-Socialist law was renewed at its expiration in 1880 and again every two years until 1890. During this period many leaders of the party were arrested, imprisoned, or exiled. Hundreds of Socialist periodicals, associations, and unions were suppressed by the police, and their assets confiscated.[17]

German-American Socialists mobilized to protest the anti-Socialist law and assist the victims of Bismarck's repression. They were joined in their protests by all other groups in the Socialist movement as well as by many non-Socialist American liberals and radicals. The Socialist Labor party's national executive committee called for protest meetings throughout the United States on January 18, 1879, and a number were held.[18] The Socialists of Chicago met in Turner Hall; after a number of speeches, according to the account in the *Chicago Socialist*, "W. B. Creech was called upon for a song, and favored the audience with a parody on 'Yankee Doodle,' as follows":

Workingmen assembled here,
No matter what your nation,
Raise your voices now against
Old Bismarck's cowardly action;
How he banished honest men,
For their love of freedom.
Far from home and fatherland,
With meanest persecution.

Yankee Doodle welcomes all
To our glorious Union,
Where from Bismarck's power you're free
Or any nation tyrant.

Bismarck and his dogs of war
Germany are searching
For our Socialist boys,
To stop their agitation;
But as soon as one is stop't,
Twenty stand defiant,
To denounce him and his chains—
This mighty prince of tyrants.

Bismarck now is badly beat
By the German people;
Better he had changed his laws,
And made them just and equal.
Give the workingmen their rights—
Some day you may need them;
Think of France—we're brothers now
In Socialistic union.

He was greeted with a round of applause, and in answer to an imperative recall, gave the following parody on "Hold the Fort":

Ho! our comrades, see our emblem
Waving in the sky!
Brighter future it betokens—
Liberty is nigh.
Raise aloft the crimson banner,
Emblem of the free!
Mighty tyrants now are trembling,
Here and o'er the sea.

Rally 'round our glorious banner,
Freedom's chosen sign,
Where amidst the din of battle
Victory does shine!
Long in dark and cruel bondage
We have suffer'd here;
Socialistic light is dawning,
Cheer, my comrades cheer!

Stand in line of battle bravely,
Gird the armor on;
Woman's faith and man's strong arm
Will right this ancient wrong.
Brightly smiles our glorious future—
Dawn, sweet hallowed morn,
On a world of love and union!
Liberty is born![19]

16Ibid., Nov. 28, 1874, reprinted in *Truth*, Sept. 29, 1883. Johann Most was a leading anarchist of the period; but his song was sung even by Socialists who objected vehemently to his anarchist doctrines.

17Koppel S. Pinson, *Modern Germany* (New York, 1954), pp. 206–9.

18*Socialist* (Chicago), Jan. 4 and 11, 1879.

19Ibid., Jan. 25, 1879.

The next song, also called "The Socialist Wagon," was attributed by the Chicago *Socialist* to Comrades Creech and Hull.

THE SOCIALISTS ARE COMING

Air—"Wait for the Wagon"

Come, all you toiling nations,
And listen to my song.
Of the trials of honest labor,
Caused by competition's wrong!
It is this slavish system
That makes you work so hard,
And live on bread and water,
And support a monied lord.

Then wait for the wagon!
The Socialists are coming;
Join in with our party, boys—
It's the only honest one.

It was in Eighteen seventy-seven
The workingmen got tired,
And thinking of their present wrongs,
With rage their hearts were fired.
They told Tom Scott they would quit work
Unless he paid them more—
And that's the only reason
Why he dyed the land with gore![20]

Chorus:

They called out their brave volunteers,
Who quickly fired on them,
And butchered full five hundred
Of true, honest, workingmen!
They brought us to submission,
But it did not make things right;
It learned us one good lesson, boys,
And that was, how to fight!

Chorus:

We're the largest in this nation,
And, if we have a mind,
We'll say who'll represent us
And who will stay behind,
We'll send good men to make our laws,
And rogues will get a slip;
We'll have good times for workingmen,
As well as for the rich.

Chorus:

So come, my friends, and join us,
And you'll never rue the day,
For we'll change this present system
To the Socialistic way.
We'll make this earth a paradise,
For so it ought to be,
And make every man a brother, boys,
As well as you and me.

Chorus:

We'll do our best, and do what's right,
And be good, honest men;
And if, perchance, we should go wrong,
We know they've done the same;
And so we'll never give it up,
But try, and try again,
Until we get a full reform
For honest workingmen.

Chorus:

There is plenty in this world
For all the sons of men,
If there were not such vultures
That are stealing all they can.
But while there is a Vanderbilt,
A Tom Scott, or Jay Gould,
The rogues will still grow richer
And honest men be fooled.

Chorus:

Then let us change the system,
And not leave it for the few,
And if these lords don't like it,
Why, they know what they can do!
So, at the next election,
Be careful how you vote,
And send good men to make your laws,
That can't be bribed or bought![21]

"Labor Song" urged Socialists to fight for women's rights.

LABOR SONG

Waken, toilers! Light is breaking,
Morn upon the mountain reigns;
In the near, prophetic future,
Lo! a trumpet voice proclaims:
Leisure for the working people,
Wealth from nature's golden store,
Justice for the waiting millions—
Herald it the wide world o'er!

Voices from across the ocean,
Wafted from Old Europe's clime,
Greeted by the Western nations,
Loud the bells of Freedom chime:
Leisure for the over-workers,
Delving in their masters' ore;
Freedom, with her morning papers,
Heralds it the wide world o'er!

[20] For the railroad strike of 1877, see pp. 126–32.
[21] *Socialist* (Chicago), Oct. 26, 1878.

Woman shall not wait forever
At the door of Senate halls,
Equal right for sex demanding,
If for JUSTICE she but calls:—
Justice for the working woman,
Time and wages to explore
Social evils and their causes—
Herald it the wide world o'er!

Yes, we'll plough the furrow deeply,
Virtue from the subsoil bring;
With a voice of living thunder,
Still upon the anvil ring;
TIME and CULTURE for the millions,
Wealth from nature's golden shore;
Riches for the men who earn them—
Herald it the wide world o'er.[22]

In light of its strong religious sentiment, "Our Cause" was a rather unusual Socialist declaration.

OUR CAUSE

(Dedicated to Socialistic Comrades)

Air—"Hold the Fort"

Comrades, up! up! and be doing
For our cause so just and grand;
Agitation is now brewing
Good for us in every land.

Raise aloft our light of justice,
Let its rays be shed all 'round,
Even on those who try to crush us—
On our side they'll yet be found.

Bravely march through every danger,
Remember, God is on our side;
And Jesus, born in the manger,
For our cause was crucified.

One for all, and all for one,
Forever will our maxim be;
With God, our Father, leading on,
Through life unto eternity.[23]

In the spring of 1879 a bill was introduced in the Illinois legislature to strengthen the state militia and require every able-bodied male above the age of twenty-one to serve in the militia. The bill, part of an employer offensive following the great railroad strike of 1877, was bitterly denounced by the Socialists as a weapon to be used to suppress workers' organizations. John M'Intosh, Socialist poet and songwriter, contributed two songs to the anti-militia bill campaign.[24] The first, below, has some of the flavor characteristic of IWW songs.

ORIGINAL SONG

By John M'Intosh

Suggested by the discussion on the Militia Bill in the State legislature, Springfield, Ill.

New Air

I'm a tramp, I'm a tramp,
Of the Socialist stamp,
And I ask you to list to my songs
Of political bums
And their sojer-boy chums,
With an echo of Socialist wrongs,
There is war in the land,
And the chaps in command
Are must'ring their men for the field;
And the foemen they'll meet
Are the men of the street,
The workmen, who never say yield.

I'm a tramp, I'm a tramp
And a Socialist scamp,
But I ask you to list to my lays,
For I sing of the Right
In its contest with Might,
Its deeds and its conquests to praise.
Though the years of the past
Like a shadow lies cast
On the struggle so manfully borne;
Still the cause that we prize
As the light of our eyes
Will shine with the glory of morn.[25]

SONG

Suggested by the consideration of the Militia Bill now before the Illinois Legislature.

By John M'Intosh

Air—"Wearin' of the Green"

Come, all you noble workingmen, and listen to my yarn;
Of joinin' the militia each one of you I warn;
They'll put a rifle in your hand and promenade you roun',
And hang you all should you refuse to shoot your brothers down.

Oh, the bosses are our enemies, I truly do declare;
The devil a bit for me and you do any of them care;
They build them costly palaces and furnish them so fine,
While we must live in tenements unfit for dogs or swine.

For them and for their families we hourly toil and sweat,

22 Ibid., Nov. 16, 1878.

23 Ibid., Dec. 7, 1878.

24 Although the militia was strengthened, the campaign defeated the provision requiring compulsory service by every able-bodied male.

25 *Socialist* (Chicago), Apr. 19, 1879.

And to support ourselves and wives we're all the while in debt;
Our little ones are poorly clad and shiver in the cold;
No better off are we, agra, than slaves that's bought and sold.

And now, since we've resolved to jine the Socialistic clan,
Demandin' in the name of God and the sacred rights of Man;
Bread for our wives and children and shelter good for all.
They point at us a bayonet and aim a rifle ball.

Oh, the curse of Cromwell on the man would seek their sojer ranks!
We'll jine the "Labor Guards" instead and earn our neighbors' thanks;
We'll raise our own battalions, boys, beneath our flag of green,
Demanding peace and plenty with the LEHR- UND WEHR-VEREIN.[26]

Now clasp your hands united, boys, and swear to Him on high,
As freemen only shall we live, as freemen only die;
Our struggle is the common good, for all and still for each,
And in the ballot-box we'll drop all difference of speech.

Now, three cheers for the Socialists, and give them with a will,
And three groans for the bosses who would work us only ill;
Upstanding and uncovered. Hip, hurrah! hurrah! hurrah!
And now the donkey groans, my lads; Eho! Eho! Eho-o-o![27]

THE EIGHTIES

FORWARD!

As long as you don't have
The courage to break the chains,
The sunlight of freedom
Will never shine on earth.
Therefore, forward, forward, into the battle,
You oppressed masses!
Whoever truly loves freedom
Must also hate slavery.

You complain speechlessly
And let your tears flow,
But at the last minute
You cannot decide to act.
Thus you alone are to blame,
That your hangman revels.
Whoever truly loves freedom
Must also hate slavery.

So hesitate no longer, prepare yourselves,
The days are already numbered,
Until the last struggle,
Until the day of decision.
Look how in the palaces
How the rich tremble.
Whoever truly loves freedom
Must also hate slavery.[28]

SONGS OF THE SOCIALISTS

H. Greulich's "Labourers' Battle Hymn," Done into English

There sounds a call from land to land,
Ye poor, give one another hand!
Then bid a "Halt" to tyranny,
And from thy slavish yoke break free!
The battle-cry low rolleth by,
The banner red doth float on high,
So labouring live or fighting die!

Now long enough have we delayed,
Now long enough have fools been made,
Then let us range ourselves for fight,
Then let us seize upon our right,
The battle-cry low rolleth by,
The banner red doth float on high,
So labouring live or fighting die!

We wish for freedom, peace, our right,
That no one slave in others' might,
That all mankind to work be bound,
That bread for each be somewhere found,
The battle-cry low rolleth by,
The banner red doth float on high,
So labouring live or fighting die!

You bring to others goods and gold,
Yet naught for self can ever hold;
Man scorning laughs you in the face,
And feareth not the judgment place,
The battle-cry low rolleth by,
The banner red doth float on high,
So labouring live, or fighting die!

Then up, then up! courageous band!
The storm breaks loose upon the land,

26 As early as 1875, a small group of German Socialists in Chicago had formed an armed club which came to be known as *Lehr und Wehr Verein.* The attack on the workers during the great strike of 1877 by the police, the militia, and the United States Army spread the movement started by the club. Although most members of these armed groups belonged to the Socialist Labor party, the party's national executive committee denounced such organizations as giving a false picture of Socialist objectives and policies.

27 *Socialist* (Chicago), Apr. 26, 1879.

28 *Vorbote,* Nov. 17, 1883. Trans. Brewster Chamberlin.

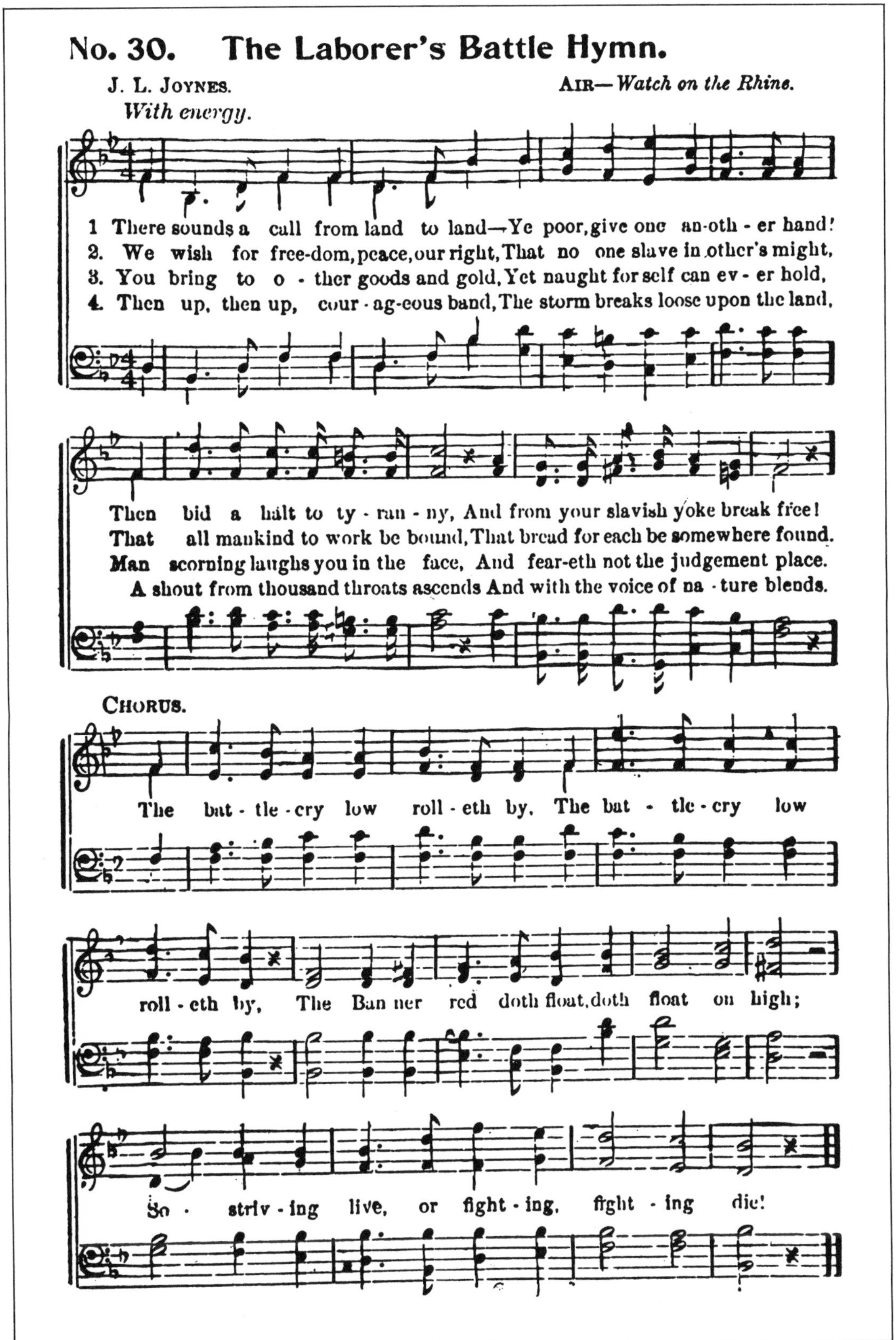

From Charles H. Kerr, *Socialist Songs with Music*, 4th ed., rev. and enl. (Chicago, 1902). Courtesy of Tamiment Library, New York University.

A shout from thousand throats assists,
And high to heaven are clenched our fists.
The battle-cry low rolleth by,
The banner red doth float on high,
So labouring live, or fighting die![29]

TO THE PROLETARIAN

Anonymous

What will become of you when you lose your strength,
When your joy of life is abated,
When your eyes weaken and your mind muddies
And the blood runs tired in your arteries—
What will become of you?

O, do not turn away your youthful head,
And do not look at me full of arrogance—
Think of the storm, which steals oak crowns.
It will touch you, too, once, and then—
What will become of you?

You lie on the ground, a broken breed,
Decayed, rotten, an obstacle to man,
And no one, even if he was aware of you,
Speaks to the question in your affliction:
What will become of me?

You worry and work. Only for your daily bread?
Does that take care of all the grief?
Crawls not once that heavy necessity
Of age with the pierced body near?
What then will become of you?

Do you believe it would be a wise decision of fate
Which sentences you to the burden of chains
In which your neighbor roots in pleasure?
And that you never have the right to ask
What will become of me?

O shake off blindness, false illusion
Which welds you in slavery to Mammon
And throw off meekness and be a man!
You have the Right, that you can ask
What will become of me?

And firmly close ranks with your brothers,
And do not listen to what betrayal says to you,
What it, in cunning and malice, thought up for you.
Head high! And boldly ask the words:
What will become of me?

An evil spirit taught you meekness
A spirit of lies for man and nature
Which dishonors you into caricature.
Destroy its traces with the question:
What will become of me?[30]

A cooperative society in Colorado, the Pioneer Group Kaweah Colony, had the following song:

OPENING SONG

"Who Would Be Free Himself Must Strike the Blow."

Dedicated to Pioneer Group Kaweah Colony

By J. J. Martin

Air—"Auld Lang Syne"

We here have now in council met,
In freedom's ranks to serve;
Our hearts and hands in union strong
No fear or threats can swerve.

For Justice is our corner stone,
And Truth, our sword and shield,
"Fraternity" our battle cry,
The World, our battle field.

To elevate humanity,
Our end and aim shall be—
To break the shackles from their limbs
And set the wage slaves free,

For Justice is our corner stone, &c.

Too long hath man upon his kind,
Inflicted wrong and pain,
And made earth's places desolate,
Where peace, and love should reign.

For Justice is our corner stone, &c.

The Age of Reason now hath dawned,
And Truth's effulgent rays
Shall lift the mists of ignorance,
And set the world ablaze.

For Justice is our corner stone, &c.[31]

The Paris Commune of 1871 was commemorated in this Socialist song:

THE SONG OF THE WORKERS

Remembering the Martyrs of Paris in 1871

By Charles E. Markham, San Francisco, Jan. 1

We drift along the streets and hear our masters in their mirth;
They've slain our friends—our martyrs—but their spirits walk the Earth.
They're moving in a silent realm of service for the race;

29*Truth*, Dec. 29, 1883. The song was published in Charles Kerr's 1902 edition of *Socialist Songs with Music* under the title "The Laborer's Battle Hymn," set to the tune of "Watch on the Rhine" and attributed to J. L. Joynes. No mention was made of its previous appearance in *Truth*.

30*Der Sozialist*, June 27, 1885. Trans. Brewster Chamberlin.

31*Labor Enquirer*, Jan. 29, 1887. The song was reprinted in Leopold Vincent, comp., *The Alliance and Labor Songster* (Winfield, Kans., 1891).

Der Sozialist.

Zentral-Organ der Sozialistischen Arbeiter-Partei von Nord-Amerika.

Herausgegeben vom National-Exekutiv-Komite.

Entered at the Post Office at New York, N. Y., as Second Class Mail Matter.

1. Jahrgang.—No. 26. New York, Samstag, 27. Juni 1885. Preis: 5 Cents.

Zweite Agitations-Nummer.

Der Sozialist. Zentral-Organ der Sozialistischen Arbeiter-Partei von Nord-Amerika.

Erscheint wöchentlich einmal und kostet per Nummer 5 Cts.; per Quartal 60 Cts.; per Jahr $2.
Kolporteure erhalten Rabatt.

Geschäfts-Lokal: No. 56 Ost 4. Straße.

Alle Beschwerden sind zu richten an die Kontroll-Kommission. Adresse: *Hugo Vogt, 56 East Fourth Street.*

An unsere Mitarbeiter und Korrespondenten! Alle Sendungen und Briefe sind zu adressiren: *DER SOZIALIST, 56 East Fourth Street, New York City.*

NB. — *Money Orders* sind zu adressiren:
DER SOZIALIST, Station D, New York City.

„Der Sozialist"

beendet mit dieser Nummer sein zweites Quartal. — Wenn auch, in Folge der schlechten Zeiten, an manchen Orten das Abonnement nicht so steht, wie es unter andern Umständen der Fall sein könnte, so kann doch die Partei mit dem Stande ihres Organs zufrieden sein.

Die jetzige feste Abonnentenzahl sichert seine Existenz.

Es muß aber noch mehr geschehen, wenn der „Sozialist" diejenige Stellung einnehmen soll, die ihm als offiziellem Partei-Organ zukommt.

Genossen! Seid daher unermüdlich thätig für die Verbreitung eures Blattes! Es wäre unser Stolz, wenn wir auf dem nächsten Kongresse einen Bericht vorlegen könnten, aus dem hervorgeht, daß die Partei mit voller Kraft für ihr Organ eingetreten ist!

Mit soz.-dem. Gruß

Das National-Exekutiv-Komite.

Bestellungen und Abonnements-Beträge für das 3. Quartal des „Sozialist" erbitten wir rechtzeitig, damit keine Unterbrechung in der Zustellung eintritt.

Die Expedition.

An den Proletarier.

Was wird aus dir, wenn deine Kraft entflieht,
Wenn deines Lebens Lust ist ausgetollt,
Wenn schwach dein Aug' und trübe dein Gemüth
Und müd' das Blut in deinen Adern rollt —
Was wird aus dir?

O, wende abseits nicht dein blühend Haupt,
Und schaue nicht voll Uebermuth mich an —
Denk' an den Sturm, der Eichenkronen raubt,
Er faßt auch dich einmal, und dann —
Was wird aus dir?

Am Boden liegst du, ein gebroch'ner Stamm,
Vermodernd, morsch, den Menschen Hinderniß,
Und Niemand selbst, wenn er dich auch vernahm,
Spricht auf die Frag' in deiner Kümmerniß:
Was wird aus mir?

Du sorgst und schaffst. Nur für des Tages Brod?
Ist damit alles Sorgen abgethan?
Kriecht einmal nicht auch jene schwere Noth
Des Alters mit dem siechen Leib heran?
Was dann mit dir?

Glaubst du, es wär' ein weiser Schicksalsschluß,
Der dich verurtheilt zu der Ketten Last,
Indeß der Nächste wühlt in dem Genuß?
Und daß du nie das Recht zu fragen hast:
Was wird aus mir?

O schütt'le ab Verblendung, falschen Wahn,
Den dir der Mammon knechtend eingepflanzt,
Und schleudre Demuth ab und sei ein Mann!
Du hast das Recht ja, daß du fragen kannst:
Was wird aus mir?

Und schließ' dich fest an deine Brüder an,
Und horche nicht, was der Verrath dir sagt,
Was er in List und Tücke dir ersann.
Das Haupt empor! Und kühn das Wort gefragt:
Was wird aus mir?!

Ein böser Geist hat Demuth dich gelehrt,
Ein Geist des Lug's für Menschen und Natur,
Der dich in dir zum Fratzenbild entehrt.
Vernichte durch die Frage seine Spur:
Was wird aus mir?

Unsere Partei besteht ganz und gar aus Demagogen.

Unter dem anrüchigen Namen, den wir hier den Mitgliedern der sozialistischen Arbeiterpartei beilegen, versteht man Leute, die das Volk politisch aufregen, um sich solche Aufregung zu ihrem Privatvortheil zu Nutz zu machen.

Zweierlei ist dabei zu merken: es gibt erstlich Demagogen im schlechten Sinne des Wortes, d. h. Leute, die das Volk zu ihrem und ihrer Herrschaft Nutzen politisch düpiren wollen, solche, denen nach Bismarck „etwas politische Heuchelei" unvermeidlich ist,

und zweitens gibt es auch Demagogen unserer Art, die das Volk heben und zur Herrschaft bringen wollen, weil das der beste, bravste, solideste und dauerndste Weg ist, sich selbst zu heben.

Auf diese zwei verschiedenen Arten müssen wir erst noch besonders hinweisen und sie zu einem Gegenstande der speziellen Auseinandersetzung machen, weil drittens ein böser Gedankenwahn durch die Köpfe geht, der eine große Zahl mit dem Krebsgeschwür der phantastischen Meinung angesteckt hat, es sei die Politik ein Feld der Interessenlosigkeit und geistigen Schwärmerei, und der eigene materielle Vortheil gehöre nicht hinein.

Auf Nüchternheit, auf nüchterne Klarheit legt die Arbeiterpartei ein großes Gewicht und muß Gewicht darauf legen, die Ideologie zu zerstören, weil sie das Mittel oder vielmehr das Loch in der Nasenwand ist, wo man bisher dem Volke einen Ring durchgesteckt und es gegängelt hat.

Die Ideologie, von der wir reden, besteht in der geringschätzigen Behandlung der realen Genüsse und der damit verbundenen übermäßigen Verehrung der Ideen, namentlich derjenigen Ideen, die sich wegen ihrer umfassenden Größe und wegen ihres unspezifizirten Inhalts zur Konfusionsmacherei besonders eignen. Es sind das die beliebten Ideen des Wahren, Guten und Schönen, des Rechts, der Freiheit und Gleichheit.

Diese schönen Dinge von ihrer realen Basis, von der Pflege des Magens und der Haut, von unserer Nahrung, Kleidung und Wohnung recht weit zu entfernen und in den siebenten Himmel zu erheben, das ist das Merkzeichen jener schlechten Demagogen, die das Volk bis dato berückt haben. Namentlich besorgen das die Pastoren und Professoren, die durchgängig in der Praxis Schlemmer und in der Theorie Ideenanbeter sind.

Die wahren Demagogen, welche die Sozialisten in's Feld schicken, belehren uns, daß nicht fernliegende Dinge, sondern die nächsten und handgreiflichsten Interessen, der wahre Jakob sind, um den es sich in der Politik handelt. Unsere Lehre muß demagogisch sein. Sie kann nicht verhehlen, daß wir nichts wissen wollen von dem duseligen unspezifizirten Allgemeinwohl, das von der eigenen Person, der eigenen Klasse, dem nächsten Bedürfniß absieht und statt dessen dem Wahren, Guten und Schönen im blauen Dunst abstrakter Allgemeinheit nachjagt.

Wir sind keine Brüder in Christo, sondern bruderliche Lohnarbeiter in der zweiten Hälfte des neunzehnten Jahrhunderts, die täglich mehr und mehr von ihren leiblichsten Interessen zusammengeschweißt werden, um dem Geschmeiß der Lohnherren, welche uns die Karre von Jahr zu Jahr tiefer in den Dreck fahren, endlich ein seeliges Ende zu bereiten.

Zu diesem materiellen Zwecke gebrauchen wir die idealen Güter, die Wahrheit und die Schönheit und Bildung. Wenn die gepriesenen Abgötter uns dazu nicht die Hand reichen wollen, mag sie die Schwerenoth holen! Eine Wahrheit, die uns nicht lehren kann, wie wir unsere Blöße decken, ein Recht, daß keine Rücksicht auf unsere fühlbarsten Bedürfnisse nimmt, eine Freiheit, die uns zu blutarmen Knechten macht, das ist keine Freiheit, kein Recht und keine Wahrheit — das ist Humbug.

Keine Egoisten dürfen wir sein; aber auch keine Phantasten, die für Andere sorgen und nicht an sich selbst denken, die von Begeisterung überfließen, wenn sie die kommenden Jahrhunderte anreden, und den Nachbar vergessen und die nächste Zeit versäumen und überstolpern. Wir sind sonderbare Kerle, die von dem Philister, der das große Wort und die Liberalität vorn im Munde, und den Eigennutz, die Beschränktheit und Kleinlichkeit im Hintersack hat, schwer verständlich sind. Wir sind egoistische Brüder und brüderliche Egoisten; wir vereinigen die Widersprüche und machen daraus das höhere Dritte: den wahren Sozialisten.

Charity begins at home, zu Haus muß man anfangen, sagt der Kleinkrämer, der auch klein angefangen und nun ein reicher Mann geworden, damit nicht wenig dick thut und wunders denkt, wie klug er ist. In seiner Einfalt glaubt er: um die Wohlthätigkeit soweit auszudehnen, wie sie der Sozialismus ausdehnt, auf die ganze Gewerkschaft, auf die ganze nationale und schließlich auch noch internationale Arbeiterklasse, da müsse ja der Mensch ein Engel werden. Deshalb will er hübsch zu Hause bleiben und seine Liebe auf Weib und Kind beschränken.

Solche Ansicht, die blind über das eigene Heil hinausfliegt und ohne Weiteres die ganze Welt umarmt, engelhaft nennen und dem Sozialismus fälschlich anhängen, ist mit rechtem Namen genannt, eine philisteriöse Bengelhaftigkeit.

Wir Proletarier dürfen nicht, jeder einzelne für sich und Gott für uns Alle, wie die Kleinbürger, mit dem Vater und der Mutter und die Kinderchen an der Hand, das Heil suchen gehen — weil die Zeit des kleinbürgerlichen Heils nun ein- für allemal vorbei und die höhere Epoche des Großbetriebs angekommen ist. Da konstituiren wir uns als Klasse und pflegen den Klassengeist, um mittels dieser klassischen Pflege aus dem persönlichen Elend heraus zur allgemeinen Menschlichkeit zu gelangen. Letztere, wenn auch „demagogisch" gescholten, ist doch weit entfernt von jenem sanguinischen „Menschenthum", welches die nebulosen Freidenker ausposaunen, wie es ihnen der Vater Uhlich vorgeblasen hat und keinen Hund hinter dem Ofen wegzulocken weiß. — Gott ja! die Freidenker und die Radikalen und Kleinbürger, Vermittler und Leisetreter sind auch gute Kerle; aber — da hilft nichts — schlechte Musiker sind es doch. Es sind keine Materialisten von der rechten Sorte, keine klassenbegeisterte Demagogen, die das Volk, klassifizirt wie es nun einmal ist, zusammenschaaren können.

Die Proletarier des neunzehnten Jahrhunderts zu Menschen machen, ist eine spezifizirte Aufgabe, welche mit Schiller'schen Versen, mit den umschlungenen Millionen und „diesen Kuß der ganzen Welt" keinen Schritt vorwärts zu bringen ist. Der Klassengeist muß das besorgen, der einer Lehre huldigt, welche die Masse ergreift, der eine Wahrheit lehrt, für die das Volk offen und empfänglich ist, die sich mit beiden Händen greifen läßt und also die Basis einer Einhelligkeit bildet, welche uns eine genügende Parteimacht geben wird, die feindliche Partei zu schlagen.

Wir sind sowenig Gegner der allgemeinen Menschlichkeit, daß gerade ihrenthalben wir den einzig praktischen Weg einschlagen, der dahinführt. Das ist der Weg der Klassenorganisation. Um denselben genau einzuhalten und alles Volk zu sammeln, das sich sammeln läßt, stellen wir den unbestrittensten Lehrsatz an die Spitze: die materiellen Güter sind und sollen die Grundlage des Geistes, der Bildung und Kultur sein.

Das ist echte Demagogie. Nur soll man uns keine schlechte unterschieben, nicht die Worte im Munde verdrehen. Weil wir die materielle Kultur zum Haupthebel machen, sollen nicht die Ideen, sondern nur die Ideologen ausgerottet werden. Aus den Ideen der Wahrheit, Schönheit und Güte bauen wir einen Triumphbogen mit der transparenten Inschrift:

„Esel bück' dich oder stoß dich."

Wer sind die Theiler?

Die Sozialisten sind Theiler, sagen unsere Gegner und die Dummköpfe; sie wollen die Güter und Reichthümer gleichmäßig unter alle Menschen vertheilen.

Dies wird gesagt, geschrieben und geglaubt. Wir aber fordern Jedermann auf, zu beweisen, ob je in einem sozialistischen Blatt, in einer sozialistischen Versammlung oder in unserem Programm solche Dinge geschrieben und gesagt wurden. Das kann Niemand, weil es eine Lüge ist.

Aber dennoch pfeifen unsere Gegner dieses Stückchen weiter, und wenn man sieht, wie viele Charlatane, Diebe und Betrüger reich werden, welchen Einfluß die Pfaffen noch besitzen, wird es Niemand verwundern zu vernehmen, daß noch Esel genug herumlaufen, um derartiges Geschwätz für baare Münze zu nehmen.

Unsere Gegner ziehen unverdrossen gegen das Gespenst der allgemeinen Theilerei zu Felde und wenden all ihren Scharfsinn daran, um dieselbe als ein Unding zu kennzeichnen; so lange das Volk im Allgemeinen sich nicht um unsere Bestrebungen bekümmert, haben sie damit natürlich auch Erfolg. Da es indessen schwer hält, die Arbeiter dazu zu bringen, unsere Schriften zu lesen, so müssen wir zuweilen die leidige Theilungsfrage separat beim Kragen nehmen, damit unsere Genossen stets frischen Stoff haben, um denen dienen zu können, welche uns die Theilerei in die Schuhe schieben wollen.

Ferne davon, die Vertheilung der Güter zu wollen, fordern die Sozialisten die Aufhebung des persönlichen Eigenthums, welches ein Ausfluß der Vertheilung der Güter ist.

Wir fordern das allgemeine Eigenthum; das will sagen: alle Produkte, Gebäude, Fabriken, Minen, Arbeitsgeräthschaften sammt dem Grund und Boden sollen der Gemeinschaft, dem Staat, gehören, damit die Güter nicht mehr zwischen Einigen vertheilt werden können, wie es jetzt der Fall ist, sondern zum Wohle aller Menschen dienen.

Heute wird ausgebeutet, geschachert und gestohlen durch die Großen, zum Nachtheil der Kleinen, und wenn diese das Ende dieser schändlichen Wirthschaft fordern, dann ruft man ihnen zu: Ihr seid Theiler!

Wir sind Theiler, weil wir den uns zukommenden Antheil an dem Ertrage unserer Arbeit verlangen und nicht haben wollen, daß solche, welche gar keine Arbeit leisten, mit uns theilen.

Wir sind Theiler, weil wir alle die Lasten, alle die Beschwerlichkeiten, alle die Gefahren der Arbeit nicht mehr allein tragen wollen, sondern verlangen, daß Diejenigen, welche fast nur den Genuß von der Arbeit haben, daran theilnehmen.

Wir sind Theiler und unser Wahlspruch ist: Alles an die Gesellschaft, Alles durch die Gesellschaft, damit den Privattheilern von heute das verderbliche Handwerk gelegt wird.

Wir sind Theiler; gab es aber je Männer, gab es je eine Partei, welche sich hartnäckiger gegen die schändliche Theilerei der jetzigen Zeit erklärten und stritten?

Wir sind Theiler und, noch einmal, wir verlangen allgemeines Eigenthum, unvertheilten Besitz.

Die Eisenbahnen sind in den meisten Ländern zum großen Theile Staatseigenthum geworden. So wollen wir es mit allen unbeweglichen Gütern, mit allen Arbeitsmitteln und selbst mit allen Arbeitsprodukten gehalten wissen.

Kann sich nun irgend Jemand etwas von diesen Eisenbahnen zueignen? Niemand.

Unter den heutigen Verhältnissen kann zwar der eine oder andere Beamte Unterschlagungen, selbst bedeutende, ausführen; in dem Staate aber, welcher auf den Grundsätzen des Sozialismus aufgebaut ist, wo der Einzelne die Garantie hat, mit seiner Familie stets in befriedigendster Weise existiren zu können, hat es für ihn keinen Zweck, sich auf unrechtmäßige Weise an dem Eigenthum der Allgemeinheit zu vergreifen.

Wie mit den Eisenbahnen, wollen wir es auch mit allen andern Gütern gehalten wissen. Sind wir nun die Theiler?

Nein, Jene sind es, welche mit dem Volke dessen unter schwerer Anstrengung geschaffenen Arbeitsertrag „theilen", ohne eine entsprechende Gegenleistung.

Da sind Fabriken, in denen tausend und mehr Menschen schaffen. Diese tausend Arbeiter bringen, nach Abzug des zu ihrem kargen Lebensunterhalt bestimmten Lohnes, einen Gewinn von Millionen auf, in den sich eine kleine Anzahl Aktionäre „theilen".

Sind wir die Theiler?

Nein, Jene sind es, und Diebe dazu, denn sie stehlen Millionen den Eigenthümern, den Arbeitenden.

Sind wir die Theiler, weil wir der schuftigen Ausbeutung ein Ende machen wollen und verlangen, daß der Ertrag der Arbeit Denjenigen zufalle, welche sie geleistet, und nicht Denjenigen, welche durch die heutige verrückte Produktionsweise, in welcher eine stete „Theilerei" vor sich geht, in die Lage versetzt sind, ihre Mitmenschen am Hungertuche zu halten?

Es giebt auch noch andere Theiler. Da habt ihr die „Schwarzen" verschiedener Schattirungen, diese ewigen Diebe und Betrüger!

Mit dem Himmel und der Hölle sind sie so freigebig, wie ein Dieb mit dem Gelde eines Andern; sie verkaufen den ersteren für einen Dollar und senden euch nach der anderen mit einer Gemächlichkeit, als sei es ein Spaß, in alle Ewigkeit mit brennendem Schwefel und Pech behandelt zu werden. Aber wagt es, an ihr Gehalt, an ihre Vorrechte, an ihren Wein und Whiskey zu gehen und von ihrem Bauch zu reden! Da wollen sie von der Theilerei nichts wissen!

Wer sind die Theiler? Wir? Nein, sondern wir führen Krieg mit den Theilern, den Kapitalisten und sonstigem Schmarotzerthum der Gesellschaft; wir wollen die Theilerei aus der Welt schaffen!

Wir sind solch verpichte Gegner jeder Theilerei, unsere ganze Literatur ist von diesem Geiste der Antitheilerei derart durchdrungen, daß es kaum glaublich erscheint, wie selbst Leute, denen man eine absichtliche Unterschiebung nicht zutrauen kann, noch auf jenem alten Steckenpferde reiten. Die Herren „Nationalökonomen" ꝛc. aber, welche ein richtiges Urtheil haben könnten, sind gleich dem Spitzbuben, welcher, von der Menge verfolgt, selbst am lautesten das Geschrei: „Haltet den Dieb!" erhebt.

Wer also nichts von der Theilerei wissen will, der komme zu uns, der trete in unsere Reihen, der stimme mit ein in den Ruf:

„Krieg den Theilern, nieder mit der Theilerei!"

Max.

From Philip S. Foner collection

Their voices now are sounding from a hush! and awful
place.

They now are calm and patient; they are for us, but can
wait;
They're moving on forever in the silent round of Fate—
Free as the winds and waters; all our earthly walls and
bars
Have crumbled into ashes; they are moving with the
stars.

We'll not forget, O comrades, how ye met the ravening
hordes—
How shone out over all the Earth the splendor of your
swords—
How they lit up all the Future, all the golden years to
be,
When men shall stand erect in God—fraternal, equal,
free.

We'll remember how ye rallied—faced the ancient wrong
in wrath—
How your swords that lie in ruins cut thro' centuries a
path,
We'll not forget your forms that loomed upon the
barricades—
Nor how ye looked from silent eyes when laid asleep
with spades.

Yours was the distant voices of the Revolution—hark!
What noise is that of hurrying feet that gather in the
dark—
The noise of pale men marshaling—look! what
tremendous form,
Looming in outer darkness, throws the shadow of the
storm?

It is the Terror marching on before the face of kings—
The light of Hope that falls upon the anvil as it rings—
The sad and haggard Spectre that begins to hush the
feast—
The Hand reached down to mortals in the furrow with
the beast,

More terrible than bugles or the roll of startled drums,
Will be their cry before us when the final battle comes,
Ring out, O voices, gather from the four winds of the
night—
Ring on as rallying music in the fearful front of fight.[32]

The Denver *Labor Enquirer* and the *Workmen's Advocate* of New Haven functioned as organs of both the Knights of Labor local assemblies and the Socialist Labor party, so that songs of the KL and socialism often appeared side by side in their pages. Here are some of the leading Socialist songs published in these papers, including a few which were reprinted from the English labor and Socialist press.

SOCIAL FREEDOM

By A. Cheesewright

Air—"Rally round the Flag"

We've gathered here together to agitate and work,
And fight for liberty and freedom;
Then shoulder to shoulder, let no one lag or shirk,
But do their duty in the cause of freedom.

Viva la humanity! Comrades hurrah!
Let it be our motto, in peace or in war;
Rally round the red flag, rally one and all;
Fight on for liberty and freedom.

The Black and Red united and climbing with a will,
Mounting the heights of Social freedom;
And we'll never get aweary until we've climbed the hill,
Shouting the cry of Social freedom.

Viva la humanity! Comrades, etc.

Our hearts are brave and true, for we know that we are
right—
Working for all and Social freedom—
And we'll never cease our shouting until we've won the
fight;
Singing the song of Social freedom.

Viva la humanity! Comrades, etc.[33]

THE LIGHT IS BREAKING

Air—"The Morning Light is Breaking"

The glorious light is breaking.
The darkness flies away,
The people are awak'ning
To see a brighter day,
From ev'ry hill and valley
Thro'out earth's wide domain,
The friends of Labor rally
To break the tyrant's chain.

The freedman's tramp is sounding,
Its echoes roll along,
By hundreds and by thousands
The people join the song.
Now joyous acclamations
Come rising on the gale;
No more with lamentations
The people will prevail.[34]

THE RED FLAG

By John P. Cosgrove

Air—"Red, White, and Blue"

O, the Red Flag, the Red Flag is flying;
Its scarlet shall flame o'er the free,

32 *Labor Enquirer*, Feb. 12, 1887.
33 Ibid., June 18, 1887.
34 Ibid., June 28, 1887.

When unfurled in dawn 'twill undying
Shed its glory o'er the land, over sea,
For the truth even now is awakening,
And 'tis dazzling men's eyes with its light;
'Tis the morning of freedom that is breaking,
Dispelling the dark clouds of night.

Then long live the Red, White and Blue!
Then long live the Red, White and Blue!
'Tis the Red Flag of Freedom that is flying,
'Tis borne by the Red, White and Blue.

See our brothers weighed down with sadness;
They are groaning 'neath never ending toil,
From their hearts has been banished the gladness,
And the robber has made them his spoil,
Shall they lie 'neath the iron heel forever?
Hark! They're calling on me and on you;
With one blow their shackles we will sever
In the name of the Red, White and Blue.

Then long live, etc.[35]

THE RED FLAG IS UNFURLED
By Arthur Cheesewright
Air—"Let the Lower Lights Be Burning"

Let us all be up and doing,
Striking hard at every wrong;
Never lagging, never shirking,
Shout the chorus loud and long.

Keep the light of reason burning,
Send its gleam around the world;
Tell the workers of all nations,
That the red flag is unfurled.

Comrades true and self-denying,
To the people bringing light;
Cowards' policy defying,
Braving everything for right.

Chorus:

Join our forces, error leaving,
Mind ye not what cowards say;
To the truth be ever cleaving,
Soon will come the light of day.

Chorus:

Keep the light of reason burning,
Send its gleam around the world;
Tell the workers of all nations
That the red flag is unfurled.

Chorus:[36]

WHEN THE REVOLUTION COMES!
Tune—"Come, Landlord, Fill the Flowing Bowl!"

Come every honest lad and lass!
Too long we've been kept under
By rusty chains of fraud and fake—
We'll snap them all asunder!

When the Revolution comes,
When the Revolution comes—
It's coming fast—our turn, at last—
The Social Revolution!

A thunderstorm of freedom shall
Go forth among the people,
Our flag shall flourish o'er the land
On every stalk and steeple!

When, etc.

The knave who lives in idleness
By plundering his neighbor,
Shall learn to use the pick and spade,
And live by honest labor!

When, etc.

That robbers' faction styled the Law
To frighten honest folk, sirs,
We'll set ablaze and fumigate,
The country with the smoke, sirs!

When, etc.

For such as contrite editors,
And penitent policemen,
We'll find nice sinecures, and say;
Go live and die in peace, men.

When, etc.

The landlord and capitalist,
If you should wish to see 'em,
You'll have to take a holiday
And search in the museum!

When, etc.

And superstition perish shall
Like flame of waxen taper;
And rank and pride and privilege
Dissolve in noxious vapor!

When, etc.

Then let us hail the coming day!
The glorious hope before us!
And with brave deeds anticipate
The good times of our chorus!

When the Revolution comes!
When the Revolution comes!
Then three cheers give off, "Long, long live
The Social Revolution!"[37]

35 Ibid., July 2, 1887.
36 Ibid., Mar. 10, 1888.
37 *London Commonweal*, reprinted in *Workmen's Advocate*, July 14, 1888. The song was later reprinted in *Socialist Songs Adapted to Familiar Tunes*, Pocket Li-

THE RED FLAG

By Alfred Ferrell

Air—"Dark Loch na Garr"

'Tis in the Red Flag true Republicans glory,
Red is the emblem of Justice and Right—
By martyr's blood dyed whose names live in story—
The victors, though fallen in Liberty's fight.
Fast flow our tears for the fettered and slaughtered,
And exiles who wander o'er valley and crag,
Too long has the earth by tyrants been tortured;
They shall crouch yet and cower before our Red Flag!

Away to the winds with the cant "moderation";
Mercy is not with king, tiger or snake;
Crush them in the dust as they've crushed each nation—
In the day of our triumph, kings tremble and quake.
"Mercy!" yes, mercy such as they gave us—
Such we'll return, and themselves will drag
From their high places all those that enslave us,
To bow, mean and abject, before our Red Flag!

"Mercy!" while Hayman riots in murder,
And tiger-like, gloats o'er the blood of mankind;
While the serfs of the Czar poor Poland encircles,
The betrayers of France Rome's chains again bind!
Sicily crushed 'neath the Bourbon lies bleeding,
And Hungary curses the Austrian rag,
The nations oppressed pray the time may be speeding
When in triumph and glory shall fly our Red Flag!

That glad time shall come, kings, though patriots you slaughter,
Fresh legions shall rise for the martyrs who fall.
Through tempest and sunshine the nations have fought for
Fair Freedom, benignant, who yet shall bless all;
We, the people, remember wrongs despots have wrought us;
Of their "divine right" not much more shall they brag;
"Moderation" is madness, experience has taught us,
When at Freedom's next summons we hoist the Red Flag![38]

THE NINETIES

Edward Bellamy's Nationalist movement gave birth to a number of songs which were published in the *Nationalist*, official organ of the Utopian Socialist movement Bellamy headed.

Songs of Brotherhood

By Allan Eastman Cross

THE BALLOT

Behold the sword the freeman wears!
Behold the brand the freeman bears!
The hilt is strong, the blade is long,
To reach and to sever the cords of wrong.

Oh, many and many a legal thong,
And many and many a civic wrong,
Shall fall in twain e'er cords of pain
Are rent from the suffering heart and brain.

For cords of custom bind our lives,
And captive Labor proudly strives
To win its worth, and free our earth,
So Life may go singing with songs of mirth.

Then seize the sword and face the foe!
Knight Roland struck no lustier blow,—
This sword hath power, did hearts not cower,
To cut as the scythe of the wind a flower;

To smite our tyrant laws and trades,
What cords may bind, what work degrades—
The sword's in hand—'tis yours—command!
And ye are the monarchs of wealth and land.

A NATIONAL HYMN

(May be sung to the tune of "America")

Thou hast ever led our people, Thou, our fathers' God!
We would tread the paths of honor that the fathers trod;
We would fight the foes of freedom till our land be free;
"One from many," consecrate us one for Liberty!

Not with foreign foe or Hessian, as in days of old,
Fight we now, but with the minions of the kings of gold;
Alien rich and Hessian poor! these have challenged Thee;
"One from many," consecrate us one for Liberty!

God of Lincoln, God of Adams, God of Washington,
Hear and heed the supplication of each loyal son!
Loose the shackle, break the bond, till the poor are free!
"One from many," consecrate us one for Liberty!

Once we shared our fight together, battled side by side,
Once we mingled tears and life-blood in a common tide;
Now in days of peace and pleasure sharers would we be;
"One from many," consecrate us one for Liberty!

Sharers of our equal birthright to the common soil,
Common sharers of the produce of our common toil,
One in wealth, in work, and leisure may we ever be!
"One from many," consecrate us one for Liberty![39]

Although anarchism received a severe blow with the Haymarket affair, *Der Anarchist* (Saint Louis) continued to publish. It carried songs

brary of Socialism, no. 10 (Chicago, 1900), with the tune given as "Yankee Doodle" and the song attributed to J. B. Glasier.

38 *London Commonweal*, reprinted in *Workmen's Advocate*, July 27, 1889.

39 *Nationalist*, Sept., 1890.

extolling anarchism, such as the following, the original of which was in German:

BATTLE SONG

By Conrad Froehlich

To battle and new struggle,
To war for the new times!
We are driven by our great
Longing for happiness—
Don't stay down there
In the cow-dung!
The drums are sounding
Swords are clashing,
The warriors are moaning,
The arrow is flying.

In every country the people
Have been crying for justice.
The priest, that pig,
Is a hypocrite,
The cowardly fobs at court
Are fawning.
Oh you busy bees
Take on arms
And give the alarm
And break your bonds!

We have waited long enough
And we've been fooled long enough.
We will no longer tolerate slavery.
A fighting force
Has been created.
The yoke is breaking;
Flee, cowards, flee!
Long live
Anarchy![40]

The vast majority of the songs of the 1890s, however, were distinctly Socialist, as distinguished from anarchist.

WORKER'S SONG

By H. Greulich

Like a spirit with fiery flames
Passes the word from land to land:
"Gather together the poor folk,
From a strong brotherly chain!"
Not from reckless striving
Comes this word of unity,
'Tis a mighty battle for life
That unites us South and North.
Whoever hears the great word
From the iron mouth of the spirit of the times
Let him enter our ranks,
Let him be welcome as a brother.

In the battle for its meager life
The people that creates everything, sighs
It must raise treasures for others—
Others only use its power.
Wife and children must starve—
Even as the man works day and night;
Because the golden sheaves of labor
Are only brought to others.
Brothers, unite full of confidence,
Give each other your hand in need—
Battle for your daily bread—
Let us build ourselves a hut.

A hut that protects us
Against the power of our masters,
A hut that supports us
When our tired body weakens.
And on its simple walls
We inscribe a new law:
"Bread for all working hands!"
"Let no man be another's servant!"
From the night of the spirit to the light,
Over the proposition of the masters in their delusions—
Unopposable in its progress
Rolls the wheel of world history.

No matter how they slander with curses and lies—
Already a pale hand writes
With powerful strokes of flames
Words of the future onto the wall
See it: "Mene, Tekel, Phares!"
Just like at the feast of Belshazar—
Like a word perennially true—
When pride is at its highest.
Undeterred by your hate,
Only strengthened by your anger,
We break with strong heart
A path for our future.

Therefore, our brothers, steadfast
To the work that lifts us up,
That striving of brotherly love
May soon pervade the entire world.
Let yourself be carried by yearning for the future,
Open wide your hearts!
Then soon the hour will strike
For a better humanity.
Tightly close your ranks!
Let the banners of your union wave,
That it may be from all heights
A battle and victory greeting of brothers.[41]

40*Der Anarchist*, June 16, 1891. Trans. Brewster Chamberlin.

41*Der Sozialist*, Feb. 21, 1891. Trans. Brewster Chamberlin.

RALLYING SONG

By Herbert Carson, Lynn

Comrades! we are all united,
One in thought and one in will,
Moving on with beacons lighted,
We shall conquer wrong and ill.

Onward, upward! On, my comrades!
In the might of Truth be true,
For our glorious cause be valiant,
Never fear to dare and do.

See, our friends are growing stronger,
More and more our host shall be,
Stand the strife a little longer,
Free our land from sea to sea.

Fear not all their learned folly
Fear not any rich man's threat;
With a cause so just and holy,
Shall we not o'ercome them yet?

Rouse to action, then, my brother,
Lend a hand in time of need,
If we will but help each other,
From our bondage we are freed.[42]

WHEN WE'RE UNITED FOR FREEDOM

By H. B. Salisbury

Air—"Marching through Georgia"

They tell us that the woods are full, they're coming right along—
The toilers of this nation—they shall sing another song,
They'll sing it as they ought to sing it, many millions strong,
When we're united for freedom.

Hurrah! Hurrah! it will bring the jubilee;
Hurrah! Hurrah! the toilers will be free;
And so we'll sing the chorus, from the mountains to the sea,
When we're united for freedom.

The ballot box contains a power no plutocrat can stay;
The toilers are uniting as they hail the happy day,
Then the reign of the oppressor, it shall vanish in dismay,
When we're united for freedom.

"These wicked social democrats will soon give up the ghost,"
So say the plutocratic press, but 'tis an idle boast,
They'll realize their impotence when soon they count our host.
When we're united for freedom.

And when we've once proclaimed the earth and all its bounties given
The inheritance of all the race who on its face have striven,
Then every willing worker shall find this earth a heaven—
When we're united for freedom.

Then shall our happy people shout, wherever they are found,
As the bounties of our common earth are leaping from the ground,
And poverty is banished from all the world around
When we're united for freedom.

O 'tis a wondrous dream of joy when toilers shall be free;
When each will have abundance, all hearts be filled with glee.
All fear of want be banished, from the mountains to the sea,
When we're united for freedom.[43]

THE NEW JUBILEE

By Andy Nesbit, Bellaire, Ohio

White slaves in the factories, we toil for our masters,
The more we produce the more they will get,
The profit goes to the Rothschilds, the Goulds and the Astors;
They're living like princes, but we—slave and sweat.
But the day is coming when the riches will perish,
And the white slaves of labor will throw off the yoke;
The morn of the commune is dawning, dispelling the night we did cherish,
When Mammon's chains of gold will be broke.

Strike, strike with the ballot for your rights, oh, ye toilers;
Strikes are a failure—at Homestead and Chicago what was our fate?
And Debs was imprisoned by the court-bribing spoilers.
If our rights we would win, workmen, we must educate.
Education is the solution of the problem of labor,
Let us study, oh, workers, and think for ourselves!
Scatter the APPEAL, and hand reform books to your neighbors,
And emancipation will come sooner—bring bread to our shelves.

Remember the White City, and Pullman, the tyrannic,
Remember our Debs who in Woodstock did languish!
Forget not the millions who're tramping, thrown out of work by the panic;
Forget not their starving babes and the fond mother's anguish!
The legislator works for god, the jurist and the preacher;
They preach not the gospel of the lowly Nazarene—

42*Coming Nation*, Jan. 27, 1894.
43Ibid., July 13, 1895.

Preaching not for the poor, but for the rich, who've the "stuff," oh, Great Teacher!
Effects of the system—but the cause must go soon, I ween.

Ere years five and twenty have passed from our vision,
The Utopia will come by poets long dreamed,
And earth shall be a paradise or bright land Elysian—
An Eden of beauty and love, as to Plato it seemed,
Crime, crime, all for the love of money; atrocities fill your daily papers;
Suicide and murder are abroad in our land.
The dude and the tramp are effects of this system that cuts such capers;
But socialism comes to deal equity with a bounteous hand.

And then shall come the jubilee!
And then the slaves shall all go free.
Hurrah, hurrah! the day is coming soon;
And pelf no more shall rule—come soon, come soon.
Hurrah! hurrah! the jubilee!
Hallelujah, hallelujah! we then shall be free,
And men can then be more like Thee,
Oh, Carpenter of Galilee!
Hurrah! hurrah! the jubilee!
Halle—hallelujah, we then shall be free.[44]

THE BATTLE SONG OF REFORM

By J. D. Steele, Los Angeles, Cal.

We are marching on to glory,
Through the darkness and the storm,
From the shades of evil hoary
To the heights with sunshine warm,
What though the way be dreary,
Our feet be bruised and torn,
Above us beaming cheery
The radiant light of morn!

We are marching on to glory,
We are marching on to glory,
We are marching on to glory,
To the light of freedom's morn.

We are marching on to glory
Where heroes trod of yore,
Where names in song and story
Are echoing evermore,
Their spirits hover o'er us,
They beckon us along,
Their voices join the chorus
Of our glorious song.

Chorus:

We are marching on to glory,
In the way our fathers trod,
Who in fields of conflict gory
With their lifeblood stained the sod,
The strife in which they perished
Is ours to wage today,
The truth they boldly cherished
Still sheds on us its ray.

Chorus:

We are marching on to glory,
Our triumph is begun,
We are marching on to glory
The fight is almost won.
The dreams of bards and sages
Our eyes shall see fulfilled
The hope of all the ages
At last shall be revealed.

Chorus:[45]

THE CRY OF THE TOILERS

By J. A. Crockett

Do you hear the cry, my brothers,
Of the toiling slaves,
Coming up from out the darkness
Of their living graves?

Of the men who, worn and weary
With the hopeless strife,
Fall, and sink, and perish, helpless,
In the noon of life?

Of the women, struggling bravely
In the homes of want,
Working till the pangs of hunger
Make them pale and gaunt?

Of the children, crying loudly
For a crust of bread?
Asking piteously their mothers
Why they are not fed?

In this bleak and dreary winter,
In the cold and rain,
They are homeless, they are naked,
Weary, sick—in pain.

Is there dearth or famine, brothers,
In our country fair?
Is the earth as poor and fruitless,
And our land so bare

That it cannot yield a harvest
Cannot furnish bread
For its toiling sons and daughters,
That they may be fed?

No, my brothers; fruitful Nature
Showers everywhere,

44 *Appeal to Reason,* May 16, 1896.
45 *Coming Nation,* Aug. 29, 1896.

All the fulness of her bounty,
And her beauty fair.

With no stinted hand she scatters
Sun and light and air,
Making field and plain and forest
Teem with riches rare.

Why, then, oh, my brothers, is it
That the toilers want,
While the ghouls of gain are reaping
Where they did not plant?

Is it not because their birthright,
God's own fruitful earth,
Has been robbed from them, His children?
That has made this dearth.

In their desolation bitter,
Have they no true friend?
Must they suffer, oh, my brothers—
Suffer without end?

Will ye heed their cry, and help them,
O! my brothers true?
Help these poor and wretched toilers?
Help them to their due?

To the rescue, oh, my brothers;
Let us strike or die!
And the God of battles guide us,
Guide us with His eye.[46]

ONWARD BROTHERS

Words by Havelock Ellis

Tune—"Silver Moonlight Winds"

Onward brothers, march still onward,
Side by side and hand in hand;
We are bound for man's true kingdom,
We are an increasing band.
Though the way seem often doubtful,
Hard the toil which we endure,
Though at times our courage falters,
Yet the promised land is sure.

Onward brothers, march still onward,
Side by side and hand in hand;
We are bound for man's true kingdom,
We are an increasing band.

Olden sages saw it dimly
And their joy to madness wrought;
Living men have gazed upon it,
Standing on the hills of thought,
All the past has done and suffered,
All the daring and the strife,
All has helped to mould the future,
Make man master of his life.

Onward brothers, etc.

Still brave deeds and kind are needed,
Noble thoughts and feelings fair;
Ye, too, must be strong and suffer,
Ye, too, have to do and dare.
Onward brothers, march still onward;
March still onward hand in hand;
Till ye see at last Man's kingdom,
Till ye reach the Promised Land.

Onward brothers, etc.[47]

BATTLE HYMN OF THE WRONGED

By Hamlin Garland

Tune—"Glory, Glory, Hallelujah"

We have seen the reaper toiling in the heat of summer sun,
We have seen his children needy when the harvesting was done,
We have seen a mighty army dying helpless one by one.
While their flag went marching on.

Glory, glory, Hallelujah,
Glory, glory, Hallelujah,
Glory, glory, Hallelujah,
While their flag went marching on.

O the army of the wretched how they swarm the city street,
We have seen them in the midnight where the Goths and Vandals meet,
We have shuddered in the darkness at the noise of their feet,
But their cause went marching on.

Glory, Glory, Hallelujah, etc.

Our slave marts are empty, human flesh no more is sold,
Where the dealer's fatal hammer wakes the clink of leaping gold,
But the slavers of the present more relentless powers hold,
Though the world goes marching on.

Glory, Glory, Hallelujah, etc.

But no longer shall the children bend above the whirling wheel,
We shall free the weary women from their bondage under steel,
In the mines and in the forest worn and helpless men shall feel,
That his cause is marching on.

Glory, Glory, Hallelujah, etc.

Then lift your eyes, ye toilers, in the desert hot and drear,

[46] Ibid., Aug. 28, 1897.
[47] *People*, Sept. 26, 1897.

Catch the cool winds from the mountains, Hark! the
river's voice is near,
Soon we'll rest beside the fountain and the dreamland
will be here,
As we go marching on.

Glory, Glory, Hallelujah, etc.[48]

WE'LL ALL HAVE ENOUGH AND TO SPARE

A Socialist Song

Written for the *People* by Peter E. Burrows

Tune—"The Red, White, and Blue"

When steam at the bidding of science,
This century's achievements began;
We thought strong old Nature's alliance
Had revoked the slave charter of man—
"That bread is the crown of endeavor,
That hope beyond that must forbear."
In the days that are coming, no, never,
For we'll all have enough and to spare.

We'll all have enough and to spare,
We'll all have enough and to spare,
From the Socialist dawn and forever,
We'll all have enough and to spare.

While labor in vision lay sleeping,
With soul looking on life's plains,
The lords of the kingdom came creeping
And bound him in wagery's chains,
Oh, who in this day will restore us?
When workers who think are so rare,
Who hope for the good time before us,
When all will have enough and to spare.

We'll all have enough and to spare,
We'll all have enough and to spare,
Oh, think of the good time before us
We'll all have enough and to spare.

And labor raised luxury's palace,
And covered with beauty its walls,
And filled the machine's master's chalice,
And lit up his banqueting halls.
But though by his skill he delighted,
And made life so wondrously fair,
He was sent to his hovel benighted
And hardly of sunshine had share.

We'll all have enough and to spare,
We'll all have enough and to spare,
With the brain and the ballot united,
We'll all have enough and to spare.

How long will ye linger, my brothers?
How long will ye labor alone?
Ye bringers of gladness to others,
When shall ye have joy of your own?
Must always your wages be sorrow?
Has labor no banner to bear?
Arise for the victory to-morrow.
When we'll all have enough and to spare.

We'll all have enough and to spare,
We'll all have enough and to spare,
Hurrah for the glorious to-morrow!
We'll all have enough and to spare.

So cast off your gloomy repining,
He misses the lark who sleeps on
Shall the Socialist day be full shining
And you not yet risen for the dawn?
Your fathers lost all while they slumbered;
But this is no time to be there
As sure as the stars are unnumbered,
We'll all have enough and to spare.

We'll all have enough and to spare,
We'll all have enough and to spare,
As sure as the stars are unnumbered,
We'll all have enough and to spare.

When hope shall have bloomed in possession,
Shall Justice with sword in her hand,
For the days of the former oppression,
Swift counting with tyrants' demand?
Ah, no! Though our faces be blighted,
Sore smitten with years of despair;
'Tis peace when the folk are united,
When we'll all have enough and to spare.

We'll all have enough and to spare,
We'll all have enough and to spare,
Farewell to the wrongs that are righted,
We'll all have enough and to spare.[49]

HOW TO BECOME RICH

Written for the *People* by a Lattimer Miner

If ye would be winners,
Ye poverty spinners,
Be meek, and obey your masters well.
Don't doubt the priest!
Or else ye'll feast
On brimstone fermented with saltpeter yeast,
And be tossed on the horns of a spear-tailed beast
Into the tropical broth of hell.

Lift never your hand
'Gainst the laws of the land.

48*Appeal to Reason*, Feb. 19, 1898. Although he was primarily the outstanding Populist literary figure, Hamlin Garland was sympathetic to the Socialist cause, as indeed were many former Populists. Garland wrote this song for the People's party; it appeared in George Henry Gibson's *Armageddon* (Lincoln, Nebr., and London, 1895, pp. 134–35) and was later taken over by the Socialists.

49*People*, May 22, 1898.

Bow in submission to things that are.
Let the rich thieves
Laugh in their sleeves,
As they pick up the statutes and turn down the leaves:
For laws were enacted for him who believes
In the justice of POVERTY, WANT AND DESPAIR.

Then, if ye are good
And are anxious for food,
They may give ye a job, now and then.
And will tell you how high
Ye will be when ye die.
In a golden paved city, far up in the sky,
With plenty of feathers and nothing to buy,
And as rich as the richest of men.[50]

OUT THEY COME

Written for the *People* by Myron Efford, Beachmont, Mass.

Nature does not produce on the one side owners of money or commodities, and on the other men possessing nothing but their own labor power.—Karl Marx

Lo, the Socialist lads are waking, hear the chantings thousand-fold.
Slaves of toil from chains are breaking, labor power no more is sold.
Now no more to market chiding,
Creeps the serf at sound of bell,
Naught expecting but a hiding,
By his labor power to sell.

Out they come from hill and valley, speaking, thinking, thoughts profound.
All the wise world swells the rally conscious of the victors crowned.
No no more in life's New Morning,
Nourishment no man shall lack,
Now no more the idler scorning,
Rides upon fair Labor's back.

Out they come from nooks and niches, hands of life, for thee and thine;
Vast emporium of riches; crowns of olive, grapes of wine.
Now no more shall bought and buyer,
To unnatural bases cling,
For the minds of men are higher
Than the merchandise they bring.

Out they march from slum and city, one grand forum of mankind;
Casting down all shame of Pity, slaves Greed no more designed.
Now no more the indolent classes,
Arrogate exclusive rights;
Now no more the half-starved masses,
Breed in anarchy of nights.

Out they come to take possession, in the ownership of lands;
Legislate, without oppression unto their collective hands.
Now no more shall purple mantles,
Stay the melody of years;
Now no more shall saintly mandrills,
Ape the form that manhood wears.

Out they come from exploitation, to a civilization NEW;
Chanting songs in exultation of the deeds now they shall do.
Now, the leisure hours beguiling,
Favorite themes of men divine;
Now the plains lie sweet and smiling,
Free this day, for thee and thine.[51]

THROW OFF THE WORKMAN'S BURDEN!

Written for the *People* by Arthur Keep, New York, with Apology to Mr. Kipling[52]

Throw off the workman's burden—
O men of every breed—
Go tell your sons of freedom
To serve your own dire need;
Wait not in heavy harness,
On bourgeois folk agape
Your longtime upper peoples
Half devil and half ape.

Throw off the workman's burden—
In patience don't abide;
The spread of cant and error
And brutal show of pride;
By open speech and simple,
One hundred times made plain,
Make clear this murderous system
Which works another's gain.

Throw off the workman's burden—
The savage wars of peace—
Fill full your mouth of famine,
And know your sickness cease;
Bring our goal one day nearer
(The end we all have sought)
Watch crime and bourgeois folly
Come on that day to naught.

Throw off the workman's burden—
The iron rules of kings,
The toil of serf and sweeper—

50Ibid., June 19, 1898.

51Ibid., Oct. 10, 1898.

52The reference is to Rudyard Kipling's poem "The White Man's Burden," an apology for British imperialism.

The tale of monstrous things,
All ports ye then shall enter,
All roads ye then shall tread,
In the glory of your living,
Long hoped for by your dead.

Throw off the workman's burden—
And reap then your reward—
The joy of men made better,
The love of those ye guard—
The cry of those ye forward
(Ah quickly!) toward the light:—
"We free ourselves from bondage—
Our long commercial night!"

Throw off the workman's burden—
Ye will not stoop to less—
Halt not but think of freedom,
Shake off your weariness.
With all your will and power,
Stand forth your share to do,
In helping into being
The time for me and you.

Throw off the workman's burden!—
Have done with slavery days—
The heartily proffered laurel,
The well earned ungrudged praise
Come soon, to prove your manhood
Through all the joyous years,
Of peace, of rest, of piety,
With no sign of crime or tears.[53]

TURN OF THE CENTURY

The following is one of the very few Socialist songs which urged black and white unity in the struggle for a new social order.

BATTLE HYMN OF THE PROLETARIAT

Written for the *People* by Stanislaus Cullen

We are lining up for battle; we are arming for the fray;
We've unsheathed the sword for action; naught can stop us, naught can stay;
Walk ye wide ye fool and fakir, give the workers right of way,
As our Class goes marching on.

Long we listened to the mouthings of the fakir and the freak;
While they preached to us submission and to turn the other cheek;
Now we're marching o'er their bodies to the battle we that seek,
As our Class goes marching on.

Arise! ye curs, and cease your fawning;
Awake, ye thieves, the Doom is yawning;
Behold! ye workers, day is dawning
As our Class goes marching on.

We have sworn to break our fetters and we've reckoned up the cost;
Life for life we'll give full measure when our firing line is crossed;
Let who lives count up the total: who has won and who has lost.
As our Class goes marching on.

Nothing stake we but our shackles, nothing lose we but our chain;
Hark! our battle-cry high swelling from the prairie to the main:
"We're the fighting proletariat with the whole wide world to gain,"
As our Class goes marching on.

Do we seek to share the plunder, are we asking to divide,
With the thieves who rob and rule us in their insolence and pride?
We will share the booty with them like the bridegroom shares his bride.
As our Class goes marching on.

All there is of art and beauty, all there is of pride and wealth,
We have wrought and carved and fashioned; yours it is by force and stealth.
We have made it and we'll have it, you can keep your gold and health.[54]
As our Class goes marching on.

What is this that makes our heart throb, we the men of every clime,
Jew and Gentile, Celt and Saxon, Black and White man in one chime?
Greater love than this has no man, this the perfect flower of Time
As our class goes marching on.

Solidarity of workers, long we sought it, firm we hold;
Nevermore shall hatred sever, never shall this fire grow cold.
In its glow the bourgeois cinders with his rule of greed and gold,
As our class goes marching on.[55]

WHEN THE GOV'NMENT MILKS THE COWS

A Socialist Jingle

A.A.H., Susanville, Calif.

Tune—"Ten Thousand Miles Away," or any other tune

Good people, I have come to bring some jollifying news;

[53]*People,* Mar. 12, 1899.
[54]Should be *wealth.*
[55]*Daily People,* July 10, 1900.

'Twill help you all to hoe your row and drive away the blues;
'Twill happen when the Socialists have settled all the rows,
When each man works and rests his share, and the gov'nment milks the cows.

When the gov'nment milks the cows, my boy, when the gov'nment milks the cows;
When each one works and rests his share, and the gov'nment milks the cows.

Then Rockefeller'll get his rest as well as sauntering Sol,
And Vanderbilt three meals a day if he does his stint like all;
No workless workers beg for bread, nor sick men's pay be stopt,
When the Socialists corral the trusts and the gov'nment gets on top.

When, etc.

When the automobiles stop and wait to carry the man with the hoe,
And Astor works three hours a day before they'll let him go;
Then the factory girl may be queen, for labor will be king
And a poor man to be senator need not consult the ring.

When, etc.

Then the white man's burden shall not be to put the natives thro'
But to give his brethren better oars to paddle their own canoe.
Then the soldier boys can stay at home and not their neighbors fleece,
For the nations all will melt their guns and smoke the pipe of peace.

When, etc.[56]

YOUR WORK, MY WORK

Words by C. H. K—Music by Rose Alice Cleveland

There's a future in store for the toilers
Who are doing the work of the world,
For the flag of the new revolution
We have raised and have gladly unfurled.

Your work, my work,
All of us working to bring the day
When the wage slaves shall be free men,
And the children shall joyfully play.

There shall be neither masters nor idlers
In the state we are striving to build,
But we all shall have work that is pleasure,
And with gladness each day will be filled.

Your work, my work,
All of us working to bring the day
When the wage slaves shall be free men,
And the children shall joyfully play.

We can hasten that day or delay it,
For 'tis coming when all the poor
Shall vote and shall struggle together,
Till they make their deliverance sure.

Your work, my work,
Work for us all to arouse the poor,
Till they stand forth in their own strength
To make their deliverance sure.[57]

MARCHING SONG

By Charles H. Kerr

Air—"Tramp, Tramp, Tramp, the Boys Are Marching"

In our poverty and toil
Lookin upon the world,
We can see the gathering armies of the Cause;
And feel ourselves a part
Of the new resistless power,
That shall sweep away oppression and its laws.

Tramp, tramp, tramp, you hear us marching,
Millions now are on the way,
And our army ne'er shall pause
Till the right to live is ours,
And the sun has risen on a fairer day.

In the shops and in the slums,
Working, suffering day by day,
We are making wealth for millionaires to hold;
But with joy we pledge our faith
To the cause of all who toil,
Till the better social order shall unfold.

Tramp, tramp, tramp, etc.

In the days that are to be
When the Cause we love is won,
We shall labor for ourselves and for our own;
Each for all and all for each,
And through many joyful years
We shall pluck the fruit that comrades brave have sown.

Tramp, tramp, tramp, etc.[58]

RALLYING SONG

By James P. Morton, Jr.

Air—"Auld Lang Syne"

Come, brothers, raise a hearty song,
To cheer us on our way;

56 *Challenge*, June 26, 1901.
57 Charles H. Kerr, comp., *Socialist Songs with Music*, 2d ed. (Chicago, 1902).
58 Ibid.

The fetters old of hate and wrong
We cast aside to-day.

In bands of Brotherhood we stand,
Determined to be free;
That love and justice hand in hand
May bring true liberty.

To all the sons of men we call,
Of every tribe and name;
The cause of each is that of all,
The hope of each the same.

In bands of Brotherhood, etc.

We need not ask another sphere,
In realms beyond the sky;
The reign of love is even here,
Behold the dawn is nigh!

In bands of Brotherhood, etc.[59]

THE LONG-HAIRED KINGS
By Charles H. Kerr
Air—"The Elephant Now Goes Round"

In the sunny land of France,
A thousand years ago,
There lived a race of warrior kings
Who were very far from slow;
They polished off the natives
In a hundred fights a year,
And the man who went against them
Found that he felt exceeding queer.
Oh, the warrior kings were great,
In the field and in the state,
And the radicals 'round
To their sorrow all found,
They were too far ahead of their date.

But the last of the warrior kings had to die,
And his son came in to rule,
And he didn't do a thing but to comb his long hair
And act like a blooming fool.
And his son's son's sons kept on that way,
And they didn't know enough to rob,
Till the rest of the warriors got tired of them
And turned them out of the job.
For the people can be stilled
While their dinner pails are filled,
But at last comes a day
When they look the other way
And their loyalty is chilled.

John D. Rockefeller is a smarter man
Than the warrior kings of old—
He takes no chances on the field of battle,
But he rules the land with gold.
He owns all the oil and the steel already
And a great university, too,
Amd all the little robbers are a-shaking in their shoes
To think what next he'll do.
And the small exploiter's dumb
Under Rockefeller's thumb,
But the Socialists smile
In their sleeves all the while,
For they know what's next to come.

The time is coming, and it's not far off,
When the people who do the work
Will run this nation to suit themselves
And not for the people who shirk.
The machinery then will belong to all,
And the land and the railroads, too,
And the labor of the people will be for themselves
And not for the profit of a few.
Do you want to see that day?
Here's the very quickest way
Cast a Socialist vote
And take off your coat
And get into the fight to stay.[60]

FOUR INFLUENTIAL SONGWRITERS

Varheit (Truth), the Yiddish-language anarchist paper of the eighties and nineties, featured many songs and ballads, a large number of which were by David Edelshtadt. Edelshtadt emigrated from Russia to the United States in 1882 and, as a worker in a Cincinnati tailor shop, experienced the exploitation of sweatshop labor. At first he voiced his anger at the misery he experienced in America with revolutionary verses in Russian, one of which was published in the *Arbeiter Freint*, the Yiddish Socialist-anarchist paper edited in London by Morris Winchevsky.[61] However, in order to communicate with the Jewish workers, Edelshtadt had to write in Yiddish, and he soon produced two of his most famous songs in that language: "In Kamf" (In battle) and "Mein Tsavoah" (The last will). Almost immediately, his verses became popular among the Yiddish immigrant workers, and they began to be featured in several New York publications, including *Varheit.* Edelshtadt became one of the most active members of the anarchist movement in this country and in 1891 was ap-

59Ibid.

60Ibid. The University referred to in st. 3, l. 6, was the University of Chicago.

61Morris Winchevsky was himself a noted working-class Yiddish poet.

No. 33. The Long-Haired Kings.

C H K. AIR—*The Elephant Now Goes Round.*

1 In the sun - ny land of France, a thou - sand years a - go, There
lived a race of war - rior kings who were ver - y far from slow; They
pol- ished off the na - tives in a hun- dred fights a year, And the
man who went a - gainst them found that he felt ex - ceed - ing queer
Oh, the war-rior kings were great, In the field and in the state, And the

The Long-Haired Kings. Concluded.

radicals 'round to their sorrow all found They were too far ahead of their date.

2. But the last of the warrior kings had to die,
   And his son came in to rule,
   And he didn't do a thing but to comb his long hair
   And act like a blooming fool.
   And his son's son's sons kept on that way,
   And they didn't know enough to rob,
   Till the rest of the warriors got tired of them
   And turned them out of the job.
   For the people can be stilled
   While their dinner pails are filled,
   But at last comes a day
   When they look the other way
   And their loyalty is chilled.

   John D. Rockefeller is a smarter man
   Than the warrior kings of old—
   He takes no chances on the field of battle,
   But he rules the land with gold.
   He owns all the oil and the steel already
   And a great university, too,
   And all the little robbers are a-shaking in their shoes
   To think what next he'll do.
   And the small exploiter's dumb
   Under Rockefeller's thumb,
   But the Socialists smile
   In their sleeves all the while,
   For they know what's next to come.

4. The time is coming, and it's not far off,
   When the people who do the work
   Will run this nation to suit themselves
   And not for the people who shirk.
   The machinery then will belong to all,
   And the land and the railroads, too,
   And the labor of the people will be for themselves
   And not for the profit of a few.
   Do you want to see that day?
   Here's the very quickest way
   Cast a Socialist vote
   And take off your coat
   And get into the fight to stay

Courtesy of Tamiment Library, New York University

pointed editor of the newly founded anarchist paper *Di Freie Arbeiterstimme.*[62]

Below are several of Edelshtadt's songs which appeared in the Yiddish anarchist press. Some of his compositions are also included in the 1972 recording *Yiddish Songs of Work and Struggle*, where they are sung in the original Yiddish.

TO THE WOMEN WORKERS

Working women, suffering women,
Women who languish at home and factory,
Why do you stand at a distance? Why don't you help
Build the temple of freedom, of human happiness?

Help us carry the red banner
Forward, through storm and dark nights.
Help us spread truth and light
Among unknowing, lonely slaves.

Help us lift the world from its filth;
Be ready, as we are, to give up what you treasure.
We'll struggle together, as mighty lions,
For freedom, equality, and our ideal.

More than once have noble women
Made the throne and his bloody hangmen tremble.
They have proven that we can entrust them
The holy flag—through the bitterest storm.[63]

AWAKE!

How long, oh how long shall your strength be sold
And a whip hang over your head?
How long shall you build the cities of gold
For those who are stealing your bread?

How long shall you stand with your eyes downcast,
Lamenting your miserable plight?
Awake! for the dawn is here at last—
Awake to your iron might!

Shackles and thrones shall be swept away
When labor takes command!
With fragrant flowers, with golden rays,
Freedom will deck the land.

And everything will blossom, and love
When freedom's May arrives!
Brothers! you've cowered long enough—
For freedom pledge your lives.

Ring bells of freedom far and near!
Assemble the slaves for war,
And fight inspired, fight without fear—
Upon your knees no more![64]

IN BATTLE

We're hated and damned and driven,
We're hounded from shore unto shore,
And all for the love we have given
To those who are hungry and poor.

We're butchered, and beaten, and branded;
They jail us again and again—
For we have sought truth, and demanded
An end to the chaining of men.

And yet we will never be frightened
By tyranny's cruel decree—
We'll work until man is enlightened
To rise up and shake himself free.

Yes, yoke us like beasts that are herded,
And drag us as long as you will—
Our bodies alone may be murdered—
Our spirit you never can kill!

Oh tyrants! you haven't the power
To kill so immortal a plant.
Its fragrant and beautiful flower
Is blooming all over the land!

Oh tyrants! although you destroy us,
New soldiers will stand in our place—
And fight for a world that is joyous,
And set free the whole human race![65]

THE LAST WILL

O comrades mine, when I am dead
Carry our banner to my grave:
The freedom-banner, flaming red
With all the blood that workers gave.

And there, the while our banner flutters,
Sing me my freedom-song again,
My "Battle Song"—that rings like fetters
Around the feet of workingmen.

And even in my grave that song,
That stormy song will reach my ears,
And for my friends enslaved so long
There, too, shall I be shedding tears.

And when I hear a cannon sound
The final siege of want and pain,
My song shall trumpet from the ground
And set the people's heart aflame![66]

62Edelshtadt joined the anarchist movement as a result of the Haymarket frame-up. For his ballad on that event, see p. 230.

63Brochure notes to *Yiddish Songs of Work and Struggle*, Jewish Students' Bund Production JS-11049. Trans. Chil Spiegel.

64*Jewish Life*, IV (Sept., 1950), 19. Trans. Aaron Kramer.

65Aaron Kramer, "Four Yiddish Proletarian Poets, III: Poems of David Edelshtadt," *Jewish Life*, IV (July, 1950), 13. Kramer prefaces these translations with a brief biographical sketch of Edelshtadt.

66Ibid., p. 14. The version of this song in the *Yiddish*

THE WORKER

The wheels whirl so quickly; machines clatter wildly;
It's dirty and hot in the shop.
The eyes become clouded with sweat and with tears
—Tears that endlessly drop.

I feel an ache in every muscle;
A heaviness lies on my breast.
My pain is so great, I can scarcely bend—
And at night I cough without rest.

The boss, like a wild beast, hurries among us;
He's driving his sheep to the stake.
Oh how long will you suffer? how long will you sleep?
Brothers of toil, awake![67]

The leading Yiddish Socialist paper during the nineties was the *Arbeiter Zeitung*, official organ of both the Socialist Labor party and the United Hebrew Trades of New York State. The paper regularly published songs and poems, especially those of the two great Jewish working-class poets, Morris Rosenfeld and Joseph Bovshover. Rosenfeld was born in Poland and came to the United States from England in 1886. In 1888 he became a contributor to the Yiddish Socialist press, and his fame as a poet spread rapidly. Working in sweatshops during the day and writing poetry and songs at night eventually took its toll, and Rosenfeld suffered a stroke which left him feeble and almost blind. We have already included several of Rosenfeld's works; here are others, which are among the best of the songs and ballads of American socialism. The songs in this section are also included in the 1972 LP *Yiddish Songs of Work and Struggle*, sung in Yiddish.

REVOLUTION

Do you know me, O you masses? Do you know my name? I teach you to love, I teach you to hate—remember me well! I help you to build, I help you to destroy—raise my flag with pride! I help to bring you freedom and equality—I am the Revolution.

I topple thrones and trample crowns like a striding giant. My spear overpowers cannons. My sweet sun rises over villages and mountains, and popes and princes fall because of me—the Revolution.

There is no equal to my wrath—but I am a tiger only to the rich. I'm tender as a child to slaves. Like a ferocious leopard, I do not spring until the final moment, when everything has been prepared by me—the Revolution.

Hear me out, you who are oppressed. Do you want to be free and happy? Then don't dream on in silence. Be a little prouder, a little bolder, put some pressure on your chains! The way to liberty is bloody—says the Revolution.

Let those who put their hope in crooked power be afraid—those who sleep and dream until the final battle. I bring naught but sharp and penetrating criticism wherever I go—that's how I'm effective, that's how I can help—the Revolution.

Blood and Knowledge then will work together—Only then can mankind hope for Liberation. So learn, consider what you have to do. For I am fervent and untamed—the Revolution.[68]

TO THE WORKER

Be proud of your labor—it gives you the right
To savor the fruits of the earth.
Be brave, be human, not a slave,
Learn your proper worth!

Your worth's beyond the price of kings.
Only Nature, your compeer,
Can properly award your toil,
Thou god of earthly spheres!

But how reward you, when the world,
Its goods, is yours to own?—
Its bread and wine, its grain and gold,
Its store of precious stones.

Take what's yours by right to take!
Be bold, base fear disdain!
Be proud, unawed! And neither make,
Nor wear, enslaving chains . . .[69]

THE TEARDROP MILLIONAIRE

My throat is not inspired to sing
In parlors rich and grand,
Nor can my voice be made to ring
At any lord's command.
I hear a worker moan in pain,
And lo! the songs awake—
And I am forced to sing again
For my poor brothers' sake.

Songs of Work and Struggle brochure appears more true to the original Yiddish. There, the third stanza reads:
And in my grave I will hear
My freedom song, my struggle song:
And even there will I shed tears
For the enslaved Gentile and Jew.

67Kramer, "Poems of David Edelshtadt," pp. 13–14.

68*Arbeiter Zeitung*, July 18, 1890. Trans. Max Rosenfeld.

69Rosenfeld, *Morris Rosenfeld*, p. 41.

And this is why I pine away,
And half-alive I linger—:
What wages can the workers pay,
What pittance to their singer?
They pay with tears for every tear—
That's all they can afford:—
I am a teardrop millionaire,
And weep upon my hoard. . .[70]

MY PLACE

Look for me not where myrtles green!
Not there, my darling, shall I be.
Where lives are lost at the machine,
That's the only place for me.

Look for me not where robins sing!
Not there, my darling, shall I be.
I am a slave where fetters ring.
That's the only place for me.

Look for me not where fountains splash!
Not there, my darling, shall I be.
Where tears are shed, where teeth are gnashed,
That's the only place for me.

And if your love for me is true,
Then at my side you'll always be,
And make my sad heart sing anew,
And make my place seem sweet to me.[71]

Joseph Bovshover was born in Russia in 1873 and journeyed to America while still quite young. He found work in the fur industry, and in protest against the conditions under which he was forced to labor, he wrote his first songs—sweatshop songs—and read them aloud to the other workers in the factory. In 1890, when but seventeen, Bovshover joined the Socialist movement, and soon his songs and poems began to appear in the Yiddish Socialist press. The songs below are among his most famous.

REVOLUTION

I come like a comet newborn, like the sun that arises at morning;
I come like the furious tempest, that follows a thunder-cloud's warning;
I come like the fiery lava, from cloud-covered mountains volcanic;
I come like a storm from the North, that the oceans awake to in panic.

I come because tyrants imagine that mankind is only their throne;
I come because Peace has been nourished by bullets and cannon alone;
I come because one world is two—and we face one another with rage;
I come because guards have been posted to keep out the Hope of the Age.

I come because tyranny planted my seed in the hot desert sand;
I come because masters have kindled my fury with every command;
I come because man cannot murder the life-giving seed in his veins;
I come because liberty cannot forever be fettered by chains.

From earliest times the oppressed have waked me and called me to lead them;
I guided them out of enslavement, and brought them to highroads of freedom;
I marched at the head of their legions, and hailed a new world at its birth;
And now I shall march with the peoples, until they unfetter the earth!

And you, all you sanctified money-bags, bandits anointed and crowned,
Your counterfeit towers of Justice and Ethics will crash to the ground;
I'll send my good sword through your hearts, that have drained the world's blood in their lust,
And smash all your crowns and your scepters, and trample them into the dust!

I'll rip off your rich purple garments, and tear them to rags and to shreds;
And never again will their glitter be able to turn people's heads;—
At last your cold world will be robbed of its proud, hypocritical glow;
For we shall dissolve it as surely as sunlight dissolves the deep snow.

I'll break down your cobweb morality, shatter the old chain of lies,
And catch all your black-hooded preachers, and choke them as though they were flies;
I'll put a quick end to your Heavens, your Gods that are deaf to all prayers;
I'll scatter your futile old Spirits, and clean up the earth and the air.

And though you may choke me and shoot me and hang me—your toil is in vain!
No dungeon, no gallows can scare me—nor will I be frightened by pain—

70 Aaron Kramer, "Four Yiddish Proletarian Poets, II: Poems of Morris Rosenfeld," *Jewish Life*, IV (June, 1950), 18.

71 *Jewish Life*, V (Apr., 1951), 25. Trans. Aaron Kramer.

Each time I'll arise from the earth, and bedeck it with weapons of doom,
Until you are finished forever, until you are dust in the tomb![72]

A SONG FOR THE PEOPLE

Lift up your eyes, oh my people: so wretchedly poor and oppressed!
Lift up your eyes to the north and the south, to the east and the west,
And look at the numberless treasures, and look at the fruit of your hands,
And see what an heirloom the earlier ages have willed to our lands!

Lift up your eyes, let them follow the ships that are laden with goods,
The smoke of the swift locomotives that race through the darkening woods,
And see how they're moving, and coming so quickly from far-away shores,
And bringing their products and wares to be bartered in far-away stores!

Lift up your eyes, and behold the great factories: heaven-ward straining,
Where workers are weaving and sewing and knitting and sawing and planing
And forging and filing and lathing and carving with skill and with speed,
And making the wares, and creating the products that people will need!

And look at the giant machines, that keep slaving from daybreak to night,
That help to amass all these riches, that make every task of ours light,
And see how the wild, mighty forces of nature are being controlled—
For Man has dug deep with his mind, and the secrets begin to unfold!

Lift up your eyes toward the flourishing, jubilant fields, and behold
The wheatstalks bowed down by their fulness, the wheatstalks of radiant gold,
And see the magnificent gardens where trees are hung heavy with fruit,
Where birds fill the quivering boughs, fill the sky with their joyous salute!

And see how all nature is ready to sweeten and brighten your lives!
And feel a compelling desire in your hearts, that arouses and drives!
Stretch forth your thin hands, and courageously join in a giant brigade—
Too long have you been the embezzled! Too long have you been the betrayed!

Lift up your eyes, oh my people! From graveyards of darkness come forth!
Lift up your eyes to the west and the east, to the south and the north,
And take the great treasures, and take what your labor deserves for a fee,
And, building—enjoy! and, enjoying—build on when the world shall be free![73]

FROM MY ALBUM

If you're trying to discover
Pearls, you do not climb a peak;
At the bottom of the ocean
You will find the gems you seek.

If you're trying to discover
Hearts whose beat is true and brave,
Do not go to see great rulers,
Go and see the simple slave.[74]

While the *People*, the *Coming Nation*, the *Appeal to Reason*, and Charles H. Kerr's *Socialist Songs with Music* tended to ignore Socialist songs published outside the particular paper or collection, each one shared a great respect for songs based on the poems of William Morris, the English Socialist poet, and each published these songs.[75] The *Coast Seamen's Journal* voiced the feeling of all workers, Socialist and non-Socialist alike, when it observed sadly in its issue of November 18, 1896: "William Morris was our best man, and he is dead." In its issue of July 8, 1900, the *People* announced it was publishing a special pamphlet, *Poems of the New Time*, by William Morris, "poet, artist, Socialist." Here are four songs by William Morris which were frequently published in the Socialist (and labor) press of the eighties and nineties, along with his "March of the Workers," which was especially popular among the Knights of Labor and the

72Aaron Kramer, "Four Yiddish Proletarian Poets, IV: Poems of Joseph Bovshover," *Jewish Life*, IV (Aug., 1950), 16. A different translation, by Joseph Leftwich, appears in *An Anthology of Revolutionary Poetry* (New York, 1929), p. 112, and is reprinted in the *Morning Freiheit*, Apr. 20, 1972.

73Kramer, "Poems of Joseph Bovshover," p. 15.

74Ibid., p. 16.

75In England the Socialist League widely distributed *Chants for Socialists*, a pamphlet of six poems by William Morris: "The Day Is Coming," "The Voice of Toil," "All for the Cause," "No Master," "The March of the Workers," and "The Message of the March Wind." The pamphlet, published in London in 1885, sold for 1d. Morris's poems, set to music, also appear in Edward Carpenter's *Chants of Labour* (London, 1891).

labor-Populists and was included in *The Labor Reform Songster.*

COME, COMRADES, COME

Tune—"Down among the Dead Men"

Come comrades, come, your glasses clink;
Up with your hands a health to drink—
The health of all that workers be,
In every land, on every sea,
And he that will this health deny,
Down among the dead men, down among the dead men;
Down, down, down, down,
Down among the dead men, let him lie.

Well done! Now drink another toast,
And pledge the gath'ring of the host—
The people armed in brain and hand,
To claim their rights in every land,
And he that will this health, etc.

There's liquor left, come, let's be kind,
And drink the rich a better mind—
That when we knock upon the door,
They may be off and say no more.
And he that will, etc.

Now, comrades, let the glass blush red;
Drink we the unforgotten dead
That did their deeds and went away
Before the bright sun brought the day.
And he that will etc.

The day! ah, friends, late grows the night,
Drink to the glimmering spark of light,
The herald of the joy to be,
The battle torch of thee and me!
And he that will, etc.

Take yet another cup in hand,
And drink in hope our little band;
Drink strife in hope while lasteth breath,
And brotherhood in life and death,
And he that will, etc.[76]

THE VOICE OF TOIL

Air—"Ye Banks and Braes"

I heard men saying, leave hope and praying,
All days shall be as all have been.
To-day and to-morrow bring fear and sorrow,
The never-ending toil between.
When earth was younger, 'midst toil and hunger,
In hope we strove, and our hands were strong;
Then great men led us, with words they fed us,
And bade us right the earthly wrong.

Go, read in story their deeds and glory,
Their names amidst the nameless dead;
Turn then from lying to us slow dying
In that good world to which they led;
Where fast and faster our iron master,
The thing we made, forever drives;
Bids us grind treasure and fashion pleasure
For other hopes and other lives.

Let dead hearts tarry, and trade and marry,
And trembling nurse their dreams of mirth,
While we, the living, our lives are giving,
To bring the bright new world to birth.
Come, shoulder to shoulder, ere earth grows older!
The cause spreads over land and sea;
Now the world shaketh, and fear awaketh,
And joy at last for thee and me.[77]

THE GOOD TIME COMING

Come hither, lads, and hearken
For a tale there is to tell,
Of the wonderful days a-coming
When all shall be better than well.

For that which the worker winneth
Shall then be his indeed,
Nor shall half be reaped for nothing
By him that sowed no seed.

Then all mine and all thine shall be ours
And no more shall any man crave
For riches that serve for nothing
But to fetter a friend for a slave.

And what wealth then shall be left us,
When none shall gather gold
To buy his friend in the market
And pinch and pine the sold?

Nay, what save the lovely city
And the little house on the hill,
And the wastes and the woodland beauty
And the happy fields we till.

And the painter's hand of wonder
And the marvelous fiddle-bow,
And the banded choirs of music,
All those that do and know.

For these shall be ours and all men's
Nor shall any lack a share
Of the toil and the gain of living
In the days when the world grows fair.[78]

ALL FOR THE CAUSE

English Air

Hear a word, a word in season, for the day is drawing
nigh,

76 *Coming Nation,* Aug. 28, 1897.

77 Charles H. Kerr, comp., *Socialist Songs,* Pocket Library of Socialism, no. 11 (Chicago, 1900).

78 Ibid.

When the Cause shall call upon us, some to live and some to die!
He that dies shall not die lonely, many an one hath gone before,
He that lives shall bear no burden heavier than the life they bore.
Nothing ancient is their story, e'en but yesterday they bled,
Youngest they of earth's beloved, last of all the valiant dead.

In the grave where tyrants thrust them, lies their labour and their pain,
But undying from their sorrow, springeth up the hope again.
Mourn not, therefore, nor lament it, that the world outlives their life;
Voice and wisdom yet they give us, making strong our hands for strife.
Some had name and fame and honor, learned they were and wise and strong;
Some were nameless, poor, unlettered, weak in all but grief and wrong.

Named and nameless all live in us; one and all they lead us yet,
Every pain to count for nothing, every sorrow to forget.
Hearken how they cry, "O happy, happy ye that ye were born
"In the sad slow night's departing, in the rising of the morn.
"Fair the crown the Cause hath for you, well to die or well to live
"Through the battle, through the tangle, peace to gain or peace to give."

Ah, it may be! Oft meseemeth, in the days that yet shall be,
When no slave of gold abideth 'twixt the breadth of sea to sea,
Oft, when men and maids are merry, ere the sunlight leaves the earth,
And they bless the day beloved all too short for all their mirth,
Some shall pause awhile and ponder on the bitter days of old,
Ere the toil and strife of battle overthrew the curse of gold.

Then 'twixt lips of loved and lover solemn thoughts of us shall rise;
We who once were fools and dreamers, then shall be the brave and wise.
There amidst the world new-builded shall our earthly deeds abide,
Though our names be all forgotten, and the tale of how we died.
Life or death then, who shall heed it, what we gain or what we lose?
Fair flies life amid the struggle, and the Cause for each shall choose.[79]

THE MARCH OF THE WORKERS
Tune—"John Brown"

What is this, the sound and rumor! what is this that all men hear,
Like the wind in hollow valleys when the storm is drawing near.
Like the rolling on of ocean in the eventide of fear!
'Tis the people marching on.
Wither go they, and whence come they? What are these of whom ye tell?
In what country are they dwelling 'twixt the gates of heaven and hell!
Are they mine or thine for money? Will they serve a master well?
Still the rumor's marching on.

Hark, the rolling of the thunder!
Lo, the sun! and lo, thereunder
Riseth wrath, and hope, and wonder,
And the host comes marching on.

Forth they come from grief and torment, on they wend toward health and mirth;
All the wide world is their dwelling, every corner of the earth.
Buy them, sell them for thy service! Try the bargain what 'tis worth.
For the days are marching on.
These are they who build thy houses, weave thy raiment, win thy wheat,
Smoothe the rugged, fill the barren, turn the bitter into sweet,
All for thee this day—and ever. What reward for them is meet?
Till the host comes marching on.

Hark the rolling, etc.

Many a hundred years, passed over, have they labored deaf and blind;
Never tidings reached their sorrow, never hope their toil might find.
Now at last they've heard and hear it, and their cry comes down the wind,
And their feet are marching on.
O ye rich men, hear and tremble! for with words the sound is rife;
"Once for you and death we labored; changed henceforth is the strife.
We are men, and we shall battle for the world of men and life;
And our host is marching on."

Hark the rolling, etc.[80]

79Ibid.
80*Workmen's Advocate,* Apr. 6, 1889.

No. 9. All for the Cause.
William Morris.
English Air.
1 Hear a word, a word in seas on, for the day is
2. In the grave where ty rants thrust them, lies their la bour
draw - ing nigh, When the Cause shall call up - on us,
and their pain, But un - dy - ing from their sor - row,
some to live and some to die! He that dies shall
spring eth up the hope a gain. Mourn not, there - fore,
p
not die lone - ly, many an one hath gone be - fore,
nor la ment it, that the world out - lives their life;
p
He that lives shall bear no bur - den heav - ier than the
Voice and wis dom yet they give us, mak-ing strong our

All for the Cause. Concluded.

f
life they bore. Noth - ing an - cient is their sto ry,
hands for strife. Some had name and fame and hon or,
e'en but yes - ter - day they bled, Young-est they of
learned they were and wise and strong; Some were name - less,
earth's be - lov ed, last of all the val - iant dead
poor, un - let - tered, weak in all but grief and wrong.

3 Named and nameless all live in us; one and all they lead us yet,
Every pain to count for nothing, every sorrow to forget.
Hearken how they cry, "O happy, happy ye that ye were born
"In the sad slow night's departing, in the rising of the morn.
"Fair the crown the Cause hath for you, well to die or well to live
"Through the battle, through the tangle, peace to gain or peace to give."

4 Ah, it may be! Oft meseemeth, in the days that yet shall be,
When no slave of gold abideth 'twixt the breadth of sea to sea,
Oft, when men and maids are merry, ere the sunlight leaves the earth,
And they bless the day beloved all too short for all their mirth,
Some shall pause awhile and ponder on the bitter days of old,
Ere the toil and strife of battle overthrew the curse of gold

5 Then 'twixt lips of loved and lover solemn thoughts of us shall rise;
We who once were fools and dreamers, then shall be the brave and wise.
There amidst the world new-builded shall our earthly deeds abide,
Though our names be al[illegible]gotten, and the tale of how we died.
Life or death then, who shall heed it, what we gain or what we lose?
Fair flies life amid the struggle, and the Cause for each shall choose

Courtesy of Tamiment Library, New York University

Bibliography

CONTEMPORARY SONGSTERS

The American Songster. Philadelphia, 1788.

The American Naval and Patriotic Songster. Baltimore, 1836.

The Blue and Gray Songster. San Francisco, 1877.

Brown, William Wells. *The Anti-Slavery Harp: Collection of Songs.* Boston, 1848.

The California Songster. San Francisco, 1855.

Carpenter, Edward. *Chants of Labour.* London, 1891.

Christy's Panorama Songster. Philadelphia, 1859.

DeWitt, R. M. *The First She Would and Then She Wouldn't Songster.* New York, 1873.

Duganne, Augustine J. H. *The Poetical Works of Augustine Duganne.* Philadelphia, 1855.

_____. *Duganne's Poetical Works.* New York, 1865.

Gibson, George Howard. *Armageddon: The Songs of the World's Workers Who Go Forth to Battle with the Kings and Captains and Mighty Men.* Lincoln, Nebr., and London, 1895.

The Homestead Strike Songster. Extra ed. New York, n.d. (Copy in Harris Collection, Brown University.)

Kerr, Charles H., comp. *Socialist Songs.* Pocket Library of Socialism, No. 11. Chicago, 1900.

_____. *Socialist Songs with Music.* Chicago, 1901.

_____. *Socialist Songs with Music.* 2d ed. Chicago, 1902.

Lawrence, Benjamin M. *George-McGlynn, Anti-Poverty Land and Labor Songs . . . Especially Prepared for the United Labor Party Campaigns.* Philadelphia, 1887. (Copy in Library of Congress.)

_____. *The National Greenback Labor Songster.* New York, 1878. (Copy in Library of Congress.)

McGovern, Michael. *Labor Lyrics and Other Poems.* Youngstown, Ohio, 1899. (Copy in Harris Collection, Brown University.)

Morris, William. *Chants for Socialists.* London, 1885.

_____. *Poems of the New Time.* New York, 1886.

Moyer, Harvey P., ed. *Songs of Socialism.* Chicago, 1905.

The National Songster. Philadelphia, 1808.

New England Songster. Boston, 1845.

The Poor Little Man and the Man in the Moon Is Looking, Love, Songster. San Francisco, n.d.

Popular National Songster. Baltimore, 1816.

Reuber, Karl. *Hymns of Labor, Remodeled from Old Songs.* Pittsburgh, 1871.

Shindler, Mary Dana. *United States Labor Greenback Song Book.* New Rochelle, N.Y., 1879. (Copy in Harris Collection, Brown University.)

Socialist Songs Adapted to Familiar Tunes. Pocket Library of Socialism, No. 10. Chicago, 1900.

Talmadge, J. D. *Labor Songs Dedicated to the Knights of Labor.* Chicago, 1888. (Copy in Library of Congress.)

Thompson, Phillips, ed. *The Labor Reform Songster.* Philadelphia, 1892. (Copy in Harris Collection, Brown University.)

Vincent, Leopold, comp. *The Alliance and Labor Songster.* Winfield, Kans., 1891. (Copy in Harris Collection, Brown University.)

Whittier, John Greenleaf. *Songs of Labor and Other Poems.* Boston, 1850.

LABOR, TRADE UNION, SOCIALIST, AND ANARCHIST PAPERS AND MAGAZINES

Alarm (Chicago)

American Federationist (Washington, D.C.)

American Socialist (Oneida, N.Y.)

American Workman (Boston)

Amerikanische Arbeiterzeitung (New York)

Der Anarchist (St. Louis)

Appeal to Reason (Girard, Kans.)

Arbeiter Freint (London)

Arbeiter-Zeitung (Chicago) (German)

Arbeiter Zeitung (New York) (Yiddish)

Awl (Lynn, Mass.)

Bakers' Journal (Paterson, N.J.)

Bee-Hive (London)

Birmingham (Ala.) *Labor Advocate*
Boston Daily Evening Voice
Boston Laborer
Boston Weekly Voice
Boycotter (New York)
Bulletin of Sovereigns of Industry (Worcester, Mass.)
Carpenter (Indianapolis)
Der Carpenter (Philadelphia)
Challenge (Los Angeles)
Champion of Labor (New York)
Cigar Maker's Official Journal (New York)
Coach Makers' International Journal (Philadelphia)
Coast Seamen's Journal (San Francisco)
Coming Nation (Girard, Kans.)
Coxey Good Roads and Non-Interest Bond Library (Massillon, Ohio) (Copy in Harris Collection, Brown University.)
Craftsman (Boston)
Daily People (New York) (followed *People*, a weekly)
Factory Girl (Exeter, N.H.) (Copy in New Hampshire Historical Society.)
Factory Girls' Album and Operatives' Advocate (Concord and Exeter, N.H.) (Copy in American Antiquarian Society.)
Factory Girl's Garland (Exeter, N.H.) (Copy in New Hampshire Historical Society.)
Factory Journal and Laborers' Advocate (Pawtucket, R.I.) (Copy in Columbia University Library.)
Fincher's Trades' Review (Philadelphia)
Di Freie Arbeiterstimme (New York)
Granite Cutters' Journal (Rockland, Maine)
Gross New Yorker Arbeiter-Zeitung
Industrial Age (Pittsburgh)
Industrial Worker (Spokane)
Irish World and Industrial Liberator (New York)
John Swinton's Paper (New York)
Journal of the Knights of Labor (Philadelphia)
Journal of United Labor (Philadelphia)
Knights of Labor (Chicago)
Labor Enquirer (Chicago and Denver)
Labor Journal (Boston)
Labor Leader (Boston)
Labor Leaf (Detroit)
Labor Reformer (Philadelphia)
Labor Standard (Paterson, N.J.)
Leather Workers' Journal (Kansas City, Mo.)
London Commonweal
Lowell (Mass.) *Working Man's Advocate*
Lynn (Mass.) *Awl and True Workingman*
Machinists' Monthly Journal (Cleveland)
Man (New York)
Mechanic (Fall River, Mass.)
Mechanics' Free Press (Philadelphia)
Miner and Artisan (St. Louis)
Miners' Journal (Pottsville, Pa.)
Miners' Magazine (Butte, Mont.)
Molders' International Journal (Troy, N.Y.)
Morning Freiheit (New York)
Nationalist (Boston)
National Laborer (Philadelphia)
National Labor Tribune (Pittsburgh)
National Trades' Union (New York)
National Workman (Boston)
New Era of Industry (Fitchburg, Lowell, and Boston, Mass.) (continuation of *Voice of Industry*)
North Star (Rochester, N.Y.) (continued as *Frederick Douglass' Paper*)
Official Journal of the Amalgamated Meat Cutters and Butcher Workmen of North America (Syracuse, N.Y.)
People (New York) (followed by *Daily People*)
Public (Chicago)
Railway Times (Chicago)
Die Reform (New York) (continuation of *Die Revolution*)
Die Republik der Arbeiter (New York)
Die Revolution (New York) (continued as *Die Reform*)
Socialist (Chicago)
Socialist (Detroit)
Socialist (New York)
Sozial Demokrat (Chicago)
Der Sozialist (New York)
Standard (New York)
Survey (New York)
Telegraph (Chicopee, Mass.)
Toiler (New York)
Truth (San Francisco)
Turn-Zeitung (New York)
Union (New York)
United Mine Workers' Journal (Columbus, Ohio)
Varheit (Chicago)
Voice of Industry (Fitchburg, Lowell, and Boston, Mass.) (continued as *New Era of Industry*)
Der Volkstribune (New York)
Vorbote (Chicago)
Woodhull & Claflin's Weekly (New York)
Working Man's Advocate (New York)
Workingman's Advocate (Chicago)
Workmen's Advocate (New York and New Haven)
Young America (New York)

GENERAL NEWSPAPERS AND MAGAZINES

Boston Evening Transcript
Boston Globe
Boston Quarterly Review
Boston Traveller
Bradstreet's (New York)
Chicago Daily Tribune
Columbian Magazine (Philadelphia)
Hartford Courant
Irish American (New York)
Lowell (Mass.) *Offering*
National Anti-Slavery Standard (New York)
Newark (N.J.) *Chronicle*

Newark (N.J.) *Eagle*
New York Copperhead
New York Courier and Enquirer
New York Daily Advertiser
New York Gazette
New York Herald
New York Journal
New York Sun
New York Times
New York World
Paterson (N.J.) *Courier*
Paterson (N.J.) *Morning Call*
Pennsylvania Gazette (Philadelphia)
Pennsylvania Packet (Philadelphia)
Philadelphia Aurora
Post (Pittsburgh)
Reporter (Lynn, Mass.)
Republican Watch-Tower (New York)
Springfield (Mass.) *Republican*
Subterranean (New York)
Tribune (New York)
Weekly Pelican (New Orleans)

OTHER PUBLICATIONS TREATING LABOR SONGS AND BALLADS

Balch, Elizabeth. "Songs for Labor." *Survey*, XXXI (Jan. 3, 1914), 408–12, 422–28.

"Ballads of Mine Regions Depict Life of the Workers." *New York World*, Sept. 11, 1927.

Barry, Phillips. "The Factory Girl's Come-All-Ye." *Bulletin of the Folk-Song Society of the Northeast*, II (1931), 12.

Barton, William E. *Old Plantation Hymns.* Boston, New York, and London, 1899.

Beck, Earl Clifton. *Songs of the Michigan Lumberjacks.* Ann Arbor, 1941.

Belden, H. M. *Ballads and Songs Collected by the Missouri Folk-Lore Society.* 2d ed. 1955. Reprint. Columbia, Mo., 1973.

Bontemps, Arna, and Jack Conroy. *They Seek a City.* New York, 1945.

Botkin, Benjamin A. *Lay My Burden Down: A Folk History of Slavery.* Chicago, 1945.

Bradford, Sarah E. *Scenes in the Life of Harriet Tubman.* Auburn, N.Y., 1869.

Brown, William Wells. *Narrative of William Wells Brown: A Fugitive Slave, Written by Himself.* Boston, 1847.

Browne, C. A. *The Story of Our National Ballads.* New York, 1919.

Burleigh, Harry Thacker. *Negro Folk Songs.* New York, 1921.

Cable, George W. "Creole Slave Songs." *Century Magazine*, XXXI (Apr., 1886), 807–28.

Carey, George. "Songs of Jack Tar in the Darbies." *Journal of American Folklore*, LXXXV (Apr.–June, 1972), 167–80.

Challinem, Raymond. *The Lancashire and Cheshire Miners.* Newcastle upon Tyne, 1972.

Coffin, Tristram Potter, and Hennig Cohen, eds. *Folklore from the Working Folk of America.* New York, 1973.

Cohen, Hennig. "Caroline Gilman and Negro Boatmen's Songs." *Southern Folklore Quarterly*, XIX (June, 1956), 116–17.

Colcord, Joanne C. *Songs of American Sailormen.* New York, 1938.

Conrad, Earl. *Harriet Tubman.* Washington, D.C., 1943.

Devine, George John. "American Songsters, 1806–1815." B.A. thesis, Brown University, 1936.

Dolph, Edward Arthur. "Ballads That Have Influenced Ballots." *New York Times Magazine*, Oct. 16, 1932.

Douglass, Frederick. *Life and Times of Frederick Douglass.* 1881. Reprint. New York, 1962.

_____. *My Bondage and My Freedom.* 1855. Reprint. New York, 1970.

_____. *Narrative of the Life of Frederick Douglass.* 1845. Reprint. Cambridge, Mass., 1960.

Du Bois, W. E. B. *The Souls of Black Folk.* Chicago, 1903.

Emrich, Duncan. "Songs of the Western Miners." *California Folklore Quarterly*, I (July, 1942), 213–32.

Evanson, Jacob A. "Folk Songs of an Industrial City." In *Pennsylvania Songs and Legends*, ed. George Korson, pp. 423–66. Philadelphia, 1949.

Federal Music Project. *Folk Songs from East Kentucky.* Works Progress Administration, ca. 1939.

Federal Writers' Project. *Cowboy Songs.* Ed. R. D. Carlson. Nebraska Folklore Pamphlets, no. 11. Lincoln, 1938.

_____. *Farmers' Alliance Songs of the 1890's.* Nebraska Folklore Pamphlets, no. 18. Lincoln, 1938.

_____. *More Farmers' Alliance Songs of the 1890's.* Nebraska Folklore Pamphlets, no. 20. Lincoln, 1939.

_____. *Nebraska Farmers' Alliance Songs of the 1890's.* Nebraska Folklore Pamphlets, no. 19. Lincoln, 1939.

Foner, Philip S. "Songs of the Eight-Hour Movement." *Labor History*, XIII (Fall, 1972), 571–88.

Gardner, Emelyn Elizabeth, and Geraldine Jencks Chickering. *Ballads and Songs of Southern Michigan.* Ann Arbor, 1939.

Gellert, Lawrence. *Negro Songs of Protest.* New York, 1936.

Gilman, Caroline Howard. *Recollections of a Southern Matron.* New York, 1838.

Gordon, Robert Winslow. *Folk Songs of America.* New York, 1938.

Gray, Roland Palmer. *Songs and Ballads of the Maine Lumberjacks.* Cambridge, Mass., 1924.

Green, Archie. *Only a Miner: Studies in Recorded Coal-Mining Songs.* Urbana, Ill., 1972.

Greenway, John. *American Folksongs of Protest.* Philadelphia, 1953.

———, ed. *Folklore of the Great West.* Palo Alto, Calif., 1968.

Hand, Wayland D. "The Folklore, Customs, and Traditions of the Butte Miner." *California Folklore Quarterly*, V (Jan. and Apr., 1946), 1–25, 153–78.

———, Charles Cutts, Robert C. Wylder, and Betty Wylder. "Songs of the Butte Miner." *Western Folklore*, IX (Jan., 1950), 1–49.

Higgenson, Thomas Wentworth. *Army Life in a Black Regiment.* Boston, 1882.

Hubbell, Jay B. "Negro Boatmen's Songs." *Southern Folklore Quarterly*, XVIII (Dec., 1954), 244–45.

Hungerford, James. *The Old Plantation and What I Gathered There in an Autumn Month [of 1832].* New York, 1859.

Johnson, James Weldon, and Rosamond J. Johnson. *The Books of American Negro Spirituals.* 2 vols. in 1. New York, 1940.

Korson, George. *Black Land: The Way of Life in the Coal Fields.* Evanston, 1941.

———. *Black Rock: Mining Folklore of the Pennsylvania Dutch.* Baltimore, 1960.

———. *Coal Dust on the Fiddle: Songs and Stories of the Bituminous Industry.* 1943. Reprint. Hatboro, Pa., 1965.

———. *Minstrels of the Mine Patch: Songs and Stories of the Anthracite Industry.* 1938. Reprint. Hatboro, Pa., 1964.

———. *Songs and Ballads of the Anthracite Miner.* New York, 1927.

———. ed. *Pennsylvania Songs and Legends.* Philadelphia, 1949.

Kramer, Aaron. "Four Yiddish Proletarian Poets, II: Poems of Morris Rosenfeld." *Jewish Life*, IV (June, 1950), 16–19.

———. "Four Yiddish Proletarian Poets, III: Poems of David Edelshtadt." *Jewish Life*, IV (July, 1950), 12–14.

———. "Four Yiddish Proletarian Poets, IV: Poems of Joseph Bovshover." *Jewish Life*, IV (Aug., 1950), 14–16.

Krehbiel, Henry Edward. *Afro-American Folksongs.* New York, 1914.

Laurie, Bruce Gordon. "The Working People of Philadelphia, 1827–1853." Ph.D. thesis, University of Pittsburgh, 1971.

Leach, MacEdward and Henry Glassie. *A Guide for Collectors of Oral Traditions and Folk Culture Material in Pennsylvania.* Harrisburg, 1968.

Leftwich, Joseph, comp. *An Anthology of Revolutionary Poetry.* New York, 1929.

Lengyel, Cornel, ed. *A San Francisco Songster, 1849–1939.* Works Progress Administration, History of Music Project, History of Music in San Francisco Series. Vol. II. San Francisco, 1939.

Levine, Lawrence W., and Robert Middlekauf, eds. *The National Temper: Readings in American Culture and Society.* New York, 1972.

Lewis, Arthur A. "American Songsters 1800–1805." Ph.D. thesis, Brown University, 1932.

Lewis, Roman, ed. *Der gesezlicher Mord in Chicago fun 11 November 1887.* New York, 1889.

Library of Congress, Music Division. *Check-List of Recorded Songs in the English Language in the Archive of American Folk Song to July, 1940.* Washington, D.C., 1942.

Lloyd, A. L. *The Singing Englishman: An Introduction to Folksong.* London, [1944].

Locke, Allan Le Roy. *The Negro and His Music.* Washington, D.C., 1939.

Lomax, Alan, and Sidney Robertson Cowell. *American Folk Songs and Folk Lore: A Regional Bibliography.* New York, 1942.

Lomax, John A. "Some Types of American Folksong." *Journal of American Folklore*, XXVIII (1915), 48–64.

Lovell, John, Jr. "The Social Significance of the Negro Spiritual." *Journal of Negro Education*, VIII (Oct., 1939), 634–43.

Lyell, Charles. *A Second Visit to the United States.* Vol. I. New York, 1849.

Marsh, J.B.T. *The Story of the Jubilee Singers.* Boston, 1880.

Miller, John. "Songs of the Labour Movement." In *The Luddites and Other Essays*, ed. Lionel M. Munby, pp. 115–42. London, 1971.

Miner, Louie M. *Our Rude Forefathers: American Political Verse 1783–1788.* Cedar Rapids, Iowa, 1937.

Moore, Leroy, Jr. "The Spiritual: Soul of Black Religion." *American Quarterly*, XXIII (Dec., 1971), 658–76.

Narrative of Sojourner Truth. Battle Creek, Mich., 1884.

Nettl, Bruno. *An Introduction to Folk Music in the United States.* Rev. ed. Detroit, 1962.

New Songs for Butte Mining Camp. Butte, Mont., n.d.

Odum, Howard W. *Negro Workaday Songs.* Chapel Hill, N.C., 1926.

———, and Guy B. Johnson. *The Negro and His Songs.* Chapel Hill, N.C., 1925.

Patterson, Cecil Lloyd. "A Different Drum: The Image of the Negro in Nineteenth Century Popular Song Books." Ph.D. thesis, University of Pennsylvania, 1961.

Pound, Louise. *American Ballads and Songs.* New York, 1922.

Ramus, Pierre. *Der Justizmord von Chicago: Zum Angedenken 11. November 1887.* Vienna, 1922.

Rosenfeld, Morris. *Morris Rosenfeld: Selections from His Poetry and Prose.* Ed. Itche Goldberg and Max Rosenfeld. New York, 1964.

———. *Poems of Morris Rosenfeld.* Ed. and trans. Aaron Kramer. New York, 1955.

———. *Songs of Labor, and Other Poems.* Trans. Rose Pastor Stokes and Helena Frank. Boston, 1914.

———. *The Teardrop Millionaire, and Other Poems.* Se-

lected and trans. Aaron Kramer. New York, 1955.
Rubin, Ruth. "Yiddish Folksongs." *New York Folklore Quarterly*, II (Winter, 1946), 15–23.
Sandburg, Carl. *The American Songbag.* New York, 1927.
Scheips, Paul J. *Hold the Fort! The Story of a Song from the Sawdust Trail to the Picket Line.* Smithsonian Studies in History and Technology, no. 9. Washington, D.C., 1971.
Siegmeister, Elie. *Songs of Early America, 1620–1830.* New York, 1944.
Southern, Eileen. *The Music of Black Americans: A History.* New York, 1971.
Spaeth, Sigmund. *Weep Some More, My Lady.* Garden City, N.Y., 1948.
Stegner, S. Page. "Protest Songs from the Butte Mines." *Western Folklore*, XXVII (July, 1967), 157–67.
Tatham, David. *The Lure of the Striped Pig: The Illustration of Popular Music in America.* Barre, Mass., 1973.
Ward, Harry F. "Songs of Discontent." *Methodist Review*, Sept., 1913, pp. 720–29.
Ward, Robert David, and William Warren Rogers. *Labor Revolt in Alabama: The Great Strike of 1894.* University, Ala., 1965.
Welsch, Roger L. *Treasury of Nebraska Pioneer Folklore.* Lincoln, 1966.
White, Newman I. *American Negro Folk-Songs.* 1928. Reprint. Hatboro, Pa., 1965.
Williams, Charlotte Fisher. "American Issues (1865–1900) as Expressed in the Songs of the People." M.A. thesis, Columbia University, 1942.
Work, John Wesley. *Folk Songs of the American Negro.* Nashville, 1915.
Yiddish Songs of Work and Struggle. Jewish Students' Bund Production JS-11049. New York, 1972.

LABOR ORGANIZATIONS, POLITICAL ACTION, SOCIALISM, STRIKES, LABOR CONDITIONS

Abramowitz, Jack. "The Negro in the Populist Movement." *Journal of Negro History*, XXXVIII (July, 1953), 257–89.
Abrams, Ray H. "Copperhead Newspapers and the Negro." *Journal of Negro History*, XX (Apr., 1935), 131–52.
Adamic, Louis. *Dynamite—The Story of Class Warfare in America.* New York, 1931.
Allen, James S. *Reconstruction: The Battle for Democracy.* New York, 1937.
Allen, Ruth A. *The Great Southwestern Strike.* Austin, 1942.
Apgar, W. E. "New York's Contribution to the War Effort of 1812." *New York Historical Society Quarterly Bulletin*, XXIX (Oct., 1945), 203–12.
Aptheker, Herbert. *American Negro Slave Revolts.* New York, 1943.
——. "American Negro Slave Revolts." *Science & Society*, I (Summer, 1957), 512–16.
——, ed. *A Documentary History of the Negro People in the United States.* New York, 1951.
Aurand, Harold W. "The Anthracite Strike of 1887–88." *Pennsylvania History*, XXXV (Apr., 1968), 169–85.
——. "The Workingmen's Benevolent Association." *Labor History*, VII (Winter, 1966), 19–34.
Aveling, Edward, and Eleanor Marx Aveling. *The Working Class in America.* London, 1891.
Bauer, Raymond A., and Alice H. Bauer. "Day-to-Day Resistance to Slavery." *Journal of Negro History*, XXVII (Oct., 1942), 388–419.
Bellamy, Ralph. *Looking Backward.* Boston, 1888.
Bernstein, Leonard. "The Working People of Philadelphia from Colonial Times to the General Strike of 1835." *Pennsylvania Magazine of History and Biography*, LXXIV (July, 1950), 322–39.
Bestor, Arthur E., Jr. "American Phalanxes." Ph.D. thesis, Yale University, 1938.
Bimba, Anthony. *The Molly Maguires.* New York, 1932.
Bower, Robert T. "Note on 'Did Labor Support Jackson?: The Boston Story.' " *Political Science Quarterly*, LXV (Sept., 1950), 441–44.
Boyer, Richard O., and Herbert M. Morais. *Labor's Untold Story.* New York, 1955.
Bridenbaugh, Carl. *The Colonial Craftsman.* New York and London, 1950.
Buchanan, Joseph R. *The Story of a Labor Agitator.* New York, 1903.
Burgin, E. *History of the Jewish Labor Movement.* New York, 1915.
Butler, Benjamin F. *Butler's Book.* Boston, 1892.
Byrdsall, Fitzwilliam. *The History of the Loco-Foco, or Equal Rights Party, Its Movements, Conventions, and Proceedings.* New York, 1842.
Cahill, Marion C. *Shorter Hours: A Study of the Movement since the Civil War.* New York, 1932.
Cale, Edgar Barclay. *The Organization of Labor in Philadelphia, 1850–1870.* Philadelphia, 1940.
Calmer, Alan. *Labor Agitator: The Story of Albert R. Parsons.* New York, 1937.
Coleman, James Walter. *The Molly Maguire Riots: Industrial Conflict in the Pennsylvania Coal Regions.* Pub. in 1936 as *Labor Disturbances in Pennsylvania, 1850–1880.* Reprint. New York, 1969.
Commons, John R. "American Shoemakers, 1648–1895: A Sketch of Industrial Evolution." *Quarterly Journal of Economics*, XXIV (Nov., 1909), 39–83.
——, David J. Saposs, Helen Sumner, et al. *History of Labour in the United States.* Vol. I. New York, 1918.
——, Ulrich B. Phillips, Eugene A. Gilmore, et al., eds. *A Documentary History of American Industrial Society.* Vol. VI. Cleveland, 1910.
Cooper, Lyle W. "Organized Labor and the Trust." *Journal of Political Economy*, XXXVI (1928), 720–39.
Darling, Arthur B. "The Workingmen's Party of Massa-

chusetts, 1833–1834." *American Historical Review,* XXIX (Oct., 1923), 81–86.

David, Henry. *History of the Haymarket Affair.* New York, 1936.

Davidson, Philip. *Propaganda and the American Revolution, 1763–1783.* Chapel Hill, N.C., 1941.

Debs, Eugene V. *His Life, Writings, and Speeches.* New York, 1920.

Destler, Charles McArthur. *American Radicalism, 1865–1901.* New London, Conn., 1946.

Ebert, Justus. *American Industrial Evolution.* New York, 1907.

Edwards, George W. "New York Politics before the American Revolution." *Political Science Quarterly,* XXXVI (Dec., 1921), 586–602.

Ely, Richard T. *The Labor Movement in America.* New York, 1886.

Ernst, Robert. *Immigrant Life in New York City, 1825–1863.* New York, 1949.

Evans, Chris. *History of the United Mine Workers of America.* Vol. I. Indianapolis, 1918.

Evans, George Henry. "History of the Origin and Progress of the Working Men's Party in New York." *Radical,* II (1842), 30–35.

Famous Speeches of the Eight Chicago Anarchists in Court. Chicago, 1910.

Feder, Leah H. *Unemployment Relief in Periods of Depression.* New York, 1936.

Feins, D. M. "Labor's Role in the Populist Movement, 1890–1896." M.A. thesis, Columbia University, 1939.

Fine, Nathan. *Labor and Farmer Parties in the United States.* New York, 1928.

Fine, Sidney. "The Eight-Hour Movement in the United States, 1888–1891." *Mississippi Valley Historical Review,* XL (Dec., 1953), 441–62.

Fitch, John A. *The Steel Workers.* New York, 1911.

Flower, Edward. "Anti-Semitism in the Free Silver and Populist Movement and the Election of 1896." M.A. thesis, Columbia University, 1952.

Foner, Philip S. *History of the Labor Movement in the United States.* Vols. I and II. New York, 1947 and 1955.

——. "Journal of an Early Labor Organizer." *Labor History,* X (Spring, 1969), 205–27.

——. *The Life and Writings of Frederick Douglass.* 4 vols. New York, 1950–52.

——. *Organized Labor and the Black Worker, 1619–1973.* New York, 1974.

——. "Samuel Gompers to Frederick Engels: A Letter." *Labor History,* II (Spring, 1970), 207–11.

——, ed. *Abraham Lincoln: Selections from His Writings.* New York, 1944.

——, ed. *The Autobiographies of the Haymarket Martyrs.* New York, 1969.

——, ed. *The Complete Writings of Thomas Paine.* 2 vols. New York, 1945.

Ford, Paul L., ed. *The Writings of Thomas Jefferson.* Vol. VII. New York, 1896.

Frumerman, Harry. "The Railroad Strikes of 1885–86." *Marxist Quarterly,* I (Oct.–Dec., 1937), 394–405.

Galster, August E. *The Labor Movement in the Shoe Industry.* New York, 1924.

Garlin, Sender. "The Challenge of John Swinton." *Masses & Mainstream,* Dec., 1951, pp. 34–39.

Geines, Maude A. "The Influence of the Labor Element in the Populist Party." M.A. thesis, University of Minnesota, 1924.

Gemkow, Heinrich. *Karl Marx: A Biography.* Dresden, 1968.

George, Henry. *Progress and Poverty.* New York, 1879.

——. *The Single Tax.* Chicago, 1887.

Ginger, Ray. *The Bending Cross: A Biography of Eugene V. Debs.* New Brunswick, N.J., 1949.

Gompers, Samuel. *Seventy Years of Life and Labor.* Vol. I. New York, 1925.

Grossman, Jonathan. *William Sylvis, Pioneer of American Labor.* New York, 1945.

Hammond, Bray. *Banks and Politics in America from the Revolution to the Civil War.* Princeton, N.J., 1957.

Handlin, Oscar. "American Views of the Jew at the Opening of the Twentieth Century." *Publications of the American Jewish Historical Society,* LX (June, 1951), 323–44.

Haynes, Fred E. *Third Party Movements since the Civil War.* Iowa City, 1916.

Haywood, William D. *Bill Haywood's Book: The Autobiography of William D. Haywood.* New York, 1929.

Hicks, John D. *The Populist Revolt.* Minneapolis, 1931.

Higham, John. "Anti-Semitism in the Gilded Age: A Reinterpretation." *Mississippi Valley Historical Review,* XLIII (Mar., 1957), 559–78.

Hofstadter, Richard. *The Age of Reform: From Bryan to F.D.R.* New York, 1956.

Hogg, J. Bernard. "The Homestead Strike of 1892." Ph.D. thesis, University of Chicago, 1943.

Huggins, Walter. *Jacksonian Democracy and the Working Class.* Stanford, 1960.

Jackson, Sidney L. *America's Struggle for Free Schools, 1827–1842.* Washington, D.C., 1941.

Jenson, Vernon H. *Heritage of Conflict: Labor Relations in the Nonferrous Metals Industry up to 1930.* Ithaca, N.Y., 1950.

Josephson, Hannah. *The Golden Threads: New England Mill Girls and Magnates.* New York, 1944.

Kauer, Ralph. "The Workingmen's Party of the United States." *Pacific Historical Review,* XIII (Sept., 1944), 278–91.

Kemmerer, Donald L., and Edward Wickersham. "Reasons for the Growth of the Knights of Labor in 1885–1886." *Industrial and Labor Review,* III (Jan., 1950), 213–20.

Kessler, Sidney H. "The Organization of Negroes in the Knights of Labor." *Journal of Negro History,* XXXVII (July, 1952), 245–76.

King, Dan. *Life and Times of Thomas Wilson Dorr.* Boston, 1859.

Klotsche, J. Martin. "The United Front Populists." *Wisconsin Magazine of History*, XX (June, 1937), 375–89.

Koht, Halvdan. *The American Spirit in Europe, A Survey of Transatlantic Influences.* Philadelphia, 1949.

Larcom, Lucy. *A New England Girlhood.* Boston, 1889.

Lemisch, Jesse, and John K. Alexander. "The White Oaks, Jack Tar, and the Concept of the 'Inarticulate.'" *William and Mary Quarterly*, XXIX (Jan., 1972), 109–42.

Lescohier, Don D. *The Knights of St. Crispen, 1867–1874.* Madison, Wisc., 1910.

Libby, O. G. "A Study of the Greenback Movement, 1876–1884." *Transactions of the Wisconsin Academy of Sciences, Arts and Letters*, XLI (1899), 370–418.

Life of Albert R. Parsons. Chicago, 1903.

Lindsey, Almont. "Paternalism and the Pullman Strike." *American Historical Review*, XLIV (Jan., 1939), 272–89.

_____. *The Pullman Strike.* Chicago, 1942.

Link, Eugene P. *Democratic-Republican Societies, 1790–1800.* New York, 1942.

Lloyd, Henry Demarest. "The Populists at St. Louis." *Review of Reviews*, XIV (Sept., 1896), 298–303.

Lorwin, Lewis L. *The American Federation of Labor: History, Policies, and Practices.* Washington, D.C., 1933.

McKee, Samuel, Jr. *Labor in Colonial New York, 1664–1776.* New York, 1935.

McMurry, Donald L. *Coxey's Army: A Study of the Industrial Army Movement of 1894.* Boston, 1929.

Mandel, Bernard. *Samuel Gompers.* Yellow Springs, Ohio, 1963.

Martin, Roscoe C. *The People's Party in Texas: A Study in Third Party Politics.* University of Texas Bulletin No. 3308. Bureau of Research in the Social Sciences No. 4. Austin, 1933.

Mittleman, Edward B. "Chicago Labor in Politics, 1877–1896." *Journal of Political Economy*, XXVIII (May, 1920), 407–27.

Montgomery, David. *Beyond Equality: Labor and the Radical Republicans, 1862–1872.* New York, 1967.

Moore, R. Laurence. *European Socialists and the American Promised Land.* New York, 1970.

Morais, Herbert M. "Artisan Democracy and the American Revolution." *Science & Society*, VI (Summer, 1952), 227–48.

Morris, Richard B. *Government and Labor in Early America.* New York, 1946.

Morris, William. *A Dream of John Ball.* London, 1888.

Mowry, Arthur M. *The Dorr's War.* Providence, R.I., 1901.

Nelles, Walter. "The First American Labor Case." *Yale Law Journal*, XLI (Dec., 1931), 165–200.

New York Public Library. Scrapbooks of clippings relating to strikes, lockouts, etc., in the United States, 1887–1888.

Nicolay, John G., and John Hay, eds. *Complete Works of Abraham Lincoln.* Vol. V. New York, 1905.

Niselson, Alex J. "The Henry George Campaign in the New York City Mayoralty Election, 1886." M.A. thesis, Columbia University, 1950.

Noyes, John Humphrey. *History of American Socialism.* Philadelphia, 1870.

Nugent, Walter. *The Tolerant Populists: Kansas Populism and Nativism.* Chicago, 1963.

Obermann, Karl. *Joseph Weydemeyer, Pioneer of American Socialism.* New York, 1947.

Pessen, Edward. "Did Labor Support Jackson?: The Boston Story." *Political Science Quarterly*, LXIV (June, 1949), 262–74.

Pinkowski, Edward. *John Siney, the Miners' Martyr.* Philadelphia, 1963.

Pinson, Koppel S. *Modern Germany: Its History and Civilization.* New York, 1954.

Pollack, Norman. "The Myth of Populist Anti-Semitism." *American Historical Review*, LXVIII (Oct., 1962), 76–80.

_____. *The Populist Response to Industrial America: Midwestern Populist Thought.* Cambridge, Mass., 1962.

Post, Louis R., and Fred C. Leubscher. *An Account of the George-Hewitt Campaign in the New York Municipal Election.* New York, 1887.

Powderly, Terence V. *The Path I Trod.* New York, 1940.

_____. *Thirty Years of Labor, 1859–1889.* Columbus, Ohio, 1889.

Rae, John B. "The Great Suffrage Parade." *Rhode Island History*, I (July, 1942), 114–29.

Rawick, George P. *The American Slave: A Composite Autobiography.* Westport, Conn., 1972.

Rayback, Joseph G. *A History of American Labor.* New York, 1959.

Revelations: The Epistle of Nathan the Wise. N.p., 1878.

Rezneck, Samuel. "The Depression of 1819–1822: A Social History." *American Historical Review*, XXXIX (Oct., 1933), 28–47.

_____. "The Social History of an American Depression, 1837–1843." *American Historical Review*, XL (July, 1935), 662–87.

Roberts, Peter. *Anthracite Coal Communities.* New York, 1904.

Robinson, Harriet H. *Loom and Spindle.* New York and Boston, 1898.

Robinson, Jesse S. *The Amalgamated Association of Iron, Steel and Tin Workers.* Baltimore, 1922.

Rowan, R. W. *The Pinkertons, A Detective Dynasty.* Boston, 1931.

Rowe, D. J. "A Trade Union of North-East Coast Seamen in 1825." *Economic History Review*, XXV (Feb., 1972), 78–98.

Roy, Andrew. *A History of the Coal Miners in the United States.* Columbus, Ohio, 1903.

Rozwenc, Edwin C. *Cooperatives Come to America: The History of the Protective Store Movement, 1845–1867.* Mount Vernon, Iowa, 1941.

Saxton, Alexander. *The Indispensable Enemy: Labor and the Anti-Chinese Movement in California.* Berkeley, 1971.

Schappes, Morris U. "The 1880's: Beginnings of Jewish Trade Unionism." *Jewish Life,* Sept., 1954, pp. 21–24.

———. "Jews and the American Labor Movement, 1850–1880." *Jewish Life,* July, 1954, pp. 17–20.

Schlegel, Marvin W. *Ruler of the Reading: The Life of Franklin B. Gowen, 1836–1889.* Harrisburg, Pa., 1947.

———. "The Workingmen's Benevolent Association: First Union of Anthracite Miners." *Pennsylvania History,* X (Oct., 1943), 243–67.

Schlesinger, Arthur M., Jr. *The Age of Jackson.* Boston, 1945.

Schleuter, Hermann. *Lincoln, Labor and Slavery.* New York, 1913.

Schuster, Eunice Minette. *Native American Anarchism: A Study of Left-Wing American Individualism.* Northampton, Mass., 1932.

Scoresby, William. *American Factories and Their Female Operatives.* Boston, 1845.

Shlakman, Vera. *Economic History of a Factory Town: A Study of Chicopee, Massachusetts.* Northampton, Mass., 1935.

Siebert, William H. *The Underground Railroad from Slavery to Freedom.* New York, 1898.

Slaner, Philip. "The Railroad Strikes of 1877." *Marxist Quarterly,* I (Apr.–June, 1937), 214–36.

Speek, Peter A. *The Singletax and the Labor Movement.* Madison, Wisc., 1917.

Stearns, Bertha Monica. "Early Factory Magazines in New England." *Journal of Economic and Business History,* II (Aug., 1939), 685–705.

Stedman, J. C., and K. A. Leonard. *The Workingmen's Party of California.* San Francisco, 1878.

Stemler, Heinrich. *Geschichte des Sozialismus und Kommunismus in Nord Amerika.* Leipzig, 1880.

Steward, Ira. *Poverty.* Boston, n.d.

Stolvey, James B. "Daniel De Leon: A Study of Marxian Orthodoxy." Ph.D. thesis, University of Illinois, 1946.

Stokes, Isaac N. P. *The Iconography of Manhattan Island 1498 to 1909.* Vol. IV. New York, 1922.

Sullivan, William A. "Did Labor Support Andrew Jackson?" *Political Science Quarterly,* LXII (Dec., 1947), 569–80.

Swinton, John. *Striking for Life.* New York, 1894.

Taft, Philip. *The A. F. of L. in the Time of Gompers.* New York, 1957.

Thompson, E. P. *The Making of the English Working Class.* New York, 1964.

Todes, Charlotte. *William H. Sylvis and the National Labor Union.* New York, 1942.

Trachtenberg, Alexander. *History of Legislation for the Protection of Coal Miners in Pennsylvania, 1824–1915.* New York, 1942.

U.S., Congress, Senate. *Report on the Condition of Women and Child Wage-Earners in the United States.* 61st Cong., 2d sess., Senate Doc. 645. Vol. IX, *History of Women in Industry in the United States,* by Helen L. Sumner. Washington, D.C., 1910.

———. Vol. X, *History of Women in Trade Unions,* by John B. Andrews and W. D. P. Bliss. Washington, D.C., 1910.

Ware, Norman J. *The Industrial Worker, 1840–1860.* Boston and New York, 1924.

———. *The Labor Movement in the United States, 1860–1895: A Study in Democracy.* New York, 1929.

Warne, Frank Julian. *History of the United Mine Workers of America.* New York, 1905.

Wesley, Charles H. *Negro Labor in the United States, 1850–1925: A Study in American Economic History.* New York, 1927.

Wieck, Edward A. *The American Miners' Association.* New York, 1940.

Wilson, Walter. "Historic Coal Creek Rebellion Brought an End to Convict Miners in Tennessee." *United Mine Workers' Journal,* Nov. 1, 1918.

Wolman, Leo. *The Growth of American Trade Unions, 1880–1923.* New York, 1924.

Yellen, Samuel. *American Labor Struggles.* New York, 1936.

Young, Alfred. "The Mechanics and the Jeffersonians: New York, 1789–1901." *Labor History,* V (Fall, 1964), 247–76.

Zahler, Helene Sara. *Eastern Workingmen and National Land Policy, 1829–1862.* New York, 1941.

Song Titles and First Lines

Song titles are enclosed in quotation marks; first lines are not.

Composers

Index